3.50 d

D0909407

A HISTORY OF
BRITISH SOCIALISM

By M. Beer

AN INQUIRY INTO PHYSIOCRACY

EARLY BRITISH ECONOMICS

FIFTY YEARS OF
INTERNATIONAL SOCIALISM

THE LIFE AND TEACHINGS OF
KARL MARX

A GENERAL HISTORY OF
SOCIALISM AND SOCIAL STRUGGLES

M. BEER

A HISTORY OF

BRITISH

SOCIALISM

ONE VOLUME EDITION

WITH AN INTRODUCTION

BY

R. H. TAWNEY

NEW YORK

THE HUMANITIES PRESS

———

GEORGE ALLEN & UNWIN LTD

LONDON

First Published in 1919
Reprinted 1920, 1921, 1923
New and Cheaper Edition 1929
One Volume Edition with a New
Chapter, 1940
Reprinted 1948

PRINTED   IN   GREAT   BRITAIN   BY
BRADFORD & DICKENS, LONDON, W.C.1

INTRODUCTION

THE book which is now published under the title " A History of British Socialism, Volume I.," was intended by the author to be the first of two volumes, the second of which would carry the story of British Socialism into the opening decade of the present century. The War intervened before the second volume was ready for the Press, and Mr. Beer, like most other students, was compelled for the time being to lay his literary work on one side. The first volume, therefore, is now published separately; the next, it is hoped, will appear on the return of peace. Together they will form the most complete account of the development of Socialist thought in Great Britain which has yet appeared. The subject of the present volume is the growth of Socialism down to the rise of Chartism, and its readers must remember that there is a sequel in which the story is completed. But the period with which it deals is sufficiently distinct to be studied separately, and the book is a unity, not a mutilated fragment.

Mr. Beer's book is a study of political thought upon the group of problems created by the rise of capitalist agriculture and capitalist industry, as it developed in the country which was the first to experience the transition, and which experienced it most completely. It is called, " A History of British Social-ism," because the particular aspect of that thought with which it is primarily concerned is the effort, partly critical, partly constructive, at once aspiration, theory, prophecy, and pro-gramme, which had as its object to substitute for the direction of industry by the motive of personal profit and the method of unrestricted competition some principle of organization more compatible with social solidarity and economic freedom. Like other summary designations of complex political forces, Socialism is a word the connotation of which varies, not only from generation to generation, but from decade to decade; and Mr. Beer has wisely refrained from trimming the edges of an experimental and combative history to fit the framework of any neat definition. Instead of formulating a canon of Socialist orthodoxy and grouping the exponents of the faith according to the different degrees of their proximity to it, he has allowed the significance of his title to emerge from the different and sometimes contradictory currents of thought which inte mingle, in their natural complexity and exuberance and crudity, in the pages of his book. His work is not the chronicle of a sect or of a party, but the analysis of a moral and intellectual movement.

As the present volume shows, that movement can claim some classics. But it has developed less through the literary succession of a chain of writers than by the renewed and spontaneous reflection of each generation upon the dominant facts and theories which confronted it. The mental atmosphere of England on the eve of the Industrial Revolution, the reactions of the French Revolution and the long War, the agitation which preceded, and the disillusionment which followed, the first Reform Bill, the influence of Adam Smith, Ricardo, and the Utilitarians form a background without a description of which English Socialism, in its seminal period, is unintelligible. Mr. Beer has set them in the high light which they deserve. He presents the main elements in the political thought of the time, not as specimens in a museum, but in the tumultuous energy and profusion with which they swept across the mind of a tormented generation. The key to the heart of an economic age lies in economics, as to that of a religious age it is religion. What he offers is a study of one side of the great debate upon the merits of modern industrial civilization, which the nineteenth century, at the climax of its triumphant self-confidence, could ignor but could not silence, and which is still unended. His feet are always planted on solid earth, and he is not of those who would convert history into a procession of abstractions. But the main theme of his book is political thought, not political events, and he is more interested in the workshops where doctrines are forged and sharpened than in their use in the field. f there are critics who regard the history of opinion as an unprofitable dilettantism, they may be invited to reconsider their judgment when they have read the second part of the present volume. For the ideas whose development and genesis it traces are not antiquarian curiosities, but a high explosive,—and an explosive which has not yet been fired.

These ideas have a long history, and the first ninety-one pages of the present volume are given to a description of the communistic elements in English thought from the Middle Ages to the beginning of the eighteenth century.   Like the Christianity of Plato, the Socialism of the *animae naturaliter socialisticae* of the pre-industrial era bears its name by metaphor or analogy, and the treatment which it receives from Mr. Beer must not be interpreted as implying that he regards a spiritual affinity as a direct affiliation. The importance for him of the earlier thinkers consists in the legacy of political principles which they transmitted. Capitalist industry arose, as he points out, in a country which was intellectually prepared to receive it. It developed, not by a fortuitous series of technical discoveries, but through the concentration of thought upon definite problems to the exclusion of others, and there is a sense in which Locke and Blackstone were as truly its pioneers as Arkwright and Crompton. The first part of the book, therefore, is in the nature of an introduction to its main theme,—the development of political thought under the stress of Industrial Revolution.

The social history of the years from 1760 to 1840 has received more attention in England than that of any other period.   Toynbee, Held, Cunningham, and Mantoux have made its main features familiar, and the brilliant books of Mr. and Mrs. Hammond have painted an unforgettable picture of the meaning of the new economic régime to the workers in village and town. The political philosophy which triumphed has been the subject of an elaborate study by Leslie Stephen.   Prof. Wallas has described it, while it still had to fight for its existence.   Prof. Dicey has shown how in the day of its power it transformed English thought and institutions between 1832 and 1870. What has never been adequately written is the history of the political philosophy which failed. For the victory of the panegyrists of the new industrial order was so complete as to obliterate the very remem-

brance of its critics, and to create the impression that Utilitarianism spoke with the voice of reason itself. That is what seemed
to be the case to the contemporaries who applauded. That is
how it still often appears to-day. There was a leaden obscurant-
ism which would not think. There was a blind movement of
misery among masses hardly capable of thought. But in the
first forty years of the century which saw the establishment of
capitalist industry intelligence was united in its approval, and
an alternative philosophy did not find expression in England
till it was imported in the forties from abroad.

That impression is natural, but the present volume shows
that it is an illusion. In the clash of political ideas in the
early nineteenth century there were not two protagonists,
but three, and the least known had not the least vitality. For
capitalism was no sooner dominant than it produced its critics,
and side by side with the economic theory of Ricardo and the
political theory of Bentham there appeared a body of doctrine
which attacked the fundamental basis of the new order. It is
not the case, therefore, as has sometimes been suggested, that
the classical land of capitalist industry had to wait for an
exposition of Socialism till a German exile disinterred dusty
bluebooks in the British Museum. As Marx himself was well
aware, there was an indigenous English Socialism which, except
for the inspiration to all creative thought given by France, owed
nothing to foreign influences. Spence, Ogilvie, and Paine, of
whom an admirable account is contained in the late Mr. P. A.
Brown's *The French Revolution in English History*, were
agrarian reformers, though Paine was much more as well. Godwin was an anarchist ; Charles Hall was a conservative critic
of capitalism rather than a socialist. But the writings of Gray,
Thompson, Hodgskin, and Bray, all published, except that of
Bray, which appeared in 1839, in the decade 1820–1830, laid
down the main lines of Socialist thought more than twenty years
before the appearance of the Communist Manifesto. Their works
are almost unobtainable. Except in Prof. Foxwell's introduction
to Anton Menger's book, *The Right to the whole Produce of
Labour*, no adequate exposition of their writings has appeared

in English. And, as readers of the present work will discover, they were not isolated eccentrics, but representatives of a current of thought which offered the working classes what in the twenties and thirties they needed most,—a philosophy interpreting the causes of their degradation, and a body of articulate doctrine which could fuse into energy their misery, their passion, and their hope.

It is this current of thought, its antecedents, affinities, and ramifications, its theoretical developments and practical effects in the world of industry and politics, which occupies the greater part of the present volume. Its immediate influence was profound. The word " Socialism " appears first to be used in the *Co-operative Magazine* of November, 1827, in which those who think that Capital should be owned, not individually, but in common, are described as " Communionists or Socialists." Its meaning was not collectivism, but co-operation ; and co-operation not in the specialised sense which it has since assumed of a particular method of conducting trade, but with the larger significance of a social order based on fraternity, not competition. In that sense it was still used by the Rochdale Pioneers of 1844, when they proposed to " arrange the powers of production, distribution, education, and government, or, in other words, to establish a self-supporting home colony of united interests."

Co-operation was a body of social principles before it was an economic device, and, if its practical application owed most to Robert Owen, the intellectual elaboration of the faith was the work of the early English Socialists. Their relation to Chartism and Trade Unionism was equally important. To the former they helped to give the anti-capitalist bias, which, as the excellent work of the late Mr. Hovell shows, was the practical motive to rally the turbulent workers of the North to the decorous political programme enunciated by Lovett and the London Workingmen's Association. Influenced partly by their teaching, which was disseminated in a popular form through the papers read by the working classes, trade unionism assumed a revolutionary and aggressive character as remote from the aims of the sober defensive associations of the sixties and seventies as from those of the local journeymen's clubs of the eighteenth century. That property not earned by labour is theft, that there is necessarily a class-war between the producers and the non-producers, that economic power precedes political power and that salvation must come, not from Parliament, but from syndicalist movements on the part of the organised workers—these were the watch words of the advanced trade unionism of the thirties. " With us, universal suffrage will begin in our lodges, extend to the general union, and finally swallow up the political power " ; " Social liberty must precede political liberty. While we are in a state of social slavery, our rights would be exercised to the benefit of our tyrants, and we should be made subservient to the parties who work us for their purposes." [1] Under the stimulus of such ideas, trade unionism became an effort directed to overthrowing the existing economic system, rather than to improving the condition of the wage-earner within it. Trade union history, which like trade union law, has suffered from the tyranny of over-rigid definitions, requires to be re-written in the light of them. When that is done, movements which now appear novel or ephemeral will possibly be found to be the re-emergence of tendencies which are fundamental and permanent. " The English intellect," writes Mr. Beer, in his preface, " from its sheer recklessness is essentially revolutionary. . . '. In periods of general upheaval, when the dynamic forces of society are vehemently asserting themselves, the English are apt to throw their mental ballast overboard and take the lead in revolutionary thought and action. In such a period are we living now." His words are more appropriate to the present moment than to that at which they were written. " Social Reconstruction " is not the invention of the twentieth century ; and those who are concerned with it to-day may find in the intellectual ferment of the period explored by Mr. Beer a medicine to chasten their hopes and to fortify their resolution.

A foreign scholar has certain advantages in writing the history of modern England. He is not scorched by the embers of living controversies. He is free from the prejudices of sect or party, and can view his subject through plain glass. The

[1] See p. 340.

snares of ready-made interpretations are not about his feet, nor conventional judgments upon his lips. His eye for the sharp outline of facts has not been dimmed by a haze of familiar words. He can find a new significance in the obvious and still be surprised at what is surprising. But only scholarship of a high order can give him the learning needed to compose a work like the present volume, and only long familiarity can save him from misinterpreting the atmosphere of a foreign nation. Mr. Beer possesses both. He is an indefatigable student, who knows the social history of England from the middle of the eighteenth century, as it is known only to Professor Graham Wallas, Mr. and Mrs. Sidney Webb, and Mr. and Mrs. Hammond. And his twenty years of residence in England have given him the working acquaintance with the unstated assumptions of English political life which is hardly less necessary than historical knowledge for the task which he has undertaken.

The present book is only part of the work which he had planned. In addition to the second volume, which was almost completed, he had begun, in conjunction with a friend, the task of reprinting the more noteworthy writings of the early English Socialists, and some of them were already in proof when he was interrupted. " I see now," he wrote, in the last week of July, 1914, " that I must use every moment for work. The War will upset all plans, if Germany gets involved in the Austrian madness. I feel more than ever that no agitation and no class-war are of any use. Man is still brutal, and despite all religion, culture, and science, not far removed from the wild animal." At a time when to speak of the unity of Europe seems a cruel jest, a work like that of Mr. Beer, the history by an Austrian scholar of the English contribution to an international movement, is not only a valuable addition to historical knowledge, but a reminder that there are intellectual bonds which preceded the War and which will survive it. English readers will thank him both for the one and for the other, and will hope that, by the publication of his second volume, he will in the near future increase the obligation under which he has already laid them.

R. H. TAWNEY.

PREFACE

FROM the thirteenth century to the present day the stream of socialism and social reform has largely been fed by British thought and experiment. Mediaeval schoolmen and statesmen, modern political philosophers, economists, poets and philanthropists of the British Isles have explored its course and enriched its volume, but left it to writers of other nations to name and describe it. The same may be said of all other philosophical and scientific achievements of Britain, and particularly of England. Mr. Kipling's heroic " Explorer " is her true symbol :—

" Well I know who'll take the credit—all the clever chaps that
    followed—
Came a dozen men together—never knew my desert fears ;
Tracked me by the camps I'd quitted—used the water-holes I'd
    hollowed.
They'll go back and do the talking. They'll be called the Pioneers ! "

This has been so all along, but it ought not to be so any longer. British students ought to work up and utilise the views which the seminal minds of England have given to the world. The nation needs now all the knowledge, ordered and systematised, of its past labours for socialism and social reform, in order to be able to cope with the social difficulties and weltering movements which are visibly coming to a head.

The English intellect, from its sheer recklessness, is essentially revolutionary, probably more so than the French intellect. But since 1688 it has been the endeavour of English statesmen and educators to impart to the nation a conservative, cautiously moving temper, a distrust of generalisation, an aversion from carrying theory to its logical conclusions. By these means they appear to have succeeded in ballasting and steadying the intellectual swiftness and restlessness of the nation and in producing well-balanced minds. In normal times this ingenious contrivance has worked well—or as Sir Leslie Stephen said, " Illogicality has saved us," and given the English a reputation for being controlled by good sense and sober judgment. In periods of general upheavals, however, when the dynamic forces of society are vehemently asserting themselves, the English are apt to throw their mental ballast overboard and take the lead in revolutionary thought and action. In such a period we are living now.

Since the beginning of the new century a new England has been springing up—" rousing herself like a strong man after sleep and shaking her invincible locks." Her men and women are all astir, their mentality has become sensitive and quickly responsive to doctrinal and moral stimuli— the people are marching on. The intellects of the nation are as bold and active as in the great crises of its stirring past. The old issues are either forgotten or forced to their final fruition, while the masses are joining issue with the classes upon the question of a redistribution of wealth and power. A new Chartist movement has arisen and is daily growing.

The period which now discloses itself to the eyes of the social inquirer exhibits some striking parallels to that of the second quarter of the nineteenth century. The consolidation of the productive and distributive forces that were brought into being by the Industrial Revolution, the contest of the then new middle classes for political power, the agitation for a new commercial policy; the surging-up of the working classes since the repeal of the Combination

Laws (1824-5), the formation of national trades organisations, the alliance between the middle and working classes
against the Tory aristocracy and in favour of the First
Reform Bill (1830-32), the disillusionment of Labour and
the consequent rise of revolutionary trades unionism or
Syndicalism (1833-4), the growth of Chartism or a Socialist
Labour Party (1836-48) ; finally, the rise of the Oxford
Movement, Young England, and Christian Socialism—all
this stupendous mental ferment in the years from 1825 to
1850 appears to be repeating itself now on a larger and
higher scale. Yet, how much do we know of the effects of
the struggle for the First Reform Bill on the then nascent
socialist and labour movement ? And how much of the
effects of the Constitutional struggle since 1909 on organised
Labour ? Or is it a mere coincidence that revolutionary
trades unionism followed in the wake of the agitation for the
Reform Bill, 1832, and that Syndicalism and general strikes
have been treading upon the heels of the Constitutional
crisis that began with Mr. Lloyd George's Finance Bill ?
And will the strengthening of the political action of Labour
which followed upon the collapse of revolutionary trades
unionism, in 1835, be repeated with regard to Syndicalism
and the British Labour Party of to-day ? And is Tariff
Reform destined to mark the close of the social ferment of
the present day as the triumph of Free Trade marked the
close of the Chartist era?

These and many other vital questions suggest themselves
from a comparison of the two periods. I do not pretend
to have supplied adequate solutions of those problems, my
aim having been to stimulate the social and political student,
rather than to offer panaceas. I have but brought together,
as completely as I could, from the vast treasure-houses
of British theology, moral philosophy, political economy,
socialist pamphlets, Labour papers, and general periodical

A2

publications, the materials relevant to our subject. I have classified them according to the theories and general concepts underlying them, and given each phase and leading personality their historical setting, thus bringing them into relation with the social events and mental developments of their time.

From 1790 to 1840 the Francis Place Collections and MSS., which are either in the British Museum Manuscript Department or at the Repository at Hendon, have been of great assistance to me. I take this opportunity to express my thanks to the librarian and assistants of the British Museum for the unfailing courtesy with which they treated my requests and for the facilities they afforded me for my research work.

The correspondence of Robert Owen is now in the keeping of the Co-operative Wholesale Society at Manchester. May I suggest to its administrators to hand it over to the Trustees of the British Museum in order to make it accessible to students?

While writing this book I often felt the want of an English work on the English schoolmen. It is rather curious that no British student of divinity has ever set himself the task of writing an exhaustive monograph on either Alexander of Hales, or Duns Scotus, or William of Ockham. Or are these leading Minorites and schoolmen regarded as foreigners because the first died at Paris, the second at Cologne, and the third at Munich?

I have likewise regretted that no English treatise exists on the currency controversies, particularly with respect to paper money, of the crucial period from 1774 to 1819.

The " History of British Socialism " is but a feeble attempt to repay the enormous mental debt which I owe to English life and scholarship. I could not have written it but for my twenty years' residence in this country, which has taught me how high an elevation of political and moral culture a nation must reach before it can embark on a socialistic reconstruction of society. I hope that British social students will assist me, by their criticisms, to make the second edition of the book less defective.

The book is based on my German *Geschichte des Sozialismus in England* (1912), which had a uniformly favourable reception from the press in Great Britain, Germany, Austria-Hungary, and Russia. The English version is practically a new book, it having been completely re-written, and enlarged by a considerable amount of original matter.

In conclusion, I express my cordial thanks to Mr. R. C. K. Ensor for having read and corrected some of the proofs, and to Dr. A. Shadwell for the encouragement and advice he gave me during the writing of the book.

NOTE TO THE REVISED EDITION

The above Preface was written in June, 1914, when the manuscript of the *History of British Socialism* was nearing completion. Owing to the Great War, however, the publication was put off till Peace was declared and public attention again turned to home affairs. The present edition is, with few exceptions, a faithful reprint of the original work which appeared in 1919 and 1920. In Volume II, the chapters XIX and XX, dealing with the years 1914 to 1919, have undergone some alterations, for they seemed to require either corrections or filling up of lacunæ. Moreover, the present edition is enlarged by a supplementary chapter (XXII), covering the years from 1920 to 1928. It is written in the same dispassionate spirit which secured for the original edition the unanimous approval of the British Press and public.

I am glad to have an opportunity of expressing my obligation to Mr. J. S. Middleton, assistant secretary of the Labour Party, to Mr. Walter M. Citrine, general secretary of the Trades Union Congress, for information and lending me the Reports of the Labour Party Conferences and the Trades Union Congresses respectively, and to Mr. Alfred Mattison, of Leeds, for his great kindness in sending me his unique notes on the life of John Francis Bray.

M. BEER.

September, 1928.

NOTE TO 1940 EDITION

THE text is substantially the same as the second edition, except for the correction of a few misprints which had escaped my vigilance.

I added a supplementary chapter to bring the book up to date. The chapter covers the decade 1929–39, which witnessed the first serious crisis of the Labour Party, the banner-bearer of socialism in this country. It deals with the economic crisis 1930–31 and its effects on the Party: the defection of its leaders, the severe electoral defeat in 1931, the controversy arising from it, then the revival and the crystallisation of the policy of the Parliamentary Labour Party.

My thanks are due to the Trades Union Congress Publicity Department for lending me the Annual Reports 1929–36, and to the Research Department of the Labour Party for supplying me the statistics of the general elections 1931 and 1935, as well as to Mr. James Middleton (Secretary of the Labour Party) and Prof. R. H. Tawney for having revised the supplementary chapter.

M. BEER.

CONTENTS

PART II

(1760–1834)

CONTENTS

PART III

CHARTISM

I. THE GROWTH OF CHARTISM

PART IV

MODERN SOCIALISM (1855–1939)

PART I

MEDIAEVAL COMMUNISM

B

PART I

MEDIAEVAL COMMUNISM

I

PRIMITIVE CHRISTIAN INFLUENCES

I.—THE LEGACY OF THE ROMAN EMPIRE

A BROAD current of communistic sentiment runs through the mental life of the Roman Empire in the age of Christ. The widening of the spiritual horizon consequent upon the growing acquaintance with Greek philosophy and oriental speculation ; the political and material forces which were operating upon the social structure since the Punic Wars ; the constant and jarring frictions and contests between the classes ;[1] finally, the increasing corruptions and complications of society, spread dissatisfaction with the existing institutions, and with traditional creeds and concepts. An unquenchable yearning for a return to the simpler past and ruder equality took hold of the minds of poets, patriots, and thinkers.

In that mood the prehistoric past, with its tribal organisation and absence of individual property, appeared to those minds as the reign of Saturn, or the state of nature, where man lived in unconscious innocence and blissful ignorance, knowing nothing of *meum* and *tuum*, good and evil, dominion and servitude. It was a state free from searchings of heart, from wearisome problems concerning social relations and ethical concepts. Vergil, mild and pensive, celebrates the reign of Saturn when—

> " No fences parted fields, nor marks nor bounds
> Divided acres of litigious grounds,
> But all was common."[2]

Strains of rude equality fall on our ear when Horace sings of Scythian institutions :

> " The Scythians of the plains
> More happy are, housed in wandering wains,

[1] Cicero, *De Rep.* I. 31.   [2] Vergil, *Georg.* I. 125–28.

3

> More blest the Getan stout,
> Who not from acres mark'd and meted out
> Reaps his fruit and grain.
> A year, no more, he rests in his domain,
> Then, pausing from his toil,
> He quits it, and in turn another tills the soil."[1]

Tacitus inquires, with romantic admiration, into the life of the Germanic tribes ; and Juvenal, conservative and patriotic, pours out his burning zeal in satires upon a civilisation that has forsaken toil and virtue and fallen a prey to luxury and voluptuousness—those insidious foes that paralyse the hands of the world conquerors.[2]

But the most pronounced admirer of primitive communism is Seneca : " The social virtues had remained pure and inviolate before covetousness distracted society and introduced poverty, for men ceased to possess all things when they began to call anything their own. The first men and their immediate descendants followed nature, pure and uncorrupt. When, however, vices crept in, kings were obliged to show their authority and enact penal laws. How happy was the primitive age when the bounties of nature lay in common and were used promiscuously ; nor had avarice and luxury disunited mortals and made them prey upon one another. They enjoyed all nature in common, which thus gave them secure possession of the public wealth. Why should I not think them the richest of all people, among whom there was not to be found one poor man ? " [3]

Josephus, a faithful index of educated opinion of his time, sees in Cain a man striving after possessions and lucre, acquisition of land, while Abel personifies the artless and innocent shepherd, moving about with his herds from pasture to pasture, without occupying any of them. Cain is also supposed by the ancients to have been the first to set bounds to fields.[4]

---

[1] Horace, *Odes* III. 24 (Theodore Martin's translation).
[2] Juvenal, *Satires*, 6 and 13.
[3] Seneca, *Letters*, 90.
[4] Josephus, *Antiq. Jud.*, l. 1, c. 2 (3). *Cf.* Wycliffe, *Civ. dom.*, III., c. 20 (vol. 4, p. 422) ; John Selden, *Mare Clausum*, l. 1, c. 4.

Private property and civil dominion thus appeared as the origin of evil.

The philosophy underlying these conceptions is of course that of the Stoa, the real origin of the doctrines of the state of nature and of natural rights.

The difficulties and problems that assailed Rome since the Punic Wars had troubled Hellas since the Persian Wars. The old society, in spite of all reforming efforts to maintain it, had given way to individualism ; the old mythology or antique theology was losing authority and its place was being taken by a philosophy that was mainly ethical. The final outcome was the Stoa, whose doctrines are partly a protest against civil society and individual property, and partly a positive guide to an ethical reform of society. It is based on an idealisation of the primitive conditions of tribal society. The appeal to nature implies a censure upon civilisation as well as a summons to mankind either to return to the past or to re-organise their institutions after the ideals drawn from the past. The urbanisation of the land, the bursting of the national bars, the growth of trade and commerce, appeared to the Stoics as an abandonment of natural pursuits, of the simple virtues of country life, and the introduction of artificial conditions, of multitudinous and complicated business, of luxury and corruption. In Stoic philosophy, God appears as the active, rational, and moral principle who saturates and vitalizes the physical nature. The world and the fulness thereof governs itself by the divine law inherent in it, which is equity and goodness. It is infinitely superior to civil law or man-made law, and it applies to all human beings, for men as participators of the divine spirit are free and equal. In the original society, as it issued from the hands of nature, the divine-natural law governed mankind, but in later times corruption set in and man enacted laws. Civil government is thus the effect of the debasement of mankind and but a vicious substitute for the reign of God and nature. From evil flows evil and it can only be cured by a return to nature and a life in harmony with nature.[1]

[1] *Cf.* Maine, *Ancient Law*, ed. 1861, pp. 53–7, 70–2 ; Pearson, *Fragments of Zeno*, pp. 11–12 ; Cornford, *Transition from Religion*

The educated Romans, in so far as they were susceptible of philosophic speculations, accepted the Stoic doctrines ; later on the Roman lawyers incorporated it as *ius naturale* into their legal system, not, however, without materially changing some of its tenets. It was in the Hellenic world that Stoic philosophy became an integral part of ethical and religious thought, and with the influx of Greeks into Christianity Stoic concepts took place among the formative elements of patristic and scholastic theology.

2.—THE PRIMITIVE CHURCH

JEWISH ethical monotheism and Stoic philosophy, both saturated either with social reform or communistic ideals, formed the mental atmosphere into which Christianity was born. As a religion of the lowly and hungry it came into the world, endowed with the sentiment that communism was capable of raising economic life to a higher moral level. The hindrance to salvation was not poverty, but riches. " Blessed be ye poor, for yours is the kingdom of God. . . . How hardly shall they that have riches enter into the kingdom of God " (Luke vi. 20 ; xviii. 24). It may fairly be doubted whether positive communistic institutions really existed amongst the primitive Christian communities, as one might infer from Acts iv. 32, but there cannot be any doubt that common possessions were looked upon by many of the first Christians as an ideal to be aimed at.[1]

Under the overpowering influence of the teachings of Christ the members of the first communities were " of one heart and of one soul, neither said any of them that aught of the things which he possessed was his own, but they had all things common " (Acts iv. 32). In this moral exaltation sacrifice was easy and renunciation of worldly possession a spiritual joy. Or as S. Cyprian says, " When at the first beginnings of the Church the mind flourished with great virtues, when the soul of the believers

to *Philosophy*, 1911 ; Voigt, *Ius Naturale*, 1857 ; Barth, *Die Stoa*, 1906 ; D. G. Ritchie, *Natural Rights*, 1895.

[1] Compare, however, Gibbon, *Roman Empire*, c. 15 (ed. Bury, II. 47) ; also Latimer, *Sermons*, First Before Edward VI.

burned with a glow of faith yet new, then they had all things common, they imitated the divine law, the equity of God the Father." [1] Barnabas enjoins the Christian, " to communicate in all things with thy neighbour ; thou shalt not call things thine own ; for if ye are partakers in common of things that are incorruptible how much should ye be of those things which are perishable." [2] Clement of Alexandria teaches, " All things are common and not for the rich to appropriate an undue share. That expression therefore, ' I possess and possess it in abundance, why should I not enjoy ? ' is suitable neither to man nor to society. . . . God has given to us the liberty of use, but only so far as necessary, and He has determined that the use should be common." [3] Tertullian argues with the Romans, " We are brethren in our family property, which with you mostly dissolves brotherhood. We, therefore, who are united in mind and soul, doubt not about having our possessions in common. With us all things are shared promiscuously, except the wives. In that alone do we part fellowship, in which alone others (Greek and Roman pagans) exercise it." [4] S. John Chrysostom preaches, " Consider the time of the Apostles. I say not the chief men, but the believers themselves generally. All, it is written, were of one heart, neither said any of them that aught of the things which he possessed was his own. There were no such words as ' mine ' and ' thine.' This is friendship. . . . It is only impossible (to-day) because we have not the will, for possible it is. If it were not possible neither would Christ have commanded it nor have discoursed so much upon love." [5]

The corollary of these beliefs was the condemnation of wealth and the exaltation of poverty. It found epigrammatic expression in the sentence, *dives aut iniquus aut iniqui heres.* " To grow rich without an injustice is impossible. But what if he succeeded

[1] S. Cyprian, *Of Works and Alms* c. 25.
[2] Barnabas, *Epistle* §19.
[3] Clement of Alexandria, *Paed.* II. 13.
[4] Tertullian, *Apol.* I. 39.
[5] S. John Chrysostom, *Homilies,* 1 Thessal. *Hom.* 2.

to his father's inheritance ? Then he receives what had been gained by injustice." [1]

The communistic ideal is evidently compatible with Christianity, provided that the methods employed for its realisation are strictly ethical and religious, and not political, seditious, or revolutionary ; they must be confined to self-reform through a moral and religious life. Therefore, it was possible for S. Paul, without offending the communistic sentiments of the believers, to exhort the Roman community to be subject to the civil authorities and obedient to their laws (Romans xiii.).

3.—CHRISTIAN THEOLOGY AND NATURAL LAW

To the teachers of primitive and mediaeval Christianity *ius naturale* must have been particularly congenial. It appeared to them to be a pagan version of the Scriptural truths of the innocence of the original man in the Garden of Eden, his Fall and the consequent corruption of man's heart, and the inferior nature of civilisation and human laws, as well as a confirmation that even Nature dictates certain commandments in conformity with divine law.[2] And they found authority for its validity in S. Paul, who argues, "For when the Gentiles, which have not the law, do by nature the things contained in the law, these . . . are a law unto themselves, which show the work of the law written in their hearts, their conscience also bearing witness " (Romans ii. 14, 15). Here the law of nature is expressly recognised. To that argument of S. Paul the Church Fathers, Schoolmen, and theologians always refer as the authority for the incorporation of *ius naturale* into their theological systems. But the *ius naturale* of the Roman lawyers lost in the process of assimilation

[1] The same, *Homilies*, 1 Tim. *Hom.* 12. Compare Pöhlmann, *Sociale Frage in der antiken Welt*, vol. 2 ; also Laurent, *Histoire du droit des Gens*, IV. 102, *seq*.

[2] William of Ockham : " *Omne ius naturale in Scripturis divinis explicite et implicite continetur* " (*Dialogus* in Goldast, *Monarchia*, II.), p. 934 ; Richard Hooker : " The Scripture is fraught even with Laws of Nature, insomuch as Gratian defining natural right . . . that which the Books of the Law and the Gospel do contain " (*Ecclesiastical Polity*, book 1, c. 12).

to the body of Roman law much of the communistic ardour which it had in the age of Vergil, Josephus, and Seneca. In Roman Law it was combined with *ius gentium*, which had grown out of the international relations and commercial transactions of the ancient world and therefore could not but be unfavourable to the social conceptions of the state of nature : the Law of Nations legalised dominion and servitude and private possessions. According to the Institutes *ius naturale* is that which nature teaches animals and man ; from it originates the joining together of male and female ; from it also procreation and education of the offspring.[1] Likewise, all men are born free ; and air, water, public and religious buildings are common possession.[2] Indeed, in Roman Law, *ius naturale* lost its old meaning and became a rudimentary organ, while in the patristic and scholastic literature it is in full vigour. This is due to the Greek Fathers, then to S. Augustine, but particularly to S. Isidore of Seville (*d.* 636), who transmitted not only the body of Roman learning to the Church, but also the primitive Christian spirit. According to him, " *ius naturale* is common to all nations and it contains everything that is known to man by natural instinct and not by constitutions and man-made law, and that is : the joining together of man and woman, procreation and education of children, *communis omnium possessio, et omnium una libertas*, the acquisition of things which may be captured in the air, on the earth, and in the water, restitution of loaned and entrusted goods, finally, self-defence by force against violence." [3] This definition of *ius naturale* contains, first, the usual characteristics as given in the Institutes ; secondly, the doctrines concerning the state of nature (communism and universal equal liberty) ; thirdly, the essence of the law of nations. It forms an integral part of the *Corpus Iuris Canonici ;* [4] the Schoolmen always refer to it ; indeed, this definition appears to them as authoritative as the reference of S. Paul to natural law. The canonic lawyers and commentators who

[1] *Inst.*, l. 1, §§ 2, 3.
[2] *Ib.*, l. 3, § 1. *Cf.* Voigt, *Ius Naturale*, 1857, vol. 1, § 57.
[3] Isidore, *Etym.*, l. v., c. 4 (ed. Migne, *tom.* 82).
[4] *Decr. Grat.*, prima pars, dist. 1, c. 7.

direct their keenest shafts against commercialism speak with evident delight of S. Isidore's additions and declare that *dulcissima rerum possessio communis* and that *meum et tuum ex iniquitate procedunt.*[1] Only from the division of things discord came, *sic inter mortales facta divisio est.* Also William of Ockham refers to the delectable words of S. Isidore.[2]

On the other hand, they meet with great difficulties when attempting to reconcile economic and political equality, or the state of nature, with acquisition of things, restitution of loans and deposits, the use of force and violence, which are foreign to the concept of the state of nature and which evidently presuppose private property, discord, and enmity. S. Isidore, of course, erroneously joined *ius naturale* to *ius gentium;* and a modern critic, despite his reverence for great and good men and their learning, would simply draw a line between those two legal concepts and show that *ius gentium* was much more akin to civil than to natural law. But the mental attitude of the Schoolmen was different. Revering authority above everything they saw in S. Isidore's definition of *ius naturale* one of those incompatibilities and contradictions which were but superficially so, and therefore called for subtle distinctions and interpretations to reconcile them.

The discovery of America and her tribal organisations added new strength to the system of *ius naturale,* and the rather romantic descriptions of natural society that followed upon the acquaintance with the American tribes are to some extent due to the preconceived notions which sprang from the concept of the state of nature. To Amerigo Vespucci, Sir Thomas More, Sahagun (a Franciscan missionary in Mexico), Hugo Grotius, Joseph Acosta, and many other scholars and travellers, the American tribes and communities appeared as striking demonstrations of the truths of natural law.[3]

---

[1] *Decr. Grat.*, sec. pars, causa 12, qu. 1, c. 2, gloss. *a.*
[2] William of Ockham, *Dialogus* (in Goldast *Monarchia* II.), p. 932.
[3] Compare particularly John Locke, *On Civil Government*, II., c 8, §§ 102, 108.

The influence exercised by that system of thought in the development of English, and generally, European social and political speculations could hardly be over-estimated. Schoolmen, theologians, statesmen, lawyers, revolutionists, and poets based their reasonings and wove their imaginings on it, and even as late as in the first half of the nineteenth century, despite Burke and Bentham who opposed it, British Socialists, poor-law and social reformers were thinking in the terms of that system. From Alexander of Hales, Duns Scotus, and Ockham to Locke, Bolingbroke, Abraham Tucker and Paley; from Bracton to Blackstone; from Wycliffe and John Ball to Hodgskin, Feargus O'Connor, and Cardinal Manning, social and political philosophy was swayed by doctrines of natural rights. And yet, during all those centuries the concept of *ius naturale* was practically always passing through divers changes and interpretations which all but obliterated its original traits.   It was, evidently, a useful hypothesis, and had to be maintained by interpretations and commentaries, which were merely adaptations of the theory to the profound mental and social transformations which English, and generally, European society was continually undergoing.

II

THE ENGLISH SCHOOLMEN

I.—DISSOLUTION OF THE MANORIAL SYSTEM

NATURAL and canonical law, as it moulded the speculations of the early Middle Ages, was in conformity with the customs and views of an agrarian, martial, and clerical society, whose units consisted of manorial demesnes, village communities, abbeys and monasteries, with towns as their appendages. Land formed the chief source of wealth, while trade and commerce were the exception and were despised as base callings ; movable capital played a negligible part, and private property in the sense of absolute individual control over wealth was little known. This natural society reached its culmination in the Crusades, the zenith of pure mediaeval spirit.

In the age of the Crusades the germs of the new social organisation had already made their appearance. Cities and towns, such as Venice, Genoa, Cologne, Augsburg, Nuremberg arose, founding their prosperity on commerce, money-changing, trade, and handicrafts. The Crusades themselves, with their need of money and their effects on the intercourse between West and East, promoted the new movement in which movable capital was destined to come into conflict with, and finally to overwhelm, the institutions and customs of feudal and clerical society.[1] The towns gradually emancipated themselves from manorial and episcopal control ; their social and economic needs and conditions became too differentiated and complicated to fit in with the communistic and anti-commercial tendencies of natural and canonical law. The growth of town economy, in its reaction on the mediaeval agrarian organisation, loosened the

---

[1] Compare H. v. Eicken, *Mittelalterliche Weltanschauung*, p. 778, sqq.

bonds between lord and vassal, manor and abbeys and village, and finally broke up the old relations. Concurrently with those events great religious and moral teachers and reformers arose, and a momentous spiritual and social ferment set in which led to (*a*) heated discussions on property and poverty (*b*) social upheavals, (*c*) changes in the doctrine of *ius naturale*, (*d*) rise of natural and moral philosophy, and (*e*) the formation of national Churches and States.

2.—THEOLOGICAL CONTEST ABOUT POVERTY

Social philosophy formed throughout the Middle Ages **a part** of theology, and the disputes concerning property, communism, and poverty were fought out by theologians. The most scholarly and influential among them were the Franciscans and the Dominicans, who from the thirteenth to the fifteenth century supplied the Church with great teachers. No member of any other Order or of the secular clergy was equal in learning and acuteness of thought to Alexander of Hales, S. Thomas Aquinas, Roger Bacon, Duns Scotus, and William of Ockham. The Dominicans were conservative and conciliatory, while the Minorites, impelled by the primitive Christian fervour of their saintly founder, were the guardians of the poor, the counsellors of the people, and the defenders of the nation against all usurping domination ; a happy people and a good king, ruling in conformity with natural and divine law, were their social and political ideals. The controversies and struggles concerning property and poverty as well as the relation between Church and State, which filled the thirteenth and, in a more intense degree, the fourteenth century, were led by Minorites and Dominicans ; and their stage was Western and Central Europe.

S. Francis of Assisi took for his rules of conduct the Scriptural texts, Matthew x. 9–10 ; xvi. 24 ; xix. 21, which command absolute poverty for the true followers of Christ. These rules were evidently a protest against the new commercial civilisation of Italy and an appeal to the pious to return to primitive Christianity, to the spirit of the Sermon on the Mount. The followers of Jesus should live a life of self-abnegation, no ties should bind them to the secular conditions of society; they should embrace poverty, practise charity, and derive their living from service, labour, and mendicancy. His doctrine of *paupertas evangelica* was uncompromising and unworldly, and although it applied to the Order only, it could not but influence the views of its adherents concerning property in general; they held in the spirit of natural and canonical law that property had its origin in iniquity.

Different in character and teaching was the greatest of the Dominicans, S. Thomas Aquinas. He was essentially a man of compromise, a great conciliator, who attempted to bring natural and canonical law into a certain harmony with the requirements of a society divided into rich and poor, agriculturists and merchants, proprietors and propertyless. He distinguished between the ideal and the possible, relegating communism to the region of the ideal and reducing it in practice to generous almsgiving and care for the propertyless. He sanctioned private property and its conditions as necessary for the peaceful existence of society. As long as man lived *in statu innocentiæ* there was no danger that community of goods would lead to discord and strife. Indeed, many good men held everything in common. But after the state of innocence had vanished and separate dominions multiplied, the division of possessions became necessary for the sake of a secure social life.[1] The division of possessions led to the division of society into rich and poor, but by natural and divine law it is incumbent upon the rich to give the whole of their superfluous wealth to the poor: *Res quas aliqui superabundanter habent, ex naturali iure debentur pauperum sustentationi*.[2] In the meaning of Aquinas the poor are not merely the destitute and paupers, but the wage-workers, the labouring poor, whose only source of living is their daily work. In times of need they must be given relief so as not to allow them to sink into destitution. Still, in the writings of the " doctor angelicus " opinions are to be found which are in complete harmony with the most uncompromising tenets of

---

[1] S. Thomas Aquinas, *Summa* 1, qu. 98, art. 1, ad. 3.
[2] *Ib.*, 2, 2, qu. 66, art. 7.

ius naturale: *In exterioribus divitiis non potest unus homo superabundare nisi alter deficiat.*[1]

The practical nature of the social teaching of the Dominicans held the Order together, while the sublimity of the Franciscan rules precluded their realisation and, therefore, gave rise to dissensions and splits.   In the main the divisions were represented by two parties, one adhering to the *usus moderatus*, the other to the *usus pauper*.   According to the first common property and common use were permitted to the Order, whose members were thus joint possessors of wealth, while according to the other practice the Order had to live in absolute poverty, without any common property, for *habere aliquid minuat de perfectione*.   Over a hundred Franciscans of the extreme wing perished at the stake in the defence of absolute poverty against the decision of Pope John XXII., who was in favour of the *usus moderatus*.   Of the English Franciscans Alexander of Hales and Duns Scotus appear to have adhered to the *usus moderatus,* while William of Ockham was one of the foremost upholders of the *usus pauper*.   He, in the capacity of the English Provincial, supported the Minister General of the Minorites, Michael of Cesena, and charged the Pope with heresy.   In 1328 he and his friends were cast into prison at Avignon, but rescued by emissaries of Emperor Lewis of Bavaria, who brought them to Munich, where Ockham composed his chief works.

3.—HALES, DUNS SCOTUS, AND OCKHAM

Alexander of Hales (de Ales, *d.* 1245), the elder contemporary and theological precursor of S. Thomas Aquinas, points out the contradiction involved in S. Isidore's definition of *ius naturale* and asks how common possessions and the rights accruing from acquisition and occupancy can be reconciled with the equity and goodness which are the basis of *ius naturale*.   And he solves the question by showing that what was equitable and good *in statu naturali* was no more so *in statu naturae corruptae*.   In the first

[1] S. Thomas Aquinas, *Summa* 2, 2, qu. 118, art. 1, ad 2.   Compare Adam Smith, *Wealth of Nations*, book 5, part 2, " The affluence of the few supposes the indigence of the many."

state communism was just, equitable and good, in the other
private property. It was quite true, he says in the words of S.
Augustine, that it was only *iure imperatoris* and not *iure divino*
that a person may say *haec villa est mea, meus est iste servus, mea
est ista domus*. The corruption of man's nature made it necessary
for civil government to introduce private property. Alexander
of Hales is however of opinion that the right of private property
could not apply to those things which belong to the whole community, and that it was not permitted to appropriate common
fields and ways : *platea aliqua, vel campus communitatis ; in
talibus non licet appropriare sibi*. In the same manner he solves
the contradiction between the doctrine of *ius naturale* that all
men are born free and equal, and the existence of dominion and
servitude which is sanctioned by S. Paul (Rom. xiii). In the
state of nature or *ante peccatum* universal liberty and equality
prevailed, while servitude came *post peccatum*, partly by God's
dispensation, which is always just though occult, partly as a
punishment of the wicked, finally, as the universal effect of
sin.[1]

Duns Scotus (*d.* 1308 at Cologne) looked upon property from
the point of view of his Order. Voluntary poverty was his ideal ;
to divest oneself of all earthly goods and use them in common
with all who strive after a perfect Christian life. The right of
private property sprang neither from natural nor divine law,
but from civil law, and was the effect of the Fall of man, when
covetousness took hold of man's heart and caused him to occupy
more than he needed.[2] The principle of natural law concerning
communism fell into desuetude, because the corruption of man
by sin no longer allowed communism to continue undisturbed.
The weak and peaceful were in danger of being wronged or were
actually offered violence by the strong and rapacious. The
common possessions were divided, but not by divine or natural
law, since such law could not cease to exist even after the original
state had disappeared ; thus it must have been civil government
that established the division of possessions. Private property

---

[1] Alexander de Ales, *Summa* 3, qu. 27.
[2] Duns Scotus, *Quaestiones super sententias* 4, dist. 15, qu. 2.

once instituted, led to changes of ownership. Civil laws were enacted to regulate the transfer of property by selling and buying, loan and hire, grant and gift. Gain or profit on such transactions is only permitted as a compensation for the sacrifice of a certain advantage, but not as a means of enriching oneself. Trade and commerce are useful to society and therefore lawful. It is however wrongful and vile to engross and forestall ; persons who are what the French call *regrattiers* are a danger to society.[1]

William of Ockham (*d.* 1347 at Munich) was the last English Schoolman of European stature. His philosophical and political front faces modern times, but his armour is mediaeval. Hence the heaviness and hesitation in his gait. His starting point is the Franciscan doctrine of *paupertas evangelica*. This doctrine led him to a life-long struggle with the Papacy, and he used it in his attempts to destroy the secular power of the Church, its claim to the supremacy over the nation. In this contest he incidentally brought out his views on property and government, some of which are strikingly modern.

His problem was, If common possessions and universal liberty are *iure naturali et divino*, and if natural and divine law is eternal and immutable, how did private property and servitude arise ? And how was it possible for S. Isidore to include institutions of private property in the definition of *ius naturale ?*

His solution is ingenious. He distinguishes three kinds of natural law, evidently corresponding to the three moral stages of man : *ante lapsum, post lapsum,* and the setting in of iniquity and corruption. Ockham puts these stages in a slightly different order—*post lapsum, ante lapsum,* state of iniquity, but as to his reasonings and conclusions it makes no difference in which order we regard the first two stages. And his reasonings and conclusions are as follows : In the state of *ante lapsum* man lived according to natural equity, without constitutions and customs ; everything was held in common and all men were free. S. Isidore, in defining *ius naturale* as *communis omnium possessio et omnium una libertas,* had this stage in view. In the state *post lapsum* right reason aided man and gave him command-

[1] Comp. Carl Werner, *Duns Scotus,* p. 585.

C

ments, as for instance, Do not commit adultery, do not tell
lies,[1] live in common and be free. The third stage was that
which followed *propter iniquitatem ;* in this stage private property
and civil dominion—economic and political inequality—were
introduced. *Ex iure naturali omnia sunt communia . . .
et si post lapsum omnes homines secundum rationem viverent,
omnia deberent esse communia, nihil proprium ; proprietas enim
propter iniquitatem inducta est.* Also dominion and servitude
sprang from the same cause. They were introduced by *ius
gentium et civile.* How, then, could the third stage of man's
history partake of the character of *ius naturale ?*

The answer to this question is the most original part in Ockham's system and distinguishes it from the *Summae* of his predecessors. He asserts that the institutions of private property
and civil government are only natural and rational if they were
introduced in the interest and with the consent of the governed.
Only in proportion to the consent of the subjects are these
institutions just and equitable, and therefore *iure naturali.*[2] Or
to speak the language of the moral philosophers, the successors
of the Schoolmen : private property and civil government are
just and legitimate if they are the effect of, and in conformity
with, the social and political contract.

All that applies to society in general, while the strict practice
of *paupertas evangelica* applies to those who desire to follow
Christ. Such poverty is superior to communism, charity, and
almsgiving. Christ and His apostles were absolutely propertyless. Evangelical poverty means abdication of all temporals.
The secular Church is as inferior to Christ's conduct as the Pope
is to the Holy Scriptures.

The tide of the Reformation and Moral Philosophy was coming
in. Ockham was its European herald.

[1] Also Sir Thomas More regards lying as against nature. *Treatise
on Passions, Works,* p. 1384.

[2] William of Ockham, *Dialogus* (Goldast, *Monarchia* II.), pp.932–34

III

EARLY ENGLISH COMMUNISM

I.—THE PEASANTS' REVOLT

THE new social forces began to make themselves felt in England in the reign of Henry II. Like islands from a receding sea the towns were emerging from their feudal surroundings, gaining an independent economic and legal existence. By the middle of the thirteenth century dozens of towns were already noted for trading and manufacturing activities, for their gilds and courts. The towns offered remunerative markets for foodstuff and raw material, and in proportion as agricultural produce grew in value and could be exchanged for money land was enclosed and the village community encroached upon. The Statutes of Merton (1235), and Westminster (1285), bear evidence of the incipient stage of the new economy. Since the middle of the twelfth century the village community was losing its ancient status,[1] and villeinage was turning into serfdom. This legal deterioration of the peasantry was taking place at an age in which the economic conditions of the peasantry were either improving or capable of improvement. For, as joint-possessors of the communal lands, the peasants could sell their produce in town and as labourers could command money-wages for their work. The contrast between a deteriorating legal status and improving economic conditions grew sharper from the effects of the Black Death and the Statute of Labourers, the first raising the value of labour to a higher level than ever, while the other sought to check the economic tendencies which were favourable to the labouring population.

It is hardly possible to do historical justice to this period if

[1] A. Réville, *Soulèvement des travailleurs en Angleterre*, Introd., *Petit-Dutaillis*, p. xxxviii.

we look upon the serf in relation to the lord only and disregard
his relation to, and his standing in, the village community. The
peasants of the later mediaeval times were not mere serfs, but
also respected members dwelling among their people, or as Locke
would say, " tenants in common," [1] who regulated their affairs
by collective customs, rights and responsibilities. They were
not atomised, propertyless proletarians, but partners of agrarian
co-operative associations, imbued with traditions of their ancient
liberties and with sentiments of communal life, and looking upon
enclosures as private appropriations of what was common, and
on the lords as usurpers,—indeed, the verb " to enclose " means
to create private property. They felt very keenly the encroachments upon their common rights and, when the Revolt broke out,
they demanded the return of their old charters of liberty and
the restoration of their rights of common, pasture, and piscary ; [2]
they destroyed hedges and fences.[3] True, they did not formulate
any communist programme, for they were not suffering from
a system of private property, but from encroachments upon
their common rights, and against those encroachments they
rebelled. It was a rebellion of obsolescent communistic associations [4] against the tightening legal and commercial grip of
lords and abbots. Theoretically, it was a rebellion of *ius naturale*
against *ius civile*, or friar against lawyer.

    In the fourteenth century, the English peasantry were not
without teachers and prophets. An age that saw Langland's
ethical writings, the Wycliffite Bible translation, and Chaucer's
poetry, must have been an age of a mentally active commonalty.
The men who prepared the minds of the people for such gifts
were Minorites, " poor priests," and other friars who toured the
country, or former friars and monks, who, impelled by Franciscan
doctrines, or swayed by a zeal for religious reform, found no

---

[1] John Locke, *On Civil Government*, II., c. 5.
[2] Walsingham, *Gesta Abbatum*, III., pp. 308, 311, 306.
[3] A. Réville, p. xli.
[4] Compare, however, Trevelyan, *Age of Wycliffe*, 1909, p. 197,
and Oman, *Great Revolt of* 1381, pp. 51-2, where contrary views
are expressed.

room in the Church for their ideals and aims. Some of them preached communism as the economic frame of society nearest to godliness, and all of them sympathised with the oppressed labouring population, and desired to see a communal and democratic peasantry, freed from the encroachments of commercialised temporal and spiritual lords. It was an age of agitation, brought about by an alliance of an intellectual proletariat with the dissatisfied labouring masses.[1] From Oxford as the intellectual and spiritual centre the light was spread by the friars to the open fields.[2] The burden of their sermons was undoubtedly the social ethics of Primitive Christianity, and of patristic and Minorite doctrines. All of them must have known S. Isidore's definition of natural law.

> " They preach of Plato and prove it by Seneca,
> That all things under heaven ought to be in common."

So writes Langland,[3] who condemns such preaching to the lewd, for Moses taught, Thou shalt not covet thy neighbour's things. The author of *Piers Ploughman* was anti-communistic ; he anticipated Protestantism far more consistently than Wycliffe, inasmuch as he was more individualistic. With great care he avoided all references in favour of communism, as may be seen from the following passage :

> Water, air, fire, and wit—these four
> The heavenly Father gave to all in common.[4]

The four elements were, of course, water, air, fire and earth. Instead of earth Langland puts wit, apparently with the purpose of not lending his authority to agrarian communism. Still, the protests of Langland against communism may serve as evidence of the widespread communistic agitation. How widespread it was among the intellectuals may be gauged by a curious variant in one of the manuscripts of Britton. Here is a case of a cleric

[1] Thomas Wright, *Pol. Poems and Songs*, I., Introd., p. lx.
[2] G. A. Little, *Gray friars of Oxford*, pp. 63–4.
[3] *Piers Ploughman*, B. xx. 273–76, quoted by Trevelyan, p. 198. For other proofs of communistic teachings of friars, compare Little, p. 84.
[4] *Piers Ploughman*, B. vii. 52–3.

playing a trick upon a lawyer. In Bracton's *De legibus* (i. 31) it is said, " All men, even serfs, are free by natural law, but civil right or the law of nations detracts from natural right, and men may be serfs under the law of nations." Britton, probably enlarging upon Bracton, declares, in his Norman French, that originally all men were free and held all things in common and lived according to the law of nature, but in ancient times (*en grant antiquité*) freedom was changed into bondage.[1] In the Manuscript F. of Britton, copied late in the fourteenth century, the words " *en grant antiquité* " are changed into " *en grant iniquité.*" It is Ockham's " *propter iniquitatem.*" Such were the sentiments of the time.

2.—JOHN WYCLIFFE

What Ockham strove to accomplish for Western and Central Europe his disciple, John Wycliffe (*d.* 1384), set himself to do for England. The stage was of smaller dimensions, the degree of economic development less advanced, and the mental capacities of the actor were less extensive. Wycliffe was, however, no mere epigonus of his revered master.[2] To the armoury of scholastic speculation on communism he added new arguments—the feudal concepts of possession and lordship. His sources of knowledge were the same as those of his predecessors—namely, the Scriptures, the Fathers, the Corpus Iuris Canonici, and Aristotle. He collects his materials with the view of solving the vital problems of his country and his age, and weaves them into a certain whole, the cohesive forces of which are an intensely ethical conception of Christianity and an overpowering interest in the welfare of England. In Wycliffe we touch English soil of the fourteenth and fifteenth century. The dissolution of feudalism gave rise to two great questions : first, How to establish a central, national authority to take the place of the feudal, decentralised order ; and, secondly, How to protect the peasantry. In his attempts to formulate an answer Wycliffe met with two

[1] Britton, ed. Nichols, I. 32 (31).
[2] Netter of Walden, *Fasc. Ziz.*, Shirley's Introd., p. liii.

difficulties. Mediaeval theology, dominated partly by *ius naturale* and partly by Hildebrandian traditions, regarded civil dominion as tainted with iniquity. This taint had to be removed if England were to emerge from the chaos consequent upon the decay of the feudal order. The second difficulty was the growing helplessness of the village community and the dispossession of the peasantry. It was no small matter for a theologian and scholastic like Wycliffe to set his face against the exhortations of the prophet Samuel concerning kingship, or against S. Augustine's view that Empire had its origin in fratricide,[1] or, finally, against a fundamental doctrine of natural and divine law. No less difficult was the defence of the village community in the teeth of powerful social forces which were undermining it. In the midst of such mental perplexities the strong lead given by his famous countryman, William of Ockham, must have greatly comforted him. And he decided for kingship and for communism; in short, a social reform monarchy. A good king using his authority to protect the peasant communities was his ideal.

Like all his predecessors Wycliffe assumes that society at its origin lived in a state of innocence and communism; natural law governed its conduct. Absence of private property and civil government was thus the distinguishing feature of the state of nature. After the Fall of man *ius naturale* became insufficient; man's moral fibre weakened and needed an artificial support. Therefore, God set up civil dominion and entrusted it with the mission of fostering love among men. The best form of such dominion is government by Judges, as among the Israelites of old. Wherever such government is impossible kingship is the next best. Civil government is thus of divine origin, though it smacks of venial sin: *Dominium civile . . . sapit tamen veniale peccatum.*[2] But if it is combined with communism it may approach to the perfect state, to the state of innocence and fatherly rule.[3] In this way it becomes natural. Wycliffe's

---

[1] S. Augustine, *Civ. dei*, l. 15, c. 5, referred to in Willmann's *Geschichte des Idealismus*, II., p. 309.

[2] John Wycliffe, *De ecclesia*, c. 14, p. 321.

[3] *Civ. dom.* I., c. 14, p. 99.

mental bent is strongly towards justification of kingship, indeed, not only justification, but sanctification of kingship, and endowing it with the supremacy over the Church. His dictum, *Deus debet obedire diabolo*,[1] may perhaps be interpreted as directed against Pope Gregory VII., who in the epistle to Bishop Herman of Metz (1081) declares, as a matter of fact, that kings and dukes derived their principle from the prince of evil, while the Church was of divine origin,[2] therefore, kings must obey the Church. In his rather bold and too finely pointed epigram, Wycliffe essentially replies, the Church must obey the king. With regard to private property, however, he is, theoretically, a decided opponent. The division of possessions arose *ratione peccati* and the taint of sin was still attached to it.

And now comes the specific addition of Wycliffe—the feudal aspect of dominion and property. God is the supreme lord. In the Scriptures, the only infallible source of knowledge, God is called Lord. He is master of all things. He is the over-lord. In contradistinction to men who do not know how to bestow gifts, He grants His fiefs to the righteous only on condition of service. And He grants them directly, there being neither ecclesiastical nor lay intermediary between God and man. The kings are His bailiffs and all the possessors His vassals. As He grants His gifts to the righteous only, nobody can hold dominion or worldly goods who is in mortal sin or who is not in grace. *Nullus est dominus civilis, nullus est episcopus, nullus est prelatus, dum est in peccato mortali.*[3] Moreover, the possessions of the unrighteous were acquired by rapine, theft, robbery, and usurpation.[4] For only to those who are in grace everything is given, and they are the lords of the earth and the fulness thereof.[5] Now, all men ought to be righteous and in grace and, therefore, ought to be lords of the earth and the fulness thereof. But how could multitudes of men be lords of everything if not by holding everything in

---

[1] *Fasc. Ziz.*, p. 278.
[2] *Gregorii VII. Opera*, ed. Migne, tom. 147–8, epistola 21.
[3] *Fasc. Ziz.*, p. 280.
[4] *Civ. dom.* I., c. 5, p. 34, c. 14, p. 101.
[5] *Ib.*, c. 6, p. 41.

common ? *Ergo omnia debent esse communia.*[1] Only through communism can the multitudes, if righteous, be lords of everything and fulfil the supreme condition of lordship—service to one another. Communism does not infringe upon Christianity. The apostles held everything in common (Acts iv. 32). Communism is as superior to private property as universal truths are to particular truths ; Christ loves the human species as a whole more than particular men. It is true that Aristotle reasons against Plato's doctrines concerning community of goods,[2] but his reasonings hold good only as regards community of wives. His objection that communism weakened the Commonwealth, inasmuch as people cared more for their own than for common goods, amounts really to the statement that there are sinful people. It must, however, be denied that communism weakened the Commonwealth. For, the greater the number of people holding possession the greater their interest in the welfare of the Commonwealth. Community of interests leads to unity, and unity is strength. Communism, then, leads to the strengthening and not to the weakening of the Commonwealth. Possessions in common being thus morally best will be best cared for. Indeed, civil dominion combined with common possessions is natural and spiritual, while dominion based on private property is artificial and corruptible.[3]

Such are the views of Wycliffe concerning monarchy and property. It is evident that he makes his communism conditional upon a high moral state of society, upon the constant effort of man to check sinfulness and to attain to that degree of grace which would render him worthy of receiving the earth as a fief at the hands of the over-lord. His doctrines preclude all sedition, rebellion, violence, and even party and faction fights, as a means to realising communism, since civil government is of divine origin, and rebellion against it is *ipso facto* treason against the supreme lord, which is punished by the forfeiture of grace and escheat of possessions.

[1] *Civ. dom.* I., c. 14, p. 96. Compare Poole, *Mediaeval Thought*, c. x.
[2] Aristotle, *Politics*, II. 1.
[3] *Civ. dom.* I., c. 14, pp. 99–100.

However, the combination of righteousness as the condition of possession with the feudal principle as the basis of dominion gave rise to a difficulty which could not easily be set aside. And it was this—What if the holders of political and economic dominion are in mortal sin? Would not, under such circumstances, rebellion be in accordance with the intention of God? It was a problem which theological communists of a revolutionary and democratic temper might not have been inclined to answer in a feudal sense. And this was actually the case with John Ball.

3.—JOHN BALL

Wycliffe's attitude towards the Peasants' Revolt was similar. to, though less violent than, that of Martin Luther towards the German Bauernkrieg (1525); and John Hus would, in all probability, have taken up the same attitude towards the Taborite wars in Bohemia, had he lived to witness them. The chief leaders of the Reformation brought their reforming zeal to bear upon ecclesiastical and national affairs and left social grievances to be removed by the operation of ethical endeavour. The times were however out of joint, and the Reformation movement was in all three countries accompanied by social upheavals. The three reformers had their revolutionary counterparts in John Ball (d. 1381), Andrew Prokop, and Thomas Münzer respectively, who, as priests, started from the same theological premisses as the reformers, but were launched on revolutionary careers by their democratic conception of mediaeval communism. Legend or tradition makes Ball a disciple of Wycliffe, Münzer a disciple of Luther, while Prokop was actually a professed adherent of Hus. The simultaneous occurrence of strong movements for national and ecclesiastical reform and of violent social upheavals in England, Bohemia, and Germany, and the rise of similar minds as Wycliffe, Hus, and Luther on the one hand, and of Ball, Prokop, and Münzer on the other, are worthy of notice, indicating as they undoubtedly do a certain regularity of historical movements. In point of time England preceded Bohemia and Germany, while in point of intensity and thoroughness Bohemia and Germany outstripped England.

The question as to whether Ball was really the disciple of
Wycliffe, as Netter of Walden states,[1] is quite immaterial. The
social thoughts and sentiments which Ball disseminated among
the peasantry were truisms in mediaeval theology. The doctrines
concerning the natural state he could have learned from
patristic and scholastic as well as legal literature, and the denunciations of the wealth and corruption of the Church were quite
in keeping with the general tenets of the Franciscans, the complaints of the peasantry and the townspeople. The same applies
to Walsingham [2] and Knighton ; [3] as far as Ball's social doctrines
are concerned there is neither external nor internal evidence that
they had any special connection with Wycliffe. Many years
prior to the Peasants' Revolt Ball was occupied in inflaming the
peasantry against the lords temporal and spiritual, adding to
the social ferment that was rapidly growing since the Black
Death and the Statute of Labourers.

According to Knighton, Ball was a most famous preacher
among laymen and disseminated the word of God " in an insipid
manner, mixing tares with the wheat." His speeches were
indeed similar to those of Thomas Münzer. Liberty and equality,
democracy and communism formed their chief theme. Ball
looked back to the origins of society and asked :—

> " When Adam dalf and Eve span
> Who was then a gentilman ? "

In consonance with the theological doctrines of *ius naturale*
he went on to discourse upon the natural state. At the beginning
men were created equal by nature ; servitude was introduced
by unjust oppression of worthless men, contrary to the will of
God. For, if it had pleased God to create serfs He would have
constituted who should be serf and who lord. The people have
now been given the opportunity of breaking the servile yoke they
have borne for a long time ; if they chose they could enjoy the
liberty so long desired by them. Therefore, they should take
good courage and like wise husbandmen should cultivate their

[1] *Fasc. Ziz.*, p. 273. [2] Walsingham, *Historia Angl.*, II., pp. 32–3.
[3] Knighton, *Chronicon*, II., p. 131.

soil and extirpate and cut off the noxious weeds that choke the fruits of the earth. They should fell the great lords, judges, lawyers, and remove everybody from the land who was injurious to the community. Then they would have peace for the present and security for the future ; for when the mighty ones are cut off all men would enjoy equal freedom, and all have the same nobility and rank.[1]

The sample which Froissart handed down of the speeches of Ball contains both democracy and communism :—

" My good people,—Things cannot go well in England, nor ever will, until all goods are held in common, and until there will be neither serfs nor gentlemen, and we shall all be equal. For what reason have they, whom we call lords, got the best of us ? How did they deserve it ? Why do they keep us in bondage ? If we all descended from one father and one mother, Adam and Eve, how can they assert or prove that they are more masters than ourselves ? Except perhaps that they make us work and produce for them to spend ! They are clothed in velvets and in coats garnished with ermine and fur, while we wear coarse linen. They have wine, spices, and good bread, while we get rye-bread, offal, straw, and water. They have residences, handsome manors, and we the trouble and the work, and must brave the rain and the wind in the fields. And it is from us and our labour that they get the means to support their pomp ; yet we are called serfs and are promptly beaten if we fail to do their bidding." [2]

In abandoning ethical propaganda for political and revolutionary agitation, Ball went outside the bounds of the communistic and equalitarian doctrines of mediaeval theology. This was his real guilt. After the defeat of the insurrection his career came to a violent end. Less fortunate than Prokop and Münzer, who fell in battle, Ball died on the gallows at St. Albans.

---

[1] Walsingham, *Hist. Angl.*, II. 32–3.
[2] Froissart, *Collection des Chroniques*, VIII., c. 106.

IV

EXTINCTION OF MEDIAEVALISM

I.—AGE OF TRANSITION

THE Peasants' Revolt collapsed, its spiritual leaders died, the town was gaining over the village, and England was gradually drawn into the vortex of international commerce. The prosperity of Flanders and its woollen trade, the rise of Antwerp, the discoveries of the Portuguese, the fall of Constantinople, the discovery of America, displaced the commercial centre from the Mediterranean to the Atlantic. English wool, cloth, and tin appeared as important articles of commerce in the markets of the world, and English merchants began to think of sea-power.[1] The Wars of the Roses extinguished many of the old feudal families and with them much of the mediaeval spirit. The new nobility partook of the character of the time in which they were created, and " besides the merchants bred, many of the country nobles were possessed by the frenzy of trade." [2]

The nobility lost its military functions, the retainers were being disbanded and let loose, with nothing but noble passions and martial instincts, upon an unstable society. Enclosures, rent-raising, conversion of arable land into sheep-drifts went on apace ; [3] the dispossessed farmers flocked into the towns, and all Acts and measures for the purpose of staying the depopulation of the country proved ineffective. The discontent of the peasantry found vent in the Kentish rebellion of 1449, of which

[1] Thomas Wright, *Pol. Poems* (*Libell of English Policy*), **II.**, pp. 161–3.
[2] Atton and Holland, *King's Custom*, I., p. 47. *Cf.* Abram, *Social Life in the Fifteenth Century*, 1909.
[3] *Cf.* Gilbert Slater, *English Peasantry*, 1907 ; Gonner, *Common Land and Enclosure*, 1912, and particularly Tawney, *Agrarian Problem*, 1912.

Jack Cade assumed command. The insurgents, like their predecessors of 1381, were longing for a strong central authority
that would be able to protect their communal rights. Shakespeare, probably following tradition, puts into the mouth of Cade
the words :—

" I have thought upon it ; it shall be so. Away, burn all
the records of the realm ; my mouth shall be the parliament of
England. . . . And henceforward all things shall be in
common." (*Henry VI., Part II.*, act 4, scene 7.)

Hardly fifty years later occurred the rising of the Cornishmen,
and in 1516 Sir Thomas More wrote his communistic criticism
of the social conditions of his age.

Concurrently with the dissolution of the old agrarian organisation the gild system loosened and finally broke down in consequence of the growing economic inequality of the members of the
gilds.

Disintegration and confusion reigned everywhere, but at the
same time there was growing up a new social organism, heralded
by the New Learning, by a quest for more adequate truths, for
knowledge as a regenerator of faith and society. Shakespeare
puts into the mouth of Lord Say, who is pleading for his life with
Cade, the following memorable arguments :—

> " Large gifts have I bestow'd on learned clerks,
> Because my book preferr'd me to the King.
> And seeing ignorance is the curse of God,
> Knowledge the wing wherewith we fly to Heaven,
> Unless you be possessed with devilish spirits,
> You cannot but forbear to murder me."
>
> (*Ibid.*)

Oxford, the old centre of scholasticism, opened its gates to
Humanism. Waynflete, the founder of Magdalen College,
included, in 1482, in his scheme of University education,
natural and moral philosophy, rather than civil and canon law,
as studies auxiliary to theology.[1]

[1] H. A. Wilson, *Magdalen College*, pp. 15, 39–40.

2.—HUMANISM : FAITH AND REASON

Although Christian faith in Europe was not, as a rule, so overpowering as to stifle reason, it was intense enough to assume the hegemony. *Credo ut intelligam* was the rule, while *Intelligo ut credam* and *Credo quia absurdum est* were its poles. Greek wisdom was subordinated to Jewish wonder. The eyes of mediaeval Christianity were turned towards heaven as the real goal. The idea was the real. The mediaeval spirit was more in harmony with Realism than with Nominalism. With the growing bulk and importance of economic activities, commercial transactions, trade processes, and geographical discoveries, secular thought began to emancipate itself from theological authority. Christians did not cease to believe, but they drew a line of demarcation between theological and secular thought. God, soul, and immortality were subjects of faith and not of knowledge ; religion could not be reasoned upon or proved by syllogisms. This was the final outcome of English Nominalism—of the philosophy of Duns Scotus and Ockham. There was, then, no use in making reason the handmaid of faith, for the province of reason was the sensual world, and its method, as another Englishman, Roger Bacon, taught, was experiment. A theological dogma might be inadmissible in logic and yet true in religion. There was thus a double truth, which however by no means amounted to duplicity and evasion, but to a division of powers. The province of faith and the province of reason were sundered. A Christian could be intensely religious and his faith pure, while at the same time he was devoted to natural philosophy and worldly politics, making unlimited use of his reason in these matters.

A rationalist element entered the life of the Christian. Reason was no more a rebellious power to be bridled by faith, but a legitimate help to man in the ordering of his affairs. However, the division of powers was destined to lead to an antagonism of powers. Indeed, reason was soon called upon to assist man in the choice of good and evil. Ethics was rationalised. Finally, reason was endowed with creative powers ; right reason acting

through great educators, legislators, or " king-philosophers,"
could call into being perfect republics, virtuous and happy
nations, and correct the fateful effects of the Fall of man.

The Humanists hardly suspected such a development, but the
tendency was there and made itself manifest when they were
dealing with intricate problems of a secular nature. Unconscious
of any contradiction the Humanists were good Roman Catholics
and lovers of Greek philosophy and literature ; they could enjoy
both S. Augustine and Lucian ; they were adherents of papal
authority and adorers of reason. Erasmus could see in reason
the ultimate control of morality and live and die as a Roman
Catholic.[1] And Sir Thomas More suffered martyrdom for his
faith after having written the *Utopia*, an apotheosis of reason and
deistic ethics.

3.—THOMAS MORE

Theologian and humanist, student of S. Augustine and Plato
and Lucian, Catholic martyr and rationalistic philosopher, un-
compromising social critic and national statesman, such was Sir
Thomas More (*d.* 1535), one of the immortal sons of England
and one of the greatest figures in the history of Communism.
Erasmus of Rotterdam, in his well-known letter to Ulrich von
Hutten, relates that More at an early age studied Greek literature
and philosophy, worked later on a dialogue in which he defended
Plato's *Republic*, and devoted much pains to the study of the
Church Fathers. As a young man he delivered public lectures
on S. Augustine's *De civitate dei*, and even priests came to hear
him propounding the mysteries of the Christian faith.[2] Had
he elected to join an Order the choice would have fallen on the
Minorites. His bent for social criticism, combined with his
education in the household of Archbishop Morton, the statesman
and counsellor of King Henry VII., and, finally, his legal career,
gave him a thorough insight into the economic and national

---

[1] Also Erasmus was in favour of communism. He asks all true
Christians " to regard their goods as common property, for Christian
love knows no private property." Quoted by Roscher, *Geschichet
der National-Oekonomie in Deutschland*, p. 42.

[2] Erasmus of Rotterdam, *Epistolae*, 1642, l. 10, ep. 30.

problems of his time. More's capacity for unravelling economic questions is amply testified to by the mission he undertook at the instance of the London mercers to settle certain litigious cases between them and the Hanseatic merchants of the Steelyard, as well as by his participation in the embassy sent by King Henry VIII. to Antwerp for the purpose of adjusting the commercial relations between England and the Low Countries.[1]

No less important was More's acquaintance with the accounts of the discovery of America and the influence they exercised on his imagination. " In a little tract of four leaves . . . entitled *Mundus novus*, Vespucci gives an account of his second voyage, on which he started from Lisbon, May 14, 1501. . . . The voyage was past the Canary Islands to Cape Verde. In those regions—the voyager names them very vaguely—' the people live according to nature, and may be called Epicureans rather than Stoics. . . . Property they have none, but all things are in common. They live without a king, without any sovereignty, and every one is his own master.' . . . In the later treatise referred to by More, in which an account is given of the first four voyages of Vespucci (*quattuor Americi Vesputii Navigationes*) it is said, ' Gold, pearls, jewels and all other such like things, which in this Europe of ours we count riches, they think nothing of, nay, they utterly despise them.' " [2]

More did not in the least doubt the moral excellence of a population which was said to live in the state of nature, since as a student of patrology and jurisprudence he was familiar with *ius naturale*. In a letter to his friend, John Colet, Dean of St. Paul's, he is full of praise of the virtues of rural life ; " in the country, as opposed to town life, the face of the earth is smiling and the sight of the sky is a delight ; one sees nothing there but the bounteous gifts of nature and the sacred vestiges of inno-cence." [3] The state of nature appeared to him as the *status innocentiae*, and how closely that state is bound up with com-

[1] Thomas More, *Utopia*, ed. Lupton, 1895, pp. 72, 79. (All references given below to More's *Utopia* apply to this edition.)

[2] J. H. Lupton, Introd. to his edition of *Utopia*, p. xxxviii.

[3] Th. Stapleton, *Tres Thomæ*, Cologne, 1612, p. 164.

D

munism we know from the patristic and scholastic writings. In his *Utopia* he also refers several times to the law of nature and life according to nature.[1]

The influence of rising rationalism must also be noticed. More, writing to Gunnell, the domestic tutor of his children, on the importance and aim of education, tells him, " that from learning they ought to derive the most sublime lessons—piety towards God, benevolence towards men, modesty of heart, and Christian humility. . . . These I look upon as true and genuine fruits of learning ; and as I acknowledge that all learned do not attain to them, so I maintain that those who begin to study with this intention may easily obtain this happy result." More, like Hooker after him, was, however, too good a Christian to put reason and philosophy in the place of the fear of God and the divine commandments.[2]   His view of the relation between reason and faith he expressed in the *Utopia*, of whose scholars he said that " they join to the arguments of philosophy certain principles of religion without which they think reason of itself weak and imperfect " (p. 188).

4.—THE *UTOPIA* : CHARACTER AND PUBLICATION

More's *Utopia* is the application of the ethics and politics of the Church Fathers and the philosophy of Humanism to the greatest secular problem—the organisation of human society, and in particular to the social England of the age of transition from feudalism to commercialism, from rural economy to money economy, from associated and regulated activities to individual enterprise.   It is mediaeval in so far as it regards communism as more favourable to virtue than private property ; and it is differentiated from the early communist doctrines by the fact that, while the Church Fathers and schoolmen reasoned from abstract morality or a Scriptural text and deplored the vices of mankind which they regarded as the effects of the disappearance of the natural and divine state, More's point of departure was that

[1] More, *Utopia*, pp. 155, 190, 192.
[2] Compare Hooker, *Ecclesiastical Polity*, book 3, c. 8.

of a Catholic and patriotic statesman, who, after an examination into the actual conditions of his country, looked for a remedy to social reform.

The book is divided into two parts, the first exposing the actual social conditions of England, the second presenting a model communist society. The first is thus given to social criticism, embracing economics, politics, and criminology ; the second is a social reconstruction.

Its form is partly dialogue and partly narrative. Its scene is Antwerp and some unknown country in South America. The *dramatis personae* are : Raphael Hythloday, Peter Aegidius or Giles, and More himself. Raphael is represented as a keen sea-farer who is supposed to have accompanied Amerigo Vespucci on his voyages ; he is a scholar of a perfect Humanist type, thoroughly familiar with Greek literature and philosophy ; he desires neither wealth nor power, and is a thoroughgoing defender of communism. On his voyages he cares nought for mythical monsters and fantastic apparitions, but inquires into the social organisation of the discovered countries, for " to find citizens ruled by good and wholesome laws is an exceedingly rare and hard thing " (p. 33) ; furthermore, he is convinced that, " where possessions are private, where money is the measure of all things, it is hard and almost impossible that the commonwealth should have just government and enjoy prosperity " (p. 104). He is the discoverer of Utopia, on the advantages of which he discourses.

The second figure is Peter Giles, an enlightened merchant, a good Christian and citizen in the usual meaning of the word, knowing how to take care of himself and family ; he is satisfied with the laws of his country and does not believe " that there is better order in that new land than there is in the countries we know," and he thinks " that our commonwealth is more ancient than theirs " (p. 111), and, therefore, more likely to possess a larger measure of social experience than Utopia.

More himself intervenes sometimes in the course of Raphael's narrative. He appears to agree in every detail with the social criticism, but not always with the possibilities of communism.

He generally enters on the scene when communism seems to offer some difficulties and is, therefore, open to objections, or where the ideal is too high for the realities of life so that a compromise between the ideal and the actual might be more practicable.

On the whole, it may be said that Raphael represents the most uncompromising aspects of communism ; he also dominates the stage. Peter Giles defends the present order, but there seems to be so little in favour of it that his part is very subordinate. More is critical, seeing both the shortcomings of the existing society and the difficulties of integral communism ; he is not a communist, but a social reformer, favouring a gradual amelioration of society and the application of all that is practicable in communism. His real attitude towards the communistic ideal is expressed in the closing sentences of *Utopia* : " In the meantime, though I cannot agree to all things that he (Raphael) said . . . I must needs express and grant that there are many things in the Utopian commonwealth which in our country I rather wish than hope for " (308–9).

As Erasmus relates in his letter to Hutten mentioned above, More first composed the second part of *Utopia* in his leisure hours while employed on his mission at Antwerp ; soon after he added the first part, which he wrote down as an improvisation, " so well stored was his mind and so great his skill in composition." He wrote it in Latin and published it at the end of 1516 in Louvain under the title *De optimo reipublicae statu, deque nova insula Utopia.* Within less than two years of its first appearance in print it was republished in Basle (1518), then in Paris (1520), and from time to time new editions have been issued in Great Britain, Germany, France, and America. The first English translation was made and published by Raphe Robynson, a London goldsmith, in 1551. But the German, Italian, and French editions preceded the English translation, and are still often reprinted, so that More's *Utopia* is one of the best known books in the literature of the world.

5.—THE *UTOPIA*: SOCIAL CRITICISM

(*a*) *Rich and Poor.*—There is no trace of equity or justice in any country which gives great rewards and fees to gentlemen, goldsmiths (bankers), usurers, and such like who do nothing or are merely the flatterers or devisers of vain pleasures of the rich, and on the other hand makes no provision for the poor ploughmen, colliers, labourers, carters, ironsmiths, carpenters, and other workers, without whom no commonwealth could exist. The lot of the working people is even harder than that of the beasts of burden ; poverty is the recompense of their toil when they are strong enough to be in employment, and destitution and misery when old age or illness renders them incapable of work. And the laws are against them. Keeping all this in mind it is impossible not to perceive that what we call a commonwealth to-day is but a conspiracy of the rich to procure their own well-being. Money and pride are the roots of all evil. All crime would die if money perished ; indeed, poverty itself, which only seems to arise from lack of money, would disappear if money disappeared. The rich undoubtedly perceive all this and would be prepared to change the constitution of society, but Pride, the queen of all mischief, hinders them ; she measures her own felicity by other people's misery (pp. 300–6). Another source of mischief, peculiar to England, are the enclosures and the conversion of arable land into pasture. The sheep, once so meek and tame, have become wild and devouring ; they consume and destroy the peasant and his land. Where the finest wool is grown there gentlemen and abbots leave no soil for tillage ; they are no more satisfied with the revenue, leisure, and pleasure that husbandry used to afford, but desire untold wealth ; insatiable covetousness causes them to depopulate the country and fill it with sheep ; and they do so by fraud and violence, legal or illegal. The decrease of tillage has for its effect a dearth of victuals ; and the rise in the price of wool makes it impossible for the poor clothmaker to continue his employment. The wealth of the country is being engrossed by a small number of persons.

(*b*) *Crime and Punishment.*—The covetousness of a few has

greatly injured the well-being of this island. The great dearth of victuals causes men to restrict their household, to curtail hospitality and dismiss servants. The nobles disband their retainers—those idle and boisterous fellows who have been used to live on the labour of others. The enclosers restrict employment and render many useful labourers idle. Hence theft, robbery, vagabondage, and all manner of crime increase. The unemployed must either beg or steal, and despite all severity of punishment crime does not diminish. The nation brings up thieves and vagabonds and then punishes them. Is this justice? Great and horrible punishments are meted out to thieves, while provision ought to have been made to enable them to get their living, so that no man should be driven to the extreme necessity, first to steal and then to be hanged for it (pp. 44–58).

(c) *Reform or Revolution.*—But is there any use in proposing reform to kings? Or, in other words, may a communist enter a non-communist government? Raphael replies, No, while More does not exclude the possibility of promoting the welfare of the realm by advising kings, " for you must not leave a ship in a tempest because you cannot rule the storm; nor must you tender advice derived from new ideals which no king, except a king-philosopher—who, however, needs no advice—would accept, but you must handle the matter subtly and diplomatically so that if you are not able to achieve the best you may at least prevent the worst; for it is not possible for all things to be well, unless all men are good, which cannot be expected for a good many years yet " (pp. 99–100). But the revolutionary Raphael replies: Princes and governments do mainly care for warlike matters— for conquests, territorial expansion, great armies, and full treasuries. And their counsellors aid them in those schemes, therefore they are tolerated; they flatter the royal self-conceit, praise the princely wisdom, and oppress and tax the people for the sake of aggrandisement of the princes. What could a social philosopher achieve in the teeth of such royal councils? He would simply be made a laughing-stock of, or worse, he would become either as bad as the government, or the people would think him so, and thus learn to despise communist philosophy.

Would a king listen to the advice of a counsellor who told him that the people gave him the crown not for his own sake but for the welfare of all ?   Or would he perceive the truth that his kingdom, small though it be, is already too big to be ruled by one man ?   No, it is no good to be subtle in such matters (pp. 80–95). All attempt at palliating evil by craftiness and reform measures must lead to nought.   The only remedy is a radical change of the whole social system.   Plato acted rightly in refusing to make laws for a country where private property reigns supreme.   Such countries may multiply laws until no lawyer could count them, and yet they will never enjoy prosperity, peace, and happiness.   For, as long as private property exists the greatest and best part of the nation will be condemned to over-work, poverty and misery.   Palliative laws may cure one part of the disease, but will at the same time aggravate the sore of another part, so that the help afforded to one will cause harm to another, for nothing can be given to Peter without taking from Paul.   To this harangue in favour of catastrophic communism More replies that communism, in withdrawing the incentive of personal gain and thus the motive of industry, might lead to the neglect of work and to general impoverishment, and when the pressure of poverty is felt and there is no law to defend the means of production and life, will not there of necessity be continual strife, enmity, and bloodshed ? (pp. 100–11). To this question, in support of which More could have quoted Aristotle and theo-logical *ius naturale*, Raphael gives no direct reply, but refers More to the example of the Utopians.   At first sight it might seem that Raphael's reply involves a *petitio principi*, in reality, how-ever, it is based on the philosophy of Humanism, which is that trained reason aided by religion and good laws will make man virtuous, dutiful, and active.   Raphael also points out that More's objection is taken from social conditions based on private property which never admits good laws and is at cross-purposes with religion and right reason, while the minds of the Utopians have been trained by a communist system of life (p. 100).

6.—THE *UTOPIA*: SOCIAL RECONSTRUCTION

(*a*) *The Republic and its founder.*—Utopus, a king-philosopher, conquered a rugged and rainless peninsula called Abraxa and changes it into a prosperous island which henceforth bears his name and merits to be called Eutopia, the abode of felicity (pp. 118, xciii.). The inhabitants, originally poor, rude, and rent by religious dissensions, are brought to a state of perfection in humanity, manners, virtue, learning, and material prosperity that surpasses anything that would be found among the other nations of the earth (pp. 132–4). The means that Utopus applied were communism and education, the latter in its broader sense as understood by the rationalists ; it includes not only schooling proper, but the training and experiences which the surroundings, occupations, customs, and laws afford. The island of Utopia consists of fifty-four shires, with a spacious and magnificent city in each as the centre of administration, public education, scholarship, handicrafts, markets, store-houses, and foreign commerce ; the hospitals are on the outskirts of the cities. The inhabitants have all the same language, manners and laws, and this similarity promotes peace and harmony. None of the shires contains less than twenty miles of land, and none has any desire to extend its boundaries, for the people regard themselves as mere tillers of the soil rather than its proprietors. In the centre of the republic is the capital city, Amaurote, the seat of the National Assembly (pp. 119–20).

(*b*) *The Constitution.*—The Republic is a democratic federation of autonomous shires. The laws are few, yet sufficient ; the inhabitants know them well and do not suffer subtle and crafty interpretations (p. 234). The Central Government is a Senate or Council consisting of 162 members, three members for each shire, who meet annually at Amaurote to discuss the common affairs of the nation (p. 119). The Senate has sometimes to settle unsolved questions of the local bodies (p. 138) ; they also keep account of the demand and supply of the commodities, so that nothing shall lack in the Commonweal (pp. 169–70). The real management of the country is, however, in the hands of the governments of the shires.   Each shire consists of 6,000 families or farms ; each family of not less than forty members and two bondmen is under the rule of a *pater-* and *materfamilias*.   Every thirty families elect annually their Phylarch or Syphogrant or head bailiff ; every ten Phylarchies or 300 families elect their Chief Phylarchs or Tranibors.   The Phylarchs of the shires, 200 in number, elect by ballot the Prince or Chief Magistrate of the shire.   The Phylarchs are elected annually ; the Chief Phylarchs likewise, but are generally re-elected ; the Chief Magistrate is elected for life, removable only on suspicion of striving after tyranny.   The Chief Phylarchs and the Chief Magistrate form the Council of the Shire ; they meet, as a rule, every third day and invite two of the Phylarchs to their meetings.   Public affairs cannot, under the penalty of death, be discussed outside the Council or the election house of the Phylarch (pp. 135–138).

(c) *Trades and Occupations.*—Agriculture is the basis of the Commonweal.   There is no person, male or female, who has no expert knowledge of it.   Agricultural instruction, theoretical and practical, is compulsory.   Every year a certain number of townspeople change places with farmers, so that city and village should keep in touch with each other.   Besides husbandry every inhabitant learns one of the handicrafts necessary for the work of the Commonweal—clothmaking, building, smithing, and carpentering ; as a rule, everybody is brought up in his father's trade.   There is no other trade besides those mentioned, the life in Utopia being simple and knowing no luxury.

(d) *Duty and hours of labour.*—The chief function of the Phylarch is to see that the citizens shall perform their duty of labour.   Idlers are expelled from the republic.   The hours of labour are six per diem.   Where all labour there is no overwork for anyone.   Only illness, old age, and devotion to study and science give exemption from labour (pp. 141–6).   Any craftsman or farmer who by devotion to learning in his leisure hours shows that he could be more useful to the community by study is promoted to the order of the scholars (pp. 146–8).

(e) *The bondmen.*—All toilsome and unclean work of the Commonweal is done by the bondmen, who are either prisoners duly

convicted of heinous offences which in other countries are punished
with death, or poor labourers from foreign lands. The first are
treated with severity, while the latter are gently treated, and are
allowed to leave whenever they like and are not sent away
empty-handed (pp. 161, 221–2).

(f) *Family and social life.*—Monogamy is strictly enforced,
and adultery is punished with most grievous bondage. Also
ante-nuptial chastity is strongly insisted upon. Matrimony is
in their eyes so solemn and holy an institution that man and
woman who are about to enter it should know all the circumstances. They have therefore a custom that a virtuous matron
shows the woman naked to the wooer, and a wise man exhibits
the wooer naked to the woman. The Utopians are given the
opportunity of taking their meals in common. For this purpose
there are in the residences of the Phylarchs large halls where
wholesome food is prepared. Every meal begins with reading
something that refers to good manners and virtue. During
the meals the elders hold conversation on serious, but not unpleasant subjects, and the younger members are encouraged to
express their opinions. The dinners are short, the suppers somewhat longer, and these are followed by music, games, and all kinds
of harmless entertainments. At eight o'clock they all go to bed
to rise at four. The morning and, generally, the leisure hours
are devoted to public lectures, study, and play (pp. 160–6).

(g) *War.*—The Utopians regard war as gross and cruel injustice.
Yet they undergo the discipline of war in order to be able to
defend themselves or to help their friends to repel invasion or to
deliver any people from tyranny (pp. 243–4). They likewise
declare war upon any nation who, possessing vacant land in
abundance, prohibit the immigration of the surplus population
of Utopia who desire to cultivate it and to form a colony there ;
such a prohibition they regard as a violation of the law of nature
(p. 155).

(h) *Education and learning.*—The constitution of the Commonweal chiefly aims at saving time from the necessary labours and
giving it to the free cultivation of the mind. Herein they
suppose the happiness of this life to consist (p. 152). Education

of the children is general and compulsory. They study music, logic, arithmetic, and geometry (p. 184), astronomy, and physical geography (p. 187). Children who show special aptitude for learning are exempted from bodily labour and are allowed to devote themselves to study ; they form the Order of the Learned.

(*i*) *Moral philosophy.*—Good and evil, virtue and happiness, soul and body, immortality and God's kindness to man are much discussed by the Utopians. Their principles are :—the soul is immortal and created for happiness by God's kindness ; virtue is rewarded and vice punished after this life. These purely religious truths, which are beyond reasoning, they think meet to prove by arguments from reason. The chief discussion, however, turns upon happiness. They think that it consists of pleasure as differentiated from lust, for it is only good and honest pleasure which they believe to produce happiness. They are opposed to the Stoics, who attribute happiness to a virtue that implies self-torture and abnegation. Life according to nature and reason they interpret as meaning a life that produces joy by good actions to others and to oneself (pp. 187–92). They distinguish between true and false pleasures. True pleasures are those which give intelligence to the mind, satisfaction to moral conscience, or which arise from the contemplation of truth and art, listening to good music, recollection of good deeds in the past, and hope of future happiness. False pleasures arise from vainglory, titles, fineries, so-called precious metals and stones, gambling, hunting, and all cruel pastimes that cause pain to beast or man.

(*j*) *Religion.*—The Utopians enjoy complete freedom of religious worship. By this means Utopus healed the wounds caused to the nation by religious dissensions. It enabled them to discuss their religious differences, carefully to weigh each other's arguments, and to arrive at a certain unity as to the essence of religion. The great majority worship under various forms one sovereign spiritual power, the Creator and Ruler of the universe, the initial and final cause of all things. Atheists, however, are not regarded as good citizens.

(*k*) *Summing up.*—Utopia is the only commonwealth which

deserves that name. It is in reality a common weal and public wealth, In all other places they speak of common wealth while everybody is trying to secure his own private wealth at the expense of his neighbour. In Utopia, where nothing is private, everybody cares for the common affairs. In other countries where nobody is secure against poverty and hunger, though the national wealth may be very considerable, everybody is compelled to make provision for himself and disregard the common interests of all. Conversely, where all things are common, nobody has reason to fear lest he should starve, so long as the public storehouses are well supplied with commodities. Therefore it is the interest of everybody to care for the community. In such a republic everybody is rich, though nobody possesses anything. This form of a republic will endure for ever, for by destroying pride and money the Utopians have uprooted the main causes of ambition, sedition, and all those vices which in other countries lead to internecine struggles, civil wars, and finally to the destruction or decay of nation and Empire (pp. 267–307).

7.—RISE OF INDIVIDUALISM

In 1549, fourteen years after the execution of More, half of the English peasantry were in insurrection. They rose up in arms to vindicate their natural right to the soil and to the fruits it yielded to their labour. It was the last great protest, the final struggle on a national scale, against the destruction of the village communities. Their defeat marks the turning point in the history of English mediaeval communism.

Robert Crowley, vicar, printer, archdeacon, and zealous Protestant, writing in 1550 on the prevalent spirit of sedition and its causes, puts the case very clearly both of the peasantry and the masters of the land and money :—

" The great farmers, graziers, rich butchers, lawyers, merchants, gentlemen, lords, and I cannot say who more," says the peasant, " men that have no name because they are doers of all things where gain is to be had . . . they take our houses over our heads, buy our lands out of our hands, raise our rents,

levy great (yea, unreasonable) fines, they enclose our commons
. . . and to go to the cities we have no hope, for we hear
that these unsatiable beasts have there all in their hands."

The lord replies :—

" The peasant knaves . . . will have no gentlemen, they
will have all men like themselves, they will have all things in
common. . . . They will appoint what rent we shall take
for our grounds. They will cast down our parks and lay our
pastures open. We will teach them to know their betters ;
and because they would have all commune, we will leave them
nothing." [1]

Bishop Latimer's sermons of that period are no less outspoken
concerning the conflicts between the agricultural population and
the lords of the land, and are imbued with great love for the
people.

That conflict must have exhibited strong communistic tendencies, since both Crowley and Latimer are at pains to repudiate
communism and only ask of the lords of the land to exercise
Christian charity and patriotic virtue towards the peasantry
as the stay of the nation. Crowley says, " I do not agitate the
people to make all things common . . . but the possessioners
must consider themselves stewards rather than lords over their
possessions." [2] And Latimer, in his fifth sermon on the Lord's
Prayer, on the verse " Give us this day our daily bread," exhorts
the people to remember that the word " our " does not mean
communism. And he adds :—

" Here I have occasion to speak of the proprieties of things ;
for I fear if I should leave it so some of you would report me
wrongfully, and affirm that all things should be common. I
say not so. . . . If all things were common there could be
no theft and so this commandment ' Thou shalt not steal,' were
in vain The laws of the realm make *meum* and *tuum*, mine
and thine. If I have things by those laws then I have them.
But this you must not forget that S. Paul says, ' Relieve the
necessity of those which have need.' Things are not so common

[1] Robert Crowley, *Select Works*, pp. 133–43.
[2] *Ibid.*, pp. 156 *sqq.*

that we ought to distribute them unto the poor . . . but we ought to help one another."

Latimer uses the same argument as Langland ; moreover, his learning is wide enough to include the opinion of S. Augustine that property has been established by civil law. He reminds the people that in the time of the apostles the believers did distribute their property among the poorer brethren and had all things in common, but he interprets this as an exceptional measure.

On the whole, with the rise of Protestantism the clear Scriptural text of the Ten Commandments prevailed over the communistic traditions of Primitive Christianity, monastic orders, and scholastic *ius naturale*. The work begun by the author of *Piers Ploughman* was accomplished by Bishop Latimer. Communism lost its sanction in Church and State, and took refuge with the extreme wing of Nonconformity, revolutionary rationalism, and working class organisations, while society at large moved towards individualism, whose first manifestation was the Elizabethan Age—an age of pioneers, men of keen initiative. Its great interpreters, Spenser and Shakespeare, were both anti-communist and anti-democratic. Spenser, in his *Faery Queen*, matches Artegall, the champion of true justice and skilled in righteous lore, against the communist Giant, who, standing on a rock near the sea, is telling the vast crowd that, with the huge pair of scales held in his hands, he would weigh equally all the world, for he saw that all was unequal and that the elements of Nature as well as the men in society were encroaching upon each other's share. He undertook to mend these things—

> " In sort as they were formèd anciently
> And all things would reduce unto equality."

The people liked to hear him discourse upon this subject and

> " Therefore the vulgar did about him flock,
> And cluster thick unto his leasings vain,
> Like foolish flies about a honey-crock,
> In hope by him great benefit to gain,
> And uncontrollèd freedom to obtain."

Artegall, seeing the mischief the Giant was causing, upbraided him for misleading the people since " All change is perilous, and all chance unsound." Upon which the Giant replies :—

> " Were it not good that wrong were then surceast,
> And from the most that some were given to the least !
>
> Therefore I will throw down these mountains high,
> And make them level with the lowly plain ;
> These tow'ring rocks, which reach unto the sky,
> I will thrust down into the deepest main,
> And, as they were, them equalize again.
> Tyrants that make men subject to their law,
> I will suppress, that they no more will reign,
> And lordlings curb, that commons overawe ;
> And all the wealth of rich men to the poor will draw."

Artegall succeeds in throwing the Giant into the sea, whereupon the people rise to revenge the blood of their leader and saviour.

> " For certain loss of so great expectation ;
> For well they hopèd to have got great good,
> And wondrous riches by his innovation."
>
> *(Faery Queen*, book 5, canto 2.)

Shakespeare deals in a similar manner with Jack Cade and the lower orders generally. Caliban, the slave or personification of Labour, is a spiritless braggart, an easy prey to ignorant adventurers ; Gonzalo, an inefficient, though noble-hearted statesman and humanist, whose description of Utopia turns out to be " merry fooling " (*Tempest*, Act 2, sc. 1). It was the spirit of the age. The labouring population was defeated and communism discredited. Its place was taken by Government action and social reform—the Elizabethan Poor Law Reform, which was much more than mere relief of destitution, for it aimed at prevention of destitution and promoting the efficiency of the productive capacities of the labouring classes.

V

CIVIL WAR AND GLORIOUS REVOLUTION

I.—RISE OF SCIENCE : NEW ATLANTIS

THE reigns of Henry VIII., Edward VI., and Mary were anything but favourable to the growth of modern civilisation. The painful birth of the Reformation out of a welter of violent religious fluctuations and baffling cross-purposes, the confiscations and cruelties and futilities of the rulers, the debasement of the coinage, the conspiracies attendant upon absolutism, impeded thought and enterprise, and kept down the energies of the nation. With the accession of Elizabeth, the triumph of the Reformation, the sack of Antwerp by the Spaniards, and the destruction of the Armada, the pent-up forces of all that was alive in England sped forth with the freshness and vigour of youth and ushered in the English Renascence—the prologue of modern England. The spirit of invention and discovery, of experiment and enterprise, the desire for sea-power and political freedom increasingly took hold of the English mind. Mediaevalism was expiring ; Francis Bacon came to bury scholasticism and heralded the advent of the Kingdom of Science, of practical work and production of wealth. His *Novum Organum* is sober positivism ; his *Nova Atlantis* is idealised scientific practice.

The *New Atlantis*, as far as its form is concerned, was undoubtedly suggested to Bacon by More's *Utopia* ; but with this the similarity ends. Bacon looks for the happiness of mankind chiefly to applied natural philosophy and productive work, More to social reform and religious ethics. These two conceptions are still at war with each other, yet the happiness of man on earth depends on the combination of both.

In New Atlantis, an island in the South Seas, a wise lawgiver established a happy and prosperous kingdom on the basis of applied science. Its centre is Solomon's House or College of Six Days, situated in the capital, Bensalem, and it aims at gaining " knowledge of causes and secret motions of things, and the enlarging of the bounds of human empire to the effecting of all things possible." [1]   It contains preparations and instruments for all kinds of physical and technological experiments ; deep caves for the investigation of the innermost of the earth, high towers for the study of the air and its phenomena ; laboratories for the experimental production of organic and inorganic matter as well as for the study of medicine ; agronomical stations ; shops for mechanical arts and manufacturing processes ; furnaces for the production of all degrees of heat ; halls for demonstrations in light and sound. " We have also engine-houses, where are prepared engines and instruments for all sorts of motions. . . . We imitate the flight of the birds, and have ships and boats for going under water." This college of science and technology sends also missions to foreign countries to study the progress of the world, it convenes meetings and conferences to discuss past achievements and new experiments ; it has its theorists who " raise the experimental discoveries into observations, axioms, and aphorisms." The inhabitants of this happy scientific Utopia adore the inventors and discoverers. " Upon every invention of value we erect a statue to its originator and give him a liberal and honourable reward." Their religious service consists of praising God for His marvellous works, and of imploring His aid and blessing for the illumination of their labours and turning them into good and holy uses. Their ethics appear to be the result of scientific training and self-respect ; chastity is regarded as an economy of force, and self-respect the bridle of vice.

New Atlantis is, in short, a model of scientific organisation of production, a commonwealth which knows how to honour inventors, discoverers, technologists, and scientists, the real creators of economic value. From the laboratories of the College of Six Days, through the multiple activities of applied science and the marvellous development of the productive forces, came

[1] Lord Bacon's *Essays*, etc. (Bohn's Library, ed. 1907), p. 297.

B

the solution of the social problem. They banished poverty by making the production of wealth easy.

Looked at from this point of view the *New Atlantis* is one of the most important contributions to the history of social science. But it is essentially materialistic, inasmuch as it presupposes human happiness to be the result of a general diffusion of wealth. It anticipates, however, the speculations of some of the acutest minds of the nineteenth century.

2.—RATIONALISM AND SOCIAL CONTRACT

The bounds which Humanism had set between the spheres of faith and reason were removed in the seventeenth century. Reason encroached upon the kingdom of faith, and in moments of revolutionary exaltation it was adored. During the Civil War the True Levellers worshipped reason, though in a less spectacular manner than the Jacobins were to do in the French Civil War. Philosophers like Locke and Leibnitz argued for religion on account of its conformity with the dictates of reason. Theological authority faded away before the glaring light of reason and the law of nature. Moral philosophy, which was in the century of Waynflete, More, and Hooker an auxiliary to theology, gained the upper hand. Mr. Worldly Wiseman had the audacity to advise Christian not to continue his tedious and health-destroying pilgrimage to the holy mountain, but to go to the village of Morality where dwelled a gentleman, Mr. Legality. In the eyes of austere Bunyan moral philosophy was pagan or heretic. It is none the less a historical fact that the transition from mediaevalism to modern times was everywhere marked by a subordination of theology to moral philosophy. As soon as faith failed to supply adequate motives for social discipline and public peace, another basis of morality was sought and, for a time, found in philosophic speculation. Francis Bacon had a fine glimmer of this crisis in human thought when he said, " Moral philosophy took with the pagans (*ethnicis*) the place of theology," [1] or rather mythology. So it was also in Christian Europe. Instead of the folios of *Summae theologicae* which every great Schoolman felt

[1] Francis Bacon, *Novum Organum*, I. 79.

bound to write, treatises on jurisprudence and moral philosophy appeared, dealing with ethics, law, particularly natural law, then with politics and economics. It thus embraced the science of morality, law, government, and wealth. Economics was originally the least and the last branch of the tree of knowledge of good and evil, but was destined to become, with the Industrial Revolution, the first and most important. The period which separates Hugo Grotius from Adam Smith clearly shows this development.

The soul of moral philosophy was *ius naturale*, which is, as we know, pure ethics in a pseudo-historic guise. Its most pronounced characteristic was the doctrine concerning the absence of private property and civil government in the original state of man. Mediaeval communistic and political thought rested on it. The final outcome of these mediaeval speculations was that personal monarchy had a divine origin and was therefore legitimate, while private property was tainted with sin. Modern English civilisation was now going to make a new use of natural law. Its material and mental conditions now demanded a reversal of the scholastic conclusions, declaring personal monarchy to be a usurpation, and private property legitimate and sacred. This task was carried out by moral philosophers, mostly Protestant jurists and political thinkers. And they did it by making the social contract and the labour value theory an integral part of moral philosophy.

The idea of contract was in the older *ius naturale* only in its incipient stage. For tribal society knew nothing of contract, its social relations having been regulated by authority and tradition. Mediaeval society had only the germ of it; apart from the relations between overlord, lord, and vassal which were supposed to rest on agreement, the great mass of the population were born into a certain status and died in it, without ever having had any chance of ordering their conditions and relations by negotiation or discussion. It was different in towns and cities. Their inhabitants settled there individually and formed corporations, gilds, clubs, and other organisations by voluntary agreements. With the growing complexity of trade and commerce, the transactions between the inhabitants became numerous and they settled them by contracts.   And in the same proportion as town life began to dominate the life of the nation, and the political centre of gravity moved from the manor to the city, the *status* gave way to the *contractus*.[1]   Custom, tradition, authority ceased to form the cohesive and vital force of society, and the concept of agreement, compact, and contract took their place.

We have previously noticed the striking arguments of William of Ockham as to private property and civil government having had their origin in the consent of those whose interests demanded such a change.   Consent means, of course, agreement, or express or tacit contract.   Richard Hooker argues also in the same manner with regard to civil dominion :—

" There being no impossibility in Nature considered by itself, but that men might have lived without any public regiment. Howbeit, the corruption of our nature being presupposed, we may not deny but that the Law of Nature doth now require of necessity some kind of regiment," for envy, strife, contention, and violence grew among men.   " To take away all such grievances, injuries, and wrongs, there was no way but by growing into composition and agreement amongst themselves, by ordaining some kind of government public, and by yielding themselves subject thereunto . . . and they gave their common consent all to be ordered by some whom they should agree upon. . . . So that, in a word, all public regiment seemeth eventually to have arisen from deliberate advice, consultation, and composition between men, judging it convenient and behoveful."[2]   Hooker does not apply his contract theory to property ; his view appears to be that, civil government once constituted, civil laws regulate the economic relations between men.   He is, however, decidedly of opinion that the contract between subjects and sovereign may be revoked, provided there is " universal consent " for such a step.   Universal consent is, however, a difficult condition to fulfil, revolutions being generally initiated by minorities.   It must also be noticed that he is not quite consistent, for he some-

[1] Compare Maine, *Ancient Law*, ed. 1885, pp. 168–70.
[2] Richard Hooker, *Ecclesiastical Polity*, Book 1, c. 10.

times ascribes the origin of civil dominion to divine appointment. Still, the contract theory dominates his reasonings.

Independently of each other moral philosophers of Western Europe and Italy put similar constructions upon *ius naturale*, the most famous among them being Hugo Grotius, who also exercised considerable influence on English political thought. Following the Church Fathers and scholastics, he assumes an idyllic state of nature, the Fall of man, the introduction of civil society, and private property. Communism was general in the natural state as well as absence of human government, but after the Fall of man vice crept in, and made a change in the social conditions a necessity. By an express or tacit agreement men abandoned the communistic mode of life and introduced private property, first with regard to movables, then immovables, and laws of property were enacted.[1] By contract they likewise constituted civil society, and by virtue of an agreement a supreme authority was set up. Grotius is, however, not quite clear with regard to the lawfulness of resistance of the people to constituted authority. He appears to be of opinion that, as a rule, non-resistance was best, yet he thinks resistance lawful if it could be achieved without endangering civil society itself, and without destroying the lives of innocent people. He is further of opinion that all depended on the tenour of the original agreement ; if the people subjected themselves unconditionally to their sovereign resistance was unlawful ; if, however, the submission was conditional resistance was lawful. But who is to decide on the tenour of the original agreement ? Grotius thinks that the decision lay with the people who happened to raise such questions. This, of course, means that the people was sovereign and had, therefore, the right to dethrone the monarch.[2] For a sober and conservative logician, like Sir Robert Filmer, it was under these conditions an easy matter to detect and expose the illogical attitude of Grotius.[3]

[1] Hugo Grotius, *De iure belli et pacis* (1625), l. 2, c. 2.
[2] *Ibid.*, l. 1, cs. 3 and 4 ; l. 2, c. 2.
[3] Sir Robert Filmer, *Observations*, on Hobbes, Milton, and Grotius, 1652, pp. 38-50.

John Selden, though inclined to favour the hypothesis that communism never existed, appears rather impressed by the communist verses of the Roman poets, whom he quotes, and arrives at the conclusion that " neither law natural nor divine . . . has expressly commanded or prohibited, but permitted both private property and common possessions." Yet he assumes that private property arose by consent of the whole body of mankind. By virtue of a compact men gave up their common interests, and ancient rights to their common possessions, and made that compact binding on their posterity.[1]

It must have been in the first quarter of the seventeenth century that a short pamphlet entitled " A Paradox " appeared, in which the state of nature is defended on ethical grounds. It attempts to prove that the inhabitants of Madagascar, or St. Lawrence, were, in things temporal, the happiest people on earth. For they knew not the " inordinate desire for riches, which is the root of all mischief—a raging famished beast that will not be satisfied, a bottomless gulf that cannot be filled." Those inhabitants set no value on gold ; their life was simple and free from the sorrows of civil society.[2]

The first attack on the communist and idyllic element of *ius naturale* came from Thomas Hobbes. He admits that in the state of nature everybody had a right to everything, " that is to say, to do whatever he listeth and to whom he listeth, to possess, use, and enjoy all things he will and can . . . and for this cause it is rightly said, *Natura dedit omnia omnibus;*" but considering the passions, rivalries, and the lust of glory, such a state was anything but idyllic. It led to perpetual strife, discord, and war, to a *bellum omnium contra omnes*, in which the strongest or craftiest prevailed, and therefore the natural rights were of no use whatsoever.[3] Laws of nature such as equity, mercy, modesty, without the terror inspired by some power to cause them to be observed, were rendered nugatory by the

[1] John Selden, *Mare Clausum*, l. 1, c. 4.
[2] *A Paradox*, *Harl. Misc.*, vol. I., pp. 263–9.
[3] Thomas Hobbes, *Elements of Law*, ed. Toennies, I., c. 14 ; II., c. 1, *et seq.*

natural passions, partiality, pride, revenge, etc.[1] Not right, but brute force ruled. Man had only the choice between natural liberty plus destructive war and subjection to authority plus security and peace. He chose the latter, since life and the preservation thereof were fundamental laws of nature.[2] Men entered into an agreement with each other to surrender their sovereignty and transfer it unconditionally to one man or an assembly of men. Thus arose civil dominion out of an inchoate and warring demos. The transfer of sovereignty having been unconditional, all must obey the sovereign's laws. " Though a monarch, a sovereign, may in his passion pursue aims contrary to the law of nature, no subject has a right to make war on him, because having authorised all his actions, and in bestowing the sovereign power, made them their own."[3] With the transfer of the natural rights to the sovereign the state of nature was at an end, and the artificial state, the Leviathan, omnipotent by the power, the sword, of concentrated sovereignty, orders the mode of property, religion, justice, and all the affairs of the organism of the Commonwealth. " The inequality that is now to be seen has been introduced by civil law . . . The constitution of ' mine ' and ' thine ' and ' his,' in one word, ' propriety,' belongs in all kinds of commonwealth to the sovereign power . . . Propriety consists in the right of a subject to exclude all other subjects from the use of the things which he possesses."[4]

We see that, apart from the principle of contract which all the moral philosophers accept, there prevails among them much difference of opinion as to its mode of application. Ockham applied it both to civil dominion and property, Hooker to the rise of civil society and civil government, but not to property. Hobbes knows only one contract, viz., between the afflicted and distracted people themselves to surrender, without any condition whatsoever, their sovereignty to one man or several men who henceforth form the civil power. The contract theory of Hobbes was exceedingly distasteful to a nation which drastically revoked their agreement with King Charles I. It was indeed a counter-

[1] Thomas Hobbes, *Leviathan*, c. 17.   [2] *Ibid.*, c. 14.   [3] *Ibid.*, c. 16·
[4] *Ibid.*, c. 15, c. 16.

revolutionary blast, a plea for absolute monarchy. The nation preferred Milton's *Tenure of Kings and Magistrates*, and, later, Sydney's *Discourse on Government*, which popularised Hooker's views on the social and political contract.

It was, however, John Locke who summed up the political and economic speculations of the revolutionary period. In his *Two Treatises on Civil Government* (1689) he popularised Hooker's reasonings on the social and political contract, but in a more rationalist and less theological manner. The great difference between Hooker and Locke is this—the first, still very near the scholastic period, fully admits that the transition from the natural to the civil state was due to the corruption of man, while Locke, in the midst of the rationalist wave, evidently dislikes the theological interpretation, and still more so the anti-idyllic theory of Hobbes, which so little tallies with Locke's belief in the inherent goodness and the power of reason of man. Still, the loss of the natural state had to be accounted for. After much hesitation Locke finally admits that the natural state had its " inconveniences," particularly in the administration of justice, and, therefore, the natural men entered into an agreement to form a civil government,[1] which, of course, was from the beginning responsible to the people. In his contract theory there is, however, nothing original ; it is all rationalised Hooker. His real contribution, and a very considerable one, is his theory concerning property.

We have seen the efforts of Ockham to demonstrate the compatibility of private property with *ius naturale*, and thus to remove the taint of sin from the division and appropriation of things. Locke makes a similar effort. His main proposition is that private property is natural and existed even in the state of nature ; it is on this account just and good. He therefore rejects altogether the theory that property had its origin in a contract, as Ockham and Grotius assumed, for this theory implies that in the state of nature there was no property. Even more important than the main proposition of Locke is his labour argument, by which he supports it. The doctrine that

[1] John Locke, *On Civil Government*, II., c. 7, § 90.

labour is the title to property and the source of value was destined to be made into the main weapon of socialism, although Locke himself used it in a contrary sense, trying to prove the legitimacy and justice of private property. He argues :—

"I shall endeavour to show how men might come to have property in several parts of that which God gave to mankind in common, and that without an express contract of all the commoners." He then goes on to say that while God gave the earth and the fulness thereof to mankind in common, He gave it for use, and, therefore, there must needs have been a means of appropriating the natural products before they could be of use to any particular man. When " the wild Indian, who knows no enclosures, and is still tenant in common," gathered eatable things and prepared them for his use, they belonged to him, and became his exclusive property. And this for two reasons :— first, man was originally free and independent ; his body belonged only to him and to nobody else ; his labour power was a part of his person, and when he removed a thing from the state of nature and made it useful, he mixed with it his labour and joined to it something that was unquestionably his own, and thereby made it his property. Secondly, the things in their natural state are generally of very little value. It was human labour which made them valuable. Nine-tenths of the value of things were created and added to them by labour. And as labour, the creator of value, was a part of man, and man was his own master and the proprietor of his person, he really took what was his own. " Labour is the title to property " ; by it a " man does, as it were, enclose the common." And only so much of land and things that he could work, and thus render useful (valuable), was rightly his own. The original meaning of value or the intrinsic value of a thing was its usefulness. In the state of nature, before the *amor sceleratus habendi* had set in, nobody appropriated more than he needed and could make useful. So there was then private property. In this respect the difference between the natural and civil state consisted only in the degree of appropriation.[1]

[1] John Locke, *On Civil Government*, II., c. 5.

Locke's doctrines concerning monarchy and property form the complete reverse of Wycliffe's. The latter aimed at sanctioning personal monarchy and defending communism, while the former attempted to condemn personal monarchy and sanction individual property. Both, the theologian as well as the political philosopher, interpreted the movements of their times.

We shall see later how Locke's labour theory of property and value was used by socialist critics, particularly after the labour value theory had been expanded and established by Adam Smith and David Ricardo. Meanwhile, we must return to the communists and social reformers of the seventeenth century.

3.—SOCIAL-REVOLUTIONARY THEORIES IN THE CIVIL WAR

In the shock of the struggle between Parliament and Monarchy, the flood-gates of revolutionary ideas opened, and a stream of religious heresies, rationalist and radical philosophy, communist theories, and social reform schemes spread over the land. The main element of this flood of ideas was *ius naturale* in one form or another. A careful observer, though zealous opponent of these movements, has left us a fairly correct summary of them. He complains :—

" Instead of legal rights, and the laws and customs of this nation the sectaries talk of, and plead for, natural rights and liberties, such as men have from Adam by birth, and in many of their pamphlets they still speak of being governed by right reason, so that look now as they do in matters of religion and conscience fly from the Scriptures and from supernatural truths revealed there, that a man may not be questioned for going against them, but only for errors against the light of nature and right reason, so they do also in civil government and things of the world go from the laws and constitutions of kingdoms, and will be governed by rules according to nature and right reason. . . . And as we are delivered of God by the hand of nature into this world, every one with a natural innate freedom and propriety, even so are we to live, every one equally and alike to enjoy his birthright and privilege."[1]

[1] Thomas Edwards, *Gangræna*, 1646, Part III., pp. 16A and

This period is also instructive for the attempt then made to determine the time of the transition of England from the natural to the civil state. That critical time was assumed to have been the Norman Conquest. Before the Conquest the Anglo-Saxons, the descendants of the Germanic tribes, so gloriously described by Tacitus, were supposed to have lived in a democratic and communal manner or in natural equality, and this natural state was destroyed by the Romanised conquerors, who divided the lands and introduced new and alien laws. This anti-Normanic agitation was partly nationalist and patriotic, and partly revolutionary and communist. The representative of the first was a certain John Hare, who published three pamphlets on the matter, the first of which was written in 1642, but published in 1647. He is strongly pro-German and anti-French. The English, he believes, had a most honourable and happy origin, viz., from Germany, but their liberties were afterwards shut up by the Normans under the name and notion of franchises ; the heraldry and the names of the nobility were nothing but inventories of foreign villages, and the royal title reminded them always of the conquest by the sword ; in short, an Englishman could not move without hearing " the chains of captivity rattle." Among other reforms Hare proposes " That all the Norman nobility repudiate their names and titles brought over from Normandy, assuming others more consistent with the honour of this nation, and disdain all right of possession here as heirs and successors to any pretended conqueror."[1] The king did not govern by law of nature and the inferences from *salus publica*, but by right of conquest ;[2] whereas the honour of Englishmen consisted of living under laws of their own choosing and under princes to whose rule they consented.

The leader of the political Levellers, John Lilburne, agitates

16D. Owing, probably, to a printer's oversight, there are between the numbered pages 16 and 17 fully sixteen pages without any number at all. In order, however, to facilitate the reference to them, I add to page 16 the letters A, B, C, D, etc., so as to cover the unnumbered pages.

[1] John Hare, *Anti-Normanism*, Harl. Misc., Vol. 8, pp. 96, 104
[2] The same, *Plain English*, Harl. Misc., Vol. 9, p. 94.

the people with the argument that "the greatest mischief of all and the oppressing bondage of England ever since the Norman yoke is a law called the common law. The laws of this nation are unworthy of a free people, and deserve from first to last to be considered, debated, and reduced to an agreement with common equity and right reason, which ought to be the form and life of every government."[1]

And Gerrard Winstanley, the fiery soul of the little body of men called Diggers, appeals to Oliver Cromwell to cast out the "Conquerors and to recover our land and liberties . . . for when the Norman power had conquered our forefathers he took the free use of our English ground from them and made them his servants."[2] In another Digger pamphlet it is said, "We do protest against all arbitrary courts, terms, lawyers, impropriators, lords of manors, patents, privileges, customs, tolls, monopolisers, incroachers, enhancers . . . against the whole Norman power, as being too intolerable a burden any longer to bear. . . . We protest against any coming to Westminster Terms, but will endeavour to have our controversies ended by two, three, or twelve men of our neighbourhood, as before the Norman Conquest."[3] In short, the whole communist movement of the years from 1648 to 1652 assumes the Norman Conquest to have marked the Fall of the Englishman and his transfer from the natural to the civil state.

4.—THE DIGGERS OR TRUE LEVELLERS

The Digger movement, although small in the number of its adherents, was an agrarian revolt on a surprisingly extensive theoretical basis. It was as if all the Peasant Wars of the past had suddenly become articulate. It aimed at making the earth the common treasury of all. The whole substance of mediaeval communism reappeared, but in a rationalist and sectarian setting. The logical theology of the Schoolmen was superseded by a mysti-

[1] John Lilburne, *Just Man's Justification*, pp. 11–15.
[2] Gerrard Winstanley, *Law of Freedom* (1652), p. 3.
[3] *Declaration of the Well-Affected in the County of Buckinghamshire* (1649).

cal religion, the axis of which was Reason; and for the Fall of mankind from the natural state was substituted the conquest of the democratic and communal Englishmen by the property-struck and iron-handed Norman. Quite in the style of Pope Gregory VII., the first manifesto of the Diggers denounces kingship as having its patent from the devil and from murder.[1] William the Conqueror is the personification of that kingship. " And all our nobility and gentry came from the outlandish Norman bastard." They all originated from cruel murder, theft, and conquest.[2] The earth and the fulness thereof were given to men in common ; it was plain that every man had a right and property in the creation, "so that for any to enclose them from its kind, to his own exclusive use, is tantamount to the impoverishment and enslavement of his fellow-men."[3] The pattern of a right commonwealth was to be found in the Scriptures, partly in the agrarian legislation of the Israelites and partly in the Gospel. " And all that believed were together, and had all things common " (Acts ii. 44).

These two pamphlets were preparatory to the propaganda by deed. A few months after, viz., on April 1, 1649,[4] a few men, led by William Everard (late of the army) and Gerrard Winstanley, took to digging and manuring land on St. George's Hill, in the parish of Walton, and later at Cobham, in Surrey, in order to encourage the people to go and do likewise and form communities, or to " restore the creation to its former condition . . . and ancient community of enjoying the fruits of the earth." On April 16, an information of their doings was given to the Council of State, who on the same day ordered Lord Fairfax to disperse the Diggers. Four days later Everard and Winstanley appeared before Lord Fairfax at Whitehall. Everard, as spokesman, said that all the liberties of the people were

---

[1] *Light Shining in Buckinghamshire*, 1648, p. 3. In Thomason's Collection of Tracts, where most of the Diggers' pamphlets are to be found. A special catalogue of that collection is in the British Museum Reading Room.　　[2] *Ibid.*, p. 9.

[3] *More Light Shining in Buckinghamshire*, pp. 2–15.

[4] *A New Year's Gift to Parliament*, p. 44.

lost through the coming of William the Conqueror, and that ever since the people of God lived under oppression and tyranny. The remedy was to dig and plough up the commons, parks, and other untilled lands. The Diggers did not intend to interfere with any man's property, or to break down the pales of the enclosures, but only to cultivate those lands that were common and untilled. When people would see the blessings of it they would come in and join the community.

The reporter of this interview adds that Everard and Winstanley stood before the Lord General with their hats on, and when asked the reason of their behaviour they replied, he was but their fellow-creature.[1]

As a movement the Diggers were unsuccessful. Although they sent missionaries to other counties of England,[2] and gained a small following in Buckinghamshire and Northamptonshire, the peasantry were against them. The settlements at Walton and Cobham were destroyed by the people ; they pulled down the few huts, cut the spades and hoes to pieces, and maltreated the Diggers. " The enemy were so mad that they tumbled the earth up and down, and would suffer no corn to grow."[3] The movement lasted only for about twelve months, but it left numerous manifestoes and pamphlets of considerable power, mostly written by Gerrard Winstanley, with whose two chief works, *New Law of Righteousness*, and *Law of Freedom*, we shall deal presently. As regards the Digger movement itself, the most characteristic manifesto is that entitled, *The True Levellers' Standard Advanced* (April 26, 1649), signed by fifteen Diggers, headed by William Everard. This declaration of their principles asserts (pp. 6-13) :

" In the beginning of time the great Creator, Reason, made the earth to be a common treasury to preserve beasts, birds, fishes, and man, the lord who was to govern this Creation. . . . The rules of Creation were, Not to enclose any part into any particular hand, but all as one man, working together, and

---

[1] *Declaration of the Levellers*, April 23, 1649, p. 3.
[2] *A Perfect Diurnal.*
[3] *A New Year's Gift*, p. 45.

feeding together as sons of one father, members of one family, not lording over another, but all looking upon each other as equals in the Creation. . . . But since human flesh began to delight itself in the things of the Creation more than in the spirit of Reason and Righteousness . . . and selfish imagination ruling as king in the room of Reason therein, and working with covetousness, did set up one man to teach, to rule over another ; and thereby the spirit was killed and man was brought into bondage. . . . Hereupon the earth was hedged into enclosures by the teachers and rulers, and the others were made servants and slaves. And the earth which was made to be a common storehouse for all is bought and sold and kept within the hands of the few." The Diggers declare that they are resolved to remove from the Creation the curse and bondage of Civil Property, not by the force of arms, but " by labouring the earth in righteousness together, to earn our bread by the sweat of our brows, neither giving hire nor taking hire . . . and lay the foundation of making the earth a common treasury for all, both rich and poor, that every one that is born in the land may be fed by the earth his mother that brought him forth, according to the Reason that rules in the Creation."

All the other manifestoes and pamphlets of the Diggers are in a similar strain, so that if we know one we know them all. The struggle is essentially against private property in land, civil law, and tyranny or oligarchy in matters of government, and for a rationalist and Christianised *ius naturale*. The Diggers looked on Jesus as the first True Leveller.

The rhymes left by the Diggers are of small poetic value. " The Diggers' Song " was evidently written in the autumn, 1649, when they met with the enmity of the people and opposition of the clergy and authorities. A few verses will suffice to learn the spirit of it :—

> " Ye noble Diggers all, stand up now, stand up now,
>   You noble Diggers, stand up now ;
>   The waste land to maintain, seeing cavaliers by name
>   Your diggings do disdain and persons all defame.
>   Stand up now, stand up now.

*   *   *   *

" The lawyers they conjoin, stand up now, stand up now,
　　The lawyers they conjoin, stand up now ;
　To arrest you they advise, and such fury they devise,
　The devil in them lies, and has blinded both their eyes.
　　Stand up now, stand up now.

" The clergy they come in, stand up now, stand up now,
　　The clergy they come in, stand up now ;
　The clergy they come in, and say it is a sin
　That we should now begin, our freedom to win.
　　Stand up now, stand up now.

　　　　　*　　　*　　　*　　　*

" To conquer then by love, come in now, come in now,
　　To conquer then by love, come in now ;
　To conquer then by love, as it does you behove,
　For He is King above, no Power is like to Love,
　　Glory here, Diggers all ! "[1]

In a long " Christmas Carol " the Diggers declare that the titles of the lords of the manors originated with the Norman Conquest, which in consequence of the execution of Charles I. had lost all value, and therefore fell to the common people. The Civil War, however, had shown that even after much bloodshed the people could have no hope in Government :—

　　　" Therefore let me advise
　　　All those who freedom prise,
　　　To till each heath and plain,
　　　For this will freedom gain,
　　　Heriots and fines this will expell
　　　A bondage great—men know full well.

　　　" Freedom is not won
　　　Neither by sword nor gun ;
　　　Though we have eight years stay'd,
　　　And have our moneys pay'd ;
　　　The Clubs and Diamonds cast away,
　　　The Hearts and Spades must win the day."[1]

And in " A Digger's Ballad," a communistic song written by

---

[1] C. H. Firth, *Clarke Papers*, II., p. 221.
[1] *The Diggers' Mirth*, 1650.

Robert Coster, only the last of the nine stanzas shows some merit :—

> " The glorious state which I do relate
> Unspeakable glory shall yield,
> The corn will be green and the flowers seen,
> Our storehouses they will be filled.
> The birds will rejoice with a merry voice
> All things shall yield sweet increase.
> Then let us all sing and joy in our King,
> Who causes all sorrows to cease."[1]

5.—WINSTANLEY'S IDEAL COMMONWEALTH

Gerrard Winstanley, the fiery soul of the Digger movement, was a peaceful John Ball.   His own writings, as well as the Digger manifestoes, which he drafted or inspired, exhibit familiarity with mediaeval communism.   In the history of English social thought he is the first sectarian communist.   He was devoted to mysticism and had visions.   Of his life little is known.   He was born at Wigan, Lancashire, on October 10, 1609.[2]   A few biographical data were supplied by Winstanley himself in the introductory epistle published in his *Watchword to the City of London* (1649).   He lived for a time in the City of London as a freeman, possessed " estate and trade," and was " beaten out of both" partly through business failure or, as he says, " by the cheating sons in the thieving art of buying and selling," and partly through the disturbances of the Civil War, " by the burden of and for the soldiery in the beginning of the war."   His friends assisted him to retire to the country, probably to the Chiltern Hills, where he evidently found leisure enough for contemplation and reading.   The progress of the Civil War, the final defeat of the King, and the feverish mental activity which set in and which manifested itself in the numerous pamphlets dealing with natural law, social and sectarian speculations on religion and ethics, mightily stirred the mind of Winstanley.   He interpreted this upheaval to be a levelling of the political mountains as a preliminary to the advent of the great reformation, the radical

---

[1] Robert Coster, *A Mite Cast into the Common Treasury*, 1650.
[2] L. H. Berens, *Digger Movement*, p. 41.

F

change of the spiritual and social conditions of England. " The
Spirit of the whole Creation (who is God) is about the Reformation
of the World, and he will go forward in his work. . . . The
great searching of heart in these days is to find out where true
Freedom lies, that the Commonwealth of England might be
established in peace." [1]

He at first wrote four pamphlets, *The Mystery of God*,
The Breaking of the Day of God, *The Saints' Paradise*, and
Truth lifting up its Head, all in 1648, interpreting Biblical
and theological subjects in a spirit of mysticism and religious
philosophy. Then he commenced to see visions which led him
to communism, and to fierce attacks on kingship and private
property. Winstanley has left us a description of his mental
state at that time. [2] " As I was in a trance not long since, divers
matters were presented to my sight, which must not be related
here. Likewise I heard these words : ' Work together : Eat
bread together : Declare this all abroad.' Likewise I heard these
words : ' Whosoever it is that labours in the earth, for any person
or persons that lift up themselves as lords and rulers over others,
and that doth not look upon himself as equal to others in the
Creation, the hand of the Lord shall be upon the labourer. I
the Lord have spoke it and I will do it. Declare this abroad.' "
This mental experience gave him a mission. He " was filled with
abundance of quiet peace and sacred joy . . . and much
pressed in spirit to declare all abroad."

The first communist treatise which he published under his
name was *New Law of Righteousness*. We find in it the usual
mediaeval communist interpretation of the creation and fall of
man. At the beginning man was created perfect, then he fell
from his estate through following self-love, covetousness, and
carnal lust. Appropriation of land followed, likewise buying and
selling, " mine " and " thine," civil laws to uphold property, and
hereby restraining men from seeking nourishment from their
mother earth. This was all the work of the unrighteous or first

[1] Gerrard Winstanley, *Law of Freedom*, pp. 4, 17.
[2] The same, *New Law of Righteousness*, January, 1649, quoted
extensively by Berens, p. 73.

Adam, who dammed up the wells of universal liberty and brought the Creation under the curse of bondage, sorrow, and tears.   For as long as there were lords who called the lands theirs and rulers who upheld this particular property, the common people would not be free.   Only by making the earth a common treasury, as it was in the beginning, could the first Adam, or covetousness, pride, and envy be got rid of,   Still, nothing was to be taken from the rich.   " If the rich hold fast to this propriety of mine and thine, let them labour their own lands.   And let the common people who say the earth is ours, not mine, let them labour together and eat bread together up on the commons, mountains, and hills."   It was with Winstanley a struggle of common against enclosure, or collective possession and co-operative work against private property and hired labour.   The ultimate remedy was the abolition of private property and civil government.

The society which was to take the place of the civil one is described by Winstanley in his *Law of Freedom* (1652).   This ideal commonwealth rests on the following principles and laws :—

" Government is a wise and free ordering of the earth and of the manners of mankind by observation of particular laws and rules, so that all the inhabitants may live peaceably in plenty and freedom in the land where they are bred " (p. 25).   This government acts according to the law of nature which is supported by reason so as not to allow the propensities of the flesh to deflect the natural law from its rational course (p. 30).   The function of governing is entrusted to a Parliament chosen annually.   It is the real court of equity.   Its duties are four-fold :—

" First, as a tender father, a parliament is to empower officers and give orders for the free planting and reaping of the Commonwealth's land, that all who have been oppressed and kept back from the free use thereof by conquerors, kings, and their tyrant laws, may now be set at liberty to plant in freedom for food and raiment, and are to be a protection to them who labour the earth, and a punisher of them who are idle.   But some may say, What is that I call Commonwealth's land ?   I answer, All that land which has been withheld from the inhabitants by the conqueror or tyrant kings and is now recovered out of the hands

of that oppression by the joint assistance of the persons and
purses of the communers of the land. It is their birthright to
them and to their posterity, and ought not to be converted into
particular hands again by the laws of a free commonwealth.
In particular, this land is all abbey lands . . . Crown lands,
bishops' lands, with all parks, forests, chases, now of late recovered out of the hands of the kingly tyrants. . . .

" Secondly, to abolish all old laws and customs which have been
the strength of the oppressor, and to prepare and then to enact
new laws for the ease and freedom of the people. . . .

" Thirdly, to see all those burdens removed actually, which
have hindered the oppressed people from the enjoyment of
their birthright. If their common lands be under the oppression of lords of manors, they are to see the land freed from that
slavery. If the commonwealth's land be sold by hasty counsel
of subtle, covetous, and ignorant officers . . . then a parliament is to examine what authority any had to sell or buy the
land without a general consent of the people. . . . They
are to declare that the bargain is unrighteous, and that the buyers
and sellers are enemies to the peace and freedom of the commonwealth.

" Fourthly, if there be occasion to raise an army to wage war,
either against an invasion of a foreign enemy, or against an insurrection at home, it is the work of a parliament to manage
that business for the preservation of common peace " (pp. 50–56).

The land having been restored to the nation it is given over to
the farmers to till it in common. " There shall be no buying
and selling of the earth, nor of the fruits thereof." For, when
mankind began to buy and sell, they fell from the state of
innocence, and began to oppress each other and discontents
and wars arose (p. 12).

"The earth is to be planted and the fruits reaped and carried into
barns and storehouses by the assistance of every family. If any
man or family want corn or other provisions, they may go to the
storehouse and fetch without money. If they want a horse to
ride, they may go into the fields in summer or to the common
stables in winter, and receive one from the keepers and when the

journey is performed, bring him back. . . . There shall be storehouses in all places in the country and in the towns to which all the fruits of the soil and the works of the tradesmen shall be brought and thence delivered again to the families and to every one who want them ; or else be transported by ships to other countries in exchange for those things which our land will not or cannot produce. All the labours of husbandmen and tradesmen within the country shall be upon the common stock. And as every one works to advance the common stock, so every one shall have free use of any commodity in the storehouse for his pleasure and comfortable livelihood, without buying or selling or restraint from anybody. . . . For as particular families and tradesmen do make several works more than they can make use of and do carry their particular works to the storehouses, so it is all reason and equity that they should go to other store-houses to fetch any other commodity which they want and cannot make " (pp. 74-5).

In order that these laws and regulations be carried out and to check the covetous, proud, and idle, there must be officers to regulate the irrational conduct of such men.

All officers of the Commonwealth to be chosen annually. " Choose such as are men of peaceable disposition ; likewise who suffered under kingly oppression, for they will be fellow-feelers of others' bondage ; likewise who have adventured the loss of their estates and lives to redeem the land from bondage and who have remained constant ; likewise men of courage who are not afraid to speak the truth ; likewise who are above forty years of age, for these are most likely to be experienced men. . . . And if you choose men thus principled who are poor men, as times go, for the Conqueror's power has made many a righteous man a poor man, then allow them a yearly main-tenance from the common stock, until such time as a Common-wealth's Freedom is established, for then there will be no need of such allowance " (pp. 37–9).

Each parish shall choose a number of peacemakers to manage the affairs of the parish, to prevent trouble and to preserve the common peace. They shall settle any matters of offence between

man and man. If the peacemakers are unable to bring about a
reconciliation of the parties, then he shall command them to
appear at the Judge's Court. Each parish shall also choose a
number of overseers to preserve peace ; to see that the young
people receive proper instruction in some labour, trade, or service
in the common storehouses ; to see that the products of labour
shall be delivered up to the storehouses and shops, and that all
who serve in the storehouses and shops do their duty. All old
men above sixty years of age are general overseers (pp. 40–6).
There shall also be chosen a taskmaster, whose office it is " to take
those into his supervision who are sentenced to lose their freedom, to set them to work and to see that they do it."

Education must be general and compulsory. After the
child is weaned the parents shall teach it a civil and humble
behaviour towards all men. Then it shall be sent to school
to learn to read the laws of the Commonwealth, the arts and
languages. But there shall be no special class of children
brought up to book-learning only. " For then through idleness
they spend their time to find out policies to advance themselves
to be lords and masters over their labouring brethren, which
occasions all trouble in the world. Therefore it is necessary
and profitable for the Commonwealth that all children be trained
to labour and to learning."

Inventions were to be promoted by all means. " Let no young
wit be crushed in his invention." Experimenting should be
encouraged. " And let every one who finds out an invention
have a deserved honour given to him." Knowledge and
experiment should take the place of believing and imagining
(pp. 68–76).

Such a Commonwealth did not mean idleness, community
of women, or anarchy. It meant labour as a duty of every
member of the Commonwealth, purity in sexual relations, and
observance of the laws. Under common management would
be the soil, workshops, and storehouses ; labour would be exchanged for labour, without the intermediary of money. Family
life must be private and strictly monogamous. " Every man's
house, furniture, and the provisions which he fetches from the

storehouses are proper to himself, likewise the wife to her husband and the husband to his wife " (p. 24).[1]

6.—THE SOCIAL REFORMERS

The years from the beginning of the Civil War to the end of the seventeenth century produced also several social reformers. As we are concerned only with those reformers whose schemes contain socialistic elements, we must confine ourselves to the pamphlets of Samuel Hartlib, Peter Chamberlen, Peter Cornelius Plockhoy, and John Bellers. The most important of them is that of Chamberlen, whose social criticism is closely related to communism, inasmuch as he makes use of the proposition that the labour of the poor, i.e., the wage-workers, is the source of all wealth. John Bellers, a member of the Society of Friends, whom Robert Owen as well as Karl Marx greatly admired, represents a combination of Hartlib, Plockhoy, and Chamberlen, making, however, a serious contribution to social-economic speculation by proposing to make labour—time, and not money, the standard of value.

In point of time, but by no means of thought and originality, Hartlib comes first. He was a German Protestant refugee from Poland, a man of much learning and some influence with his English friends on account of his endeavours to promote education and agriculture. He wrote, in 1641, a small treatise, *A Description of the Famous Kingdom of Macaria*, reminiscent of readings in Sir Thomas More's *Utopia* and Francis Bacon's *New Atlantis*. The name Macaria actually occurs in More's Commonwealth : " The laws of the Macarians are not far distant from those of Utopia."[2] The main characteristic of the constitution of Macaria is that the government, consisting of departments of agriculture, fishing, home trade, foreign trade, and colonisation, manage the economic affairs of the commonwealth. No man may hold more land than he can improve ; the death duties amount to the twentieth part of the goods left, and are

---

[1] *Cf.* Bernstein, *Sozialismus und Demokratie*, 1905. Gooch, *Democratic Ideas*, 1898.

[2] More, *Utopia*, ed. Lupton (1895), p. 95.

used for the improvement of agriculture, highways, and bridges ;
the home trade is so regulated as to correspond to the needs
of the people ; crown lands are so carefully tilled and cultivated
that they yield considerable revenues and lighten the burden of
taxation.[1]

Of considerably higher historical value is Peter Chamberlen's
Poor Man's Advocate (1649). It combines " Nature, Reason,
and Religion " with the doctrine of labour as creator of wealth,
and makes use of these theories to advocate the justice of the
claims of the working classes. Chamberlen argues that the
wealth and strength of all countries were the poor (labouring
poor, or the propertyless workmen), for they did all the necessary
works of society and formed the main body of the armies. They
had the same right to the earth as the rich. Moreover, they
provided for the rich. The latter must, therefore, regard
themselves merely as stewards whose main duty it was to care
for the poor and enable them to produce wealth. The end of
wealth was not enjoyment for the rich, but to banish poverty
from the land. And that was also in conformity with religion,
which commands to love our fellow-man. " For if we love not
our brother whom we have seen, how can we love God Whom we
have not seen ? " And the same commandment was the basic
principle of organised society. There could be no peaceful and
healthy social life as long as the many were poor. In order
to get rid of poverty Chamberlen proposes to nationalise (*a*) the
estates of the King, bishops, deans and chapters, and delinquents ;
(*b*) the commons, wastes, heaths, woods, forests, etc. ; (*c*) the
mines, which are not worked ; (*d*) parish charities ; (*e*) unearned
increment[2] of agriculture, trade, and manufactures, arising from
improvements and inventions and colonisation ; (*f*) treasures
found in sea and land. Finally, he proposes the establishment
of a national bank, like those of Amsterdam and Venice,
likewise of academies for higher learning in arts and sciences
in order " to prevent youth from going abroad, in the

[1] *Harl. Misc.*, I., pp. 580–5.
[2] Chamberlen does not use this term, but the sense of his proposal
amounts to that.

blossom of their years, to be corrupted there in religion and manners."

This national stock of wealth should be organised by the Commonwealth with a view to employment of the poor. The land was to be cultivated on a co-operative basis ; still, if any farmer desired to work individually, a certain number of enclosed acres should be let to him on an annual rental of £5. The government of the Commonwealth should procure implements and raw material for the farmers and handicraftsmen and generally assume those duties which employers performed.

In creating this national stock the former owner's claims should be considered, except of those who legally forfeited their rights. The revenue that would accrue to the Commonwealth from those enterprises would be used for the needs of the government. It might be objected that only unworthy and ignorant men were poor, or by the improvement of their social condition the poor might become untractable, insolent, and idle. To these and similar objections, Chamberlen replies : " Let no man say that men were poor because they were unworthy. Some of the greatest philosophers, also Christ and the apostles, were poor. Besides, the poor would not be so poor, if the rich were honest, so as to let the poor have their own ; the riches of the rich are oftentimes but trophies of their dishonesty, of having robbed the poor, or cozened the Commonwealth " (p. 12).

And as to idleness it might be said that, if wealth made idleness to be a reason why the poor should be kept poor, then it was also a reason why rich men should not be rich, since " Edel "-man (gentleman) is idle-man. There was no necessity in " Nature, Reason, and Religion why they that are rich should continue so, and they that are poor should always remain so. Is aught of thine taken from thee ? O, envious man ! The demands of the poor are but food and raiment, and to be disposed into such an order that they and their posterity should not lack the necessaries of life nor be exposed to slavish labour." Finally, as regards insolence there was no greater incitement to insolence than poverty face to face with flaunting wealth.

The reforms, if carried out, would bring the poor into a condition of regular employment, instruction, and good, orderly government, such as they had never known before. Such conditions would engender love for the country, obedience to the laws, and stability of government. The new order would act as a good Samaritan and pour oil and wine into the wounds of the nation.

Far less revolutionary was the proposal of Peter Cornelius van Zurik-Zee, or Plockhoy (sometimes written Plockboy), in his pamphlet, *A Way to Make the Poor in these and other Nations Happy* (1659). He was a Dutchman, who lived for some time in England, evidently attracted by the social ferment of the Civil War and Commonwealth period. The reforms he proposed aimed at the establishment of " Little Commonwealths." They amounted essentially to the formation of co-operative societies for trade and commerce on a voluntary basis. His main idea was that co-operative production was cheaper than individualised enterprise, and could therefore more efficiently compete in the markets. Wholesale buying of raw material, co-operative work and common householding would result in a decrease of the prime cost of the commodities, in lessening the household expenses, and therefore in a greater ability to undersell the competitors. These " Little Commonwealths " should establish the most efficient schools and educational institutions, so as to induce the rich to send their children to those schools and thereby to spread the knowledge of co-operative enterprise. Also, the most skilled surgeons and physicians were to be engaged, who would treat the poor free of charge, and by this means advertise the blessings of co-operative labour. The regulations of the " Little Commonwealths " were to aim at uprooting covetousness, excesses, lying and deceit and all other vices that sprang from riches and poverty. In the schools the children were to be taught no particular form of religion, but to read the writings of the saints, study arts, sciences, languages, " and learn to follow those that have the spirit of God, doing miracles as the prophets."

Plockhoy's idea of combining voluntary social reform, philanthropy, and business was particularly congenial to the Society of Friends, a prominent English member of which was John Bellers (1655–1725). In his pamphlet, *Proposals for Raising a Colledge of Industry of all Useful Trades and Husbandry* (1696), he aimed at affording the poor co-operative and remunerative work, the rich a fair rate of interest, the youth good education. All social revolutionary enthusiasm, all millennial vision had vanished, and prosaic business enterprise began to dominate the life of the nation. The sobering process had set in with the Restoration, and went on at an accelerating rate after the Glorious Revolution. Bellers saw that " What sap is to the tree, profit is to business," or, if social reform was to succeed, it had to be put on a business footing. He did not denounce the rich, but spoke of their pity for their poor, among whom " crime, misery, idleness, and lewdness " prevailed. He believed that there were many rich who would like to see the poor reformed in manners and better provided for, and who, therefore, would be willing to contribute money for the establishment of co-operative agricultural colonies.

Each agricultural colony was to consist of 300 persons who would be so selected as to be able to perform all the labours necessary for farming. The cost of establishing such a colony, inclusive of acquiring land, he estimated at £18,000, which could be raised by shares. In all trading centres of the country co-operative workshops for arts and crafts should be established. The advantages of co-operative labour, by eliminating competition and waste, would be considerable, and would ensure a remunerative rate of interest to the shareholders. But the main benefit would be moral, such colleges of industries affording the best opportunity of educating the children of the poor to useful work, industrious habits, and good manners. Bellers does not attach undue importance to learning, for " though learning is useful, yet a virtuous, industrious education tends more to happiness here and hereafter." The life in those agriculture and trade colonies would be communistic. " The poor thus in college will be a community like the example of primitive Christianity that lived in common, and the power that did attend it bespeak their excellency ; but considering the constitution of mankind that have estates (but it is not so with the poor), it was none of the least miracles of that age." In these colleges or fellowships the standard of value of all necessaries would be labour, and not money. Bellers evidently means labour-time, and thus anticipates Robert Owen and John Gray, who in the years from 1820 to 1850 advocated labour-time notes as a means of exchange instead of money tokens. Bellers goes on to say that " though money has its conveniences, it being a pledge among men for want of credit, yet it is not without mischiefs, and called by our Saviour the Mammon of Unrighteousness. When the rich lose their money they can't employ the poor, though they have still the lands and hands to provide victuals, which are the true riches of the nation and not money. Money in the body politic is what a crutch is to the natural body, crippled ; but when the body is sound, the crutch is troublesome. So when the particular interest is made a public interest, in such a college, money will be of little use there." A college thus constituted " cannot so easily be undone, for if plundered, twelve months' time will recruit again ; like the grass new mowed the next year supplies again, labour bringing a supply as the soil does. When men work together they assist one another, but when scattered are useless, if not preying upon another." Bellers reminds the rich that they had no other way of living but by the labour of others, as the landlord by the labour of the tenants, and the merchants and tradesmen by the labour of the mechanics, unless they turned levellers and took to work together with the poor (p. 35). Labour being the monies of the rich (p. 10) it behoved them to see the poor work under the most advantageous conditions, both for the creation of wealth and the moral elevation of the poor.

Bellers was only one of a long and honourable series of Poor Law reformers, who, in the years from the Restoration to the reign of Queen Anne, were dealing with the question of utilising the labour power of the poor for the welfare of the nation. Some of the greatest men of that age, viz., Sir Josiah Child, Sir Matthew Hale, John Locke, Dr. Davenant, and Daniel

Defoe, devoted much attention to that problem,[1] but in none of them was the spirit of social criticism so reminiscent of the Commonwealth period as in Bellers.

As a reaction against all those proposals for raising the material, intellectual, and moral condition of the poor must be regarded Bernard Mandeville's *Fable of the Bees* and *On Charity and Charity Schools*, in which he pleaded for letting the poor alone, for " in a free nation, where slaves are not allowed, the surest wealth consists in a multitude of labouring poor . . . ignorant as well as poor." Their wants should be relieved, but it were folly to cure them.[2]

[1] Compare Sir Frederick M. Eden, *State of the Poor*, 1797, I. 184–264.

[2] Mandeville, *Fable of the Bees*, etc., edition 1724, pp. 328 and 280.

VI

THE ANTI-COMMUNIST PERIOD

I.—EVE OF THE ECONOMIC REVOLUTION

LOOKING at England of the seventeenth century, with her mighty ferment and titanic clash of forces, her intellectual and spiritual giants who filled the national arena, her immortals who illumined the path of human history, it is exceedingly difficult to believe that we are dealing with a numerically small nation—a country of something over one million families only.   And they overthrew personal monarchy, established the sovereignty of Parliament, produced Harvey, Milton, Hobbes, Petty, Locke, Newton, Cromwell, and Marlborough, and a host of lesser stars who, in any other age or country, might be counted as of first magnitude.

Gregory King, a political arithmetician of no mean value, left us, in his *Natural and Political Observations* (1694), a statistical view of England in 1688.   The population of England and Wales consisted of five and a half million souls, or 1,360,000 families. The national income amounted to £43,500,000 ; the annual increase of wealth to £1,800,000.   How narrow the circle of life then was, may be gauged from the remark of King that Lichfield was " a large town in the Midlands of nearly 3,000 souls."   The number of families of the various classes and groups of the nation were then as follows : Nobility and gentry 16,586, officials 10,000, oversea traders 12,000, home traders 2,000, law 8,000, clergy 10,000, yeomanry 48,000, farmers 150,000, liberal professions 16,000, small traders and shopkeepers 40,000, handicraftsmen and mechanics 60,000, officers in army and navy 9,000, seamen 50,000, workmen and servants 364,000, cottars and paupers 400,000, soldiers 35,000.   The income of the nobility and gentry was between £2,800 and £180 per family, oversea traders £400, home traders £200, yeomanry between £84 and £50, shopkeepers £45, handicraftsmen and mechanics £40, workmen, labourers and servants £15, cottars and paupers £6 10s. According to King, all families whose income was above £40 belonged to the productive classes, and increased the national income, while the labourers and workmen were non-productive, and decreased the national wealth, for their earnings had to be supplemented by parish relief in order to allow them to meet the cost of living. King appears to have looked upon society from the point of view of distribution ; statistics and not economics was his proper field. There is still another important feature in his statistical view of the nation, viz. that the size of each family depended on its income ; the number of the members of each family was large or small in proportion to the large or small income ; he computes for instance, the number of the members of a noble family to have been between sixteen and forty, of a merchant family eight, of a yeoman family between five and seven, of a workman's family between three and four. In short, the means of subsistence determined the size of the family. This view is confirmed by Adam Smith, who declares : " Poverty, though it does not prevent the generation, is extremely unfavourable to the rearing of children. . . . It is not uncommon in the Highlands of Scotland for a mother who has borne twenty children not to have two alive. . . . Every species of animals naturally multiplies in proportion to the means of subsistence, and no species can ever multiply beyond it. But in civilised society it is only among the inferior ranks of people that the scantiness of subsistence can set limits to the further multiplication of the human species ; and it can do so in no other way than by destroying a great part of the children which their marriages produce."[1]

English society as it emerged from the Glorious Revolution consisted of a population fifty per cent. of whom were relatively well-to-do. But the bulk of the national income fell to the agricultural proprietors. Of the 43·5 millions sterling only 2·4 millions fell to the great merchants, a similar sum to the craftsmen, and 1·8 millions to the small traders and shopkeepers.

[1] Adam Smith, *Wealth of Nations*, book 1, chap. 8.

Agriculture was the main occupation of the nation, while the industries played a relatively small part and were chiefly in the hands of small masters and mainly dependent upon the skill of handicraftsmen and artificers using human power. Even in the larger factories the skilled workman, and not the mechanical contrivance, was the dominant labour factor. The handicraftsman, the artificer, the mechanic appeared as the creator of wealth. This was the period when Sir William Petty and John Locke formulated their labour value theories.

From 1688 to about 1750 the progress of agriculture, trade, commerce, and population was slow and even halting. It by no means corresponded with the great exertions of the statesmen, diplomats, and generals of the nation. As regards home politics and economics, the period was altogether counter-revolutionary and conservative. The stream of life flowed quietly and cautiously, avoiding rapids and eddies, and though it was sometimes caught by the whirlpool of speculation, like the South-Sea Bubble, or by the delusions of the decadence-mongers, the population lived, on the whole, peacefully and enjoyed a certain amount of contentment. Poor Law rates were comparatively small, oscillating between £600,000 and £800,000 sterling annually, the inconsiderable number of enclosures hardly touched the yeomanry and farmers, the harvests were good, the cost of living was low, and, therefore, the real wage satisfactory. Philosophers and essayists busied themselves with ethics and natural religion, believing in a rational government of mankind and expecting virtue to be rewarded. Addison's prose, Pope's *Essay on Man*, Richardson's novels are the mirrors of the age, while Swift and Fielding are the rebels. The doctrines of natural law were made to tally with and to strengthen the constitution and the institutions of England. Pope, Burke, Blackstone, Robert Wallace, Adam Smith and Abraham Tucker's populariser, Paley, either use and interpret natural law in a conservative sense or draw its social-revolutionary teeth.

2.—POPE, BOLINGBROKE, AND BURKE

Inspired by Henry St. John, Lord Bolingbroke, who, in his retirement from public life, inquired into the system of *ius naturale* from an ethical-religious point of view, Pope sought to reconcile the state natural and civil, to teach man that happiness, the great aim and end of life, did not depend on equality of goods and station, but on virtue, on the rule of reason over passion, on the harmony between self-love and social, on the identification of individual with social interests. The state of nature was undoubtedly a state of innocence, in which the whole creation was united in peace. But man's passion got somehow the upper hand and ordered society became a necessity. Then nature spoke to man to take instruction from the ants' republic and the realm of bees, " how those in common all their wealth bestow, and anarchy without confusion know." Thus arose paternal government and common possessions. " True faith, true policy, united ran, that was but love of God, and this of man." Then came force and conquest, ambition, lucre, and lust, and destroyed the paternal and social state. In the reign of self-love, conflict and rebellion made all life impossible, until " forced into virtue thus, by self-defence, even kings learned justice and benevolence." Men learned to restrain each other, and join order to liberty. They ceased to fight about constitutions and religions, but desired good order and right behaviour :

> " Order is Heaven's first law ; and this confessed,
> Some are, and must be, greater than the rest,
> More rich, more wise." [1]

Although Pope's description of the state of nature and social equality is, in comparison with the apology for the existing order, the more poetical, Edmund Burke thought that Bolingbroke was not satisfied with it. " Pope cannot bear every truth. He has a timidity which hinders the full exertion of his faculties, almost as effectually as bigotry cramps those of the general herd of mankind." [2] And when, in 1754, Bolingbroke's *Philosophical*

[1] Pope, *Essay on Man* (1734), epistle 3, c. 4–6 ; epistle 4, c. 2.
[2] Burke, *Vindication of Natural Society*, ed. 1905, p. 41.

G

Works were published, in which natural religion and the simple teachings of Jesus are defended against artificial religion, revelation, and Christian theology, Burke set himself the task of finishing, once for all, with natural law. For this purpose he wrote his pamphlet, *A Vindication of Natural Society* (1756), which was supposed to have been left, in manuscript, by Lord Bolingbroke. It is a disturbing essay. Burke intended it as a *reductio ad absurdum* of Bolingbroke's doctrines, as an incisive condemnation of the dangerous tenets of natural law, yet its tone is so serious and its criticism of civil society so keen that it has often been taken as a genuine justification of the state of nature. Also, the bad reputation of its author among revolutionary writers has contributed to the misunderstanding of its purpose. It has been thought that Burke, having found his critique of civilisation inconvenient, " burked " its true character.[1]

The author exhibits a wide knowledge of the literature of natural law, but his main sources are Pope's *Essay on Man* and Bolingbroke's *Works*. The luminous features of the state of nature stand out against the dark and dismal background of civil society. Peace fled, and war transformed the world into an Aceldama. " Leviathan or civil power overflowed the earth with a deluge of blood, as if he were made to disport and play therein." And the cause of all that slaughter was the division of mankind into nations, created by artificial society, natural liberty was lost, and coercion made dungeons, whips, chains, racks, and gibbets a necessity. And there was no essential difference between despotism, oligarchy, and democracy. Everywhere the people, in an artificial or civil society, were sacrificed to the passions of the few. " In proportion as we have deviated from the plain rule of nature, and turned our reason against itself, in that proportion have we increased the follies and miseries of mankind." The same happened in law and religion. Laws multiplied and confusion increased, until it could be discovered no longer what things were held in property and what in common.

The professors of artificial law had always walked hand in

---

[1] I may add that I was of the same opinion myself, until a study of the whole period convinced me of my error.

hand with the professors of artificial theology. " As their end in confounding the reason of man, and abridging his natural freedom, is exactly the same, they have adjusted the means to that end in a way entirely similar." It might be said that in a state of nature the strong could rob the weak, but then the weak had at least full liberty to defend himself, or make reprisal by surprise or cunning, or by any other means in which he thought to have a superior advantage ; in political society, however, the poor man could not defend himself, since the only weapon he was allowed to use was money, and if he tried to avenge himself the whole force of that society would be directed against him. " The most obvious division of society is into rich and poor ; and it is no less obvious that the number of the former bears a great disproportion to those of the latter. The whole business of the poor is to administer to the idleness, folly, and luxury of the rich ; and that of the rich, in return, is to find the best methods of confirming the slavery and increasing the burden of the poor. In a state of nature it is an invariable law that a man's acquisitions are in proportion to his labours. In a state of artificial society it is a law, as constant and invariable, that those who labour most enjoy the fewest things ; and those who labour not at all, have the greatest number of enjoyments. . . . I suppose that there are in Great Britain upwards of a hundred thousand people employed in lead, tin, iron, copper, and coal mines ; these unhappy wretches scarce ever see the light of the sun ; there they work at a severe and dismal task, without the least prospect of being delivered from it. . . . A hundred thousand more, at least, are tortured without remission by the suffocating smoke, intense fires and constant drudgery necessary in refining and managing the produce of those mines. If any man informed us that two hundred thousand innocent persons were condemned to so intolerable slavery, how we should pity the unhappy sufferers, and how great would be our just indignation against those who inflicted so cruel and ignominious a punishment ! " All those miseries came upon men in consequence of having abandoned the laws of nature and reason.

Burke's argument is clear. By laying open the foundations of society, as Pope and Bolingbroke did, by contrasting natural with political society to the disadvantage of the latter, the poor, *i.e.* the great majority of the nation, might shake the whole fabric of the existing order.   It was no use replying that the theorists and poets of *ius naturale* confined themselves to religion and abstract ethics.   The masses, once awakened to their grievances and wrongs, would not stop there.   In short, the popularisation of the doctrines of natural law might lead to a social upheaval. English history, since the days of John Ball, confirmed those misgivings.   And Burke lived long enough to witness the French Revolution—that great experiment in *ius naturale*.

3.——ROBERT WALLACE

As a preacher in the royal chapel at Edinburgh and a man of liberal culture and learning, Robert Wallace devoted his leisure to the study of problems of population, scientific progress, and Utopian constitutions.   Some of the results of his researches and speculations he published in a series of essays under the collective title *Various Prospects* (1761), which deal also with the idea of perfect government, its great advantages and obstacles.   He was the first social-economic student who expressed the opinion that a communist republic, while it would at first banish poverty and promote the welfare of the people, would eventually come to grief from over-population.

Wallace's point of departure is the glaring disproportion between the capacities of man and nature on the one hand and the miserable and backward condition of the masses in particular and society in general.   Mankind, evidently, did not take advantage of the opportunities offered to it.   How little care did society take either of the souls or bodies of men !   Great numbers of the poor were but slaves and beasts of burden to the rich.   Ignorance toil, a scanty and unwholesome diet were their share.   Yet all these unhappy mortals were as much qualified by nature as the most fortunate of their kind, for a more agreeable life and nobler enjoyments.   Society as a whole made very little progress Even the most civilised nations knew little of the mysteries of nature.   No experiments were made to discover the essence of life. The advance in morality was hardly perceptible ; lust of wealth and power set man against man, nation against nation. Even the increase of population fell far short of the necessities for an adequate cultivation of the earth and the pursuit of useful arts, and yet the sexual appetites and human fertility were enormous.

It would appear that these evils and shortcomings could not be removed as long as private property and individual work prevailed, for without united efforts and harmonious endeavours neither agriculture nor arts and sciences would be cultivated. The great inequality which private property involved must necessarily lead to overwork and idleness, and both were unfavourable to acquisition of knowledge and self-culture. In order, therefore, to enable man to lift human affairs to a higher level new maxims of property and education must be introduced. The best models for such society were presented by Plato's *Republic* and Sir Thomas More's *Utopia*, and they essentially consisted of common possessions, co-operative labour, agriculture as the chief occupation, and education as the main care of society. The advantages which joint labour and the simple life of all the members of society might offer, were sufficiently known. Only such a society could provide for the improvement of the happiness of mankind.

The introduction of such government was, however, a difficult task now, for the minority who possessed wealth and power would use all means to prevent it. No amount of preaching and moralising could persuade them to acquiesce in a change of private property into common possessions. Such a transformation could only take place in times of a general revolution, when mental exaltation, love of equality, and a spirit of sacrifice took hold of all ; if in times like these a great legislator arose he might lead the nation to perfect government. Or it could be established by the example of small communist colonies formed by men of exceptional abilities ; the advantages reaped by them might stir up their neighbours to imitate their constitution and thus gradually spread the ideas of a communist and equitable constitution. There was nothing in the human mind which was averse from such a mode of life. There would be room enough in a communist society for any one to distinguish himself and satisfy his ambition and desire for distinction, by excelling in his work or by invention or discoveries. The love of liberty implanted in man's heart could find no higher satisfaction than in a society of the free and equal. The love of ease and pleasure would not be disappointed in a society where labour was moderate and more in the nature of healthy exercise than of toil. Idleness, one of the sources of poverty and decay, could not exist to any appreciable extent in a society where labour constituted the main basis ; public opinion would soon brand it as one of the worst vices. The equitable distribution of labour and its produce would remove the main cause of envy, jealousy, discord, hardship, and intrigue. Finally, general and careful training of the mind and body would steadily be directed towards developing those propensities, abilities, and forces of mankind which were favourable to, and suppressing those passions which were destructive of, communist life.

Such government was not only the happiest, but the most worthy of man. Poverty, ignorance, vice, could thus effectually be removed, and education, knowledge, health, and security afforded to everybody.

But there frowned one tremendous rock ahead on which the communist ship would be dashed to pieces. Under a perfect government the inconveniences of having a family would be entirely removed ; children would be so well taken care of and everything become so favourable to populousness that the earth would be overstocked with the human species and become unable to support it. The increase of mankind would outstrip the fertility of the soil. And these facts constituted the primary determinants in social affairs. To them all other things must be adjusted. A limited earth, a limited degree of its fertility, and the continued increase of mankind were the primary determinants. Poverty, war, vice, in short, the evils which we were complaining of were but the means of adjusting society to its primary determinants. The speculations of the social philosophers who framed a perfect constitution were only useful in so far as they might suggest some particular reform, but as a whole they were doomed to remain charming fiction, serving to enlarge our views and amuse our fancies.

Needless to say that Robert Wallace is the forerunner of Thomas Robert Malthus.

4.—BLACKSTONE, ADAM SMITH, AND PALEY

In his *Commentaries on the Laws of England* (book 2, chap. 1), Sir William Blackstone has left a summary of the critical attitude of *ius naturale* towards private property as well as of the wisdom of civil law in promoting order and ownership. The whole chapter, although by no means original, is curious ; the idea is still lurking therein that private property was more in the nature of a politic expedient than a right principle. Blackstone declares that, while people were pleased and charmed with the right of property, they were fearful of some defect of their title. It was none the less necessary to examine more deeply into the rudiments and grounds of the institutions of property. In the beginning of the world the all-bountiful Creator had given to man dominion over the earth and the fulness thereof. This gift was the only true and solid foundation of man's dominion over external things. As long as the population was insignificant in numbers all things were common, and every man took from the public stock to his own use such things as he required. In the same state of primeval simplicity lived also the American nations when they were discovered by Europeans ; and the Europeans themselves had once lived under similar conditions, or, as tradition related, in the golden age of the poets. By the law of nature and reason, he who first began to use a thing acquired a kind of transient property that lasted so long as he used it and no longer. Thus the soil was held in common, and no part of it was a permanent property of any man in particular, yet whoever was in occupation of any particular spot of it acquired for the time a sort of ownership. But when mankind increased in number, craftiness, and ambition, it became necessary to change occupation into ownership, otherwise innumerable disturbances might have arisen. In order, therefore, to secure peace private property was introduced, first in movables, partly by possession, but principally by the bodily labour bestowed upon them by the possessor ; then, in the soil, which was vested in the sovereign of the State or in his representatives, *i.e*, the lords of the manors. " And thus the legislature of England has universally promoted the grand order of civil society, the peace and security of individuals, by steadily pursuing that wise and orderly maxim of assigning to everything capable of ownership a legal and determinable owner."

After the great legal authority came the great economist to prove the necessity of private property. With Adam Smith it was not peace and security but the productivity of labour and the increase of wealth which justified private property. The most considerable improvements in the productive powers of labour were made after the appropriation of land and accumulation of stock. As professor of moral philosophy Smith knew all the phases through which natural law had passed. In his time the laws of nature, natural order, and natural liberty, came to signify freedom of trade and commerce from the regulations and interferences of Mercantilism, freedom for the natural promptings of the economic man. With the physiocrats, he assumed the existence of a natural order of things, which, if not interfered with by State laws and subtle regulations, would result in the happiness of mankind.[1] He never misses the opportunity of pointing out that civilisation or the improvement of society was not the product of human foresight and calculation, but of the natural propensities of economically active men.[2] *Laissez faire* did not mean licence or anarchic confusion, but a settled confidence in the laws inherent in nature and man, and distrust of State-made laws. But Smith was also fully cognisant of the communist interpretation of natural law. " In the original state of things," he declares, " which preceded both the appropriation of land and the accumulation of stock, the whole produce of labour belongs to the labourer. Had this state continued, the

[1] Adam Smith, *Wealth of Nations*, book 3, chap. 1 ; book 4, chap. 9.
[2] *Ibid.* Introduction ; book 1, chap. 2.

wages of labour would have augmented with all those improvements in its productive powers to which the division of labour
gives occasion." For "the produce of labour constitutes the
natural recompense or wages of labour. . . . But this
original state of things .   . could not last beyond the first
introduction of the appropriation of land and the accumulation
of stock. It was at an end, therefore, long before the most considerable improvements were made in the productive powers of
labour, and it would be of no purpose to trace further what
might have been its effects upon the recompense or wages of
labour." [1]

It was, then, under the system of private property
that improvements in the production of commodities were
introduced and it was no use speculating upon a dead past.
Besides, the poorest labourer in a civilised society enjoyed a
greater share of the necessaries and conveniences of life than any
member in a natural society, though the distribution of labour
and its produce was very unequal in the former, and equitable
in the latter society.[2] Private property was thus justified by the
increase and improvements in the production of wealth. And
were it not for the passions, such as envy, malice, or resentment,
society could exist with some tolerable degree of security, even if
there were no civil government to protect life and property from
the injustice of those passions. " But avarice and ambition in
the rich, in the poor the hatred of labour and the love of present
ease and enjoyment, are the passions which prompt them to invade
property. . . . Wherever there is great property, there is
great inequality. For one rich man there must be at least
five hundred poor, and the affluence of the few supposes the
indigence of the many. The affluence of the rich excites the
indignation of the poor, who are often both driven by want and
prompted by envy to invade his possessions It is only under
the shelter of the civil magistrate that the owner of that valuable
property, acquired by the labour of many years or perhaps many
successive generations, can sleep a single night in security.

[1] Adam Smith, *Wealth of Nations*, book 1, chap. 8.
[2] *Ibid.* Introduction.

. . . The acquisition of valuable and extensive property necessarily requires the establishment of civil government."[1] It was thus through the inequality engendered by the increase and appropriation of wealth that the civil state became a necessity. And the civil state itself was justified by the protection it afforded to private property as the basis of the production of wealth. Lest it should be inferred that Adam Smith was prepared to sacrifice everything to the growth of wealth we must point out that his attitude towards the working classes was full of humanity. Like most philosophers who were familiar with the doctrines of *ius naturale* he was favourable to the claims of labour, and he urged the employers to listen to the " dictates of reason and humanity " and to consider the health and welfare of their work-people.

Archdeacon Paley was greatly preoccupied with the theoretical problems of the origin and justification of private property. " There is a difficulty in explaining, consistently with the law of nature, the origin of property in land, for the land was once, no doubt, common." Altogether, the whole system of economic life under private property appeared to him unnatural. In his famous chapter " On Property " he gave rein to his sentiments in the following parable : " If you should see a flock of pigeons in a field ; and if (instead of each picking where and what it liked, taking just as much as it wanted, and no more) you should see ninety-nine of them gathering all they got into one heap, reserving nothing for themselves but the chaff and the refuse, keeping this heap for one, and that the weakest, perhaps worst, pigeon of the flock ; sitting round and looking on all the winter, whilst this one was devouring and throwing about and wasting it ; and if one pigeon more hardy or hungry than the rest touched a grain of the hoard, all the others instantly flying upon it and tearing it to pieces ; if you should see this, you would see nothing more than what is every day practised and established among men."[2] That was human society on the basis of property.

[1] Adam Smith, *Wealth of Nations*, book 5, chap. 1 (part 2).
[2] William Paley, *Moral and Pol. Philosophy*, 1785, book 3, part 1, chaps. 1-4.

Did it not appear paradoxical and unnatural? Yet it existed and people did not mind it. There must, therefore, have been some very important advantages which counterbalanced those miseries and imbecilities and kept the world going. What were they? (1) Private property increased the produce of the earth. (2) It preserved the produce of the earth to maturity. (3) It prevented contests. (4) It improved the conveniences of life. Upon these accounts it may be pronounced that, with a few exceptions, even the poorest and the worst provided were, under the system of private property, better provided with the necessaries of life than any of the people who lived in societies where most things were held in common. The earth and the fulness thereof were given to mankind for use, and the system of private property made a better use of them than communism did. Paley, in effect, says the same as Adam Smith—the justification of private property lay in the improvements of production, accumulation of stock, and the growth of wealth or the necessaries and conveniences of life.

At the time when Smith and Paley were writing, the economic revolution was beginning to unchain or call into being productive forces which were destined to surpass the greatest economic achievements of the past.

PART II

1760-1834

I

THE ECONOMIC REVOLUTION

I.—INVENTIONS : ENCLOSURES

THE last half of the eighteenth century will ever be memorable in the history of England in particular and of mankind in general. What philosophers and scientists had dreamt, handicraftsmen and legislators had feared, came to pass. Invention after invention penetrated the enclosed dominions of arts and crafts, and transferred human skill and deftness of hand to passive and lifeless matter, changing it into a multitudinous host of ceaselessly active forces and all-powerful creators of riches beyond the dreams of the political economists.

" .   .   . I exult to see
An intellectual mastery exercised
O'er the blind elements .   .   . almost a soul
Imparted to brute matter. I rejoice,
Measuring the force of those gigantic powers
That, by the thinking mind, have been compelled
To serve the will of feeble-bodied Man."
(Wordsworth, *Excursion*, book 8.)

In the wake of the triumphant march of the iron giants the social and political face of England changed. Ancient cities and boroughs lost their glamour ; insignificant hamlets rose to splendour ; a resettlement of the population went on apace.

" .   .   .   . At social Industry's command,
How quick, how vast an increase ! From the germ
Of some poor hamlet, rapidly produced
Here a huge town, continuous and compact,
Hiding the face of the earth for leagues—and there,
Where not a habitation stood before,
Abodes of men irregularly massed
Like trees in forests—spread through spacious tracts,
O'er which the smoke of unremitting fires
Hangs permanent, and plentiful as wreaths
Of vapour glittering in the morning sun."   (*Ibid.*)

The long and amazing series of inventions, particularly the improvement of the steam engine, inspired also the imagination of Erasmus Darwin, the poet-thinker, who saw in his mind the steam engine applied to sea and land and air transport, and " as the specific levity of air is too great for the support of great burdens by balloons there seems no probable method of flying conveniently but by the power of steam or some other explosive material, which another half century may probably discover." [1]

At the same time a wide net of canals, connecting the shipping, manufacturing, and commercial centres of the kingdom, were built.

> " So with strong arm immortal Brindley leads
> His long canals, and parts the velvet meads ;
> Winding in lucid lines, the watery mass
> Mines the firm rock, or loads the deep morass,
> Feeds the long vale, the nodding woodland laves,
> And Plenty, Arts, and Commerce freight the waves." [2]

Simultaneously with these revolutionary changes in manufacture and commerce a no less revolutionary transformation took place in agriculture. While in the period from 1710 to 1760 the process of enclosing farms and lands was slow and imperceptible, amounting altogether to about one-third of a million acres, its pace was enormously accelerated in the following sixty years, when no less than 5,700,000 acres were withdrawn from the common-field-system or small cultivators. The traditional regulations and tangled customs of the village community, which impeded production and nursed inefficiency, were swept away like cobwebs, and the new agriculture, carried on with improved methods and tools as well as scientific experiment, began to cope with the rapidly growing home demand. Wide tracts of waste land were brought under the plough, and the experiments in stock-raising yielded results as remarkable as those of the mechanical inventions. The economic superiority of enclosed or private agriculture over the open-field or communal agriculture was so striking that nobody denied it. Rents and prices rose, and the wealth of the landowners multiplied.

[1] Erasmus Darwin, *Botanic Garden*, ed. 1799, I., p. 31, note.
[2] *Ibid.*, canto III. 351–7.

Rapid as the changes were in England, they lacked the suddenness and catastrophic character which they exhibited in Scotland. The transition in England took centuries—in Scotland decades. Sir Walter Scott witnessed the sunset of mediaevalism of his country and with all the power of his mind attempted to bring it again to life in his poetry and romance. Instead of a preface, which he was afraid the reader would skip, he wrote an epilogue to his *Waverley*, explaining his innermost thought : " There is no European nation which, within the course of half a century, or little more, has undergone so complete a change as this kingdom of Scotland. The effects of the insurrection of 1745, the destruction of the patriarchal power of the Highland chiefs, the abolition of the heritable jurisdictions of the Lowland nobility and barons . . . commenced this innovation. The gradual influx of wealth, and extension of commerce, have since united to render the present people of Scotland a class of beings as different from their grandfathers as the existing English are from those of Queen Elizabeth's time."

It was this suddenness that produced so many Scottish social reformers, particularly land reformers. From 1775 onwards the pioneers of land reform have been Scotsmen.

2.—SOCIAL EFFECTS

In the midst of this economic revolution the statistician, Patrick Colquhoun, wrote : " An era has arrived in the affairs of the British Empire, discovering resources which have excited the wonder, the astonishment, and perhaps the envy of the civilised world " ; and spoke of " the accumulation of property, extensive beyond all credibility and (during a war of unexampled expense) rapid in its growth beyond what the most sanguine mind could have conceived." [1] Looked at from the angle of vision of production and wealth the exultation of Colquhoun, an adorer of Adam Smith, was justified. In 1688, as we know from Gregory King, the national income amounted to £43,500,000 ; in 1770,

[1] P. Colquhoun, *Resources of the British Empire*, 1814, pp. 49, 110.

H

Arthur Young [1] estimated the national income at £119,500,000 ; according to Colquhoun it amounted, in 1812, to £430,000,000.

Profound and comprehensive changes in the economics of society could not come to fruition without shaking the social structure to its foundations. " Domestic handicraftsmen and small farmers alike were overwhelmed ; industry, both manufacturing and agricultural, was re-organised on the new commercial lines which seemed best adapted for the greatest possible production at the least possible cost. The completion of the work of enclosure destroyed the inherited traditions of the peasantry, their ideals, their customs and habits, their ancestral solutions of the problems of life—all, in fact, that made up the native homebred civilisation of rural England." [2] The economic revolution resulted in the concentration of land and manufacture in fewer hands, in production on a large scale at the expense of the small independent producers ; it collected large numbers of propertyless people as wage-earners or proletarians into factories, mines, and fields. Out of heterogeneous masses of labourers, artizans, domestic craftsmen, coming from different surroundings, with different habits and feelings, a working class gradually arose, compact and militant. The social stratification, built up by centuries of a stirring history, broke into a jumble of fragments which in stress and turmoil changed positions. The rise of new classes, the submerging of old social strata, and the re-valuation of traditional worth in society, rendered a long and painful process of re-organisation and readjustment an urgent political necessity. The transformation was, however, so new and unprecedented a phenomenon that none of the contemporary statesmen and political students saw it whole or perceived the wide ramification of its effects. They were still thinking in old political terms, busying themselves with parliamentary franchise, poor laws, foreign and colonial affairs while the social confusion was being aggravated by the powerful effects of the French Revolution and Napoleonic Wars.

[1] A. Young, *Tour Through the North of England*, 1771, IV., p. 393.
[2] R. A. Prothero, *English Farming*, 1912, p. 407. *Cf.* also Robert Southey, *Letters from England*, 1807, III., pp. 114–9, and Sir Walter Scott, *Familiar Letters*, II., p. 78.

3.—AGGRAVATION BY NAPOLEONIC WARS

England as the pioneer of the transition from the agrarian to the manufacturing state suffered more than any other nation which, in the course of the nineteenth century, followed her on the same path of development. The experience necessary to mitigate the miseries and pains attendant upon such a re-adjustment of society was wanting, and the empirical, go-ahead, not to say, recklessly daring nature of the English mind was not apt to pause and inquire into the operation of the new economic phase the nation was entering upon. While crossing an uncharted sea England was caught by the tornado of the French upheaval. She was involved in a long war which emptied her treasury and withdrew the attention of her best minds from home affairs at a time when every ounce of gold and silver, when every thought, was necessary to help her in overcoming the difficulties of the economic transition. The terrible decade 1810–20, the Luddites, the Spenceans, the Blanketeers, the conspiracies, Peterloo, and Cato Street, were largely due to the errors, perhaps inevitable errors, committed in the years from 1790 to 1800. One-sixth of the expenditure raised for war purposes might have been sufficient to lay the foundation of a healthy social reform, to provide for old age [1] and illness of the factory workers, to regulate child labour, to assist the small farmers and handicraftsmen, to protect agricultural labour, and generally to render the social readjustment less fortuitous and, therefore, less painful. We need not accept as wholly true all the alleged horrors that are so often ascribed to the rise of the

[1] Dr. Priestley advocated, in 1787, the establishment of an old age and sickness fund by means of deductions from the wages. He argued that, " since the labour of the husbandman or manufacturer is the only source of all gain or property in any country, even that of the gentleman, it is their own labour that, more circuitously and ineffectually, now maintains them in their wretched and dependent state, whereas upon this plan, their own labour (and probably much increased) will be more immediately employed for their own advantage " (*An Account of a Society for Encouraging the Industrious Poor*, Birmingham, 1787, p. 15).

factory system. Communist and Tory prejudices, particularly those of Charles Hall, Robert Southey, and Robert Owen, go some way to account for the gloomy impressions which that period still evokes. The most cogent proof against their accusations is to be found in the rapid growth of the population and the decrease of the rate of mortality, which set in with the development of the industrial revolution. Such facts cannot be gainsaid ; they are irrefragable evidence of growing prosperity. Up to 1806 wages were high, employment was plentiful. The displacement and depreciation of labour by machinery began about that time. Still, such a catastrophic change as the economic revolution implied was bound to shake society, to produce widespread discontent, and to create problems, perils, and crises which only far-seeing statesmanship and recognition of causes and effects might have mitigated or forestalled. Peace, watchfulness, and social reform were necessary. Instead of which came war, repression of the discontented elements, suspension of the Habeas Corpus Act, high treason trials, indiscriminate poor relief, and Malthus's population theory as a salve to the agitated conscience of the nation. And the drain of precious metals caused by the payment of subsidies and war expenditure as well as by the needs of expanding agriculture and trade, led, in 1797, to the suspension of specie payment and issue of a paper currency, giving rise to a high gold agio, high prices, fluctuations of trade, Socialist and Radical schemes of paper money and paper notes. For want of coin of the realm manufacturers paid their employees with money tokens, and the delusion was created that paper could completely displace precious metals as a circulating medium, and that gold as legal tender (established in 1816) was merely the invention of Lord Liverpool, Sir Robert Peel, and the Jews. Finally, the enormous national debt and the Funding System, to which the wars had given rise, caused much perturbation among reformers.

All these chaotic events, while playing havoc with men's fortunes and lives, combined to create problems which occupied two generations of social philosophers, economists, and poets, and produced a period of intense thinking and glowing emotion.

II

COMMUNIST AND DEMOCRATIC FERMENT

I.—PHASES OF THOUGHT

FROM a sociological point of view, the period from 1760 to 1825 exhibits four phases. The first phase was purely parliamentary and constitutional; its protagonists, Wilkes and "Junius," fought against the oligarchy and the remnants of personal monarchy; this phase is outside the plan of our work. The second phase was mainly agrarian; the effects of the rapid rate of enclosing farms and commons as well as of the improvements in agriculture turned the attention of revolutionary minds towards agrarian reform; its writers were Spence, Ogilvie, and Paine. The third phase was caused by enthusiasm for the French Revolution on the part of English intellectuals and London artizans, whose minds had been prepared by the theories which were current in the antecedent two phases; its writers were William Godwin, the youthful Coleridge, Southey, Wordsworth, and John Thelwall. The fourth phase was that of the industrial revolution proper, the first critical writer of which was Charles Hall, followed by Robert Owen and his school, and the anti-capitalist critics, Ravenstone, Hodgskin, and several anonymous writers; the poet of this phase was Shelley.

The common basis of all those writers consisted mainly of natural law as they found it in Locke's *On Civil Government*. This small treatise became their Bible, particularly after its theories had been consecrated by the success of the American Revolution, and had come back to England from France endowed with the fiery soul of Rousseau. The purely constitutional reformers took from Locke the theories of the social and political compact and of original society whose members were supposed to have been free and equal. The agrarian reformers appealed to Locke for the truth of their first principle that the land was originally held in common. The communists and socialist, or anti-capitalist writers, based themselves, in addition to those self-evident truths, on Locke's theory that labour was the real title to property, or, as Adam Smith puts it, " the produce of labour constitutes the natural recompense or wages of labour." The industrial revolution had shown, however, that the produce of labour belonged, not to the labourer, but to the capitalist. This experience, joined to Adam Smith's emphasis on labour being the source of wealth and the standard of value, and Ricardo's apparently irrefragable logic of the theory of labour value and the inverse ratio of wages and profit, gave to Locke's argument on labour and property a social-revolutionary turn, and converted it into a weapon against the social system which was emerging from the economic revolution.

We shall have occasion to point out the cardinal error that underlay those reasonings ; meanwhile, let us see the logical conclusions at which the communists, socialists, and anti-capitalist critics arrived. They were as follows :—

(1) Common possession was natural and therefore just and equitable ; (2) Labour was the only title to property or wealth ; (3) Nature, including human nature, was governed by inherent, divine, and rational laws.

Hence it followed :—

(1) That private property was unnatural and pernicious, and ought to be abolished ; (2) That all deductions from the produce of labour, in the shape of rent, profit, and interest, by non-labourers, constituted a violation of natural law ; (3) That all reform must be directed towards the restoration of, or be in harmony with, natural law.

This was the main current which pervaded social and political criticism in the period from 1760 to 1850. Its theorists became the teachers of the Chartists, who spread it among the masses.

However, though it formed the main current, it was not the only one on which the revolutionary writers floated their theories. We have already seen that Burke realised the danger which lurked behind the system of *ius naturale*—a system which assumed that the horde of human animals were born into the world, receiving the earth and the fulness thereof as their common inheritance, but that a few of them, endowed with cunning and strength above the rest, disliked labour and scanty fare, and therefore appropriated the earth for their own exclusive use, and made all the other human animals work for them. Burke saw the meaning of this theory, but not until 1790 did he attempt to formulate an alternative social theory. The essence of his *Reflections on the Revolution in France* (1790), written with the view of stemming the tide of revolutionary ideas that were pouring into England from Paris, was that social systems and constitutions were neither manufactured by theorists nor suddenly called into being by a vote of popular assemblies, but were an organic growth; the past was not a stupendous error or imposture to be wiped off the national slate, but an organism grown in the course of ages and containing both living and sloughy matter, the former to be preserved and further developed, the latter to be removed. This theory of organic development of social institutions, while it gained approval among conservative publicists and jurists (Savigny), did not commend itself to the revolutionary writers. Yet the course of the French Revolution made it impossible to adhere to natural law, and thinking men were searching for a new social theory. Philosophically, the French Revolution appeared as a great experiment in *ius naturale;* all its declarations were written in its spirit and terms, and its inspirer was Rousseau. The terroristic acts and wars into which that social earthquake degenerated had the effect of discrediting the whole system of natural law. Robespierre and Bonaparte destroyed the halo of Rousseau. A painful void was created in the minds of the poets and philosophers who had welcomed the events of 1789 to 1793 as the dawn of the rights of man. The light of nature and right reason failed. What was now to take its place as the guide of human affairs? Some writers accepted Burke's organic theory, or Schelling's evolutionism, to which Erasmus Darwin's *Zoonomia* (translated into German in 1795-6) had probably given the impulse; others turned to romanticism and mediaevalism, for which Sir Walter Scott found the most adequate literary forms, while the advanced English reformers found in Bentham's utilitarian philosophy a substitute and leading principle.

It was Bentham who, for a time, supplanted Locke. From the beginning of his legal career he rebelled against the abstract, unempirical, and pseudo-historical state of nature. As far back as 1780—his *Introduction to the Principles of Morals and Legislation* was printed in 1780, but published in 1789—he was convinced of the unscientific character of the theories on which jurisprudence was based. He had a historical sense, and greatly admired Montesquieu's *Esprit des Lois*.[1] Still, it was not history, but psychology, from which he took his leading principle. Following Priestley, Holbach, Helvetius, and Beccaria, he saw in utility or in the greatest happiness of the greatest number the moral test of individual and government actions. This test was accepted by political reformers and socialist writers. Happiness was thought to be the aim and end of man and human society, to which constitutions and laws should conform. Bentham himself was aggressively anti-communist and preferred security of property to equality of distribution ; he regarded private property as the only possible basis of social life, and whenever it came into conflict with equality, the latter should forthwith be abandoned.[2] But in the hands of the communists or socialists the felicific formula was converted into as effective a weapon

---

[1] Bentham, in his essay on the " Influence of Time and Place on Matters of Legislation," declares : " Before Montesquieu, a man who had a distant country given him to make laws for, would have made short work of it. ' Name to me the people, reach me down the Bible, and the business is done at once. The laws they have been used to shall be superseded by mine ; manners, they shall have mine, which are the best in nature ; religion, they shall have mine too, which is all of it true, and the only one that is so.' Since Montesquieu, the number of documents which a legislator would require is considerably enlarged. He would say, ' Send the people to me, or me to the people ; lay open to me the whole tenor of their life and conversation ; paint to me the face and geography of the country ; give me as close and minute a view as possible of their possible laws, their manners, and their religion.' "

[2] The same. *Works*, I., chap. 7–12, also Appendix.

against private property as natural law had been before. The founders of co-operative communities and advocates of Owenite views simply revelled in the idea of happiness, regarding it as the major premise of all social reasonings, as if it were a self-evident truth that man was born for happiness. They argued that private property was wrong, since under its sway the labouring masses, the greatest number of the nation, were condemned to misery. Nor did the institution of private property lead to security, for the produce of the exertions of labour was not secured to the labourer, but was taken from him by the land-owner, capitalist, and money-lender. With Bentham, the bar to happiness was the oligarchy, which should be removed by democratic reform. With the communist, the bar to happiness was the proprietor of the means of production, who should be discarded for the communist co-operator. The principal representatives of social reform based on happiness are Robert Owen, William Thompson, and John Gray. From about 1828 the utilitarian doctrine, as one of the principles of communism, gradually gave way to a revival of natural law. The social critic who accomplished the restoration of Locke was Thomas Hodgskin. Also the question of Poor Law reform, which at that time became increasingly urgent, contributed a good deal to the rehabilitation of natural law, the advocates of the old Poor Law arguing that men, by renouncing their community rights, reserved to themselves, or could not have abandoned, the right to existence ; the maintenance of the poor was thus guaranteed by the social compact, or by the law of nature. Theoretically, natural law formed the link of connection between the working class social reformer and the Tory who opposed the abolition of the old Poor Laws, while the same doctrine separated the socialists from the Benthamites, who worked with might and main against the old system of poor relief.

This outline of the theoretical controversies and their phases may serve as an introduction to the following chapters dealing with three groups of social critics, viz., (1) the agrarian reformers —Spence, Ogilvie, and Paine ; (2) the communists who received the strongest impulse from the French Revolution—William

Godwin, Coleridge, Southey, and the London Corresponding Society ; (3) the communists and anti-capitalist critics—Hall, Owen, Thompson, Ravenstone, Gray, Hodgskin, and several anonymous writers, whose criticisms and schemes were connected with the rise of the factory system and the unfolding of class warfare between Capital and Labour.

2.—SPENCE, OGILVIE, AND PAINE

Thomas Spence (b. June 21, 1750, d. September 1, 1814), the originator of the single-tax reform, was of Scottish origin, his father having left Aberdeen, in 1733, for Newcastle, where he followed the trade of net-making, shoe-making, and shop-keeping. Thomas, one of a family of nineteen children, was taught by his father, who appears to have been a capable educator and a man of wide reading. At first, Thomas learned the trade of his father, but on showing some talent for mental work, he was given opportunity for reading, and successively became a bookkeeper and private tutor. During his leisure hours he must have read a good deal of natural law in Locke, Grotius, Blackstone, and others, which studies gained in practical importance by a lawsuit then pending between the freemen and the corporation of Newcastle. Following the trend of the time the corporation enclosed the town moor or common, and let it for agricultural purposes. The rental was divided between the members of the corporation, to the exclusion of the freemen, whereupon the latter brought an action, demanding a share of the rent, since the town moor was common. A similar lawsuit was pending in Durham. The controversies to which these lawsuits gave rise decided the future career of the obscure schoolmaster, and turned him into a lifelong missionary for land reform on the basis of parochial partnership.

As a member of the Newcastle Philosophical Society he developed his plan in a lecture delivered on November 8, 1775, which contains all the ideas he propagated to the end of his life. Believing that the doctrines of natural law were axioms which everybody accepted, he takes it for granted that in the state of nature the earth and the fulness thereof were common and that everybody

enjoyed equal liberty.   The land was as necessary to human existence as light, air, and water ; to deprive a man of the land was to
deprive him of his life.   Jurists argued that private property in
land originated from agreement.   No agreement, however, could
bind posterity, unless it be renewed by each successive generation.   Of such a renewal nobody knew or heard anything.
Besides, civil society did not arise for the purpose of rendering
the conditions of mankind worse than they were in the natural
state, but to remove the inconveniencies which had arisen from
the absence of conscious organisation.   Civil society was, indeed
an agreement between free and equal to guarantee their mutual
rights and liberties of nature against aggressions and usurpations.
From these premises it might be concluded that the earth was
still the common heritage of mankind.   Yet, the actual conditions told quite a different tale.   The land had been allowed
to be usurped by comparatively few people, who called themselves
the aristocracy, and who were actually worshipped as demi-gods.
Another argument in favour of private property was labour.
It was said by Locke that labour bestowed on things was the
real title to property.   That argument held good as to manufactured goods, the manufacturer being their real creator.   But
who could seriously argue that the earth was manufactured
by the aristocracy ?   No !   It was usurpation on the one hand,
and ignorance on the other, which led to the flagrant violation
of natural law, and to the establishment of the usurpers.   An
enlightened nation, conscious of its natural rights and liberties,
could resolve to restore the land to its rightful heirs, and join
the advantages of the state of nature to those of civil society.
Public meetings all over the country would carry such a resolution.   The people being sovereign would transfer the land to
the parishes, for the purpose of erecting not a complete communist republic, but a mixed state between communism and
private use—Spence called it later (1798) a state between More's
Utopia and Harrington's *Oceana*—*i.e.*, where the land belonged
to the parish, which would let it to farmers on a moderate rental.
The revenues from the rent would form the only tax, from
which the expenses of the local and central government would be

defrayed. No other taxes and duties to be levied. A complete democratic constitution in parish, borough, city, and national affairs was, as a matter of course, the only one worthy of such a commonwealth. This republic, based on justice and reason, and protected by the virtue and prosperity of large masses of farmers against all disturbers of the public peace, as well as by a well-trained citizen army against foreign aggressions, would endure for ever and ever, serving as a model and an inspiring example to all the nations of the earth. That is the substance of the lecture and the teachings of Spence, in general. He added, in 1800, a new idea to the body of his doctrines, viz. that the real struggle was not about forms of government, but for " a system of society capable of delivering us from the deadly mischief of great accumulations of wealth, which enable a few rich unfeeling monsters to starve whole nations."[1]

Spence, being an agitator rather than a scholar, published his lecture and hawked it himself in the streets of Newcastle at a halfpenny a piece. The Philosophical Society, evidently disgusted with this way of spreading the light of nature and reason, cancelled his membership. Also his reputation as a teacher suffered, for soon after this event the number of his pupils began to dwindle. Spence left for London, where he was successively a number-carrier, street bookseller, and editor of a democratic periodical, *Pig's Meat* (1793–95), consisting of extracts from various advanced writers, for which he was kept in prison from May to December, 1795. He was at the same time implicated in the conspiracies of the London Corresponding Society. In 1797 he published a pamphlet, *Rights of Infants*, in 1798 a Constitution for his Spencean Commonwealth, which consists of two parts, the first being a reprint of the French *Declaration of the Rights of Man and Citizen*, the second a codification of his agrarian proposals contained in his Newcastle lecture, adding the new provision of female suffrage. In 1800 he wrote, in the form of letters to the " Citizens " of England, *The Restorer of Society to its Natural State*, consisting of a revolutionary formulation

[1] Thomas Spence, *Restorer of Society to its Natural State*, 1801, Letter 14.

of his agrarianism and democracy.   This publication brought him into conflict with the law, and he was sentenced to twelve months' imprisonment. He was his own counsel, and treated the jury to a long and laborious exposition of his theories, reading all his pamphlets and giving a history of his life and work. Shortly before his death he attempted to publish a new periodical, *The Giant Killer, or Anti-Landlord*.   He had a small but very active group of adherents, who made themselves noticeable in the stormy years from 1816 to 1820 ; they were the leaders and banner-bearers of all great demonstrations of the working classes in London in those years.   Even in the Chartist Movement of 1838 and 1839 the name of Spence was held dear. Francis Place, who knew him well and acquired some of his correspondence, describes him as a man of short stature, " not more than five feet high, very honest, simple, single-minded, who loved mankind, and firmly believed that a time would come when men would be virtuous, wise and happy.   He was unpractical in the ways of the world to an extent hardly imaginable." [1] Spence republished his Newcastle lecture several times, in 1796, under the title *Meridian Sun of Liberty or Rights of Man*, a new edition of which was published by H. M. Hyndman in 1882.

The critical apparatus of natural law used by Spence was handled with incomparably greater skill and erudition by William Ogilvie (1736-1813) in his *Essay on the Right of Property in Land* (1781).   Ogilvie, a professor of humanity at the Aberdeen University, and a successful agriculturist, was evidently distressed at the sight of the misery, ignorance, and stagnation of the labouring classes, and regarded private property in land as the source of all evil ; the monopoly in land, " by the operation of which the happiness of mankind had been for ages more invaded and restrained than by all the tyranny of kings, the imposture of priests, and the chicane of lawyers taken together, though these are supposed to be the greatest evils that afflict the societies of human kind " (§ 28–9).

[1] Place, Add. MSS. 27808, Vol. 1, Part 3 (British Museum). *Cf. Quarterly Review*, 1817 ; Mackenzie, *History of Newcastle*, 1826 ; Davenport, *Life of Thomas Spence*, 1836.

The rumblings of the French Revolution are distinctly heard in that denunciation. Yet Ogilvie was no revolutionist. "It is natural to the mind, when new ideas arise on important subjects, to open itself with fondness to the pleasing impressions which they make. Yielding to the seducing enthusiasm, the author has been led to speak with freedom of great changes, suddenly to be accomplished, as practicable in some cases, and to be desired in many. Yet he is well aware that great changes, suddenly accomplished, are always pregnant with danger and evil, and ought, on almost no occasion whatever, to be desired or brought forward by the friends of mankind. Partial reformation, gradual progressive innovation, may produce every advantage which the most important and sudden changes can promise, yet without incurring those dreadful hazards and those inevitable evils with which great and sudden changes are still attended " (Introduction).

His critical shafts are, nevertheless, exceedingly keen. The earth having been given to mankind in common, every man possessed a natural right, an inalienable birthright to an equal share in the land. This right could not be renounced by any express or tacit compact on man's entering into civil society, and therefore could still be claimed. Rude societies, like the ancient German tribes, or the Irish up to the sixteenth century, acknowledged it. In short, the first maxim of natural law was that every man had an equal share in the land. But there was a second maxim of natural law, " that every one, by whose labour any position of the soil has been rendered more fertile, has a right to the additional produce of that fertility, or to the value of it, and may transfer this right to other men. On the first of these maxims depends the freedom and prosperity of the lower ranks. On the second, the perfection of the art of agriculture and the improvement of the common stock and wealth of the community " (§ 10). Natural law was destroyed by the progress of trade and commerce or by conquest Municipal (civil) laws took its place and confirmed and extended private property and the monopoly in land, thereby causing misery to the lower ranks of society. The interest of society was completely subordinated to the interest of the land owners, who were permitted to enjoy revenues out of all proportion to their services rendered to agriculture or society. All property ought to be the reward of industry ; all industry ought to be secure of its full reward ; the exorbitant privileges of the landholder subverted both these principles of good policy. And " whoever enjoys any revenue, not proportioned to such industry or exertion of his own or of his ancestors, is a freebooter, who has found means to cheat or rob the public, and more especially the indigent of that district in which he lives. The hereditary revenue of a great landholder . . . increases without any efforts of his . . . it is a premium given to idleness " (§ 39). The real problem was, how to abolish that monopoly and to combine the two maxims of natural law, *viz.*, equal share in the land, and right of property to the additional value produced by man's labour, so as to banish poverty and, at the same time, promote improvement of cultivation ?

Revolutionary as Ogilvie is in his critique, he becomes conservative when dealing with reform propositions. Very little remains of man's natural and inalienable right to an equal share in the land. The utmost that a propertyless citizen might claim was a farm of forty acres for which he was to pay to the landlord a rent, fixed by arbitrators, besides " certain aids and services of a feudal nature, so regulated as to produce that degree of connection and dependence which may be expedient for preserving order and subordination in the country without danger of giving rise to oppression and abuse " (§ 71, number xv.). The farm or allotment thus acquired should be perpetual. The occupier should have the right to transmit it to his heirs or assignees, but could not sublet it ; if he sold it to another man who did not reside upon it, but annexed it to some other farm, one-tenth part of the price or reserved rent should go to the community. The occupier of such a farm was not given any right in the commons, moors, woodlands, private roads, or other appendages of the manor. Ogilvie also advocated the appointment of a special board, with powers to purchase estates which were in the market and might be had for a reasonable price (twenty-five to thirty years' purchase), and divide them into small farms of a single plough only, to be let for a full reserved rent in perpetual property.

Ogilvie's *Essay* was reprinted in 1838 for the instruction of the Chartists, and the following preface appended to it :—

" The present reprint is submitted to the public at a time when the demands of the labouring classes are beginning to be heard from the deep degradation to which they have been submitted ever since the Norman Conquest. They will see here the cruelty, absurdity and tyranny of man monopolising the labour of thousands ; and they will also see the means whereby they may extricate themselves from so miserable a bondage." The editor, however, knew nothing of the life of the author, whom he calls John Ogilby, " who lived about the year 1778." He also declares that the book was then suppressed and the author bribed by the government. Still, the doctrines contained therein " are the same, unchanged and immutable, and will afford the only remedy for the existing miseries and oppressions of the labouring and useful classes of England."

A third edition was published in 1891.

Thomas Paine (1737–1809), a radical politician and moderate social reformer, who, in the present age, would have been a respected member of the Liberal Party, sketched in his *Agrarian Justice* (1795–96) a plan of social reform, based on arguments of natural law, particularly of Locke's *Civil Government*, part second. It may be regarded as the economic supplement to his *Rights of Man* (1791–2), which was written with the purpose of refuting Burke's *Reflections*. The division of society into rich and poor, he argues, was the effect of civil government or civilisation. In the natural state, such as the Indians in America still presented, there were not to be found any of those spectacles of human misery which met the eye in the great cities of Europe. On the other hand, the natural state lacked the advantages that sprang from agriculture, arts, science, and manufacture. As it was not possible for a civilised man to return to the life of an Indian and thus to escape misery, some means must be found to bring to him the advantages which he enjoyed in the natural state and join them to those of civilisation. And this could be effected by accepting the principle of natural law that every man and woman was entitled to an equal share in the land. But the land in its uncultivated state was of small value. It was cultivation and improvement which made it valuable, but at the same time made it property of the agriculturist. Still, only the improved value was the property of the cultivator, while the ground itself belonged to all. Each cultivator owed, therefore, a ground-rent to the community. The absolute right of property in land sprang from identifying the improvement of the land with land itself. This identification was, in reality, confusion, and ought to be removed, for it had been the source of evil. The community as the owner of the land must reclaim the ground-rent in the shape of a 10 per cent. death duty on estates, and turn its revenues into a national fund, out of which should be paid to every propertyless person, in compensation for the loss of his or her natural rights, the sum of £15 when arrived at the age of twenty-one years, and £10 annually as an old age pension for life. The surplus should be used for the upkeep of the blind, lame, and incapable. Paine had, in 1792, proposed a similar plan of reform. In the second part of the *Rights of Man*, he asked for the abolition of the poor laws, remission of indirect taxation, imposition of a surplus tax on the wealthy, out of which a fund should be created for the support of the poor, unemployed, and old, as well as to defray the cost of popular education.

Paine's reform plan displeased Spence, who severely criticised it in his pamphlet entitled *Rights of Infants* (1797), charging him with trying to sell the birthright of the people for a pottage of lentils.

3.—WILLIAM GODWIN

The wealth of ideas created in the simple, rude forges of the English mind in the seventeenth century flowed to France, where Cartesians and Encyclopædists endowed them with new elements and with *esprit*, logic, and grace. Then the reflux began. The apparently simple constitutional doctrines of Locke reappeared in the dazzling shape of Rousseau's *Discours sur l'inégalité* and *Contrat Social;* the empiricism of Bacon,

I

Hobbes and Locke returned in the machine-like perfection of Lamettrie's and Holbach's materialism, and English ethics was transformed by Helvetius into utilitarianism.

In the thunder and lightning of the French Revolution the English intellectuals eagerly opened their minds to the various enunciations of the Encyclopædists, and desired a systematic exposition of those theories which appeared to reveal themselves as creative fiats. The man who satisfied that desire was William Godwin. He was anything but an original social philosopher ; his mental make-up was that of a first-rate journalist, but his intellectual adventures as a nonconformist theologian and unfrocked preacher, combined with a rich vocabulary and flowing style, enabled him to recast political science for the younger generation of feverish enthusiastic intellectuals. Nothing less satisfied them than political anarchy, abolition of private property, absolute reign of reason, universal benevolence and joyful devotion to social duty and justice. And he supplied it to them in two quarto volumes for three guineas. What Burke's *Reflections* were for the upper classes, Paine's *Rights of Man* for the masses, that was Godwin's *Enquiry Concerning Political Justice* (1793) for the intellectuals. Godwin suddenly woke up one morning as the most famous social philosopher of his time. Youthful poets, like Coleridge, Southey, and Wordsworth, all of them University students, looked upon their studies as a useless dust heap, but read Godwin with avidity.

Political Justice went through four editions ; the first appeared in February, 1793, the second in 1796, the third in 1798, the fourth in 1843 at the culmination of Chartism. The most characteristic is the first edition, which was written in the heat and fever of the French Revolution, and also at the time when some of the author's opinions were still in a ferment, or, as he says, " The ideas of the author became more and more perspicuous and digested as his enquiries advanced " (Preface),[1] and his enquiries advanced during the printing of the book. The second edition is more systematic, but in less revolutionary language. In the interval between the first and second edition a revolutionary

[1] Our references are throughout to the first edition.

movement made itself noticeable in London and in the industrial centres of Great Britain, initiated by the London Corresponding Society, which consisted of workmen, small traders, and intellectuals, and alarmed the Government.   Mr. Pitt took at once repressive measures and some of Godwin's friends were arrested and charged with high treason.   Likewise the terror in France revealed the fact that revolutions were apt to silence reason and philosophy.   These circumstances induced Godwin to soften the attacks on government and property, to emphasize the evil of physical force, and to point, in the most unmistakable manner, to reason, persuasion, and argument as the sole instruments of social changes.   Some critics saw in those emendations a betrayal of the cause of justice, but, in reality, Godwin remained what he had been, a peaceful revolutionist, peaceful even to the point of non-resistance, believing in the omnipotence of reason and truth (book 4, chapter 2, section 2) ; still, his unmeasured invectives against the institutions of government and property must have left on the readers of the first edition the impression that Godwin had identified himself with the Jacobins and levellers.   The irritation caused by the second edition was aggravated by his pamphlet entitled *Considerations on Lord Grenville's and Mr. Pitt's Bills*," published anonymously (by a " Lover of Order ") in 1795, in which he approved of the government's repressive measures and denounced the agitators and democrats, *i.e.* his own friends.[1]

In order to understand Godwin it must always be borne in mind that he was essentially a Calvinist preacher.   His materialism is inverted Calvinist theology.   God is reason ; predestination necessity or determinism, Providence causation, the Kingdom of God ethical communism.   His criticism is one long Nonconformist sermon, vivacious, diffuse, and sometimes powerful, but always based on abstract reasoning.   He held the historical view of society as of little use compared with the philosophical view, which he considered to be " of a higher order and more essential importance " (*Political Justice*, book 2, ch. 1).

Political Justice is divided into eight books.   The following

[1] Cestre, *John Thelwall*, p. 136; Coleridge, *Letters*, 1895, I., p. 162.

thoughts pervade the whole. The human mind in action, or human psychology, is a mechanism, a combination of phenomena, operating strictly according to the law of causation (b. 4, ch. 7). It has no innate ideas nor good or bad propensities (b. 1, ch. 3), but is endowed with the passive capacity of receiving sensations which turn into impressions, and with the active faculty of reason which turns the impression into thought, the real motor force of animal life. On thought depends volition or moral action (b. 4, ch. 7 and 8). Were the external world based on justice the impressions that the mind receives would be good, consequently the thoughts and motives good, and vice would be eradicated (b. 1, ch. 3), all the more so as the influence of reflection on man is incomparably greater than that of physical factors (b. 1, ch. 7). Reason is favourable to virtue and is potent enough to overcome error. It would thus lead man on the way of perpetual improvement and perfection ; the great series of inventions and discoveries sufficiently show the perfectibility of man. But government, originating in force and violence, darkens counsel and strengthens error, by supporting and defending all those institutions that are opposed to justice or utility or happiness. It perpetuates the alarmingly great inequality of property (b. 1, ch. 5; b. 8, ch. 1), and puts man in chains of authority. It thus prevents renovation and checks the operation of reason— the sole legislator. All government, no matter what its form is, is evil, while society is natural. With Thomas Paine [1], our author is of opinion that government springs from our wickedness, society from our wants (b. 2, ch. 1). But how will society keep together if government, law, and authority are abolished ? By equity and the common deliberations on general welfare, which is the law of reason. Society cannot legislate, but can interpret the inherent law of reason (b. 3, ch. 5). And this law implies those actions and conditions that contribute most to the enlargement of understanding, stimulation of virtue, and awakening of the independence of man (b. 2, ch. 2). It is the duty of every man to apply his capacities to the general welfare. The fulfilment of that duty is virtue—

[1] Thomas Paine, *Common Sense*, p. 1.

the sole source of happiness. The sum total of those actions and conditions is political justice.

Having instituted a no-government society, there still remains property to be dealt with. Indeed, the solution of the question of property is the keystone of the system of political justice. It enables man to leave artificial or complicated government-society for natural or simple society. Errors with regard to wealth preclude the attainment of freedom, virtue, and happiness. For private property leads to inequality, and this renders all mental improvement impossible. The possession of wealth produces vanity, ostentation, depravity, while poverty stunts the mind, turns man into a slave, ruins his reason and morality. The effects of the present distribution of wealth are by far more pernicious than those of government, priestcraft, and lawyers.[1] They lead men to extol selfishness, teach them to adore their oppressors, and to strive after luxuries and vice. Even the distribution which to-day is thought to be just is not consistent with justice. If a man renders greater service he receives a hundred times more than he needs. Is this really just ? No ! For nobody has a right to superfluities. If one man possesses ten loaves of bread while another has nothing, justice demands that the hungry should get from the former bread enough to satisfy his hunger. And yet we see to-day superabundance on the one hand and privation on the other, without any attempt being made to equalise distribution (b. 8, ch. 1). What magic is there in the pronoun " my " to overturn the decision of ever-lasting truth (b. 2, ch. 2). " If justice reigned a state of equality would prevail. Labour would become light as rather to assume the appearance of agreeable relaxation and gentle exercise. Every man would have a frugal, yet wholesome diet ; every man would go forth to that moderate exercise of his corporal functions that would give hilarity to the spirits. None would be made torpid with fatigue, but all would have leisure to cultivate the kindly and philanthropical affections and to let loose his faculties in the search of intellectual improvement. How rapid would be the advances of intellect, if all men were admitted into

[1] This is evidently a reminiscence from Ogilvie's *Essay.*

the field of knowledge. And the moral progress would be as great as the intellectual. The vices which are inseparably joined to the present system of property would inevitably expire in a state of society where all shared alike the bounties of nature. The narrow principle of selfishness would vanish. No man being obliged to guard his little store, or provide, with anxiety and pain, for his restless wants, each would lose his individual existence in the thought of general good. No man would be an enemy to his neighbour, for they would have no subject of contention, and of consequence philanthropy would resume the empire which reason assigns her."

But how would such a distribution of commodities be effected in any particular case ? As soon as law was abolished, men would begin to inquire after equity, " which bids giving to each according to his needs." Godwin is not unmindful of the objections raised against equality, and he answers them with a series of arguments similar to those of Wallace, whose *Various Prospects* evidently impressed him (b. 8, ch. 7). He differs however from Wallace on three points. Godwin gives no outline of any Utopian scheme, but merely argues that equality, established by persuasion and the reasoned consent of all, would endure ; the only hint he gives of the form or constitution of his future society is when he declares that small societies or aggregates of men were preferable to large societies, since on a small surface the waves of popular commotion would soon subside. Secondly, Godwin does not desire economic co-operation nor any closer communist life nor lasting relations between man and woman, his ideal being an aggregate of free, independent persons, mainly bent on the utmost development of their individuality (b. 8, ch. 6). Finally, he has no misgivings whatsoever as to the increase of mankind beyond their means of subsistence. The whole question of population was to him either too remote a contingency to be considered or of no importance in the face of the omnipotence of reason. The time would surely come when mind would control matter. The reign of reason would not only deal with so trivial a matter as increase of population and means of life, but would make man immortal (b. 8, ch. 7). The main task of all who desire to establish political justice was therefore the cultivation of reason through independent thinking, free and fearless enquiry into all ideas and opinions, and careful education.

In 1797, Godwin published the *Enquirer*, a collection of essays, two of which are relevant to our subject. One is entitled "Riches and Poverty," the other "Avarice and Profusion." In the former he warns against an intemperate use of philosophy, and then proceeds to declare that the real evil of poverty was not bodily privation, but lack of leisure to cultivate the mind. Real wealth was leisure. In the other essay he refutes the idea that capital, by giving employment to the poor, was their benefactor. The growth of manufactures aggravated the misery of the poor by prolonging their working time from eight to ten hours, and by fastening the yoke of slavery upon the working classes. The rich did not pay the poor, since there was no wealth but labour. The only way for the rich to help the poor was to take off their shoulders a part of the burden of labour.

Godwin's communist position was discussed, in 1797, between Thomas Robert Malthus and his father ; the latter was favourable to some of its elements, while the former opposed it. The result of this discussion was the *Essay on the Principle of Population* (1798), the most formidable weapon against communism and social reform in the first half of the nineteenth century. Its main thesis is essentially that of Robert Wallace, whose *Various Prospects* are referred to by Godwin in the following manner : "An author who has speculated widely upon subjects of government, has recommended equal, or, which was rather his idea, common property, as a complete remedy to the usurpation and distress which are at present the most powerful enemies of human kind. . . . But, after having exhibited this picture, not less true than delightful, he finds an argument that demolishes the whole and restores him to indifference and despair, in the excessive population that would ensue." [1] In his argument against social reform Malthus goes farther than that : according to him

[1] William Godwin, *Pol. Justice*, book 8, chap. 7 ; Malthus, *Essay*, Preface and book 3, chap. 2.

there was no need to wait for communism in order to detect the law of population, for it was in full operation to-day.

4.—WORDSWORTH, COLERIDGE, SOUTHEY, PANTI-SOCRACY

Carried away by the moving spectacle of the French Revolution William Wordsworth hoped to see the reorganisation of society on the basis of freedom and justice. He regarded the travails of the time as the forebodings of the moral rebirth of humanity, and the establishment of Utopia not on " some secreted island, but in the very world, which is the world of all of us—the place where, in the end, we find our happiness or not at all." His poetic imagination was all aglow and filled his whole being with an enthusiasm which seemed to render him capable of any sacrifice for the salvation of mankind :—

> " Bliss was it in that dawn to be alive,
> But to be young was very Heaven ! . . .
> I had approached, like other youths, the shield
> Of human nature from the golden side,
> And would have fought even to the death, to attest
> The quality of the metal which I saw . . .
>   I began
> To meditate with ardour on the rule
> And management of nations, what it is
> And ought to be ; and strove to learn how far
> Their power or weakness, wealth or poverty,
> Their happiness or misery, depends
> Upon their laws, and fashion of the State."

And when the acts of terrorism began to shake his belief in the emancipating mission of the Convention, Godwin's book restored his confidence and taught him " to look through all the frailties of the world, and with a resolute mastery . . . build social upon personal liberty." By Godwin's book " a strong shock was given to old opinions ; all men's minds had felt its power, and mine was both let loose and goaded." [1]

Samuel Taylor Coleridge and Robert Southey, young students

---

[1] William Wordsworth, *Prelude*, book 11. *Cf.* Leslie Stephen, *The English Utilitarians*, II., pp. 368-73.

at Cambridge and Oxford, felt the same shock, wrote hymns on the author of *Political Justice*, and welcomed the dawn of human liberty and equality.   Projecting their revolutionary sentiments on English history both wrote dramas, of which Southey's *Wat Tyler* is the more important.   Wat Tyler and John Ball are brought on the scene as natural law communists, and Tyler tells Piers :—

> " No fancied boundaries of mine and thine
>   Restrain our wanderings ! Nature gives enough
>   For all ; but Man, with arrogant selfishness,
>   Proud of his heaps, hoards up superfluous stores
>   Robb'd from his weaker fellows, starves the poor,
>   Or gives to pity what he owes to justice ! "

And Piers replies :—

> " So I have heard our good friend John Ball preach."

The peasantry sing the song, " When Adam delved and Eve span ; " finally, John Ball preaches his sermon on Blackheath.

Coleridge, not satisfied with hymns, odes, and dramas, proposed to Southey, in 1794, the establishment of a communist colony, where all-equality should reign.   " Pantisocracy ! Oh, I shall have such a scheme of it ! My head, my heart, are all alive.   I have drawn up my arguments in battle array " (Coleridge, *Letters*, 1895, I. p. 81).   It is not enough to write about equality and justice, they must be practised.   " The heart should have fed upon the truth, as insects on a leaf, till it be tinged with the colour, and show its food in every minutest fibre.   In the book of pantisocracy I hope to have comprised all that is good in Godwin . . . I think not so highly of him as you do " (*Ib.* p. 91).   Southey, less enthusiastic and more cautious of communist experiments, for he was the only one among the prospective pantisocrats who possessed some property, gradually abandoned the whole scheme, whereupon Coleridge wrote to him :—

" You are lost to me, because you are lost to Virtue.   As this will probably be the last time I shall have occasion to address you, I will begin at the beginning and regularly retrace your conduct and my own. In the month of June, 1794, I first became acquainted with your person and character. Before I quitted Oxford, we had struck out the leading features of a pantisocracy. While on my journey through Wales you invited me to Bristol with the full hopes of realising it. During my abode at Bristol the plan was matured, and I returned to Cambridge, hot in the anticipation of that happy season when we should remove the *selfish* principle from ourselves, and prevent it in our children, by an abolition of property. . . . But alas ! a short time passed ere your departure from our first principles became too flagrant. . . . Your conversation scorched my throat. Your private resources were to remain your individual property, and everything to be separate except a farm of five or six acres. In short, we were to commence partners in a petty farming trade [in Wales]. This was the mouse of which the mountain Pantisocracy was at last safely delivered. . . . Thus your system of prudentials and your apostasy were not sudden ; these constant nibblings had sloped your descent from virtue. . . . My indolence you assigned as the reason for your quitting pantisocracy. Supposing it is true, it might indeed be a reason for rejecting *me* from the system. But how does this affect pantisocracy, that you should reject *it ?* " (Coleridge, *Letters*, 1895, I. pp. 137-51).

However, the time was to come when this fiery apostle of all-equality would follow the example of Southey. Before the eighteenth century expired the French Revolution was discredited and Godwin was sinking into oblivion. Disillusionment and despair took hold of the spirit and heart of those who had been so full of hope, enthusiasm, and exaltation, and " sick, wearied out with contrarieties, yielded up moral questions in despair" (Wordsworth, *Prelude*, II. 304–5), and returned to the institutions of government, law, and authority. Wordsworth, Coleridge, and Southey became, in the course of time, the spiritual leaders of the new conservatism, imbuing it with a sense of social righteousness and love of the people. They are the fathers of the Tory Democracy and Christian social reform. Of the anti-capitalist spirit Southey possessed the most ; he was an assiduous reader of the socialist literature of his time, and one of the keenest and most one-sided critics of the industrial revolution. Some of his *Letters from England* (1807) might have been written by a communist. Manufactures appeared to him as the source of misery, depravity, and rebellion, threatening England with destruction.[1] Coleridge worked by fits and starts on a philosophy which was diametrically opposed to that of the Radicals. And Wordsworth was, to the end of his life, in sympathy with the social movements of the masses. There is a curious utterance reported of him by Crabb Robinson : " I recollect once hearing Mr. Wordsworth say, half in joke, half in earnest, ' I have no respect for Whigs, but I have a great deal of the Chartist in me.' To be sure he has."[2]

5.—LONDON CORRESPONDING SOCIETY : JOHN THELWALL

The same agitated period saw the beginning of the independent political action of the working classes, the London Corresponding Society (L.C.S.) forming the preface of its history.[3] The programme of the L.C.S. was democracy and social reform. Its founder was Thomas Hardy (1752–1832), a Scotch shoemaker, who had come to London from Stirlingshire in the year 1773. Its intellect was John Thelwall (1764–1834), an orator, poet, and journalist of considerable power. The L.C.S. was formed in March, 1792, and soon attracted the attention of the democratic and revolutionary intellectuals who supplied the working class organisations with speakers and lecturers, among them being Horne Tooke, Thomas Holcroft, John Richter, and John Thelwall. Holcroft and Thelwall were friends of Godwin, and Thelwall lectured before the working men of London on Godwin's " Political Justice." Hardy was not only moved by the ideas of the French Revolution, but by the views which had gathered

[1] Robert Southey, *Letters from England* (1807), I. 306–8 ; II. 139–44, 147-151 ; III. 114–19, 132–4.
[2] H. C. Robinson, *Diary*, ed. 1872, II., p. 290.
[3] Francis Place, Add. MSS. 27808, 27814 (British Museum) ; E. Smith, *English Jacobinism*, 1881 ; *State Trials*, vols. 24, 25 ; Graham Wallas, *Life of Francis Place*, pp. 20–8 ; Charles Cestre, *John Thelwall*, 1906.

round the agitation of Wilkes, " Junius," the American War of Independence, Major Cartwright and the Duke of Richmond. Also Thomas Spence was very active in the interest of the L.C.S., two branches of which used to meet in his lodgings in Holborn. The connection of the L.C.S. with the French Convention, their attempts to hold, in conjunction with the Scottish Reformers, a National Convention at Edinburgh (1793), finally their growing and insurrectionary activity among the industrial population of London and the Midlands, alarmed the Government. Mr. Pitt, informed by spies of the turmoil produced by the L.C.S., took at once measures for their suppression. In May, 1794, Hardy, Horne Tooke, Thelwall, etc., were arrested ; at the same time the Government prevailed upon Parliament to agree to the suspension of the Habeas Corpus Act ; and in October, 1794, the leaders of the L.C.S. were tried at the Old Bailey for high treason. The redoubtable Erskine was chief counsel for the defence, and the prisoners were acquitted. John Thelwall had prepared a speech in his defence, which, however, he had no opportunity of delivering ; he published it, in 1795, under the title " Natural and Constitutional Rights," which is a defence of universal suffrage and the rights of labour. He ascribed the power of property and monopoly to the fact that the richer classes were represented in Parliament. " If, once in every year, the poor man's vote were as important as his employer's, the poor could not be forgotten. But it is property, we are told, that ought to be represented, because by property government is supported. What ? Does property man the navy or fill the ranks of the army ? . . . Let us not deceive ourselves ! Property is nothing but human labour. The most inestimable of all property is the sweat of the poor man's brow ; the property from which all other is derived, and without which grandeur must starve in the midst of supposed abundance. And shall they who possess this inestimable property be told that they had no rights, because they have nothing to defend ? . . . No ! Man and not movables is the object of just legislation. All, therefore, ought to be consulted where all are concerned, for not less than the whole ought to decide the fate of the whole. And if the few are to be the ultimate organ of that decision . . . then only the few are free, the rest are helots, bondsmen, slaves. The few, are, in fact, the owners of the life and liberties and possessions of the many " (pp. 42–3). Thelwall was connected by bonds of friendship with Coleridge, at least in the last decade of the eighteenth century. They exchanged many letters, in which Coleridge took great pains to cure Thelwall of his atheism. Both came to despise Godwin, although Thelwall remained to the end of his life a democratic reformer, while Coleridge became one of the formative minds of New Toryism. Thelwall delivered the funeral oration at the grave of Hardy (October, 1832), and was denounced by the Government spy, named Poppay, whom old Cobbett exposed in the first Reform Parliament.

Hardy's last years were, from a financial point of view, not happy. He retired in 1815, at the age of sixty-three, from business, with a competency which he reckoned would last him another ten years. But Providence ordained otherwise. He outlived his resources, and, but for the generosity of Francis Place and Sir Francis Burdett, would have had to spend the evening of his life in the workhouse and die a pauper's death.

The L.C.S. constituted a sort of democratic and social reform seminary for labour leaders. From it issued most of the ideas and men that made themselves conspicuous in popular movements up to the year 1820. Thomas Evans, leader of the Spenceans in the fateful years 1816–18, Colonel Despard (executed for high treason in 1805), John Gales Jones, later a supporter of Owen, Francis Place, and many others received their education, or impulses, from the L.C.S. The United Irishmen, when preparing for the insurrection, entered into communication with its leaders.

By the Corresponding Act, 1799, which prohibited all communication between political societies, the L.C.S. was suppressed, but it had already done its work ; the movement had spread to Lancashire and Yorkshire.

6.—CHARLES HALL

The sources of information concerning the life of Charles Hall are but few and scanty. Even the years of his birth and death are uncertain. It is only known that he published his book, *Effects of Civilisation*, in 1805, in the preface of which he relates that he practised as physician in the West of England. In the last years of his life he made the acquaintance of John Minter Morgan, a Christian Owenite, who left a few notes about him. " Hall's book," says Morgan, " contains an able analytical examination of the errors of the existing system. The author was in very reduced circumstances ; his work was published without funds to make it known. . . . Dr. Hall reached the age of eighty years, but he died in the Rules of the Fleet Prison, where I frequently saw him ; occasionally, when he could obtain a day-rule, he dined at my chambers ; his conversation was particularly animated and intelligent ; although learned in the classics, he was more distinguished for attainments in natural philosophy. He had friends who would have released him from prison, but he was confined through a lawsuit, as he considered, unjustly ; and rather than permit the money to be paid, he had resolved to remain incarcerated for life."[1] In the collection of Francis Place, there are two letters written by Hall to Thomas Spence. In one of the letters, dated Tavistock, August 25, 1807, he writes that he was nearly seventy years of age, a widower, and father of eight sons and two daughters ; his intention was to leave the country for London and get rooms at Furnival Inn.[2] From the reminiscences of Morgan and the letter to Spence it may be inferred that Hall was born about 1740, and died about 1820.

Hall's book [3] is evidently based on personal observations of the effects of the Industrial Revolution in particular, and private

---

[1] J. M. Morgan, *Hampden in the Nineteenth Century*, 1834. I., pp. 20–1.

[2] Place, Add. MSS. 27808 (British Museum).

[3] Only the second edition, published by J. M. Morgan in 1850, is extant, and here quoted or referred to.

property in general, but it also shows distinct traces of wide reading in economic and socialist literature, particularly Adam Smith, David Hume, Thomas Paine, and Godwin. The author is a determined opponent of manufacture, trade, and commerce, and regards agriculture as the most useful and beneficial occupation. He elaborates the doctrine of the antagonistic interests between the capitalist and working class, a doctrine found in embryo in Adam Smith's *Wealth of Nations* (book 1, ch. 8), but developed to a revolutionary stage by Hall, who was the first socialist to make a statistical attempt at demonstrating the enormous injustice of profit, which he regards as a wholly illegitimate deduction from the produce of labour and the natural reward of labour.

Hall's position in the history of socialism is an intermediary one between natural law or ethical socialism and proletarian or revolutionary socialism. It is the first interpretation of the voice of rising Labour.

Following, evidently, Thomas Paine, Hall defines civilisation as that state of society in which, on the one hand, science, knowledge, trade, and manufacture flourish, while, on the other hand, the large majority of the population is poor, or sinking into poverty, and therefore excluded from enjoying its advantages. It is a state opposed to natural and simple life, where there is neither riches nor misery. The division of society into rich and poor is, for the social investigator, the most striking mark of civilisation. The life of the poor is short, hard, and deprived of all bodily and mental care. No government thinks it worth while to examine into their conditions, though they form the large majority of the population. It was mainly the establishment of manufactures that brought about this state of things, and is now aggravating it by withdrawing the mass of the population from agriculture, and thus starving the land of the necessary labour. The results are scarcity of agricultural produce and continual rise of the cost of living, which reduce the purchasing power of the wages and further depress the condition of the poor (pp. 25–37).

The motor power of these changes is wealth or capital. Economists have hitherto looked upon it from one side only; they have but seen its workings and effects on production, and have neglected to investigate it with regard to its effects on the structure and welfare of society. In this rôle it reveals itself as a tremendous political power. Wealth is pre-eminently power; in it resides the real sovereignty of the nation. It has the absolute command of the labour of those who are propertyless. This power of the rich is as strong and effective as that of the most despotic monarch, and probably more so. To condemn so many to the mines, to confine such numbers to such nauseous, irksome, unwholesome, destructive employments in factories and workshops, is more than equal to any kingly power on earth (pp. 39–40). The possessors of wealth govern the distribution of the whole produce of labour and the lion's share falls to them. The so-called contract of labour is a sham, since the poor have only the choice between starvation or slavery (pp. 58–9). The interests of Capital and Labour, of the non-producers and the producers, are absolutely opposed to each other. The acquisition of the one is the spoliation of the other. What the possessor has the non-possessor is deprived of. " The situation of the rich and the poor, like the algebraic terms plus and minus, are in direct opposition to, and destructive of each other " (pp. 53–4). If every one had an allotment of land from which he could live and on which he could fall back in times of need, the accumulation of the few could have no such injurious effect on the masses, for there being no destitute the rich would be unable to force anybody to work for them at their discretion. Wealth, without labour to fertilise it, represents a harmless heap of goods, giving no power to its possessor. It is, then, the poverty of the many that results in the despotism of the capitalists. Altogether, manufacturers are the cause and symptom of the poverty of the masses, they render them more ignorant and barbarous and weaken the nation.

How is wealth produced and distributed? Trade and commerce consist in buying and selling articles already produced by the poor, and gaining a profit on them. These goods are all the products of the hands of the workmen, from whom they are bought for less than their full value, else a profit could not be realised. The tradesman shares or takes part of the fruits of the labour of the poor. The means enabling tradesmen to share in the product of labour is their capital, from which they furnish materials and immediate subsistence to the artificers to work on. This loan of capital to the workman is supposed to give the capitalists the right to direct the distribution of the produce (p. 56–7). How the distribution is accomplished, the following data may help us approximately to ascertain. The rent of all lands in England about twenty years before was supposed by Adam Smith and others to have been twenty millions; since that time the amount of rent had considerably increased; the rapid rise of rent in the last thirty years was a well-known fact. Smith also supposed that the rental represented one-third of the value of the produce. Dr. Grey, in his late treatise on the income-tax, estimated the value of agricultural produce to amount to £112,000,000. The amount of exported manufacture according to Mr. Pitt's statement was the previous year (1804) about £50,000,000; the home consumption was supposed to be treble the foreign. The total produce of labour in agriculture and manufactures was therefore £312,000,000. The labouring population forms eight-tenths of the whole; supposing their families to consist of five persons each, in a nation consisting of ten millions there will be 1,600,000 working men's families; the average annual income of such a family is £25. This multiplied by the number of families give a total wage bill of £40,000,000.

Result : Eight-tenths of the population—or the large majority who produce all the wealth—receive one-eighth of it, while two-tenths who produce nothing receive seven-eighths of the produced wealth.

Or, a working man labours seven days for the capitalist, and one day in eight for himself, wife, and children (pp. 94–6).

> " Sic vos non vobis mellificatis, apes ;
> Sic vos non vobis fertis aratra, boves."[1]

The sum total of civilisation is to enable a few of mankind to

[1] You make the honey, but not for yourselves, bees ;
You make the land fruitful, but not for yourselves, oxen.

attain all possible enjoyments both of mind and body that they are capable of, but at the expense of the bulk of mankind, by which a great proportion of them are destroyed, and the remainder stunted in body and mind. All this is brought about in a regular, orderly, silent manner, under specious forms, with the appearance of law, order, and liberty, and even charity.

Wealth which is so injurious to national life is also the principal cause of one of the most fateful international calamities—viz. war, the objects of which are to increase trade and territory or to stifle internal revolutionary movements provoked by the infinite lust of the rich for power. The education given by the rich to the children of the poor is calculated to impart to them a warlike spirit ; the books they read are little else than a glorification of bloodshed ; the most destructive battles are called brilliant and glorious, but the horrid spectacle presented by the " field of glory," the day or the night after the battle—the mangled carcases, the groans of the dying, the ghastly aspect of the hospitals full of wounded and dying, are not mentioned. How overwhelming then must be the power of wealth that it is able even to extinguish the light of reason and morality, to suppress the feelings of the human heart, and cause man to slaughter his fellow-man !

This state of things was not brought about by the express design or contrivance of any set of men, but was the result of forces working unconsciously. The division of the land into large dominions, and the inequality consequent upon that division, gave to the rich an absolute power over the non-possessors, whom they use for the purpose of increasing the stock of wealth. Private property in land led to manufactures, trade, and commerce, by which the poor are made poorer still, and the small possessors are deprived of the little they possess and thrown into poverty.

The division of the land being thus the original cause of the evil, the reform of society must evidently start by removing the cause. The land, therefore, should be nationalised and settled with small farmers. The land to be restored to the nation, and the nation to the land. Agriculture should be the main occupa-

tion of all. Of the sciences and arts only those should be preserved and promoted that are necessary for the prosperity of
agricultural pursuits.

The significance of Hall's book is, however, not to be sought in
its reform schemes, which are evidently nothing else but an
elaboration of the sentimental reaction against industrial progress.
Its place in the history of socialist thought is assured to it by its
critical part, in which the rising opposition of the working classes
against the factory system found so keen an expression. It is
the edge-like sharpness and mathematical precision of the nascent
class antagonism which makes it into a herald of the approaching
revolutionary period. At first the book remained unheeded.
It was published in the year of Trafalgar and in the midst
of internal inaction. The youth of the nation, the strong
and adventurous, were either in the army and navy or
profitably employed in the factories, mines, and commercial houses ; glory and prosperity kept them quiet. The course
of the French Revolution and the repressive measures of Mr. Pitt
either damped the ardour of the intellectuals or brought them
back to a more conservative frame of mind. Hall's book fell
flat or was regarded as a paradox by the few papers which thought
it worth while mentioning or reviewing it.[1] These reviews had
only the effect of calling the attention of Thomas Spence to
Hall as a fellow-labourer. He sent him his Newcastle Lecture
and other pamphlets and asked for his opinion. Hall at first
replied with a few polite commonplaces, but after having been
urged again and again to speak freely, Hall told Spence that his
scheme was worth little, since it left capital and wage labour
untouched. The capitalist system was so complicated and
injurious an arrangement that it could not be mended, but must
be completely abolished.[2]

Hall's book is also mentioned by George Mudie, an Owenite

[1] *Monthly Review*, 1806, Vol. 51 ; *Monthly Magazine*, May, 1807.
[2] Place, Add. MSS. 27808. Reply of Hall to Spence, June 7,
1807 ; Letters of Spence to Hall, June 28, Aug. 13, 1807 ; Reply of
Hall, Aug. 25, 1807.

and journalist, in the *Economist* (1820-1, No. 4), who points out that Hall had not taken sufficient account of the evil of competition, and that the remedy was not a return to simpler conditions, but co-operation.

On the whole it would appear that in socialist and reform circles the book was read.

III

STORM AND STRESS

I.—REBELLIONS OF LABOUR

ONCE a communist, always a communist. This applies, as far as social criticism is concerned, to Robert Southey. His *Letters from England*, published two years after Hall's book, contain as destructive and one-sided a criticism of the new industrial era as the *Effects of Civilisation*. Southey only saw the poverty of the masses and he argued that, " if religion were out of the question, it would have been better for them (the lower classes) to have been born among savages than in a civilised country, where they are in fact the victims of civilisation " (*Letters*, I., pp. 306–8). This is curiously reminiscent of Hall. The wealth which the new era brought in its train was " not equally and healthfully distributed through the whole system ; it sprouts into wens and tumours, and collects in aneurisms which starve and palsy the extremities " (*Ib.*, II., p. 147). It needed the pen of a Dante to describe the horrors of the Manchester factories (*Ib.*, II., pp. 139–44). The result of that system would be a violent revolution. " The introduction of machinery in an old manufacturing country always produces distress by throwing workmen out of employ, and is seldom effected without riots and executions. . . . A manufacturing population is always ripe for rioting. They have no local attachments ; the persons to whom they look up for support they regard more with envy than with respect, as men who grow rich by their labour ; they know enough what is passing in the political world to think themselves politicians. . . . Governments who found their prosperity upon manufactures sleep upon gunpowder. . . . If the manufacturing system continues to be extended, increasing as it necessarily does the number, the misery, and the

133

depravity of the poor, I believe that a revolution must come, and in the most fearful shape. And the tendency of the present system is to lessen the middle classes and to increase the lower ones " (*Ib.*, II., p. 157, III., pp. 132–3).

Three years later the *Edinburgh Review* diagnosed the condition of the nation in no less gloomy colours. " The great body of the nation appears to us to be divided into two violent and most pernicious factions : the courtiers who are almost for arbitrary power ; and the democrats who are almost for revolution and republicanism. . . . If the two opposite parties are once permitted to shock together in open conflict, there is an end to the freedom and almost to the existence of the nation. In the present crisis, we have no hesitation in saying, it is to the popular side that the friends of the constitution must turn themselves. If the Whig leaders do not first conciliate and then restrain the people ; if they do not save them from their leaders they are already choosing in their own body . . . the Constitution itself, the Monarchy, and the Whig aristocracy will, in no long time, be swept away. . . . The nation is on fire at the four corners. . . . That the number of democrats is fast increasing with a visible and dangerous rapidity, any man may satisfy himself by the common and obvious means of information. It is a fact which he may read legibly in the prodigious sale, and still more prodigious circulation of Cobbett's *Register*, and several other weekly papers of the same description ; he may learn it in every street of the manufacturing and populous towns in the heart of the country. . . . The storm is most evidently brewing over our heads at this moment, and if it cannot be dispersed before it bursts upon them, we do not know where is our chance of being saved from destruction." [1]

And the storm burst. First in the form of Luddism. The infuriated workmen destroyed machinery. In March, 1812, Parliament passed a law for the protection of machinery, punishing Luddite actions with death, and in the second week of January, 1813, eighteen workmen died on the gallows at York.[2] Lord

[1] *Edinburgh Review*, 1810.
[2] Henry Brougham, *Life and Times*, II., pp. 76–7.

Byron, who had opposed that law in the House of Lords, evidently regarded this movement as one for freedom, and composed, in December 1816, the following song of the Luddites :—

" As the Liberty lads o'er the sea
Bought their freedom, and cheaply, with blood,
  So we boys, we
  Will die fighting, or live free,
And down with all Kings but King Ludd !

" When the web that we weave is complete
And the shuttle exchanged for the sword,
  We will fling the winding sheet
  O'er the despot at our feet,
And dye it deep in the gore he has pour'd.

" Though black as his heart its hue,
Since his veins are corrupted to mud,
  Yet this is the dew,
  Which the tree shall renew
Of liberty, planted by Ludd ! "

Quite different from the attitude of the rebellious aristocrat was that of the fighting democrat, William Cobbett. Though in his cheap weekly edition of the *Register*, begun in the autumn, 1816, he represented Labour as the creator of all wealth and the foundation of the State (*Political Register*, November 2, 1816), he soon appealed to the Luddites to desist from destroying machinery, and to join, instead, the movement for Parliamentary reform. Not machinery, but oligarchic rule, the debased state of currency, the heavy load of taxation consequent upon the enormous expenditure for war, pensions and sinecures, borough-mongering and Jewish Stock Exchange jobbery, were at the bottom of the misery of the working classes. These evils could only be removed by a popularly elected Parliament (*Ib.*, November 30, 1816). Indeed, soon after Waterloo, Radicals began to revive the democratic traditions of the years from 1760 to 1794, and to undertake the political education of the working classes. The City of London became again one of the foci of Liberal thought, and on December 9, 1816, the Common Council told the Prince Regent that the

Government was corrupt and wasteful, and that the late war was unjust and senseless. Following Cobbett's cheap *Register*, a Radical and popular press, mostly weeklies, appeared, such as Wooler's *Black Dwarf*, John Wade's *Gorgon*, Carlile's *Republican*. An alliance between the middle and working classes was being formed ; Cobbett, Hunt, Major Cartwright, Sir Francis Burdett, took the lead, and the working men, abandoning sporadic revolts, which only led to executions and to the suspension of the Habeas Corpus Act, joined the Hampden Clubs, the first of which was formed at Westminster in 1812. This club was, however, exclusively for rich reformers, while the Hampden Clubs formed after the war bore a popular character, and demanded not only Universal Suffrage and the abolition of the Corn Laws, but also the abrogation of the Combination Acts.

While Cobbett and Hunt were beginning to dominate the popular platforms, a writer of vastly superior intellectual and literary powers was meditating upon the problems of the time— Samuel Taylor Coleridge composed his *Lay Sermons*. He retraced " the progress of things from 1792 to 1813, when the tide was at its height . . . and the ebb from its first turn to the dead low-water mark of the last quarter," *i.e.*, end of 1816, and then generalised the events under the following heads: " Fluctuations in the wages of labour, alternate privation and excess, consequent improvidence, and, over all, discontent and a system of factious confederacy—these form the history of the mechanics and lower ranks of our cities and towns. In the country a peasantry sinking into pauperism, step by step, with the rise of the farmer's profits and indulgences." The trading and huckstering spirit predominated everywhere, and to excess within its own sphere. How should this state of things be remedied ? First, as to agriculture : This " requires principles essentially different from those of trade." A gentleman ought not to regard his estate as a merchant his cargo, or a shopkeeper his stock. The marketable produce of the land ought to be made a subordinate consideration to the living and moral growth that was to remain on the land—a healthful, callous-handed, but high-hearted tenantry, twice the number of the present landless, parish-paid labourers.

" Our manufacturers must consent to regulations ; our gentry must concern themselves in the education as well as in the instruction of their natural clients and dependents ; must regard their estates as secured indeed from all human interferences by every principle of law and policy, but yet as offices of trust, with duties to be performed, in the sight of God and their country. Let us become a better people, and the reform of all public griev-ances . . . will follow of itself. . . . Let us palliate where we cannot cure, comfort where we cannot relieve ; and for the rest rely upon the promise of the King of Kings by the mouth of His Prophet, ' Blessed are ye that sow beside all waters.' " [1]

This was the first voice of Christian Socialism.

2.—STRIKES AND DEMONSTRATIONS

Andrew Ure, in his *Philosophy of Manufactures*, goes to the root of strike movements when he declares that the concen-tration of industry brought them in its train. " The textile manufactures consist of two distinct departments ; one carried on by multitudes of small, independent machines belonging to the workmen ; another carried on by concentrated systems of machinery, the property of the masters. The workmen of the first class being scattered over a wide tract of country, and being mutual competitors for work and wages, can seldom conspire with one another, and never with effect against their employers. . . . The operatives of the other class are necessarily associated in large bodies, and have no capital sunk in machinery and work-shops. When they choose to strike they can readily join in the blow, and by stopping they merely suffer a loss of wages for the time, while they occasion to their master loss of interest on his capital, his rent, his taxes, as well as injury to the delicate moving parts of metallic mechanism by inaction in our humid climate." [2]

As soon as the textile industry reached a sufficient degree of concentration the struggle between Capital and Labour began,

[1] S. T. Coleridge, *Lay Sermons* (in *Constitution of Church and State*), 1830, pp. 414–30.
[2] A. Ure, *Philosophy of Manufactures*, Bohn's Library edition, 1861, p. 281.

and that was at the commencement of the nineteenth century.[1] Both parties soon formed separate and mutually hostile organisations, and by 1810 the North of England was in the throes of large strike movements, the cotton spinners and miners leading. Sporadic turn-outs occurred in the following years, which culminated in the great Lancashire strike of 1818, the textile workers fighting not only for higher wages, but for factory legislation, and particularly for the regulation of female and child labour. From Lancashire the movement spread to Scotland, where the weavers, taught by their English brethren, formed trade organisations and entered with zest into the struggle.

These agitations, occurring at a time of political crisis, drew the trade unionists into the vortex of radical reform. Hunt and Cobbett fraternised with the trade union leaders ; the organised workmen formed the bulk of their audiences or readers, and even the female workers formed Female Reform Associations, at whose meetings not only the thoughts and vigorous utterances of Cobbett were repeated, but also the particular demands of Labour found expression. On July 5, 1818, the Female Reform Association of Blackburn held a mass meeting of working people of both sexes, in which a woman was the chief speaker. The meeting carried the following characteristic resolution :—

" By means of the improvement of machinery, the means of producing most articles of agriculture and manufacture have been increased in an astonishing degree ; it necessarily follows that the industrious labourer ought to have a far greater quantity of produce than he had previous to those improvements ; instead of which, by means of taxation and restrictive laws he is reduced to wretchedness. Borough-mongering and tyranny must be exterminated. If this is not done, thousands of our

---

[1] " It is well known that the seeds from whence these troubles have sprung up, first began to vegetate amongst the weavers of Lancashire, in the latter end of 1799 and the beginning of 1800, changing the aspect of the manufacturing districts from that of wealth, peace, and godliness to that of complaint against masters, murmurs against ministry, and a general cry for peace ! "—i.e., against the war with France (W. Radcliffe, *Origin of the New System of Manufacture*, 1827, p. 73).

countrymen must starve in the midst of plenty. No man can have a right to enjoy another man's labour without his consent. And we do contemplate with horror the many placemen and pensioners, whilst at the same time we live in poverty, slavery, and misery. We protest against those unjust and unnatural regulations—the Corn Laws and the Combination Acts. We demand Universal Suffrage, annual Parliaments, and the ballot."[1]

A week later the men of Birmingham assembled in public meeting, and, as protest against borough-mongering and the restricted franchise, " elected " Major Cartwright and Sir Charles Wolseley to Parliament. The culminating point of these demonstrations was Peterloo (August 16, 1819), which led to the Six Acts, and put a stop to the public agitation in England. In Scotland, however, the agitation went on at an accelerating pace. English Radicals from the South and trade union leaders from Lancashire and Yorkshire won the ear of the Scottish working men and tradespeople, particularly of Paisley, Glasgow, and Carlisle, and formed unions in most of the manufacturing districts. " The devil seems to have come among us unchained," wrote Sir Walter Scott at that time to one of his correspondents, " and bellowing for his prey. In Glasgow, Volunteers drill by day and Radicals by night, and nothing but positive military force keeps the people under." The workmen had formed societies, and were led by the cleverest and most impertinent fellows, " bell-wethers in every sort of mischief." [2] In March, 1820, considerable unrest and alarm began to prevail in Scotland, and on April 2 the alarm grew into extreme anxiety by a proclamation, posted on the walls of many houses in the commercial and manufacturing centres, calling upon the people to close their factories and workshops, and to desist from work until Universal Suffrage was granted. " Equality of rights (but not of property) " was the cry. The proclamation, which the authorities considered as " highly seditious and treasonable," was signed by " The Committee for Organisation of a Provisional Government." Many workmen obeyed the appeal and struck work. At Paisley, Glas-

[1] *Black Dwarf*, July 14, 1818.
[2] Sir Walter Scott, *Familiar Letters*, II., p. 78.

gow, Carlisle, and in the colliery district the strike was all but general. Small bands of people took up arms, but only at Bonny-muir did some of them come in contact with a military detachment. After a short skirmish the insurgents suffered defeat ; many of them were wounded, and nineteen made prisoners. Numerous arrests in other parts of the country soon put an end to the rising. In July and August the prisoners were brought to trial for high treason, and many of them found guilty, but only three, among them being Andrew Hardie, a forebear of Mr. James Keir Hardie, suffered the extreme penalty.

3.—THE SPENCEANS

In 1812 Thomas Spence formed an association of his adherents and friends, who became known later as Spencean Philanthropists. This association consisted of four groups of ten persons each, all of them skilful propagandists and agitators, who by their organising activities created the impression that they were controlling the whole working class democratic movement in the metropolis. The most prominent members were : Thomas Evans, a traces-maker, who after the death of Spence became the literary mouthpiece of the Spencean doctrines ; Thomas Preston, a leather worker ; John Hooper, a labourer ; Dr. James Watson, physician ; and Arthur Thistlewood, later of Cato Street fame. Evans had been a member of the London Corresponding Society and its secretary in 1798 when the whole Executive were arrested and kept in prison, without any trial, for nearly three years. In 1816 he published a pamphlet entitled *Christian Policy*, which went through a second edition in the same year. It is devoted to a demonstration of the necessity of a reform or rather " revolution of property " by giving back the land to the people as the only means of removing the distress caused by the war. The people in possession of the land would become consumers of industrial commodities, and extended consumption would promote production. Instead of a revolution in the land system the ruling classes were treating the poor with Malthus's theory that they had no claim whatsoever to the smallest portion of food, " and, in fact, had no business to be where they are."

Also, the whole foreign policy was wrong. The Napoleonic Wars had only served the interests of Russia, which had become overwhelmingly powerful by swallowing Poland—the granary of Europe. The right policy would have been an alliance between England and France with the purpose of checking Russia.

The same author published, probably in 1817, another pamphlet entitled *Christian Policy in full practice among the people of Harmony, a town in the State of Pennsylvania . . . to which are subjoined a concise view of the Spencean system of Agrarian Fellowship, and some observations on the manifest similarity between the principles of the system and the truly practical and Christian establishment of the Harmonites.* It contains a description of the communist colony of the Rappists, which Robert Owen bought up seven years later.

While Evans was spreading the socialistic doctrines of his master, the other Christian philanthropists were busily engaged in organising popular demonstrations for political and social reform. They were the organisers of the Spa Fields meetings (November–December, 1816), which led to rioting and to the high treason trial against Dr. Watson and his son, Preston, Hooper, and Thistlewood. Their acquittal was due to the advocacy of Sir Charles Wetherell, who in a severe cross-examination exposed the chief witness for the Crown as a spy. In March, 1817, Parliament carried a Bill for the suppression of clubs and associations known as Spenceans or Spencean Philanthropists, for they were aiming at the confiscation and division of the lands as well as at the repudiation of the national debt. Parliament at the same time renewed the Corresponding Act, 1799, which prohibited all communication between political societies. Of the Spenceans only Thistlewood remained active. For a defamation of Lord Sidmouth he was sent to prison for twelve months After his release he was active more than ever for reform, but his past experience and the events on the St. Peter's Fields in Manchester (Peterloo) caused him to abandon all peaceful methods, and with the help of Government spies he organised the Cato Street conspiracy, for which he and four of his fellow-conspirators paid with their lives on the gallows at Newgate, on May 1, 1820.

Peterloo, Bonnymuir, and Cato Street closed one of the most agitated and terrible and at the same time mentally most active and prolific decades in British history. The chaotic fires of popular rebellions and aspirations, in passing through the preternatural imagination of Percy Bysshe Shelley, flamed up in fury and splendour in " Queen Mab," " Poems of the Time," and " Prometheus Unbound." The baffling problems of the Economic Revolution and financial distresses excited the logical and concentrated thought of David Ricardo. The new conditions of the working classes found in Robert Owen a reformer of exceptional energy and constancy. All men of understanding were searching for knowledge of social affairs, the modes of distribution of the national income, the cause and cure of the nation.

IV

THE ECONOMISTS

1.—PATRICK COLQUHOUN

THE first writer who attempted to satisfy the desire of the educated classes for information concerning the new economic conditions of the country was Patrick Colquhoun. As a trained jurist, municipal administrator, director of commercial enterprises, and London magistrate, he possessed the requisite knowledge and opportunity for such a work. The circle of his friends and acquaintances included Adam Smith, Robert Owen, and probably also David Ricardo. As a loyal supporter of the Government and staunch adherent of the existing order he had access to contemporary State documents. In possession of these advantages he wrote his *Treatise of the Wealth, Power, and Resources of the British Empire,* published in 1814, in which he gave a statistical account of the population, agriculture, manufactures, commerce, and distribution of the national income among the various classes of the United Kingdom and the British Colonies in 1812. A second edition appeared in 1815, so great was the curiosity of the nation with regard to its economic position.

But even apart from this legitimate curiosity the thought of the nation became increasingly economic. The industrial revolution appeared to reveal the new truth that the basis of society was economic rather than philosophical or spiritual. The idealists lamented the new turn which mental speculations were taking. "Absorbed in the contemplation of material objects," lamented Isaac D'Israeli, " and rejecting whatever does not enter into their own restricted notions of utility, these old arithmetical seers, with nothing but millions in their imaginations, . . . value the intellectual toils of library and studio by the law of supply and demand. In their commercial, agricultural,

and manufacturing view of human nature . . . they confine
the moral and physical existence of man in tables of population.
Planning and levelling society down to their carpentry of human
nature, they would yoke and harness the loftier spirits to one
common and vulgar destination. Man is considered only as he
wheels on the wharf, or as he spins in the factory. But man as
a recluse being of meditation, or impelled to action by more
generous passions, has been struck out of the system of our
Political Economists.''

Colquhoun's treatise was the book of revelation after which
the nation thirsted. It gave statistical tables and glowing descriptions of the new wealth of the country. But also the critical
socialist found in it what he wanted. In fact, the book may be
regarded as one of the most important bases of economic and
socialist researches and criticisms during the Ricardian and
Owenite period. This applies particularly to its tables on the
distribution of the national income.[1] The socialist interpretations of Colquhoun's distribution tables played in working class
agitation of those times a rôle similar to that of Mr. Chiozza
Money's *Riches and Poverty* in our time.

Colquhoun was fully acquainted with the revolutionary
movements. As London magistrate since 1792 he studied the
doings and proclamations of the Corresponding Society and the
revolutionary intellectuals. He appears to have had a hand in
the composition of the secret reports with which the Government
justified, in Parliament, the measures they proposed for checking
those movements. He also knew his Adam Smith and told his
readers that labour was the source of wealth. '' Millions of
individuals,'' he declares, '' pass through life without being aware
that the food, clothing, and the other conveniences and comforts
which they enjoy, proceed entirely from the labour of the people
employed in agriculture, mines and minerals, in manufactures
and handicrafts, in trade, commerce, navigation, and fisheries.
It is by the labour of the people . . . that all ranks of the

---

[1] *Life of Robert Owen*, 1857, I., pp. 150, 125–7 ; J. Gray, *Lecture
on Human Happiness*, 1825 ; *Midland Representative*, June 25, 1831 ;
Bray, *Labour's Wrongs*, 1839, p. 85.

community in every condition of life annually subsist ; and it is by the produce of this labour alone that nations become powerful in proportion to the extent of the surplus which can be spared for the exigencies of the State." The people who produced all these things were poor, and it was quite true that " every State is supported by the poverty of the community composing the body politic. Without a large proportion of poverty there could be no riches, since riches are the offspring of labour, while labour can result only from a state of poverty. Poverty is that state and condition of society where the individual has no surplus labour in store, or, in other words, no property or means of subsistence but what is derived from the constant exercise of industry. Poverty is therefore a most necessary and indispensable ingredient in society, without which nations and communities could not exist in a state of civilisation. It is the lot of man. It is the source of wealth, since without poverty there could be no labour, no riches, no refinement, no comfort, and no benefit to those who may be possessed of wealth, inasmuch as without a large proportion of poverty, surplus labour could never be rendered productive in procuring either the conveniences or luxuries of life." [1]

What is the amount of wealth produced annually, and how is it distributed ? The question of distribution began at that time to interest the bulk of the nation. This curiosity arose from two sources—first, from the manufacturing and commercial class, who felt that, for all their efforts and risks, the largest part of the national income fell to the landed interests ; it was the beginning of the struggle for the abolition of the Corn Laws ; secondly, from social critics who, as we have seen from Hall, were quite sure that Labour was the producer of all wealth and received very little, but wanted accurate data to base their arguments upon ; it was the beginning of economic socialism or the agitation for the abolition of Capitalism.

Colquhoun appeared to satisfy this quest for facts and figures of distribution by giving approximately correct, at any rate,

[1] Patrick Colquhoun, *Resources of the British Empire*, 1814, p. 110 ; the same, *Treatise on Indigence*, 1806, pp. 7-9.

L

authoritative replies drawn from official records and papers. The new wealth produced, in 1812, in the United Kingdom, he found to have amounted to over 430 millions sterling. The number of the population was then 17,096,803. The distribution of the national income was as follows :—

The higher and lower nobility (numbering with their families 416,000 persons) received fifty-eight millions sterling, or from 200*l.* to 400*l.* each member, including women and children ; the yeomanry (1,400,000 persons, including women and children) received forty millions, or from 20*l.* to 50*l.* each ; farmers (1,540,000 persons, including their families) received over thirty-three millions, or 22*l.* each member ; merchants (194,000 persons, including their families) received twenty-seven millions, or from 112*l.* to 260*l.* each member ; shopkeepers (700,000 persons, including their families) received twenty-eight millions, or 40*l.* each member ; manufacturers (264,000 persons, including their families) received thirty-five millions, or 134*l.* each member ; agricultural labourers, including miners (3,154,142 persons, including families) received 33,400,000*l.* or 11*l.* each ; industrial workers, mechanics, artisans (4,343,389 persons, including their families) received over forty-nine millions, or 11*l.* each member. The remainder was distributed among royalty, the services, professional classes, clergy, small tradespeople, commercial assistants, finally among the paupers, who numbered 1,647,900 persons, and received either allowances or full relief.

The stress laid by Colquhoun on labour producing all the wealth could not but painfully emphasise the small reward that fell to the share of Labour. The contrast was striking. Likewise, the profits of the manufacturers compared unfavourably with the rent of the landowners, all the more so as Colquhoun sometimes regarded the work of the manufacturers and, generally, the manufacturing capital as productive labour (*Resources*, p. 109). The indefiniteness of the concept of Productive Labour, as we shall see later, is one of the weakest points of classical Political Economy and has been a fruitful source of error. Still, the general impression which Colquhoun's treatise left on the mind of its readers was that labour formed the source of wealth.

Reasoning from this premise there appeared to be no justification for the mode of distribution. Where lay the error ?

This problem was taken up by Ricardo and by Owen. Ricardo asked, what were the principles that ought to govern the distribution, and why were they ineffective ? How did it come that such a large part of the national income was absorbed by Rent ? And Owen asked, why did Labour receive so small a share, and why was the nation, as a whole, in the face of the enormous productive forces created by invention and science, still so poor that poverty fell to the lot of the great majority ?

Ricardo believed he had discovered the source of mischief in the Corn Laws and Poor Laws ; Owen in the new machinery being exploited exclusively in the interest of the capitalists, and, generally, in the ignorance of the rationalist truth that man did not make his own character, but that it was made for him by the past and present conditions.

Other reformers, like Thomas Attwood and John Gray, believed the medium of exchange (gold) and the whole process of circulation of commodities were at the root of all social misery. They were, therefore, currency reformers, or proposed a different form of exchange.

The Radicals, as we know, thought the cause of discontent and social unrest was the oligarchic form of government.

All those streams of opinion intertwined or crossed and formed, in their courses, large movements which filled British history from 1815 to about 1850.

2.—DAVID RICARDO

Among the theorists of Political Economy there has been none more inductive, and less abstract in method, than Ricardo. The misconception regarding his method arose, first, from his assumption that the problems which preoccupied him were known to everybody, and that, therefore, his main business was to supply the commentary and solution ; secondly, from the erroneous view prevailing until recently, that a great writer was enunciating eternal truths, instead of merely attempting to interpret a minute segment of the passing waves of human history.

But, taking Ricardo as he really was—viz. the economist of the latter phase of the Economic Revolution and the transition from the Napoleonic Wars to peace, there is no difficulty in judging his work.

Ricardo's problem was distribution. It engrossed his attention to such a degree that he regarded it as " the principal problem of Political Economy,"—a view in which Adam Smith would not have concurred, for, in his time, it was production which formed the principal economic problem ; and Thomas Mun, in his turn, would surely have opposed the opinion of Smith, and maintained that the balance of trade was the principal problem of Economics. Time and place control economic theory, and the England of the first half of the nineteenth century desired to know how the wealth produced by the new industrial system was divided. Ricardo, being a rationalist, lacked the historical sense and assumed that there was a natural law which regulated distribution and would, if not deflected by class or government legislation, equitably divide the produce of labour into rent, profit, and wages (*Principles of Political Economy and Taxation*, third edition, Preface, and conclusion of chapter 4). Ricardo, in speaking of natural law, has nothing to do with the state of nature. He, like Adam Smith, held the system of private property as far superior to any other system. In his eyes, property was sacred,[1] and he, like Smith and the Physiocrats, assumed the commercial system to be governed by inherent laws, acting through the nature of man. So, too, had Edmund Burke, the great opponent of the state of nature, assumed that commerce was governed by inherent laws, " which are the laws of nature, and, consequently, the laws of God." [2] There was, further, in the mind of Ricardo, not a shadow of doubt that Capital was the creator of civilisation, progress, and all that was good in society. He never regarded Labour as a separate and independent factor. Labour was the instrument of Capital. Only on one point there appeared to him a divergence of interest between Capital and Labour,—viz. in point of machinery (*Principles*, chapter 31),—

[1] Hansard's *Parliamentary Debates*, 1820, Vol. II., p. 122.
[2] E. Burke, *Thoughts on Scarcity*. 1795, p. 157.

and at this view he arrived comparatively late (about 1819), through the propaganda of Owen and the Owenites. On the other hand, he always believed that there was an irreconcilable opposition of interests between Capital and the landed aristocracy who lived on ground rent.

Although Ricardo was profoundly convinced that Capital was the creative and driving power of society, and that Labour was merely the appendage and instrument of Capital, he nevertheless made labour the foundation of his theories, without defining, in an unambiguous manner, the concept of labour. We shall deal, in the following chapter, with the erroneous inferences caused by that ambiguity; meanwhile, let us consider the law which, according to Ricardo, governed economic life.

It is the law of exchange-value.

Given utility, the exchange-value of a commodity arises from labour, and is measured by the quantity of labour necessary to produce the commodity. Political Economy deals, as a matter of course, with commodities that can be increased at any time and in any country, by human industry. The quantity of labour which measures value, is that which is necessary under the most unfavourable circumstances of production. It is, to use a modern economic term, marginal labour, or final utility labour, that measures value or forms the standard of value (*Ib*. I. 2, II.). Exchange-value and natural price are identical.

Value and riches are not identical. Riches or wealth consist of utilities, of an abundance of useful things, while value depends on the difficulty or facility of production. A person may possess for a period of, say, ten years, the same quantity of useful things, or the same quantity of wealth, yet its value may have increased or diminished according to the changes that have taken place during that period in the quantity of labour necessary for production. If, in the meantime, new machinery had been brought into operation which displaced a certain quantity of human labour, the exchange value of those goods will have decreased ; or, conversely, if, in the meantime, a larger quantity of labour will have to be employed in order to produce the same amount of wealth as ten years ago, its exchange-value will have increased (*Ib.* ch. 20.).

It is thus marginal human labour that forms the standard of exchange-value. It measures the volume of wealth of a person or country. Machinery, or natural agents used as motor power, may increase the volume of wealth or useful things, but add nothing to exchange-value ; they rather decrease it, since they displace or save human labour.

In order to produce commodities three things are necessary— land, labour, and capital.

The most important factor is capital, or accumulated labour. It is the motor power of social life. It consists of tools, implements, machinery, buildings, raw materials, food, and clothing, used for purposes of manufacture, agriculture, trade, and commerce. It is divided into two portions—fixed and circulating. Fixed capital consists of machinery, buildings, raw materials ; circulating capital is that which is spent on wages. Capital used in such a manner yields a profit or a surplus over the prime cost. Prime cost, plus profit, is the cost of production. The movement of capital, particularly circulating capital, determines the increase or decrease of population ; for, the larger the circulating capital, the greater the opportunity for steady work and good wages, and, therefore, the possibility of bringing up large families, and *vice versa* ; growth of population results in a greater demand for agricultural produce, consequently, in an extension of agriculture and rise of rent (*Ib.*, ch. 2 and 5). [1]

Rent is a surplus profit on the cultivation of land, paid by the cultivator to the owner. It presupposes private property in land, and arises from three causes—(1) Land is limited in quantity ; (2) it varies in quality and advantages ; (3) with the progress of population inferior soils are taken into cultivation. Suppose there are, in a new country, three qualities of land— Nos. 1, 2, 3. Land of the first class is abundant relatively to the population. It is, therefore, taken first into cultivation, and it yields a hundred quarters of corn. With the growth of the population, however, the cultivated area proves inadequate, and

[1] See also *Essay on the Influence of Low Prices of Corn*, 1815.

therefore, the farmers have recourse to soil No. 2, which yields but ninety quarters of corn. As soon as this is accomplished there is a surplus profit on No. 1, amounting to ten quarters. With the further increase of capital and population the soil No. 3 must be cultivated, which yields but eighty quarters. In this case the rent of soil No. 1 will be twenty quarters, and that of No. 2 will be ten quarters. And in the same proportion as we descend the scale of land qualities and reach marginal land which just covers the cost of production and thus produces no surplus profit, the rent of the superior qualities rises.

It is, as we have seen, marginal land that determines rent, and marginal labour that determines exchange-value. And as the inferior qualities of agricultural land require a greater quantity of labour to reproduce the cost and yield a profit, the exchange-value of agricultural produce must rise.

Had Ricardo thought out his theory of marginal labour to its last consequences, he would have come to the conclusion that the profits of all better equipped manufacturing establishments also partook of the nature of rent. For, if labour under the most unfavourable circumstances forms the standard of exchange value, all establishments which work under more and more favourable circumstances must yield surplus profits or rents. But he has not gone beyond stating the theory of marginal labour.

Having dealt with value and rent, we must consider Ricardo's theory of wages. Wages are not the price paid to the workman for the produce of his labour, but they represent a certain amount of food, clothing, shelter, and conveniences of life according to the habits and customs and the degree of civilisation of the country or district in which the workman lives, in order to enable him to exist and perpetuate his race without increase or diminution Or, in other words, wages are intended to restore to the labourer the physiological wear and tear caused by his exertions in field, factory, mine, office, and shop. In progressive countries the money wages have a tendency to rise, since the price of agricultural produce, according to the law of value, must rise, and the bulk of wages consists of agricultural produce. The only

factor which depresses wages is machinery, for through its introduction a part of the capital which would have been allotted to
the circulating portion (for wages) is added to the fixed portion.
But the introduction of machinery is only profitable when
money wages rise, and this rise is the effect of the extension of
agriculture to inferior soils, or the rise of agricultural prices.

On the whole, in a progressive country, rent and money wages
have a tendency to rise.

How does this rise act on the reward of Capital?

The value of the produced commodities, after deducting the
cost of the fixed capital, is divided into profit and wages. And
as wages have the tendency to rise, profit must have the tendency
to fall. For, if one whole consists of two portions, one portion
must decrease when the other increases. Wages and profit stand
in an inverse ratio to each other. Experience shows also that
the rise of agricultural prices is more prompt and rapid than that
of wages. The workman is therefore less benefited than the
landowner.

Before we sum up Ricardo's theories, in so far as they
are relevant to our subject, it must be pointed out that we
have been dealing with pure theory, leaving out of account such
factors as supply and demand, and fluctuations in the market
which lead to deviations from the theoretical laws and which
cause the natural price to become the market price. Ricardo
has not neglected those disturbing factors, but he always assumes
that the natural price forms the centre of gravitation round
which the market price fluctuates. The exchange-values or
natural prices are, in John Stuart Mill's simile, the sea level,
while the market prices are the ripples and waves.[1]

Ricardo's theories may be summed up as follows: The centre
of his system is the law of exchange-value. Labour, under the
most unfavourable circumstances, is the foundation of value;
the quantity of such labour, or marginal labour, is the standard
of value or the natural price. This price is represented in the
cost of production (fixed capital used, wages paid, profit). Higher
or lower wages do not appreciably affect the price, but they do

[1] J. S. Mill, *Principles of Pol. Econ.*, book 3, ch. 3, § 1.

considerably affect the volume of profit. Wages rise or fall according to the movement of agricultural prices, and if wages rise profit sinks, and *vice versa.* With the development of capitalist activities, the population increases, agriculture extends to inferior soils, rent rises, corn prices go up, wages go up, but profit sinks. The more Capital risks and undertakes, the less its relative income, the greater the income of the landowning class, which does nothing for the growth of civilisation. Moreover, manufactured commodities are losing in value, since the improvement in machinery lessens the quantity of labour, and, therefore, decreases their value, while the corn prices rise, since inferior soils are taken into cultivation which, as a matter of course, require larger quantities of labour. The result of the progress of civilisation is prosperity of the landowning classes and severer struggle of the capitalist classes. And yet it is Capital which creates civilisation ! Were this result the natural outcome of economic life nobody would have any right to complain. But it is not the natural effect. It is produced artificially by class legislation,—viz. the Corn Laws. By closing the English markets to foreign corn English agriculture is forced to have recourse to inferior soils, and thus to larger expenditure of labour quantities, which, by the law of value, raise the natural price. Diminished supply, limited competition, marginal labour and marginal lands combine to produce that effect. The interests of the landowning classes are thus opposed to the interests of the whole community.

This is the Ricardian interpretation of the Economic Revolution and the social turmoil produced by it. The middle classes found in it a clear and logical exposition of their own feelings ; they knew now their real enemy ; and they gained some insight into the movement of population, prices, profits, rents, and wages. The agitation for Parliamentary reform and the abolition of the Corn Laws appeared theoretically established and justified. Ricardo's treatise, while it undoubtedly contributed to the aggravation of the warfare between the people and the Tory aristocracy, softened the antagonism between Capital and Labour. The manufacturers learned the cause of strikes and the reason of the desire of Labour for coalition, and Labour discovered that oligarchic legislation, and not capitalism, was at the root of their distress. And that was essentially what Cobbett taught them. For the next fifteen years the capitalists and the mass of the working classes marched hand in hand in the struggle for Radical reform. And it was the sympathy of the middle classes which enabled the working classes to arrange demonstrations, to get rid of the Combination Laws, and to appear on the scene as a political factor. Without that sympathy such an event, for instance, as Peterloo would have passed comparatively unnoticed, or as little noticed as the Luddite hangings in January, 1813. Liberalism stood godfather to Labour politics. Most of the leaders of the organised workmen were cognisant of that fact.

But at the same time the socialists appeared and began to make use of the Ricardian theory of value as a weapon against the middle classes and to teach Labour that not the Tory landowner but the Liberal capitalist was their real enemy. Ricardo made labour the corner-stone of his system and yet he permitted the capitalist to appropriate accumulated labour and to decide the fate of the working classes. Ricardo looked upon social life from the point of view of Capital, the socialist looked upon life from the point of view of Labour. Ricardo asserted that the capitalist was everything and the landowner nothing, and yet the latter received the lion's share of the national income. Rent swallowed up profits and wages :—

> " See these inglorious Cincinnati swarm,
>   Farmers of war, dictators of the farm ;
>   *Their* ploughshare was the sword in hireling hands,
>   *Their* fields manured by gore of other lands ;
>   Safe in their barns, these Sabine tillers sent
>   Their brethren out to battle—why ? for rent !
>   Year after year they voted cent. per cent.,
>   Blood, sweat, and tear-wrung millions—why ? for rent !
>   They roar'd, they dined, they drank, they swore they
>   meant
>   To die for England—why then live ?—for rent ! "
>   (Byron, *The Age of Bronze*, xiv.)

While Byron was voicing the sentiments of rising Liberalism, the socialists asserted that the capitalists and the landowners were nothing, the working men everything, and yet the latter, even under the most favourable circumstances, received but food, clothing, and shelter as a compensation for the produce of their labour or for the national wealth they created : Society rests on injustice, on the robbing of Labour, and ought to be either radically mended or ended :

> " Men of England, wherefore plough
> For the lords who lay ye low ?
> Wherefore weave with toil and care
> The rich robes your tyrants wear ?
>
>   *   *   *   *
>
> " Wherefore, Bees of England, forge
> Many a weapon, chain, and scourge,
> That these stingless drones may spoil
> The forced produce of your toil ?
>
>   *   *   *   *
>
> " The seed ye sow, another reaps ;
> The wealth ye find, another keeps ;
> The robes ye weave, another wears ;
> The arms ye forge, another bears."

Shelley created the song of rising socialism. Ricardo, Byron, and Shelley were ushering in a period of social warfare, in which England was transformed from an Oligarchy into a Democracy. Manufacturing and trading capital found its theorist in Ricardo ; Liberalism its bard in Byron ; Communism and social justice found in Shelley, a poet,—visionary, passionate, and transcending reality.

3.—CURRENCY AND SOCIAL REFORM

The period of the Economic Revolution and Napoleonic Wars gave rise to prolonged and intricate controversies on currency which also influenced the social agitators for many years and played no small part in the Owenite and Chartist literature. Up to the foundation of the Bank of England the media of exchange were gold, silver, and bills of exchange. With the establishment of the Bank the nation soon realised that paper, even when only partly covered by gold and silver, could be made into money. This was a new experience which, at first, met with difficulties, but finally won the day. Since 1774, gold began gradually to be regarded as the only proper and legal basis of money, and in 1816 Parliament declared it to be the only legal tender—England accepted monometallism. It was this period (1774–1816) which bristled with difficulties, theoretical and practical, about money. The expansion of agriculture (rapid enclosing of lands), manufacture, and commerce, on the one hand, and the enormous expenditure and loans for war purposes on the other, led to the Bank Restriction (1797) which made paper the legal tender. The country was suffering from a lack of gold and silver, the Bank suspended specie payment and issued one-pound-notes, and many private business men issued token money for the purpose of paying wages to their workmen. Although the price of gold gradually rose and paper money suffered depreciation, many currency reformers could not rid themselves of the new and astonishing experience that paper could be made into money even if totally deprived of its metallic basis.

As far as our subject of social reform is concerned there were two kinds of currency writers. Some of them argued that the proper basis of money was the productive power of the nation. Money being the medium of exchange of goods and labour there ought to be as much money in the country as to facilitate the exchanges. No good standing business man ought to be hampered by lack of the circulating medium in his transactions. The banks which were licensed to issue notes should issue and lend him as much paper money as he needed. Other reformers were of opinion that money was merely a receipt for goods produced, which receipt enabled the producer to exchange them for goods of equal value.

The former writers on currency were numerous and had their representatives in Parliament, who, in the first decade of the nineteenth century, spoke in favour of their theories. One of their most active followers was Thomas Attwood (1783–1856), the son of a Birmingham banker, who in the years from 1816 to 1819 issued several pamphlets on currency reform, and in the years from 1829 to 1839 was prominently associated with, and often the leader of, all popular movements in Birmingham and the Midlands. In 1816, the year of the final victory of gold over silver and the year of the beginning distress, he published a pamphlet entitled *The Remedy, or Thoughts on the present Distress;* one year later he issued *A Letter to Mr. Vansittart on the Creation of Money,* and in 1819 a pamphlet *Observations on Currency, Population, and Pauperism,* in form of a letter to Mr. Arthur Young ; the latter pamphlet being intended to show that the resumption of specie payment by the Bank of England in conformity with the so-called Peel's Act (1819), *i.e.,* on the basis of gold, was injurious also to the landed interests.[1] Attwood's theory may be outlined as follows :—

All riches come from labour in agriculture, manufacture, and trade. All labour comes from the population. With the increase of the population the needs multiply, and also the resources and exertions of society to satisfy those needs. Increase of the population means therefore increase of production and wealth. This progress has no limits. But the employment of labour and the production of wealth are only rendered possible through the agency of the circulating medium. The invention of money has done more for the progress of society than any other. It facilitated division of labour and thus led to all the other inventions and improvements of which Adam Smith speaks. Hence it follows that if the population increases the quantity of the circulating medium must be increased, else it becomes unequal to its increased duties, and the population becomes redundant, which really means a shortage of the circulating medium. Labour and employment cannot be brought together, goods remain unexchanged, with the result that stagnation and misery overtake society. It is therefore evident that the well-being of the society depends on the facility with which capital is exchanged for industry, and consumption for production. The medium which facilitates this process of circulation is money, which not only must exist in an adequate quantity, but must be elastic enough to expand with the expansion of population,

[1] A summary of these currency theories and an elaboration of their arguments are given in *Gemini Letters*, 1844.

labour, and wealth. Has the Government, whose chief business is supposed to be the promotion of the welfare of society, given us such an expansive currency? No! Instead of an elastic circulating medium it took great pains to establish a restricted and restricting currency. Were gold a home commodity easily procurable there would be nothing to object to it ; such a commodity would be capable of satisfying the needs of an expanding productive population. Gold is, however, the product of oversea countries ; it is not easily procurable ; moreover, it is subject to fluctuations which are beyond our control. We are thus suffering from the contradiction of an expanding society and a restricted medium of exchange. Population, trade, and commerce are being strangulated. Hence the distress.

Attwood belongs to the usual type of revolutionary thinkers, who are possessed with one idea which they use for the interpretation of past and present history. They bend, stretch, and break the facts until they are made to prove that that idea underlies or controls the whole course of human history. Attwood argued that it was the paper currency following upon the Bank Restriction which enabled England to carry the Napoleonic Wars to a successful issue. In his eyes this period was prosperous, trade and commerce flourished, and the working classes were peaceful. But as soon as the Government, giving way to the financiers, jobbers, and Jews, began to prepare measures for the resumption of specie payments, business slackened and distress set in. After 1819 it was Peel's Act to which he ascribed every evil, and when, in the course of the trade cycle, distress gradually disappeared and the country enjoyed years of prosperity, Attwood was quite sure that they were preceded by a large issue of paper notes. On the whole, he refused to believe that England could ever prosper as long as Peel's Act remained in force. The remedy for this deplorable state of things was of course a return to the period of the Bank Restriction and creation of paper money on the basis of the productive power of the nation. To make gold the basis of the circulating medium, he argued, was tantamount to making the social pyramid stand on its apex.

To the objection that England was not suffering from a shortage of money, but of markets, Attwood replied with the question, What were markets ? Markets were created by our needs, and most of the needs of the productive classes or the great majority of the nation remained unsatisfied. The home market should be first supplied. The productive classes were the creators of wealth and would form a most profitable home market if the opportunity were given to them to employ their skill at remunerative wages. The capitalists were comparatively few in number and their whole work consisted in accumulating property. The labouring classes, on the other hand, formed the great majority of the population and would consume most of the goods if capital could be readily converted into industry. And this would be the case if the currency were based on reasonable principles. The cry of the nation should therefore be, Break the strangulating gold chains from our body politic ! Let the circulation move freely and easily ! Without such measures all other reforms must prove futile. Parliamentary reform, abolition of the Corn Laws, reduction of taxes, emigration, sexual restraint, etc., etc. would avail nought as long as the circulation was fettered.

The establishment of gold as legal tender had also caused much harm to the farmers, debtors, and taxpayers. For, in consequence of the gold basis of money, the prices fell considerably, while the contracts, national debt, and private debts, made during the war period, when prices ruled high, remained, and no corresponding abatement was arranged.[1]

The influence of the currency controversies on Owen and John Gray will be dealt with in a subsequent chapter.

[1] For a refutation of the paper money theorists see J. S. Mill, *Principles of Political Economy*, book 3, chap. 13, § 4.

V

ROBERT OWEN

THE central figure of British Socialism in the first half of the nineteenth century was distinguished neither by original philosophic speculations nor outstanding literary achievements, but by strength of character and untiring reform activities. He witnessed and took part in the rise and development of the industrial revolution, the social agitations, the struggles of the working classes for economic and political power. His influence on the movements of this period was considerable, and is still being felt. His strong and simple intellect, perfect bodily health and even temper, always under the control of reason, resulted in an unbroken, energetic, and straight-aiming volition, in a self-confidence and rapidity of resolution which destined him for the leadership of men. These qualities, mostly the result of heredity and natural gifts, were ascribed by Owen to his having early gained the conviction that the character of man was formed for him by the circumstances into which he was born, and in which he lived. As soon as Owen had attained to that truth, which was with him one of his few leading principles, his " mind became simple in the arrangement of ideas," and " in consequence, gradually became calm and serene, and anger and ill-will died within " him.[1] But he has failed to explain why so many of his brother rationalists, who were imbued with the same opinions, never attained to that simplicity of reasoning, serenity of mind, capacity for leadership, and social reform activities, which made him so conspicuous a personality.

That was one side of Owen's character.

Beneath his armour of dispassionate logic burned a

[1] *Life of Robert Owen* (Autobiography), 1857, I., p. 30.

heart with the glow of compassion for the labouring poor, and an imagination fed by social visions. He united in his personality the shrewdness and keen eye of the business man with the emotionalism and ecstasies of the prophet. As long as the management of textile workers and the business of cotton spinning in Manchester and New Lanark were uppermost in his mind, his emotions and imaginings were controlled by his strong and cool reason. He then marched from success to success ; the apprentice in a drapery shop at Stamford became, at the age of twenty years, manager of one of the largest factories in Manchester, then factory owner, finally partner of one of the greatest manufacturing establishments in Scotland and rationalist educator of his numerous employees. Wealth and fame were his. Without any conscious effort on his part, he exacted cheerful obedience from his subordinates, and even men of incomparably superior education and higher station of life than Owen's willingly paid their tribute of respect to his understanding and sterling worth. Princes, dukes, and lords admired his educational and philanthropic work, and New Lanark became, for a time, particularly from 1815 to 1820, the Mecca of reformers. The son of a Welsh saddler and ironmonger, with a scanty education at a village school, became one of the best public speakers and writers of lucid and vigorous English.[1] As soon, however, as he had left the sphere of trade, commerce, and philanthropy, and dedicated himself to the mission of a saviour of mankind, his shrewd realism, exactness of statement, and wonderful executive capacity came to an end. Of his long life from 1771 to 1858, the years from 1817 onwards increasingly exemplified to the second phase of his career, which was strewn with failures, material losses, disappointments. His outlook on society became blurred, his social criticism marred by exaggeration, his inferences degenerated into prophecies, and his charming and disarming naïveté had much of the credulity of a child.

Still, his infinite charity and love of humanity cover a multitude of shortcomings ; and his insight into some of the meanings of the new inventions, the services rendered to infant education,

[1] Robert Southey, *Sir Thomas More, or Colloquies*, 1829, I., p. 144.

M

factory legislation, and the co-operative efforts of the working classes have secured for him one of the foremost places in the history of socialism.

Owen was the first British socialist who did not turn to the past for inspiration, but attempted to put the productive forces, unlocked by modern science, into the service of collective production and distribution, first on behalf of the unemployed, and afterwards of society as a whole. He was immensely impressed by the facilities for wealth production which the new machinery afforded. It seemed to him that inanimate machinery, tended by a comparatively small number of manual labourers, would soon be capable of supplying the needs of mankind. What was, then, to become of the working classes ? Yet, for all his propaganda among the labouring population he was no democrat. He was always with them, but never of them. He could be their self-sacrificing father and teacher, their authoritative adviser and leader, but never the *primus inter pares*. He was perfectly free from all demagogy. In telling the working classes that labour was the source of wealth, he never failed to qualify it by adding that only " well-directed " or " properly-directed " labour was the fountain of riches and standard of value. Moreover, it was only modern machinery which caused the sources of wealth to flow abundantly.[1] He, at first, used to speak of them as " lower orders " ; then, with the rise of co-operation, trade unionism, mechanics' institutes, and Chartism, he called them " productive classes." From him they learned socialism, but it was essentially co-operative socialism and not militant socialism. He was strongly opposed to strikes, trades-unionist policy, and class warfare. His struggle was not primarily against usurpation and wickedness, but against error and ignorance, of which both the possessing classes and the labouring poor were the victims.

Which was that cardinal and fateful error ?

[1] *On the Proposed Arrangements of Mr. Owen*, 1819 (Three Letters to Mr. Ricardo).

2.—LEADING PRINCIPLES

Bentham's formula is Owen's premise. The object of all human exertions is happiness. Yet, happy individuals are rare exceptions, and happy nations do not exist at all. This state of things cannot have been caused by a perversion of the human will, since volition is not the prime mover of human actions. Like all rationalists, Owen is of opinion that reason, the prime materials of which are impressions, governs man. Reason, badly or falsely trained, creates evil. Hence the cause of the failure of man to achieve his object must be sought in some error of judgment. It consists, according to Owen, in the current and generally accepted belief that man makes his own character, while the truth is that man's character is made for him by the circumstances into which he is born and in which he lives and works. Inferior conditions produce inferior men ; good circumstances create good characters. Evil conditions are those that favour ignorance, selfishness, misery, illness, fear, untruthfulness, hypocrisy, superstition, enmity, and war. These conditions prevail to-day, and their fruit is unhappiness,

The first business of the reformer is, manifestly, to spread the truth concerning the formation of character in order to gain universal consent for such a change of circumstances that would create good characters. These views he elaborated in his four *Essays on the Formation of Character*, written in the years 1813-15.[1]

The creation of good circumstances depends, next, on an abundance of wealth. Without such an abundance the lot of the many must be poverty, and poverty is one of the evil circumstances, for it causes ignorance, bad health and cowardice. These ideas are dealt with in Owen's pamphlets, *Observations on the Effect of the Manufacturing System, Report on the Poor, Memorial to the Allied Powers,* and *Report to the County of Lanark,* written in 1815-20.[2]

Rationalist psychology and social economics are Owen's main fields of research. The spreading of the principles of both

[1] Reprinted in *Life of Owen,* I., pp. 257-332.   [2] *Ib.,* IA.

are alike important. For as long as the old conception of character-building prevails the infinite multiplication of wealth will only be exploited by the few to the detriment of the many, while as long as the material resources are scanty the opposition of the possessing and ruling minority to any reform will be overwhelming, and poverty will remain the lot of the majority.

The great importance of our times is that both requisites for universal happiness are at hand. The new truth concerning the formation of character is being revealed, and wealth is being produced at an unprecedented rate. The time for human emancipation has arrived. Owen, as the new character-builder, on the one hand, and the inventors of the industrial machinery, on the other, are creating that great crisis or turning-point in human history. He has shown what could be done by education and benevolent care for the working people, and under modern industrial conditions, with the machinery created by science, wealth can be made as plentiful as water. The rich will therefore sacrifice nothing by consenting to a change of conditions by social arrangements in favour of all. And the poor need no more envy and hate the rich, since the opportunity will soon be given to them to produce as much wealth as they liked.

Owen exclaimed : " Any general character, from the best to the worst, from the most ignorant to the most enlightened, may be given to any community, even to the world at large, by the application of proper means ; which means are, to a great extent, at the command and under the control of those who have influence in the affairs of men." Given the proper circumstances, it is best to begin with the formation of the character of the infants, for these being " passive and wonderfully contrived compounds . . . can be trained to acquire any language, sentiments, belief, or any habits and manners, not contrary to human nature " (*First Essay on the Formation of Character*). Side by side with training must go the opportunity for " honest and useful employments to those so trained," by which means " some of the circumstances which tend to generate, continue, or increase, early bad habits " will be withdrawn. This truth, combined with the evident fact that the world is now being saturated with wealth, render the emancipation of mankind possible. And it is high time to prepare the way for it, for, " those who have duly reflected on the nature and extent of the mental movements of the world for the last half century, must be conscious that great changes are in progress ; that man is about to advance another important step toward that degree of intelligence which his natural powers seem capable of attaining. Observe the transactions of the passing hours ; see the whole mass of mind in full motion ; behold it momentarily increasing in vigour, and preparing, ere long, to burst its confinement " (*Third Essay on the Formation of Character*).

Owen was evidently a careful observer of the growing ferment and agitation among the working classes, and the knowledge gathered therefrom accelerated his reform activity. He gradually entered upon his missionary career of emancipating mankind from misery. It must have been a moment of ecstasy when the full import of his mission flashed upon his mind. The elements had been slowly gathering, and in 1817 they coalesced. The shrewd cotton spinner of New Lanark was reborn as a socialist. Private initiative, he saw, would give to the labouring poor neither education nor employment, " for the children of commerce have been trained to direct all their faculties to buy cheap and sell dear ; and, consequently, those who are the most expert and successful in this wise and noble art, are, in the commercial world, deemed to possess foresight and superior acquirements ; while such as attempt to improve the moral habits and increase the comforts of those whom they employ, are termed wild enthusiasts " (*Third Essay*). Owen, therefore, asked the Government to carry out the task of national education and national employment in order to create those circumstances which were favourable to the formation of good characters. It was in 1817 that he began to see the evil and good circumstances, in the shape of an antithesis of capitalism and socialism or competition and co-operation.

3.—FACTORY LEGISLATION.

Prior to 1817, Owen's definition of bad circumstances did not go beyond sweating, ignorance, and enmity. It did not imply any radical change of the system of property, but amelioration through private initiative and legislative action. In 1813 or 1814, Owen exhorted his fellow-manufacturers and superintendents to devote more attention to the welfare of the operatives. " Experience has also shown you," he told them, " the difference of the results between mechanism, which is clean, well-arranged, and always in a high state of repair ; and that which is allowed to be dirty, in disorder, without the means of preventing unnecessary friction, and which, therefore, becomes and works out of repair. In the first case the whole economy and management are good ; every operation proceeds with ease, order, and success. In the last, the reverse must follow, and a scene be presented of counteraction, confusion, and dissatisfaction among all the agents and instruments interested or occupied in the general process, which cannot fail to create great loss. If, then, due care as to the state of your inanimate machines can produce such beneficial results, what may not be expected if you devote equal attention to your vital machines, which are far more wonderfully constructed ? . . . Will you not afford some of your attention to consider whether a portion of your time and capital would not be more advantageously applied to improve your living machines ? " [1]

In the years 1815–18 Owen devoted a great deal of his time and money to the propaganda of Factory Legislation and relief of the unemployed. His success was by no means equal to his efforts, but his insight into the effects of the Industrial Revolution widened and deepened from the necessity imposed upon him of proving the truth of his propositions and the practicability of his demands. He had started as a rationalist educator and psychologist, he now became a social economist. In order to interest his fellow-employers in his plans, he, in 1815, convened a meeting in Glasgow of the Scotch manufacturers, with a view to consider

[1] *Life of Owen*, I., pp. 260–1.

the advisability and policy of asking the Government to remit the heavy duty on the importation of cotton, and, further, to consider measures for the improvement of the condition of the young children and others employed in the various textile manufactures. Owen spoke on the objects of the meeting, but while the audience was enthusiastically in favour of the remission of the cotton duties, not one person rose to second his motion for the protection of the textile workers. The preparations he had made for the address to this meeting and the experience he had gained from the attitude of the audience enabled and impelled him to write his first economic pamphlet, *Observations on the Effect of the Manufacturing System* (1815). Having shown the growing preponderance of trade and manufacture over agriculture, he proceeds to describe the cause of those changes. " The change has been owing chiefly to the mechanical inventions which introduced the cotton trade into this country." The foreign trade extended, and the wealth, industry, population, and influence of the British Empire increased so rapidly that by their aid the nation was able to carry on the war against France for twenty-five years. But " these results have been accompanied with evils of such a magnitude as to raise a doubt whether the latter do not preponderate over the former. Hitherto, legislators have appeared to regard manufactures from the point of view of wealth. The other mighty consequences which proceed from extended manufactures when left to their natural progress have never yet engaged the attention of any legislature. The general diffusion of manufactures throughout a country generates a new character in its inhabitants ; and as this character is formed upon a principle quite unfavourable to individual or general happiness, it will produce the most lamentable results, unless the tendency be counteracted by legislative interference and direction."

Owen then proceeds to draw a dark picture of the deterioration of the character of the commercial and working classes, through the lust of gain and exploitation, and urges upon the Government to limit the regular hours of labour in mills of machinery to twelve per day, including one and half for meals ; to prohibit the employment of children under ten years, or for longer than six hours daily, until they reach the age of twelve years ; after a time to be named, children shall not be admitted into any factory until they can read and write and understand the first four rules of arithmetic.   For the success of this legislative measure he worked for three years, until it was embodied, in form of a compromise with the opposing interests, in the Factory Act, 1819.

Owen always believed that he had been the main driving power of that Act.   On the other hand, Alexander Ure, whose knowledge of the history of the factory system was considerable, ascribed that law to the " strikes and turmoils " of the Lancashire cotton spinners in the years 1817 and 1818.[1]

Owen's pamphlet contains also a curious prophecy.   He thought it was highly probable " that the export trade of this country has attained its utmost height, and that by the competition of other States possessing equal or greater advantages it will soon gradually diminish.   The direct effect of the Corn Bill lately passed will be to hasten this decline and prematurely to destroy that trade.   It is deeply to be regretted that the Bill passed, and I am convinced that a repeal will be ere long absolutely necessary in order to prevent the misery of the people."

This was written in 1815, and during the whole of the nineteenth century the export trade was increasing and is still increasing.   Of the unfulfilled prophecies concerning the downfall of capitalism there is no end.

4.—UNEMPLOYMENT AND SOCIALISM

The distress which set in towards the end of 1816 was the first crisis caused, not by scarcity, but by over-production.   The supply was outstripping demand.   The number of unemployed increased at an alarming rate, public opinion became agitated, meetings were convened and committees appointed to investigate the cause of the distress and find a remedy for it.   The demands of the poor for parish relief increased to such an extent that the House of Commons appointed a Committee on Poor Laws. Robert Owen, having found it impossible to explain his views

[1] Ure, *Philosophy of Manufactures*, Bohn's Library, p. 288.

upon the matter to a committee appointed by a meeting of the leading men of London, wrote a report for the Parliamentary Committee on Poor Laws, March, 1817.[1] A year later he further elaborated his reforms on behalf of the working classes in a Memorial to the Allied Powers assembled in Congress at Aix-la-Chapelle,[2] and in 1819 he caused one of his literary friends, probably George Mudie (editor of the *Economist*, 1821-2), to write a number of open letters to Mr. Ricardo on the same subject.[3] The gist of these pamphlets is that machinery facilitated production to such a degree that the world was becoming saturated with wealth. As long as manual labour was the main source of wealth demand and supply balanced. Production and population were to each other as 1 to 1. In the years 1792 to 1817 the proportion changed enormously. Production and population were now as 12 to 1. As machinery worked cheaper than manual labour, the latter was being depreciated or displaced. The total wage bill of the country diminished ; the working classes lost, therefore, much of the fund from which they satisfied their needs, the home market contracted, and the produced commodities remained unsold in the barns and warehouses. When the invention of the steam engine and other machines was made, either the greatest blessing or the greatest curse was bestowed upon society. At present, the latter prevailed, and a considerable portion of the British population was doomed to pauperism. It was in vain for manual labour to contend, under the present conditions, with the sinews of mechanism. On the other hand, if it were possible to make consumption keep pace with production, labour and capital would be beneficially employed, and distress would be unknown. But this could not be the case as long as private gain, and not social welfare, ruled economic life. As things stood now, production would more and more outstrip consumption, for the export trade must gradually decrease, and the home market contract, and, therefore, unemployment and insecurity of existence increase, until the working classes, finding their remuneration either gone or reduced below the means of

---

[1] *Life of Owen*, IA., pp. 53-63. [2] *Ib.*, pp. 212-22.
[3] *Mr. Owen's Proposed Arrangements*, 1819.

subsistence, would be goaded into fury and despair, and suddenly overwhelm our noble and beneficent institutions and lay them in ruins. " We resemble individuals standing on the narrow causeway of a surrounding abyss." And all that happened because the human mind, after countless ages of struggle with poverty and ignorance, finally succeeded in unlocking the sources of wealth ; in multiplying the productive forces ; in rendering the production of goods easy. It was abundance that brought upon us misery ! Large masses of producers were being thrown upon the Poor Laws because they had produced too much wealth ! How paradoxical it all looked ! What was the remedy ? Some said Poor Law Reform ; others advised emigration. But all remedies of that kind would do no good, for they did not touch the problem. The real cure lay in arrangements that would enlarge consumption and make it tally with production. Such arrangements were conditioned upon combined labour and expenditure, or communism.

However, the remedy could only be applied gradually. First of all, the problem of unemployment must be dealt with. " Under the existing laws the unemployed working classes are maintained by, and consume a part of, the property and produce of the wealthy and industrious, while their power of body and mind remain unproductive. They frequently acquire the bad habits which ignorance and idleness never fail to produce ; most of the poor have received bad habits from their parents ; and as long as this present treatment continues those bad and vicious habits will be transmitted to their children, and through them to succeeding generations." The care of the unemployed must therefore include education, and circumstances must be created for them in which duty and interest would coincide. The bodily and mental power of the poor should be used for their own benefit as well as for that of society as a whole. All those advantages could be realised by establishing Villages of Unity and Co-operation, consisting each of 500 to 1,500 persons and 1000 to 1,500 acres of land for agricultural and manufacturing purposes, with blocks of houses erected in such a manner as to enclose large squares. The establishment of such a co-operative village would require a capital outlay of £96,000. This sum, divided by 1,200 (the number of persons), gave £80 per head, or, at 5 per cent. interest, the sum of £4 per annum. With so small an expenditure, an unemployed workman could be made to maintain himself and family, educate his children, and even repay the capital charge. In the squares of the Co-operative Villages would be erected public buildings so as to divide the squares into parallelograms or quadrangles.

Owen's unemployed reform remained on paper, and became known jocularly as Owen's Parallelograms. He was opposed practically by the whole nation. Even the working men of London voted against his string of resolutions on Unemployment, which he had laid before two public meetings, in August, 1817, in the City of London Tavern. The London artisans sided at that time with the advocates of Parliamentary reform as against social reform of a coercive or patriarchal nature. An Owenite complained that the " lower orders are quite assured that a radical reform of the House of Commons must prove the grand panacea for all our woes." [1] Owen ascribes his defeat to machinations of the Churches and the Political Economists. Owen always regarded these two London meetings as the turning-point in his life.[2] Speaking on August 21, 1817, in the City of London Tavern, he denounced all religions of the world as now taught as gross errors. It was they that prevented mankind " from knowing what happiness really is." And the Political Economists, " including Malthus, Mill, Ricardo, Colonel Torrens, Hume, and Place . . . were all well-intentioned, clever, acute men, close reasoners, and great talkers upon a false principle. . . . I was most desirous to convince them that national education and employment could alone create a permanent, rational, intelligent, wealthy, and superior population, and that these results could be attained only by a scientific arrangement of the people, united in properly-constructed villages of unity and co-operation. While they, on the contrary, strongly desired to convert me to their views of instructing the people without find-

[1] *Mr. Owen's Proposed Arrangements*, 1819, p. 4.
[2] *Life of Owen*, IA., p. 161.

ing them national united employment, and of a thorough system of individual competition. The one may be called the system of universal attraction ; the other, that of universal repulsion." [1]

Owen was now fast drifting into socialism. On September 6, 1817, he wrote a letter to the press on " Relief of the Poor and Emancipation of Mankind." Soon after he published a brief sketch, written by Mr. Warder, a Philadelphian Quaker, dealing with the communistic arrangements of the Shakers, in order to show that " even with an inferior communistic life, wealth could be easily created for all "; he also republished John Beller's *Colledge of Industry*, to which Francis Place had called his attention.[2] Owen was now clear in his mind that the first step of social reform was to create a superior physical and mental character for all ; the second step was to produce abundance of wealth for all ; the third step would be to unite the two first by basing society on its true principle, *i.e.*, " by placing all within such arrangements of surroundings as will well-form the character, create the wealth, and cordially unite all in one interest and feeling over the world." [3]

Undeterred by the failure of his plan to form villages of co-operation for the unemployed, he laboured assiduously in London for his ideas, and, in 1819, a committee consisting of the Duke of Kent, Sir Robert Peel, David Ricardo, and W. Tooke, was formed in order to raise subscriptions for an experimental establishment of a " Parallelogram," but no adequate amount of subscriptions came in, and the committee dissolved in November, 1819. Robert Southey, evidently grieved at the failure of Owen's committee, comments upon it, saying that if Owen " had not alarmed the better part of the nation by proclaiming, upon the most momentous of all subjects [religion], opinions which are alike fatal to individual happiness and the general good," he might have, ere this, seen the firstfruits of his labours. " For the connection between moral truth and political wisdom is close and indissoluble ; and he who shows himself erroneous upon one

[1] *Life of Owen*, I., p. 129.   [2] *Ib.*, IA., pp. 119–60.
[3] *Ib.*, I., p. 243.

important point, must look to have his opinions properly dis-
trusted upon others." [1]

5.—SOCIAL RECONSTRUCTION AND CURRENCY REFORM

The enormous efforts made by Owen in the years 1815–19
produced no tangible result. Apart from the Factory Act,
1819, the honours of which he must undoubtedly share with
the Lancashire cotton operatives, nothing was achieved in the
way of the relief of the unemployed or communist experiment.
In 1819, he issued an *Address to the Workmen*, offering them
his whole-hearted assistance in their striving for emancipation
from misery and ignorance, but under the condition that they
should first accept and imbue themselves with his doctrine of
the formation of human character in order to renounce all
violence and hatred against the possessing and ruling classes. As
long as they showed themselves impervious to that truth, there
was no hope of saving them from the depths of misery and
darkness ; the new light which he had to reveal might then
prove too strong, and cause more mischief than good. Owen
was evidently of opinion that it would do no good to society to
reveal to the workmen the mysteries of wealth-making and the
principle of communism before they had made a successful
attempt to re-moralise their character, to extinguish their
violent class-warfare against the rich. He therefore explained
to them his psychological theory, and told them that (a) Rich
and Poor, the governors and the governed, had in reality the
same interests ; (b) The upper classes had no more the desire to
degrade the workmen or to keep them in subjection ; (c) The
labouring masses possessed now the means for emancipating
themselves and their posterity from economic misery, but that
the knowledge of those means must be withheld from them until
they fully comprehended that rich and poor were alike the
creatures of circumstances, and that, therefore, all personal enmity
was senseless ; (d) The past ages belonged to the history of human
irrationality, and that now the dawn of reason was beginning. [2]

[1] Robert Southey, *Sir Thomas More, or Colloquies*, 1829, I., pp. 130–2.
[2] *Ib.*, IA., pp. 224–31.

The working classes, however, were at that time fully occupied with the agitation for Parliamentary Reform, and Owen's exhortations remained unheeded. He then returned to Scotland, where he twice stood as a Parliamentary candidate, and was defeated. In 1820, the County of Lanark applied to him for a remedy against lack of employment and falling wages. Owen wrote his *Report to the County of Lanark* (1820), in which he gave a full exposition of his communist teachings as well as of currency reform.

This document deals also with one of his minor proposals— the discarding of plough cultivation for spade cultivation, but for the understanding of Owenism it is of no importance, it being accidental and logically unconnected with communism, although it played, later, some part in the Owenite movement.

As far as the communist teachings are concerned, there is nothing new in the Report ; they present a good and clear summary of Owen's economic views, which he had treated in his pamphlets in the years 1815–19. They are only bolder and more complete as coming from a courageous thinker who had passed the Rubicon, and who, moreover, had come to the conclusion that agriculture and manufacture on commercial lines were " on the eve of bankruptcy." [1] On the other hand, the views on currency and value, which this Report contains, are a substantial addition to Owenism. They exercised a considerable influence on the later movement, and led to practical experiments. Prior to 1820, Owen believed that the sources of evil were the error of character-building and mal-distribution of wealth ; he now began to disseminate the view that the form of exchange and the circulating medium were also at the root of social misery. His premise was the same as Attwood's, but the opinion of John Bellers on money appears also to have influenced him. In his *Colledge of Industry* (1696) Bellers declares that the " colledge fellowship " or communistic establishment " will make labour, and not money, the standard to value all necessaries by." Money had its mischiefs, and was called by

[1] *Report to the County of Lanark*, in *Life of Owen*, IA., p. 270.

the Saviour the Mammon of Unrighteousness ; although land and labour were the true riches, yet they could not be made productive if money was lacking. In reality, " money in the body politic is what a crutch is to the natural body, crippled ; but when the body is sound the crutch is but troublesome. So when the particular interest is made a public interest, in such a colledge money will be of little use." [1]

Owen, stimulated by Attwood, Bellers, and the public discussions on money which were caused by the introduction of monometalism (1816) and resumption of specie payment (1819), treated also currency and standard of value reform in his *Report*. He argues that the distress for which the County of Lanark was looking for a remedy showed that, under present arrrangements, no remedy was procurable. The wealth of the country had grown too rapidly and no measures had been taken for directing the overflow into proper channels. Society was suffering from an excess of production and weakened by maldistribution, caused partly by the mode of property, and partly by bad circulation. Effective measures must, therefore be taken for a re-arrangement of the system of property and the standard of value or the circulating medium. In taking such measures the following principles must be borne in mind : (*a*) " Manual labour, properly directed, is the source of all wealth and national prosperity ; (*b*) When properly directed, labour is of far more value to the community than the expense necessary to maintain the labourer in considerable comfort ; (*c*) Manual labour, properly directed, may be made to continue of this value in all parts of the world under any supposable increase of its population for many centuries to come ; (*d*) Wealth will grow faster than population." There need be no fear of change. With reasonable measures, such a change would literally " let prosperity loose on the country." One of the measures was a change in the standard of value. It was quite true that, in the civilised parts of the world, gold and silver had long been used for this purpose, but they had changed the intrinsic values of all things into artificial values, promoted fraudulent commerce and specula-

[1] Reprint in *Life of Owen*, IA, pp. 164 *et seq.*

tion, and, in consequence, materially retarded the general
improvement of society. It was fortunate, however, that the
Bank Restriction (1797) had taught Englishmen that gold and
silver could no longer represent the increased wealth. Paper
became legal tender, but this measure at the same time placed
the community at the mercy of a trading company, which was
ignorant of the mighty machine it wielded. Gold was restored
to its ancient dignity, but, being inadequate for the circulation
of the increased wealth, it aggravated the crisis, poverty, discontent, and danger. The restoration of the metallic currency
was like forcing a grown-up person to put on the swaddling-
cloth of its infancy. It cramped the body politic. Hence the
unparalleled depression of agriculture, commerce, and manufacture, and the total annihilation of the value of labour. The
remedy was a change in the standard of value. " The natural
standard of value is, in principle, human labour, or the combined
manual and mental powers of man called into action." A
certain quantity of such labour should form the unit of value,
and the labourer who performed it should get a paper note
certifying the number of units of value he had produced, with
which note he would be able to obtain the necessary goods
containing an equal number of units of value.

It might be objected that human labour was unequal, and
therefore could not form the measure of value. Against this it
was only necessary to point out that horse power was also unequal, and yet served as the measure of mechanical power.
Surely, average human power could be found out, and, as it formed
the essence of all wealth, its value in every article of produce
might be ascertained and the relation of its exchange-value to
other values fixed accordingly ; the whole to be permanent for
a given period, until progress of science had brought further
facilities for wealth production and made a revaluation necessary.
Human labour would thus acquire again its natural or intrinsic
value, which would increase as science advanced ; and this was,
in fact, the only useful object of science. The demand for human
labour would no longer be subject to caprice, nor would the support of human life be made a perpetually varying article of

commerce, and the working classes made the slaves of an artificial system of wages, more cruel in its effects than any slavery ever practised by society. This change in the standard of value would immediately open the most advantageous home markets, until the wants of all were supplied, nor, while the standard continued, could any evil arise in future from the want of markets. For, if the labourer was rewarded according to a natural standard of value, he would receive a fair proportion of the product of labour. Consumption would keep pace with production.

There is much confusion of thought in these reasonings. Owen believed money and standard of value to be identical, whereas money but expresses the standard of value. He regarded gold and silver as artificial values, and did not see that they could only serve as measures of value because they are real values in themselves. Owen applied his reform also to conditions of private property. If, then, a labourer is to be remunerated according to the standard of labour value—*i.e.*, if a labourer received for six hours' work a certain quantity of goods embodying six hours' work, he would really receive also the additional value produced by machinery, management, organisation, or the profit of capital. Where should, then, the new capital come from? Or the cost of maintenance, of science, and of administration?

It seems, however, that Owen did not mean that the labourer should receive the full product of labour, but a fair wage, or a fixed proportion of the product, for after much discussion he finally arrives at the conclusion that a fair proportion of the product would be for the labourer sixpence an hour. The truth appears to be that Owen was caught in the whirlpool of the currency controversies in the years 1816–19, without having been able to extricate himself. A discordant and fissiparous character was hereby imparted to his social economic reasonings, which made itself felt in the course of development of the Owenite movement. Some Owenites became merely currency reformers, and busied themselves with remedies for the improvement of exchanges and the circulating medium. From the Owenites it

N

passed to the Chartists, and from the latter to the International Working Men's Association (1864-73).

There are thus in Owen's social system two currents of thought: (a) Social misery arises from the error concerning the formation of character, the excess of production over effective demand, and consequent mal-distribution; (b) Social misery springs from or is considerably aggravated by artificial currency, deficient circulation. Against the former evils he recommends communism; against the latter, labour notes as the circulating medium, and he leaves private property untouched. Owen undoubtedly preferred communism, but some of his followers regarded circulation and currency as the main point.

Although Owen and Attwood started from the same premise, and had the same views regarding the history of currency in the years 1790-1819, they differed considerably as regards the remedial measures. Attwood and his school desired a paper currency in order to enable manufacturers and merchants to get loans and to facilitate production. Owen, on the other hand, desired labour notes in order to enable the community to fix a fair rate of wages and to render the exchanges equitable.

The *Report to the County of Lanark* was held by Owen to be one of his best publications; it gave, as he thought, " a full view of society in its whole extent, including every department of real life necessary for the happiness of our race. It was the first time that the outlines of a science of society were given to the world; . . . and it was after the circulation of this report that the imaginative Fourier imagined his notions for forming a practical community society, mixing old and new principles and practices, which never can continue long to work together." [1]

In 1821, Owen wrote a treatise, *Social System*, published in 1826-7, in the *New Harmony Gazette*.[2] His way of thinking is completely communist, without any admixture of private property institutions. He was then already determined to retire from business and form a community in order to act by example. He directs his critical shafts against the political

---

[1] *Life of Owen*, I., pp. 238, 234.
[2] *New Harmony Gazette*, February 14, 1827 (note).

economists. They had totally misunderstood their subject. They had, in all cases, supposed that the sole object of society was the accumulation of riches and that men would necessarily obtain all they required in proportion as their wealth increased. They had always reasoned as though man were an inanimate machine, without the capacity of suffering, understanding, or enjoying. They had led the nation from error to error, until it had become evident that production was easier than distribution. At this moment the main sufferings of mankind arose from the excess of wealth and the excess of ignorance; the political economists were powerless to alleviate the lot of the greatest number of the population; their praise of individualism, competition and foreign trade had resulted in the degradation of the many by mal-distribution. The main problem was, therefore, not production, but proper distribution.

The real object of political economy or a science of society should be happiness for all. This object could only be attained to by a system of mutual aid and co-operation, or communities with equality of labour and equality of distribution. The achievements of science would then be accessible to all, and therefore cease to be a curse for the many. Every new mechanical invention would lead not to the displacement of the labourer, but to the abridgment of labour time. It would not aggravate the opposition of interests, but strengthen the community and harmony of interests, since under a system of equality of labour every member would have the interest of abridging and facilitating the process of production. Ignorance could not exist in such a society, since it was in the interest of all to educate and train every member and make him an efficient producer. Abundance of wealth joined to equal distribution would put an end to all economic crises. Equality of distribution would under such conditions appear quite natural. " With means thus ample to procure wealth with ease and pleasure to all, none will be so unwise as to desire to have the trouble and care of individual property. To divide riches among individuals in unequal proportions or to hoard it for individual purposes, will be perceived as useless and injurious as it would be to divide air or light into unequal quantities for different individuals, or that they should hoard them."[1]

In the years 1812–21, Owen was at the zenith of his mental powers. His activities in the following forty years, or from 1821 to his death in 1858, were either reiterations and propaganda of his views, at which he had arrived in the second decade of the nineteenth century, or attempts to put them into practice.

The leading representatives of the country of Lanark having refused to put the *Report* into operation, Owen made an effort to form a community at Motherwell, but failed to interest a sufficient number of wealthy people to subscribe the necessary capital. For all his authority and persuasive powers, he did not succeed, at that time, either in getting in touch with the leaders of the working classes, or in bringing his communist views to the test of experience. Baffled in his ardent desire for immediate and tangible results, interfered with even in his educational experiments in New Lanark, he failed to notice that he was making proselytes among intellectuals, stimulating several critics, and creating an Owenite school of thought destined to leave a deep impress on the movement of the working classes and their socialist leaders. His first adherents were Scotsmen, Irishmen, and Welshmen—George Mudie, Abram Combe, Archibald James Hamilton, William Thompson, John Gray, J. M. Morgan, who subsequently became the pioneers of Owenism, spreading its doctrines among the working classes and forming communities.

However, the disappointments and defeats which Owen had suffered since 1815 induced him to retire from business, and to leave Great Britain for America, where he thought to find free men, brought up in the spirit of the Declaration of Independence, and to form there a community. In 1824 he carried out his plan. He bought the Rappist community " Harmony," in the State of Indiana, for £30,000, and converted it into a New Harmony after his own model. His attention to that community had been drawn by reports of travellers, which were

[1] *The Book of the New Moral World*, 1836, Introduction, xxi.

reproduced by Evans, the Spencean, in his *Christian Policy* (1818), and by the anonymous writer of *Mr. Owen's Proposed Arrangements* (1819), at the end of the third letter to Ricardo. The Rappists, simple religious peasants from Germany, had bought, in 1814, about 30,000 acres of land, then a mere desert, and converted it, within a few years, into a flourishing communist settlement. Thither Owen repaired, and about 900 people, a motley of idealists, adventurers, and craftsmen, joined him. Only very few of them were capable of sustained effort or animated by the true pioneering spirit. After three years of much disharmony and constitution-making, the communist experiment ended in dismal failure. Owen lost his money, and finally returned to England, where, in the years 1832–44, he displayed great activity among the working classes. This period of his eventful life belongs, however, to the history of Chartism.

VI

OWENITE AND RICARDIAN INFLUENCES

I.—SOCIALISM BASED ON CO-OPERATION

IN the years 1820 to 1830 the doctrines of Owen, supported by anti-capitalist deductions from Ricardo's theory of value, entered the wide field of working-class agitation, and coalesced into a system of socialism. The industrial, commercial, and political life of the nation favoured the dissemination and growth of the new views. The reign of George IV. marks the rise of Liberalism and the birth of the modern Labour Movement, political and socialistic. This decade saw the repeal of the Navigation Act, of the Combination Laws, of the Corporation and Test Acts ; it witnessed the destruction of the last remnants of the yeomanry, and the bulk of the handloom weavers ; in it occurred a short, but phenomenal spell of manufacturing and commercial pros- perity (1824–5), accompanied by the biggest and hardest-fought strikes which the country had until then experienced ; after which one of the severest commercial crises overtook the nation, and the temper of agrarian and industrial labour became restive and rebellious. " King Ludd " reappeared in the manufacturing centres, and " Captain Swing " devastated the counties by fire. Capitalism appeared to be on its trial. Thinking people began to read Adam Smith again, to pore over Ricardo, with a critical eye, and even Owen, the visionary, found favour with some intellectuals. An era of economic criticism and co-operative experiment was ushered in, which laid the foundation of modern socialism, in the midst of a gloomy atmosphere and full of fore- bodings of the impending bankruptcy of capitalism. Socialism, at its birth, imbibed the dogma that industrialism meant short spells of prosperity, followed by chronic crises, pauperisation of the masses, and the sudden advent of the social revolution.

182

Two sets of social reformers and critics made then their appeals to the nation, and, particularly, to the working classes, whom they were beginning to designate producers or industrious classes. They were making their appeals to the workers, not as wage-slaves, but as producers of the wealth of the nation. One set consisted of individualists, who, whilst unsparing in their criticism of the capitalists, whom they regarded as non-producers, were not favourable to socialism, and practically demanded a return to the pre-capitalist era, but completely freed from the fetters of mercantilism ; they demanded, in short, a society of free, independent, small producers, agricultural and manufacturing, governed by natural laws of exchange—without any Government interference. The other set of reformers, though in agreement with the former as to the injurious effects of capitalism and State regulations, recommended socialism as the remedy for the wrongs of Labour and the ills of the nation at large. With the former we shall deal in a subsequent chapter. Our first business is the exposition of the doctrines of co-operative socialism.

This movement as it issued from purely Owenite sources, though supplemented by deductions from the Ricardian theory of value, was pacific, constructive, educational, and non-political. Class warfare, passionate appeals to the feelings of Labour, demands for legal enactments, and government reforms were regarded not only as utterly futile, but directly detrimental to the cause of the people ; even trade union activities, strikes, and coercion, were often condemned, and they were but tolerated in so far as they could lead to co-operative-socialist unions. The Owenites believed that all social evils and wrongs had their origin in error, in the neglect of natural rights, but not in ill-will and class antagonisms. Society was suffering because the nation allowed itself to be actuated by erroneous conceptions. The most mischievous effect of error regarding society was competition. Hence the proper methods of removing evil and wrong were the spreading of truth and the formation of co-operative communities, or other co-operative forms of economic life. The main representatives of these views were George

Mudie, Abram Combe, William Thompson, John Minter Morgan, and John Francis Bray, writers of ability and men of action. The most distinguished among them was William Thompson. The views they were spreading and practising may be called Orthodox Owenism. After the failure of Owen to enlist the sympathies of the ruling classes for his plan, he and his faithful adherents mainly appealed for the sympathies of the working classes, or rather of the more intelligent and better situated elements of Labour, and as these were generally organising themselves for fighting purposes into trade unions, the orthodox Owenites made great efforts to persuade them to convert these unions into co-operative-socialist societies, and to invest their funds in production on socialist lines, instead of wasting their money on bitter and futile strikes.

Organised labour never accepted complete Owenism. As a rule, they added to certain parts of it political action or trade union action. One of their most gifted leaders, William Lovett, relates that he and his friends, after having read and admired the writings of Robert Owen, Peter (probably a mistake for William) Thompson, Morgan, Gray, and others, " resolved to be instrumental to the extent of their means and their abilities in spreading a knowledge of these works throughout the country. They intended, however, to avoid the course taken by Robert Owen. He had all along, though in his mild manner, condemned the radical reformers, believing as he did, that reform was to be effected solely on this plan ; the radical reformers of the working classes believing that his plan could only be carried out when the reforms they sought had been accomplished. . . . They resolved to take up such parts of his (Owen's) system as they believed would be appreciated by the working classes, and be the means of uniting them for specific purposes, taking care that these purposes should not interfere more than was possible with opinions in the proceedings to be adopted in matters on which great differences of opinion prevailed."[1] In short, the leading spirits of the working classes took up only certain parts of Owen's teachings, at the same time adhering to the Radical

---

[1] *Lovett's Memorandum* in Place, Add. MSS. 27791, III.

movement for Parliamentary reform. They believed that only through political power would the labouring masses be able to bring about the co-operative commonwealth, while the orthodox Owenites emphasised the priority of economics, arguing that forms of government and legislatures were the superstructure and economics the basis of society; the main business of socialists consisted therefore in changing the forms of wealth production, for as soon as this was accomplished the superstructure would adjust itself to the new basis.

Finally, parallel with these two main streams of Owenism ran a third which concentrated its activity on the process of exchange and the function of currency. Its foremost representative was John Gray, who attempted to combine individualisation of production with a socialisation of the exchange of commodities through national storehouses and labour notes.

Common to all Owenites was the criticism and disapproval of the capitalist or competitive system, as well as the sentiment that the United Kingdom was on the eve of adopting the new views. A boundless optimism pervaded the whole Owenite school, and it filled its adherents with the unshakable belief that the conversion of the nation to socialism was at hand, or but a question of a few years. Commercial crises, plethora of wealth, and widespread misery, dissatisfaction and general ferment, proved that society was out of joint. "And when these things begin to come to pass, then look up, and lift up your heads ; for your redemption draweth nigh."

2.—RISE OF THE TERM "SOCIALIST"

The centre of co-operative socialist thought was the London Co-operative Society, founded in the autumn, 1824, for the purpose of "formation of a community on the principles of mutual co-operation," and to restore "the whole produce of labour to the labourer." The founders declared that happiness was the true object of human exertions, and that it could not be attained to without a knowledge of the principles of society ; the inventions and discoveries that led to the production of an abundance of wealth could not produce happiness unless corresponding progress was made in moral and political science. Only through such knowledge could man come to see that competition and private accumulations or excessive inequality could never produce happiness ; society must, therefore, be built up on a system of mutual co-operation, community of property, equal labour, and equal enjoyment. Accordingly, the members of the London Co-operative Society resolved to " renounce all the evils of trafficking or mere commerce, likewise profit, which implies living on the labour of others ; all our exchanges being proposed to be for fair equivalents, representing equal labour, and destined for immediate or gradual consumption, and not for accumulation to command the labour of others."

The best periodical publication of orthodox Owenism was *The Co-operative Magazine* (1826–30), which contains a great amount of instructive matter. It was the central organ of co-operative thought and experiment of the time. It expressed the views, arrived at by serious and long discussions, of the London Co-operative Society. This Society and its organ were the common meeting-place of the adherents of communist co-operation. Here are some of the subjects of their debates :—

" May not the greater part of the moral and physical evils which afflict mankind be traced to individual competition in the production and distribution of wealth ? "

" Is the labourer entitled to the whole produce of his labour ? Why is, in the present state of society, the lot of the producing classes poverty and wretchedness ? "

" What are the objections to a state of voluntary equality of wealth and community of property ?   And can they be satisfactorily answered ? "

" Is the position of Mr. Owen correct, that man is not properly the subject of praise or blame, reward and punishment ? "

" Would the arts and sciences flourish under the co-operative system ?'"

" Is there any principle in human nature which presents an insurmountable obstacle to the co-operative system ? "

"Can the working classes permanently improve their condition by combinations to raise the rate of wages, or by benefit societies and similar means now adopted by them?"

"Is the right of property derived from nature, or from social compact?"

"Are the present distresses of the country attributable to redundant population?"[1]

In these debates the term "Socialist" must have been coined. It is found for the first time in *The Co-operative Magazine* of November, 1827—in the same year in which Robert Owen published, in *The New Harmony Gazette*, a series of articles under the heading "Social System." The adjective "social" in juxtaposition to self-love is of course much older; its origin may be traced back to Alexander Pope's well-known verses in the *Essay on Man* :—

> "So two consistent motions act the soul ;
> And one regards itself, and one the whole.
> Thus God and Nature linked the general frame,
> And bade self-love and social be the same."

With Owen and his adherents, however, self-love and social were not only not the same, but in direct opposition to each other. Self-love found its expression in individual competition, while social meant communist co-operation. In a footnote to a communication of the Brighton co-operators, the editor of *The Co-operative Magazine* observes that the value of a commodity consisted both of present and past labour (capital or stock), and the main question was "whether it is more beneficial that this capital should be individual or common." Those who argued that it should be in the hands of individual employers were the modern political economists of the type of James Mill and Malthus, while those who thought it should be common were "the Communionists and Socialists"[2] They based their demands on moral grounds, on the doctrines of Robert Owen,

[1] *Co-operative Magazine*, 1826, 1827 ; John Gray, *Lecture on Human Happiness*, 1825, Appendix ; William Thompson, *Labour Rewarded*, 1827, p. 106.

[2] *Co-operative Magazine*, 1827, p. 509 (footnote). *Cf. Archiv. für die Geschichte des Sozialismus*, 1912, 2 und 3 Heft, pp. 372, *seq.*

and on the theory of labour value, from which they deduced the injustice of the existing order.[1]

3.—SOCIALIST DEDUCTIONS FROM RICARDO : A CRITICISM

It is hardly possible for an Englishman of to-day to form an adequate idea of the charm which Ricardo's *Principles* exercised on his ancestors of nearly a century ago.   Only a German is still able to feel it, for he lives nearer the industrial revolution and all the social ferment that it produces, and he has to study also Karl Marx—the last great disciple of Ricardo who developed the labour value theory to its final consequences.   Most of the controversies of German and Eastern European scholarship concerning Marx's *Capital* were, in their essence, fought out in the years between 1820 and 1830 in England round Ricardo. Englishmen, at that time, still liked a good logical tussle, and found pleasure in economic theories.

Adam Smith and David Ricardo, in assuming that labour was " the original purchase money that was paid for all things," and that in the " early and rude state of society which precedes both the accumulation of stock and the appropriation of land," [2] exchange-value was known, committed the error of transferring concepts of advanced commercial societies to an age and social state in which economy was self-sufficing and exchange a rare exception.   Any Christian missionary or traveller in non-civilised lands could expose that error by relating his experience with members of tribal societies.   When a " savage " gives handfuls of gold nuggets for a necklace of glass beads, or a bag of diamonds for a cart and a span of oxen, he merely follows desire or utility, without any reference to the quantity of labour embodied in the goods exchanged.   The meaning of worth or intrinsic value is utility, or the virtue of a thing, a quality which resides in it and renders it desirable.   Aristotle regarded the utility of a thing as the foundation of value.   He held barter or exchanging things for use as proper and natural, while trading or

---

[1] See *supra*, pp. 175–177.

[2] Adam Smith, *Wealth of Nations*, book 1, ch. 5 ; Ricardo, *Principles*, ch. 1, sec. 1.

buying things for the purpose of selling them at a higher price than they cost was improper or unnatural. Aristotle thought that a trader was buying up utilities in order to extort a profit from the people who need them.[1] In regarding trade as unnatural he implicitly showed that he had no idea of exchange-value, which really means exchanging equal quantities of labour to the mutual benefit of both buyer and seller.

Shakespeare's view of value is similar to that of Aristotle. In *Troilus and Cressida* (act 2, scene 2), Hector and Troilus are discussing the meaning of it.

> *Hect.* Brother, she is not worth what she doth cost
> The holding.
> *Tro.* What is aught but as 'tis valued ?
> *Hect.* But value dwells not in particular will ;
> It holds his estimate and dignity
> As well wherein 'tis precious of itself.

John Locke also held " intrinsick value " to mean utility.[2]

The concept of exchange-value arose only with the ascendancy of the commercial classes, who had to defend and justify their property against mediaeval views. Labour, as the title to property and the foundation and measure of exchange-value, is a theory in opposition to feudal conceptions of property. Ethically, the theory of exchange-value justifies commerce against Canon Law and against Aristotle by demonstrating that trading meant an exchange of equal quantities of labour and was, therefore, equitable and just and good.

This theory, having its origin in a comparatively advanced trading and manufacturing society, where capital and labour were largely united in the same hands, means capitalist labour, *i.e.*, labour exercised by the craftsmanship and skill as well as organising, managing, and superintending capacities of the capitalist. It is an English theory, and it arose in the seventeenth century, and no English economist ever thought of propertyless labour as the foundation and measure of value. From Sir William Petty to Ricardo the great English leaders of political

---

[1] Aristotle, *Politics*, I. 8 (Jowett's translation).
[2] John Locke, *Of Civil Government*, II. 5.

economy were so clear in their minds about the meaning given here of labour-value that they neglected to emphasise it. Hence the confusion that arose when that theory was taken up either by their less discriminating followers or by the socialists. Only a careful analysis of the history of that concept will reveal its original meaning.

The author of the exchange-value theory is Sir William Petty, the son of a clothier, the observer of many arts and crafts, and a realistic intellect of the highest order. His economic reasonings do not form a separate treatise, but are interwoven with enquiries concerning public affairs. His *Treatise on Taxes* and *Political Arithmetic* contain his most original thoughts. The latter book was written in refutation of one of those periodic panics occasioned by cries and lamentations about the decay of England and the overwhelming and increasing power of foreign nations. Living in the seventeenth century, when middle-class economics, trade and commerce were growing, when the whole life of the nation was being commercialised, Petty asked himself, What was money, and what did it measure ? And he replied :—

" Our silver and gold we call by several names, and in England by pounds, shillings, and pence. But that which I would say upon this matter is that all things ought to be valued by two natural denominations, which is land and labour ; that is, we ought to say, a ship or garment is worth such a measure of land with such another measure of labour, . . . for Labour is the father and active principle of wealth as Lands are the mother."[1] But what labour ? Is it only labour in factory, mine, and field, done by propertyless hands ? Petty's reply was :—

" Suppose a man could, with his own hands, plant a certain scope of land with corn, that is, could dig, plough, harrow, weed, reap, carry home, thresh, and winnow ; and had withal seed wherewith to sow the same. I say that this man after having subtracted his seed out of the proceed of his harvest, and also what himself has both eaten and given to others in exchange for clothes and other natural necessaries, the remainder of corn is a

[1] Sir William Petty, *Economic Writings*, Hull's edition, 1899, pp. 68, 44–5.

natural and true rent of the land for that year. . . . But a further, though collateral, question may be, How much English money this corn or rent is worth ? I answer, so much as the money which another individual can save within the same time over and above his expense, if he employed himself wholly to produce and make it, viz. let another man travel into a country where is silver, there dig it, refine it, bring it to the same place where the other man planted his corn ; coin it, etc., the same person working all the while for his silver, gathering also food for his necessary livelihood and procuring himself covering, etc., I say, the silver of the one must be esteemed of equal value with the corn of the other ; the one, perhaps twenty ounces, and the other twenty bushels. From whence it follows that the price of a bushel of this corn to be an ounce of silver."[1] Trade and commerce thus consist in exchanges of equal quantities of labour. Or " if a man can bring to London an ounce of silver out of the earth in Peru in the same time that he can produce a bushel of corn, then one is the natural price of the other. Now, if by reason of new and more easy mines a man can get two ounces of silver as easily as formerly he did one, then corn will be as cheap at ten shillings as it was before at five shillings, *caeteris paribus*. . . . Natural dearness and cheapness depends upon the few or more hands requisite to the necessaries of life."[2]

It is clear that Petty, in formulating his exchange-value theory, had in mind a man with capital who works and manages his business. All this work, comprising outlay of capital, planning, managing, production of commodities, transport, and exchange, constitutes the value of a thing. Such labour is the foundation, and the quantity of such labour is the measure of value.

And now, what was the opinion of Petty with regard to wage labour employed under the management of the capitalist, at any part of the process of production, transport, and exchange ? Petty said, " It is observed by clothiers and others who employ great numbers of poor people that when corn is extremely plentiful the labour of the poor is extremely dear, and scarcely to be had at all, so licentious are they who labour only to eat or rather

[1] *Ib.*, p. 43.   [2] *Ib.*, p. 51.

to drink. Wherefore, when so many acres sown with corn
. . . shall produce perhaps double to what is expected or
necessary, it seems not unreasonable that this common blessing
of God should be applied to the common good of all people . . .
much rather than the same should be abased by the vile and
brutish part of mankind to the prejudice of the commonwealth."[1]

Wage labour was, evidently, regarded by Petty as something
inferior or a necessary evil, and by no means as a creator of value.

Exceedingly instructive, in this respect, is the view of Gregory
King. In his treatise on the various classes of society, in 1686,
he drew up a table of the national income and expenditure,[2] in
which he stated that there were at that time, in England and
Wales, 511,586 families who increased the national wealth by
2,447,000*l* annually, and 849,000 families who decreased the
national wealth by 622,000*l* annually, among the latter being
the families of wage-labourers—*i.e.*, the masses of propertyless
working men, who thus not only created nothing, but actually
decreased the national income. King was no economist, but
merely gave expression to the opinions that prevailed in the
seventeenth century. Labour, as the foundation of value, was
the labour of the capitalists or of handicraftsmen and artisans,
who worked in their own workshops and with their own tools,
and generally managed their business of buying, producing, and
selling ; and the same applies to the yeomen, farmers, and other
land-possessing peasantry.

John Locke, in speaking of labour as making things valuable,
does not discriminate between capitalist labour and wage labour,
but his whole point of view was that of the proprietors of land
and workshops, since his arguments were intended to establish
the truth of his proposition that labour was the only legitimate
title to property, for " 'tis labour which puts the greatest part
of the value upon land, without which it would scarcely be
worth anything. . . . I think it will be a very modest computa-
tion to say that of the product of the earth useful to the life of

---

[1] Sir William Petty, Economic Writings, Hull's edition, 1899,
pp. 274-5.

[2] Gregory King, *Natural and Political Observations*, 1694, p. 3.

man, nine-tenths are the effects of labour . . . in most cases, ninety-nine hundredths are wholly to be put on the account of labour," and by this creation of value labour became the real title to property. Middle-class property was, therefore, justi-fied. This was the inference which Locke drew from his labour theory. For the labouring poor he only asked parish relief. The labourer's share being but rarely more than a bare sub-sistence, he must, in times of unemployment, come to the parish. Also, when the prices of commodities rise the labourer's wages " must rise with the price of things to make him live, or else, not being able to maintain himself and family by his labour, he comes to the parish." [1]

In the eighteenth century, many popular writers, not being trained economists, failed to discriminate between capitalist and wage labour, and merely wrote of labour being the source of wealth.

Adam Smith, by his great and well deserved authority, spread the confusion, although he was fully aware of the meaning of the labour concept. In treating of wages he speaks of wage labour as the creator of that fund which supplies the nation with the necessaries and conveniences of life. " It is but equity," he says, " that they, *i.e.*, the wage labourers who feed, clothe, and lodge the whole body of the people, should have such a share of the produce of their own labour as to be themselves tolerably fed, clothed, and lodged " (*Wealth of Nations*, book 1, ch. 8, section 4). In treating of the different employment of capital, he holds, as a matter of course, that " the persons whose capitals are employed in any of those four ways *i.e.*, in procuring the raw materials, in manufacturing those raw materials, in trans-porting raw and manufactured materials, in distributing those goods, are themselves productive labourers ; their labour, when properly directed, fixes and realizes itself in the commodity upon which it is bestowed, and generally adds to its price the value at least of their own maintenance and consumption. The profits of the farmer, of the manufacturer, of the merchant and retailer, are all drawn from the price of the goods which the

[1] John Locke, *Works*, 1812, Vol. 5, pp. 57, 71, *seq.*

o

two first produce, and the two last buy and sell. . . . No equal capital puts into motion a greater quantity of productive labour than that of the farmer. Not only his labouring servants, but his labouring cattle are productive labourers. . . . The labourers and labouring cattle," etc. (*Ib.*, book 2, chap. 5). In this chapter we have a transformation of the scene and actors. As the main agents in the creation of wealth and value, appear the capitalists, while wage labourers are put on the same level as cattle. The further we proceed in our reading of Adam Smith, the clearer grows the conviction that he meant that capitalist labour constituted the source of wealth and value. In dealing with the rise of civil government, Smith unhesitatingly states his opinion that the owners of property acquired it " by the labour of many years, or, perhaps, of many successive generations," while the labouring poor are described as swayed by the passions of " hatred of labour and love of ease and enjoyment," and driven by these passions " to invade property " (*Ib.*, book 5, chap. 1, part 2). It is but necessary to collate these passages in order to perceive, at a glance, the inconsistencies and confusions in which Adam Smith was entangled.

The same remarks apply to Colquhoun. On page 109 of his *Treatise*, the manufacturers, proprietors and farmers, are accounted as productive labourers, while on page 110 he sings the song of poverty as the creator of the wealth of nations.

David Ricardo is free from these inconsistencies and confusions, but fails to think out his theories to their final consequences. He regarded labour, as directed and managed by the capitalist, as the foundation and measure of exchange-value. But which labour ? The labour of wage-earners and cattle, *i.e.*, living labour, or circulating capital, to the exclusion of fixed capital. Ricardo assumed that capital employed in manufacture, agriculture, etc., was composed of two portions—viz. fixed and circulating ; the fixed capital or machinery and raw materials do not create any new value, but only add to the produced or handled commodity as much value as they lost by their being used up, or written off, in the process of production and distribution. On the other hand, circulating capital was the real source of exchange-value, and from it flowed the new values. Not machinery, but living labour augments the values or the annual fund which supplies the nation with all it needs. This theory is, however, quite incapable of explaining the problem of the distribution of profit. Suppose two capitalists start cloth manufacturing with equal capitals. But one possesses more expensive machinery, or a higher portion of fixed capital, and, therefore, has less to spend on living labour, since his circulating capital is smaller. The other capitalist, following the theory of Ricardo, cares more for circulating capital, and makes it as large as possible. Were Ricardo right, the latter manufacturer would create a larger amount of new values and earn higher profits than the former. Experience, however, shows that equal capitals employed in the same industry, or in the whole field of industry, yield, or tend to yield, equal earnings. In the market all differences in the composition of capital, all differences between the amounts of fixed and circulating capital, disappear, while the total amount of the employed capital determines profit and price. It is no use replying that supply and demand or competition equalise price and profit, for Ricardo knew all that, and regarded it as a disturbing, but not an invalidating factor of his theory. Moreover, were Ricardo's theory in consonance with the realities of economic life, the enormous and astonishing increase of wealth, as measured by exchange-values, since the Economic Revolution, would be inexplicable. Ricardo himself admitted that the introduction of machinery displaced living labour, i.e., diminished circulating capital, and yet the national income grew by leaps and bounds. China and India employ relatively and absolutely more living labour than either Great Britain or the United States of America ; none the less the former countries are suffering from lack of capital, while the latter countries are constantly on the look-out for new markets and investments in order to place their surplus capitals. Or take the development of England since the end of the seventeenth century. According to King, England and Wales, with a population of five millions, had then a national income of about forty-three millions sterling. In 1913, England and Wales, with a population of thirty-seven millions, had a national income of about fourteen hundred millions sterling. The population and the manual labour increased sevenfold, the national income thirty-three times. What had happened in the meantime to account for this growth of wealth and value ? The advent of applied science, new discoveries, and higher organisation. It is altogether an absurd belief that an illiterate boy and female worker tending a machine should create new values, while steam, electricity, chemistry, the embodiments of genius, and the highest exertions of countless ages of collective human thought and endeavour, should be barren of economic values.

The surplus earnings over the prime cost, or the new wealth produced annually, can therefore not be the result of living labour (circulating capital) only, but of the accumulated labour (fixed capital) as well. A factory, a modern farm, a commercial establishment, embody the labour of centuries of invention, discovery, organisation, management, transport, production, and distribution. Indeed, the periods of technological inventions, scientific and geographical discoveries, and introduction of new forms of economic organisation constitute epochs in the history of wealth and value. And these are mainly the work of mental qualities of a high order. The active agent, then, in the production of wealth is mind, and as it was mainly under the system of private property that the human mind brought about those inventions, discoveries, and organisations, the new wealth which they have been yielding takes therefore the form of property and capital. And by the expenditure and new creations of capital the exchange values of the commodities are measured. Exchange-value has just as much to do with wealth as the yard or the pound has to do with the length or weight of things. It is merely a measure, and its expression, under the present system, is money. In order to preclude error it is necessary to add that just as the yard can only measure dimensions because it has itself certain dimensions, or just as the pound measures weight because it has itself gravity, so money measures value because it is itself valuable or based on valuable things, *i.e.*, on things which embody a certain quantity of capital.

We have seen the confusions into which such writers as Smith and Ricardo have fallen with regard to the concept of productive labour. Errors of great minds are generally but a degree less instructive than their truths. There is reason in such errors. Smith and Ricardo erred, because they had not seen and could not have seen the developed form of capitalist production. They were still thinking of domestic industries, farmers, small traders, and independent craftsmen, rather than of wage-labour divorced from the mental functions and tools of labour, which is the main characteristic of the factory system and large agriculture. This can be clearly perceived from the reasonings of the social critics of the time of the Economic Revolution. All of them saw in the capitalist, who was then re-organising the economic basis of society, a mere speculator and cunning money-monger, and in the labourer the real producer. It is remarkable that by " manufacturer " the writers of those times mean a " workman employed in manufacture." Manufacturer, as meaning the owner of the factory and employer of labour, is of later origin. " Trade or traffic," says Charles Hall, " consists in buying and selling articles produced by the poor, and gaining a profit by them. These articles are all the products of the hands of the labourers, manufacturers, etc., from whom they are obtained for less than their full value ; a profit otherwise could not be made. The tradesman, therefore, shares or takes part of the fruits of the labour of the poor. . . . The means enabling tradesmen to share or take a part of the product of the labour of the poor, is their capital, which puts it into their power to furnish materials to the artificers to work on, and to provide them with immediate subsistence, and on that account is supposed to give the tradesman a just claim to a part of the production of the workman's hands."[1] Substantially the same views are to be found in the whole socialist and anti-capitalist literature since 1820 onwards. Ravenstone, Gray, Hodgskin, William Thompson, and the leaders of Chartism, assumed that the capitalist as such was non-productive and was merely a lender of the means of production to the wage-labourers, from whom he extorted a usurious rate

[1] Charles Hall, *Effects of Civilisation*, edition 1850, pp. 56–7.

of interest on his capital. Moreover, they either misunderstood or corrected Ricardo by assuming that the foundation of value and source of wealth was exclusively the labour in field, factory, and mine, while the labour of transport and distribution was not productive of value. This is not the opinion of Ricardo, for he includes in the definition of labour-value all kinds of labour necessary " to manufacture (the commodities) and bring them to market." He says : " First, there is the labour necessary to cultivate the land on which the raw cotton is grown ; secondly, the labour of conveying the cotton to the country where the stockings are to be manufactured . . . ; thirdly, the labour of the spinner and weaver ; fourthly, a portion of the labour of the engineer, smith, carpenter, who erected the buildings and machinery . . . ; fifthly, the labour of the retail dealer, and of many others. . . . The aggregate sum of these various kinds of labour determines the quantity of other things for which these stockings will be exchanged " (Ricardo, *Principles*, chap. I, sec. 3).

So much as to value. Another critical conclusion was drawn by the more revolutionary socialists from the Ricardian concept of wages. " Labour, like all other things which may be purchased and sold," says Ricardo, " has its natural and its market price. The natural price of labour is that price which is necessary to enable the labourers to subsist and to perpetuate their race, without either increase or diminution. . . . With a rise in the price of food and necessaries, the natural price of labour will rise ; with the fall in their price, the natural price of labour will fall." From this statement, which is by no means complete, the conclusion was drawn that, under the capitalist system, the wages of labour could never amount to more than a minimum of means of subsistence. No matter how much the workman produced, his real wages would always tend to that minimum. Moreover, by this Ricardian law of wages, the poor must get poorer and the rich richer. If, for instance, the workman produced necessaries enough for two persons, he would get half the produce ; if, by reason of inventions and improvements, he produced enough for ten persons, he would only get one-tenth of the produce of his labour, while his employer would get nine-tenths. Thus, the more goods he could create the smaller the proportion of his reward. It really did not matter to the workman how the country was governed, what the taxes were, or what the political parties did, for the main thing that concerned him was the law of wages, which, being inherent in the capitalist mode of production, could only perish with it. All reforms that did not touch the wage problem were mere tinkering, and therefore not worth the attention of Labour.

This criticism, which bears all the marks of a mechanical conception of social life, must, however, not be laid at the door of Ricardo. He clearly points out that " notwithstanding the tendency of wages to conform to their natural rate, their market rate may, in an improving society, for an indefinite period, be constantly above it " (*Principles*, chap. 5). And even his natural price includes conveniences as well as necessaries of life. But the revolutionary socialists simply refused to believe that capitalist society could be improving, or progressive. Their outlook was statical, and they failed to perceive the dynamic forces that were operating on social life. By their exaggerations and one-sided assertions they hampered rather than promoted the recognition of the rights of Labour and the moral essence of Socialism.

The truth appears to be that most writers on subjects of moral philosophy, social and economic science, and history of nations, form their conceptions not from phenomena which are in the process of shaping themselves, but from phenomena which already belong to the past. The external world moves faster than the operations of the human mind. Objective creation precedes subjective logic. Or, as Hegel says, " the owl of Minerva emerges from its hiding after sunset." [1] To this purely objective and, perhaps, inevitable source of error must be added all those sources of error that have their origin in the passions and prejudices of man. They combine to turn the dominion of history, politics, economics, ethics, and religion into arenas of warring doctrines, contradictory hypotheses, and heated controversies.

[1] G. W. F. Hegel, *Philosophie des Rechts* (Preface).

VII

THE CO-OPERATIVE SOCIALISTS

I.—GEORGE MUDIE AND THE "ECONOMIST"

ROBERT OWEN's failure to win the confidence and the ear of the London artisans was retrieved by George Mudie, a Scotch journalist and printer, who came to London about 1820. There are but few biographical data of this Owenite pioneer. He studied at Edinburgh, where he made himself obnoxious by his opposition to established ideas, and apparently did not finish his studies. He gradually drifted into journalism, and in 1818 or 1819 was employed at a newspaper in Glasgow. At that time he was already acquainted with Owen's teachings and ideals. By the end of 1820 he was reporter to the *Morning Chronicle*, then the great Liberal daily of the metropolis. It appears from notes left by Francis Place that Mudie owed his position to a recommendation of James Mill, who was an intimate friend of Mr. Black, the editor-in-chief of that paper. Place speaks disparagingly of Mudie, from which it may be inferred that the latter was from the beginning an Owenite agitator among the working men. From January, 1821, to January, 1822, he edited *The Economist*, a weekly paper devoted to the propaganda of Owenism and co-operation. It describes itself as " A periodical paper, explanatory of the New System of Society projected by Robert Owen, and of a plan of association for improving the conditions of the working classes during their continuance of their present employment." Its leading principles were : (1) That poverty was not necessarily the lot of civilised societies, but afflicted them merely from their ignorance of true principles and the influence of other principles based on error ; (2) that while the erroneous principles prevailed, poverty must necessarily increase, and the bulk of human misery grow ; (3) that the knowledge and practice of true principles would assuredly banish poverty, and place mankind above the fear and danger of want; (4) that the power of producing superabundance of all the goods of life was so great, even in this thickly populated country, that England was capable of sustaining several times the number of the present population in security and comfort; (5) that the application of the true principle would also disseminate knowledge as certainly as it would diffuse plenty for all; (6) that knowledge and plenty would build up the physical and intellectual strength of the nation, would in a great measure subdue vice, destroy misery, promote virtue, and lead to happiness—the aim and end of all human effort.

Looking at the productive capacities of nature and man, there was no reason why misery should exist. Even in a very early stage of society each individual had been capable of producing more than several individuals could consume. The first progressive steps in the cultivation of the soil and the making of implements had already raised production, and taught man how to protect himself against poverty. And this was all the more so in the present stage of society in England, where science and mechanism were creating all the facilities for the production of wealth; one Englishman was now capable of producing more than twenty individuals could consume. None the less, misery and distress were rife in the land, for the productive powers had been misapplied and distribution vitiated.

Some people ascribed this condition to the spread of machinery. It was, however, clear that the natural or the theoretical tendency of mechanical inventions and the progress of science was not to increase the number of the poor, but to increase the number of the rich, and every addition made to the number of the rich must be taken from the ranks of the poor. The natural tendency of mechanical inventions was not to render the poor poorer, but to enrich them and render all mankind rich, by furnishing all with an abundance of goods. The realities appear to belie that theoretical tendency, and to justify the assertion of those who saw in mechanism an enemy of the labouring classes.

Which was the truth? The truth was that society was based

on erroneous principles, the effects of which were counteracting the natural tendencies, and did not allow them to assert themselves. The fatal error was that " the interest of each individual has been placed, in almost every circumstance and situation, in direct opposition to the interest of other individuals, and to the interest of society." In consequence of this error the productive powers of society were never brought into full and healthful operation, but on the contrary, production, particularly of really useful and necessary articles, was ever kept within the bounds of demand. The possessors of the means of production always had in view, not the interests of society, not the needs of all, but only of those who could pay remunerative prices. Consumption governs production ; not a single wheel was set in motion unless it promised to promote the interests of capital. And as, in present circumstances, the circle of consumption was narrow, the productive forces could not expand to their full capacity. The result was poverty. Quite apart from the wretched condition of the labouring classes, it must be asserted that even the possessing classes were not nearly as rich as the facilities for the production of riches would warrant. The opposition of interests, the waste that competition brings in its train, were paralysing production, and impeding the progress of knowledge.

The civilised nations did not, in reality, form societies, but aggregates of warring individuals. Everybody cared only for himself ; there existed no bond of union ; the nations were kept together by force and compulsion, press laws, militarism, prisons, and gallows. The constitutions and institutions rested on anti-social principles. The imperfections of government or the misconduct of rulers were not the causes of the multifarious evils from which mankind was suffering, but the consequences of the anti-social principles on which society was based. As long as they prevailed there was no remedy for poverty. No addition to our productive powers and no reduction of the population could avert the calamities that threatened us. If Providence were to bless our plains with double fertility, if foreign nations were to pour a superabundance upon us, they would but accelerate the arrival of our greatest woe. For they would cause unemployment, and, consequently, a shrinkage in the consumption of the masses and a narrowing of the circle of production.

Having recognised the source of evil, it was easy to discover the remedy. It consisted in basing society on a harmony of interests or on co-operation, instead of antagonism and competition. The working classes being the greatest sufferers from that system must follow the advice of Robert Owen and form villages of unity and co-operation. But how could that be accomplished without the aid of capital? Was not capital the source and power of production? The belief in the creative powers of capital had been spread by the political economists, but, in reality, capital was neither the true source nor the true power of production. The source of production was the land, and the real power of production beyond the spontaneous gifts of nature was the labour of man, rendered infinitely more productive when combined. Capital, far from being the source or power of production, was the product of labour, or rather of human co-operation. Capital did not precede, but follow, production. Labour might go on without capital, but the latter had no power of multiplying itself without labour.

These views, developed in the first numbers of *The Economist*, Mudie had spread, in 1820, among the London journeymen printers and he succeeded in persuading the most enterprising of them to make an experiment. This happened towards the end of 1820, and it seems that it was this success that encouraged Mudie to issue *The Economist*.

2.—THE CO-OPERATIVE AND ECONOMICAL SOCIETY

The London printers, influenced by Mudie, appointed a committee to investigate a co-operative scheme by which they would be able to continue their usual employment, and save enough money for the purpose of establishing a co-operative society of production. The first stage of the experiment was to be an association of co-operative householding. By clubbing together their household expenses they would be able to buy larger quantities of the means of subsistence for the same money, and enable their wives to perform their domestic duties more skilfully and in less time than now. The householding community would have its own school for the children, its library, its infirmary and medical practitioners, and thus promote co-operative habits and harmonious action. Detailed estimates of the cost of living of 250 families on private and co-operative lines showed that by co-operation they would save nearly £8,000 per annum and thus establish a fund for co-operative production and become their own employers.

Much more interesting than this plan is the Report which the committee issued. The editor of *The Economist* thought it " the most important document that has ever proceeded from a body of workmen." They argued that " if foreign nations will not take our manufactures in exchange for agricultural produce, we trust that agricultural customers will spring up at home, and that we shall ere long find means to divide among ourselves, by a fair exchange of produce, all the goods and provisions that our domestic industry and ingenuity can create, and indeed so to open, renovate, and enlarge the home market as to render it much more valuable to all the interests of the State, to the labourer, the farmer, the manufacturer, the merchant, and the landowner. The country abounds with means and materials of wealth, and possesses unemployed productive powers (in manual and mechanical energy) of vast extent, and capable of almost unlimited increase. By what fatal error, then, is it that in this land of abundance there is so much wretchedness and want ? . . . By what hitherto unaccountable fatality has it been that this country has been kept dependent on foreign nations for a large portion of its food, though its own soil required only increased culture in order to furnish a redundancy, that the agriculturists complain of inadequate remuneration for their industry and capital, while they are surrounded by so many hundreds of thousands of half-starving consumers ? " Similar questions are directed to the manufacturers and scholars. The working men only desired the opportunity of exchanging their articles for those they were in need of. " Let us but be placed together in contiguous dwellings, and with the command of a small portion of the land, for which we will pay the usual rental, and we shall soon show our legislators what we are capable of doing for ourselves, for our children, and for all." Poverty could only be banished by combined labour and expenditure and by education. Such associations would injure nobody, and, if once in full action, would be stable. As to the objection that the success of co-operation might lead to an excessive increase of population, and, consequently, to a recurrence of poverty, the committee replied that if a taste for comfort could be diffused over the whole community, it would constitute a much more effective check upon excessive population than the misery which resulted from blind improvidence could do. They summed up their social ideal with a verse from Robert Southey :—

" Train up thy children, England,
    In the ways of righteousness and feed them
        With the bread of wholesome doctrine.
    Where hast thou thy mines—but in their industry ?
    Thy bulwarks where—but in their breasts ?   Thy might
        But in their arms ? . . ."[1]

These lines of Southey enjoyed great popularity in co-operative circles, but, of course, they put on them their own construction. Training of children they meant in the sense of Owen, and " wholesome doctrine " was that of the " New View of Society."

The London printers established the Economical and Co-operative Society and drafted the following Constitution :—

" The ultimate object of this society is to establish a village of Unity and Mutual Co-operation, combining agriculture, manufacture, and trade upon the plan projected by Mr. Owen, of New Lanark. The immediate object of the Society is to form a fund for the purchase of food, clothing, and other necessaries at wholesale prices ; and (where the members reside near each other) to form arrangements for co-operating in the care of their dwellings, the superintendence, training, and education of their children. The Society also proposes, as early as possible, to provide productive employments for such of its members as may

[1] *The Economist* (1821), No. 3.

be without work and to make provision for the members and their families in sickness and old age.

" The fundamental principle is, in proportion as every member shall endeavour to promote the good of the whole Society, will be the amount of respect and happiness enjoyed by each individual.

" Religious and political opinion are a private matter." [1]

Towards the end of 1821 the Society was in full action, but the majority of its members were " men of fortune and individuals of liberal professions."[2] The last number of *The Economist* (end of January, 1822) was printed by that Society. However, the co-operative experiment proved a failure. Robert Southey, who had followed it with close and sympathetic attention, explained the course of the failure. " The founders proposed to raise £12,000 in shares of £100 each. . . . The capital was not forthcoming. The experiment was commenced with insufficient means, and under circumstances every way inconvenient. Of necessity, therefore, it failed." [3]

3.—ABRAM COMBE'S PARABLE OF THE CISTERN.

The first British Socialist who formed an Owenite community was the Scotsman Abram Combe (1785–1827). He was less original and less comprehensive than Robert Owen, but equal to him in devotion, singleness of purpose, love of humanity, and organising capacity. He possessed, moreover, one great quality which his master lacked—a sense of humour. If the great majority of mankind consisted of men like A. Combe, integral socialism would either be possible or superfluous. In 1820 he visited New Lanark and came at once under the spell of Owen. He was then a well-to-do and prosperous leather manufacturer, and gradually decided to sink his money in an Owenite experiment. How intense his studies of Owenism were may be seen from his *Metaphorical Sketches of the Old and the New System*

[1] *The Economist* (1821), No. 1.
[2] *Ib.*, No. 46.
[3] Robert Southey, *Sir Thomas More, or Colloquies*, 1829, I., pp. 134–9.

(1823), in which he attempted to illustrate, by flashes of genuine humour and good-natured satire, the difference between capitalism, as he saw it, and the ideal of communism. The essence of his views is contained in the following parable or " metaphorical sketch," which applies particularly to the British people of the period of the Economic Revolution.

 The wealth of this great people was contained in the Cistern of their national resources. This Cistern was supplied from three streams—agriculture, mining, rivers, and seas. These streams were purified and made fit for consumption at special stations by human labour, before they reached the Cistern; and when they were all put together they contained all that was necessary and desirable for the supply of human wants, and it was called Wealth. At the stopcock of the Cistern stood a guardian by the name of Competition, whose duty it was to see that each individual should only draw out in proportion to what he put in, lest the Cistern should become empty, to the injury of the whole people ; it was also his duty to see that, if any particular stream was deficient, encouragement should be given to those who supply it.

Those who conducted the streams received a metal order on the Cistern, which they might draw or retain at pleasure. The labourers who attended the streams received an order for about an eighth part of what they put in ; with this remuneration they were quite satisfied. The other parts went to the proprietors of the streams, to those who directed the labourers, to the merchants who exchanged the produce of the native streams for that of of foreign streams, and to those who managed the affairs of the nation. Owing to the difficulty of furnishing the supplies there was no lack of employment for the labourers, since the demand was equal or even greater than the supply. Things went on in this manner for a long time, till the progress of knowledge pointed out a way by which one stream could be made to flow into the cistern with a tenth part of the labour formerly required ; or, in other words, a discovery was made, by means of which each labourer could furnish ten times the quantity that he did formerly. The individuals whose business it was to furnish the supplies through this stream were compensated by orders on the Cistern, in some degree corresponding to the quantity they sent in. The high remuneration they received stimulated their minds to greater exertions. Those who furnished the supplies from the other streams were also put on the alert by the success of their neighbours.

The streams were augmented from all sides, and the Cistern would have been over full had not this wise people employed force to settle a dispute with a neighbouring nation, and made for this purpose large demands on the Cistern. The wise men of the people drained extraordinary quantities of wealth from the Cistern, but they were unable to see how it had come about that the streams flowed so abundantly. The supplies came into the Cistern so fast, and the demands upon it were so great that metal orders could not be found in sufficient quantity to let the supplies out, and without producing such an order it was believed the stopcock would not open. Moreover, ignorant as most of the people were, they firmly believed that the metal orders were the sources of wealth, and they looked upon the contents of the Cistern as of comparatively little importance. But when these orders were exhausted, a crisis broke out. The wise men of the nation fancied ruin to be inevitable, and, necessity being the mother of invention, they introduced paper orders. To their great astonishment they found that a piece of paper let out the supplies just as well as the piece of metal had done.

For upwards of twenty years did these wise men carry on a destructive war at enormous cost. What industry and ingenuity created, waste and extravagance destroyed; the one pouring supplies into the national Cistern, the other drawing them off at a great rate. But industry and ingenuity obtained so much aid from art and science that the Cistern was kept brimful. Finally, the war came to an end; waste and extravagance ceased; the paper orders were withdrawn, and metal ones again resorted to. The sudden shrinkage of the demands on the Cistern, consequent upon the conclusion of the war and the reintroduction of the metal orders, nearly proved fatal to those who attended the streams. As the Cistern was overflowing and the streams were gorged, guardian Competition dismissed the labourers, who, being deprived of metal orders, could not open the stopcock and draw what they wanted. The labourers then applied to him again, saying that it would not in the least hurt him if he allowed them to pour their stream into the Cistern so that they might be able to draw instantly from there what they wanted, for by doing so the cistern would, in the end, not be fuller than it was at that moment. In this way they could go on working their stream and satisfy their needs, while injuring nobody. Competition, hearing this argument, got into a passion and asked them if they were such fools as to suppose that they would be able to draw from the cistern without metal orders? And as to giving them any of these, it was what he could not and would not do ; for, he declared, he had already more wealth on his hands than he knew what to do with. So he turned them away, showing no mercy to the poor producers who were starving. Disaffection grew apace, and the country was in a turmoil.

A crisis overtook the nation, and its wise men were at a loss to account for it. Mr. Commonsense, seeing all parties at a standstill, gave the people a hint that a remedy for the distress, occasioned by an excess of supply of all they wanted, might easily be found. He said, " The Cistern contains all that your minds desire, why then do you hesitate to give orders to the producers corresponding to the quantity they send in ? You are in distress because waste and extravagance have ceased to dissipate the contents of your Cistern ; but why not divide the surplus among those who supply the whole, since no one need feel want while the Cistern can be so easily kept up ? You say, guardian Competition would not allow it. Well, why not dismiss him ? You say, further, there were not sufficient metal orders to go round,—why not use paper orders which for over twenty years had served the purpose well and kept the circulation between the streams, the Cistern, and the people in some order ! "

However, the people, not having been accustomed to listen to Commonsense, did not understand what he meant. They rather believed those who told them that Commonsense was a visionary and Utopian who imagined impracticable things.

P

They advised the people to listen to the teachings of the political economists. The latter, being called upon to come forward and explain to the people the cause and remedy of the distress, said that the sources of production were woefully scanty, and what they had been yielding was destroyed by the long and ruinous war ; and even the wealth which would be produced in the next future was, by anticipation, wasted, since the national debt had grown to enormous proportions. There was, then, no other remedy for the producers but strict sexual restraint and emigration. And those who remained in the country should strain every nerve to reform the Government in order to render it impossible for them to fall again into extravagance.

Mr. Commonsense, hearing this interpretation of the crisis, could no longer contain himself, and put the question to the political economists, " Why not give the producers orders on the Cistern equal to what they put in, instead of an eighth part only ? " Whereupon the political economists cut him short by saying, they did not wish to " enter into a controversy on such a subject." [1]

This was Combe's interpretation of the effects of the Economic Revolution, the Napoleonic Wars, the Bank Restriction, and the crisis which overtook the nation in the years 1816-20. As soon as he had grasped the doctrines of his master he began to think of co-operative experiments, and he found a fellow-labourer in Archibald James Hamilton (1793-1834), an ex-officer, who had served under the Duke of Wellington in the Peninsular War and at Waterloo. Hamilton was the son of General John Hamilton, of Dalzell and Orbiston. He met Robert Owen at dinner in Dalzell House, discussed with him the new views of society and, finally, adopted socialism. He fully identified himself with the aspirations of the labouring classes and attempted to educate them in the theory and practice of co-operation. In 1821 he made the acquaintance of Abram Combe, and both decided to establish a co-operative store at Edinburgh. They formed a society which from the beginning enjoyed much popularity It grew in numbers and prosperity, about five

[1] Abram Combe, *Metaphorical Sketches*, 1823, pp. 40-51, 184.

hundred families joined it, but within a year it collapsed owing to the dishonesty of a storekeeper. Undismayed by this failure, Combe immediately thereafter formed a community in his tanyard. He encouraged his workmen to live in common and to share in the profits of the factory. This experiment also failed; dissensions among the working men rendered community life impossible. In 1825 Combe made the largest and last socialist experiment of his life: He bought Orbiston (near Motherwell), which belonged to the Hamiltons of Dalzell, and formed a community. Warned by his previous failures he proceeded warily and arranged for a gradual transition from private property to communism. This displeased the communists and they began to look at Combe with suspicion. Also the London Co-operative Society, the theorists of nascent Socialism, became impatient with the slow progress of Orbiston ; only John Gray, of whom more presently, warned against the adoption of complete communism, but his voice was unheeded. While all these murmurings and complaints of the onlookers and beneficiaries went on, Combe quietly devoted all his time and energies and sacrificed, to the irreparable injury of his own family, all he possessed—a sum of over £20,000 —to the building up of the first British communist establishment. Enmity from opponents, who gave to Orbiston the name of Babylon, zealous criticism from friends, and the labour and anxiety which the scheme entailed, impaired the health of this truly noble socialist pioneer, and after an illness, which lasted exactly twelve months, he passed away in August, 1827. Combe died a ruined man, leaving his family destitute. Orbiston then went from bad to worse. Deprived of its master-mind and guiding and helping hand, it was doomed to rapid extinction. At the end of 1827 it was bankrupt.[1]

4.—JOHN GRAY

The idea underlying Combe's Parable of the Cistern forms the subject of the elaborate economic treatises of John Gray (1799–

[1] Register for Orbiston, 1825-7 ; John Gray, *Social System* 1851, Appendix ; Alex. Cullen, *Adventures in Socialism*, 1910.

1850 ?). He was of Scottish origin, but spent his boyhood in Derbyshire, his school days at Repton, and his youth in London. He left Repton at the age of fourteen years, when he was sent as an apprentice to a wholesale merchant in Cheapside. Being a thoughtful youth, he observed the doings in the metropolis in the agitated years, 1816 to 1820 ; he was probably a careful reader of the newspapers of the day, followed the discussions on the crisis, on currency, on over-production, and " came to the conclusion that the commercial system was at variance with the whole system of nature, and that God could never have intended His creatures to be mere stumbling-blocks to each other," as he saw them at every step he trod. The final result of his observations and meditations was as follows : " I saw clearly that goods of every description are made either because they are ordered or because there is every prospect of their being so ; and continual reflection satisfied me that this state of things ought to be reversed—that production, instead of being the effect of demand, ought to be the cause of it."[1] The main conclusion of Gray is, as we see, the same as Mudie's.

After an abortive attempt to put his ideas in a readable form on paper he read Owen, and in 1825 published the first instalment of his system, under the title, *Lecture on Human Happiness*, which was intended to be the first of a series of lectures dealing with the evils of the existing order of society, and the development of means by which they might be permanently removed. This pamphlet, though Owenite in spirit, betrays also influences of other socialist, social reform, and economic writers. Its author knew Ricardo, Colquhoun, and probably also Attwood. The leading ideas are : Society is a natural phenomenon, since nature has implanted in man the desire to associate himself with his fellow-man ; it has likewise implanted in man the desire for happiness. If this is so, how comes it that society is afflicted with so many evils, so much misery and wretchedness ? The answer is, the principle on which the association of man with man is founded has been misapplied. The principle which satisfies the natural desire of man to live in society is barter.

[1] John Gray, *Social System*, 1851, p. 340.

"Barter, and barter alone, is the basis of society, all other institutions are built wholly and solely upon it." The right application of this principle is giving and taking equal quantities of labour. Were this fundamental principle acted upon, society would have attained to happiness. But it is not acted upon. Under the existing conditions the labourers are robbed of four-fifths of their produce, which are distributed among the non-producers who give no equivalent to society. The whole principle of exchange is falsified, the basis of society vitiated.

And here we come to the main critical consideration of Gray, which exercised considerable influence on the subsequent socialist agitation. The Ricardian concept of labour as the foundation and measure of value was taken by Gray to mean exclusively wage-labour in field, factory, and mine. Only these labourers produced the wealth of the nation. All the other members of society were either useful, if they rendered services, or useless, if they rendered no services. Employers, merchants, traders, physicians, artists, scientists, were non-productive, though some of them useful, while the remainder were both non-productive and useless. But the useful as well as the useless lived on the wealth produced by wage-labour in field, factory, and mine. Gray took Colquhoun's table of production and distribution, and re-classifying it under the heads of Producers and Non-Producers, he arrived at the following conclusion: In 1812, the population of the United Kingdom numbered 17,096,803 persons, and the new wealth produced amounted to £430,521,372. This wealth was produced by 7,897,531 labouring persons, who on the principle of equal exchanges ought to have received £54 each, but had actually received £11 only, or one-fifth of the produce of their labour. Or, in other words, about eight million producers received £90,500,000, and nine million non-producers received £340,000,000. "The rich man, who, in point of fact, pays nothing, receives everything, while the poor man, who, in point of fact, pays everything, receives nothing. We put it to the candour of every honest man whether such a state of society as this ought to be preserved! Whether it is not at variance with every principle of honesty!" (*Lecture*, pp. 15–20).

Gray leaves no doubt whatsoever as to his meaning.   He believes he has shown " that from human labour every description of wealth proceeds ; the productive classes do now support, not only themselves, but every unproductive member of society. Only these are productive members of society who apply their own hands either to the cultivation of the earth itself, or preparing its materials for the uses of life ; that every individual not so employed is a direct tax upon those who are so employed ; that the whole merchant class are either directors of production or distribution of wealth who are paid by those who create it ; only a sufficient number of all such persons are useful.   We have shown that the wealth annually produced is taken from its producers, chiefly in form of rent, interest, and profit.   Profit being obtained by buying labour cheap and selling it dear " (*Lecture*, p. 69).

The non-producers and useless will, of course, reply that they live upon their property.   But Gray rejoins : " This we positively deny, and, on the contrary, affirm that they live upon the property of others."   The foundation of all property is labour or accumulated labour.   Property not acquired by labour is injustice.   The landed proprietor has no right to the land, for the earth is the habitation and natural inheritance of all mankind. And the capitalist, who lives on the interest of money, lives likewise on injustice.   " By what principle can a man lend £10 and receive £12 for them ? " (*Ib.*, pp. 34–5).   All just exchanges can only be based on equal quantities of labour, while between the possessing and labouring classes no just exchanges can take place.   From these unjust relations spring the irrational luxurious and unnatural living of the rich, and the misery and wretchedness of the poor.   " And yet people think Owen a visionary whose plan is to abol'sh the circumstances which now limit production, and to give the producers the wealth they produce.   It has nothing to do with turning men into angels, but it is simply the employment of mankind upon the principle of co-operation " (*Ib.*, p. 56).

The evils which flow from the misapplication of the principle of exchange are aggravated by competition.   It is competition which puts an unnatural limit upon production. In order to show the restraining influence of competition on the production of wealth, let us assume that society determines to call into action the whole industry of the country, and put all the marvellous mechanical inventions and contrivances at its disposal. Under these circumstances the production of wealth would only be limited either by the amount of productive powers extant or by the full satisfaction of the wants of everybody ; and as the productive forces and the wants of society are great, the volume of wealth will be large. The limits thus imposed upon production would be natural. Under the present system neither the power to produce nor the capacity to consume limits wealth. It is competition that does it. At present, production is limited by effective or profitable demand. This demand depends on the amount of wealth which all the classes of society have for purposes of consumption. And the distribution of this amount of wealth among the various classes is regulated by competition. It is competition that fixes the quantity of wealth obtained, in the form of wages, by the productive classes ; the competition among the workmen for an opportunity to labour presses down the rate of wages. The competition among manufacturers and other employers lowers the rate of profit. The same applies to rent. Thus the consumable income of every individual and consequently of the whole country, except those who have fixed incomes, is lowered.. And this national income forming the effective demand, this demand is lowered ; and limited demand means limited production, for, in the present state of society, not a single commodity is produced unless it promises a profit. No matter, therefore, how great the wants of the people are, no matter how enormous the facilities for wealth production are, nothing will be done to remedy these defects, so long as labour is brought into competition with labour, capital with capital, instead of being brought to act in conjunction with each other.

Gray concludes : " In a further Lecture we shall endeavour to explain another set of arrangements on the basis of a national capital, by the introduction of which the only limits to our wealth would be the exhaustion of our productive powers, and the satisfaction of our wants. The plans to which we allude are altogether different from those proposed by Mr. Owen, and we willingly admit that they are altogether inferior to them ; but we entertain a hope that they will be useful in proving to the world that unity of interest is in every way consistent with individuality and distinctions of property, and at a period like the present, when, we hesitate not to say, society is on the eve of relinquishing for ever the commercial principles on which it has hitherto acted, we think that too many modifications of the same fundamental principle cannot be laid before the public, from out of which something advantageous may perhaps be selected."

No further Lecture appeared. Gray invested some money in Combe's Orbiston venture and, of course, lost it, though it must be said that he warned his friends against the adoption of complete communism. Gray removed to Edinburgh, where, in company with his brother, he published a newspaper, at the same time meditating upon his reform plan. In 1831, he published his *Social System*, which shows him to have been, in his way, a lucid thinker and vigorous writer. He abandoned socialism as far as production was concerned, and based his system solely on a plan of equitable exchange. Also his opposition to the existing order of things lost much of its acerbity, and his book is quite free from the bitter invective and moral ardour which characterise his *Lecture*. The exposition of his reform plan is summarised as follows :—

As it is by labour that all things valuable to mankind are produced, so it is by exchange that individuals are enabled to get a variety of things which their own labour could never have commanded without it. Without exchange man could have never emerged from a state of rudest ignorance and barbarism. The present application of the principle of exchange is faulty. It forms the hiding-place of that giant mischief which bestrides the civilised world, rewarding industry with starvation, exertion with disappointment, and the best efforts of the rulers to do good with perplexity and failure. It is this system of exchange which has produced a confusion of ideas on social matters, which find expression in the various demands for parliamentary reform, universal suffrage, annual parliaments, vote by ballot, free trade, repudiation of the national debt, reduction of taxation, repeal of the union, etc., etc. Even if all these demands are granted, nothing will be altered for the better as long as the present form of exchange is left unreformed.

The medium of exchange is money ; its use is the same as that of scales, weights, and measures ; it is to measure and apportion exchanges, to facilitate the giving and obtaining of equivalents. Money, therefore, ought to be as cheap, as accessible and easily attainable by those who have anything to exchange, as a pair of scales or a pound weight, or a yard. If this proposition is true, gold is totally unfit for this purpose : it does not fulfil these conditions ; moreover, it is itself subject to fluctuations of value. It is no exaggeration to say that ninety-nine out of every hundred marketable articles are easier of production and attainment than gold. For this reason money, when based on gold, renders exchange difficult, and thus checks demand, which, in its turn, checks production. Bank notes are exposed to the same objections as gold, for they are uniformly issued upon securities, which, in the aggregate, contain more value than the money advanced upon them. Therefore the nation suffers constantly from a deficiency of money ; the medium of exchange falls always short of the amount of goods waiting for exchange, though the object of money is to enable any man, at any time, to exchange any article of any value for an equal value of any commodity he desires to have in its stead.

Which kind of money would answer this purpose ? Money should be merely a receipt, an evidence that its bearer has contributed a certain value to the national stock of wealth. The use of the receipt should be to enable the bearer to re-obtain the value that was given for it, whenever he pleases, and in whatever shape he may require. But money should not be intrinsically valuable. For the purpose of carrying out such a reform a National Bank should be established, possessing the sole power of manufacturing paper money, and of issuing it to the accredited agents.   Another, and the only other, business of the Bank should consist in keeping the national books, and separate accounts with all the agents.   All goods should be transmitted from their respective manufactories and workshops to the national warehouses, where their direct cost or price of material and labour expended is to be ascertained, and a certain percentage or profit, fixed by the Chamber of Commerce, added, to pay the various expenses of rent, interest, depreciation of stock, incidents, and taxes.   This would form the retail price of goods.   All the warehouses to be under the supervision of agents who give receipts of the goods delivered with the money received for this purpose from the Bank.   Thus the amount of money would always be in exact proportion to the goods.   The producers would get the exact amount of money value for their goods, and be able to get in exchange from the warehouses any goods they may need.

The accomplishment of this reform will render exchange smooth and equitable.   It will then be as easy to sell as to buy. Under this system, the more one will produce the more will he get.   The national warehouses will, in the aggregate, form one large reservoir, into which a constant stream of wealth, arising in different places and partaking of different qualities, will drain ; and from that reservoir every producer will draw according to the labour values he sends in.[1]

Gray evidently presupposed a simple society of small producers, and he never attempted to show that his plan could apply also to a complicated society, with large manufacturing, commercial, and agricultural establishments, working not only for the national but international markets.

5.—WILLIAM THOMPSON

The ethical philosophy of Jeremy Bentham, the labour economics of David Ricardo, and the social views of Robert Owen, were united into a system of socialism by William Thompson (d. 1833).   As a prosperous landed proprietor of Cork, with an

---

[1] John Gray, *Social System*, 1831, particularly chap. 5 ; *An Efficient Remedy*, 1842 ; *Lectures on Money*, 1848.

inquiring intellect and philanthropic disposition, he at first turned to the Utilitarian school for enlightenment. He adored Bentham as the Francis Bacon of moral philosophy, and adopted his doctrines and, unfortunately, also his style. His faith in these doctrines was, for a time, strong enough to make him regard Owenism merely as " an improved pauper management," totally unsuitable for society as a whole. This was about the year 1818. Gradually, however, he came to a different conclusion. " Patient study of the subject of distribution led me to mutual co-operation."[1] The year 1822 marked the turning-point of his life, and he sat down to think out how and why he left Bentham for Owen. His excogitations he published, in 1824, in a large volume under the title, *Inquiry into the Principles of the Distribution of Wealth most conducive to Human Happiness*. Its diffuse style and its reiterations—the effects of the author's painful efforts to satisfy his scientific conscience, make the book tedious reading. Still, it is instructive to watch how a Utilitarian becomes a Socialist.

Thompson starts with the concept of Utility, or the pursuit of the greatest possible sum of human happiness. This is the aim of man and the test of the institutions of society. This aim cannot be attained without the physical means of enjoyment or objects of wealth. An abundant production and a just distribution of commodities are therefore the indispensable conditions of happiness. To make the production of wealth abundant, security is necessary, for nobody will undergo the toilsome labour of producing an abundance of goods unless he is sure that he will enjoy them. But abundance of wealth is, by itself, not sufficient to bring about the greatest sum of happiness. For, the British nation is rich in all materials of wealth, in machinery, inventions, intelligence, and industry, and is none the less not happy ; moreover, poverty and misery are really the lot of the majority of the producers. The truth is that to abundant production must be joined a just or equal distribution, *i.e.*, the abundance of wealth must be distributed over the whole population so as to allow every member of the community to satisfy

[1] William Thompson, *Labour Rewarded*, 1827, pp. 98–9.

its needs, instead of leaving the wealth in the hands of the few. By a just distribution only can the total sum of happiness be greatest, for the whole is greater than a part.

But, are security and equality consistent with each other ? Will equality of distribution not defeat all efforts to make production abundant ? If the industrious and skilful will only receive as much of the wealth as the less industrious, less skilful, or idle and unskilled—or, in other words, if they are deprived of the security of enjoying the fruits of their exertions, they will cease to produce in abundance, and thus render happiness altogether impossible of attainment.

It is the old problem which occupied Bentham and still occupies all those who discuss socialism.   It really amounts to the question whether, under socialism, people will work as hard as they do under the system of private property.   Bentham, as it is known, replies that security is more important than equality, and wherever they cannot be reconciled with each other equality must be abandoned ; the proper policy is to base society on the foundation of private property, and by gradual reform to approach equality.

At this point Thompson turns away from Bentham, and joins the orbit of Owen.   He takes from the Utilitarian school utility, or the test of happiness and the anti-governmental creed.   All Radicalism was in theory completely libertarian ; all government was compulsion and force ; but in practice their libertarian view really meant opposition to a Tory government.   On the other hand, the co-operative socialists completely adhered to the creed of anti-government.   The difference in the respective attitudes to the State or Government has an important bearing on the respective views concerning distribution.   Bentham, in adhering to security or private property, needs government laws to regulate distribution in order to secure to the owner of the means of production his rent, interest, and profit.   Thompson, in adhering to equality, rejects government laws and looks for those natural laws that govern distribution.   His whole *Inquiry* is devoted to a quest after those natural laws.   However, at the bottom of this difference of attitude lies the question as to the identity

of the producer and the creator of value. Bentham, like Ricardo
and James Mill, regards the capitalist as the real creative power
of production and value, and therefore desires to see the capitalist
well remunerated for his all-important function in keeping society
going. Thompson, on the contrary, regards the labourer and
craftsman as the real producer. He, therefore, argues that
the system of private property does not give security to the
producer, since at least half of the produce of his labour is taken
away from him in the shape of rent and profit. And it is precisely
this lack of security that does not allow the productive forces
to be exerted to their utmost capacity, and produce an abundance
of wealth—hence the poverty of the nation. It is the unjust
and unnatural distribution which checks production ; moreover,
the little that is produced is being monopolised by the few.
Excessive wealth and luxury on the one pole of society, abject
misery and privation on the other, with the result of almost
general unhappiness. The present society, brought to the test
of Utility, is found wanting.

The gist of the economic criticism applied to the existing mode
of distribution is to be found in chapter 1, section 14, of his
Inquiry. Thompson argues that the entire use of the products
of labour is the strongest stimulus to universal and continual
production. But under the present conditions the labourer
must offer some part of his produce to those who possess the
means of production, and who put them at his disposal. The
proportion of his labour demanded by the capitalist for the use
of the means of production he lends him is, however, so great
that the real operative producer is deprived of most of his reward.
The idle possessor of those inanimate instruments of production
not only secures to himself as much of enjoyment as the most
diligent and skilful of the real efficient producers, but in proportion to the amount of his accumulations he procures ten times,
a hundred times, a thousand times, as much of the articles of
wealth, the products of labour, and means of enjoyment, as
the utmost labour of such efficient producers can procure for
them." This is done by means of rent and profit. Is this situation of the productive labourer irremediable ? Are there no

limits to these enormous taxes on industry, and to these exactions
by capitalists ?

There are two points of view from which this most important
matter may be considered. First, do these deductions from the
produce of the labourer's exertions tend to increase production
or the enjoyments derived from production ? Secondly, can
they, without preponderant evil, without the employment of
force, be avoided ? In answer to the first question, it is evident
that every abstraction from the produce of the labourer's exertions, whether by open force or by compulsion of want, must
proportionately diminish his motive to production ; they lessen
security and therefore the stimulus to efficient work. Not the
cheerful desire of increasing happiness, but the fear of want
becomes the stimulus to labour, when the use of its products is
withdrawn from the labourer. Still, these abstractions continue,
and they amount at least to one-half of the produce of labour.
They are called profit. But the source of profit is " the value
added to the raw material by the labour, guided by skill, expended on it. The materials, the buildings, the machinery,
the wages, can add nothing to their own value. The additional
value proceeds from labour alone." But, it will be said, without
the capital in the shape of machinery, materials, etc., mere
labour will be unproductive ; and therefore it is but just that the
labourer should pay for the use of that, without which his mere
productive powers would be ineffective. Doubtless, the labourer
must pay for the use of these, when he is so unfortunate as not
himself to possess them ; the question is how much of the products of labour ought to be deducted for their use ?

Two measures of value of this use present themselves : the
measure of the labourer and the measure of the capitalist. The
measure of the labourer consists in the contribution of such
sums as would replace the waste of the capital consumed in the
production, with such added compensation to the owner and
superintendent of it as would support him in equal comfort
with the more actively employed productive labourer. The
measure of the capitalist, on the contrary, would be the additional value produced by the same quantity of labour in conse-

quence of the use of machinery and other capital ; the whole of such surplus value to be appropriated by the capitalist for the superior skill and intelligence in accumulating and advancing to the labourers his capital or the use of it.

We must pause here for a few moments in order to clear away an obscure, or contradictory, statement of Thompson.   In arguing for the labourer the author assumes that capital is unproductive of any new values ; he thinks that labour produces the additional value, while it is only the amount of consumed or depreciated capital that enters into the new commodities.   This is in accordance with the opinion of Ricardo.   On the other hand, when arguing for the capitalist, Thompson assumes that it is the machinery that produces the surplus value or the new value—or, in other words, mere labour always produces a certain minimum, while the abundance of wealth is produced by capital.   Were the latter opinion that of Thompson himself there could be no reason for him to complain of unjust deductions from the produce of labour, for under these conditions capital merely takes what it produces.   He evidently intended, for the nonce, to look upon the whole question from the point of view of the capitalist.   In this case it was his duty to argue the question on economic grounds and decide which of the two measures of profit and wages was in accordance with economic science and history.   Thompson, however, does nothing of the kind.   He falls back on the doctrine of utility and declares : " The difference of the amount paid by the labourer for the use of the capital necessary to enable him to exert his productive powers, according to these two measures, is enormous.   It is the difference between almost perfect equality and excess both of wealth and poverty. . . .   What says justice, what says utility, to these rival claims ? "   If the measure of the labourer prevail, wealth would increase rapidly, since the productive labourer, being sure of the whole produce of his labour, would employ the utmost energy in production ; wealth would be diffused among the masses, and thus create the opportunity for the greatest happiness of the greatest number, and society would be nearing its goal.   If, on the contrary, the measure of the capitalist prevail, excessive inequality would ensue. Whetted by the stimulus of unbounded wealth, of superiority over the mass of society, he would turn into a despot. The evils of inequality would be pushed to their utmost limits. Happiness would sink to its lowest level. For, first, excessive inequality diminishes the sum total of enjoyment by depriving the greatest number of happiness. Secondly, it does not add proportionately to the happiness of the rich ; only a certain portion of wealth being necessary to satisfy our needs and desires, every successive portion added to the former portions of wealth, though all of equal value, adds less and less to our happiness. Excessive inequality engenders positive vices in the excessively rich, and it spreads these vices to the rest of the population. It lessens the stimulus to efficient production. It encourages futile arts and trades, mainly intended to minister to the whims and love of pleasure of the idle rich. Finally, it necessarily leads to the usurpation of powers, legislative, executive, and judicial, by those who have no other qualification for them than the patronage of the rich.

Hence it follows that on grounds of utility and justice the measure of Labour must prevail.

The foregoing argumentation leads us necessarily to the conclusion that of all causes which operate on human character and human happiness, none is as potent as the distribution of wealth. Therefore, on the principle of utility, every generation ought to have the right to arrange the distribution in such a manner as to produce happiness. No existing distribution ought to be upheld unless it is shown to promote preponderating good. Considering the fertility of the new productive powers, there need be no hesitation to undertake a redistribution of wealth. The accumulated wealth is really insignificant as compared with the possibilities of creation of new wealth which a just distribution would effect.

According to what principles or natural laws is the new social system to be arranged ?

In order to extract from wealth the greatest happiness which it is capable of affording, it is necessary that (1) Labour shall be free and voluntary as to direction and continuance ; (2) All the products of labour shall be secured to the producers of them ; (3) All exchanges of these products shall be free and voluntary.

These principles carried into effect will result both in security and equality.

Thompson, when working on his *Inquiry*, was not yet quite clear as to the form of society which could best follow up these principles. It is quite conceivable that he had then in view a society consisting of small independent producers, working on individualist lines. But his predilection for Owen's scheme of socialist co-operation was already strongly asserting itself. " Owen of New Lanark has shown how to reconcile equality of distribution with perfect security. Mutual co-operation and equal distribution are the instruments by which he operates " (*Inquiry*, chap. 6, sec. 1). However, at that time he was still hesitating between a free, primitive, democratic society of independent producers, and united labour under a system of voluntary socialism. The latter form soon got the upper hand, and Thompson adopted socialism. In his second book, *Labour Rewarded*, written in 1826 and published in 1827, there is no trace of any hesitation. Here he pleads for a co-operation against any other system of society, particularly against the scheme of free and competing small producers, suggested in Thomas Hodgskin's *Labour Defended* (1825). While the latter is written in an anti-capitalist spirit, full of fight and class warfare, Thompson devises a constructive plan for the emancipation of labour by establishing co-operative societies of production.

With Hodgskin, trades unions are fighting organisations ; he saw them as such in the years 1824–5. With Thompson, trades unions should have for their aim the saving and accumulation of funds with a view to establishing, by a series of successive steps, the co-operative commonwealth. He admits that trades unions, or voluntary associations openly and legally organised by the industrious classes, are likely to be useful ; they can help those who are thrown out of employment ; they will operate as a check on the caprice and selfishness of employers ; they will keep up wages and keep down profits. Moreover, trades unions

Q

will tend to call the intellectual powers of the industrious classes
into full activity, for questions of remuneration are closely
connected with political economy, statistics, nature of legal
institutions, and moral philosophy—subjects which the working
men have hitherto thought to be beyond their ken.   Finally,
they will lead them to the discovery that all their methods are
inadequate to secure to them the full produce of their labour,
so that they will be forced to investigate the teachings of the
political economy of co-operation.   The trades unions, in raising
the wages and the intellectual and moral level of the working
classes, will have achieved all they can ever achieve.   With the
funds saved by them they will then embark on the real work
of redemption, and build up, first, trade manufactories of their
own on the following plan :—

In those trades which require large buildings and machinery,
the funds of the trades unions, comprised in a general union,
should be permanently devoted to the erection of suitable
buildings, and the purchase of the best machinery to give employment to the industrious who might be thrown out of employment
through disagreement with their employers ; the general union
approving of their conduct and entitling them to work at the
trade manufactories, instead of granting them aid from the
Unemployed Funds and supporting them in their enforced idleness.   Near the largest seat of every extensive branch of manufacture these buildings and workshops should be erected—a
kind of industrious refuge for the victims of capital.   Out of the
products of the labour of those employed in these trade manufactories, nothing should be withheld from the labourers but the
cost of management and depreciation of capital.   The unions
should encourage those who are thus employed to become
shareholders of the trade manufactories.   Every individual
labourer paying the amount of a share should become a capitalist-
labourer, and would thus enjoy an increased part of the products
of his labour.   The same facilities for independence should,
of course, be opened in every department to women as to men ;
no person being permitted to purchase more than one share.
As these trade manufactories would thus come to be possessed

by joint-stock companies of the labourers themselves, other buildings and always improved machinery should be erected with their funds by the unions to keep up a constant refuge for the honest and industrious losing their employments. These establishments of capitalist-labourers would be something approaching to an efficient check on the exactions of mere capitalists. They would prove that capital can be accumulated without the aid of capitalists. But let not the industrious classes think that trade manufactories, even supposing them established in every branch of industry, would secure the labourers from the vicissitudes of the capitalist system. No, for they would still be burdened with payments of rent on the land on which their buildings stand, and profits on the raw materials —cotton, metals, etc.—which they use ; and they would still be exposed in their transactions to all the uncertainties of competition, the rivalries of similar establishments conducted by capitalists, and the fluctuations of trade dependent on the general markets. The workmen engaged in those trade manufactories would then find themselves under the necessity to have recourse to more advanced measures—to buy land, form agricultural associations, and finally form communities of co-operative production for their mutual wants. The progressive advance of Labour is from trades unions through knowledge and moral character to mutual co-operation.[1]

Thompson was at that time already one of the pillars of the London Co-operative Society, and one of the most assiduous contributors of the *Co-operative Magazine*. In 1830, he published a manual for co-operators under the title, *Practical Directions for the Establishment of Communities*, in which he laid down the principles of the political economy of co-operation : " Want or uncertainty of employment for the industrial classes is the master-evil of society as now constituted. What immediately causes want of employment ? Want of sale or market. Goods when produced cannot be sold at all or not at a price that would repay the cost of production ; therefore manufacturers cannot give permanent and remunerative employment. The remedy

[1] *Labour Rewarded*, 1827, pp. 87–93.

evidently is to find an unfailing market for all sorts of useful produce. The system of co-operative industry accomplishes this, not by the vain search after foreign markets throughout the globe which are no sooner found than overstocked or glutted by the restless competition of the starving producers, but by the voluntary union of the industrious classes in such numbers as to afford a market to each other by working together for each other, for the direct and mutual supply by themselves of all the most indispensable wants in the way of food, clothing, dwelling, and furniture."

Thompson took part in all the co-operative meetings and congresses. He was also one of the most thorough-going advocates of equality of rights for women, and wrote with this view a pamphlet entitled, *An Appeal of one-half of the Human Race* (1825). In fact, the whole co-operative-socialist movement identified itself with this demand. Thompson desired his property to be devoted to co-operative purposes, but his will was contested by his relatives in an action which outlasted the whole period of experimental socialism.[1]

6.—JOHN MINTER MORGAN

" In acute analytical investigation, in just and comprehensive views of society, and in bold uncompromising exposition of error, the *Distribution of Wealth* by Mr. William Thompson is perhaps unrivalled ; it is the most able work upon Political Economy that has appeared since the *Wealth of Nations*." This enthusiastic eulogy was passed by John Minter Morgan (1782–1854), a Christian Owenite, in his *Revolt of the Bees* (p. 81), which appeared in 1826. Morgan belongs to the popularisers of Owenism, and was eminently fitted for his task in virtue of his poetic style, singleness of purpose, and complete lack of originality. He was one of the earliest adherents of Owen, and published in 1819

[1] William Thompson's main teachings are to be found in his *Inquiry*, Preface, chap. 1, sections 6, 9, 11, 14, and Concluding Remarks ; then in *Labour Rewarded*, and *Practical Directions*, Introductory Remarks. *Cf. Poor Man's Guardian*, February 1, 1834.

a booklet entitled *On the Practicability of Owen's Plan.* His most popular work was the *Revolt of the Bees ;* it was much read by working men, and popular writers ; Harriet Martineau, quite a power in those times, knew it,[1] and the *Co-operative Magazine* published lengthy extracts from it. The author looks upon society as a hive of bees which had left its instinctive communal order, the state of nature, and instituted private property and competition, in the train of which came poverty and strife, super-abundance and misery, crime and punishment, lawyers and judges, moral precepts and immoral deeds. They had forgotten that under the primitive system, when each had its moderate portion of honey, there was no repletion, no destitution, and consequently neither theft nor murder. The miseries now occasioned by selfishness, folly, and ambition, to which the new system gave birth, excited the commiseration of the more reflecting bees, and from time to time there would arise individuals who devoted themselves voluntarily to the relief of the distressed. Once it happened that an ingenious bee invented a contrivance by which honey and wax could be made in large quantities with the aid of a few workers only. This scheme was imitated by others to such an extent that the poor working bees lost much of their employment. Then came the political economists, who argued that the misery could only be alleviated by greater accumulations of honey in the hands of the few rich, while one of their cleverest drones declared that the misery was due to the fact that there were too many working bees, and no matter how much honey was accumulated, the increase of the number of bees would always be much greater. This opinion became general, and there appeared to be no other alternative for the unemployed and hungry than to commit suicide. At that juncture a wise bee (Owen) appeared and showed them a way out of all misery, but its advice was regarded as visionary. It therefore flew away to a far-off land. However, since 1824 the poor bees began to shake off the despondency into which they had been thrown by the clever drones and to take to the teachings of the wise bee.

[1] *Poor Man's Guardian,* 1832, p. 383.

No lengthy explanations are needed to show that Morgan intended to give an outline of the state of nature, the introduction of private property, the coming of the inventions, the theory of Malthus, and the doctrines of Owen.

Dropping metaphor Morgan assumes that man had gone through four revolutions, and was now entering on the fifth. In the first stage mankind appeared as a noble savage; in the second, as a shepherd; in the third, as an agriculturist; in the fourth, " science enabled man to produce riches in superabundance, but as yet the right to use them was unknown; there might have been seen immense wealth in the midst of a starving population, more strife and contention than when less wealth prevailed, and infinitely more discord and crime." In the fifth stage a far greater change was taking place than in any of the preceding. Wealth, which had before lain in masses, was now being beneficially diffused and greatly increased, and with it invaluable riches of mind, knowledge, and virtue were spreading over the land.

7.——THOMAS ROWE EDMONDS

The author with whom we are going to deal cannot be said strictly to belong to the Owenite school of co-operative Socialism, but he is closely related to it by postulating happiness as the object of society; further, by using Ricardian economic concepts; finally, by advocating the social system. He differs from that school only by his appealing to the higher classes, and not to the working men, to introduce socialism, and by his belief in the efficacy of political methods. Edmonds (1803-89) was a Cornishman who graduated at Cambridge and soon after wrote a treatise, entitled *Practical, Moral, and Political Economy most conducive to Individual Happiness and National Power* (1828). For all its dispassionate and sober reasonings it is in its effect as condemnatory of the system of private property as any book which emanated from the Owenite school. Edmonds appears to have been influenced by Paley's *Moral and Political Philosophy*, then by Ricardo's *Principles*, whose views on value and wages he fully accepts, and by the whole socialist and anti-capitalist current of the time. Also Malthus's population theory was not without influence on him, though it was rather disturbing than positive. He argues for socialism in the following manner :—

Every man is in pursuit of happiness, yet he is still very far from having achieved it. The obstacles which stand between him and his object are ignorance, private property, competition, and a relative excess of population. Man, therefore, requires, before all, knowledge—knowledge of the physical and moral world. Useful physical knowledge has for its object the diminution of labour required to provide a given quantity of the necessaries of life, as food, clothing, lodging, and national defence, while mental or moral knowledge has for its object the exploration of the faculties and affections of the mind with the view of their being applied to the improvement of physical and social knowledge, and, consequently, the increase of human happiness (p. 264). But man is prevented from acquiring this knowledge by the love of money. This has become the predominant passion and excludes all really useful mental pursuits. It has even infested the minds of men of cultivated understanding whose opinions rule the opinions of all other men ; and the possessing and ruling classes are not slow in making use of this passion of scholars, and thus array the men of talent against truth (p. 262). Likewise, the Government does not favour freedom of discussion on the subject of social happiness. In consequence, minds of the highest order in England cannot publicly express themselves on subjects most vital to the community. All this is the effect of private property, and the division of society into two classes, masters and labourers.

The labourers work as hard as horses and produce all the necessaries and luxuries of life. The labourers who produce the necessaries are productive labourers, but receive only one-third of the produce of their toil, while two-thirds are taken away from them by the masters (p. 108–9). It is productive labour that supplies the nation with wealth, and it is the quantity of labour that measures the value of all commodities, but labour itself is measured by the necessaries of life. No matter how much a labourer may produce he will only get as much thereof as is necessary to keep him alive. If the arts of a country are so advanced that one labourer can produce necessaries for two men, he gets as wages half of it ; if the arts are so advanced that one labourer produces necessaries for three, as it appears to be the case in England, he will get one-third (p. 100-1) ; and should the arts and sciences advance to such a degree that one labourer could produce for ten, he would but receive one-tenth (pp. 122, 288).

The effect of this division of the produce is in the highest degree deplorable. The labourers, condemned to a life of a beast of burden, follow a principle of action similar to that of a horse, in being always ready to propagate, though they know that the result can only be semi-starvation and pauperism for themselves and their offspring. Pauperism, although apparently it is the effect of over-population, and can only be obviated by sexual restraint of the workmen,[1] is in reality the effect of private property, for there is hardly a country in Europe which could not sustain ten times as many people as they do sustain now (p. 107).

Finally, trade and commerce are at present regulated by competition. There is, therefore, a tendency in all capitals to undersell one another, that is, to diminish the rate of profit, and thus to reduce the revenue of the smaller capitals, while the larger capitals are amply compensated by quicker returns, with the result that, although by lowering the price of the commodities they lower the rate of profit, their total profit is larger than before.

Those are the causes that thwart man in his efforts to attain to happiness.

There are, however, in man and capital, certain tendencies that counteract those causes, and, aided by human endeavour, might lead to happiness. There is the social instinct. " Sociality," or the collecting together of many men for the purpose of united action, is a natural desire and necessity. Nature has so ordered it that the majority of pleasures and improvements depend on

---

[1] Edmonds was so disturbed by the view that over-population was the immediate cause of pauperism that he regarded as " the best cure for pauperism a tax on marriage both of masters and labourers " (*Practical, Moral, and Political Economy*, p. 113).

society. As the number of men forming one society increases the saving of labour increases, happiness increases, and the rapidity of progress made in the physical and moral arts and sciences increases (pp. 238, 268). Then there is the tendency of capital to concentrate or unite together and form one great fund under a single management. Competition soon teaches the merchant and shopkeeper and trader that only by collecting together many small capitals he will be able to reap high profits. By the increase of the size or the amount of single capitals the national wealth or power is increased, because by this increase, and united action, a greater quantity of commodities may be produced by a given quantity of labour. By the decrease of competition in consequence of the decrease of single capitals acting independently of each other, the profits become more regular and secure. When the labour employed in the different arts and crafts has been collected into very large and distinct capitals, all will probably unite and form a single corporation (pp. 128-30).

To these two natural tendencies, viz. sociality of men and association of capital should be added the principle of improved propagation of men and women. " The breed of men, like that of all other animals, is capable of infinite improvement in mind as well as in body. The bodies of the coming generation may be rendered superior in health, strength, activity to the present generation by selecting for the purposes of propagation the individuals of both sexes possessing those qualities, and not allowing the weak and diseased to transmit their diseases and miseries to posterity." The same principle of propagation should be applied to mental qualities. And with the help of training and education the human race could be made fit for the highest tasks.

Finally, there is a law of God and nature " that no man or class of men can increase their happiness by oppressing, or by diminishing the happiness of other men or other classes of men. The law of nature is that the interests of individuals and the interests of the public shall always be inseparably linked together " (p. 261).

If we enlist for our purpose these tendencies and principles we can devise a plan of rendering society happy and powerful. Such a society may be denominated the " Social System " on account of its being based on sociality and equality (p. 281). By way of illustrating the social system the author assumes that about a thousand people, agriculturists, craftsmen, and scientists, decide to settle in some distant isle which contains about 5,000 acres of land. They do not commence by dividing the land into a thousand equal parts and isolate each man on his five acres, but resolve to work together in order to enjoy the benefits of large capital, proper division of labour, mutual defence and assistance. All matters of administration they put into the hands of a small number of elected persons distinguished by the clearest judgment and most firmly rooted principles of justice. These persons form a representative assembly who select from their midst the best and fittest as justices, for no social system can exist if the administration of justice does not command the confidence of all. This secured, the members of the community will direct their attention to the organisation of production. All the men of the same trade will collect together, in one mass, each man's machinery, stock, and labour, in other words, all the capitals of any one trade will be collected into one single capital. At least one half of the community will consist of agriculturists, who, besides their fixed capital (machinery, stock), must possess necessaries (circulating capital) to be consumed by the five hundred men during the process of production. Since all the agriculturists have an equal right to govern their collective capital, the government, or management of this capital must be performed by a small number of their representatives. The management of the capitals of the other trades will be regulated on the same principle. And the governments of all capitals will be subject to the general government.

After providing for equal administration of justice and for the management of collective labour, the community will turn its attention to fostering the gregarious instinct and the increase of sociality by erecting large apartment houses, common dining-rooms, sitting-rooms, lecture halls, theatres, concerts, dancing-halls, libraries, open to the whole population.

The community will then be united by the threefold cord of equal administration of justice, collective labour, and sociality. When these social bonds will have reached a high degree of perfection, injustice will disappear, and with it the necessity of the Courts of Justice. Collective labour and sociality will then be of sufficient strength to keep the community closely together and perpetuate happiness. The only pressure which the assembly of representatives might have to apply would be in matters of propagation. Should over-population threaten, then it would be necessary to prevent the weak in body or mind from multiplying, and to take the quota of children necessary for the existence of the community from the stronger members only.

The benefits to be derived from the social system will be so considerable that the nation which first adopts it will so far exceed in power all other nations that they will fall an easy prey to it and be compelled to adopt the same system. The British nation is the one which, in all probability, will soonest arrive at the social system and which will spread it over the world. England is more powerful than any other nation because its system approaches nearest to the social system. There is equal administration of justice, concentration of capital, division of labour ; only sociality is lacking. The population of English towns is divided and split up into a multitude of different ranks, sets, groups, with no intercourse between them. This lack of sociality is manifest in the pride, self-consciousness, and ferocity of the English. And this is the main cause of the unhappiness so prevalent among them (p. 250). And nowhere are the working classes so degraded as in England, for the upper classes keep them in ignorance. All reform in England must be directed towards fostering sociality.

The social system is the ideal towards which all governments tend, and at which they cannot fail to arrive sooner or later. It is in harmony with nature and the doctrines of Christianity (pp. 270–288). The establishment of the social system should be the work of the thinking and richer classes, for only to them would the bulk of the population pay attention, while any reform undertaken by the working classes would be insecure and finally

fail. Changes proposed by the working classes " even if con-
formable to truth, or conducive to happiness, could not be carrried
by them into effect ; the exceptions to the general truth would
stagger them, they would reject the truth in despair, and things
would return to a worse state than before " (303–4). In other
words, the author is evidently of opinion that working men, by
assuming that a theory must uncompromisingly be carried out,
are bound to fail in their efforts for reform ; they do not see that
a theory can only become workable when it is corrected by, or
enters into a compromise with, practice. This is, indeed, one of
the causes of failure of revolutionary movements.

8.—JOHN FRANCIS BRAY

The synthesis of Owenite teachings and anti-capitalist criticisms
was effected by John Francis Bray in his *Labour's Wrongs and
Labour's Remedy* (1838–9), a book written with great knowledge
and genuine rhetorical fire. He was born June 26, 1809, in
Washington City, U.S.A., as son of John Bray, comedian and
writer, a native of Yorkshire. Father and son returned to
England in 1822 and settled with their relatives at Leeds, where
John Francis attended school and then worked as compositor
at the *Leeds Times*, edited by Samuel Smiles (*Self Help*)[1]. He
was active in the labour movement, read Owen, Gray, and
Hodgskin, and was profoundly grieved at the constant efforts
of the working classes to ameliorate their condition, or to accomplish their emancipation, by trade unionist and political methods,
notwithstanding all the failures and disappointments which
attended their feverish activities in the political and trade
unions. And when he finally witnessed the rising tide of Chartism he summoned up all his energies and his store of philosophic
and economic knowledge for the purpose of demonstrating to the
working classes that the only remedy for their wrongs was
mutual co-operation in production, distribution, and exchange.
His book is the last and most powerful manifesto of Owenism.

[1]Bray returned in 1842 to U.S.A., lived in the state of Michigan
as printer, journalist, and farmer, later on, with his relatives and
grandchildren in and near Boston, and died in 1895. (Compare also
Socialist Review, London, Sept., 1916.)

The doctrines concerning happiness, natural rights, circumstances as builders of character, capitalist production, labour-value, co-operative enterprise, socialisation of exchange, and the priority of economics to politics, are combined and fused into one whole by the concentrated heat of an intensely thinking mind. He argues :

Were we able to take an unprejudiced survey of the human race we should compare it to a group of shipwrecked men thrown upon an almost desert island. There is sufficient room for all to live and move, plenty of materials necessary to support existence, but nothing can be done without labour. It requires labour to gather even the wild fruits from the trees, or the shell-fish from the shore. Without labour we die. Surely, the most rational mode of action for men so circumstanced would be to unite in parties, work and share alike, and render to each other mutual assistance and protection. But men have hitherto done nothing of the kind. They have pursued different tracks, and have moved on alone, each for himself, although they have all been in search of the same object—happiness. The result has been complete failure to achieve it. And it could not be otherwise, since men have neglected the first principles of society, or the rights of nature. We live in an unnatural society. All this restlessness and yearning and dissatisfaction of a great part of humanity is due to that fact. Our whole social fabric is one vast Babel of interests, in which true charity, morality, and brotherly love are absent. The hand of every man is raised against every other man ; the interests of every class are opposed to those of every other class, and all other interests are in opposition and hostility to those of the working class. This unnatural state of things was originally brought about and is now maintained by man's ignorance of the first principles promulgated in the great book of Nature, which may be thus interpreted :

(1) All men are alike in regard to their substance, their creation, and their preservation, the inequalities in men's nature mostly arising from the different circumstances in which men are placed, and from the inequalities produced by the artificial state of things.

(2) The materials requisite for the preservation of life—food, clothing, and shelter—exist everywhere around us, but they are naturally valueless or unobtainable until labour intervenes ; therefore, as the life of man cannot be maintained without a due provision of food, clothing, and shelter, and as these cannot be procured without labour, it follows that every human being ought to labour.

(3) As the nature and wants of all men are alike, the rights of all must be equal ; and as human existence is dependent on the same contingencies, it follows that the great field for all exertions and the raw material of all wealth, the earth, is the common property of all its inhabitants.

Equality of men, equality of rights and duties, common ownership of the soil, are the laws of nature.

Further, it is labour alone that bestows value. Every man has an undoubted right to all his honest labour can procure him ; when he thus appropriates the fruits of his labour he commits no injustice upon any other human being ; but if any individual appropriates the field on which all labour is exercised, he clearly infringes the common equality of rights. And these rights have been destroyed by the appropriation of the land. Or, as the author puts it, " From the very nature of the thing, and the position in which man stands with regard to his fellows, he never did, and never can, individually, possess any exclusive right to one single inch of land. Wherever such an assumed right is set up and acted upon, there will always exist injustice, tyranny, poverty, and inequality of rights, whether the people be under the monarchical or the republican form of government ; for all the wrongs and woes which man has ever committed or endured, may be traced to the assumption of right in the soil by certain individuals and classes to the exclusion of other individuals and classes. Equality of right can never be enjoyed until all individual claims to landed property are subverted, and merged in those of the nation at large " (p. 33–4).

From this prolific source of evil have arisen despotisms, governmental power, domination of class over class, riches and misery—in short, the wrongs of Labour must be traced back to inequality of possessions. No change of forms of government or laws, no struggles for higher wages and a shorter number of working hours can remove those wrongs, for government and laws or conditions of employment are the effects, and not the causes, of the evil. Wherever inequality of possessions prevails, inequality of rights and duties must necessarily exist. Our politicians have always been wont to make laws for rich men as such, and poor men as such, without ever inquiring how it came to pass that some men were rich and some were poor ; or how it happened that one class toiled away, generation after generation, without becoming any richer, and the other class ate, drank, and were merry, generation after generation, without becoming less rich. The politicians have almost always taught the workmen to look for relief to governmental changes and reforms ; but the majority of these advisers have not belonged to the working classes ; and, connected as they are with the rich, and living as they do on rents and profits, they are necessarily hostile to the interests and wishes of labour. The politicians who always descant on the load of taxation, cost of royalty, etc., do not know that taxes form a relatively small fraction of the social burden of Labour. The amount of taxation is now (1838) about fifty millions sterling. On the other hand, the value of the goods produced by the working classes of the United Kingdom is no less than five hundred millions, of which they receive in wages about two hundred millions ; thus the capitalists and landlords deprive them of three-fifths of their labour produce. A right understanding of the tables of production and distribution, as given by Colquhoun and Gray, could teach the working classes more than all the speeches of the politicians and taxation reformers (pp. 76, 85) The insufficiency of political measures to remedy social grievances was long since seen by thousands of the working classes ; they had some sort of conception that the gain of the capitalist was the loss of the producer ; and therefore sought relief by the institution of trade societies and trades unions. But these also had the same ultimate object in view as the political unions—namely, the partial amelioration of the condition of the working class as such.

Likewise, factory legislation can, at best, have no other effect. All these remedies will reduce neither the number of the rich nor the poor ; and therefore they are not capable of curing the evils which this relative position and this division of society inflict upon the workman. The capitalist or employer, by his very position in society as the purchaser and controller of the labour of the working class, has it in his power to suck from them the greater part of the wealth which they produce. Indeed, capital arises from unpaid labour.

" Every accumulation of the capitalist or employers, as a body, is derived from the unsurrendered earnings of the working class, or persons employed ; and wherever one man thus becomes rich, he does so only on condition that many men shall remain poor " (p. 56). All this is done by means of unequal exchanges. The workmen have always given the capitalist the labour of a whole day for the value of only a half day, and even this value had been previously taken from Labour, since the capitalist, being a non-producer, can have nothing to exchange. It is this inequality of exchanges, and not the supposed inequality of bodily and mental powers, that makes the rich richer and the poor poorer (pp. 48-9).

The division of society into two classes, into capitalists and labourers—into those who produce everything and get little, and into those who produce nothing and get the most—is the root of evil. It perpetuates the division of interests, and by bringing individuals into hostile contact in the common scramble for subsistence, destroys those germs of social sympathy which naturally exist in all men, while the germs of self-love are fostered and even forced to a riotously profuse growth and unnatural development. To apply to an evil of this potency the measures advocated by politicians is to equip men with pop-guns for a hunting expedition in a jungle.

However, while reviewing their wrongs and devising remedies, the working class must never lose sight of the fact that their warfare is not against men, but against a system,—not against capitalists as individuals nor against capital itself, but against the present mode of applying capital, against that system which gives to irresponsible individuals the power of grinding masses of labour between masses of capital. There is no remedy for this except a change of system. Without such a change, the cause of the redemption of the working class is a hopeless one!

From the nature of the evil it follows that the remedy can only be found in the establishment of equal exchanges—exchanges of equal quantities of labour. Such an equality, once established, would necessarily lead to universal labour, or to the extinction of the idle classes. The social burden will then be taken off the shoulders of the working classes (p. 110).

This change must be undertaken with a view to a reconciliation of interests, to uniting all into one interest. And this is only possible in a social system based on community of possessions, as devised by Robert Owen. Such a form of society is in every respect the most perfect which is in the power of man to institute, but it cannot be called into existence at one stroke, for it requires a degree of excellence of character and reasoning capacities which but few enjoy to-day. We are all tainted by, and more or less imbued with, the depravity and ill-feeling which the present system generates. The failures which have hitherto attended co-operative experiments have been due either to those causes or to lack of capital. If, then, a changed character be essential to the success of the community system in its most perfect form, and if the present system affords no circumstances and no facilities for effecting the requisite change of character, it is evident that things must necessarily remain as they are, unless one of the two methods are adopted. Either those who commence a new system must possess accumulations of capital sufficient to overcome the drawbacks imposed by the present system until the superior circumstances created by the new system shall have done their work, or else some preparatory step must be discovered—some intermediate resting-place, to which men may go with all their faults and follies, and from which they may move forward, imbued with those qualities without which the system of community and equality cannot exist.

After having dealt with all the familiar objections to com-

R

munism and proved them to have emanated either from prejudice and ignorance or from the failures of rashly undertaken communist experiments, the author devises, as a preliminary step to the perfect social system, the formation of communities in form of joint-stock companies, based on the following principles : Society is to consist of one class only, labourers, mental and manual, united together in an indefinite number of communities or joint-stock companies, in which labour is to be universal and the remuneration in proportion to the time of labour.   These communities would hold possession of the land and the productive capital of the nation ; they would likewise possess a circulating bank-note or paper medium, amounting to two thousand million pounds sterling ; they would mutually and universally produce and distribute wealth, exchanging their labour and their productions on one broad principle of equality. This vast confederation of labour would have somewhat the character of a modern joint-stock company, and would bring forth its results by means of similar appliances. There would be general and local magazines of food and necessaries ; this produce would be distributed by means of large markets or bazaars instead of through innumerable petty tradesmen ; and every commodity would be procurable in any part of the country for its wholesale cost of production, neither depreciated by abundance—social statistics based on the national accounts would preclude gluts—nor enhanced by the artifices of speculators.   The production and transport, and, generally, the affairs of society at large, would be regulated by national and local boards of various kinds, the members of which would be elected by the communities.   A national bank would create the circulating medium, and issue it to the managers of various companies in proportion to the number of members of each company, or the character of their occupation. With this money, all individuals and companies would purchase commodities and transact their exchanges, on the present principle of trade ; and, either by the imposition of a direct tax on persons, or a percentage on commodities, necessary funds would be forthcoming for the expenses of administration.   The money issued would always keep within the limits of actual effective capital existing.   The money would always be at hand to pay for the labour—the labour would always be ready to exert its power for this universal representative of capital, and thus, while the money would insure the labour, the labour itself would insure the creation of commodities. Production, accumulation, distribution, and consumption would naturally be adjusted to each other, thus precluding confusion, gluts, unemployment, and poverty.

For the rest, no accurate and detailed description of future arrangements can be given by any human being. For, as the knowledge of every man is acquired either through his own experience or the experience of others, he can never accurately foretell and determine how individuals will feel and act, in every instance, when placed in new circumstances. We can only judge from the past and present, and keep in view principles, actions, and incentives to action ; by combining experience with principle, or practice with theory, we can make an approximation to the results sought for. The efforts of the communists are of this character ; although they may not be able to point out every trivial arrangement which might be adopted by a people acting upon such a system, the principles on which it is founded, and the general outline of it, will serve as a standard with which to compare and test existing social arrangements. And it is not the communists or any other individuals who are preparing the change of the social system. " The present crisis is no more than a natural movement attending the course of things—it is but one move of that mighty ocean of events, the billows of which have rolled on from eternity, and will progress in unchecked power for ever . . . it was advancing even when polished Greece and Rome degenerated into semi-barbarism—it was coming on when the French Revolution took place . . . and it is at this moment passing before our eyes and bearing us along, destroying and reinstituting political and social institutions of every character and kind. The present is not a merely local movement, it is not confined to country, colour, or creed—the universe is the sphere in which it acts . . . and whatever may be its immediate prospect, there are to be seen harbingers of brighter and better times. The light of Mind is beaming through the gloomy boundaries of the Age of Might, and ushering in the Age of Right."[1]

[1] Bray's book was regarded by Socialists and Chartists as a standard work (*Northern Star*, May 20, 1843); *O'Brien's National Reformer and Manx Weekly Review*, Oct. 24, 1846; Karl Marx, *Misère de la Philosophie*, 1847.

VIII

ECONOMICS OF ANTI-CAPITALISM

I.—"A LETTER TO LORD JOHN RUSSELL"

The revolutionary ferment consequent upon the rise of the new manufactures and aggravated by the Napoleonic Wars, the distress which had set in at the end of 1816, and the propaganda of Owen, produced a revulsion of feeling and reasoning against the capitalist mode of production and its economic theories, particularly as formulated by Ricardo, whose concise statement of principles and verbal inaccuracies in details offered a favourable front to attack. The writers who led the attack were, as already stated in a preceding chapter, by no means socialists. They only saw in capitalism a destructive or subversive force dangerous to the welfare of the working-classes in particular, and to the nation in general. The comprehensive and sweeping character of their criticism is out of all proportion to their indefinite and halting proposals for reforms. Their leading idea is, capital is really preserved labour ; the foundation of value is labour ; and yet, socially, Capital is everything and Labour nothing ! The reverse ought to be the case. No socialist has ever surpassed these writers in the emphasis they laid on the opposition of interests and the irreconcilable antagonism between capital and labour. Most of their thought was communicated to the rising Labour Movement by Thomas Hodgskin, of whom we shall treat later on. One of the first critics of capitalism was an anonymous writer of an open letter to Lord John Russell on *The Source and Remedy of the National Difficulties* (1821).

Our country, he says, is suffering, and the revenue of the nation is rising. Political economists count those nations richest where the greatest revenue can be raised, " as if the power of compelling or inducing men to labour twice as much at the mills of Gaza for the enjoyment of the Philistines were a proof of anything but a tyranny or an ignorance twice as powerful " (p. 1).

This is the arsis. And now comes the thesis. Labour, either our own or of others, is the source of wealth and revenue. The wealth of a nation consists in its preserved labour, or rather in its preserved surplus labour, that is, labour beyond its usual and necessary consumption. Surplus labour, then, means all the labour of the individual beyond what is exclusively appropriated to the maintenance and enjoyment of himself and family. Such labour is capital (p. 3).

And as this surplus labour is not owned by those who produced it, but by those who allowed the labourer the necessaries while he was producing it, therefore, capital is surplus labour taken away from the producer.

Capital has the power of reproduction. All political economists have for their object to suggest means to increase capital. But it will be shown that the accumulation of capital is very limited if we look at the condition of the whole population, and not at the opulence of the few, or at the high rate of interest which the labourers have to pay to the capitalist for the loan of the means of production.

The author assumes that profit is merely another name for interest ; the usurer lends money, the capitalist lends fixed and circulating capital to the labourers, who only leave to themselves as much of the produce of their labour as to enable them to subsist and perpetuate the race, while the rest goes as surplus labour to the lender of capital, *i.e.*, the capitalist.

Notwithstanding these appropriations, capital accumulates but slowly, since a high rate of interest has to be paid by the producer for its use. And this slow accumulation of capital is the immediate cause of the distress of the nation.

In order to grasp the meaning of this cause and find out its source, let us suppose a simple society where the whole labour of the country is just sufficient to support the whole population. In this case there is no surplus labour, and consequently no accumulation of capital. Suppose now the whole labour of the country can raise as much in one year as would maintain it two years, then either one year's produce must perish or the population must cease work for one year. But, of course, nothing of the kind will take place. The appropriators of the surplus produce or capital will, for one year, employ the labour on commodities not directly consumable, *i.e.*, on buildings, machinery, roads, etc. But the third year will again be devoted to productive labour, and, with the aid of the machinery built last year, the population will produce much more than in the first year, and consequently the surplus labour will be greater. It would follow still more that either the surplus commodities should perish or the population cease labour until the commodities were consumed. However, the labouring population will never be asked how to get rid of the surplus produce, but the capitalists will accumulate it. Looking at the reproductive power of capital and at the readiness of the great mass of the people to apply their labour to it, capital ought to go on increasing until no man would have any difficulty in getting it. And the falling rate of interest shows the tendency in that direction, but so long as capital can command interest at all, society cannot have arrived at the maximum production of wealth. When that maximum is reached society will not go on to exert its productive power as before, but will reduce its hours of labour from twelve to six. This beginning of general ease would be the beginning of real prosperity.

Wealth of the nation does not mean the opulence of the few, but facilities of living for all. " Wealth is liberty—liberty to recreation—liberty to enjoy life—liberty to improve the mind. Wealth is disposable time, and nothing more " (p. 6).

Considering all the facilities for production and the great benefits which would accrue from it to the nation at large, the question is, why has society never arrived yet at this prosperous situation ?

The first dead weight that impedes the progress of production is the possessor of capital who, as soon as surplus labour is available, ceases to work and maintains himself on the interest, or the surplus labour of others. He becomes an idle consumer. The increase in the production of wealth is marked by an increase of idle persons, and their menial servants and parasites. Thus, the momentum of wealth production is slackened. Moreover, the idle classes, besides exacting surplus labour for lending real capital, inflate the capital of the country by issuing fictitious paper money and stock,—fictitious because not covered by gold and silver or increase of real capital ; and for this fictitious paper capital they exact interest from Labour. Finally, they destroy enormous amounts of real capital by wars, and they waste real capital by exporting it to foreign countries in exchange for luxuries. We may safely assume that if capital does not decrease in value as it increases in amount, the capitalist exacts from the labourer the produce of every hour's labour beyond what is possible for the worker to subsist on. The less useful the capitalist becomes, the stronger his lust for appropriating and accumulating the surplus labour of others ; the more he wastes, the greater the exactions from the producers.

What are the exactions from Labour ? These can only be roughly estimated. According to Patrick Colquhoun's *Resources of the British Empire*, a labouring family consisting of four persons receives £45 annually, or £11 per head. We may, therefore, assume that the mere labour of any member of society is not worth more than £11 per annum ; and all income beyond that sum represents interest on the capital outlay for education, apprenticeship, training, etc. If a clergyman or a lawyer receives two, three, or four hundred a year, it is because two, three, or four thousand pounds is presumed to have been expended on his education. Taking now from Colquhoun the number of the heads of families of other classes and allowing to each the worth of mere labour, £45 per annum, we are able to separate the worth of this labour, or the just wages, from the interest they derive from capital, as the following table shews :—

The total income of these classes amounts to about 276 millions sterling, the value of their labour is about 41 millions' sterling. Consequently, they exact as interest on capital no less a sum than 235 millions, or six times as much as their labour is worth (pp. 35–6).

Number of Heads of Families.	Rank, Degree, Occupation.	Total Income.	Just Wage Total.	Interest on Capital.
		£	£	£
68,937	Royalty, Nobility ...	67,753,590	3,102,165	64,651,425
621,000	Professions, Farmers ...	92,830,000	27,945,000	64,885,000
35,000	Bankers, Merchants ...	30,064,000	1,575,000	28,489,000
9,250	Shipowners, etc. ...	5,652,000	426,250	5,225,750
44,900	Manufacturers, etc. ...	36,099,600	2,020,500	34,079,100
183,750	Shopkeepers, Traders ...	35,875,000	4,268,750	31,606,250
35,874	Teaching profession ...	7,664,400	1,614,330	6,050,070
	Total ...	275,938,590	40,951,995	234,986,595

The effect on society is deplorable.

" The increase of trade and commerce opened a boundless field to luxuries ; the splendour of the luxurious enjoyments of the few excited a worthless, debasing, and selfish emulation in all. The attainment of wealth became the ultimate purpose of life.` . . . Their appetite was corrupted in their infancy that it might leave its natural and wholesome nutriment, and feed on the garbage of Change Alley. . . And the consummation of their hopes was characterised by misery and ignorance, the dissolution of all social virtue and common sympathy among individuals, and by a disunited, feeble, despotic, and despised government " (p. 18–19).

We have reached a stage of social life when Colquhoun wants the working men to feed on potatoes instead of bread. To such a pass has the nation been brought through injustice and bad policy. None the less, the political economists do not cease to write about the wealth of the nation and to exalt capital. In reality, the progress of a nation is marked by reduction of the hours of labour and rise of wages. These are unmistakable signs of prosperity ; and growth of capital would bring this about if we could eliminate the factors that retard and check it. Moreover, the emancipation of labour depends on abundant capital. When capital is increased in such masses that the rate of interest sinks to zero, the hour of freedom for all mankind will have arrived.

As to the measures to bring this flood of wealth over the earth the author hardly suggests any. He denies that he is " for levelling all classes and distinctions, or reducing the pay of a judge to the wage of a labourer, or any other such foolish speculations." He merely demands abolition of the Corn Laws, reduction of the interest on the National Debt, " for the loans to the Government were made in depreciated currency, which has now been restored to its full value," reduction of rentals and a general rise of wages.[1]

This anonymous pamphlet may have had some influence on John Gray.

[1] *Cf*. Karl Marx, *Theorien über den Mehrwert*, III., pp. 281–305.

2.—PIERCY RAVENSTONE

One of the seminal minds of the period was the author of the remarkable book, *A few Doubts as to the Correctness of some Opinions Generally Entertained on the Subject of Political Economy* (1821), and of a pamphlet, entitled *Thoughts on the Funding System and its Effects* (1824). He signed himself " Piercy Ravenstone," but it is very doubtful whether this was his real name ; it is rather probable that it is a pseudonym. Of his life nothing has been ascertained. In the Goldsmiths' Economic Library (London University) there are two copies of the book, one bearing the autograph " Henry Brougham, Esq. From the Author." The other copy is from the library of Sir Robert Peel. However, no matter what the name and history of the life of the author were, his works exercised a great influence on that group of writers and working class agitators, who, though averse from socialism, were intensely anti-capitalist, and laid the foundation of the class-warfare theory.

Ravenstone was essentially a Tory Democrat, but without any ulterior motives, without any other end to serve than what he considered justice and national welfare. Of an ardent temperament, a religious and cultured mind, his whole being was in revolt against capitalist and Stock Exchange dominion. He must have been in an advanced age when he wrote his first book, for the experience which he brought to bear upon it was full of pessimism, caused evidently by the French Revolution, the Napoleonic Wars, and the terrible years 1816 to 1820. He was then firmly convinced that England had run her course, and, loaded with debt and torn with dissensions, was tottering to the brink of the grave-trap in which exhausted nations disappear from the scene of history.

His ideal was a nation consisting in the main of peasant proprietors, handicraftsmen, and other useful labourers, with a minimum of government and taxation under the control of those who serve the community by hand and head. Like Cobbett, he hated the " accumulating, centralising, and amalgamating band of Malthusians and political economists." He was indeed Cobbett *édition de luxe*—a Cobbett who could think systematically and consistently, whose knowledge of history was more comprehensive and accurate and less vitiated by prejudice, and whose style was as vigorous as that of the *Political Register*, but of a polish and refinement which only a superior classical education can produce. We can imagine him an independent squire with an Oxford or Cambridge education, who knew his Thucydides, Tacitus, Montesquieu, Gibbon, the histories of the Italian republics, and the deeds of the Dutch, and who was impelled by a burning zeal to warn his countrymen of the impending fall of England, and to analyse and define the economic and social causes of it.

The events of the last hundred years, he declares, the changes they have wrought in the mode of existence of every nation of Europe, and the complications they have introduced into all relations of society, have given to the science of political economy an importance to which it could have never before pretended. As the classes into which nations are divided have multiplied, as the space allotted to the movements of each individual has been more circumscribed, their different interests have brought men more frequently into collision, and it has required no small amount of skill to state and regulate the claims of each (*Funding System*, p. 1). Political economists, or the scientists of the essentials of society and government, have undertaken to interpret those changes and to teach us how to re-adjust society. What is the system they have built up ? " A cold and dreary system which represents our fellow-creatures as so many rivals and enemies, which makes us believe that their happiness is incompatible with our own, which builds our wealth upon their poverty, which would persuade us to look on the world in the light of a besieged town, where the death of our neighbours is hailed with secret satisfaction, since it augments the quantity of provision likely to fall to our own share " (*A Few Doubts*, p. 17). It is time to put an end to that cheerless system which represents society as a jungle of wild animals always ready to devour each other.

In searching for the fundamental principle of society we find that every man brings into the world the capacity for procuring his own sustenance. Man gives existence to food, clothing, and shelter. Subsistence grows with the growth of numbers, or with the amount of labour employed on its production ; where the population is most numerous wealth is abundant. The increase of population allows of division and subdivision of labour, which, in their turn, raise production, and give leisure to some, who employ it to extend the bounds of knowledge. Increase of population, division of labour, opportunity for research, and the necessity of easing the labour of production, lead to inventions which result in an infinite multiplication of the productive powers (*Ib.*, pp. 23, 119, 177). Without detracting from the merit of a Watt or an Arkwright, inventions are seldom due to the man who brings them forward ; they arise from the spirit, the experience, knowledge, and needs of the age. Had not the predecessors of Watt studied the power of steam and built contrivances to utilise it, had not the population grown faster than sheep, had there still been enough wool for clothing, the steam engine and the spinning-jenny would have never reached that stage of perfection which permitted them to revolutionise our manufactures. Invention always sleeps in thinly populated countries. Human ingenuity awakens and is impelled to activity by the growing needs of a growing population. Where population is making great advances, every day presents new combinations of machinery and calls into action powers that a few years before none would have dared to dream of. The elasticity of nature and mind, the constant tendency in every people to increase its numbers and to give more profitable employment to its industry, this exhaustless capacity of improvement is the true capital of nations ; thence flows, if properly understood and acted upon, their wealth (*Funding System*, p. 43). God, in bidding man increase and multiply, and eat bread by the sweat of his brow, pointed out to him the true source of the wealth of nations. Growth of population and industry is the real cause of riches and welfare (*Ib.*, p. 76).

If, then, the experience of particular nations appears to controvert this theory, if the means of subsistence have not increased as rapidly as the population, the defects and errors must be sought in their own institutions.   Not the principles of society are wrong, but the human regulations of society are at fault.   Such a state of things is decisive evidence that the constitution of that society is defective and therefore requires to be re-cast.

Which are the defects and errors that have led to the dispro-portion between the means of subsistence and the population ?

Rent, taxes, and capital (profit) are the great engines for bringing about this unfortunate change in the condition of society.   And rent, taxes, and profit have their origin in the right of property.

We do not condemn property as such, but there are two kinds of property, natural and artificial.   The natural right of property is identical with the reward of labour.   Ravenstone, following Locke, says that he who renders things useful and valuable by his labour and skill is, as it were, their creator and they are rightly his property.   This species of property is, however, very different from that " artificial right " which grows up in the progress of society, by which a man is enabled to appropriate to himself the ownership of lands which he does not occupy, and on which he has never exercised any industry ;   a right which enables him to live in plenty, without any labour of his own, and to exact from others a large portion of the fruits of their industry, for the permission to employ their labour in rendering productive lands in which all appear to have an equal right of property (*A Few Doubts*, p. 99).   This pretension of the landowner is the basis of the property of every description which is seen to multiply with the growth of civilisation.   On it are built the pretensions of the master manufacturer, tradesman, and capitalist.   No sooner has the landowner established his claim to share in all the earnings of those who exercise their industry in the cultivation of the soil, than the master manufacturer sets up a similar claim to a share in all the earnings of those whose industry is employed in wool, cotton, timber, iron, or any of the productions of human ingenuity.   From this moment labour ceases to be free.   The exercise of industry is effectually barred ;   everywhere the toll must be paid before industry is allowed to go to work. This toll is rent or profit, or the idle men's shares in the labouring men's earnings (*Ib.*, p. 225). These idle men live on the surplus produce of the workers (p. 311).

Ravenstone does not clearly show how and why these rent and profit gatherers succeeded in raising themselves to that position, but he appears to suggest that man is naturally weak and desires some sort of leadership. Leaders are appointed to regulate and promote the affairs of society, but finally end by tyrannizing society and promoting their own interests. Or, as he says : " In a well-regulated society, the landowner, the trades-man, and the manufacturer perform merely the functions of channels in a system of irrigation. They do not produce water, their business is only to distribute it equally through every part of the field. But if these channels be made so numerous that all the water is absorbed in its passage, they will rob the soil of its nourishment, they will destroy the fertility they were meant to assist, their existence must prove injurious " (p. 352). At first, rent and profit constitute a very small proportion of the income of a nation, but gradually the proportion comes nearly to constitute the whole. In the early stages of society, when men, bound to-gether by few ties, contribute little to each other's aid, it is as much as each can do with all his industry to keep himself from starving. In every subsequent stage of society, as increased numbers and better tools add to each man's power of production, the number of those who labour is gradually diminished. When one man's labour is barely sufficient for his own subsistence, there can be no property nor idle men. When one man's labour can maintain five, there will be four idle men for one employed in production. They appropriate his surplus produce. The usurpers come to be considered as proprietors of the whole. Finally, the industrious are supposed to live on the bounty of the idle, the producers to owe their existence to the loving-kindness of the appropriators. The productivity of labour results in the undoing of the labourers. They sink to the level of horses, the reward of whose efforts is a wage just sufficient to keep them in working order. On the other hand, the interests of the rich are identified with those of the nation ; they frame the laws, which of course sanction all these usurpations (p. 201). For it may be accepted as a rule that economics rule politics.

And yet labour is the reality, while capital is a metaphysical concept, and one of the cabalistic signs of political science. Its incorporeal nature for ever eludes our grasp. Where the political economists are at a loss to explain any of the problems of social progress they have recourse to the miracles supposed to be performed by capital. According to the political economists capital is at once the child and the parent of labour. It is preserved labour and yet labour can achieve nothing without capital. Capital builds our towns, cultivates our fields, it mans our ships, it marshals and feeds the army, it fills the world's markets with goods, it turns a desert into flourishing habitations of man. But whence came capital that creates all these prodigies ? Adam left none to his children. Capital is the creation of labour, it is the result of accumulation of preserved labour. How then can it be the cause of labour ? (*Funding System*, pp. 38–9. *A Few Doubts*, pp. 293–4.) Capital is merely an instrument of exchange ; it exchanges preserved labour for new labour. And exchanges can add no value to the produced goods. The only source of value is productive labour, particularly labour employed on necessaries. " How ridiculous, then, the alarm which has been attempted to be raised that if the employers are not sufficiently attended to they would leave the country, and carrying with them their capitals, would deprive it of the advantages afforded to industry ! " (p. 352). Much more real is the dread that if labour left the country the source of all wealth would be gone ; no amount of capital could save us from destruction. Notwithstanding all these considerations capital is extolled and labour downed. " It is, however, hopeless to expect that industry will be able to rescue herself from the oppression of capital when once the latter has firmly established its dominion. The contest is that of feebleness against power. It is the struggle of the horse against the rider. . . . Capital, when it has once got its legs round the neck of a nation, never loosens its hold till it has strangled its victim. It is only by a revolution in its state, by a new casting of its constitution that a people can ever escape from its thraldom " (p. 357). England is, indeed, on the eve either of a revolution or a total eclipse. The Napoleonic wars, with their legacy of a crushing national debt, funding system, paper commercialism, suppression of the old nobility in favour of a money aristocracy of low-bred upstarts and Jews, have infinitely aggravated her condition. " The struggle she is now making serves but to show her weakness. The weather-beaten hull of her commercial system still floats on the waves, . `. . but every scheme to relieve her distress has failed. The straining of her beams, the exhaustion of the pilot, explain but too clearly even to the most inexperienced passengers that if the wind should at all freshen, she must either throw overboard her cargo or perish in the storm " (p. 366).

What's to be done ? The remedy cannot be looked for in communism. A communist society is an artificial and over-governed society. Such a community can never be upheld but either by angels or by the strictest regulations and the most vigilant police. It is, in fact, a tyranny exercised by fanatics (pp. 196–7). But some may reply that men are improving and ever tending towards perfection. This is quite true, but communism depends for its success on a perfection of human character, which, if attained to, would bring men to the final term of their existence. " When the procession arrives at the temple of the gods, the victim without spot is offered on their altars " (*Funding System*, p. 51).

The most ordinary and most rational principle on which society can be formed is that which, leaving every man master of his own requirements, only puts forth the united strength of the community to check the encroachments which each individual may be disposed to make on the acquisitions of his neighbours. In order to enable the present society to re-arrange its affairs in conformity with that principle, the following measures appear to be required—Reduction of the national debt by taxing the income of the stockholders, taxation of profit, reduction of rents, abolition of indirect taxation, representation of Labour in Parliament. The rights of Labour will be neglected so long as the

s

working classes have no share in electing the House of Commons. People who live on rent, interest, and profit will never legislate for Labour. There is no reason to fear the influence of the people on legislation. The great body of the nation can never have an interest distinct from and opposed to that of the nation. It is a contradiction in terms. They cannot adopt a foolish measure without themselves feeling the consequences. The cry against democracy has no foundation in historical experience. If historians represent popular governments as turbulent, it is only because they have misapplied the term ; they have considered government as democratic which had no claim to that character. The republics of Greece were essentially aristocratic, for even the most popular of their constitutions was based on slavery. Rome had no pretension to be regarded as a democracy ; for though all had the right of voting, the mode in which their suffrage was given secured all power to the possessors of property. The constitutions of the Italian republics of the Middle Ages were still more objectionable. In short, experience does not speak against democracy, and reason is in favour of it. A Parliament consisting of a majority of men acknowledging the right of property, and labour as its source, will guard the nation against excessive wealth and excessive poverty. In securing to each the fruits of his labour they will not impede the production of wealth, but will correct the maldistribution of it. They will not allow capital to fasten itself on industry.

Such legislation involves changes in the economic constitution of present society. But change is inseparable from our condition ; it is a law of nature, from whose operation we cannot escape. All the works of creation are continually assuming new forms ; so rapid are the shiftings that the eye is scarcely fixed on their contemplation when already they appear other than they were.

It should also be remembered that, in the end, the greatest innovators are those who oppose timely reforms.

3.—THOMAS HODGSKIN

(a) His Activity and Principles.

Circumstances and temperament turned the young naval officer Thomas Hodgskin (1783–1869) into a social critic, and the books of Piercy Ravenstone gave him, for a time, an anti-capitalist direction.[1] He was, however, too original a thinker to be a mere populariser of Ravenstone. He studied the political economists, particularly Ricardo, whom he, at first (about 1820) misunderstood and disparaged, but afterwards regarded as " an ingenious and profound writer " (*Labour Defended*, p. 24). Besides Ravenstone and Ricardo, John Locke's natural rights doctrines, laid down in the famous treatise on *Civil Government*, exercised a lasting influence on his social speculations.

Hodgskin's part in the history of British socialist thought is not inconsiderable. He supplanted Bentham by Locke. Instead of the formula of happiness as the test and end of human institutions he emphasized the rights of nature and grounded his reasonings on the antithesis of natural and artificial rights of property. Although a friend of Francis Place, the Benthamite, who endeavoured to attach him to the Utilitarian circle, Hodgskin withstood all temptations, and reasoned in all matters concerning government and property in the sense of Locke. He was, further, one of the principal founders of the London Mechanics Institution[2] (1823), whose first director was Dr. George Birkbeck. And in that Institution, which was attended by the most active minds of the metropolitan mechanics and artisans, Hodgskin lectured on political economy and spread his anti-capitalist and natural rights philosophy. Some of these students became later the leaders of the Chartist Movement ; for instance, Lovett and Hetherington, to name only the most prominent. What George Mudie did for Owenism, Hodgskin

[1] For a biography of Thomas Hodgskin, based on original research, see Élie Halévy, *Thomas Hodgskin*, Paris, 1903. Ravenstone is mentioned by Hodgskin in *Popular Political Economy*, p. 77.

[2] Francis Place, Add. MSS. 27823 ; *Mechanics' Magazine*, June 16, 1827 ; *Mechanics' Weekly Journal*, 1823–4, p. 112.

accomplished for Ravenstone, Locke, and the anti-capitalist deductions from Ricardo. He transmitted the teachings of these pioneers to the British working classes who were soon to enter on one of their revolutionary periods.

Hodgskin's most active years were from 1820 to 1830 ; in this decade he wrote the pamphlet *Labour Defended Against the Claims of Capital, or the Unproductiveness of Capital Proved*, published anonymously in 1825 ; two years later, *Popular Political Economy*, based on his lectures delivered at the London Mechanics' Institution ; and, in 1832, he published anonymously *Natural and Artificial Right of Property Contrasted*, which had appeared, in 1829, in the shape of newspaper letters addressed to Henry Brougham. In February, 1833, he was still in touch with the Labour Movement and encouraged the editor of the *Poor Man's Guardian* in his journalistic exposition of the natural rights doctrines. And this is the last trace of his career as a popular agitator. He disappeared from the public scene at a moment when the working men, inspired by the doctrines of Owen and natural rights, organised themselves in huge federations and unfurled the banner of class warfare and social revolution.

(b) *His Labour Economics.*

Through the intercession of James Mill, the friend of the editor of the *Morning Chronicle*, Hodgskin was engaged, at the end of 1822, as reporter of that paper. His start was similar to that of Mudie. He soon came in contact with the metropolitan mechanics, took an interest in the struggle of Francis Place for the abrogation of the Combination Laws,[1] and attended the House of Commons in 1824-5, when the Bills concerning that subject were debated and passed. The speeches which Hodgskin heard were on the whole not favourable to the claims and prospects of the working classes. None the less, the repeal was carried through, and the forward movement of the working classes began. The rising spirit of Liberalism in the council of the nation undoubtedly accounts a good deal for this legislative measure in favour of the

[1] Graham Wallas, *Life of Francis Place*, chap. 8.

wage workers. The policy of concession in preference to force becomes from that time one of the main characteristics of the history of the relations between Liberalism and Labour. The idea of political equality, flowing from a purely doctrinal and humanitarian source, expresses itself in Parliamentary measures and softens the clash of antagonistic interests, which originates in field, factory, and mine, and finds its expression in trade unionist action. Hence it comes that the economic action of Labour, in passing through the atmosphere of Liberal Parliamentary politics, loses its revolutionary edge and temper. The hard-bargaining and unsentimental capitalist-employer becomes in Parliament a Liberal, and the revolutionary Labour leader, when elected to Parliament, turns into a reformer. This is the cause and source of the frictions between Labour in the workshop and Labour in Parliament. And this is the cause of the hatred of the ultra-conservative and the revolutionary against Liberalism. On the one hand, Liberalism facilitates the rise and movement of Labour, and is, therefore, hated and branded as subversive by Conservatives ; on the other hand, Liberalism prevents the rising and moving working classes from falling into the extremes of purely economic and revolutionary action, and is, therefore, hated and branded as hypocritical, by Revolutionists.

Hodgskin was, of course, unable to foresee this development, which required a century to mature. He reasoned on the basis of economics and cared little for politics. To him, all the Parliamentary debating proved but too clearly the irreconcilable opposition between capital and labour, as he was taught by the deductions from Ricardo's theory of value and wages, fortified by the doctrines of Ravenstone. In this mood and sense he wrote *Labour Defended*, one of the most aggressive and closely reasoned pamphlets of the labour and socialist movement.

Throughout the country, he declares, there rages at present a contest between capital and labour. The workmen of almost every trade have combined to obtain higher wages, and their employers have appealed to Parliament for protection. The contest will be decided not only by physical endurance, but by argument and reason.   To suggest some arguments in favour of labour and against capital, is the main purpose of the pamphlet.

The workman does not receive as wages the produce of his labour ; he only receives and has ever received as much as will enable him to subsist.   Although, by his increased skill and knowledge, he produces now probably ter times more than two centuries ago, he must be contented with the same reward as two centuries ago.   All the advantages of the improvement go to the capitalist and landlord. And when the workmen claim their share and combine in order to give weight to it, they are punished or regarded as a danger to the nation.   " Capital," says Mr. Huskisson, " will be terrified out of the country, and the misguided workmen, unless they are stopped in time, will bring ruin on themselves and on us."   And the Marquis of Lansdowne says, " Capital must be protected, else it will leave for some more favoured country." The political economists, like McCulloch, James Mill, and Malthus, hasten to confirm the surpassing importance of capital, and assert that without circulating and fixed capital no wealth could be produced.   Under the influence of such ideas Labour is forced back to its old position of a bare subsistence wage, and all the rest of the produce of labour goes to the capitalist under the name of profit and rent for the use of his capital (pp. 1–6). Capital thus appears to be a substance of some wonderful properties, considering the fact that it has so many advocates and that Labour pays so exorbitantly for it.

Let us see what it does, whether it does anything, or whether it has any independent existence at all.

Without circulating capital, or food and clothing, say the economists, the labourer could never engage in any undertaking which did not yield an almost immediate return.   The advantage, then, of circulating capital is that by it the labourer is enabled, he being assured of his present subsistence, to direct his power to the greatest advantage.   The fact, however, is that that assurance is not the effect of circulating capital, but of co-existing labour.   The capitalist does not possess any such stock of commodities necessary to feed and clothe the labourers.   He only possesses money or credit, by which he commands the labour of the poor, of whom one set of workers produces machinery and raw materials, and the other set produces food and clothing. This gives the employer as well as the employed the assurance that they will be fed and clothed. It is thus co-existing labour, and not circulating capital, which makes it possible for the labourer to bend his energies on the production of wealth (pp. 9–11). The labourer, having no stock of commodities, undertakes none the less to bring up his children and teach them some useful art, always relying on his own labour. And various classes of persons undertake tasks, the produce of which is not completed for a long period, relying likewise on the labour of other men to procure them in the mean time what they require for subsistence. All classes of men carry on their daily toils in the full confidence that while each is engaged in his particular occupation, some other will prepare whatever he requires, both for his immediate and future wants. Co-existing labour is a fundamental fact of social life, and is made use of by the capitalist to magnify his own importance. So much as to circulating capital.

Fixed capital consists of tools and instruments of labour, or means of production. But what produces these instruments, and in what degree do they aid production independent of the labourers, so that the owners of them are enabled to receive by far the greatest part of the whole produce of the country? Are they, or are they not produced by labour? Are they not so much inert, decaying matter, of no utility whatsoever, but as they are guided, directed, applied, and vitalized by skilful hands? It is admitted by the advocates of capital that fixed capital is the product of previous labour, and is entitled to profit on account of having been stored up or preserved or saved. But the manufacture of machinery, tools, and instruments is quite as uninterrupted and constant as that of food and clothing. They are not stored up, and are not intended to be so, but are brought into use, and the quicker they are brought into use the better for the capitalist, for only when used do they yield a profit. They are made solely for the use of the labourers, and directly they come into the hands of the labourers, they return or repay the sum they cost him, and over and above this the labourers must give him an additional sum corresponding to the prevailing rate of profit.   It is plainly not the previous creation which entitles them to profit, for most of them diminish in value by being kept in storage.   Fixed capital does not derive its utility from previous, but present labour ; and does not bring its owner a profit because it has been stored up, but because it is a means of obtaining a command over labour (p. 15).   The capitalist lends it to the labourers and they pay him a compound interest (p. 22).   To make the evil effect of capital more apparent let us take the following simple example :—

The real price of a coat, or a pair of shoes, or a loaf of bread— all that nature demands from man in order that he may have any of these necessary articles—is a certain quantity of labour. But, for the labourer to have either of these articles he must give over and above the quantity of labour which nature demands from him, a still larger quantity to the capitalist.   He must pay interest to the owner of the sheep, the buyer of the wool, the owner of the spinning mill, the owner of the weaving shed, the cloth-merchant, the master of the tailoring shop.   How much more labour the working man must give to have a coat, or a loaf of bread, than the coat or the loaf cost, is impossible to say, but it is probably six times more (p. 22).   Here is the source of evil, and not in taxation or Corn Laws ; these exactions do not concern the labourer ; they but diminish the profit of the capitalist, for if food and clothing are made dearer by reason of those exactions, the wages must rise, and profit and wages vary directly.   But no matter how great or small the taxes are, the labourer will have to pay the same quantity of labour for his loaf or coat.

Hodgskin, as we see, is of opinion that there is an iron law of wages, and all socialists or social critics who believe that law to be operative must needs reject all palliatives.   If the labourer receives no more than a mere subsistence wage it does not matter to him how high or low prices, taxes, and house rents are, for if they rise wages must also rise to the subsistence level ; and if they fall wages must also fall correspondingly   All reform agitation appears thus as an attempt to divert the working classes from their revolutionary aim of getting the whole produce of their labour, or abolishing the capitalists.

Hodgskin continues to say that the power of the capitalist is so great that he mobilizes the greatest part of the nation to hurl anathemas against the Corn Laws and imbue it with respect and awe for capital, the most injurious enemy of labour (pp. 22–3). The capitalist permits the labourers to have but the means of subsistence, because he cannot do without labour, contenting himself very generously with taking every particle of produce not absolutely necessary to that purpose. It is the overwhelming nature of the demands of capital, sanctioned by the laws of society, which keep, which have ever kept, and which will ever keep, as long as they are allowed and acquiesced in, the labourer in poverty and misery (p. 24).

And yet, capital, both circulating and fixed, has no independent existence. It is nothing but a cabalistic sign used by certain men to stultify the labouring masses in order the better to deprive them of their surplus produce.

For a nation to acquire wealth and to make good use of it, three things seem to be requisite. First, knowledge and ingenuity for inventing machines. Secondly, manual skill and dexterity for carrying these inventions into effect. Thirdly, skill and labour to use them after they had been made. All these requisites of genius, talent, and labour have been attributed with an extraordinary perversion of thought to fixed and circulating capital, in order to justify the existing order of society, which is founded on property or possessions, and oppression of the labourers who form unhappily part of these possessions. It is therefore evident that the interests of the capitalist, or master-manufacturer who performs no labour, are decidedly opposed to those of the labourers (pp. 17–19, 27).

How should this sort of distribution be righted? That the whole produce of labour ought to belong to the labourer is quite evident and true, but how to apply this principle in practice, is difficult to say. Each article is the result of combined labour, and no individual labourer can put his hand on any commodity and say that it was made by him only. It is hard to find a satisfactory principle or rule for dividing the produce of joint labour among the various individuals who concurred in its production, but the judgment of the individuals themselves ; that judgment, depending on the value men set on different species of labour, can never be known nor dictated. As well might we dictate to others what they shall like or hate. There is no other way of deciding but by leaving it to the unfettered judgment of the workmen themselves. If all kinds of labour were perfectly free, if no prejudice invested some parts with great honour, and branded other parts with disgrace, there would be no difficulty on this point, and the rewards of labour would be justly settled by competition or what Adam Smith calls the " higgling of the market " (p. 24-5). Our labourers possess already in a high degree the skill to execute, and they are acquiring also the skill to contrive ; they are forming Mechanics' Institutions, studying physical and moral science ; they will soon engage in the investigation of the problem, why they only, of all classes of the nation, have always been poor ; they will examine into the foundations of society and see whether they were laid in justice and are worth preservation. And it is certain that the contest between labour and capital will go on and ought to go on, that there will be neither peace on earth nor good will among men, until the triumph of labour is complete, until productive labour is rewarded with wealth and idleness with poverty, until he who sows shall reap, in short, until labour shall possess and enjoy the whole of its produce (pp. 29-33).

This is the substance of Hodgskin's pamphlet, which may be said to have been the Manifesto of British Labour in the memorable year 1825, the commencement of the organized and systematic struggle of the British working class, either in the form of large trades unions, or Chartism, or labour politics, co-operation and Socialism.

Hodgskin himself was no socialist. He preferred competition in the midst of institutions and opinions as free as man can form them. For this attitude he was taken to task by William Thompson, who regarded the difficulties which the author of *Labour*

Defended pointed out with regard to just distribution as a confession of failure. He, therefore, wrote *Labour Rewarded, or the Claims of Capital and Labour reconciled through Co-operation.* As a true Owenite he saw in competition one of the main sources of evil, and therefore, could not but scornfully reject the " higgling of the market " as a solution. He calls Hodgskin " my friend and fellow-labourer," with whose defence of the right of labour to the whole produce he fully concurs, saying that all the industrious " are indebted to him for the step he has made," but he tells him that, in adhering to individual competition, he is in bad company, since all the advocates of it are on the side of capital and against the claims of labour (*Labour Rewarded*, pp. 1, 5, 97).[1]

(c) *His Philosophy of History.*

The economic teachings contained in *Labour Defended* are further elaborated, and somewhat softened, in the *Popular Political Economy*, but the latter book includes also some speculations on the natural laws of human society or science of history, which are dealt with more comprehensively in *Natural and Artificial Right of Property contrasted.*

Society, according to these theories, is a natural phenomenon endowed by the Creator with laws which regulate it. The business of the political economist, or, as we should say to-day, the business of the sociologist, is to inquire into and ascertain these laws, and to warn against their being infringed. Were they acted upon by men, were their operation not impeded by human laws, the moral and material improvement of social conditions would have been much greater. For, the natural laws are beneficial, human laws a mere interference and injurious meddling.

The foundation of all national greatness is the increase of the people ; it renders division of labour possible, and promotes observation and knowledge, thus augmenting the productive forces in a compound ratio of the increase of labourers multiplied

[1] *Cf.* Karl Marx, *Theorien über Mehrwert*, 1910, III., pp. 313–80.

by the effects of division of labour and increase of knowledge. The increase of the people in this country within the last century, by creating a demand for agricultural produce, has led not merely to an extension of cultivation, to enclosures and breaking up of heaths, but also to improved agricultural processes. The growing wants of society act as a stimulus on the mind of the inventor— necessity is the mother of invention. The endeavour to trace the discoveries and inventions to natural laws does by no means detract from the merits of genius, it merely attempts to place him as a link in the endless chain of causation. For every individual has his character, sentiments, passions, thoughts, yea, even his intellect itself, fashioned by the time in which he lives and by the society of which he is a member. Every man is deeply indebted for whatever he possesses of knowledge, skill, inventive power to his present and past generations. Inventors and discoverers gather and accumulate within themselves the nascent truths, the products of numberless previous researches and improvements, and connect them by a comparatively small additional dis- covery or invention. Such minds arise naturally and necessarily from the general progress of knowledge and increase of human wants (*Pol. Econ.*, pp. 87–9).

Hodgskin, then, appears to regard increase of population, wants, knowledge, and inventions as the dynamic factors of human society.

The political organisation of society depends very largely on the mode in which property is distributed. Wherever the right of property is placed on a proper foundation, slavery, oppression, and legalised robbery cannot exist ; wherever this foundation is rotten, freedom cannot exist nor justice be administered. Economics precedes politics. Property makes laws, and not laws property. And this is the difference between Locke and Bentham. According to the former property was anterior to government ; it is a natural law that useful labour shall be rewarded with wealth. According to the Utilitarian, government or human laws make property. With Locke, the legislator's task is to prevent natural rights being transgressed, while the Utili- tarians deny the existence of natural laws and look to government to determine the welfare of mankind (*Nat. and Art. Right*, pp. 35, 42, 152).

In accepting Locke's theory of property, Hodgskin separates himself expressly from the Owenites and declares that he regards individual property as natural and essential to the welfare and existence of society (*Ib.*, pp. 35, 41).

Neither socialism, nor capitalism, but the natural right of the labourer to his whole produce, is the remedy. This natural right has been violated by human legislation. Legislation has originally been founded in conquest, and it has ever continued in utter ignorance of its results. It is hostile to the course of nature. Who are the law-makers ? Men who do not labour ; the law is actually made by those who derive from nature no title whatever to any wealth (*Ib.*, pp. 63–7). Laws are always made by others than labourers, and are intended to preserve the power of those who make them, or to enable them to appropriate wealth to themselves. The law-makers are the landed aristocracy, the bishops, and the capitalists, or rent, tithes, and profits. To this violation of the natural right of property, to this creation of the artificial right of property we owe most of our social miseries, and as long as plunder and oppression last, there will be misery, fraud, mistrust, crime, and murder.

Who will make an end to the artificial right and restore the natural right of property ?

Hodgskin's reply is rather halting and contradictory. In *Labour Defended* he attributed that mission to the working-classes. In his *Natural and Artificial Right* he thinks it will be the middle-classes who will accomplish it. At any rate, it will not be done by law-makers. All real progress to freedom has been caused by the development of history and forced on the law-makers. Hodgskin may have meant that progress was effected by a sort of re-assertion of the outraged divine-natural laws. In attempting to explain his meaning he gives a short and very fragmentary outline of the stages of historical development. He begins by putting the question, " Who brought the capitalists to power ? " The law-makers ? No, for they upheld the landed interests against the monied interests. " It came about by itself." The changes form an interesting part of the history of civilisation. When feudalism weakened, the serf gradually outgrew his bondage, ceased to be the property of the warrior noble, and acquired a right of property in what he created. The capitalist then emerged into notice and, obtaining from the landlord interest and profit on his property, shared his power. Now we find that a large middle class, completely emancipated from bondage and destitution, has grown up in every part of Europe, uniting in their own persons the character both of labourers and capitalists. They are fast increasing in numbers, and we may hope that, as the beautiful inventions gradually supersede unskilled labour, they will gradually reduce the whole society to equal and free men, and extinguish all that still remains of slavery and oppression. Changes are going on which are over-throwing injustice. All these changes are sometimes attributed to the discovery of America, the rounding of the Cape of Good Hope, the sagacity or rulers and philosophers, or to any thing else rather than to the divine government of the moral world.

IX

SOCIAL CONSERVATIVE CRITICS

I.—COLERIDGEAN INFLUENCES

SEVEN years after Edmund Burke, in his *Reflections on the Revolution in France*, had defended the organic view against the mechanical conception of society, and two years after Erasmus Darwin, in his *Zoonomia*, had laid the foundation of the evolutionary view of nature, the German philosopher, F. W. J. Schelling, in his *Ideen zu einer Philosophie der Natur* (1797), began to spread in his country the concept of organism, the inner growth and connection of living matter as opposed to the mechanical atomism, and gradual evolution in opposition to sudden creation. The same thoughts, which, in England, had a historical and a scientific setting, assumed in Germany a mystical appearance and an idealistic meaning. It was no longer nations that developed organically their institutions, nor nature that evolved from stage to stage to higher forms, but the Absolute who in ceaseless productivity brought forth natural formations and historical periods. Nature was the Odyssey of the Absolute, and History His epic poem. Religion, tradition, intuition, and mysticism gradually gained predominance over sober science, critical reason, and logical prose.

The rapid transition from the liberal philosophy of Kant and the national socialism of Fichte to the romanticism of Schelling was the effect of reaction against and dire disappointment with the course of the French Revolution. The intellects of Germany, who had hailed the storming of the Bastille and the victory at Valmy as the dawn of human freedom, who had expected external actions and spectacular dramas to bring salvation to humanity, now immersed their minds in the inner depths of things and looked inwardly to the eternal forces which, inscrutable to the reason of man, mould and govern this infinite Universe.

Coleridge, who had gone through similar mental experiences, visited Germany at the time when that transition took place. He at once felt its vibrations and remained all his life in harmony with them. And, like Schelling, who never succeeded in formulating a systematic philosophy of history, Coleridge never did go beyond enunciating religio-philosophical aphorisms, which since about 1820 began to attract the inquiring minds of the British youth ; since about 1820—the same date when Owen's co-operative schemes and the anti-capitalist economics began to find adherents. Thomas Carlyle has left us a short sketch of this period of Coleridge's life. He relates : " Coleridge sat on the brow of Highgate Hill, in those years, looking down on London and its smoke-tumult . . . attracting towards him the thoughts of innumerable brave souls still engaged there. His express contributions to poetry, philosophy, or any specific province of human literature or enlightenment had been small and sadly intermittent ; but he had, especially among young inquiring men, a higher than literary, a kind of prophetic or magician's character. . . . The practical intellects of the world did not much heed him, or carelessly reckoned him a metaphysical dreamer ; but to the rising spirits of the young generation he had this dusky sublime character ; and sat there as a kind of Magus, girt in mystery and enigma, . . . his Dodona oak-grove whispering strange things, uncertain whether oracles or jargon." [1]

But while Carlyle goes on entertaining his readers with Coleridge's " sum-m-jects " and " om-m-jects," a far superior thinker, John Stuart Mill, tells us the real reason of Coleridge's attraction. The awakening of the spirit of philosophy and of inquiry into the laws of human existence and the growth of society, was the work of the Germano-Coleridgean school. " This doctrine expresses the revolt of the human mind against the philosophy of the eighteenth century. . . . They were the first who inquired, with any comprehensiveness and depth, into the

[1] Thomas Carlyle, *Life of John Sterling*, I., chap. 8.

inductive laws of the existence and growth of human society. . . . They thus produced not a piece of party advocacy, but a philosophy of society, in the only form which is yet possible, that of a philosophy of history. The brilliant light which had been thrown upon history during the last half century, has proceeded almost wholly from this school. The disrespect in which history was held by the Encyclopædists is notorious ; one of the soberest of them, D'Alembert, we believe, was the author of the wish that all records whatsoever of past events could be blotted out."[1]

This Germano-Coleridgean school brought the political and philosophic thought of England in touch with socialistic schools and the aspirations of the masses, either by leading men's minds back to the pre-individualistic times when society was organised in corporate bodies with special responsibilities towards their members, or by turning the attention of the possessing and ruling classes to the social ethics of Christianity, or by showing history to be a long and continuous process of the development of social institutions, in which the concept of property and the relation of the classes changed, and have been changing from period to period. It taught men that such laws as those of supply and demand, wages, capital, and other economic categories were by no means eternal and immutable, nor was their absolute rule desirable. Finally, it induced some of the noblest spirits of the nation to look at Chartism as not a mere rebellion of drunken helots to be ruthlessly suppressed by bullets and gallows.

Coleridge inspired Frederick Denison Maurice, later the guide and philosopher of Christian Socialism, particularly of Charles Kingsley. And Cardinal Newman, in his controversy with Kingsley, relates that the "Oxford Movement," too, owed much to Coleridge, who, "after all, instilled a higher philosophy into inquiring minds than they had hitherto been accustomed to accept. In this way he made trial of his age, and succeeded in interesting its genius in the cause of Catholic truth."[2] Hurrell Froude, one of the founders of that Move-

---

[1] J. S. Mill, *Dissertations*, I., article Coleridge ; *Autobiography*, 1873, pp. 160–2.

[2] J. H. Newman, *Apologia*, 1864, p. 185-6.

T

ment, undoubtedly read Coleridge; his poem " Farewell to
Toryism " is distinctly Coleridgean.[1]   And there was much
social reform and even democratic sentiment among its
leaders.[2]

These were the influences of Coleridge. But he has left no
book which would give an adequate summary of those teachings.
The nearest approach to such a book is his *Constitution of Church
and State* (1830), which, besides a trenchant criticism of utilitarian
liberalism, contains some of his views of an ideal commonwealth.
He desired to see an English realm, " where the integral parts,
classes, or orders are so balanced, or inter-dependent, as to constitute, more or less, a moral unit, an organic whole."   The landed
interests, or the principle of permanence and law, should work
harmoniously with the monied interests, or the principle of progression and freedom.   The possessions of both orders, taken
collectively, should form the Property (pp. 117–18), which must be
connected with especial duties and should be regarded as a trust
rather than as arbitrary and unconditional ownership (p. 45).
The Church should comprise the whole scholarship and the
educators of the nation, which means, that the arts and sciences
should be headed by theology.   In short, his ideal commonwealth
was a nation ruled by the spirit and letter of Christianity.   Only
in such a State will the conquests made by reason redound to the
moral benefit of the nation.   To-day reason governs in opposition
to Christianity.   And what are the results ?   " My eye at this
moment rests on a volume newly read by me, containing a well-
written history of the inventions, discoveries, public improvements, docks, railways, canals. . . .   We live, I exclaimed,
under the dynasty of Understanding : and this is the golden age.
It is the faculty of means to medial ends.   With these the age,
this favoured land, teems ; they spring up, the armed host,
from the serpent's teeth sown by Cadmus. . . .   Sea and
land, rock, mountains, lake and moor, yea, nature and all her
elements, sink before them, or yield themselves captive !   But
the ultimate ends ? . . .

[1] R. Hurrell Froude, *Remains*, I., p. 429.
[2] *Ib.*, p. 312.

> O voice, once heard
> Delightfully, increase and multiply !
> Now death to hear ! For what can we increase
> Or multiply, but woe, crime, penury.

. . . We have game laws, corn laws, cotton factories, Spitalfields, the tillers of the land paid by poor rates, and the remainder
of the population mechanised into engines for the manufactory of
new rich men ; yea, the machinery of the wealth of the nation
made up of the wretchedness, disease, and depravity of those who
should constitute the strength of the nation " (pp. 63–7). The
history of a century of wealth-making is a history of vulgarisation of thought and politics : " The mechanico-corpuscular
theory raised to the title of the mechanic philosophy. . . . A
state of nature, or the Ourang Outang theology of the origin of
the human race, substituted for the first ten chapters of the Book
of Genesis. . . . Our state-policy a Cyclops with one eye,
and that in the back of the head ; our measures become either
a series of anachronisms, or a truckling to events. . . . Meantime, the true historical feeling, the immortal life of the nation,
generation linked to generation by faith, freedom, heraldry, and
ancestral fame, languishing and giving place to the superstitions
of wealth and newspaper reputation. Talents without genius ;
a swarm of clever, well-informed men : an anarchy of minds, a
despotism of maxims. Hence despotism of finance in government
and legislation. . . . and hardness of heart in political
economy." And he saw " government by clubs of journeymen ;
by saint and sinner societies, committees, institutions ; by reviews, magazines, and above all by newspapers " (pp. 67–70).
The cure for this vulgarisation and anarchy is religion, moral
discipline—Christian ethics and faith.

2.—SOUTHEY'S PROSPECTS OF SOCIETY

While Coleridge was thundering against the mechanisation of
the country and creating an anti-liberal phraseology which made
the fortune of many an anti-capitalist writer after him, Southey
was communing with the spirit of Sir Thomas More on the evils
of the time. The trend of conservative and religious minds to-

wards mediaevalism became pronounced, as it always will in
Christian countries in times of spiritual and social anarchy, or
after a surfeit at the feasts of reason and materialist conceptions
of nature and life. The great European minds have, since the
Renascence, been oscillating between Olympus and Golgotha,
moving to and fro in search either of happiness or redemption.
According to Cardinal Newman also Southey contributed much
to the stock of ideas and sentiments that led to the Oxford
Movement.

Both Sir Thomas More and Robert Southey speculated in
the joy and freedom of their younger years upon the possible
improvement of society ; and both in like manner lived to dread
the effects of that restless spirit which insults Heaven and disturbs
the earth. In the eyes of Southey, the nineteenth century exhibited characteristics similar to those of the age of the Reformation, and he thought to hear the voice of the author of *Utopia*,
saying, " By comparing the great operating causes in the age of
the Reformation, and in this age of revolutions, going back to the
former age, looking at things as I then beheld them, perceiving
wherein I judged rightly and wherein I erred, and tracing the
progress of those causes which are now developing their whole
tremendous power, you will derive instruction " (*Sir Thomas
More, or Colloquies*, I., p. 19).

To him, as the representative of Catholicism who could not
believe in the salvation of any Protestant nation, is assigned
the part of the social critic, while Southey himself represents the
optimistic social reformer who believes in the moral and material
progress of man. Sir Thomas warns him against short cuts to
the Millennium, for this has always " been the ruling fancy of the
most dangerous of all madmen " (p. 34). And there is hardly.
anything in the present age to warrant such a belief. " The
prevailing opinions of this age go to the destruction of everything that has hitherto been held sacred. They tend to arm the
poor against the rich ; the many against the few ; worse than
this, for it will also be a war of hope and enterprise against
timidity, of youth against age. . . . You surely do not expect
that the Millennium is to be brought about by the triumph of

what are called liberal opinions ; nor by enabling the whole of the lower classes to read the incentives to vice, impiety and rebellion, which are prepared for them by an unlicensed press " (p. 35). But, even granted that there is now more knowledge and more wealth in England than there was in former times, surely there is also less wisdom and less happiness. Finally, Southey accepts the assumption that the condition of the labouring classes was, perhaps, better in the age of More " than it ever has been either before or after. The feudal system had well-nigh lost all its inhuman parts, and the worse inhumanity of the commercial system had not yet shown itself." To which More rejoins that " it was, indeed, a most important age in English history, and till the Reformation so fearfully disturbed it, in many respects a happy and an enviable one. But the process was then beginning, which is not yet completed."

This remark gives Southey the occasion to present the Catholic view of the social development of English history from the Reformation to the first quarter of the nineteenth century, in which the Factory system took its rise. On this point both More and Southey are at one in condemning it, but they differ as to its origin. Southey is of opinion that " it has been the growth of circumstances, not a system fore-planned, foreseen and deliberately chosen. Such as it is we have inherited it, or rather have fallen into it, and must get out of it as well as we can. We must do our best to remove its evils, and to mitigate them while they last, and to modify and reduce it till only so much remains as is indispensable for the general good." More, however, replies : " The fact will not warrant you in saying that it has come upon the country unsought and unforeseen. You have prided yourselves upon this system, you have used every means for extending it ; you have made it the measure of your national prosperity. It is a wen, a fungous excrescence from the body politic ; the growth might have been checked if the consequences had been apprehended in time ; but now it has acquired so great a bulk . . . that to remove it by absorption is impossible, and excision would be fatal " (pp. 171–2). Fraud and gamble have taken the place of work and wealth. Paper notes, stock, and the funding system, or the so-called securities, have rendered the whole system insecure. It is but certain that the poverty of one part of the people seems to increase in the same ratio as the riches of another part. This is the effect of competition. Every man oppresses his neighbour ; the landlord racks his tenant ; the farmer grinds the labourer ; great capitalists ruin the small traders,—like pikes in a pond which devour the weaker fish. There is no stability anywhere. A nation on the move—from village to town, from town to oversea countries. The great majority of these poor people are willing to work, to go anywhere where they may be able to provide for themselves. Whatever means may be devised for their benefit, they are ready to co-operate, and perform their part. They can dig and sow, weave and spin, forge and mould iron and steel, make bricks and build houses. But how they should be set to work, how the beginning should be made, is what we must not expect to learn from any professor of political economy. And Sir Thomas More adds : " The wisdom of the heart is wanting there. Statesmen . . . have not yet had faith enough in goodness to believe in the moral miracles which benevolence and zeal are able to perform ! If at any time they have entertained a serious wish for bettering the condition of their fellow-creatures, the difficulties which they see before them have appeared like mountains in the way ; and yet, had they faith but as a grain of mustard seed, these mountains might be removed. There is abundant room in this country and its colonies for any possible increase of population till the end of time ! Only let the poor be placed where they may ' labour for that which satisfieth,' and ' the earth will give seed to the sower and bread to the eater—they shall build houses and inhabit them ; and the solitary place shall be glad, and the desert shall rejoice ' " (II., pp. 263–5).

Meanwhile the evil is growing and the revolution is spreading. Society has its critical periods, its climacterics. The present age is a critical one. " A new principle, a *novum organum* has been introduced, the most powerful that has ever yet been wielded by man. If it was first *Mitrum* that governed the world, and then

Nitrum, both have had their say—gunpowder as well as the triple crown. Steam will govern the world next, and shake it too before its empire is established " (I., p. 199).

And the shake came in the form of Chartism, the first social-democratic and revolutionary movement of the British working classes as the pioneers of European and American Labour. Southey heard their tramp and the voices of their commanders. Austin, then a famous jurist, lecturing in 1829 on the condition of England, complained that the working classes were not favourable to the system of private property. And two years later the London artisans were taught that " Property is the cause of all evils. Create it not ; make it but sufficient for yourselves— and that not to possess it, but to enjoy it. . . . No personal liberty or happiness for the people can exist until at least there is no individual property in the soil."[1]

[1] *Poor Man's Guardian*, June 4, August 20, 1831. *Cf.* Graham Wallas, *Life of Francis Place*, p. 274, for similar views expressed by London artisans in 1831.

X

THE BIRTH OF CHARTISM

I.—ESSENCE, AIM, AND NAME

THE two currents of social economic thought generated and developed by the school of Owen and the anti-capitalist criticism reached, in the years from 1825 onwards, the thinking portion of the British working class and created Chartism, which constituted a series of social revolutionary attempts to re-organise the United Kingdom on a socialist and labour basis. This movement assumed gradually national proportions, and was in full activity in the second quarter of the nineteenth century, but it was only in the year 1838 that it received the name " Chartism," which merely signifies democratic parliamentary reform. The name, like that of many of the great movements and parties of the United Kingdom, does not cover, either chronologically or intrinsically, the history and essence of this movement. The years 1825 to 1830 were the period of its incubation ; from 1831 to the end of 1834 it developed its theories and exhibited great intellectual vigour ; from 1837 to 1842 it received, as far as the Corresponding Act permitted, its practical and organised form ; and from 1849 onwards its vitality was rapidly ebbing away and it died in 1855, leaving only here and there scattered stragglers who obstinately refused to believe that Chartism was extinct. Its theories, traditions, and legacies were either taken up by continental socialists, like Karl Marx and Frederick Engels, who, ten years later, formed the International Working Men's Association, or by the co-operators and trade unionists of Great Britain, who transformed them according to their education and experience.

Chartism, in its essence and aim, resembled the international socialist and labour movement of the present day. But, having had no precedent to be guided by, and, indeed, forming a kind of socialist seminary and an experimental laboratory of working-class revolution, it was deficient in coherence of thought and systematic policy. It presents itself as an elemental class-war, rising and falling in curves between enthusiastic upheavals and apathetic inertia, between riotously profuse creations of ingenious ideas and pitiful relapses into barren and obsolete theories ; only its immediate aim—the conquest of political power— appears to have been grasped with unmistakable distinctness and energy, but owing to lack of a national organisation and popular education it was impossible for it to become a permanent and victorious movement. To the eye of the historian it takes the form of a pioneer movement of socialists and masses of work-men—a valiant and desperate contest for the material, moral, and intellectual uplifting of Labour. From its experimental and, on the whole, practical character it follows also that there could be no uniformity of opinion as to the ultimate shape of the social revolution and social reconstruction. During its theoretical period (1831–34) illuminating ideas flashed out with meteoric suddenness and disappeared just as abruptly, leaving scarce a trace behind ; and even to the present day doubts, erroneous assumptions, and misunderstandings are still prevalent with regard to the originators and the import of their ideas. And during the practical period (1837–49) theoretical discussions were not favoured, lest they should be a hindrance in the struggle for the immediate aim—to seize the reins of government as quickly as possible : " Peaceably if we may—forcibly if we must."

As already indicated, the ultimate socialist aim was not estab-lished with unanimity. A judgment on this point can only be formed by a study of Chartist newspapers and pamphlets, and of their intellectual sources and ramifications. There were three lines of policy in the question of the ultimate aim : one was communistic and parliamentary, at any rate up to the year 1845, until the disastrous break-up of Queenwood, the last Owenite colony ; it strove for political power in order to trans-form Great Britain into a certain number of communist colonies ; and with its adherents the question of the common ownership of the land took precedence of every other consideration. This line of policy dominated among the working classes of the North of England. The second was, indeed, Owenite in its critical attitude to social problems, but it aspired after political power in order to utilise it for paving the way for social reform, for trades unionism and the political organisation, education and enlightenment of the working classes, so as to fit them for reforming the country in a socialistic sense. These were the ideas which centred in the intellectual working men of London and Scotland, who probably did not form more than ten per cent. of the British working classes. The third line of policy was in the direction of trades unions, and adhered to the theory of natural rights, viz. that the workman should receive the full produce of his labour, and in actual practice made the demand : " A fair wage for a fair day's work." A sharp separation of these lines of policy was never attained. Excepting for the years 1833 and 1834, in which economic action in the syndicalist sense was most strongly marked, the organised workers and the Chartists were of opinion that the fundamental condition for emancipation from wage slavery lay in the conquest of political power, and that therefore all their energies ought to be concentrated on this purpose. The parliamentary and democratic idea dominated the movement so completely as to give it its name. The movement received the name Chartism from its democratic programme : the People's Charter, which was originated in the year 1837 to 1838 by the London Working Men's Association, and was drawn up by the joiner, William Lovett. The People's Charter was nothing more than a plain and clearly written Bill, containing the following six points in the form of sections and paragraphs : (1) Universal Suffrage, (2) Equal Electoral Districts, (3) Abolition of Property Qualifications for parliamentary candidates, (4) Annual Parliaments, (5) Ballot, (6) Payment of Members of Parliament.

2. STAGES OF DEVELOPMENT

Chartism, as a collective term for the revolutionary struggle of the British working class, passed through several stages, as already stated in the preceding section. The years 1825 to 1830 formed its period of incubation. They were years in which Great Britain cast off its agricultural character, and passed over to industrialism on a large scale. To the revolution in production was added that in commerce and transport. Through the repeal of the Bubble Act (1719) in the year 1825, capital could henceforth form joint-stock companies and inaugurate the era of extensive and collective enterprise which revolutionised commence and transports. The middle classes became intoxicated with the prospect of infinite possibilities ; and it flashed upon the working men that, as a class, they played a more indispensable part even than capital in the process of production. At the same time the operatives gained the depressing conviction that there was no possibility of their ever becoming capitalists themselves ; they saw the vast scale of industrial production, with which no independent craftsman could compete. The middle classes hastened towards their political victory, the working classes began their class war. This great transition period was depicted by a Conservative writer in 1826 in a naïve yet broad and fascinating manner :

" The age which now discloses itself to our view promises to be the age of industry, to which no monarch shall affix his name —it shall be called the age of comfort to the poor,—if the phrase had not been so ill applied of late, we should say—the age of the People. By industry alliances shall be dictated and national friendships shall be formed. . . . The prospects which are now opening to England almost exceed the boundaries of thought ; and can be measured by no standard found in history. . . . The manufacturing industry of England may be fairly computed as four times greater than that of all the other continents taken collectively, and sixteen such continents as Europe could not manufacture so much cotton as England does. . . ."[1]

At the same time the working classes appeared upon the stage of history, self-conscious economically, but with hesitation from a political point of view. The following declarations are charac-

[1] *Quarterly Review*, June to August, 1826, pp. 92–99. *Cf.* also Ure, *Philosophy of Manufacture*, Introduction.

teristic of this appearance. A meeting of the unemployed in
Leeds, passed the following resolution on November 23, 1829[1] :—

" We, the Operatives, by no means wish to assume a situation
that does not belong to us, yet we are well aware that labour is
the only source of wealth, and that we are the support of the
middle and higher classes of society."

The first political weekly newspaper of the working classes of
Lancashire announced in its programme :

" Labour is the source of wealth ; the working men are the
support of the middle and upper classes ; they are the nerves
and soul of the process of production, and therefore of the
nation."[2]

The same paper, however, declared at the same time for
joint political action with the Liberals.

On the other hand they were taught that " the natural tendency
of wealth " was " for the rich to become richer, and for the poor
to become poorer.   Trade carried out on a large scale has driven
out trade on a small scale.   The result is that a large proportion
of the community has to depend on their labour only, whilst
machinery is superseding labour. . . . The effect of wealth
is to divide society into classes, between whom the distance is
so great that they have lost touch with each other, and are in
danger of becoming enemies to each other." [3]

The first result of this knowledge was that from a trade unionist
point of view the workmen strove for comprehensive class-
organisations, but politically for an alliance with the middle
classes.   In the years 1830 to 1832, when the struggle for the
Reform Bill was raging, the workers for the greater part marched
as allies of the middle classes.

The alliance between the working and the middle classes was
the first stage of Chartism.   But already during this period of
alliance there was a small minority of workers who defended the
standpoint of class-war with extreme acrimony, and were opposed

[1] *Leeds Patriot*, November 29, 1829.
[2] *Voice of the People*, Manchester, January 1, 1831.
[3] *Sheffield Courier*, quoted by the *Midland Representative*, September 17, 1831.   The latter paper was edited by Bronterre O'Brien.

to every alliance with the middle classes. Regardless of consequences, they transferred the economic antagonism of the middle and working classes into the political arena and pointed with inexorable logic to the fact that labour and capital must always remain irreconcilable opponents. This minority existed in London ; its organisation was the " National Union of the Working Classes," and its paper was the *Poor Man's Guardian*. This remarkable organ was one of the first unstamped newspapers ; it appeared first of all as *Penny Papers for the People*, from October 1, 1830, to the end of December, 1830 ; then it received the sub-title, *By the Poor Man's Guardian ;* from July 9, 1831, until it ceased on December 25, 1835, it appeared as the *Poor Man's Guardian*. It refused to pay the newspaper stamp. " Unstamped " at that time meant the same thing as illegal. By reason of the " Six Acts " of the year 1819 every periodical which published news had to pay a stamp-tax of fourpence a copy, and since paper was also burdened with a high tax and the publisher had to give security, the publication of a newspaper involved heavy expenses. The stamped papers could not be sold at less than sevenpence a copy,—a price which only few working men could pay. Henry Hetherington, the publisher of the *Poor Man's Guardian*, defied the law and published the paper at the price of one penny. Below the heading of every number was the announcement : " Established contrary to Law to try the power of Might against Right." The editor of the *Poor Man's Guardian* was after the middle of 1831 or the beginning of 1832, Bronterre O'Brien. Most of the social-revolutionary thinkers of those years contributed either anonymously or under a pseudonym to the paper, and made it an arsenal of revolutionary ideas. Among the anonymous contributors there was one who championed the idea of class-war with a determination which few followers of Marx could have surpassed. For a long time the articles of the anonymous correspondent were ascribed to the editor, but it will be pointed out later on that they proceeded from the pen of a self-educated weaver, most probably a hand-loom weaver, who had been ruined by machinery. He hurled polemics against the alliance between the working and middle classes. The best of his articles were reprinted later on as standard documents. They initiated the schism between the workers and the middle class ; they made a profound impression upon the thinkers of the working class of Great Britain.

At the same time the idea of a general strike came into being ; a London shoemaker, publisher and coffee-house proprietor, called William Benbow, gave expression to it in a pamphlet that appeared in January, 1832. Benbow likewise belonged to the minority which rallied round the *Poor Man's Guardian* and the National Union.

Finally, Owen in 1831 took up an attitude to parliamentary action which not only signified disdain, but even contempt and abhorrence.

The combined effect of these influences became all the stronger from the fact that the Reform Bill, which had become law after a year of violent conflict, agitating the whole country, left the workers as unenfranchised as before. The working class which had to a great extent furnished the physical energy for the movement of reform came away with empty hands.

Disappointed and embittered by the negative result of the agitation for reform ; their self-consciousness strengthened by the help they had given to the middle classes ; influenced by the class-war idea of the anonymous weaver, by the general strike advocated by Benbow and by Owen's anti-parliamentary attitude, the organised working class turned syndicalistic. The tempestuous course of the class-war idea and of direct economic action not only swept away all notions of the solidarity of the classes or of alliances between them, but, at least for two years, it destroyed all ideas of parliamentary action or of democratic parliamentary reform. The organised workers became revolutionary and anti-parliamentary, and hoped for everything from the direct economic action of the masses. This period embraced the year 1832 to 1834 ; it formed the second stage in the history of the growth of Chartism ; its characteristic was *Syndicalism*. At this stage of development strenuous intellectual efforts were made to emerge from the socialism of natural rights, to make an end to Utopian experiments and to form a conception of history based on class-war and evolution, in short, to accomplish what Karl Marx took in hand ten years later. In 1833 discussions took place in English working men's clubs about the descent of man from the animal kingdom, or as it was called at that time : the Simian theory.[1] And a year later the *Pioneer and Official Gazette* (September 20, 1834),[2] the organ of the revolutionary trades unions, published an essay which pointed out that class-war is the necessary consequence of the natural evolution of Society from capitalism to socialism, and that it heralds in the growth of a new form of society. The intellectual history of this period has remained unknown to the present time. It is essentially the history of the separation of the workers from orthodox Owenism. Its documents lie scattered in the weeklies, the *Crisis, Pioneer,* and *Pioneer and Official Gazette.* But at that time no thinker arose to strike the intellectual balance of those remarkable years. In the summer of 1834 British syndicalism broke down, and at the same time its mental activity sank into complete oblivion. However, mental struggles are never wholly fruitless. Even if their results are only appreciated by posterity, yet they also furnish their contemporaries with suggestions and ideas which are turned to good use for future progress. This, indeed, was the case in Great Britain in the years subsequent to 1834, when social reform, trades unionism, and parliamentary action became re-united. Only the orthodox Owenites remained as sectarian independents, and they were known at that time as socialists, and were few in number. The gist of the contests and discussions of the years 1825 to 1835 consisted of the following declarations :

The workers form a class whose interests are opposed to those of all the other classes ; their ultimate emancipation can only be obtained by a revolution in the socialist sense ; the means for this purpose is to seize political power. The embodiment of these

---

[1] *Crisis*, September 28, 1833.

[2] Only one number of this weekly journal has been preserved. All that we know about it otherwise occurs only in extracts printed by the *Poor Man's Guardian* in August, 1834.

ideas constitutes Chartism from 1837 onwards.[1] The struggles, disappointments, Owenite experiments and syndicalist efforts which preceded it were the cause of the last stage of Chartism assuming in the main the character of *independent parliamentary action*. In addition to these principal causes the following secondary causes were contributory, viz. the dissatisfaction with the Poor Law of 1834 in the North of England, and the demand for factory legislation for the protection of women and children.

3.—ORGANISATION AND DOCTRINE

From 1837 onwards Chartism became a movement of the masses, a revolutionary struggle implying many a sacrifice, for the purpose of seizing political power. It suffered, however, up to the very last from the following weak points : the impossibility of conferring upon the masses a firm and unified organisation, since the Corresponding Act (1817) did not permit of founding a national organisation with branch societies. The Chartists were only allowed to form local societies, but not to enter into union with each other. This led sometimes to the formation of secret leagues, which only caused the government spies to promote existing insurrectionary tendencies, and to bring the Chartists to trial for high treason, and resulted in heavy sacrifices. As a rule the leaders and the speakers were the connecting links between the local organisations. On this account such a preponderating part in the movement fell to the share of the leaders that it would hardly be possible to write a history of Chartism without a thorough study of the life-histories of the leaders and of the trend of their thoughts. The leaders and speakers were, however, only human, and afflicted with human weaknesses. Disunion in their ranks implied the splitting and breaking up of the Chartist societies, the formation of cliques and hero-worship, which raised serious difficulties in the way of any well-organised progress of the Chartists on a large scale.

The other source of weakness lay in a relapse into the historical

---

[1] These ideas were later secured for Socialism by Engels and Marx. Both expected great things from this movement, if not from its leaders. *Cf. infra* XIII. 2 ; also the *Northern Star*, December 4, 1847.

conception of natural law. The following are a few characteristic extracts and references on the subject, occurring in the authoritative organs and documents of Chartism :

" We base our demands upon natural equity : All men are equal and can demand equal rights and liberties.[1]

" A receipt for making eye-water for the benefit of Englishmen, Irishmen and Scotchmen : Take of the Law of Nature, 6 drams ; of the Rights of Man, 4 drams ; of Reason, 3 drams ; of Agrarian Justice, 5 drams ; of Commonsense, ½ grain. Mix them up in the Cup of Liberty."[2]

" The abstract political rights of man are founded on natural and moral justice. All presumed rights not founded on the above are usurpations. . . . Every community has a right to be governed by the concentrated wisdom and intelligence of its members."[3]

Even a Tory and Social Reformer, like Richard Oastler, exclaimed :

" Every man born in England has a natural right to live well in England. It is a law of nature and a law of God that the husbandman that laboureth must be the first partaker of the fruit."[4]

The central organ of the Chartists treated the law of nature almost from the commencement as the foundation-stone of the movement.[5] All the great manifestoes of Chartism, e.g., the Declaration of Rights of 1831 and 1839, the three petitions of the Chartists of 1839, 1842, and 1848, refer to the law of nature as the irrefutable proof of the justice of their democratic demands. The leading spirits of Chartism : O'Brien, O'Connor, Lovett, M'Douall, always had recourse to the law of nature as the source of their knowledge and action. And most of the Chartist speeches for the defence on the trials for high treason in 1839 and 1840 bore the impress of the law of nature.

[1] *Poor Man's Guardian* (Penny Paper), May 26, 1831.
[2] *Ibid.*, January 12, 1833. The names of the specified ingredients are the titles of Thomas Paine's works.
[3] *Carpenter's Monthly Political Magazine*, February, 1832, p. 229.
[4] *Poor Man's Guardian*, August 15, 1835.
[5] *Northern Star*, May 14, 1842.

U

The whole trend of Chartist thought was dominated by the idea that the weal and woe of society depends in the last resort upon the character of the laws of the State. The law can build up and destroy, can both heal and wound. With the exception of the germinating idea of evolution in history in the year 1834 Chartism lacked the faintest trace of any insight into the growth and decay of right and law, or the dependence of legislators upon social forces and changes. And this insight is of necessity absent in adherents of the law of nature. According to this conception of history it was originally men who, after having made a social contract, promulgated laws, because they enjoyed sovereign power. Simply by human decrees corporate society and private property were brought into being. Subsequently a single individual or a small minority of men made the laws after having usurped the sovereign power. But what is the essential nature of sovereignty ? What enables it to produce revolutions wholesale ? What is it that enables it quite arbitrarily either to further the common weal or to degrade the masses ? To these questions the law of nature gives the answer, Force. Whoever possesses force exercises sovereign power and can make laws at will. Force, sovereignty, and legislation form, according to natural law, the Trinity of the State, all-powerful and absolute : it can change public property into private property, or private property into public property, or can mould society into any form it likes.[1] Accordingly, the main object of revolutionaries and reformers must be to obtain power. If they possess the forces of the State the main problem is solved. They considered sovereign power to be creative.

The law of nature holds also another answer to our question. Since the time of the Physiocrats and Adam Smith, the old Stoic opinion of the law of nature held the ground, viz. that definite laws are inherent in the universe, and that if these laws of nature were not hindered by human laws, they would ensure the happiness of all. The originators of human laws were the despots and the oligarchs. If they could be swept away then

[1] This idea is very clearly expressed in Pascal's *Pensées*, ed. 1850, **Pt. I.** Ch. XII. § 7.

the inherent laws of nature would resume their functions. Accordingly the work of the revolutionaries and reformers was purely negative. Their real work lay in the removal of usurpers and their laws. As soon as this takes place the social problem is solved. In any case—so the Chartists reasoned—the main task of the movement lay in seizing the power of the State, so as to destroy the oligarchy and then at least to approximate to the law of nature.

4. LINES OF POLICY

The Chartist movement revealed two different lines of policy, the advocates of which were known as the Physical Force Party, and the Moral Force Party. They were opposed to each other, and between the two there existed elements which oscillated backwards and forwards. The policy of Physical Force was insurrectionary and militant, with proclivities to conspiracies, secret societies, and violent talk. The policy of Moral Force directed its aim towards slow and thorough organisation within the law, towards peaceful trades unions, political and educational societies. The militant party were more revolutionary in their phraseology, more determined in their attitude, and much more hostile to the middle classes than the adherents of moral force. The mass of the proletariat supported the militants, whilst the smaller number of intellectual workers associated themselves with moral tactics. The representative of the militant tactics was the Irish landowner, Feargus O'Connor, who indeed always condemned on moral grounds the abortive attempts at insurrection, yet continually fostered them anew by his insurrectionary language. The representative of moral tactics was the London carpenter, William Lovett. The contest between the two lines of policy lasted for several years, and was decided in favour of militant tactics: Lovett had to give way to O'Connor.

The insurrectionary policy seems to have originated from the historical conception of the law of nature. The following considerations may throw some light upon the question of Jacobinism and Blanquism.

The whole democratic and socialist movement, which is based on considerations of the law of nature, considers the evil of the existing order of things to be the result of bad laws based on usurpation. Certain cunning despots are supposed to have got hold of society in order to oppress and to exploit it for the benefit of a small minority. This whole system of government is therefore a misuse and violation of the social contract and of natural equity. This conception appeared with classic clearness in the conspiracy that is connected with Babeuf's name. The people are justified and in duty bound by all great principles to do everything in their power to sweep away the unnatural, unjust, and pernicious state of things. The fight against this condition is a holy war for the restoration of the law of nature, the social contract, the ancient constitution, innate rights and liberties,—a holy war against usurpers, who destroyed and subverted the old conditions. What need is there of further arguments ? What is the use of philosophising, of educating and enlightening the masses when everything is all as clear as day-light ? The aim of society is the happiness of all and the pro-tection of all. This aim would have been realised if despotism and oligarchy had not destroyed the ancient rights and pledges. The existing order is full of manifest evils ; each of the evils is an indictment against the usurpers and an argument against the minority who gained their power by robbery and destruction. Nature created men in a state of freedom, the rulers threw them into chains.

Such conceptions are just as much calculated to incite violent insurrections of the mass of the people as the feelings of the robbed against the robber. The passions become much more easily roused to action if claims are made upon ancient rights which have once been possessed than if new rights are demanded. In the first case no further evidence or further arguments are required ; force alone is necessary to overthrow the robbers *i.e.*, the Physical Force argument. On the other hand, if rights are demanded which have not hitherto been enjoyed, or if indeed reliance is placed upon new rights in order to contest obsolescent and moribund rights, then the demand for these rights must be based on theory. In this case the feelings play a much smaller part than reason, research, and education.

O'Connor's victory was inevitable ; his tactics corresponded more exactly than Lovett's to the fundamental ideas of Chartism.

The history of Chartism as outlined in the preceding four sections will be treated in detail in the following chapters.

XI

THE ALLIANCE BETWEEN THE WORKING CLASS AND THE MIDDLE CLASS

I.—THE REFORM BILL AND THE POLITICAL UNIONS (1830 to 1832)

From the last third of the eighteenth century until 1830 Great Britain was in the throes of a transformation, which altered the face of the country, brought new classes into being and created men with new interests. Scattered hamlets became vast industrial districts ; trading villages became populous centres, feverish with activity. The increase in the population of the towns is illustrated by the following figures :

			1801	1821	1841
London	...	...	959,000	1,379,000	1,950,000
Liverpool	...	...	82,000	138,000	286,000
Manchester	...	...	77,000	129,000	243,000
Birmingham	...	...	71,000	102,000	183,000
Leeds	...	...	53,000	84,000	152,000
Sheffield	...	...	46,000	85,000	125,000
Nottingham	...	...	29,000	40,000	52,000
Bradford	...	...	13,000	26,000	67,000
Newcastle	...	...	33,000	—	70,000

Yet in spite of this increase the parliamentary representation of the nation in 1830 remained the same in character as it was in 1760. The entire economic revolution appeared incapable of affecting the composition of parliament in the slightest degree. Even in November, 1830, at the opening of William the Fourth's first parliament, the Duke of Wellington, the head of the Tory government, explicitly declared that the existing franchise could not be altered. The time was, however, ripe for a political change. In a debate on a subject of minor importance the ministry was defeated and had to resign. A Whig ministry took its place with Lord Grey and Lord John Russell for its chief members.

A premonition of a coming political crisis swept over the country. No one exactly gauged the significance of the coming events; there was only a general feeling that English history had reached a crisis. A Radical press came into being to give expression to these feelings; enthusiasm was rife, and when news reached London of the July revolution in Paris, the people burst into a frenzy of delight that knew no bounds.

On February 18, 1830, the Marquis of Blandford introduced a Reform Bill in the House of Commons, to confer the franchise on householders. The Bill was thrown out. It was a whole year later that Lord John Russell introduced the great Reform Bill. It passed the second reading by a majority of one, and was thrown out in Committee. It was followed by a dissolution of parliament, and the fresh elections gave the government a majority of over 130 votes. A second Reform Bill was introduced; it passed the House of Commons and was thrown out by the Lords on October 8, 1831, but the government answered them by re-introducing the Bill. The attitude of the Lords roused the whole country to a pitch of indignation that increased from day to day, and led to rioting and the Bristol conflagration.

In the meantime political unions had been formed in most of the towns and by speeches and writings hastened on the agitation for reform. The first political union was founded by Thomas Attwood and his adherents in Birmingham, and it comprised members from both the middle and the working classes. The paper-money reformers in Birmingham had endeavoured for over a decade to press their views upon government, but without any result, and they now saw no other way out of the difficulty than to agitate for a reform of parliament itself and to call in the workers to their help. On January 25, 1830, a meeting took place in Birmingham of 20,000 people, to whom Attwood, the principal speaker, expounded his views. The working men attended the meeting in great numbers, since they were in agreement in demanding that parliament should be reformed. Their idea, however, was less to reform the currency than secure legislation for the protection of labour. Moreover, the fact that they possessed no franchise was unendurable, and they were seeking for the means of obtaining it.

Attwood, in the course of his speech, outlined the scheme of a political alliance between the middle and the working classes. He had already observed the growing independence of the workers and the development of antagonism between capital and labour. He therefore utilised the general demand by the masses for reform to restore harmony between the two classes. The following was the programme he drew up for the political union :—

" 1. To obtain by every just and legal means such a Reform in the Commons House of Parliament as may ensure a real and effectual representation of the lower and middle classes of the people in that House.

" 2. To enquire, consult, consider, and determine respecting the rights and liberties of the industrious classes, and respecting the legal means of securing those which remain and recovering those which are lost.

" 3. To prepare petitions, addresses, remonstrances to the Crown and legislative bodies, respecting the preservation and restoration of public rights, and respecting the repeal of bad laws, and the enactment of good laws.

" 4. To prevent and redress, as far as possible, all local public wrongs and oppressions, and all local encroachments upon the rights, interests, and privileges of the community.

" 5. To obtain the repeal of the beer and malt taxes ; and in general to obtain an alteration in the system of taxation, so as to cause it to press less severely upon the industrious classes of the community and more equally upon the wealthy classes.

" 6. To obtain the reduction of each separate tax and expense of the government in the same degree as the legislative increase in the value of money has increased their respective values, and has reduced and is reducing the general prices of labour throughout the country.

" 7. To promote peace, union and concord among all classes of His Majesty's subjects and to guide and direct the public mind into uniform, peaceful and legitimate operations, instead of leaving it to waste its energies in loose, desultory, and unconnected exertions, or to cater to its own objects, unguided, unassisted, uncontrolled.

" 8. To collect and organise the peaceful expression of the Public Opinion, so as to bring it to act upon the legislative functions in a just, legal, and effectual way

" 9. To influence by every legal means the election of Members of Parliament so as to promote the return of upright and capable representatives of the people.

" 10. To adopt such measures as may be legal and necessary for the purpose of obtaining an effectual Parliamentary investigation into the situation of the country, and into the cause of its embarrassments and difficulties, with the view of relieving the National Distress, of rendering justice to the injured as far as practicable, and of bringing to trial any member of either House of Parliament who may be found to have acted from criminal or corrupt motives."

Nearly the whole of the English press published long reports of this meeting, and all over the country political associations of the middle and working classes came into being, adopting the Birmingham programme. By electoral reform the workers understood universal suffrage, or at least a very wide extension of the franchise which would include a great part of the workers. The organised operatives of the North of England held the same opinion as their comrades in Birmingham. When the committee of the Birmingham political union supported the Marquis of Blandford's proposals to enfranchise house owners and tenants, the operatives of Birmingham protested against this unfriendly attitude of the middle class to the working class. A working man called Bibb, who spoke on behalf of his comrades against the action of the committee, declared :

" . . . . If the suffrage be confined to householders the poor would almost entirely be shut out from the exercise of the rights of the people to annual parliaments or universal suffrage.

People say we should have no right to vote because we don't pay direct taxes. But who are the classes of the people who pay taxes ? The working men. The source of taxation is the produce of labour. What the master pays in taxes is taken off the produce of labour. Profit on capital, profits on trade come from labour. Even those small shopkeepers who pay rates recoup themselves on the consumers for taxation. Finally it is the workmen who pays. In this manner taxes are dragged out of the vitals of the workmen. (Loud cheers) . . . I ask therefore what can the poor expect from the middle classes should they obtain the desired rights, if when there ought to be a similarity and union of feeling from common wrongs, they shrink from their support ? "

During the discussion Attwood and other speakers defended the action of the committee, whereupon Bibb withdrew his protest and at the same time declared :—

" I took this step reluctantly, for I am convinced the declaration you are going to sanction would ultimately destroy the chief, the most important means by which the lower classes might expect to obtain equal rights with their superiors." [1]

Among the Birmingham workers we find the same consciousness of their economic *rôle* and of their political dependence as in the case of the operatives in Leeds and Manchester. From January 1, 1831, the operatives of Lancashire ran their own paper, the *Voice of the People*, which was also the organ of the trades unions as well as of radicalism and Owenism. The Lancashire workers, who aspired after comprehensive economic class-organisation and coquetted with co-operative experiments, came under the political influence of the Benthamites. Only the hardest thinkers of the Lancashire workers, in particular John Doherty, the leader of the textile operatives, dreamed of creating a political Labour Party with the trades unions for its units. According to this plan the local and district unions were to be affiliated for the sole purpose of dealing with matters affecting trades unions, but all the unions should together

[1] *Birmingham Journal*, January 31, 1830.

form a National Association to undertake the emancipation of the working class by means of parliamentary and socialistic action.[1] This plan only became realised in the year 1899–1900 by the formation of the Labour Party. It is obvious that the founders of the Labour Party had no conception that seventy years earlier the idea of a similar organisation had originated. At that time it remained a mere dream, for during the agitation for the Reform Bill the workers formed a part of the political union of the middle and working classes.

It was only in the summer of 1832 that organised Labour dissolved its alliance with the middle classes, and this was partly owing to the stormy character and negative result of the agitation for the Reform Bill, and partly to the propaganda of the intellectual section of the workers of London, who banded together in opposition to the political unions founded on the Birmingham plan and in hostility to the reforms suggested by the Whigs.

2. THE LONDON NATIONAL UNION OF THE WORKING CLASSES

This union, founded in the year 1831, was the birthplace of Chartism. Here the first contests took place between class-war and the solidarity of classes, and here after a long struggle the ideas were formulated of independent action on the part of the operatives, of decisive democratic reform, of revolutionary agitation by the masses and of the general strike.

This union stood in the most intimate connection with the *Poor Man's Guardian*. The development of the movement can be closely followed in its discussions, and their sounding-board was formed by the whole of the thinking portion of the working men of Great Britain. Its immediate history extends as far back as the year 1829, when the British Union for the Diffusion of Co-operative Knowledge was founded. In a manuscript document that is still extant one of its founders makes the following remarks on the subject :—

" During Owen's absence in America, the leaders of the working men who were in favour of Owenism and also of political

[1] *Voice of the People*, June 11, 1831.

Radicalism, met together and opened co-operative shops ; finally they founded the British Union, for enquiries reached London from all sides for information concerning co-operative matters. A special office for supplying information became necessary therefore ; for the correspondence connected with the co-operative establishments had increased to such vast proportion that it could no longer be grappled with after business hours. Our work was both practical and theoretical and we extracted from Owenism as much as we had in common and discarded all points of difference. All the leading men were workmen. When Owen returned from America and saw our co-operative undertakings, he disapproved of them and contemptuously called them Trading Associations, frankly declaring that buying and selling had nothing in common with his co-operative commonwealth. But when he discovered that numerous members of these unions were inclined to support many of his views, he entered into relations with them and took a keen interest in their deliberations." [1]

The meetings of the workers took place at that time either in the large hall of the Mechanics' Institute or in Carlile's Rotunda (Blackfriars). One of these meetings—the fourth quarterly meeting of the British Union for the Diffusion of Co-operative Knowledge—was held at the Mechanics' Institute in October, 1830 ; the report yields a good insight into the mental progress which the workers had made in socialistic thought.

The fundamental ideas were Owenite, but the tone of the speeches was full of a fighting spirit and revolutionary verve. The wage system was condemned root and branch, capitalism was denounced as obnoxious and execrable, whilst labour and co-operation were regarded as the pillars of civilisation. " We by our labour produce all and we ought to enjoy it." The committee's report laid stress upon the rapid rise of the co-operative idea ; the main point was to eradicate the belief from the workers' heads that they were dependent on money or on the possession of capital. Labour was to supplant capital, co-operation was to take the place of individual competition.

[1] Lovett's *Memorandum* in Place MSS. 27791, III.

When the report had been read and discussed, a debate was opened on the subject : " Machinery under competition and under co-operation." Among the speakers were Hetherington, Lovett, Cleave, and Watson, all of them subsequently leaders of Chartism, and their speeches resounded with the theme that machinery is a curse under the system of capital, since all the advantages of mechanical progress fall to the share of the capitalists ; machinery on the other hand will become a blessing under the system of co-operation, since in this way the acquirements of the human mind will benefit the whole of society. Side by side with ideas of co-operation and attacks on capitalism most of the speeches contained hostile aspersions on the Church. If the word socialism were substituted for co-operation, it would be easy to imagine that this report referred to any large social-democratic meeting of workers at the present day.[1]

These were also the doctrines which the leaders of the British Union disseminated in 1829 and 1830 all over the country in the furtherance of co-operation.

In February or March, 1831, the leaders of this association were requested by some joiners to assist them in founding a general union of London operatives. The joiners were acquainted with the doctrine of co-operation and to all appearances were bent on founding a political trades-unionist organisation based on the ideas of the leaders of the Lancashire working classes. Hetherington and his friends immediately met them half way, and in March, 1831, the " Metropolitan Trades Union " sprang into life. Hetherington wrote out a prospectus for it, laying down two aims for the organisation, viz. to obtain universal suffrage and to carry out trades-unionist and co-operative measures.[2]

The prospectus was despatched to 150 working men's clubs in London, many of which joined the Union. In a few weeks its meetings were so largely attended that the Union moved to larger premises, and met in the Rotunda, which could accommodate 1000 people. The meetings in the Rotunda were always

[1] *Magazine of Useful Knowledge and Co-op. Misc.*, October 30, 1830.
[2] *Penny Papers* (*Poor Man's Guardian*), March Numbers, 1831.

overcrowded, so that hundreds could not obtain admission. The subjects which were discussed immediately after the foundation of the Union hinged upon universal suffrage and questions of organisation. In a few weeks the name " Metropolitan Trades Union " disappeared to give place to the name " National Union of the Working Classes and Others." It is obvious from this addition that non-workers were also received within the Union. But the words " and others " were only used at the very beginning. Afterwards we read only of the " National Union of the Working Classes." The non-workers found themselves in a dwindling minority ; among them were Julian Hibbert, a member of a rich Liberal philanthropic family ; T. J. Webb, a practical surgeon ; William Benbow, at that time a coffee-house proprietor ; Benjamin Warden, formerly a saddler's apprentice, but now an independent master.

The National Union rapidly increased in members and prestige, so as to justify Hetherington's exclamation that the Union was on the right road to become national. On May 25, 1831, it received its constitution, which had been drawn up by Lovett and Hetherington, and to all appearances with O'Brien's assistance. The main declaration was a nearly verbal copy of the first part of the French " Rights of Man," 1789. It merely contained the following alteration—emphasised here by spacing : " The members of the National Union of the Working Classes are convinced that forgetfulness of and contempt for the Rights of Man in a municipal state of society[1] are the only causes of the crimes and misfortunes of the world."

This was followed by the aims and objects of the Constitution :—

" 1. To avail itself of every opportunity in the progress of society, for the securing for every working man the full value of his labour and the free disposal of the produce of his labour.

---

[1] " Municipal state of society " means the same as " civilised or artificial state of society," in contrast to the original or natural state. This expression, so far as social criticism is concerned, is only used by Ogilvie and O'Brien (*Carpenter's Political Letters*, January 18, 1831).

2. To protect working men against the tyranny of masters and manufacturers by all just means as circumstances may determine.

3. To obtain for the nation an effectual reform in the Commons House of the British parliament : annual parliaments, extension of the suffrage to every adult male, vote by ballot, and especially no property qualification for members of parliament.

4. To prepare petitions, addresses and remonstrances to the Crown and both Houses of Parliament.

5. To concentrate into one focus a knowledge of moral and political economy, that all classes of society may be enlightened by its radiation, the National Union feeling assured that the submission of the people to misrule and oppression arises from the absence of sound moral and political knowledge amongst the mass of the community."

Finally the constitution of the National Union took over most of the provisions from the statutes of the "Birmingham Political Union." The addition of the statutes of the Birmingham Political Union shows that the London National Union at the time of its foundation held no decided opinion in favour of class-war. The very first discussion, however, evoked a declaration on the subject. In electing the committee some of the workers proposed the following motion :

" Since the Union aims at rescuing the workers from their degradation and in raising them to a higher level, it is necessary that the workers should set themselves the task of attaining this object. Therefore no member of the Union shall be elected on the Committee who is not a producer, or who does not earn his living by labour."

Warden and Hetherington opposed this resolution. They expressed the opinion that holding office did not depend on a man's trade but on ability, talent and allegiance to principles, and that the National Union had not been founded in order to lay stress on differences of class. The meeting agreed with these views, and the resolution was rejected. The leading men in the Union were Owenites, and consequently opposed to class-war. This position, which Hetherington and Warden had taken up.

drew upon them a sharp attack by the anonymous champion of class-war (to whom reference has already been made) in a communication addressed to the *Poor Man's Guardian*. His first letters allow the critical reader to form an estimate of the personality of their author. In the first place solecisms escape from his pen which could not possibly proceed from a practised writer like Bronterre O'Brien, who had received a college education, but might very well be written by a self-taught working man. For instance, the anonymous writer interchanges the verbs " teach " and " learn ; " in the second place he mentions "his loom" on one occasion ; thirdly he opposed co-operative enterprises, whilst O'Brien even in 1830 was one of Owen's admirers ; fourthly, he regards trade unionism as one of the foremost weapons of the fighting working class, while O'Brien, in 1831, held the opinion that trade unionism was " a folly and waste of money and time, leading but to discord and riots ; "[1] finally, the anonymous writer was hostile to any joint action between the operatives and the lower middle classes, whilst O'Brien was in favour of an alliance between them. This correspondence could, therefore, not have proceeded, either in its wording or its tenour, from O'Brien, but must have come from a hand-loom weaver, ruined by modern machinery, who had had the advantage of a little schooling in his youth. The most determined fighters of Chartism came from the handicraftsmen who were ruined by the growing Factory System.

Now for the " communication."

The anonymous correspondent inveighed in long diatribes against the Reform Bill, which he considered to be even more reactionary and pernicious than the old franchise. Then he addressed himself to Hetherington (the publisher of the *Poor Man's Guardian*) and Warden :—

" People who live by plunder will always tell you to be submissive to thieves. To talk of *representation*, in any shape, being of any use to the people is sheer nonsense ; unless the people have a House of working men, and represent themselves. Those

[1] *Midland Representative*, May 28, 1831, p. 8.   (Review of *Knight's Working Men's Companion*.)

who make the laws now and who are intended, by the new reform bill, to make them in future, all live by profits of some sort or other. They will, therefore, no matter who elect them, nor how often they are elected, always make the laws to raise profits and keep down the price of labour. Representation, therefore, by a different body of people to those who are represented, or whose interests are opposed to theirs, is a mockery, and those who persuade the people to the contrary are either idiots or cheats. . . . The people should drop all contention, therefore, about electing a legislature in its present shape, and contend night and day, every moment of their lives for a legislature of their own, or one made up of themselves. This is the *primum mobile*, the grand *desideratum*, and in the absence of this there is not a shadow of a chance of getting a shadow of justice, but that of keeping the plunderers in continual dread, thereby raising a sufficient portion of fear to counteract their vicious desires. They will then respect the people for the sake of themselves. . . . Co-operation is of no use, unless the people would get the raw materials without going to the land-stealer, then dispense with the use of money, and live by bartering their manufactures with each other. No one could then get either rent, tax or profit out of them, but as they cannot do this, co-operation has little or no other effect than that of feeding the rich, and starving those who can scarcely live. . . . As soon as it becomes generally understood that the co-operators can live a shilling a week cheaper than before, their employers will reduce their wages to that amount ; and thus will their employers reap all the advantages of their co-operation. . . .

" *The Trades Union.*—This was a most important union, but unfortunately strangled in its birth. The first resolution of the Union that was proposed was to this effect—' That as this Union is intended to raise the working classes from their present degraded condition, it is necessary that it *be done by* themselves. No person, therefore, shall be eligible to act on the committee unless he be a wealth-producer, that is, one who gets his living by labour.' This resolution spoke a volume, by showing the people's desire to take the lead in favour of themselves. This

w

resolution you and Mr. Warden destroyed. . . . You and
Mr. Warden then will do well in withdrawing yourselves from
their committee, and every one else who is not absolutely a man
who works for a master, or working man. Attend their meetings,
hear what they have to say, report their proceedings, and encourage them to go on ; but at the same time give them the lead,
learn them to go alone, and encourage them to be no longer slaves,
but men." [1]

The anonymous correspondent addressed to the *Poor Man's
Guardian* other letters full of the logic of the working man.
From the very beginning this organ advocated universal franchise, but it considered the alliance between the middle and
working classes to be necessary. A few days after the introduction of the Reform Bill this newspaper wrote :

" . . . In conclusion, we hope and trust this reform measure
will not be carried ; at the same time we feel convinced, that
even those who are now so more than satisfied, will soon find out
its complete inefficiency even for their own purposes ; but it
will retard the progress of real reform considerably ; for a time,
the middle classes will be removed from the side of the people at
large, and, it must be admitted that they are a great loss, inasmuch, as when united in one common cause, they can afford to
give publicity to their wants, which the people cannot." [2]

This attitude appeared to the anonymous writer to be dangerous. He protested in a blazing letter to the editor against any
compromise between workers and capitalists. The economic
contrasts between the two classes were so deep-seated that the
workers could not possibly expect any political help from the
middle class. And he addressed himself to the working people
as follows :—

" What justice or what mercy can you expect at the hands of
the employers when they shall have acquired their elective
privileges of forming the legislature, whose very preliminary step
consists in divesting you of your dearest and most *sacred right ?*
We have a hundred rotten boroughs at the present day, but

[1] *Penny Papers* (*Poor Man's Guardian*), April 29, 1831.
[2] *Poor Man's Guardian,* March 12, 1831 (leading article).

pass this Bill with this obnoxious clause and the whole kingdom will be rotten to the very core. . . . The landowner, the merchant, and the tradesman will hereafter possess the sole right (or rather privilege) of making the laws. The interest of all these people is directly opposed to yours. Mark then what I say: If this Bill pass in its present shape, that is, with this obnoxious clause, *house rent will rise*, wages will be still further reduced, and the prices of everything else will be advanced. You are now to be forsaken, rejected, and to become entire outcasts in the world. . . ."[1]

" As a proof of what kind of materials the House of Commons is to be composed, two candidates have already been named by the profit-men or middlemen, for our town. One of them everybody knows, and therefore I shall say nothing about him ; the other, I am informed, is a Cockney, of the name of Young, a shipbuilder, who possesses as much information as *my loom*. . . . It is but common justice that the people who make the goods should have the sole privilege of making the laws." [2]

During the discussions and the enormous mass demonstrations of the people in favour of the Reform Bill, the Whigs succeeded in intimidating the Lords, and in exacting from the King a promise to create a batch of peers if necessary. In March, 1832, a decisive victory for the Reform Bill was at last in sight. The anonymous writer took all his knowledge and ability in both hands and wrote the following article for the *Poor Man's Guardian* :—

" TO THE WORKING PEOPLE OF ENGLAND "

" FELLOW COUNTRYMEN.

" I have given you my opinion in several letters, at various times, on the present measure of Reform. I have in these letters uniformly told you that that measure, if carried into effect, will do you an incalculable deal of harm. I have told you that the evils under which you labour are not produced by taxation. I have shown you that the whole expense of the government, from

[1] *Penny Papers* (*Poor Man's Guardian*), April 9, 1831.
[2] *Poor Man's Guardian*, November 19 and 26, 1831.

the King to the common soldier, does not amount to more than one halfpenny a day upon each individual in the two kingdoms ; and that the abolition of the whole government would relieve you to the amount of only that one halfpenny a day. I have told you that the remote cause of your poverty is your not having seats, personally, in that which ought to be your house ; and that you are thereby prevented from assisting, like the land-stealers, the merchants, the manufacturers, and the tradesmen, in your own persons, to make the laws by which you are governed ; and I told you that the *immediate* cause of your poverty is the exorbitant rents, tithes, interest on money, profits on labour, and profits on trade, which are imposed on you by laws made by the land-stealers, merchants, manufacturers, and tradesmen in that house from which you are excluded, and by which exclusion you are prevented from making laws to regulate your wages. I have told you that the government taxes are only a natural consequence arising out of the rents, interest, and other profits which are imposed on you—that those taxes are, in short, only a sum of money given to the government to beat and torture you into a submission to those rents, tithes, interest, and profits, by which you are robbed to more than twenty times the amount of those taxes. I have told you these things before, and I tell you the same now, and in so doing I tell you the truth.

" I have told you that the influence of those men who impose those rents and profits, is to be increased in making the laws, and that your influence is to be diminished by this Bill. I told you, and I shewed you that every increase of these rents, tithes, and profits is equal to a reduction of your wages to the same amount ; and that by this Bill these rents and other profits will be still farther increased, and your wages, in consequence, still farther reduced. I told you these facts before, and I repeat it again now, that this Bill will augment your poverty to an incalculable degree.

" I told you, and I shewed you existing facts to prove that the taxes, in every country in the world, are always increased in exact proportion as the influence of the land-stealers, merchants, manufacturers, and tradesmen is increased in making the laws ;

and as I am determined to assert nothing without proof, I will now shew you the reason why those taxes are so increased. For instance, as soon as the land-stealers, merchants, manufacturers, and tradesmen acquire the privilege of law-making, they begin to legislate for their own individual interest ; that is, to increase their rents and profits, by which they deprive you of the produce of your industry ; and in proportion as their influence in law-making is increased, so are those rents and profits increased, and so likewise is your burden increased accordingly. In proportion as your poverty is increased, so do you become more and more tumultuous for the want of food. In proportion as you become tumultuous, so do these land-stealers and others strengthen the government to keep you down ; and in proportion as they strengthen the government to keep you down, so do they increase the taxes to support the government. So here then you *see*, in a few words, the real cause of that increase of taxes in all countries, which I only *told* you of before—that these taxes are nothing more than the natural consequence or offspring of exorbitant rents, tithes, interest, and other profits ; and that these rents, and so on, are the real cause of your poverty ; yet the influence of these men who live by these impositions, is to be increased in making the laws, by this Bill, more than ten-fold ! ! Will you believe now that you have any interest in the passing of this Bill, or that your interest does not consist in its being kicked out, as it was before ? I am told that you cannot be worse off than you are now. I say yes. The Irish people are three times worse off than you are, bad as you are, and that you are capable of being as bad off as they. I therefore conjure you to prepare your coffins if you have the means. You will be starved to death by thousands, if this Bill pass, and thrown on to the dung hill, or on to the ground, naked, like dogs. I now proceed to other matters connected with this measure.

" Of all the Bills, or plots (for it is nothing else), that ever was proposed on earth, this is the most deceptive and the most mischievous. This Bill proposes to extend the number of electors to about five times the present amount. This, on the face of the measure, appears, at first sight, a most liberal alteration What !

extend the number of voters from 150,000 to 600,000 or 700,000 ?
Most liberal indeed ! ! ! But now, when we come to see that the
liberality is all on one side, and none on the other—when we
come to see that those whose influence is already tenfold too
great, are to have that influence tenfold increased, while you
whose influence is already tenfold too little, are to have that
influence (through the great increase of the other) incalculably
diminished, it is the most *illiberal*, the most *tyrannical*, the most
abominable, the most infamous, the most hellish measure that
ever could or can be proposed. Your number is four-fifths of the
whole population. Your influence, therefore, at elections (in
addition to your right of being elected yourselves) ought to be
four times as great as all the rest of the community. Yet your
influence will not be more than *one-twentieth part* of that which
will be exercised by those who live on the fruits of your labour.
You will in reality, therefore, from fear and fewness of number,
have no influence at all.

" This Bill proposes to disfranchise a number of rotten boroughs,
and to transfer the elective franchise to large populous towns.
This is another of the supposed liberal features of the Bill.
Do you not see that the interest of a few wealthy individuals at
Gatton, and Old Sarum, who live on the fruits of your labour, is
the same as the interest of as many millions, in any other part of
the kingdom, who live by the same means, and that the interest
of one working man is the same as that of all others—that is,
to get rid of his burdens ? But then it will be said : those
wealthy individuals at Gatton and Old Sarum live by high rents,
while the same description of people in the large towns live
by profits on manufactures, and on trade. Oh ! then these
individuals in these large towns want to get as large profits on
their manufactures as the others do on corn, and thereby im-
poverish you three times as much as you are. Their profits,
already, are three times as great, aye, ten times as great, in those
towns, as they ought to be. These profits are the main cause
of your poverty in those towns now. So much for the liberality
of disfranchising small towns to enfranchise large ones ! The
increase of poverty by this *liberality* will be in exact proportion

to the increased number of working men who will be affected by those profits. What liberality !

"When I hear master manufacturers and tradesmen say—We must get large profits to enable us to pay you high wages, my blood curdles within me, and I wish at once that I were a dog, or anything else, rather than a man. Those large profits are the sole cause why wages are low. They are got by keeping wages down. Shall I say anything more on this subject ? Is it necessary, seeing that we are rational beings and ' lords of the creation ! ' . . . The profit is that which is retained and never paid back. The manufacturer's profits, therefore, like the land-stealers' rent, and tithe-stealers' tithes, and all other profits, was obtained solely by keeping wages down. . . . There is no common interest between working men and profit-makers. This fact, like the sun, for ever stares us in the face—that in exact proportion as these large capitals are obtained, so is the poverty of the working people most *capitally* increased. . . .

" It is supposed that the members for the manufacturing towns will be enabled successfully to attack and abolish the corn-laws. Nothing can be more delusive. They must be holders of stolen land themselves before they can become members. Besides, if they were not, a sufficiency of land-stealing members has been secured by the division of counties to make head against the large towns, and for the loss of the rotten boroughs, so that, in short, the corn laws will be equally as secure as ever, while the manu-facturing members will increase their profits like the profits of the land-stealers, and therefore I am justified in saying that the Bill will retrograde from, instead of approaching towards Reform.

" Do you not see then that all that you want is high wages and low profits ? You must get your own wages up, and then these rents, tithes, interest, and other profits must fall. The Reform Bill has nothing to do with this policy of the working man. I therefore warn you, if the Bill be kicked out, be you as peaceable and as still as mice. I know you will never get anything without exertion ; but then the example of France, Belgium, and all other countries, will convince you that no sudden convulsion will relieve you. Your exertion must be constant, uniform, and as silent and as perpetual as the conduct of your enemies, till they pay you as much wages as will purchase you your fair proportion of everything you produce. If you want to know who is your greatest enemy—it is he who has the greatest income, no matter what he may say to deceive you, nor to what sect or party he may belong, nor from what source his income may be derived. With this warning I take my leave with the assurance that if the Bill pass, I will tell you something of greater importance than anything else I have told you before.

" ONE OF THE OPPRESSED."[1]

Manchester, March 19, 1832.

The power of the style and the argument of this anonymous social thinker are so striking that little comment is necessary. The article reveals all the strong and weak points of a keen but one-sided brain : ruthless logic, transparent clearness, inclination to prophecy, the omission of all factors not bearing on the economic side of the question, however important they might be in themselves, which, however, subsequently prove strong enough to overturn all the economic prophecies. The essay shows distinct traces of Hodgskin's way of thinking. Its author was obviously influenced by the latter.

It is highly probable that the same anonymous writer is responsible for the following verses which were printed in the *Poor Man's Guardian* (January 7, 1832) :—

" Wages should form the price of goods ;
    Yes, wages should be all,
Then we who work to make the goods
    Should *justly have them all ;*
But if their price be made of rent,
    Tithes, taxes, profits all,
Then we who work to make the goods
    Shall have—*just none at all.*"

The verses contain the entire theory and deduction of natural rights, viz. that the price of work is by right the product of the work ; but under civilised conditions the worker only receives

[1] *Poor Man's Guardian,* April 14, 1832.

for his wages the minimum of the means for existence, since capitalism, landlordism, State and Church appropriate the greater part of the proceeds of labour.

The *Poor Man's Guardian* also published opinions drawn from labour and socialist circles in support of the Reform Bill. A labouring man wrote :—

" You are certainly correct in your opinion of the ' Reform,' which literally does *nothing* for us, the labouring classes ; but are you not wrong in advising us to have all we demand or nothing ? Should we not get as much as we can ? I do not say, accept this reform, which gives us worse than nothing, but let us get any advantage, however trifling it be, by the aid of which we might benefit ourselves more and more, step by step. This strikes me to be better advice than what you offer."

Allen Davenport, an old Spencean, wrote to the paper as follows :—

" I feel inclined to support the present Reform Bill in spite of all that can be said against it. I consider the Reform Bill, if carried into law, will be the commencement of a legal revolution, whose movement will not be so easily arrested as some persons imagine. I calculate more on external than internal energy, when every thing has changed around us it will be impossible for us to remain stationary." [1]

The National Union fostered international solidarity with particular ardour. It celebrated the anniversaries of the French Revolution and of the Polish insurrection, and opposed Palmerston's foreign policy, which it severely stigmatized as dictated by the Tsar. From the summer of 1831 onwards the influence of the National Union upon the *élite* of the British working class was

[1] *Penny Papers* (*Poor Man's Guardian*), March 18 and May 27, 1831. Allen Davenport was born in 1775, as the son of an agricultural labourer. He grew up without having been to any school, served in the army, became converted to Spenceanism in 1817, subsequently to Owenism, wrote poems, pamphlets, and a short biographical sketch of Thomas Spence (1836). He died in London in 1846, poor but universally esteemed (*Reasoner*, 1847, pp. 16, *sqq.*).

very considerable.[1] Delegates from the Midlands and North of England appeared at their meetings. The whole mental activity of British socialism was disseminated thence by the leaders of the British working men. In October, 1831, their members were already regarded as communists holding the opinion that " private property had no right to exist at all, since it could only be harmful to the worker." [2] They were not Owenite communists but socialists, waging class-warfare ; they were unable to dissociate themselves from militant tactics, and at the end of October, 1831, the *Poor Man's Guardian* published instructions on making barricades and on street-fighting against soldiers. That was the time also in which the Reform Bill agitation reached its greatest height and in which the social-revolutionary idea of the general strike and of convoking a national convention began to take root and was soon formulated by William Benbow.

3.—WILLIAM BENBOW AND THE GENERAL STRIKE

The later months of 1831 saw the birth of the idea of a social-revolutionary general strike. Its originator was William Benbow, shoemaker, publisher, bookseller and coffee-house proprietor, a man of great eloquence and mental energy, but with a violent temperament and exaggerated self-consciousness. The pathological trait of his nature was in all probability the result of a nervous affection, partly due to his ceaseless self-tuition under unfavourable material conditions, mostly to persecution on account of his violent agitation and speeches. Hitherto, little has been known of his life history. The movements in which he was engaged used him up without caring for his personality. William Benbow represents the same mental type as Richard Carlile and Thomas J. Wooler. This type was a product of a mental tendency, characterized by democratic radicalism, free thought and the law of nature, which prevailed in the last decades of the eighteenth century and the first decades of the nineteenth century. At that period the cleverest artisans and operatives

[1] Place MSS., 27,791, pp. 333, *sqq.*, 343, 412.
[2] *Ibid.*, 27,790, p. 23.

acquired considerable literary and political knowledge by dint of iron will-power and unquenchable enthusiasm, and they utilised this knowledge to enlighten the masses. Benbow appears to have been born in Manchester in 1784. In April, 1840, when he had to defend himself before a jury in Chester for having made seditious Chartist speeches, he stated at the end of a ten-hour speech in his defence that he was already an old man and at the very best had only ten years more to live.[1] He was apprenticed to a shoemaker,[2] showed capacity for public speaking, and preached in Nonconformist chapels. He took part, after 1815, in the Radical movement and was arrested. He is also known to have been a printer and publisher from 1817 to 1825. His publishing house had Lord Byron's head for a sign and was called " Byron's Head " in consequence. Here he printed for Richard Carlile the drama *Wat Tyler*, by Robert Southey, which drew upon him the latter's eternal enmity.[3] Benbow printed cheap editions of the English poets, especially of Byron. In 1823 he brought out a work in parts which was a chronicle of clerical scandals. It bore the title, *Crimes of Clergy*, and belongs to the class of scurrilous literature. Two years later he published a polemic against Southey and in defence of Byron. This pamphlet, *A Scourge for the Laureate*, is well written and shows that Benbow was a man with a trenchant style and with no inconsiderable literary knowledge. At that time he had already served a term of imprisonment. In 1831 and 1832 we find him to be a member of the National Union and one of the most violent speakers in the Rotunda. At that time he owned a coffee-house at No. 205, Fleet Street, where he penned his pamphlet on the social-revolutionary general strike. It bears the title : *Grand National Holiday and Congress of the Productive Classes.* It appeared towards the close of 1831 or in January, 1832, and was dedicated to the workers in the following brief sentences :—

[1] *Northern Star*, April 25, 1840; *Chester Gazette*, April 11, 1840.

[2] *Gaols and Prisons :* Accounts and Papers, Vol. 38, 1840, No. 600, pp. 691, *sqq.*

[3] This statement is based on Benbow's evidence only. I could find no *editio princeps* of Southey's *Wat Tyler*, and therefore I am unable to confirm it.

" Plundered Fellow-sufferers ! I lay before you a plan of freedom ; adopt it and you rid the world of inequality, misery and crime. A martyr in your cause, I am become the prophet of your salvation. A plan of happiness is pointed out and dedicated to you. With it I devote to you my life and body, my soul and blood.

" Commercial Coffee House,   " WILLIAM BENBOW."
    205, Fleet Street."

His speeches in the National Union were often printed in the *Poor Man's Guardian*. From 1834 to 1838 we hear nothing of him. It is only in 1838 that he appears again in Lancashire, where he travelled about with horse and cart, holding open-air meetings and pushing the sale of his pamphlet on the general strike. He must have left London about the year 1837, in order to betake himself to the centre of the Chartist agitation. For at that time the leading radical and socialist agitators, such as O'Connor and Owen, left London for Yorkshire and Lancashire, whither the political centre of gravity had followed the industrial centre. In the beginning of August, 1839, Benbow was arrested in Manchester and spent eight months in prison awaiting his trial since he could not give security ; it is curious that he could not induce any one to bail him out. He was popular enough among the workers, without, however, receiving any degree of confidence at their hands. Positions of trust were not conferred upon him. In all the many conferences, conventions and other functions of the Chartists he never appeared as a delegate. All this neglect greatly contributed to embitter him still further. He believed himself to be persecuted alike by friend and foe. Yet his pamphlet on the general strike exercised a powerful influence between 1838 and 1842. There were probably few Chartists who had not read it ; its phrases were on every lip ; Chartist speakers made use of it ; and all the debates on a general strike and all attempts at its realisation in that decade are to be traced to Benbow's pamphlet.

Benbow's main ideas are as follows :—

The labour of the mass of the people is the source of wealth, but it is only a privileged few that obtain it. The people is the source of all power, but the oppressors of the people make use of it ; the mass of the people fight both by land and sea, but the usurpers carry off the laurels and the booty. How has this become possible ?

By the ignorance and disunion of the people.

The worst result of ignorance is the assumption that others will do for us what we ought to do ourselves. It is sheer lunacy for working men to ask their masters to undertake the task of emancipation.

The working men must emancipate themselves. And if the working-men understand this they will win. From Wat Tyler to Thistlewood the martyrs of truth have always been found among the people.

But how can the people obtain this knowledge and unity of action ? By proclaiming a national holiday ; by stopping work. We suffer from overproduction, so we are told. Good. Let us stop producing. The masters will soon find out that an over-abundance of goods is no misfortune. We suffer from over-population, so we are told. Good. Let us count ourselves ; let us find out the large numbers of the working men and the small numbers of the privileged class. The very act of the masses stopping work will give the latter the consciousness of their strength, the magnitude of their united action. The month's holiday must be a month's congress of the working men ; a people's month for taking stock of the social conditions ; a national congress to put tyranny to flight.

Before the national holiday is proclaimed, preparation for it must be made. Every locality will elect a committee to direct the agitation and to enlighten the masses concerning the objects and significance of the national holiday and of the national congress.

Every family of workers must provide food for a week. A longer period is not necessary. If the working class of the whole country is united and resolute for only a single week, success is certain.

All money and property which were originally destined for the support of the people and have been appropriated by various corporations and churches must be restored to their original destination. Land and live stock originally belonged to all. The committees appointed by the people will have to see that the present owners restore part of the fruits of the earth and the live stock to the masses resting from their toil. And behind the committees there must stand a people strong in morals and resolute in action. Above all the masses must not be squeamish. Both right and might are on the side of the people.

The object of the national congress is to reform society root and branch by a better division of wealth, by a uniform circulation of goods so as to set the whole body of society in a state of harmonious activity.

Benbow's plan can therefore be reduced to the following ideas : The general strike is the best means of bringing the workers to a sense of their power ; the object of the agitators is to make use of a propitious moment to induce the workers to act together *en masse*. Consolidated action on the part of the workers would transform their power into violence which would lead the people on to victory and happiness by producing economic equality.

Benbow himself never used the term " general strike," but spoke always of the national holiday ; the Chartists generally used the term " sacred week " or " sacred month " ; it was the trades unions who discarded all those terms and spoke of the general strike. We find this term for the first time in the *Herald of Rights of Industry* (April 5, 1834, p. 66. col. 2). This paper was edited by John Doherty.

4.—THE REFORMED PARLIAMENT AND DISILLUSIONMENT

In June, 1832, the Reform Bill was made law and in the middle of August parliament was dissolved. The posting of the lists of electors and the preparations for the elections had a sobering effect. The exhilaration of the Reform agitation had evaporated, the wildest hopes gave way to the deepest disappointment. In November and December the elections took place, but they only resulted in a great victory for the Whigs. In February, 1833, the first Reformed parliament was opened by a King's speech, which, as Thomas Attwood, the member for Birmingham, remarked, might just as well have been read by the Emperor of China, since it had so little connection with the problems of the day or the wishes of the people.

The first year of the Reformed parliament was, however, not quite so barren as its critics maintained ; negro-slavery was abolished in the West Indies and a factory act was passed for the textile industry of Great Britain, which marks the actual commencement of legislation in protection of the working man. It was absolutely forbidden to employ children under nine years of age, the working hours for children from nine to thirteen years were restricted to eight hours, a maximum of sixty-nine working hours a week was established for young people, night-work was forbidden for both categories and an inspection of factories was introduced. The law, however, only affected the North of England and had hardly any application except for textile-workers. Not a single labour paper of the day printed a leading article on the factory law. On the other hand, ample use was made of the material of the Committees of Inquiry, which had preceded this law and had revealed the frightful exploitation of child-labour. The feeling of disillusionment was intensified by the Act of 1834 amending the Poor Law, which swept away the old Poor Law administration, erected bastilles for the poor, and stigmatised poverty as a crime. The old Poor Law had a social reform character ; the support of the unemployed out of the parish-rates was regarded as a duty, the claim to support was considered as the right of the citizen who had fallen on evil times. The new law completely reversed this conception and asserted the individualistic idea by which it was the duty of every one to look to himself and to make no claim whatever to the help of his fellow-men. The majority of the Reformed parliament swore by Malthus and the political economists, who knew no other remedy for poverty than celibacy and regarded unemployment as the result of laziness or as an unavoidable evil with which no social remedy could contend.

The new franchise, which conferred parliamentary representation upon the middle classes, but left the working classes unenfranchised, disclosed at one blow the apparently unbridgeable chasm that existed between capital and labour. The operatives had realised the economic antagonism for decades, but owing to the middle classes being just as much without representation up to 1832 as the working classes, the opposition between the classes was to some extent obscured and, accordingly, both classes fought side by side for reform as allies. After 1832 this alliance was no longer possible. The division was obvious in every direction. To cap it all, the severity of the new Poor Law changed the estrangement into open enmity.

The anonymous champion of class-war in the *Poor Man's Guardian* had, so it seemed, predicted all this in advance! And a working class poet expressed the feelings of Labour in the following lines :—[1]

'Tis twelve months past, just yesterday, since earth, and sky, and sea,
And rock, and glen, and horse, and man rang loud the jubilee;
The beacons blazed, the cannons fired, and war'd each plain and hill
With the Bill—the glorious Bill, and nothing but the Bill!

Our taxes, by the glorious Bill, were all to sink and fade,
Our shipping was to prosper, and think, oh ! what a trade !
Our agriculture and our looms, our pockets were to fill,
By, ah ! you rogues, the Bill, the Bill, and nought but the Bill!

But now each holds up his hands in horror and disgust
At this same document, once termed the people's trust,
That at last was to bring grist to all the nation's mill.
Ah ! curse the Bill, ye rogues, the Bill, and nothing but the Bill!

The working men in their desperation condemned not only the Reform Bill but the whole institution of parliament. The workers now asked the question : " What have the political unions done for us ? "

Nothing at all ! Worse than nothing ! And they shattered their gods of reform and even turned away from the prophets who had warned them against the false gods. The London National Union lost its members and prestige so rapidly and the *Poor Man's Guardian* its readers, that both of them only carried on a precarious existence and died out in 1835.

[1] *Glasgow Liberator and Trades Union Gazette*, September 14, 1833.

The people again looked for their salvation to Owen, who had become entirely anti-parliamentary, and to trades unions, which gradually assumed a revolutionary or syndicalist character. The operatives looked to them not only for an amelioration of the conditions of labour but for emancipation from wage slavery.

Yet an alliance between Owenism and syndicalism presented difficulties both in theory and practice. Owenism depended on the co-operation of classes; it only distinguished between erring and enlightened human beings. Trades unionism, with its social-revolutionary character, depended on class-war and only recognised exploiting and exploited classes. Owen made the attempt to displace private industry and competition by means of peaceful co-operative establishments and wherever possible by a union between the workers and the capitalists. The object of syndicalism was to expropriate the capitalists by continued hostilities and to get the factories, workshops and agricultural industries into the hands of the trades unionists. The intrinsic opposition between the two aspects of society was not immediately recognised. The fusion of Owenism and syndicalism led to conflict and confusion; and this period did not last long enough to furnish investigators with the opportunity of producing a clear separation of the two points of view.

XII

SEPARATION OF THE MIDDLE AND WORKING CLASSES

I.—LABOUR EXCHANGES AND CO-OPERATIVE SOCIETIES

AT the time when the Reform Bill agitation reached its high-water mark and Great Britain was brought to the verge of civil war, Owen again took up his plan for guiding the country into the path of a peaceful economic revolution. He interpreted the whole political agitation as the blind yearning of the nation for redemption, and as the tempestuous approach of a momentous crisis in history.

Without delay he grappled with his task. First of all labour exchanges were to be instituted, in order to enable producers suffering from a stagnant market to exchange their goods for others which they might require. Then the individual producers were to be induced to band themselves together in co-partnership, so as to emancipate the operatives from their dependence on capital. As a first step in this work of emancipation Owen in November, 1831, conceived the idea of founding an association for the intelligent working men of London in order to initiate them in the doctrine of co-operation, and to train up leaders for carrying out his great work. A committee for this purpose was formed as early as December 3, and a certain Bromley placed at Owen's disposal, without any compensation, his business-premises in Gray's Inn Road, known as the " Royal Bazaar." On December 12 and 19, 1831, a crowded public meeting was held in these premises, and led to the foundation of the " Association of the Intelligent and Well-disposed of the Industrious

---

[1] The plan of labour exchanges is mentioned, for the first time, in the *Co-operative Magazine*, 1827, p. 511.

Classes for removing Ignorance and Poverty."[1] The objects of the association were announced to be the education of the children of working-men, and the purchase of land for agricultural schools, as well as " to receive provisions, clothing and other property, and services of every description to be exchanged on the equitable principle of labour for equal value of labour, through the medium of labour notes ; also to establish a bank in which to exchange the labour notes for the currency of the country." [1]

The ideas on value and money which Owen had expounded in the Lanark *Report*, published in 1820, were now to be put into practice. The committee accepted Bromley's offer without securing it by a contract. The Institute was opened. Its organ was a weekly, the *Crisis*, of which the first number appeared on April 14, 1832. Its first editor was R. Dale Owen. From the very beginning, not only in the association but also in the *Crisis*, active propaganda was set on foot in favour of the labour exchanges which Owen regarded as only introductory to the work of emancipation. The following ideas were at the root of the scheme of the labour exchanges :

The producers suffer from the drawback of not knowing the markets for their produce ; they are not acquainted with the people who would be ready and willing to exchange their goods for others. Therefore, they betake themselves to contractors, middlemen, and retailers, who pay them money for their goods after deductions for profits and rents. With the money thus obtained they have recourse again to middlemen to procure the goods they require, and in their purchase they have again to pay profits and rents to the non-producers. Before the producer, therefore, can obtain what he wants he has to hand over to non-producers the major part of the produce of his labour. In order to guard against these evils labour exchanges were to be set up where the producers can deposit their goods and can estimate the average amount of time taken in their production. When this is done, the producers receive vouchers stating the amount

[1] *Times*, December 20, 1831 ; Carpenter, *Co-operative Congress*, 1832, p. 128.

of labour time on deposit. By means of these vouchers they can obtain, at the same place, at any time, goods to the same average amount of labour time that has been expended in their production. In this manner supply and demand are brought into close relation with each other, and an exchange takes place without any loss.

Owen's labour exchange was not the first of these institutions. Even at the close of 1831 a bank of exchange was founded at the Gothic Hall in Marylebone ; the second was situated in the northwest of England. Owen's was the third, but was the most notable of its kind, owing to its founder's reputation. The Institute in Gray's Inn Road became the Mecca of all interested in co-operation and peaceful social reform. During the last week of April, 1832, the third Co-operative Congress was held in its rooms. The first congress sat in Manchester in May, 1831, the second in Birmingham in October, 1831. In the third Congress, in London, 65 co-operative societies were represented, and 29 of these were manufacturing societies. Here Owen expounded his plan of a labour exchange and proved at the same time that he himself was the originator of the idea and not John Gray. Gray's ideas were indeed anticipated in the Lanark report. William Thompson, too, was present as a delegate, and confirmed Owen's opinion of his priority over Gray.[1] In this congress a clash of views occurred for the first time between the parliamentary, democratic socialists and the non-political, co-operative socialists, and in general Owen's Institute and the *Crisis* on the one hand were often in conflict with the Rotunda and the *Poor Man's Guardian* on the other hand. It was in this Congress also that Owen demanded State-assistance to the tune of five million pounds for co-operative undertakings.[2]

On September 3, 1832, the labour exchange was opened at the Institute. During the first four months its success was not inconsiderable. Every week goods to the average value of £600 were deposited and exchanged, and the Institute received 8.5 per cent. of this sum for covering the expenses of administration.

[1] Carpenter, *Co-operative Congress*, 1832, p. 43.
[2] *Ibid.*, p. 42.

LABOUR EXCHANGES, ETC.

At the same time a branch institute was started in Blackfriars Road near the Rotunda. Several trades unionist organisations of London also proceeded to engage their unemployed members in co-operative undertakings and to exchange in the Institute the goods which they made. These undertakings could, however, only benefit the operatives who were in fairly good circumstances. The really poor workers could neither attend the meetings and socials at these institutes, since they had to pay for admission, nor could they enjoy the advantages of the labour exchanges, since they were unable to produce any article at their own cost. These institutes offered a great advantage to Owen, for they brought him into close relations with the intelligent members of the working classes.

Owing to misunderstandings between Owen and Bromley, the Institute had to vacate the premises in Gray's Inn Road about the middle of January, 1833. The enterprise moved for the time being to the branch institute near the Rotunda. The disturbance of moving, adverse rumours in the London newspapers, and the resultant losses caused a moral disorganisation from which the association never quite recovered. Finally it moved to 14, Charlotte Street, Tottenham Court Road, and was opened on May 1, 1833, by Owen in an apocalyptic speech. This district has ever since served as a resort for all political refugees who, on account of their political or communist convictions, have been forced to seek asylum in London.

In June, 1833, the operatives and the Owenites opened a labour exchange in Birmingham, which also enjoyed only a moderate degree of success.

For the whole year Owen lived in a state of ecstasy. The rapid rise of the trades unions, the diffusion of the idea of co-operation, the thorough contempt for parliamentary action, and the growing solidarity of the working classes were all considered to be harbingers of the imminent emancipation of the world from error and injustice. He handed over the labour exchanges to the workers, and went on a tour of propaganda to Lancashire, Yorkshire, and Staffordshire, where he came in touch with the workers' leaders. His propagandist tour revealed to him the possibility of uniting all the trades unions and co-operative societies of the United Kingdom—the productive classes, as he called them—into a single organisation, and of transforming them in a communistic sense so as to place the whole country upon a co-operative basis.

A colossal plan ! A few years were to see the completion of the work. Its entire creation lay all ready made in his constructive brain. But ideas and facts soon began to come into conflict with each other.

2.—THE SYNDICALIST PHASE

Up to the year 1832 the trades union movement passed through the following stages of development : organisation for the purpose of mutual support, organisation of a single trade for purposes of strikes and mutual support, finally organisation of allied trades (trades unions). These economic unions were non-political ; their members were either Tory or Whig, or adhered to Radicalism and vied with the members of the other classes in struggling for a definite political programme. In any case, the economic unions of the workers only pursued aims which did not go beyond daily interests, and which did not seriously affect the stability of the prevailing system of society.

From 1832 onwards the position was changed. The organised workers became anti-parliamentary for a time. They cut themselves off from parliamentary politics, not for the purpose of observing neutrality, but in order to fight against parliamentary action, and to attain by means of trades unions what had hitherto been only considered possible of attainment by legislation. At the same time Robert Owen came on the scene with his anti-parliamentary views and placed before the trades unions the aim of converting society from capitalism to socialism by means of productive co-operation.

Owing to its alliance with Owenism, however, trades unionism assumed a Utopian character antagonistic to its essential nature. The economically organised working class possessed no preconceived system of society. It regarded class-warfare as a means of raising wages and lowering profits.

For the time being it was not concerned with what would happen if the profits sank to zero. As soon as the struggle had strengthened the workers' organisation sufficiently for them to checkmate capital, they would take over the business of production and would conduct it for the benefit of the workers. They are, to use Henri Bergson's or Belfort Bax's phraseology, *alogical*.

Owen did not understand this point of view. His system was the product of rationalist logic. It rested, moreover, on the idea of the solidarity and co-operation of Capital and Labour. His remedy and his aim were in point of fact the reconstruction of society.

Convinced of the absolute truth of his views, and buoyed up by the conviction that absolute truth is irresistible, when uttered at the right time distinctly and resolutely, Owen communicated his plan to the leaders of the workers. He found the relatively highest degree of understanding to exist among the operative builders, who at that time formed one of the most powerful organisations. This was no mere chance. The builders suffered greatly at the hands of middlemen, contractors, and sub-contractors, who intervened between the employers and the workers, and derived their profit entirely at the expense of the working man. " Down with the middlemen and the contractors " was the watchword of the operative builders. Why should profit-hunters push their way in between the producer and the consumer so as to diminish the just wages of the workers ? We, the workers, said the operative builders, could just as well make the contract so as to receive the full amount of pay for our work.

These ideas and precepts were closely allied to Owenism. Owen's economic doctrine for the major part laid stress upon the parasitic nature of the middle man, upon the necessity of close relations between producer and consumer, and finally he considered that the actual solution of the social problem consisted in the producers taking over the management of production.[1]

As soon as Owen received information of this state of things

[1] *Pioneer*, September 7, 1833. *Cf. Character of Trades Unions*, 1834, p. 45.

from his adherents he entered into communication with the builders' organisations. The leaders called a conference, which met in Manchester in the last week of September, 1831. No less than 500 delegates were present, and after long discussions Owen's plans for labour exchanges and co-operative societies were adopted.[1] Owen, however, remained in ignorance of the fact that the workers still adhered to their policy of class-war.

Three weeks after the conference of the operative builders they started a weekly, *The Pioneer*; its motto, "The day of our redemption draweth nigh." Its editor was James Morrison, a young, self-taught operative builder, who began with Owenism and ended with syndicalism. Beyond all doubt Morrison must be regarded as the originator of the syndicalist conception of class-antagonism on the part of the working-classes. Little is known of his life. He came from Birmingham, but was of Scottish descent. In 1832 he was active in the workers' movement and after two years of intense intellectual work he died, owing to overwork and poverty, at the end of September, 1835, in Manchester. His wife continued to work for a long time afterwards as a socialist agitator in Salford.[2] His friend and intellectual companion, James E. Smith (1801–1857),[3] was more fortunate. Smith came of a family of weavers; he was a mystic, a theologian with broad views, and a metaphysician, and came to London from Glasgow in September, 1832. He became converted to Owenism, gave lectures in the Owenite Institute, and became editor of the *Crisis*. Smith was an original thinker. His main line of thought was mysticism and opposition to dogma. His mind was extremely active but somewhat lacking in stability, and was susceptible to all heterodox theories. The tenets of socialism soon captivated him, at least for some time, so long as they presented him with fresh problems and roused his incessant search after truth. He exercised a great influence as a speaker in the Owenite community in 1833 and 1834 on account of his philosophical culture, his remarkable power of

[1] *Crisis*, October 12, 1833.
[2] Holyoake, *History of Co-operation*, 1875, I. 211.
[3] W. A. Smith, *Life of J. E. Smith*, London, 1892.

oratory and his artistic style. He soon exhausted Owenism and pursued his search in other directions. He met Morrison, who, in his capacity of editor of the *Pioneer*, frequented the same printing-office. Smith became fascinated with the syndicalist ideas of the young operative builder, and gave them definite shape in his lectures and leading articles. Morrison and Smith, therefore, gradually withdrew from orthodox Owenism, and in 1834 became actively opposed to Owen. Smith then became a follower of Saint-Simon, subsequently of Fourier, and finished as an ordinary journalist; but to the very end he retained an attitude hostile to parliament, and friendly towards trades unionism. Indeed, his belief in the efficacy of trades unions was one of the few positive ideas which this restless spirit was able to assimilate. His philosophical and historical writings show clearly traces of Schelling's influence. Smith evidently believed in a theory of evolution, tinged with mysticism. Up to the present time little was known of this man's activity in the co-operative and syndicalist period. His biographer accumulated a mass of material which concealed rather than revealed this activity.

The first duty of the editor of the *Pioneer* was to comment upon the great conference at Manchester :

" Our Union Bark is once more safely out at sea. She has proudly triumphed over the troubled waters. . . . The new arrangements are likely to insure the permanent prosperity of the Union. We are not permitted to go into detail, but from what we have seen of the regulations, we believe they will produce an immediate effect on the district lodges. The builders' parliament have had a long session, but we hope the result of their labours will give satisfaction to the whole of their constituents. There has never been a period when the working classes were so intent on bettering their condition, and the silent progress they are making in legislation will secure them from ever being gulled with the party politics of the old school. . . . We are in earnest in saying that the builders have initiated the task of the emancipation of the world."

The chief result of the conference seems to have been the

unanimous resolution that the operative builders should form a co-operative body in order to "render the employer superfluous."[1]

In the second week of October, 1833, a Congress was held in London of delegates of co-operative societies and trades unions in order to discuss the question of amalgamation. On the evening before the congress a mass meeting took place at Charlotte Street, where Owen was the principal speaker and discussed the relations between socialism and trades unionism. According to the information he had obtained during his tour of propaganda the workers would be won over within six months' time to the great truths of co-operation. He added : " I will only briefly sketch the outlines of the great revolution in preparation, which will come upon society like a thief in the night."[2]

Everything was to be consummated without strife or violence : the unions would be transformed into co-operative societies, and would combine into associations to exchange goods reciprocally by means of labour exchanges. A general congress, to sit in London, was to take the place of parliament and to regulate the production of the whole country.

A great part of the time of the congress was taken up with reports. The main task, viz. the amalgamation of the co-operative societies and trades unions, was deliberated with closed doors. The congress must have made a very favourable impression upon all who visited or participated in it. Even the

[1] *Pioneer*, October 5, 1833.

[2] It may not be without some interest to compare this theory of sudden development in sociology with the analogous theory in biology. Just eight days before this speech of Owen's the *Crisis* printed a report by the Owenite and geologist, W. D. Saull, on the progressive development of man from the animal world. Saull had spoken on this subject in meetings of working men. The *Crisis* called it the " Simian hypothesis," with which it could not agree. The editor declared : " Man, it is allowed, is of recent origin ; and as is also evident that he has come suddenly into existence ; and this suddenness of appearance is rather a formidable argument against the supposition that Nature gradually converts one species of animals into another " (*Crisis*, September 28, 1833).

Poor Man's Guardian (October 19, 1832), was full of praise and admiration for the proceedings :

" A spirit of combination has grown up among the working classes, of which there has been no example in former times. A grand national organisation, which promises to embody the physical power of the country, is silently, but rapidly progressing ; and the object of it is the sublimest that can be conceived, namely—to establish for the productive classes a complete dominion over the fruits of their own industry. Heretofore, these classes have wasted their strength in fruitless squabbles with their employers, or with one another. They have never sought any grand object, nor have they been united for those they sought. To obtain some paltry rise, or prevent some paltry reduction in wages, has been the general aim of their turn-outs ; and the best result of their best combinations, even when successful, was merely to secure their members against actual want in the day of sickness, or of superannuation. These and the like objects were only worthy of slaves ; they did not strike at the root of the evil ; they did not aim at any radical change ; their tendency was not to alter the system, but rather to perpetuate it, by rendering it more tolerable ; nay, they in some respects only aggravate the evils of the workman's condition, as for instance, in benefit societies, of which the tendency is to pinch the bellies and backs of the contributors to the fund, in order to save the poor-rates, that is to say, the pockets of the affluent classes, from the just claims of broken-down industry. . . . But far different from the paltry objects of all former combinations is that now aimed at by the congress of delegates. Their reports show that an entire change in society—a change amounting to a complete subversion of the existing ' order of the world '—is contemplated by the working classes. They aspire to be at the top instead of at the bottom of society—or rather that there should be no bottom or top at all ! "

Morrison exclaimed : " Well, brothers, we have now macadamized the road to success, or rather, we have laid a railroad to prosperity. . . . The crisis of our condition is at hand—close upon us. The contest affects all alike ; and woe unto the man who deserts his post. The question to be decided is, Shall Labour or Capital be uppermost ? "[1]

The delegates and agitators returned to their districts or started on missionary tours : the committees of the trades unions sent out circulars and the secretaries and organisers set about the task of realising the plan which had been drawn up in London. At the present day it is difficult to realise exactly what took place at this juncture. The trades unions experienced a growth that was more rapid and comprehensive than any before or since. Battalions of trades unionists seemed to rise out of the ground ; the spirit of redemption swept through the working classes and intoxicated them with boundless hopes. In November, 1833, as many as 800,000 workers are said to have been organised,[2] and the continual additions to the organisations showed no signs of decrease. The boundless hopes at one pole of society were counterbalanced by excessive apprehension at the other pole, viz. among employers and all who were interested in capital. The centres of industry, trade, and commerce became transformed into hostile camps. Class-war raged from south to north, and from east to west. Strikes, lock-outs, coercion of the men to join the trades unions or to leave them, were all in the order of the day. The part played by the agitation for the Reform Bill in 1831 and 1832 was now transferred to the struggle for and against the trades unions. The excitement was even greater than before, since it concerned no longer a political, but a social revolution.

The vigour with which such large numbers of operatives threw themselves into the cause of class-war filled their friends partly with enthusiasm, partly with dread, but it only inspired their enemies with fear and hatred. The whole press of the kingdom busied itself with the question and took up various attitudes to the trades unions according to their interests in class or party. The Whig newspapers poured the vials of their wrath upon the class they had hitherto despised ; the papers of the radical middle class were fairly friendly but expressed the wish that the operatives should not disdain politics ; the Tory press called

[1] *Pioneer*, October 12, 1833.   [2] *Crisis*, October 12, 1833.

for the police and the public prosecutor or else they tempted the operatives to join their cause so as to lead them against the Whig government.[1]

In this atmosphere charged with enthusiasm the operatives adopted Benbow's plan of a general strike. On October 5, 1833, a resolution to this effect was passed in a large meeting of Glasgow operatives. The idea of a general strike was the subject of much discussion :—

" There will not be insurrection ; it will simply be passive resistance. The men may remain at leisure ; there is, and can be, no law to compel them to work against their will. They may walk the streets or fields with their arms folded, they will wear no swords, carry no muskets ; they will present no multitude for the Riot Act to disperse. They merely abstain, when their funds are sufficient, from going to work for one week or one month ; and what happens in consquence ? Bills are dishonoured, the *Gazette* teems with bankruptcies, capital is destroyed, the revenue fails, the system of government falls into confusion, and every link in the chain which binds society together is broken in a moment by this inert conspiracy of the poor against the rich." [2]

A journeyman shoemaker writes at this time to the *Poor Man's Guardian* :—

" If organisation goes on like that there will soon be no more than two classes : non-producers and producers—the first will no longer be permitted to revel in wealth, for by law of nature and common justice wealth and power belong only to those who produce it." [3]

The idea of class-war finds its clearest expression in an anonymous letter to the *Poor Man's Guardian* of August 30, 1834 :—

" The battle of labour against capital is not to be fought with guns and swords ; the capitalists themselves do not go into the fight ; they send ignorant labourers against enlightened labourers.

[1] *Tait's Edinburgh Magazine*, January, 1834, p. 389 ; *Cobbett's Political Register*, December 7, 1833 ; *Newcastle Press*, December 21, 1833 ; *Times*, November 4, 1833.

[2] *Glasgow Liberator* (*Trades Union Gazette*), February 1, 1834.

[3] *Poor Man's Guardian*, November 2, 1833.

The people's press must be the chief weapon of our warfare. When the labourer knows his wrongs, the death-knell of the capitalist has been sounded. In order to work out the salvation of the working classes I would recommend that strikes should be repeated as often as possible, especially against employers who stand forth most prominently as the enemies of labour. The men cannot lose by a strike, for the work wanted must be done at some future time ; and the men ought to exercise their power of annoyance against their enemies by choosing their own time for doing the work. The great advantage of a strike is that it increases the enmity between labourers and capitalists, and compels workmen to reflect and investigate the causes of their sufferings. There are thousands of labourers in England who go on from year to year in perfect contentment with masters who allow them a bare subsistence in exchange for their incessant toil. A strike of a week's duration among such labourers would make them ask the question by what laws they were compelled to toil and to starve in order that their masters may idle and roll in wealth. The fruit of such reflections would be a violent hostility against the capitalist class ; and the new converts would be prepared to second the efforts of emancipation made by labourers in other quarters of England. Such a movement would inspire the capitalists with fear and would make them yield."

All this has a remarkably modern sound. In general, ever since 1833, the whole phraseology is modern. The terms social democrat, trades unionism, strike, general strike, bourgeoisie and proletariat, politics and anti-politics, class-warfare and solidarity of classes, etc., have been in general use ever since that period. Occasionally, and especially in reading the *Poor Man's Guardian* and the *Pioneer*, it is possible to imagine one's self transferred to the present day.

As soon as organised workers entered into the socialist agitation it ceased to be an Owenite sect and became a great movement of the working classes. Owing to special circumstances, it shunned parliamentary action for the time being and staked everything upon the direct action of trades unions.

Owen was horrified to see the masses abandoning his aims

and his policy. The spirits which he had helped to call up from the deep began to refuse obedience. He therefore redoubled his exertions to prove that the redemption of the country could only be obtained by the united action of the operatives and the propertied classes. He urged that capital was also a producer and that it deserved to receive friendly overtures from the operatives instead of meeting with hostility.[1] Alarmed at the rapid revolutionary growth of the trades unions, Owen, on the suggestion of John Fielden, founded the " National Regeneration Society " at a meeting in Manchester on November 25, 1833. Its object was to introduce an eight-hour day on March 1, 1834, by the joint action of the employers and the operatives. But the trades unions believed that the general strike would commence on March 1 in order to wrest the eight-hour day from the manufacturers. Owen soon began to throw the whole blame upon Morrison and Smith, and considered that the whole state of confusion was to be ascribed to their machinations and class-war policy. The incompatibility between peaceful socialism and fighting syndicalism, hitherto hidden and unrecognised, began to make itself noticeable from about the end of 1833.

Morrison and Smith had now to fight on two fronts, against Owen and his adherents on the one hand, and against the parliamentary socialists on the other hand. Smith considered Owen's influence on the trades unions to be pernicious,[2] and Morrison lost all respect for Owen.[3]

Owen's authority was, however, still considerable among the masses and many of their leaders. Syndicalist ideas were still of so recent growth and were known to so few of the working classes that Morrison and Smith were unable to achieve any success in opposition to Owen, for when the conflict came to a head Owen secured the dismissal of both (June, 1834). They, meanwhile, found greater opportunities and a more favourable scene of action in their polemics against the parliamentary socialists, who were headed by O'Brien, the editor of the *Poor Man's Guardian*.

[1] *Crisis*, December 7, 1833, January 11, 1834.
[2] W. A. Smith, *Life of J. E. Smith*, p. 104.
[3] *Pioneer*, January 25, 1834.

3.—CONTROVERSIES BETWEEN SOCIAL DEMOCRATS AND SYNDICALISTS

J. E. Smith, prior to his conflict with Owen, declared in his lecture of August 25, 1833, that parliamentary politics could not suffice for the people either from an intellectual or practical point of view, since they furnished no opportunity for action. The political unions merely developed a power of eloquence in their members and the drafting of useless resolutions. The main point is economic action :

" Politics must gradually change as the working men rise into importance ; and the operatives will then soon discover that, by looking exclusively to their own affairs, they will control the movements of the government, as a rudder controls the movements of the vessel to which it belongs."

Smith had in his mind's eye both co-operative societies and trades unions. After the congresses of the working classes in September (Manchester) and October (London), anti-parliamentarism assumed a purely syndicalist character both for Smith and for Morrison who in the meantime had become the editor of the *Pioneer*. The *Crisis* and the *Pioneer* became the organs of the intelligent section of the proletariat, whilst the *Poor Man's Guardian* lost its old prestige. O'Brien protested as follows :—

" In viewing the struggle which is now in progress between labour and capital there is one circumstance which fills us with astonishment and regret—we mean the disposition of the chief leaders of the workmen to disconnect their cause altogether from politics. This is the most futile and ill-judged proceeding that can be conceived. They see that if the workmen combine against the employers, the soldiers are called in. By whom are the troops paid ? By the people ! Who commands the troops ? The Government ! And in the composition of the Cabinet, just as in the making of the whole machinery of the State, the people have no share. Universal suffrage would place the magistracy and Parliament and consequently the disposal of the military

[1] *Crisis*, August 31, 1833.

and police forces in the hands of the entire body of the people, the workmen as well as employers. The Parliament being thus the representative of the whole, and the magistracy its principal executive, no particular part would receive more than its due share of protection. The present objects of the Trades Unions can never be attained under the existing Government. . . . Universal suffrage does not signify meddling with politics, but the rule of the people in the State and municipality, a Government therefore in favour of the working men. What seek the Trades Unions ? *Increase of wages* and a *diminution of the hours of labour;* that is to say, *to work less,* and to *get more for it*—in other words, *to produce less wealth,* and to *enjoy a larger portion of it.* Who does not see that this is to attack ' property ? ' But do *we* find fault with this ? Far from it ! To attack ' property ' is to attack robbery. But the question is, how are we to attack the capitalist in the safest and most expeditious manner ? We cannot attack him by *law,* for he holds the ' law ' in his own hands. How are we to attack him then ? We say, *in the way of the Trades Unions,* provided only that they add Universal Suffrage to their present avowed objects." [1]

These polemical statements were regarded by trades unionists as an attack upon trades unionism. The *Poor Man's Guardian* was treated by the workers as obnoxious and O'Brien was stigmatised as their opponent. An ordinary working man answered him (*Poor Man's Guardian,* December 28, 1833).

" Your remarks on the trades unions show lack of knowledge of trades unionism. The working people have found that political unions have not as yet been able to produce anything but the Humbug Bill, nor do they think they will ever be able to do anything. There are men mixed up with these unions whose interest it is to hinder the working man from enjoying the fruits of his labour. They are of opnion that in unions where all sorts of people are mixed up there never will be one united opinion or determination to do any real good. A remark has fallen from you last week that the workman in asking for higher wages and shorter labour time was attacking property. Now the trades

[1] *Poor Man's Guardian,* December 7 and 21, 1833.

Y

unions do not seek to produce less wealth, but to equalise it by giving employment to the unemployed and full employment to the partially employed. Now I ask you, will this produce less wealth? With regard to the attack on property, I would ask whose property is it but the producers? And consequently why should he have no right to take his own? Also the whole talk about capitalists giving higher wages is nonsense. They never did and never will. What the working men mean by getting better wages is to enjoy the produce of their labour."

This was the opinion of ordinary working men in 1833. It was not difficult for O'Brien to show that he too was in essential agreement with these objections, but that " the natural claim of the working man to the product of his work must be recognised by the artificial law of the State," and this could only be effected by the help of universal suffrage. But at that time the working men of the trades unions were so permeated with distrust of the State and so full of the consciousness of their power and of faith in their own organisations that they treated every reference to the necessity of seizing political power as a depreciation of trades unionism. Both sections of thought ceased to understand each other, as if they had suddenly begun to speak two different languages. Such expressions as government, universal suffrage, self-government received different meanings. The parliamentary party referred these terms to political institutions, the syndicalists applied them to trades-unionist organisations. The former desired a democratic House of Commons ; the latter strove for a general Labour Chamber to direct the interests of the productive classes and of the whole nation. The former regarded the electoral districts as political units, the latter found them in the separate trades unions. Parliamentary politics and trades-unionist economics diverged completely from each other. The *Crisis* wrote :—

" A struggle is awaiting us, but it is a struggle in which we are sure to conquer. At present we are within the laws, and still we are making our rulers tremble. By and by they will make new laws and then reproach us for breaking them. Shall we consider it our duty tamely to submit to any new laws which may be made to check our progress to prosperity and social happiness ? Let them make laws for themselves if they are so fond of legislating. If they are so fond of imposing taxes let them tax one another ; but let them first ask our consent before they prescribe pills for our disease which we ourselves know much better how to cure. No ! The immediate consequences of any attempt to crush the efforts of the popular mind, at this present juncture, will be a most resolute determination on the part of the people to legislate for themselves. This will be the result. We shall have a real House of Commons. We have never yet had a House of Commons. The only House of Commons is a House of Trades, and that is only just beginning to be formed. We shall have a new set of boroughs when the unions are organised : every trade shall be a borough, and every trade shall have a council of representatives to conduct its affairs. Our present commoners know nothing of the interests of the people, and care not for them. They are all landholders. How can an employer represent a workman ? There are 133,000 shoemakers in the country, yet not one representative have they in the House of Commons. According to the proportion they bear to the population they ought to have twenty-five representatives. The same is with carpenters and other trades in proportion. Such a House of Commons, however, is growing. The elements are gathering. The character of the Reformed Parliament is now blasted, and like the character of a woman when lost, is not easily recovered. It will be substituted by a House of Trades."[1]

The democratic press misunderstood the opinions of the *Crisis* and the *Pioneer*, and this attitude evoked the following reply from Morrison :—

" . . . The political economists are so short-sighted that they look only to partial release,—the diminution of taxation, separation of Church and State, revision of pension list and such other milk-and-water favours ; and when they have received their boon, pray where are they ? Is the power of private capital and monopoly in any wise impaired ? Is the commercial system paralysed ? And finally, have the working classes ob-

[1] *Crisis*, April 12, 1834.

tained any practical knowledge by scrutinising the measures of government ? No, nothing valuable is gained. There is only one way of gaining them, and that is by a general association of the people for the purpose of initiating themselves into the practice of conducting those affairs in which they have some experience. The Unions are of all the other means the only mode by which universal suffrage can safely be obtained, because it is obtained by practice, by serving an apprenticeship. Here they start to manage their own affairs on a small scale before they get management of larger affairs. The growing power and growing intelligence of trades unions, when properly managed, will draw into its vortex all the commercial interests of the country, and, in so doing, it will become, by its own self-acquired import- ance, a most influential, we might almost say dictatorial part of the body politic. When this happens we have gained all that we want ; we have gained universal suffrage, for if every member of the Union be a constituent, and the Union itself becoming a vital member of the State, it instantly erects itself into a House of Trades which must supply the place of the present House of Commons, and direct the industrial affairs of the country, according to the will of the trades which compose the associations of industry. This is the ascendant scale by which we arrive at universal suffrage. . . . With us, universal suffrage will begin in our lodges, extend to the general union, embrace the management of trade, and finally swallow up the political power."[1]

Two weeks later Smith, who contributed to the *Pioneer* under the pseudonym " Senex," gave expression to this idea in the following classic words (*Pioneer*, June 14, 1834) :—

" Social liberty must precede political liberty. While we are in a state of social slavery our rights would be exercised to the benefit of our tyrants, and we should be made subservient to the parties who work us for their purposes. No, before the horse is turned out to enjoy freedom in the green meadow, he must be unharnessed from the shafts of the wagon ; the galling rein that holds back his neck in the collar must be loosened, the bit must be taken from his mouth, and the collar itself from his shoulders ;

[1] *Pioneer*, May 31, 1834.

nor will he go forth in the valley rejoicing in his strength, while the limber of the gear hangs over his loins and encumbers his feet. To say, indeed, we shall never be free until we have universal suffrage is saying nothing more than we never shall be free until we are free. . . . Our position, brethren, is not political, and it cannot become political with any benefit to ourselves until we have found means to obtain a greater independent weight in society. This can only be the result of Unions."

At the time that Morrison and Smith wrote these articles, the "Grand National Consolidated Trades Union," with which we shall deal presently, had come into existence. They endeavoured to complete the edifice of this great organisation in a syndicalist sense, whilst Owen exerted himself to endue it with a co-operative character and a spirit of national solidarity so that it should form the basis for a peaceful revolution of society.

4. GREATER UNIONISM.

In the third week of February, 1834, the delegates of the trades unions met in London for the purpose of founding the "Grand National Consolidated Trades Union." The proceedings took place in secret. So far as can be gathered from the statements in the *Pioneer* a number of delegates were opposed to centralisation ; in the same way the assumption is warranted that the Consolidated Union only comprised about one half of the organised operatives of Great Britain. The committee appointed by the conference resolved to waive the question of a consolidation of the funds of the different trades unions, but to secure a unity of action and management, especially in the spending of sums of money in support of members or individual unions who might fall victims to the relentless persecution of capitalists. Moreover, the committee drew up the following propositions, forming a kind of programme of future action :—

"1. That as many different Trades Unions as possible do mutually agree under a perfect understanding with each other, to maintain a unity of action in all their proceedings with respect to their general laws and government, and also with regard to the levying and disposing of all funds raised for objects of presumed permanent utility.

" 2. As land is the source of the first necessaries of life, and as, without the possession of it, the producing classes will ever remain in a greater or less degree subservient to the money capitalists, and subject to the deterioration of the money value of their labour consequent upon the fluctuations of trade and commerce, this committee advise that a great effort should now be made by the Unions to secure such portions of it on lease as their funds will permit, in order that in all turn-outs the men may be employed in rearing the greater part, if not the whole, of their subsistence under the direction of practical agricultural superintendents, which arrangements would not have the effect of lowering the price of labour in any trade, but on the contrary would rather tend to increase it by drawing off the at present superfluous supply in manufactures. . . .

" 3. The committee would, nevertheless, earnestly recommend in all cases of strikes and turn-outs, where it is practicable, that the men be employed in the making or producing of all such commodities as would be in demand among their brother union-ists ; and that to effect this, each lodge should be provided with a workroom or shop in which those commodities may be manu-factured on account of such lodge which shall make proper arrangements for the supply of the necessary materials.

" 4. That great advantages would accrue by the formation, in each district lodge, of a fund for the support of the sick and aged.

" 5. That in all cases where it be practicable, each district or branch lodge should establish one or more depots for provisions and articles in general domestic use ; by which means the work-ing man may be supplied with the best commodities at little above wholesale prices.

" 6. That each lodge do make arrangements for furnishing the means of mental improvement to their members, and for the cultivation of good habits among them, by affording them every facility for meeting together for friendly conversation, mutual instruction and rational amusement or recreation ; which arrangements might be rendered in a short period infinitely more enticing and agreeable than the delusive, pernicious, and dearly-bought gratifications sought after in the tap-room or the gin-shop.

" 7. That we should offer the females among the industrious classes every encouragement and assistance to form themselves into lodges for the protection of their industry."

The programme was therefore a compromise between the Owenite and trades-unionist aims, and kept closely in view the object of " freeing the working men completely from the tyranny of the capitalists."

Morrison's *Pioneer* was officially adopted as the central organ to start with.

Whilst the accoucheurs and nurses of the Grand Consolidated Union shouted for joy, the new-born babe hovered between life and death. The employers, the Press, and the State made every effort to deprive it of light and air. Lock-outs and strikes exhausted the funds of the Union, the Press demanded a strict inquiry into the union's by-laws, the law passed draconic sentences upon trades unionists. The conviction of the six Dorchester labourers for swearing and administering oaths on the admission of members was a deterrent example.[1]

The main policy of the employers was not to wait until the Labour forces were concentrated, but to attack at once and beat the separate columns of the Labour army before they had reached the converging point where the grand assault on property was to take place.

The unprotected condition of the funds of the Union was another obstacle. Defaulting officials could embezzle money with impunity, and this actually happened in the case of the " Grand Consolidated Trades Union," shattering the confidence of working men. As early as April the position of the organisation was critical. This was followed by the differences between Owen, Morrison, and Smith, who were no longer able to work together. Owen viewed everything from the standpoint of co-operation and solidarity of the classes and regarded all class strife as pernicious, whilst Morrison and Smith, on the other

[1] Webb, *History of Trade Unionism*, pp. 113. *seq.*, 1896.

hand, rejected all Utopian ideas and wished to utilise the instrument which the working class had forged in the Consolidated Trades Union by wielding it as a sword to overthrow the old state of society and to set up labour in the place of capital. In June, 1834, the antagonism between the thinkers of the working class could no longer be bridged over. Owen stopped the publication of the *Crisis* in order to turn Smith out of the labour movement, and he induced the committee of the Consolidated Trades Union to disown the *Pioneer*, to discharge Morrison, and to found a new paper as the central organ.

Owing to the secrecy of the committee's proceedings nothing further can be stated concerning this national confederation of labour. When the *Pioneer* ceased publication the committee founded its own paper, i.e. *The Pioneer and Official Gazette.* In September the committee broke off all relations with Owen [1] and refused his request for an interview. The organisation fell to pieces, but even in its dissolution it has handed down an important document of the intense activity of thought of this period. It occurs in the *Pioneer and Official Gazette* of September 20, 1834, the only copy extant of this newspaper. The leading article is obviously a kind of final survey of the struggles of 1832 to 1834, and they could not have received more suitable treatment. The article runs as follows :—

" *Thoughts on the growing spirit of union among the labour holders or operative classes.*—The spirit of union among the operatives of the industrious classes in the most advanced nations of Europe is the manifestation of a strong natural feeling, the remote causes of which are of greater magnitude and of more serious influence on the happiness of mankind than most people are disposed to acknowledge. From time immemorial this creation moves on, and works on, with us and within us. Man individual is at different times more or less actuated by the temporary arrangement of localities, or by the artificial circumstances that surround him ; but nature acting incessantly upon man species by the constant laws of assimilation which develop all organised substances, they consequently vary from

[1] Frank Podmore, *Robert Owen*, 1906, II., 453.

themselves imperceptibly at each instant of time, and no sub-stance can rationally be said to BE, since all are passing from one modification to another modification. The condition of society at any given moment must always be considered as modifying itself, because the human species being composed of organised substances, generating new ideas by the successive modification of their nature, whilst the artificial rules of life (laws and regulations) do not undergo a corresponding gradual modification of their nature, man individual soon begins to feel new wants ; he finds, after a period, that he can no longer move in comfort and liberty in the same localities, under laws and regulations framed long since for substances and circumstances which no longer exist : hence it is that radical reforms in all things artificial become indispensable after a certain period of time. The most important duty expected by reason from all rational government is undoubtedly that of watching the effect of the natural changes thus operated upon whole populations, in order that after having ascertained the nature of the new ideas which have actually created new imperative wants, the laws and regulations may be so modified *in time* as to maintain political equilibrium. The performance of that important duty requires that rulers should possess three qualities most essential to sound legislation : 1, a knowledge of the age they live in ; 2, sagacity to discriminate right from wrong ; 3, impartiality to act with justice from a *national* point of view *only*. . . .

" The increasing competition between great and small masters has compelled some to become the unwilling petty tyrants over the operatives ; and the unionists appear to be equally unjust in compelling others not to work under a minimum of wages, fixed by no acknowledged authority. But in truth no one is actually to blame—it is nature all through. It is the Creator's law of progress working on for the greater happiness of mankind through the mind and the difficulties of individuals. . . . A new system of labour is coming into the world. The new system and the struggles between the classes are positive signs of new social arrangements. Boards of labour or committees of industry must assume the place now occupied by the great masters. Such arrangements will gradually pave the way to community of property.

" Meanwhile the struggle goes on and the operatives are suffering. But we must have patience. The spirit of the age is an irresistible power—unions will continue ; more strikes and more blunders will succeed each other. However productive they may be of temporary mischief and misery, better associations shall be formed, and from the difficulties of the time the nation will learn. A new world will gradually unfold itself ; the financial delusions and blunders which clog and shackle society will become evident to every one ; a new kind of knowledge and of liberty will arise and spread itself, from that single reason that no remedy can be found in the old, worn-out basis of thought and action far too narrow for the mental fecundity and for the mechanical powers of the age now begun ! "

This was the last syndicalist manifesto. The movement collapsed, dragging down with it in the dust labour exchanges, co-operative societies, the movement for the Eight Hour Day, syndicalism, and even a great part of the Owenite Utopias and tenets of salvation. Among the ruins of the shattered syndicalist laboratory the labouring class lay in a state of exhaustion. John Francis Bray, the author of *Labour's Wrongs* (1839), has left us a vivid picture of the doubt and disappointment of that time :—

" The great body of the working classes believed that their late trades unions would be omnipotent in effecting their deliverance from the dominion of the capitalist ; for a more powerful engine was never made use of by the producers. From there being many trades united together, and supporting each other, when one struck a blow at tyranny, that blow fell with the accumulated monetary force of the whole mass. But, whether victorious or defeated, the workman was alike involved in losses and in difficulties—all his efforts for the permanent bettering of his condition were uneffectual—and this vast confederation was at length broken up and dissolved into its primitive trade societies. These have continued at times a desultory and unequal contest with capital—sometimes with partial success, but oftener with defeat and ruin. The capitalist and the employer have always ultimately been too strong for them ; and trades unions have become, amongst the enemies of the working class, a by-word of caution or contempt—a record of the weakness of Labour when opposed to Capital—an indestructible memento of the evil working of the present system in regard to the two great classes which now compose society."[1]

Two years of recuperation and reflection enabled the working classes to rise up again into activity. They were awakened and roused from their apathy by the intelligent section of the London operatives, who were parliamentary Owenites and were convinced more than ever of the necessity for independent parliamentary action. In their meetings which were held either in favour of the liberation of the Dorchester labourers or in favour of the people's press, Lovett, Hetherington, Watson, Cleave, Hartwell, etc., spoke on the position resulting from the events of 1830 to 1838, and drew inferences for future guidance. Their main doctrines were : an independent labour policy, socialist aims, peaceful and educational methods.[2] The threads of social democracy which had been snapped by the events of 1833 and 1834 were now to be taken up again. Circumstances came to their help ; the Municipal Reform Act (1835) which adapted the parliamentary franchise to the municipalities and was intended to put an end to the old system of cliques, was opposed by the Lords and led to a conflict between the two Houses. This aroused once more the public interest in constitutional questions. The introduction by stages of the new Poor Law Bill incited the working class to political activity. The impending reduction of the newspaper stamp from fourpence to one penny put fresh life into the people's press. At the end of 1835 the approach of Chartism proper was perceptible.

[1] J. F. Bray, *Labour's Wrongs*, p. 100.
[2] Place, MSS. 27819, pp. 24, 229, *seq*.

INDEX

(PARTS I. AND II.)

349

VOLUME II

VOLUME II

PART III

CHARTISM

THE GROWTH OF CHARTISM

I.—THE CENTRES AND LEADERS OF THE MOVEMENT

In 1836 the revival of the working class activities was clearly discernible, and it was everywhere connected with parliamentary politics. There were at that time four centres of the movement, which supplied thought and enthusiasm to all that was alive among the industrial population—London for the South of England, Birmingham for the Midlands, Newcastle and Leeds for the North of England, Glasgow for Scotland. With the exception of London, where intelligent artisans stood at the head of the revival, all the other centres were, at first, managed by middle class extremists, idealists, and revolutionists. Since about 1839 Manchester became the focus of Chartist thought and action in the North, while Bradford gave to the movement some of its most zealous and orthodox adherents, always hunting for heretics and " traitors."

London was the centre of the Moral Force section, though representatives of Physical Force were not lacking. The latter, who only came to the fore in moments of great excitement, had their seats in Spitalfields and in the district round Lincoln's Inn Fields. On the whole, the Moral Force men had the upper hand, because they had the most intelligent members, able writers and speakers. The most distinguished among them were William Lovett, Henry Hetherington, James Watson, and Henry Vincent.

In the Midlands, Thomas Attwood dominated the scene up to 1840. Surrounded by his lieutenants, Scholefield, Muntz, Salt, and Douglas, he worked with might and main for his paper currency schemes until the movement had outgrown his control and his aims.

In the North, Feargus O'Connor, Taylor, Stephens, and Lowery were the protagonists of the Physical Force party—the largest and most determined section of the Chartist movement. Their influence was also distinctly felt in Wales.

The movement in Scotland exhibited mental characteristics similar to those of London. The Moral Force men prevailed over the adherents of O'Connor. The Scottish movement has not produced any great leader who would bear comparison with Lovett or O'Connor or Attwood, but it possessed a relatively great number of able writers and serious propagandists.

There was no Chartist organisation in Ireland, her working men were too poor and little educated to be able to grasp the meaning and support the movement of a Labour Party. Besides, all the Irish Radical writers and orators who could have organised Chartist associations lived in England and worked either for Repeal or Revolution. Ireland supplied to the Chartist movement its greatest orator, O'Connor, and its most trenchant writer, Bronterre O'Brien.

The adherents of Chartism belonged, as a rule, to the better paid and mentally active sections of the working class. This was particularly the case in the years from 1836 to 1842. Contemporary evidence leaves no doubt that it was not a movement of the lowest strata of society, but of the best elements of the industrial population.[1]

2.—THE LONDON LEADERS

The author of the Charter and the most sympathetic leader of Chartism was William Lovett (1800–1877), a Cornish workman, who came to London in 1821. Originally a ropemaker, he turned to cabinetmaking and became an efficient artisan. He read and learned much, attended the Mechanics' Institution and debating societies, joined the Metropolitan Political Union in 1826, and was gradually converted to Owenism. He was one of the first founders of co-operative shops, and spread the doc-

[1] Thomas Carlyle, *Chartism*, 1839, c. 4 ; *Westminster Review*, April, 1839, p. 496 *sqq.* ; J. S. Mill, *Dissertations and Discussions*, vol. 2, p. 188-9;

trines of Owenite Socialism among the working men, but always
in conjunction with Radical politics. His activity as secretary
of the Society for the Diffusion of Co-operative Knowledge and
as a political worker brought him into close relation with Owen,
Hunt, Cobbett, and the Socialist leaders, and made him one of
the best known and most respected of the leaders of the London
workmen. " Possessed of a clear and masterly intellect, and
great powers of application, everything that he attempted was
certain of accomplishment." [1] This opinion was fully shared
by all who knew him. His numerous manifestoes and other
writings as well as his continual struggle for the working classes,
lasting for nearly thirty years, testify to the intellectual and
moral strength of this man. His autobiography, entitled *Life
and Struggles*, is still worth reading. A profoundly ethical
strain runs through all his writings. There is not the least
trace of demagogy in his character. The essence of his convictions, acquired under the fire of the social battlefield, he summed
up in the following advice to the working classes : " You must
become your own social and political regenerators, or you will
never enjoy freedom ; for true liberty cannot be conferred by
Acts of Parliament or decrees of princes, but must spring from
the knowledge, morality, and public virtue of our population." [2]

In his capacity as a leader of revolutionary movements Lovett
did not escape attacks from both friend and foe. In July, 1839,
he was sentenced to a year's imprisonment for seditious libel and
treated like a common criminal. His sufferings affected him incomparably less than the attacks made upon him by O'Connor
and his adherents for keeping his agitation within legal and
peaceful limits, for his warm advocacy of education for the
masses, and for the plan he devised during his imprisonment for
completing a system of popular education. Lovett, who sur-
vived Chartism by two decades, was an Owenite and democrat
from about 1826 to 1842. He afterwards gradually abandoned
Owenism and class warfare and came to consider democratic and

[1] Gammage, *History of the Chartist Movement*, ed. 1894, p. 10.
Compare Graham Wallas, *Life of Francis Place*, pp. 362–5.
[2] Lovett and Collins, *Chartism*, 1840.

I A

educational reform as the best means of improvement of the condition of the working classes.

Henry Hetherington (1792–1849), a compositor, was one of the first pupils at the Mechanics' Institution, and he followed the current of the intelligent working men of the metropolis by becoming an Owenite, free-thinker, and democrat. In 1828 he published a pamphlet in defence of free-thought. In October 1, 1830, he undertook the publication of *Penny Papers for the People*, which subsequently became the *Poor Man's Guardian*. In this action he followed the example of William Carpenter (afterwards editor of *Lloyd's Newspaper*), who published his *Political Letters* without a newspaper stamp, and initiated the struggle against the taxes on knowledge. In this campaign Hetherington showed himself to be an extraordinarily able, pertinacious, and dauntless leader of men. In 1831 three indictments were framed against him, and he was sentenced to six months' imprisonment. After having served his sentence he continued his campaign without interruption, and found a valiant supporter in Bronterre O'Brien as editor of the *Poor Man's Guardian*. In 1832 he published the *Republican*, an extremely mordant weekly paper, quite in the style of the speakers at the Rotunda ; King William IV. is always called Mr. Guelph in its columns and the Queen Mrs. Guelph. Towards the end of 1832 he spent another six months in prison, whence, by means of letters and articles, he stirred up public opinion against the newspaper stamp. In 1833 he undertook the publication of the *Destructive*, or *People's Conservative*, which was edited in exactly the same tone as the *Poor Man's Guardian*, and later on *Hetherington's Twopenny Despatch* and *London Despatch*. The latter gave expression to the agitation for the fundamental ideas of the Charter and for a peaceful policy restricted to moral weapons. All these papers were issued unstamped and forced the Government to reduce the stamp duty from 4d. to 1d. Hetherington did yeoman service to the movement as a missionary of the London Working Men's Association in 1837.[1]

[1] Gammage, *op. cit.*, p. 7.

Hetherington's views of Chartism were similar to Lovett's. He was a Puritan in morals, Spartan in simplicity, a total abstainer and humanitarian to the point of self-denial. By his death Chartism lost one of its most unselfish, valiant, and resolute adherents. He left a will, in which, after a deistic confession of faith, he declares :—

" These are my views in quitting an existence that has been chequered with the plagues and pleasures of a competitive, scrambling, selfish system ; a system by which the moral and social aspirations of the noblest human being are nullified by incessant toil and physical deprivations ; by which, indeed, all men are trained to be either slaves, hypocrites or, criminals. Hence my ardent attachment to the principles of that great and good man—Robert Owen. I quit this world with a firm conviction that his system is the only true road to human emancipation ; that it is, indeed, the only just system for regulating the affairs of honest, intelligent human beings—the only one yet made known to the world that is based on truth, justice, and equality. While the land, machines, tools, implements of production and the produce of man's toil are exclusively in possession of the do-nothings, and labour is the sole possession of the wealth-producers—a marketable commodity, bought up and directed by wealthy idlers—never-ending misery must be their inevitable lot. Robert Owen's system, if rightly understood and faithfully carried out, rectifies all these anomalies. It makes man the proprietor of his own labour and of the elements of production—it places him in a condition to enjoy the entire fruits of his labour and surrounds him with circumstances that will make him intelligent, rational, and happy.

" Grateful to Mr. Owen for the happiness I have experienced in contemplating the superiority of his system, I could not die happy without recommending my fellow countrymen to study its principles and earnestly strive to establish them in practice. I freely forgive all who have injured me in my struggle ; and die in the hope and consolation that a time is approaching when the spirit of antagonism will give place to fraternal affection and universal co-operation to promote the happiness of mankind."

" London, August 21, 1849." [1]

In the last year of his life he was acquainted with Frederick Denison Maurice.

James Watson (1799–1874) resembled Hetherington both in character and disposition. He was born in Yorkshire, of working class parents. His mother taught him to read and write. In 1819 he became a free-thinker by reading Cobbett's and Carlile's newspapers. In 1823 he was sentenced to three years' imprisonment for circulating seditious and free-thought literature. In 1826 he became an Owenite, and two years later he was the storekeeper of the first co-operative association in London, where he made friends with Lovett. Watson was the first itinerant preacher or missionary of co-operation, and greatly contributed to the rise of the co-operative movement of that period. In 1831 he started a publishing office and bookshop for works on free-thought and Owenism. He joined the National Union, pushed the sale of the *Poor Man's Guardian*, and in 1832 opposed, in public discussion, Owen's anti-parliamentarism and the orthodox Owenites. In 1833 he was again sentenced to six months' imprisonment, and once more in 1834. He belonged to the Charter Committee, and worked for Chartism on the same lines as Lovett and Hetherington.[2]

The fourth in the band of workers was Henry Vincent (1813–1879), a compositor, who joined the Chartist movement at its inception. He was the most popular speaker among the London working men and one of the most prominent orators of Chartism. In February, 1839, he founded a weekly, *The Western Vindicator*, and transferred his activities as an agitator to Wales. The longer his absence from London, the more rapidly he forgot the peaceful, moral tactics recommended by Lovett and Hetherington, and he followed O'Connor's and Stephens's example in dropping into violent phraseology, and into predictions of the

[1] G. J. Holyoake, *Life of Hetherington*, 1849.
[2] W. J. Linton, *James Watson*, 1879; Holyoake, *History of Co-operation*, 1875, vol. 1.

imminence of their victory. On May 7, 1839, he was arrested for taking part in riotous assemblies, and on July 31 he was sentenced at Monmouth to a year's imprisonment. On March 26, 1840, he stood again before a jury for taking part in riotous assemblies, and received an additional sentence of eight months, so that he spent altogether twenty months in prison. From 1842 onwards he was active as a temperance lecturer and Radical politician.

3.—THE NORTHERN LEADERS

It was from Ireland—economically the most retrograde and nationally the most disturbed corner of the United Kingdom— that the socialist and revolutionary movement of the masses of the most industrial country of the world received its orator and leader. Yet he was alien to it, both by race and language : " I am a foreigner by language and blood," he told the operatives of Yorkshire ;[1] the causes of his rebellion bore no relation at all to theirs ; his dreams by night and thoughts by day were an independent Ireland,[2] whilst their aspirations moved towards a social revolution. O'Connor's dominant position in the Chartist movement is one of the most difficult problems in the history of British labour. A glance at the history of Ireland of the years from about 1750 to 1840 as well as at the life history of O'Connor may help us to solve this problem. In the latter half of the eighteenth century, when cattle-breeding in Ireland became more profitable than agriculture, the ground landlords fenced in numerous small farms to form large grazing farms, and even where commons still existed they were enclosed to form part of the pastures. In this way many Irish small-holders lost their means of subsistence altogether ; they formed secret leagues such as the Whiteboys, who tore down the fences and stopped at no violence. The secret organisation of the Whiteboys still existed in the first three decades of the nineteenth century, and Feargus O'Connor belonged to it. The impression which this secret organisation made upon O'Connor was indelibly engraved

[1] *Northern Star*, October 16, 1838.   [2] *Ibid.*

upon his mind ; the Whiteboys were his type of revolutionary activity.[1]

In the same period a change of opinion swept over a section of the Irish Protestants, which exercised a profoundly revolutionary influence on Irish thought. Owing to bad government and financial mismanagement the English colonists of Ireland became disaffected. Protestants and Catholics found that they had interests in common against England. In this rebellious mood they came under the influence of the ideas of the Radical movement in England, the American War of Independence, and finally the French Revolution. The educated Protestants of Ireland absorbed the revolutionary ideas and furnished the Irish with thinkers and leaders for an insurrection against England. The Catholic Irish also contributed some of the leaders, of whom Arthur O'Connor, an uncle of Feargus, was one of the most influential. In October, 1791, they formed the organisation of the United Irishmen, read Rousseau, Paine, Locke, came into touch with the London Corresponding Society, and five years later conspired with the French Government for the purpose of freeing the Irish people, with their help, from the yoke of the English. The insurrection failed. A few of the leaders were condemned to death, whilst Arthur O'Connor escaped and entered the French army, in which he ultimately became a general. Arthur was also a political writer and an admirer of Condorcet, whose name he adopted ; in 1798 he published an essay on the " State of Ireland," in which he pointed out that the granting of Universal Suffrage was absolutely necessary in order to make it possible for the people to alter the rights of property according to the wishes of the majority. Arthur O'Connor was idealised by his nephew Feargus. During the first year's issue of the *Northern Star* (1837–8) Arthur O'Connor's biography appeared in several serial parts, and in June, 1843, Feargus brought out a new edition of Arthur's aforesaid essay, and commended it to the Chartists as the quintessence of all political and economic wisdom. Arthur and Feargus O'Connor vividly recall to mind

[1] *Northern Star*, March 28, 1840 ; May 29, 1841 ; May 13, 1848. *Cp.* Thomas Frost, *Forty Years' Recollections*, 1880, p. 137 *sqq.*

the generals and democrats of the gentry of Poland, who took part in all popular movements from the last partition of Poland down to 1871, and who were very greatly influenced by ideas of a social revolution.

These national, family, and social revolutionary traditions gave Feargus O'Connor a historical outlook that was closely allied to that of British Socialism and Chartism, viz., agrarian reform on socialistic lines, the sovereignty of the people, the law of nature, hatred of oligarchy, the absolute necessity for Universal Suffrage. This mental affinity with the revolutionary movement of the British working classes he combined with great oratorical powers, which could not fail to impress the inarticulate masses of the factory towns. What they attempted to express by passionate outbursts of temper, impulsive strikes, and clumsy conspiracies, the Irish agitator gave utterance in thunderous rhetoric, sometimes trenchant, but always vulgar. His mental culture was surprisingly limited, his legal education was neither comprehensive nor profound enough to separate him from the masses. There was no need for him to descend from any scientific heights to the madding crowd, nor was it necessary for them to make any effort to understand him. Charles Kingsley's O'Flynn in *Alton Locke* is not a bad representation of O'Connor, while Charles Dickens's labour leader, Slackbridge, in *Hard Times*, is rather too much of a caricature of the same personality.

After a short political career in the first Reform Parliament (1833–4), in which he mostly spoke on Irish affairs and generally voted with the Radicals, except on their motions for the modification or abolition of the Corn Laws, he began to attend working class meetings and to advocate the cause of democratic reform. But he never succeeded in gaining the confidence of the metropolitan artisans. To the thinking workmen of London he was a blustering demagogue, a backwoodsman with plenty of ready-made phrases at his command. When they came into open conflict with him and told him their opinion of him, O'Connor replied, " You must fight it out ; you shall either crush me or I will annihilate your association." The highly skilled artisans of the large towns only aroused O'Connor's derision ; he did not regard them as working men at all, and declared, " Let those with unshorn chins, blistered hands and fustian jackets read the occupations of some of the subscribers to the document, and the bubble bursts ! "[1]

Whenever O'Connor came into conflict with the intellectuals of the working classes, ne inevitably made the appeal to the fustian jackets, unshorn chins, and blistered hands. The *Northern Star* is full of these appeals of O'Connor. An appeal of this nature was always an indication of its author being about to oust one of his rivals. In the course of time this conflict occasionally softened, the Londoners could not fail to recognise O'Connor's tireless activity, whilst O'Connor, in his turn, learned much, especially in the years 1842–44, and attained a certain degree of comprehension of modern industrial problems. For instance, he declared that :

" The ten hour proposals will later on be regarded as a measure of the power of the working men. It is an attempt to initiate a series of laws which will curb the new order of things that has been produced by machinery, and which will place it at the service of the whole of society, instead of letting it act solely to the advantage of a single class."[2]

Still, the rupture between O'Connor and the London artisans was never healed. O'Connor was not able to find a footing in London. He, therefore, removed his sphere of activity to Yorkshire, where the operatives in the autumn of 1837 were making preparations to issue a newspaper of their own, and had contributed £800 for this purpose. O'Connor became the editor, and on November 18, 1837, the first number of the *Northern Star* saw the light. The existence of the paper was assured from the very first. O'Connor was the editor-in-chief ; the sub-editor was William Hill, a Swedenborgian preacher and a grammarian, from whom O'Connor acquired the power of writing a correct and trenchant style of English. Towards the end of 1842, Hill fell out with his chief, and George Julian Harney entered the

---

[1] *Northern Star*, February 10 and 24, 1838 ; March 3, 1835.
[2] *Ibid.*, April 6, 1844 ; June 29, 1844.

editorial office. In November, 1844, the paper was moved from Leeds to London, where it existed till 1852. The largest circulation of the *Northern Star* reached a total of 45,000 copies, but each number was read by at least ten people.

The founding of the Great Northern Union was another of O'Connor's ventures. In Leeds there already existed a Working Men's Association on the lines of the London Association. O'Connor exerted himself to make this association the central union of all the Radical working men's societies of the North of England. He chose the term " Union " in imitation of the Birmingham society, but the words " Great Northern " showed that he contemplated from the very beginning the inclusion of the whole of the North, although the Corresponding Acts did not allow any such federation. On April 26, 1838, a general meeting of the Leeds Working Men's Association took place, which appointed a committee to draw up a programme for the Great Northern Union. O'Connor was elected secretary of the committee, who outlined a programme in which stress was laid upon the importance of democratic parliamentary reform and trades unionism. The following was one of the objects of the Great Northern Union :—

" The last but not the least object which your Committee confidently anticipate the Northern Union will constantly keep in view is the uniting together, upon the general principle of justice all those who, though loving peace, are resolved to risk their lives in the attainment of their rights. Your Committee deem it, therefore, expedient that before joining the Union every member should distinctly understand that in the event of moral force failing to procure those privileges which the Constitution guarantees but which a party would abrogate, and should the Constitution be invaded, it is resolved that physical force shall be resorted to, if necessary, in order to secure the equality of the law and the blessings of those institutions which are the birthright of free men. That as the object of yielding allegiance is to receive protection, the fact of withholding protection is a violation of the bond which should bind subject to monarch ; and, therefore, the Union should recognise no authority save that which emanates from the legitimate source of all honour, namely, from the people."[1]

The outlined programme was adopted at a great meeting in Leeds on May 3, 1838, at which numerous delegates were present from Huddersfield, Halifax, Elland, Dewsbury and other smaller places. The meeting pledged itself to acknowledge Feargus O'Connor as their leader—or, as Francis Place remarks, as the apostle of the North.

A new policy was introduced into the movement by his recommending the use of physical force against the Government as well as by the summons to the working men to prepare for such eventualities. There can be no doubt that O'Connor meant no more than he said, viz., opposition to the constituted authorities as a last resort, but his insurrectionary manner of speech, his references to the " heroic " deeds of the Whiteboys, and his glorification of Arthur O'Connor caused disastrous misunderstandings.

The work which O'Connor began was carried on by other agitators—Joseph R. Stephens, Richard Oastler, John Taylor, George Julian Harney; the lawyer, August Harding Beaumont, the tailor, Robert Lowery, and the publican, Peter Bussey. The great mass of the factory hands of the North of England adopted the policy of physical force.

John Taylor (1804–1841) came of a prosperous Scotch family, studied medicine, and became a surgeon in the navy. He received a legacy of £30,000, which he spent almost entirely on fitting out a ship to assist the Greeks in their war of liberation against the Turks. He also lived a few years in Paris after the July Revolution, and came into contact with the revolutionary leaders and conspirators. He was a born fighter, and had little or no inclination for protracted political talk and speechifying. When the Radical movement had made itself felt in Great Britain he returned to Scotland, settled in Glasgow, and founded the *Glasgow Liberator*, which had only a short existence. His sphere of action was not in a close and confined study. He threw himself body and soul into the agitation and was drawn under O'Connor's

[1] *Northern Star*, May 5, 1838.

influence. Of the London working men he had the same opinion as his chief; it was only in 1840, after having witnessed William Lovett's determination and capacity for self-sacrifice, that he altered his opinion. Here is the conclusion of a speech which he made at Newcastle at the end of December, 1838 : " I shall part with my sabre only with my life, and my own hand shall write the epitaph upon a tyrant's brow in characters of blood and with a pen of steel."[1] In 1838 and 1839 he stood at the head of the secret league of the extreme Chartists.

August Harding Beaumont (1800-1838) was an English lawyer, whose family were inclined to Radicalism. Even as a young man he entered into relations with the Irish Radicalism and founded a Radical newspaper in London, which had only a brief existence. He then moved to Newcastle, where he assisted in founding the *Northern Liberator* and edited it. The first number appeared on October 21, 1837. The *Northern Liberator* pronounced for democratic parliamentary reform, for the repeal of the Poor Law of 1834, and in general for the interests of the working men. Beaumont was out and out in favour of the policy of physical force. In a public meeting in Newcastle on January 1, 1838, he demanded the execution of Lord John Russell, Lord Melbourne, and Sir Robert Peel.

In energy of expression, in a strict logical sequence of ideas, and mastery of homely sentiment, J. R. Stephens, a Nonconformist minister, was head and shoulders above both Vincent and O'Connor. In the extreme impetuosity with which he called for opposition by force of arms he surpassed Beaumont and Taylor, without descending to their exhibitions of bad taste. During 1837 and 1838 he gave utterance, with a display of volcanic energy, to the whole gamut of feelings of right and wrong, justice and injustice, love for the poor and hatred of the rich. His sources were the Bible and the doctrines of the law of nature. He was the avenging preacher of the God of wrath, a prophet from the old books of Israel, inflammatory and inciting to violence. He was in his element when speaking in public. Standing on the platform in the open air, on some town moor or common, sur-

[1] *Northern Star*, December 29, 1838.

rounded by thousands of colliers, weavers, stockingers, and metal workers, cheering and applauding, a feverish and frenzied enthusiasm took hold of him and all the powers of his mind became enhanced, concentrated, and transformed into winged words, which sped forth tempestuously, and yet with rhythm and order. His was a short-lived but heroic adventure. The first rude contact with the mailed fist brought him back to the sober realities of life. The spirit of the prophet of Yahve departed, and Stephens turned into a conservative and mild-mannered preacher.

When the new Poor Law was put into force he, following Oastler's example, actively opposed it; and when Chartism, in 1837, began to grow in power he took up its cause. He declared himself a convinced partisan of Universal Suffrage, and in September, 1837, he helped to finance the *Northern Star*; he took twenty £1 shares.[1] He cannot, however, be regarded as a strict adherent of the Chartist movement. His main object was the repeal of the new Poor Law and the improvement of the material condition of the working people. The Charter seemed to him to be a fit means to this end, but he always subordinated politics to social reform.

Towards the end of the year 1838, his agitating reached boiling point. The nocturnal gatherings must have presented a solemn and fantastic scene, held as they were in the open air, attended by thousands of working men, many of them with flaming torches in their hands, others armed with muskets, all of them eagerly listening to Stephen's violent oratory. The propertied classes became alarmed, and on December 12, 1838, the torchlight meetings were declared illegal by royal proclamation.[2]

Richard Oastler (1789–1861)—the "factory king"—considered the new Poor Law to be subversive of the Constitution, and instigated the masses to oppose by force of arms the administration of the Poor Law   He exhorted them in the following terms:

[1] G. J. Holyoake, *Life of J. R. Stephens*, 1881, p. 181, where the receipt for £20 is reproduced.
[2] For a description of the torchlight meetings, see Disraeli, *Sybil*, book 4, chapter 4.

" Arm then, arm, my fellow-countrymen, against this most execrable law of tyrants ! Arm ye, sons of Britain, whose souls are in the Ark of the Constitution ! Arm, and make the traitors pause and tremble. . . . Let no other ornaments be cared for in your houses but bright and well-made arms. Arm then, arm for peace and justice. If the tyrants know that you possess arms, there will be no need for you to use them. . . Be sober, be vigilant, be *men !* "[1]

Oastler never definitely declared himself in favour of the Charter. Radical democracy was repugnant to his Tory conscience. He entertained a particular hatred for Liberal philosophy—the anti-dogmatic character of liberal thought. He stood, however, in close relation to O'Connor and Bronterre O'Brien. When the latter undertook the London correspondence for the *Northern Star*, Oastler wrote to Stephens : " Tell O'Brien to put the *Poor Man's Guardian's* soul into the *Star*."[2] He meant the hatred which O'Brien felt for the middle classes.

Oastler and Stephens were on friendly terms with Robert Owen. On May 17, 1837, they spoke at a meeting in Huddersfield in favour of a resolution, in which the government was called upon to provide State-aid for founding agricultural co-operative societies for the unemployed ; the land was to be tilled in common and to remain the common property of the workers.[3] Owen had a high opinion of Stephens, and said : " Although Stephens is a clergyman, he is a most ardent friend of the working classes and a very liberal man."[4]

4.—THE CHARTIST SCHOOLMASTER

Among all the Chartist leaders there was not a single one who so thoroughly embodied the movement as James Bronterre O'Brien (1805–1864). His admirers and followers were to be found everywhere. His best known disciples were Harney and Gammage. The Chartists regarded him as their schoolmaster. O'Brien held the same position to the thinkers in the Chartist movement as O'Connor to the masses.

[1] *Northern Star*, August 25, 1838.   [2] G. J. Holyoake, *op. cit.*, p. 86.
[3] *New Moral World*, May 27, 1837.   [4] *Ibid.*, April 29, 1837.

O'Brien was under the deepest obligation to Owen, Ogilvie, and Gray. At a somewhat later date he received great inspiration from Hodgskin's *Labour Defended*. He added nothing to the ideas of these four men. They formed his arsenal whence he procured his weapons in his contests for political and social reforms. The influence of Spence, Godwin, and J. F. Bray is also clearly visible. He was a most extensive reader, but always with a view to his journalism. His trenchant articles, which he often signed " Bronterre," procured for him the nicknames Brimstone O'Brien or Bronze O'Brien.[1] Land reform, currency reform, and the conflict between capital and labour are the fundamental ideas of his journalistic labours.

His school days he spent in his native country and studied law at Trinity College, Dublin. In 1830 he came to London to complete his studies. Here he rapidly plunged into the Radical movement, joined Cobbett and Hunt and gave up his legal career.

In January and February, 1831, O'Brien published three essays in Carpenter's *Political Letters*, on the condition of England—written in a Radical and Owenite sense. Owen's communist plans were to be realised by means of a parliament elected by universal suffrage, whilst the State was to acquire the necessary land and machinery in order to turn the operatives into independent producers.

These articles attracted Hetherington's attention, who was at that time looking out for a capable editor. Hetherington appointed him to the post.[2] The exact date when O'Brien became the editor of Hetherington's weekly is not known. To all appearance he lived at that time in Birmingham, where he was editor of the *Midland Representative*. In addition, a letter from O'Brien, dated from Birmingham, March 27, 1832, occurs in Owen's manuscripts, and in it the writer describes himself as Owen's admirer and adherent. O'Brien advised Owen to make his institution in Gray's Inn Road the centre of a popular movement where his ideas could reach the masses. Owen was to take Attwood for a pattern and to form a compre-

---

[1] *Northern Star*, April 11, 1840.   [2] *Ibid.*, March 29, 1845.

hensive organisation, for the masses had already begun to turn away from the Reform Bill agitation, and were sick and weary of public meetings. But Owen would be well advised to keep his own views on religion, responsibility, and other such matters in the background, at least for a short time, since the people were still frightfully superstitious.[1]

In reading the *Midland Representative* and the *Poor Man's Guardian* it is possible to follow O'Brien's mental evolution. In 1831 he was still an Owenite and Radical, defending co-operation against capitalists as well as against trade unionists. He thought trade unionism to be a folly and waste of money, leading but to discord and riot. He distinctly refused to accept Hodgskin's views of the class-struggle as propounded in *Labour Defended*.[2] Having settled in London and learned the ideas of the National Union of the Working Classes, he became one of the champions of the class struggle theory also. He quotes Hodgskin, especially his *Natural and Artificial Right of Property*, which corresponded most of all to O'Brien's own way of thinking. Hodgskin himself wrote to O'Brien and congratulated him on his efforts. Also Godwin, Spence, and several French social critics are referred to by O'Brien. Even Richard Oastler had recourse to the *Poor Man's Guardian* to ventilate his ideas.[3]

From 1833 onwards O'Brien took a deeper interest in the French literature of social reform. Three years later there appeared from his pen an English translation of Buonarroti's *Conspiration pour l'égalité,* in which he found his own ideas embodied. Two years later he published the first volume of a work on the life of Robespierre; no further volumes appeared. In the meantime he was active in journalism, had much intercourse with Irishmen—with O'Connor from 1836— and in 1837 he published *Bronterre's National Reformer* for a few months. In 1838 he contributed to the *Northern Star*; at the end of 1838 he became the editor of the *Operative,* a weekly, belong-

[1] Frank Podmore, *Robert Owen*, 1906, II., 430–431.
[2] *Midland Representative*, May 28, 1831, p. 8 (Review of Knights' Working Man's Companion).
[3] *Poor Man's Guardian*, February and March, 1833.

ing to a group of working men who disagreed with Lovett and
Hetherington. When this paper ceased publication he joined
forces with William Carpenter towards the end of 1839, and
they jointly published the *Southern Star* during the first months
of 1840. From April, 1840, to the middle of 1841 he was in
prison. In the latter half of 1842 he edited the *British Statesman* ;
in 1845, 1846, and 1847 he published the *National Reformer and
Manx Weekly Review*, at Douglas, in the Isle of Man, which
enjoyed complete freedom of the press, and in its columns he
waged violent warfare against O'Connor. In the 'fifties he wrote
for *Reynolds' Newspaper* ; the articles he contributed to it were
published posthumously under the title *Rise and Progress of
Human Slavery* (1885). During all these decades he was actively
engaged in lecturing to the remnants of Chartism.

In contradistinction to O'Connor, who, in 1845, abandoned
agrarian socialism, O'Brien remained a socialist to the very last,
and he only differed from the orthodox Owenites in making
the journey to the final goal by several stages—viz., Spenceanism,
the Charter, and the reform of credit and currency according to
Gray and Bray. He thought that " with the Charter, national
ownership of land, currency, and credit, people would soon discover what wonders of production, distribution, and exchange
might be achieved by associated labour, in comparison with the
exertions of isolated individual labour. Thence would gradually
arise the true social state, or the realities of socialism, in contradistinction to the present dreams of it. And doubtless the ultimate consequences would be the universal prevalence of a state
of society not essentially different from that contrived by Owen.
But the idea of jumping at once from our present iniquitous
and corrupt state of society into Owen's social paradise, without
any previous recognition of human rights and without establishing a single law or institution to rescue the people from
their present brutalised condition of ignorance and vassalage, is
a chimera."[1]

He died on December 3, 1864, two months after the founding
of the International Working Men's Association in London.

[1] *National Reformer and Manx Weekly Review*, January 30, 1847

George Julian Harney (1817–1897), like his master, participated in the Chartist movement from beginning to end as one of its leaders. He was educated at the Royal Naval School at Greenwich from his eleventh to his fourteenth year. His career as a sailor soon came to an end. In 1833 he began to read the *Poor Man's Guardian*, joined Hetherington in his fight against the newspaper tax, was arrested several times for acting as agent of unstamped newspapers, and in 1836 was sentenced to six months' imprisonment. He adored O'Brien as " his guide, philosopher, and friend," [1] from whom he derived his liking for the revolutionary literature of France. Marat was his revolutionary ideal ; he had a predilection for calling himself a " friend of the people," and signed his articles " Ami du peuple." His attitude from 1838 to 1840 was insurrectionary and revolutionary. He knew Benbow's pamphlet by heart. He became more moderate in his views after 1840, when he had recognised the dire results of this policy. Towards the end of 1842 or the beginning of 1843 he joined the staff of the *Northern Star*. In the same year Friedrich Engels came from Bradford to Leeds, in order to enter into relations with the Chartist movement. At that time he was collecting materials for his book, *Die Lage der arbeitenden Klasse in England* (Condition of the Working Class in England).[2]

At the end of November, 1847, Harney also made the acquaintance of Karl Marx, who at that time had come over to London from Brussels in order to attend the conference which led to the drawing up of the " Communist Manifesto." Harney formed the connecting link between the British Chartists and European revolutionaries and leaders of the proletariate. Nevertheless he stood much nearer to O'Brien and Louis Blanc than to the Marxian policy. Harney was a facile journalist and a good speaker, but he was not an original thinker.

R. G. Gammage, the author of the *History of the Chartist Movement*, came from Northampton, and was successively a cartwright, shoemaker, and finally a medical practitioner. From

[1] *Northern Star*, May 19, 1838, p. 6.
[2] *Social Democrat*, London, January, 1897.

I B

the very beginning of his Chartist career he was one of O'Brien's admirers, and regarded his writings as the last word in wisdom. He stuck to his master through thick and thin, especially in his quarrel with O'Connor. Gammage was an opponent of the ultimate aim of the communists. His programme consisted of an independent labour policy for setting up a democratic government and for carrying out social forms as expounded by O'Brien. In other words : the Rights of Man and the Rights of Labour.

II

THE POLITICAL ORGANISATION OF THE MASSES

I.—THE LONDON WORKING MEN'S ASSOCIATION (L.W.M.A.)

IN the later months of 1835 and the early part of 1836, independent attempts were made to organise Labour politically,
on the one hand by Feargus O'Connor and on the other hand
by the friends of Francis Place. These attempts were abortive,
for the workmen were unwilling to accept any leaders who did
not belong to the working class. Place deplored " the complete
estrangement of the working men from the middle classes," [1]
whilst O'Connor accused the leaders of the London artisans
of dreading his rivalry and of alienating the men from him in
order to sell them to the Radicals. Place's friends relaxed their
endeavours, and O'Connor transferred his activities to the North
of England and Scotland. Now that the pretenders had vacated
the political arena belonging to the London operatives, Lovett
and his friends met on June 6, 1836, at No. 14, Tavistock Street,
Covent Garden, for the purpose of forming an association for
London working men as the nucleus of an independent Labour
party.[2] Lovett drew up a prospectus and the rules of the
association, and a public meeting was convened ten days later,
in which the association was founded and the rules adopted.[3]
The association grew rapidly and was imitated in the provinces.
The members were required to belong to the industrious classes,
to " be of good moral character," to strive for education and
enlightenment and to declare for the democratic reform of parliament. The cards of membership bore the following motto :

[1] Place, MSS., 27819, pp. 24, 229, and *sqq.*
[2] *Northern Star*, September 19, 1846 (O'Connor's sketch of the
history of Chartism).
[3] William Lovett, *Life and Struggles*, 1876, p. 91 *sqq.*

" Whoever does not perform his share of work, diminishes the store of public wealth and lays his duty upon the shoulders of his neighbour."

The committee did not let the grass grow under their feet, but immediately took steps to bring the new organisation to the notice of the working men. The executive published an address to the working men of the United Kingdom and the nation, in which it subjected the Reformed Parliament to a critical examination :

" There is at present a contest between the two great parties both in and out of parliament—between the agricultural and privileged classes on the one hand and the moneyed and commercial classes on the other. We have little to expect from either of them. There are persons among the moneyed classes who, to deceive their fellow-men, have put on a cloak of reform ; many boast of freedom while they help to enslave us, preach justice while they help to oppress us. Many are for step-by-step improvement, lest we should see our political degradation too soon, and make an advance towards depriving them of their privileges. These persons, under various pretences, enlist some portion of our deluded countrymen—and, by opposing them to each other, accomplish their object of deceiving and fleecing the whole. So long as we are duped this way and we continue to seek political salvation through the instrumentality of others, so long will corrupt legislation prevail, so long must we continue to be the cringing vassals of a proud, arrogant, speech-making few. The men who are in parliament have interests opposed to yours. . . . Yet such is the description of persons composing that House, and whom we in our simplicity expect will sacrifice their interests by beginning the great work of political and social reformation. Working men ! Enquire into this matter, and if you feel with us, stand apart from all projects and refuse to be the tool of any party that will not, as a first and essential measure, give to the workmen equal political and social rights so that you may be able to elect men of your own who will take care that the interests of the working classes, ' who are the foundation of the social edifice,' shall not be sacrificed. . . .

There are in the United Kingdom 6,023,752 males over 21 years of age, only 840,000 have a vote, and owing to the unequal state of representation about one-fifth of that number have the power of returning a majority of members." [1]

The Working Men's Association held public meetings, and always took care that working men had control of the meetings. The officers of the association were also ordinary working men, so as to convince the public of the parliamentary capacity of the working classes. Until that time it had always been the custom to call in some well-known politician or parliamentary "lion" to take the chair at any large public demonstration. The L.W.M.A. broke through this rule, and this breach of custom created a greater sensation than the most brilliant speech of any Labour leader. Public opinion regarded it as a declaration of independence on the part of the working classes. The working men of Manchester followed London's example, and associations of working men were founded in several towns in the north and south of England and in the Midlands.

At the commencement of 1837, Lovett, Hetherington, Watson, Hartwell, Vincent, and their friends had made such progress that they planned a great meeting at which the Charter was to be publicly formulated. The meeting took place at the Crown and Anchor, Strand, London, on February 28, 1837, and was attended by 3,000 working men, the *élite* of the London working class. Prominent Radical politicians were also present. Feargus O'Connor travelled on purpose from Exeter to London to attend this meeting. He was not among those whom the London organisers delighted to honour, but he did not wish to be ignored ; Lovett's popularity was distasteful to him.

In the memorable meeting of February 28, 1837—the birthday of the Charter—Hartwell took the chair. After thanking the meeting for the honour shown in electing him chairman he continued as follows :—

" I express gratification that you placed a working man in the chair, rather than running after a man with a high-sounding

[1] *Rotten Parliament*, 1836 ; Place, MSS., 27819, p. 195 and *sqq.* ; *Bronterre's National Reformer*, February 4, 1837.

title or of great ability but little honesty. This great mass meeting will remove the stigma from the working classes that they do not attend meetings to support their principles, but to gaze on a 'lion' or to applaud and swallow the dogmas he may give utterance to. It also shows the great progress of democratic education among the workmen. The greatest danger for the workman is to remain attached to so-called political leadership of the men of culture and wealth. We need democracy, political and social rights for the producing millions. It seems to me to be an anomaly that in a country where the arts and sciences have been raised to such a height, chiefly by the industry, skill and labours of the artisan, where the principle that labour is the source of all wealth is generally acknowledged, that in such a country only one adult male in seven should have a vote, that in such a country the working classes should be excluded from the pale of political life. How can we emancipate ourselves from this state of political bondage ? Not by pandering to the fears of that timid and irresolute class of politicians who have lately appeared among the Radical ranks, not by relying on the dastardly Whigs, not by placing faith in the tyrannical Tories, but by a full reliance on our own strength—upon the inherent justice of our claims."

Lovett was the second speaker :—

" The exclusive power of wealth and privilege has in all ages been the greatest obstacle to human improvement. When their baleful influence failed to bind down effectually the swelling power of thought, when art and industry burst their slavish bands, when the despotism of the few could no longer prevail, they became kind patrons and leaders and promoters of all improvements. By their careful training and watchful attention they soon made knowledge subservient to their purposes, by embracing within their circle the master-spirits of intellect. By fictitious honours and glory they rallied to their aid the brave, the resolute, the ambitious ; by hopes of preferment, rank, riches and pleasure, they formed a powerful phalanx around them, and by the frowning terror of the law scared back all the rest of mankind. Therefore, working men, you must trust to yourselves."

He then proposed the following resolution :—

"This meeting is of opinion that so long as political power is vested exclusively in the few, will they seek to perpetuate their power and to render the multitude subservient to their purposes; they will continue to make them machines and instruments of production, toiling from youth to old age to procure a scanty portion of food and clothing, and having neither time to cultivate their mental powers nor means of enjoying rational comforts."

Lovett was followed by Henry Vincent, who after a republican harangue, moved the second resolution :—

"We believe that the only security against the corruption of the few and degradation of the many is to give to the great body of the people their equal political and social rights by the exercise of which they will improve their condition, gradually acquire knowledge and by experience learn wisdom. To obtain these rights it is necessary that every male above 21 years of age have the power to choose his representative without loss or injury, which can only be effected by secret voting. To have all classes represented equal representation is necessary. To purify the system from all remnants of corruption annual parliaments are necessary."

Other working men spoke, among them the saddler, Richard Cameron, who condemned the new Poor Law. The object of this reform was not only to prevent the population of the working classes from increasing, but to starve and exterminate those who were incapable of finding a new market for their labour. Finally Feargus O'Connor spoke, but only a few words, as the meeting had given him a cool reception.

The meeting resolved to adopt the petition to parliament which had been published by the committee on February 25, containing the following reforms: universal suffrage, annual parliaments, secret ballot, equal electoral districts, abolition of the property qualification for parliamentary candidates, payment of members.[1]

The next step was to present the petition to parliament and

[1] *True Sun*, March 1, 1837.

to introduce it in the form of a Bill. The members of the Working Men's Association called a meeting for the purpose and a resolution proposed by Hartwell was adopted, which appointed a committee to get into communication with those Radical members of the House of Commons, who by their activity in parliament had shown themselves friendly disposed to the people, and to invite them to co-operate with the committee of the London Working Men's Association to draft a Bill embodying the six points.[1] The committee carried out this request, and on May 31 and June 7, consultations took place between the Radical members of parliament and a delegation from the L.W.M.A., at which Francis Place was also present. The former comprised Daniel O'Connell, John A. Roebuck, Colonel Perronet Thompson, and Sharman Crawford, who pledged themselves to take part in drawing up the People's Charter and to represent it in parliament.

Since the Corresponding Act rendered it impossible to communicate the result of these conferences to the working men's associations in the provinces, Lovett published an address, which was printed in the Radical press, and in which he informed them of the result. The address then continued :—

" In the course of a few weeks these Bills will be prepared and printed for circulation under the title of " The People's Charter," and will form a rallying point for Radical reformers, a standard by which to test all those who call themselves the friends of the people. . . . Working men's associations should be established in every town and village throughout the country, and the wise and good of every class should be enrolled among them. We caution you not to branch your associations, because the Corresponding Act is still in power, not to correspond privately, but through the press."[2]

The movement extended everywhere so rapidly that the committees of the working men's associations in the provinces applied to the London Working Men's Association to send down agitators (missionaries) to the North of England in order to organise the masses of working men who had taken up the movement. Hether-

[1] *British Statesman,* June 5, 1842.   [2] *True Sun,* June 29, 1837.

ington, Vincent and Cleave undertook this mission. They were received everywhere with enthusiasm, and Lancashire, Yorkshire, Durham, and Northumberland were organised.

The London Working Men's Association was also deeply persuaded of the necessity for the international solidarity of the working men and of all oppressed peoples. It took up the cause of the oppressed British colonies and agitated for the self-government of Canada. When the Polish refugees turned for sympathy to the London Working Men's Association, the latter immediately seized the opportunity of stigmatising Palmerston's anti-Polish policy and at the same time of calling upon the workers of all countries to organise themselves internationally and to acquire political knowledge.[1]

2.—THE PEOPLE'S CHARTER

Fourteen months elapsed from the meeting on February 28, 1837, until the publication of the Charter. The six members of parliament who had pledged themselves in the meetings of May 31 and June 7, 1837, to co-operate in the composition of a bill embodying the six points were obliged to return to their constituencies, owing to the dissolution of parliament and the new elections of the summer of 1837. It was only in November that they returned to London. Lovett and his friends had their time too fully occupied with their struggle for existence, with their manifestoes and their trade unionist work, to be able to complete in so short a time the drafting of a large and complicated Bill—no easy task for men without legal training. Out of the twelve members of the committee who had been appointed for the task Lovett was the only man who undertook the work and gave all his spare time to it.[2] According to all canons of historical criticism, Lovett must be regarded as the author of the Charter. Francis Place also laid claim to its authorship,[3] but his share in the preparation of the Charter was quite insignificant ; it was restricted to a transposition of the headings.

[1] Lovett, *Life*, p. 150.   [2] *British Statesman*, June 12, 1842.
[3] Place, MSS. 27820, pp. 89–99.

Even during Place's lifetime it was the generally accepted opinion that the Charter was mainly the work of Lovett. No one raised any protest against this assumption, not even Place himself, although he read the newspapers in which this statement was made.[1]

On May 8, 1838, the People's Charter was published. It contained the following main points :—

" The People's Charter : A Bill to provide for the just representation of the People of Great Britain and Ireland in the Commons House of Parliament.

" Whereas, to insure, in as far as it is possible by human forethought and wisdom, the just government of the people, it is necessary to subject those who have the power of making the laws to a wholesome and strict responsibility to those whose duty it is to obey them when made. And whereas, this responsibility is best enforced through the instrumentality of a body which emanates directly from, and is itself immediately subject to, the whole people, and which completely represents their feelings and their interests. And whereas, the Commons House of Parliament now exercises, in the name and on the supposed behalf of the people, the power of making the laws, it ought, in order to fulfil with wisdom and with honesty the great duties imposed on it, to be made the faithful and accurate representation of the people's wishes, feelings and interests. Be it therefore enacted : "

This preamble, written by J. A. Roebuck, is followed by the six points containing the provisions in legal phraseology arranged in paragraphs, setting forth the granting of the franchise to every male person over twenty-one years of age, provided that they are of sound mind and not convicted of any crime. Naturalisation of foreigners was to be permitted after two years' residence in the United Kingdom. The country should be divided into 300 electoral districts, and every constituency was to contain as nearly as possible an equal number of inhabitants. No other qualifications for candidates was to be required than election by the electors. Parliaments were to be restricted to *annual*

[1] *British Statesman*, June 12, 1842 ; *National Association Gazette*, June 4, 1842.

periods. The ballot was to be secret. Every member of parliament was to receive £500 for his work in the public service.

Henry Hetherington bore the cost of printing the Charter.
Lovett wrote the following manifesto to announce the publication
of the Charter :—

" The Working Men's Association of London to the Radical
Reformers of Great Britain and Ireland !

" Fellow-countrymen ! We hold it to be an axiom in politics
that self-government, by representation, is the only just foundation of political power—the only true basis of Constitutional
Rights—the only legitimate parent of good laws ; and we hold
it as an indubitable truth that all government which is based
on any other foundation has a perpetual tendency to degenerate
into anarchy or despotism ; or to beget class and wealth idolatry
on the one hand, or poverty and misery on the other. While,
however, we contend for the principle of self-government, we
admit that laws will only be just in proportion as the people are
enlightened ; on this, socially and politically, the happiness of
all must depend ; but as self-interest, unaccompanied by virtue,
ever seeks its own exclusive benefit, so will the exclusive and
privileged classes of society ever seek to perpetuate their power
and to proscribe the enlightenment of the people. Hence we
are induced to believe that the enlightenment of all will emanate
from the exercise of political power by all the people. A strong
conviction of these truths, coupled as that conviction is with
the belief that most of our political and social evils can be traced
to corrupt and exclusive legislation, and that the remedy will be
found in extending to the people at large the exercise of those
rights now monopolised by a few, has induced us to make some
exertions towards embodying our principles in the Charter. . . .
Fellow-countrymen, the object we contemplate in the drawing
up of this Bill is to cause the Radicals of the kingdom to form,
if possible, a concentration of their principles in a practical form,
upon which they could be brought to unite, and to which they
might point, as a Charter they are determined to obtain. . . .
We hope that electors and non-electors will continue to make
it the pledge of their candidates ; will seek to extend its circu-

lation, talk over its principles, and resolve that, as public opinion forced the Whig Reform Bill, so in like manner shall this Bill eventually become the law of England.

" London, May 8, 1838."

The impression which the Charter made upon the working men's associations throughout the country was extremely favourable.[1] The publication of the Charter came at a time when the country was already seething with political agitation. Even at the end of 1837 it was becoming increasingly clear that a political storm was brewing among the people. About the middle of November, 1837, the newly-elected House of Commons assembled. On November 20 the young Queen read the Speech from the Throne—a colourless and non-committal document that gave rise to bitter disappointment in the circles of the hopeful reformers. In the debate on the address that immediately followed the Queen's Speech the Radical member for Finsbury, Thomas Wakley, an old friend of the National Union, moved an amendment in which he regretted that the Queen's Speech made no reference to an extension of the franchise and other parliamentary reforms which were desired by the people. Some of his Radical colleagues supported him. Lord John Russell replied in the name of the government that the agitation for further parliamentary reform could not be supported by the government. The authors of the Reform Bill of 1832 went to the furthest bounds of possibility ; they regarded that Bill as final ; they had made no concealment of their views, and it was, therefore, impossible for them to alter the limits which had been set once and for all or to act contrary to the intentions of the legislators.[2]

Lord John Russell's declaration that the government regarded the Reform Act of 1832 as the final word in parliamentary reform earned for him the nickname of " Finality Jack." It caused absolute dismay in the circles of reformers, and roused the Radical and working men's associations to a feverish pitch of

---

[1] R. G. Gammage, *History of the Chartist Movement*, 1894, pp. 8–9.
[2] Hansard's *Parliamentary Debates*, 3 series, vol. 39, pp. 11–12, 69–70 ; *Annual Register*, 1837, p. 392.

activity. Of course, the progressive leaders of the working men were prepared for a declaration of this sort, and when it was actually made they only regarded it as a justification of their attitude and an incitement to greater activity. In Leeds the *Northern Star* appeared from November 18 under the direction of Feargus O'Connor and became the central organ of the Chartists. In Newcastle the *Northern Liberator* had made its appearance fully a month previously. In December, 1837, the Birmingham Political Union declared for Universal Suffrage and took measures for mobilising the masses in the Midlands and the North of England.

3.—THE BIRMINGHAM POLITICAL UNION

The years 1836 and 1837 witnessed a financial crisis of a rather severe, though sporadic, character. Over-speculation in railway and foreign stock, as well as the reaction of the crisis in the United States of America, resulted in a panic, especially affecting those towns and districts which depended on the export trade to America, India, and China. Credit became short; the Bank of England raised the bank rate in order to check the depletion of gold; in the autumn of 1836 numerous joint stock companies became bankrupt, and the Bank of England declined to discount the bills of the provincial banks of issue. The towns which suffered most were Birmingham and Sheffield with their metal industries, and Liverpool and Glasgow with their shipping.

Attwood and his adherents, who regarded Peel's Bill of 1819 as the cause of the whole evil, and found a panacea in a paper currency, sent three deputations in 1837 to the government to call their attention to these causes and the remedies.[1] Attwood and his friend Scholefield sat in parliament as members for Birmingham, and did all they could to induce the government to give a hearing to their theories and proposals, but all their efforts were in vain. At the same time they saw that the working men were entering once more into the arena of politics and were demanding reforms. In the place of the old Political Union, which had died out at the end of 1834, but which had done so

[1] *Birmingham Journal*, June 19, 1841.

much to insure the success of the Reform Bill of 1832, the working men of Birmingham founded a Reform Union.   Distress was rife in that town ; many operatives lost their employment owing to the financial crisis and the consequent stoppage of business ; and many of them could only be employed for shorter hours and lower wages.   The operatives as well as the smaller masters suffered and therefore began to turn their attention to political reforms.

On January 15, 1837, a dinner was given in honour of Attwood and Scholefield in order to induce them to enter once more into the movement for reform.   Both of them declared in their after-dinner speeches that nothing was to be expected from the parliament which had assembled as the outcome of the Reform of 1832.   They drew up the following programme of reform : household suffrage, secret ballot, triennial parliaments, abolition of the property qualification for parliamentary candidates, payment of members of parliament.   On May 23, the old Political Union was reorganised and this programme was handed over to it.[1] In consequence of the agitation of the working men belonging to the Union, universal suffrage was substituted for household suffrage. The Birmingham programme, as we have seen, contained *five* points only.   Attwood would have nothing to do with equal electoral districts.   His reasons for his attitude were highly remarkable and only came to light on May 7, 1839.   On that day a deputation of Chartists, including O'Connor and Lovett, waited on Attwood to induce him to introduce the Charter into parliament.   The following dialogue took place :—[2]

LOVETT : As representatives of the Chartist movement we request you, Mr. Attwood . . . to move for leave to bring in a Bill to parliament, entitled the People's Charter.

ATTWOOD : That I refuse.   I agree with the five points in what was called the People's Charter, but there was one which went to alter the ancient mode of taking the suffrage in the electoral districts.   The objection to it was : if the distribution of the elective franchise were carried out in full, according to the People's Charter, it would have the effect of giving to Ireland

[1] *Birmingham Journal,* June 10 and 17, 1837.
[2] Place, MSS. 27821. p. 213.

one-half of the representation. If the Irish people went on increasing and the English people diminishing, it would give to the most miserable people on earth the power of making laws for this generous and industrious nation.

LOVETT : ᜵ We do not give way on the People's Charter. The people of England and Scotland are unanimous upon it. . . . and we look upon the Irish as our brethren and as one family with ourselves.

ATTWOOD : So do I, and I look on the Hindus as brethren, but I do not believe there is one man in England who would give Ireland 200 and England only 400 members of parliament.

This was Attwood's actual point of view. He regarded democracy as an evil, even if it were a necessary evil, which he had to take into consideration in order to be able to repeal Peel's Act. His interests lay solely and entirely in the sphere of currency reform.

Immediately after the Birmingham programme was drawn up the committee of the Union decided to send out emissaries to agitate in all the centres of industry and trade in the Midlands, the North of England and Scotland. The most important among the itinerant orators of Birmingham was John Collins (1800–1850), a mechanic, who had worked 14 to 16 hours a day in steel pen factories from his tenth year until 1836. Later on he became Lovett's friend and colleague, and was a fellow-prisoner with him in 1840.

4.—THE NATIONAL PETITION

The committee meetings of the Political Union were held regularly every week, and testified to the indefatigable and feverish activity at the centre of the movement. The main result of the consultations was the resolve not to rest content any longer with local petitions of sporadic unions, but to get up a comprehensive and national manifesto, including every part of the country ; a national petition was to be drawn up and signed by millions of male and female operatives and reformers and presented to parliament. In March and April, 1838, the petition was drawn up by R. K. Douglas, the editor of the *Birmingham Journal*, and published on May 14.

The text of the national petition was as follows:—

TO THE HONOURABLE COMMONS OF GREAT BRITAIN AND IRELAND

" Your Petitioners dwell in a land whose merchants are noted for enterprise, whose manufacturers are very skilful and whose workmen are proverbial for industry. The land itself is goodly, the soil is rich, the temperature wholesome ; it is abundantly furnished with the materials of commerce and trade ; it has numerous and convenient harbours ; in facility for internal communication it exceeds all others. For 23 years we have enjoyed a profound peace.

" Yet, with all these elements of natural prosperity, and with every disposition and capacity to take advantage of them, we find ourselves overwhelmed with public and private suffering. We are bowed down under a load of taxes, which notwithstanding falls greatly short of the wants of our rulers ; our traders are trembling on the verge of bankruptcy ; our workmen are starving, capital brings no profit and labour no remuneration, the home of the artificer is desolate and the warehouse of the pawnbroker is full, the workhouse is crowded and the manufactory is deserted.

" We have looked on every side, we have searched diligently in order to find out the causes of distress, so sore and so long continued.

" We can discover none in Nature, none in Providence. Heaven has dealt graciously with our people, but the foolishness of our rulers has made the goodness of God of no effect. The energies of a mighty kingdom have been wasted to build up the power of selfish and ignorant men, and its resources are squandered for their aggrandisement.

" The good of a party has been advanced to sacrifice the good of the nation ; the few have governed for the interest of the few ; while the interests of the many have been neglected or insolently and tyrannously trampled upon.

" It was the fond expectation of the people that a remedy for the greater part, if not the whole, of their grievances would be found in the Reform Act of 1832. They were taught to regard that Act as a wise means to a worthy end ; as the machinery of an improved legislation where the will of the masses would be at length potential. They have been bitterly and basely deceived. The fruit which looked so fair to the eye has turned to dust and ashes when gathered. The Reform Act has effected a transfer of power from one domineering party to another, and left the people as helpless as before. Our slavery has been exchanged for an apprenticeship of liberty, which has aggravated the painful feeling of our social degradation by adding to it the sickening of a deferred hope.

" We come before your honourable House to tell you in all humility that this state of things must not be permitted to continue ; that it cannot long continue without very seriously endangering the stability of the Throne and the peace of the kingdom ; and if by God's help and all lawful and constitutional means an end can be put to it, we are fully resolved that it shall speedily come to an end. We tell the honourable House that the capital of the master must no longer be deprived of its due profit ; that the labour of the workman must no longer be deprived of its due reward ; that the laws which make food dear, money scarce, labour cheap, must be abolished ; that taxation must be made to fall upon property, not on industry ; that the good of the many must be made the sole end, as it is the legitimate end of government.

" As a preliminary essential to these and other requisite changes, as means by which alone the interests of the people can be effectively vindicated and secured, we demand that those interests shall be confided to the people. When the State calls for defenders, or for money, no consideration of ignorance or poverty can be pleaded in refusal or delay of the call. Required as we are to obey the laws, nature and reason entitle us to demand that, in the making of the laws, the universal voice shall be implicitly listened to.

" We perform the duties of free men, we must have the rights of free men.

" We demand : Universal Suffrage . . . the Ballot . . . Annual Parliaments . . . Payment of Members . . . Abolition of Property Qualification." [1]

The object was now to make the petition a national question : to have it taken up by the masses of the United Kingdom. It was the same idea which the London Working Men's Union had held with regard to the Charter. The Birmingham men anticipated them, and the rivalry between them was soon noticeable. Attwood's prestige and that of the Political Union of 1832 gave precedence to the Birmingham Petition in the first place. But in the course of about six months the Charter had become the standard of the movement, giving it its name and objective, whilst the Birmingham Petition was only regarded as an instrument in the warfare. The victory achieved over Attwood by Lovett, a nearly unknown man, in the Midlands and in the North of England was to be ascribed, solely and absolutely, to the concrete form with which he clothed democratic principles.

[1] *Birmingham Journal*, May 19, 1838.

III

THE CHARTIST MOBILISATION

I.—THE LINE OF ACTION

The events of the year 1837 made themselves felt with surprising swiftness. In 1838 a rapid mobilisation of the working classes was the outcome of the preparation of the Charter and National Petition and of the foundation of the Chartist press. The whole populace seethed in a state of fermentation. Attwood and O'Connor took over the management of affairs and were supported by a brilliant staff of orators, such as Stephens, Vincent, Taylor, Lowery, Douglas, and Collins. The demonstrations of the Midlands and the North of England became military reviews.

The masses of the working men marched everywhere in serried columns, accompanied by bands and standard bearers to the places of assembly. Mass meetings were held in all the industrial centres. And towards the end of the year sensational nocturnal gatherings took place, lit up by flickering torches, at which Stephens and O'Connor inflamed the masses with their speeches. The *Northern Star* declared for Owen's communist experiments and for the doctrines of Thomas Spence.[1]

The year 1838 seemed to Bronterre O'Brien to mark the actual commencement of the emancipation of the people.[2] And Francis Place expressed the greatest astonishment at the rapid ebullition of popular sentiment :—

" The great excitement,which had already become noticeable at the commencement of 1838, swept over the southern and eastern counties of England and over South Wales. Birmingham was the centre of the Midlands ; Manchester and Newcastle

[1] *Northern Star*, June 16, 1838 (leading article and page 4).
[2] *Operative*, November 18, 1838.

38

were the hotbeds of the northern countries ; Edinburgh and Glasgow the foci of Scotland. The excitement spread rapidly in all directions."[1]

Birmingham was the actual starting-point. The tour of agitation undertaken by its missionary, John Collins, in Scotland resulted in an immediate success. The meetings which he held were thickly attended, to a far greater extent than those of Daniel O'Connell or O'Connor. " In Scotland alone," Collins reported to Birmingham, " there is misery enough, intelligence enough and zeal enough to realise our aims." The trade unions everywhere took the most active part in the agitation, and worked hand in hand with the intellectual section of the working classes. The Scottish reformers then expressed the desire to arrange for holding a great demonstration in Glasgow, and to invite the leading reformers from London and Birmingham. The invitation was issued in the last week of April, 1838. It was accepted, and the Glasgow demonstration was fixed for May 21. The object of the demonstration was to cause the Scotch people to adopt and sign the National Petition.

The committee of the Birmingham Political Union now began to deal with the question as to how the moral power of the people could be organised to the best advantage in order to press the five points of the Petition upon the attention of parliament. It was well aware of the fact that parliament takes very little heed of petitions. In the meantime the government had appreciably restricted the time which had previously been reserved for the reading and discussion of petitions. Moreover, petitions up to this time were only local in their nature ; they proceeded from separate towns or from small groups united by a common interest. The Birmingham Petition was to be national in character, embracing all shades of popular opinion, and to be a manifesto of the masses. Yet it was to be feared that the government would disregard a manifesto of this nature. The result of these deliberations was the outline of a plan to convoke a National Convention, a parliament of the people, which should bring the whole moral power of the people in support of the petition.

[1] Place, MSS. 27820, p. 7.

The final weapon in the armoury of the Convention was to be a proclamation of a week's national holiday, of a general strike during a week. The plans formulated by Benbow and the National Union between 1832 and 1834 appeared to have finally arrived at the point of being realised.

This was the plan of campaign which Attwood and his friends drew up during the latter part of April and the first two weeks of May, 1838, and which they disclosed at the Glasgow demonstration on May 21. This demonstration was the signal for mass-meetings to be held all over Great Britain. In all parts delegates were elected for the coming Congress. The London meeting took place on September 17, 1838, in Westminster Palace Yard, not far from the Houses of Parliament. It was not by any means so noisy as the demonstrations in the Midlands and the North of England. It was precisely for this reason that it made a powerful impression upon the nation. During the meeting in Birmingham (August 6, 1838) it was also resolved to raise a so-called " National Rent " or money contribution from those localities which sent delegates to the Convention, viz., fifty shillings for every 1000 inhabitants. In reality the demand was made to the working men's associations and to the political unions, but since the Corresponding Act did not permit any alliances between the organisations these meetings were convoked as town meetings, the towns were pledged to make the payment of the " National Rent," and the delegates were regarded as the representatives of the towns. According to another regulation of the Corresponding Act, the Convention could not comprise more than 49 members.

The working classes had hardly wakened into vigorous political existence than the first conflict arose with regard to party policy.

2.—QUESTIONS OF POLICY AND INTERNAL DISSENSIONS

The speeches delivered by O'Connor, Stephens, and Taylor, as well as by their friends in the North of England and in Scotland, roused misgivings in the Birmingham Union, the London Working Men's Association, and the great majority of the Scotch organisations. They considered the continual appeals to armed opposition to be prejudicial. The Birmingham Union laid the chief stress upon the organisation of the masses and their subordination to the leaders. The Londoners expected everything from the organisation, education, and independence of the working men and from democratic reform, and they were opposed to Chartism being mixed up in any way with the agitation against the new Poor Law, against Peel's Currency Acts or against any other social evils and abuses. Their watchword was : the concentration of all efforts in order to obtain democratic rule. The Scotch were convinced adherents of a peaceful policy, and considered every appeal to physical force to weaken the influence of moral power, and to be a vote of censure upon the invincible power of truth. Stephens took very little heed of these protests, whilst in the case of O'Connor and O'Brien both of these principles of policy ebbed and flowed according to events and the circumstances with which they had to deal.

During the last two months of 1838 Stephens was the apostle of terrorism. In a public meeting of 6,000 operatives at Norwich he exclaimed :—

" I tell the rich to make their will. The people are with us, the soldiers are not against us. The working men have produced all the wealth and they are miserable. They want no more than a fair day's wage for a fair day's work. There is one pin on which the title of all property is hung, and that is the unchangeable right of the working men to a comfortable subsistence. . . . The working man is the ground landlord of all the property in the kingdom. If he has it not he has a right to come down on the rich until he gets it."[1] The central organ of the Chartists reported these speeches fairly completely every week.

Particularly violent or incendiary phrases must, however, have been suppressed, for John Collins, who occasionally spoke from the same platform as Stephens, reported to the committee of the Birmingham Political Union that Stephens incited in the plainest language to the burning down of factories and to the murder of any particularly obnoxious police. Also in the form in which his speeches were printed in the *Northern Star* they

[1] *Northern Star*, November 10, 1838.

sound sufficiently terrorising. The Birmingham Union demanded the exclusion of Stephens from the movement. Also the newspapers of the middle classes made a great outcry against the agitation of terrorism. On the other hand, O'Connor stood by Stephens all the more steadfastly, and called upon the working men to form a bodyguard for Stephens and to defend him against his enemies with all their physical strength. At the close of 1838, O'Connor was nervous, exhausted, and mentally unbalanced as the result of his incessant, harrying agitation. In supporting Stephens's tactics there is no doubt that he exceeded the dictates of his reason. For he was of opinion that his energies were coming to an end, so that he aimed at some violent action to obtain the Charter in the shortest possible time. He even fixed a definite limit, viz., September 29, 1839, on which date the British people were to have attained the fulfilment of its desires.

He had barely heard of the dissatisfaction in Birmingham when he went there to defend Stephens and himself. In two meetings he laid down his point of view and made a determined appeal to working men " with fustian jackets, blistered hands and unshorn chins." On December 1 the Birmingham Political Union adopted, however, the following resolution :—

" This Union expressly and in the strongest manner condemns all exhortations to physical force for the purpose of procuring Universal Suffrage and the other objects of the National Petition."

A reconciliation actually took place between O'Connor and the Birmingham men, but the former decided to sever his connection with Attwood's society.

At the end of December O'Connor spoke in London and defended his line of action. Lovett opposed him, saying :—

" The whole physical force agitation is harmful and injurious to the movement. Muskets are not what are wanted, but education and schooling of the working people. Stephens and O'Connor are shattering the movement, in setting secondary demands in the foreground. Violent words do not slay the enemies but the friends of our movement. O'Connor wants to take everything by storm and to pass the Charter into law within a year.

All this hurry and haste, this bluster and menace of armed opposition can only lead to premature outbreaks and to the destruction of Chartism. If Stephens, O'Connor, and their adherents cannot realise this, many will leave the movement. What happened to the London National Union ? Benbow's violent phrases crushed the life out of it. Agitation by moral weapons will never succeed so long as they are considered ineffectual in comparison to physical weapons."[1]

In December also a conference of the delegates from the Scotch organisations was held in Edinburgh in order to deal with the dissension. It adopted the following resolution :—

" This meeting deems it quite unnecessary to express any opinion on the question whether it be constitutional or no for the people to have arms and to use them in their own defence, because they have a full conviction that in the present struggle for liberty the exercise of moral power is completely adequate to obtain it in spite of all opposition.

" Relying with unshaken confidence on the efficacy of the many moral means the people possess for the achievement of their rights, we unequivocally denounce in the strongest terms any appeals to physical force, any exhortations to buy arms, being fully persuaded such appeals tend to diminish the vast influence of moral power. If the people would only use, with wisdom, vigour and perseverance, constitutional and peaceful means in the present struggle, no government whatever could long resist their just claims to civil and political equality. We disclaim any connection with those who use violent language, which is both illegal and injurious. The chief thing is organisation, payment of members' dues, part of which should be devoted to literature and lecturing, and to teach self-reform as the great and only source from which can spring social and political happiness, good government, pure and virtuous institutions."[2]

In spite of all the resolutions and statements, no decision was arrived at, which held good for the whole movement. Its policy continued to oscillate backwards and forwards, for owing to the obsolete Corresponding Act it was not possible for a

[1] *Northern Star*, Dec. 29, 1838.   [2] *True Scotsman*, Dec. 8, 1838.

movement to possess unity of action. The only watchword that was universally accepted was : " Peacefully if we may ; forcibly if we must." Under the circumstances of the time the " must " was a much more probable contingency than the " may."

3.—SOCIALIST AIM AND END

As the Chartist movement progressed increasing interest was shown in its ranks in the ultimate object to be attained and in social and economic problems. All the Chartists entertained definite aims, or, as they were called at the time, ulterior motives, for which they entered into the struggle for the Charter as a means to the end.

Owenism, which since 1835 had fallen to quite an unimportant position, received a fresh impetus in the years 1837–8, which it maintained until 1842. Its central organ, the *New Moral World*, which came into existence at the extinction of the *Crisis*, was removed to Manchester and Leeds. Owenite congresses and meetings again became well attended.

Letters from working men were very often directed to the editors of the Chartist press, asking them to print articles on capital and wage labour. On this point Bronterre O'Brien wrote as follows :—

" I am repeatedly urged by friends and correspondents to write some articles on wages or, what amounts to the same, on the conflicting claims of labour and capital. I would gladly comply, but what is the good of discussing what we have no power of interfering with ? Of what possible use to broach theories which are incapable of being reduced to practice under the present condition of society ? Besides, were I just now to promulgate what I believe to be the truth respecting capital, I should of necessity alarm and offend many parties which are zealously co-operating with us for universal suffrage. I think that until the question of universal suffrage is settled, we cannot with advantage enter deeply into that of labour and capital."[1]

[1] *Operative*, November 25, 1838 ; similarly in the *National Reformer*, February 25, 1837.

When O'Brien, by O'Connor's desire, condescended to write an article on questions affecting property, the issue of the paper in which it occurred had a record sale.[1] Most of the leaders held the same opinion as the expounder of Chartism. The ultimate aim was, therefore, designated by the characteristic expression, Ulterior Motives. There is no possible room for doubt as to the social-revolutionary aim of Chartism up to the year 1845. A Radical politician of the middle classes to whom this state of affairs was repugnant, wrote in 1839 :—

" Owenism, as those are aware who habitually watch the progress of opinion, is at present in one form or another, the actual creed of a great portion of the working classes."[2]

And in writing a survey of the year 1839 a Conservative politician philosophised as follows :—

" Apart from the political demands of the Chartists, the movement is characterised by other noteworthy conceptions. The hostility of the Chartists is directed less against the privileged condition of society, which up to the present was the particular object of democratic indignation, than against capitalists in general. The movement is, in fact, an insurrection which is expressly directed against the middle classes. A violent change in the system of government is demanded by the Chartists not for the purpose of receiving more power and privileges, but— as far as their aim permits of any definition—for the purpose of producing a hitherto non-existent condition of society, in which wage labour and capital do not exist at all."[3]

The Central organ of Chartism declared in the plainest terms : " Socialism and Chartism pursue the same aims, they only differ in their methods."[4] Nevertheless, there was one section of the orthodox Owenites, most notably Robert Owen himself, who remained unsympathetic or even hostile to Chartism. How is this strange phenomenon to be explained ? How did this attraction and repulsion originate ?

[1] *Northern Star*, June 2 and 16, 1838.
[2] *Westminster Review*, April, 1839, pp. 496 and *sqq.*
[3] *Annual Register*, 1839, I., 304.
[4] *Northern Star*, January 21, 1843 (leading article).

It is useless to seek for a satisfactory answer in the papers belonging to these two movements. At the best, the answer might by chance be discovered that it was parliamentarism that divided the two factions. The answer mistakes the symptom for the cause. In both camps there was a lack of thinkers on social philosophy who were in a position to work out the problem to its logical conclusion.

Both the problem and its solution are the result, however, of the difference that had arisen between a Utopia and a class movement, between a sect and a political party. The syndicalist phase (1832 to 1834) revealed the chasm existing between Utopia and class movement, whilst the commencement of the Chartist and parliamentary phase disclosed the contrast between sect and party. The masses of the working class who adhered to Chartism adopted the social criticism of Owenism, but they rejected its dogmas of salvation, which Owen considered as precisely the most important of his whole system, and he regarded Chartism therefore as a retrograde step.

The years 1839–45 mark the period when Owenism as a social system fell to pieces.

There is no doubt that the silence observed as to the final aims, in addition to the dissensions and polemics between the Owenite Socialists and the Chartists, were responsible for the social revolutionary character of Chartism being sometimes misunderstood. Another factor contributory to this misunderstanding was the demand of the trade unions : " A fair day's wages for a fair day's work." Quite apart from the fact that the logical consequence of this demand, as understood by the Chartists, implied the abolition of capitalism and the enforcement of the doctrine of natural law that the labourer ought to receive as his wage the whole product of his labour, the schoolmaster of Chartism allowed no doubt to exist as to his opinion that this demand could only be realised by parliament being ruled by the mass of the working men, that is to say, that they should make use of political power for the purpose of effecting an economic revolution in the interests of the proletariat. He informed his readers that : " ' A fair day's wage ' is a very captivating sort of phrase, but may be moulded into as many different meanings. Under present conditions there is no possibility of realising that demand. The combined power of capital, machinery, and competition must continually reduce the wages and prospects of working men to promote their interests by trades union means alone. Trades unions, at best, can only prevent the employers cutting down the wages of mechanics and artisans to the level of agricultural labour. The trade union is only in some degree efficacious in those branches of labour in which the personal skill of the mechanic still plays an important part. Is there any hope that without an entire change of the system the operative will be able to command a fair day's wage for a fair day's work ? The thing is, in my opinion, impossible."[1]

Even Lovett's declaration that capital, land, and labour belong to one another and render production possible[2] must not be interpreted in a middle class sense. The English working men considered capital to mean stored-up labour. Even at the present day they adhere to this definition.[3]

The full meaning of the Charter for the Chartist masses of the North of England was most clearly defined by Stephens in the great meeting on Kersal Moor, near Manchester :—

" The principle of the resolution on which I have to speak is a principle which every man was obliged to acknowledge—the principle which acknowledged the right of every man that breathes God's free air and trod upon God's free earth to have his home and his hearth, and his wife and his children, as securely guaranteed to him as to any right the aristocracy has created. This question of universal suffrage is a knife and fork question, after all, a bread and cheese question, notwithstanding all that has been said against it ; and if any man should ask me what I mean by universal suffrage I should reply : That every working man in the land has the right to have a good coat on his back, a comfortable abode in which to shelter himself and his family, a good dinner upon his table, and no more work than is necessary

---

[1] *Operative*, November 4, 1838. [2] *Sun*, September 13, 1838
[3] *Daily Herald*, May 12, 1912.

to keep him in good health, and so much wages for his work as should keep him in plenty and afford him the enjoyment of all the blessings of life, which a reasonable man could desire. . . . Behind universal suffrage I want to see that knowledge in the mind, that principle in the heart, that power in the conscience, that strength in the right arm that would enable the working man to meet his master boldly, upright on his feet, without the brand mark of the bondman upon his brow, and without the blush of shame and slavery upon his cheek. I want to see the working man as free in the mill as when he goes into the wilderness —as free spoken when he goes for his wages as he is when he spends a part of it with his companion. I want to see every man so free as to speak his mind, act according to his conscience, and do no one any injury. . . . I second the resolution, and shall support it with heart and soul, so far as I can, and as far as you can with me if you acted the same way, and we shall ultimately carry the Charter."[1]

No lengthy explanation is necessary to arrive at the conclusion that Stephens's ideal could not be realised under capitalist conditions and that it implies a transitional period from Capitalism to Socialism.

These were the aims cherished by the working men when they entered into the Chartist struggle and elected delegates to the National Convention.[2]

[1] *Northern Star*, September 29, 1838.

[2] Stephens was also elected a delegate, but he was arrested at the end of December, 1838.

IV

THE GENERAL CONVENTION

I.—THE OPENING OF THE CONVENTION

THE immediate result of the efforts made during 1838 was the National Convention, which met in London on February 4, 1839, for the purpose of inducing parliament to adopt the National Petition and the People's Charter. The Convention was the first Labour Parliament in Great Britain. Its original title was the National Convention, but since that name revived recollections of the French Revolution and contributed to increase the enmity of the ruling classes towards Chartism, the Chartist leaders agreed to alter it. From this time it was called : " The General Convention of the Industrious Classes of Great Britain."

The number of the delegates elected in the various towns and districts was 56, 53 of whom accepted their mandates. The delegates were not by any means united in their views and plans. They gradually formed three parties, a Right, a Left, and a Centre. The Right, to which J. P. Cobbett, Hadley, Salt, and Wade belonged, was dead against any serious contest or any violent speech, and was in favour of the Convention acting strictly within the letter of the law. The great majority of the Convention, including O'Connor, Lovett, and O'Brien, were for legal and constitutional means ; by " constitutional " they understood struggles and resistance to constituted authority interpreted by O'Connor, on the one hand, probably as street fighting, whilst Lovett, on the other, would be thinking of demonstrations and protests, possibly leading to trials and imprisonment of delegates. The Left consisted of Taylor, Cardo, Ryder, Harney, Frost, Burns, Bussey, Marsden, and Lowery, who by degrees arrived at the firm conviction that insurrection was to be preferred to any number of speeches or petitions.

Few indeed of the delegates entered the Convention with clearly defined views of the policy to be adopted. Broadly speaking, there was first of all a distinct endeavour to promote the objects of the Convention ; to encourage the masses to sign the Petition, to enlist the interest of members of parliament for the Petition and the Charter, and to enlighten the public opinion of the Charter by their discussions. All of them were well aware of the fact that strong divergences of opinion as to policy existed amongst the delegates ; they exerted themselves, however, to gloss over in silence their points of difference, to lay stress on their common principles and to work together in harmony. This was particularly evident in the election of Lovett to the secretaryship of the Convention. For this office he had been proposed by John Collins. The Convention seemed to be practically unanimous in adopting this proposal, when O'Brien rose and opposed it. He indicated that Lovett's policy might not be acceptable to the delegates of the North ; he urged the difference between the views of the London Working Men's Association and those of the organisations in the North of England, and he moved that other names should be proposed. Delegates from all parts of the country spoke in opposition to O'Brien, and recommended that Lovett should be elected as secretary. O'Brien then withdrew his motion, whereupon Lovett was unanimously elected to be permanent secretary of the first labour parliament in Great Britain. John Taylor, in his materials for a history of the Convention, refers thus to the circumstance :—

" While I am bound to confess that I came to London much prejudiced against Lovett and all who belonged to the Working Men's Association, looking upon them as no better than tools of the Whigs. . . . I will unhesitatingly affirm now that no appointment could have given more satisfaction to the Convention or to the country, nor could any man have surpassed William Lovett in talent, in energy, and in honesty." [1]

[1] Place, MSS. 27831, p. 143. Taylor's materials appeared in one of the Chartist papers of the North of England or of Scotland ; Place collected the cuttings, but did not quote the title of the newspaper.

During the first week of the Convention £700 odd was collected in party contributions. The Convention appointed its most prominent orators to be " missionaries," in order to enlighten the masses of the working classes concerning the nature and significance of the Charter and to complete the organisations. It also appointed a committee upon whom the task devolved of getting into communication with members of parliament and winning them over to support the Petition and the Charter, and to elicit information from them as to the attitude of parliament to the Charter. The views of many of the members of parliament were unknown to the labour leaders; on the other hand, the government lost no time in announcing its position with regard to Chartism.

On February 5, 1839, one day after the meeting of the Convention, parliament was opened with a Queen's Speech, in which the following statement was made among others :—

" I have observed with pain the persevering efforts which have been made in some parts of the country to excite my subjects to disobedience and resistance to the law, and to recommend dangerous and illegal practices." [1]

This was a distinct hint to the Chartists that the government was only waiting for an opportunity to set the forces of the State in movement against the reformers. The Convention replied with an address to the people, in which the attention of the Queen and the government was called to the impropriety of their warning. The address also contained a threat of armed resistance :

" If forced to resort to self-defence, even to that last tribunal we are prepared to appeal rather than continue in bondage, and rather to lay our heads upon the block as freemen than to rest them on the pillow as slaves. Interference by force, however, depends not upon us ; and if the infatuation of those in power prompt them to have recourse to it, so surely as in the exercise of it they dare to trench upon the liberties of Britons, so surely shall they be met with that stern resolve which prompts men either to conquer or die." [2]

[1] *Times*, February 6, 1839.   [2] *Charter*, February 17, 1839.

The Convention was denuded of nearly half the number of its members by the appointment of the delegates sent on tour as missionaries for the purpose of agitating, and also by the withdrawal of members to serve on committees. On this account the discussions in the public sittings were seldom exhaustive or systematic. The Convention sat with interruptions until September 14, 1839 ; yet there were only two subjects which occupied the time of the Convention, viz., the attitude towards the free trade agitation and the question of the " ulterior measures " which were to be adopted if parliament rejected the Petition and the Charter. The rules for the attitude of the working classes towards the Anti-Corn Law agitation were laid down by the Convention without opposition. It was quite a different matter with the ulterior measures ; in the discussions of this critical question, which also included that of arming and the general strike, the opposing views were sharply divided, leading finally to secessions, divisions, and imprisonments.

2.—DISCUSSION ON FREE TRADE

In 1836—the year when the London Working Men's Association was founded—some Radical members of Parliament, George Grote, J. Hume, Molesworth, and Roebuck, met one day and called the Anti-Corn-Law Association into being. In spite of the great literary reputation and oratorical gifts of its founders, and notwithstanding their political prestige, the association made no progress. The working men were turning their attention to Universal Suffrage and to the political organisation of their class. The London middle classes, such as the shopkeepers, traders, tradesmen, and financiers, were not particularly interested in a question which mainly affected the industrial classes of the Midlands and the North of England. Moreover, London had ceased to be the centre for popular agitations. The great political period of the metropolis of the British Empire extended from 1770 to 1831, when the issue was the overthrow of the oligarchy and the rise of the middle classes to power. Whilst the struggle for this reform was in progress the economic and political centre of gravity was shifted to the North of England, to the great centres of industry, which had been called into existence between 1770 and 1830 by the Industrial Revolution. London acquired in the main a commercial, intellectual, administrative, and financial character; its interests increased in diversity and variety, scattering its representatives apart. This tendency became intensified by the migration to the suburbs, by extensive building, and the wide area occupied by the group of towns which goes by the name of London. The London Working Men's Association had already experienced the disruptive and dispersive influence of London life. The Owenites gradually had the same experience; and even the Radical free traders soon discovered that they were not in a position to create a popular agitation in favour of their idea. The Anti-Corn Law Association pined away, and could neither live nor die, for on the one hand it was born in unfavourable surroundings, whilst on the other hand it corresponded to certain economic interests of the country and without doubt justified its existence. It possessed an ably and cleverly managed organ in the *Sun*; it had popular leaders; all it lacked was the backing of the masses. In 1837, when the political agitation of the working men, known a year later as Chartism, began to arrest the attention of the nation, the *Sun* made the attempt to win over the working men to the side of the Anti-Corn Law Association. The Radical operatives had at all times opposed the landed interests; even the *Poor Man's Guardian* had often declared for free trade; the chief Labour leaders saw eye to eye with the Radical members of parliament. Why, then, should it not be possible to induce the masses to enter the fight against the Corn Laws? To be sure, the working men stood above all for the introduction of universal suffrage. It was not possible, however, for this demand to be realised immediately in spite of its inherent justice; let the working men therefore assist the middle classes first of all in their fight against the Corn Laws; a victorious issue of this struggle would also be beneficial to the working men and would in addition weaken the economic position of the landed nobility; in this manner the political power of the latter, which was always opposed to progress, would be severely crippled. When the

I D

Corn Laws had been abolished the middle classes would work for the introduction of universal suffrage.

This attempt on the part of the *Sun* missed fire, and its arguments deepened the mistrust of the London Working Men's Association towards the free traders. The working men knew the value of the promises of the middle classes from their experiences in the years 1830–1832, and the attempt to enlist them in the free trade campaign appeared to them to be an underhand trick to divert their attention from the fight for universal suffrage.

The distrust, moreover, was mutual. The leaders of the Anti-Corn Law Association were in favour of universal suffrage, but they were of opinion that circumstances were not yet in its favour. The operatives were in a bad material condition, and would therefore vote against the propertied classes, regardless of consequences, and overwhelm them by force of numbers. In the United States of America, where differences of class were not so accentuated, universal suffrage might indeed work well. Not so in England, however, where wealth and poverty were sharply contrasted and divided society into antagonistic classes. England was standing on the eve of a great trial of strength between Capital and Labour ; it would therefore be advisable to bring the working men into a calmer state of mind by a sounder trade policy, and to provide them first of all with cheaper means of subsistence and with good employment. After this policy had led to the desired results then universal suffrage might be granted to them.

Both parties, in their mutual distrust, misunderstood each other, and O'Brien and O'Connor did their utmost to increase the distrust between the working men and the Radicals.

About two weeks before the London meeting of September 17, 1837, in favour of the Charter, the *Sun* printed a leading article, in which it was stated that :—

" The 17th inst., on which the Chartists are to hold their great meeting at Westminster, rapidly approaches. According to our view, that meeting will lead either to immediate benefit, or much mischief, as it is conducted to promote a repeal of the Corn

Laws or to procure the establishment of the People's Charter. All those who wish to stave off, as long as possible, the trial of strength between the proprietary and working classes, ought, we think, to direct that meeting to the attainment of the former object. Should resolutions be passed in favour of now agitating for the People's Charter, the question of the Corn Laws will for the moment be stifled, and the capitalists, who are known to dread the labourers, will at once unite to oppose them to the utmost of their power. Not only will the opportunity be lost of effecting a great practical good by procuring the repeal of the Starvation Laws, but angry agitation and great confusion, it is to be apprehended, will ensue." [1]   The *Sun* advises those people who attend the meeting to move an amendment that it would be better to direct the energies of the people to " the abolition of the accursed Corn Laws, this aim having more prospect of being attained than the Charter."

A few days later the same newspaper declared :—

" It is said by some of the speakers at popular meetings that the observations made of late on the subject of the Corn Laws are designed to divert the attention of the people from the discussion of the more important question of the Charter. Even the *Spectator* of last Saturday asserted that there is an attempt on the part of the ministerial press to divert the attention of the working classes from political changes to the overthrow of the Corn Laws ; the desperate Whigs throw their cry of the Corn Laws amongst the working classes as a tub to a whale. This is totally without foundation. The assertion is borrowed from the *Times* and the *Standard*. . . . We admit the justice of universal suffrage, but we deny the prudence of bringing it forward now, when there is no earthly chance of its being carried by this parliament, instead of bending all their energies to get rid of the Corn Laws."

Lovett rejected with scorn this advice of the free traders, and stoutly maintained that free trade was merely a tub for the proletarian whale. He was of opinion that universal suffrage

[1] *Sun*, September 5, 1837.
[2] *Ibid.*, September 10, 11, 12 and 18, 1837.

stood first and foremost ; when this had been obtained, then there would be a possibility of securing reforms in the cause of freedom, and among them the abolition of the corn taxes.

The London Anti-Corn Law Association was incapable of accomplishing anything. Its place was taken by the Anti-Corn Law Association founded in Manchester in October, 1838, which a year later became known throughout the world as the Anti-Corn Law League. Richard Cobden soon joined it and became the most important of its agitators and leaders. He was opposed to compromise and preached a class war against landowners. He considered the corn duties to be the greatest hindrance in the way of any progress in English industries. He immediately drew up a petition to parliament, in which he referred to the increase in foreign competition, and argued that it could be successfully countered by England only if it decided to abolish the Corn Laws.

Two answers were given to the question as to how free trade could neutralise the effect of foreign competition. The answer given by the leaders of this agitation can be summarised as follows : The more the masses have to pay for the means of subsistence, the less they are able to spend on manufactured goods. On this account the internal demand for manufactured articles is low. The abolition of the corn taxes would in itself reduce the price of food, and the people would therefore be in a position to spend more on manufactured goods and to increase the demand for them. An increase of this demand implies a greater industrial activity, more employment, and higher wages. Contentment would again visit the masses, and would make an end of all the struggles for trades unionism and for social reform. The abolition of the corn taxes would then open the English market to foreign corn, foreign agriculture would obtain a higher revenue, and the agricultural nations would have less reason to turn to industrial pursuits, thereby entering into competition with Englishmen. In return for their corn they will be able to obtain articles of English manufacture at a cheaper price than if they produced them themselves. It was only the English corn duties, and not, as the Tories argued, the Continental system of

Napoleon[1] that induced Prussia to build factories and to drive out English trade by extremely low wages. If foreign countries remain predominantly agricultural in character they will purchase English goods, thereby ensuring industrial prosperity for England, and industrial prosperity signifies high wages for working men and contentment in their homes. The abolition of the corn taxes would, therefore, bring happiness and social peace to England.

The other answer to the question was to the effect that free trade means low prices for means of subsistence, and cheap food means low wages, and it is only low wages that can put England in a position to meet foreign competition successfully, for foreign competition is based upon the low wages which are paid to operatives abroad.

The principle of political economy that was at the bottom of both of these answers was at that time uncontested, viz., that wages depended on the prices of the necessaries of life, or in other words, that wages are nothing else than the amount of the necessaries of life which are required by the working classes. The former answer, however, included also the idea that supply and demand exert some additional influence upon the scale of wages : the greater the demand for operatives, the higher the rise of wages above the level of the minimum of the necessaries requisite to life.

Judging by the first answer, the working men would be particularly interested in the abolition of the corn taxes ; this was the view adopted by Cobden and the majority of the Liberal free traders. According to the second answer, the whole question of free trade was entirely without significance for the working man : the iron law of wages would prevail, with or without free trade, until the working men should replace the whole capitalist system by the Socialist system, or until the working man should exercise a powerful influence in parliament by means of universal suffrage, and could protect the produce of their work by legislative powers.

These statements of divergent views were voiced in meetings and in the press as early as 1838.

[1] The Tory view of the beginning of German manufactures appears to be historically correct.

As already mentioned, parliament met on February 5, 1839, and the Chartist Convention on the previous day. At the same time the leaders of the Anti-Corn Law agitation met in conference in London, in order to present their petition to parliament, to bring on a debate by means of concerted action on the part of the Liberal members, such as Villiers, Molesworth, Clay, and Hume. The debate took place in the middle of March ; it lasted four days, and was concluded, as in previous years, by a rejection of the free trade motion. Clay, a Liberal member, made a particularly remarkable speech, in which he disposed of the allegation that the people took no interest in the free trade agitation, and that the free traders were speculating on a reduction of wages. On this point he made the following rejoinder :—

" Wages would not fall because the Corn Laws were repealed, but because, in our struggle with foreign manufactures, it would be impossible to get a profit enabling us to pay high wages. . . . It is said the working classes kept aloof, but why ? Is it because they believe in the Corn Laws ? No ! but because they don't expect relief from a parliament as at present constituted. Again, they say, if we refuse to join the middle classes in procuring repeal they will join us in demanding the People's Charter. Let the House beware lest they make good that prophecy, lest in the utter hopelessness of seeing justice done in this matter it drives the middle classes to make common cause with the working classes, and to force on a change in our form of government as the only means of ridding themselves of what they feel to be an intolerable oppression. As yet the members of this House had the time to prevent the alliance—as yet they might withdraw all the better portion, even of the working classes, the honest and well-intentioned, from the guidance of the visionary, the fanatic, the revolutionist, and the incendiary." [1]

Naturally, Clay comprised in this category Stephens, Oastler, Owen, O'Brien, and O'Connor. The spokesmen of the Chartist opposition against the free trade agitation were O'Connor and O'Brien. O'Connor argued as follows :—

[1] *Times*, March 14, 1839 ; Hansard's *Parliamentary Debates*, third series, vol. 46, pp. 516–519.

" The Anti-Corn Law Association is composed principally of
master manufacturers, whose interest is to buy labour at the
cheapest market and sell the produce of labour at the dearest
market.   Machinery will always help the employer to buy labour
cheap. . . .   The League is composed of the owners of
machinery, and machinery is the great, the monster enemy of
an unrepresented people.   It is the new-born influence of the
master manufacturers which forced the Reform Bill from the
Tory Party.   And for the last ten years they have gone on
establishing the details by which the Bill should be made beneficial to their order.   Poor Law, Corporation Reform Bill, Rural
Police Bill, appointment of Whig magistrates, and now they
require the abolition of the Corn Laws.   Since machinery and
capital became represented in the House of Commons the
hostility between master and man has become greater every year,
and this has arisen from the discovery made by the working
classes that capital thinks of nothing else but of the subjugation
of labour.   Landlords treat their labourers as a rule well, and are
controlled by the public opinion of their order, while manufacturers have no other rule but buying cheap and selling dear.
. . .   Trade and industry have denationalised Englishmen and
made them cosmopolitan." [1]

This was the strain in which the most popular of the Chartists
spoke.   It was not without reason that O'Brien reproached
O'Connor with arguing like a country squire, whilst the subject
ought to be approached from a democratic standpoint.[2]

O'Brien wrote a great deal against the free trade agitation ;
but there were not many ideas underlying his articles.   His
arguments may be thus summed up :—

The difference in the interests of the middle and the working
classes cannot be bridged.   Free trade is a policy of the middle
classes and, therefore, can be of no use to the working men.
The rate of wages depends on the prices of the necessaries of life ;
it rises and falls with them.   The abolition of the Corn Laws will

[1] O'Connor, *The Trial of Feargus O'Connor*, 1843.   Introduction,
v.–viii.
[2] *British Statesman*, November 12, 1842.

lower the price of food, and hence will lower wages ; and in the interests of the working man we cannot desire this contingency. It may be admitted that free trade will revive industry, and that business will be brisker—but were wages raised by the enormous increase in trade which has taken place since 1688 ? No ! Therefore, free trade cannot bring the working men the blessings promised by its advocates.[1]

The hostility between Chartists and free traders increased rapidly. The Chartists dubbed the free trade agitators " Political Pedlars," and the latter accused the Chartist leaders of being in the pay of the landowners. From 1841 to 1844 there was not a single free trade meeting at which Chartists were not also present, in order to move amendments to the free trade resolutions and to call upon the audience to work first of all for the Charter. Not infrequently the partisans of the two agitations came into open collision with each other, especially when the Chartists were of the opinion that free speech was denied to their speakers at free trade meetings. The Chartists got on the nerves of the Anti-Corn Law agitators, and Cobden believed the Chartists had made him the particular object of their hostility.[2]

Thus from the very beginning these strained relations prevailed between Chartism and the free trade agitation. The Convention, therefore, considered it necessary to lose no time in defining their position on this question, and to give a clear lead to the working classes. James Bronterre O'Brien was entrusted with drawing up a report. He submitted the following resolution :—

" The Convention is convinced that at the present eventful crisis it is indispensably necessary that the people's undivided attention should be concentrated upon the National Petition alone, to the exclusion of all others ; being also convinced that the present agitation for a repeal of the Corn Laws was intended, and does actually tend to divert the working classes from their paramount object ; and being further of opinion that such an unconditional repeal as would alone be likely to receive the

[1] *Operative*, November 5, 1838 ; *British Statesman*, October 29, November 5, 12 and 26, 1842.

[2] Thomas Frost, *Forty Years' Recollections*, 1880, pp. 33–34.

sanction of the Anti-Corn Law agitation would be rather injurious than otherwise to the interests of the poorer classes : we, the delegates of the Convention do, therefore, most earnestly recommend our constituents in particular and the unrepresented classes in general to deprecate and oppose all and every agitation for or against a repeal of the Corn Laws until the fate of the National Petition and People's Charter shall have been determined by the legislature, so far as the legislature is able to determine it."[1]

In moving his resolution O'Brien denounced the free trade agitators as stockjobbers and tricksters, whose agitation was only calculated to enrich speculators and Jews, to lower the wages of working men, and to divert the attention of the masses from the Chartist agitation.

O'Brien's speech was received with general applause. His resolution was supported by all the speakers, but more especially by Attwood's adherents. We may omit their speeches ; they were full of satisfaction with the triumph of their master's doctrines ; Attwood's mantle had fallen upon O'Brien, the teacher of Chartism. John Collins was, moreover, of opinion that the whole aim of the free traders was to reduce the wages of the English workmen to the level of the Prussian, since Prussia had become a serious competitor of English textiles.

O'Brien's resolution was carried unanimously. The Chartists were guided by it during the whole period of the Anti-Corn Law agitation. Here and there a few workmen indeed followed Cobden, but the majority kept apart. Nevertheless, it was the Chartist agitation, as we shall see later on, that broke down the opposition of the Whigs and of a section of the Tories to the abolition of the Corn Laws and paved the way for the victory of free trade. If it had not been for the revolutionary agitation of the British working classes, Cobden and Bright would never have attained their object.

3.—DISSENSION IN THE CONVENTION

Even during the first few weeks of its existence dissensions broke out in the meetings of the Convention, in spite of the

[1] *Charter*, February 10, 1839.

avoidance of all theoretical discussions and in spite of the unanimity of opinion as to the importance of the Charter to the
exclusion of all other subjects. The cause of the dissensions was
to be sought in the differences of opinion on the "ulterior
measures" to be adopted, in the event of Parliament rejecting
the Petition or the Charter. The old contrast between moral
and physical force did not permit of any compromise. The
question of ulterior measures occupied the attention of the
great majority of the delegates, who either felt or were convinced
that the Charter had no chance whatever of being adopted by
Parliament.

What was to be done ? What measures were to be taken if
the moral influence of the discussions of the Convention, of the
petitions of the people, of the meetings and great manifestoes
of the masses were all to be of no avail ?

In reading the reports of the Convention, it is possible even at
the present day to realise the mental anguish endured by the
delegates in attempting to answer these questions. On the
one hand, they felt a repugnance to an open and full exchange
of opinions, on the other hand they made the most anxious efforts
to obtain an answer to their enquiries. There was no question
of any dread of legal consequences, any dread of the power
of the government, but of solicitude for the stability of the
Convention and for the united action of the Chartist agitation.
Discussions on this point commenced in the second week of the
Convention (February 11 to 17, 1839) ; they were deferred,
resumed, and again deferred until the course of events rendered
it impossible to postpone a decision.

Hugh Craig, one of the Scotch delegates, proposed the following
motion on February 8 :—

"That on an early day the Convention take into consideration
what ulterior means they would employ, or what measures they
would resort to or recommend to the industrial classes for speedily
obtaining and firmly securing their political rights, should it
unfortunately happen that the delegates fail in their attempt
to convince the members of the House of Commons of the
justice of the principles of the People's Charter."

The motion came on for discussion on February 11. Craig moved it with merely a brief comment that a clear pronounce-ment on the subject would assist in winning over those who were still in doubt as to the Chartists being in earnest. Taylor opposed, for it should not be assumed in advance that parlia-ment would be likely to oppose the wishes of the people ; a pronouncement of this sort would only place unnecessary impedi-ments in the way of the delegates appointed by the Convention to influence members of parliament in favour of the Petition and the Charter. O'Connor supported the motion, for the best way was to go with the National Petition in one hand and with the ulterior measures in the other and to approach parliament with both hands. O'Brien supported Taylor's views ; the Convention ought to act as if it expected a successful issue for the Charter. It would be absurd to talk of ulterior measures unless two or three million signatures backed up the Petition. If parliament were then to reject it, the indignation of the people would soon furnish materials for ulterior measures. Salt was also of opinion that the main point was the organisation of the people ; if this were strong enough the tyrants would be forced to adopt views more consonant with liberty. Vincent moved an amendment, recommending the appointment of a committee to consider and determine what measures should be adopted in the event of failure with the legislature, and to report thereon to the Convention.

Vincent's amendment proved to be a good way out of a delicate situation and was therefore adopted.

Cobbett expressed dissatisfaction with this expedient, and regarded it as indicating the resolve of the majority of the Convention not to acquiesce in the rejection of the Petition ; and he therefore resigned from the Convention.

J. P. Cobbett, a strict legalist, was the first to strike a note of discord in the Convention, and he was followed by Harney, the fiery revolutionist, who at that time was barely twenty-two years old, and had got obsessed with the idea of being a second Marat in the English Convention. He soon drew comparisons between the French and English Conventions, much to the disadvantage of the latter.   He had set his mind on action, on deeds of heroism, whilst the delegates, on the other hand, were busy with the Petition, avoided sharp words, and were careful not to give the slightest cause of offence to the Queen and the Girondists. " *Nous sommes trahis !* " We are betrayed ; the traitors are ruining the revolution ! He donned the Phrygian cap and called the people into the meetings. The delegates Ryder and Marsden rallied to his side, and came to the conclusion that " there were only eight honest men in the Convention."[1] They did not reveal the names of the other five.   " The truth is," exclaimed Harney, " that there is only one way of obtaining the Charter, namely insurrection " ![2] From the month of March his tongue could no longer be curbed.   In April one of his friends founded the *London Democrat*, a weekly, which is a mine of Anarchist phrases. Here is a sample :—

" Organisation won't do it. It won't be the organised masses that will carry the victory. Oh, no ! That depends upon the outcast, friendless beings, who have no house to go to, no food to satisfy the cravings of hunger, no covering to keep them warm, or even to make them look decent, no wherewithal to render their lives worth preserving ? The battle will be fought and won by those who hide themselves from the gaze of the world, through the cruel operations of unjust laws. The battle will be fought by brigands as they are called."[3]

Harney himself gave the people the following advice :—

" When parliamentary elections take place let all the unrepresented elect Chartists. There is no doubt that nine-tenths of the elected will be Universal Suffrage men. To elect representatives without enabling them to take their seats in the legislature would be the veriest farce imaginable. To complete the good work it will be necessary that each representative should be furnished with a bodyguard of sturdy *sans-culottes*, some thousands strong. By the time the whole of the representatives arrived in the environs of the metropolis they would have with them not less than a million men. This would settle the matter.

[1] *Charter*, April 28, 1839.   [2] *London Democrat*, May 4, 1839.
[3] *Ibid.*, May 18, 1839.

They would encamp for one night on Hampstead Heath and then march to Parliament Street. Should the plutocratic-elected scoundrels be fool enough to have taken their places in the tax trap, the voice of the people, crying, ' Make place for better men ! ' would scatter them like chaff before the wind, or should they hesitate to fly the job will soon be settled by their being tied neck and heels and flung into the Thames.''[1]

He was aided and abetted by Major Beniowski, a refugee from the Polish insurrection of 1831. Beniowski contributed articles regularly to the *London Democrat* on the Polish revolution, on strategy and tactics, on the possibility of an invasion of England, and on the worthlessness of the Convention. Later on he was singled out by the extreme Left of the Convention to head the insurrection in South Wales.

From March, 1839, onwards the delegates Harney, Ryder, and Marsden held meetings in London, and encouraged the people to arm themselves and to make other preparations for opposing force by force. They sent a resolution to the Convention to the effect that if the delegates really had the courage the Charter would become law in four weeks' time.[2] A motion to expel Harney and his associates was rejected, on the ground that the Convention was not armed with the authority to declare the mandates of the people to be null and void. On the other hand a vote of censure was passed upon them, but this did not mend matters. On March 11 a crowded meeting was held in London at the " Crown and Anchor," Strand, London, W.C., in which the delegates Frost, O'Connor, Harney, and other speakers adopted a threatening tone. The speakers called upon the masses to prepare for the coming fight. This incitement to arms furnished an opportunity to the anti-Chartist newspapers to draw attention to the true character of the agitation and to point out to the nation the dangers with which it was threatened. The newspaper reports had a deterrent effect and were the cause of the resignation of three of the Birmingham delegates, Hadley, Salt, and Douglas.[3]

[1] *London Democrat*, April 27, 1839.   [2] *Charter*, March 10, 1839.
[3] *Ibid.*, April 7, 1839.

Although the vacant places were soon filled up again, the Convention suffered both in power and prestige. The withdrawal of the adherents of constitutional tactics left the field open to the advocates of armed resistance, and discussions in the Convention became long and frequent on the constitutional right of the people to carry arms. Several delegates were of opinion that the whole discussion was superfluous, since this right was beyond all question. One of the delegates asked tersely and curtly : " What would we think of a nation of slaves asking legal opinion as to the right of arming themselves ? " Most of the delegates were in agreement with this view. Only one delegate, Alexander Halley, made the attempt to bring his colleagues to a calmer frame of mind. He appealed to them as follows :—

" What purpose has this discussion ? Can we make this question a practical one ? Was it, in fact, of any use in this question of universal suffrage ? Can we have a commissariat department ? Was it intended to have drilling masters and to prepare for actual war ? I feel truly surprised that such a question should occupy us so long when so small a proportion of the people are with us. We are accused of being violent men, who would adopt violent means to accomplish their purpose. Will not the adoption of such a motion afford confirmation of this charge ? "

The Convention finally adopted a motion of Dr. Fletcher, declaring that the right of the people to arm was beyond all question and needed no discussion.

The actual cause of this discussion was the conviction that had been arrived at that the Petition had no chance of being accepted by parliament. This was the upshot of the report which was furnished to the Convention by the committee appointed to enter into communication with members of parliament.[1] The statements made on the right to arm were a demonstration and a protest against parliament. In the fourth week of April the Convention issued a short manifesto to the people, containing the information that it was in vain for the people to expect any relief from those in authority. " The Convention

[1] Compare Disraeli, *Sybil*, book 4, chapter 5.

have no hopes other than in the firmness and energy of the people. Public meetings should be holden in as many places as possible during Whitsun week, to direct what ulterior measures shall be adopted. Delegates from the Convention will attend as many of these meetings as their numbers will allow."

At the same time the delegates Patrick Matthew and Dr. A. S. Wade handed in their resignations, since they regarded a peaceful policy to be the only right line of action. In Lancashire and Wales numerous Chartists provided themselves with pikes and muskets ; in other districts the workmen engaged in military exercises ; but there was no organised plan, and their proceeding was more likely to weaken the agitation than to strengthen it. On April 29 the Welshmen rose up in revolt at Llanidloes, but it naturally proved abortive, and ended in the arrest of seventeen Chartists. Owing to the absence of any strong organisation it was not possible for the leaders to obtain exact information concerning the arming of the people, and there was free play for the imagination on this point. The agents of the government sent in reports on the extent of the armed preparations, with the result that the Cabinet took special precautions for the army and police to be in readiness for emergencies. The garrisons of the Midlands and the North of England were strengthened and placed under a single command. On May 3 Lord John Russell, in his capacity of Home Secretary, authorised the magistrates and justices of the peace to confiscate the weapons of civilians in all suspicious cases, and also to declare all meetings illegal to which people came armed with weapons. Finally, he encouraged all well-intentioned citizens to form " societies of volunteers for the protection of life, liberty, and property."

In the second week of May the excitement of the masses in the Midlands and the North of England rose to a dangerous pitch. A contributory cause was the introduction of a rural police, which up to that time was not only unknown in the rural districts, but even in many towns. Birmingham, for instance, had no police. The Chartists regarded this arrangement as a blow directed against themselves, and on this account they made a call to arms. A formidable conflict between the people and the armed forces of the State seemed to be unavoidable. On the one hand, the Convention began to take precautionary measures for its own safety, on the other hand it wished to be nearer to the seat of war. On May 10 O'Connor, therefore, brought forward a motion to adjourn the sittings of the Convention from London to Birmingham. Brown, the Birmingham delegate, declared that " the people of Birmingham were ready for anything, and would stand forth as a wall of brass in protection of the Convention." The Convention resolved upon this step.

During the sitting of the Convention in London the National Rent steadily poured in. In the week ending May 12 it amounted to £86.

The Petition had already been signed by 1,250,000 people ; it weighed six hundredweight, and was two miles long. It was placed on a huge wagon decorated with banners.

4.—THE SESSION AT BIRMINGHAM AND THE ULTERIOR MEASURES

On May 13, 1839, the delegates of the Convention arrived in Birmingham, and were enthusiastically received by 50,000 working men, who formed a square, put the delegates in the middle, and marched to the place of meeting. The working men indicated by this action that they were ready to protect their delegates from the police and the soldiers. The authorities had also made preparations ; even at an early hour in the morning infantry and artillery marched in and were held in readiness for action. On the following day the Convention published the report of the committee on ulterior measures in the form of a manifesto, which, after a fierce onslaught on the Whigs and their ambiguities, proceeds :—

" From numerous communications we received we believe you expect us to collect the will and intentions of the country respecting the most efficient means for causing the People's Charter to become the law of the land. Anxious, therefore, clearly to ascertain the opinions and determinations of the people in the shortest possible time, and doubly anxious to secure their righteous objects bloodless and stainless, we respectfully submit the following propositions for your serious consideration :

" That at all the simultaneous public meetings to be held for the purpose of petitioning the Queen to call good men to her councils, as well as at all subsequent meetings of your unions or associations up to the 1st of July, you submit the following questions to the people there assembled :—

" 1. Whether they will be prepared, at the request of the Convention, to withdraw all sums of money they may individually or collectively have placed in savings banks, private banks, or in the hands of any person hostile to their just rights ?   Whether, at the same request, they will be prepared immediately to convert all their paper money into gold and silver ?[1]   (2) Whether, if the Convention shall determine that a sacred month (general strike) will be necessary to prepare the millions to secure the Charter of their political salvation, they will firmly resolve to abstain from their labours during that period. (3) Whether they would refuse payment of rents, rates, and taxes ? (4) Whether, according to their old constitutional right, they have prepared themselves with the arms of free men to defend the laws and constitutional privileges their ancestors bequeathed to them ?   (5) Whether they will provide themselves with Chartist candidates, so as to be prepared to propose them for their representatives at the next general election ; and if returned by show of hands, such candidates to consider themselves veritable representatives of the people, to meet in London at a time hereafter to be determined on ?   (6) Whether they will resolve to deal exclusively with Chartists ; and in all cases of persecution rally around and protect all those who may suffer in this righteous cause ? (7) Whether, by all means in their power, they will perseveringly contend for the great objects of the People's Charter, and resolve that no counter-agitation for a less measure of justice shall divert them from this righteous object ? (8) Whether they would abstain from purchasing newspapers which opposed them ?   (9) Whether the people will determine to obey all the just and constitutional requests of the majority of the Convention ? "[2]

[1] This form of pressure would mean a run on the banks and on the Bank of England.   [2] *Charter*, May 19, 1839.

I E

These questions contained the ulterior measures, concerning which the Convention wished to ascertain whether they could be carried out.

The Convention resolved, in addition, to adjourn from May 16 to July 1, in order to give the delegates the opportunity to hold mass meetings in Whit week, and to learn whether and to what extent the ulterior measures could be carried out with any degree of certainty.   Before the adjournment the Convention issued the following directions (drawn up by O'Brien) for the impending mass meetings :—

" 1. That peace, law, and order shall continue to be the motto of this Convention, so long as our oppressors shall act in the spirit of peace, law, and order towards the people ; but should our enemies substitute war for peace, or attempt to suppress our lawful and orderly agitation by lawless violence, we shall deem it to be the sacred duty of the people to meet force with force, and repel assassination by justifiable homicide. 2. That in accordance with the foregoing resolution, the Convention do employ only legal and peaceable means in the prosecution of the great and righteous objects of the present movement.   Being also desirous that no handle should be afforded to the enemy for traducing our motives, or employing armed force against the people, we hereby recommend the Chartists, who may attend the approaching simultaneous meetings, to avoid carrying staves, pikes, pistols, or any other offensive weapons about their persons. We recommend them to proceed to the ground sober, orderly, and unarmed.   As also to treat as enemies of the cause any person or persons who may exhibit such weapons, or who by any other act of folly or wickedness, should provoke a breach of the peace.   3. That the marshals and other officers who may have charge of the arrangements for the simultaneous meetings are particularly requested to use every means in their power to give effect to the recommendation embodied in the preceding resolution.   We also recommend that the aforesaid officers do in all cases consult with the local authorities before the meetings take place. 4. That in case our oppressors in the middle and upper ranks should instigate the authorities to assail the people with armed force, in contravention of the existing laws of the realm, the said oppressors in the upper and middle ranks shall be held responsible, in person and property, for any detriment that may result to the people from such atrocious instigation."

It was necessary to issue these directions, for every day witnessed a more and more widespread acquisition of pikes, old muskets, and other weapons of defence. William Benbow's pamphlet on the National Holiday as well as Francis Maceroni's book on street fighting reached a phenomenal sale.[1] From the beginning of May, 1839, the Chartists of the North of England who were in favour of physical force were convinced that the outbreak of the insurrection could not be deferred much longer.[2]

It was a fortunate circumstance for the British working classes that Lord John Russell appointed General Sir Charles J. Napier to be commander-in-chief of the troops in the North of England. Napier was a born leader of men, humane and enlightened, a lover of liberty, a hater of all plutocratic civilisation, sympathising to a certain degree with the political and social ideas of Chartism. He belonged to a family conspicuous in mental ability and nobility of character, which furnished the British nation with gifted generals, admirals, and writers on military subjects. The task was laid upon him to keep the Chartists in check. He was in sympathy with the people, and yet, in obedience to military discipline, he had undertaken the task of suppressing Chartism. In 1839 he wrote in his diary as follows :—

" As matters stand, I am for a strong police, but the people should have universal suffrage, the ballot, annual parliaments, farms for the people, and systematic education. I am opposed to landlordism and capitalism. . . . Manchester is the smokey chimney of the world. . . . If the path to hell is paved with

[1] Maceroni was an Italian colonel who lived in London as a refugee. In 1832 he wrote a pamphlet for the London workmen, entitled " Defensive Instructions for the People," which dealt specially with street fighting and the erection of barricades. A second edition appeared in 1834.

[2] Lloyd Jones, *Life of Robert Owen*, 1905 edition, p. 346.

good intentions, it is certainly laid out with Lancashire cotton goods. . . . The people must have rights to be able to protect themselves. Good government consists in having good laws well obeyed. England has an abundance of bad laws, but is every man to arm against every law he thinks bad ? No ! Bad laws must be reformed by the concentrated reason of the nation gradually acting on the legislature, not by pikes of individuals acting on the bodies of the executive."[1]

But the miseries of the people were heartrending. The suppression of Chartism must not lead to the triumph of militarism. However, the world does not stand still :—

" Truth is marching on, sadly shackled indeed, but the press will set her free, and the next hundred years will produce more change in the condition of men than the last thousand."[2]

Dominated by these ideas, Napier took over the command-in-chief of the North of England.

On May 16 the delegates separated. In the fourth week of May mass meetings were held at Newcastle, Sheffield, Monmouth, Bath, Liverpool, Hanley, Hull, Birmingham, Kersal Moor (near Manchester), Peep Green (near Huddersfield), Sunderland, Northampton, Preston, Glasgow and numerous smaller industrial towns. Everywhere they were well attended, if not in such masses as the Chartist papers asseverated. At most of these meetings several delegates of the Convention were generally present. The speeches were devoted to a clear exposition of the ulterior measures ; but they also contained much violent rhetoric, partly expressing the revolutionary sentiments of the speakers, partly as a means of inflaming the masses and to gain their assent to the proposed measures. The meetings everywhere passed off without any disturbance of the peace. The meeting on Kersal Moor was attended also by General Napier and Colonel Wemyss, and they found nothing of a dangerous character in the speeches to which they listened . Both of the commanding officers were indeed supporters of the most complete freedom of speech, but they regarded the policy of physical

[1] W. Napier, *Life of Sir Charles J. Napier*, 1857, II., 63, 74, 75.
[2] *Ibid., op. cit.*, pp. 77 and 85.

force to be a delusion, since the physical force was wielded by the State and not by the poor people.

To all appearance the Chartists did not understand the reason for the restraint of the military. They were not acquainted with Napier and knew nothing of his mental struggles. They considered the restraint of the armed forces was due to their fear of the Chartists. As soon as the delegates returned to Birmingham on July 1, 1839, and the deliberations of the Convention were resumed, their revolutionary ardour came uppermost. In most cases there was no longer any question of regarding the situation as it really was. They reported on the large meetings at which the ulterior measures had been adopted with unanimity and enthusiasm. The numbers of the audiences were unconsciously greatly exaggerated, and they calculated the numbers of the men who were ready to fight by their estimates of those present at the meetings. Taylor and his special clique had raked up five old brass cannon from somewhere or other, and had buried them to be dug up again in case of need. They imagined that the English artillery which had not been in action since Waterloo would be useless. In addition there was the fact that a number of soldiers under Napier's command attended Chartist meetings and were adherents of Chartism. Under these circumstances how easy it was to give way to illusions and to consider them to be palpable facts! Napier was kept informed of these occurrences and invited a representative Chartist to inspect the English artillery and its prompt handling. He also formed up his battalions in Manchester, so as to bring back the revolutionary elements of the Lancashire working men to a true understanding of the actual position. On the advice of Lord John Russell, the soldiers who were adherents of Chartism were not punished, but, through discussion, were made to realise the folly of the policy of physical force.[1]

In the meantime the Convention was deliberating and Taylor declared :—

" The people have got muskets, but they require bayonets in order to be able to resist cavalry charges. I move that the Con-

[1] W. Napier, *Life of Sir Charles J. Napier*, pp. 62 *sqq.*

vention issue, without delay, a request to the country at large
to withdraw all the moneys from all banks or from persons hostile
to the People's Charter ; to convert all paper money into gold ;
to abstain from all excisable articles of luxury ; to commence
exclusive dealings, prepare arms ; and that the members of the
Convention meet on July 15 for the express purpose of appointing
a day when the sacred month or national holiday should commence."

O'Connor seconded the motion, and declared :—

" I strongly approve of the sacred month when the people might
act the part of honourable plunderers instead of being arrant
slaves."

Bussey was equally of the opinion that it was time to take
serious action ; his constituents were resolved immediately to
carry the ulterior measures into effect. Dr. Fletcher gave
expression to the same view, whilst M'Douall desired a stricter
organisation after the manner of the United Irishmen. Burns
supported M'Douall's proposal by saying: " Such an organisation is necessary. If the Government Peterlood the people, we
should Moscow the country." [1]

When Napier heard of these resolutions he wrote :—

" The Chartists say they will keep the sacred month. Egre-
gious folly ! They will do no such thing ; the poor cannot do
it ; they must plunder, and then they will be hanged by the
hundreds ; they will split upon it, but if they are made to attempt
it they are lost. . . . Physical force ! Fools ! *We* have
the physical force, not they. They talk of their hundred thousands
of men. Who is to move them when I am dancing round them
with cavalry and pelting them with cannon-shot ? What would
their 100,000 men do with my rockets wriggling their fiery
tails among them, roaring, scorching, tearing, smashing all they
come near ? And when in desperation and despair they broke
to fly, how would they bear five regiments of cavalry careering
through them ? Poor men ! How little they know of physical
force ! "[2]

Education was what the workmen needed, said Napier, but

[1] *Charter*, July 7, 1839.   [2] W. Napier, *op. cit.*, p. 69.

above everything they wanted bread. And he bestirred himself to bring influence to bear upon the magistrates to mitigate the severity of the Poor Law. He notes with pleasure that his officers felt a repugnance to fire upon fellow-citizens. The advocates of energetic measures were the magistrates, whose activity Napier had to be continually restraining. He had a poor opinion also of the Chartist leaders. He considered Taylor to be the leader of the physical force section.

In the meantime the magistrates of Birmingham, among whom were the ex-Chartists Muntz and Scholefield, took extensive precautions to keep the agitation in check. On May 16 they arrested two of the Chartist leaders, viz., Brown (a delegate) and Fussell. In the beginning of July they issued a proclamation forbidding workmen to meet in the evening in the Bull Ring. Since the town had no police force, the magistrates sent to London on July 4, for a hundred policemen, who marched to the Bull Ring between eight and nine o'clock, and used their truncheons on the crowd. At first the workmen took to flight, but in a few minutes they returned to make an attack. Their counter-attack was so violent that the police were scattered in all directions and sought refuge in houses. Three policemen were left severely wounded in the Bull Ring and two more remained in the hands of the workmen, who were determined to wreak their vengeance on them. But Taylor came quickly on the scene, and saved the life of the two policemen. Rioting lasted for some hours in Birmingham, until the delegates of the Convention succeeded in calming the people. Early in the morning of July 5 several Chartists, including Taylor, were arrested.

At nine o'clock the Convention met in order to discuss the events. Lovett immediately rose to speak and moved the following resolution :—

" 1. That this Convention is of opinion that a wanton, flagrant, and unjust outrage has been made upon the people of Birmingham by a blood-thirsty and unconstitutional force from London, acting under the authority of men who, when out of office, sanctioned and took part in the meetings of the people ; and now, when they share in the public plunder, seek to keep the people in social

and political degradation.   2. That the people of Birmingham
are the best judges of their own right to meet in the Bull Ring
or elsewhere ; have their own feelings to consult respecting
outrage given, and are the best judges of their own power and
resources to obtain justice.   3. That the summary and despotic
arrest of Taylor, our respected colleague, affords another convincing proof of all absence of justice in England, and clearly
shows that there is no security for lives, liberty, or property
till the people have some control over the laws they are called
upon to obey."

The resolution was adopted unanimously ; it was then printed
and posted up all over the town.   All the delegates were ready
to subscribe their names to the poster, but Lovett warned the
Convention to consider that the people ought not to be deprived
of all its representatives at one blow ; it would suffice if there
were only one signature to the poster, and he would gladly
make the sacrifice.   He signed it alone and, accompanied by
Collins, took it to the printer.   By the afternoon it was printed
and posted up.   On the evening of July 6, Lovett and Collins
were arrested and brought before the magistrate late at night.

It was only to be expected that Lovett's statements were frank
and manly, and they immediately gained for him the magistrate's
respect.   He assumed entire responsibility for the resolutions,
and for their publication by means of posters, and he declared
that he stood by every word they contained.

Lovett, Collins, and Taylor were set at liberty on bail in the
course of a few days.

At the same time Harney was arrested in Northumberland
and brought to Birmingham.   He had made inflammatory
speeches on May 14, and had called upon the people to arm,
to proclaim the sacred month, and to follow William Benbow's
recipe for living at the expense of the landlords and capitalists.
The charge against Harney was finally dropped, as well as the
charge against Taylor.   Only Lovett and Collins were brought
before a jury at a later date.

In the meantime the streets of Birmingham were in the
hands of the military and police ; the shops were shut, and all

meetings were forbidden or dispersed by force. Martial law prevailed, where seven years ago the heart of the British Reform agitation had pulsated. In the course of the next few days the soldiers came twice into collision with the working men. The wrath of the people increased in intensity, until it gave vent to acts of violence on July 15. The houses and business premises of well-known enemies of Chartism were set on fire. Gold and silver goods were thrown into the street, but no working man picked them up ; no one plundered, no one considered his own interests. The rich took to flight, since they were unable to obtain protection from either the military or the police. Thereupon the workmen made full use of their right to meet in assembly, and since they were no longer interfered with, Birmingham again returned to its normal peaceful condition. Protest meetings were held by working men all over the country against the arbitrary action of the authorities in Birmingham. Whilst Sir Charles J. Napier agreed with the people, and ascribed the blame to the magistrates, the Iron Duke, when speaking in the House of Lords, bewailed the malicious and horrible acts " of the Birmingham mob, which has wrought more havoc than the cruellest enemies."

Already on July 8 the Convention had resolved to return to London, since the second reading of the Petition was to take place on July 12 in the House of Commons, and since the ulterior measures could be more successfully carried out from the capital. On the 10th, the delegates arrived in London.

5.—THE NATIONAL PETITION AND PARLIAMENT

The shadow of the fate of the Petition lay across all the debates of the Convention and all the meetings and resolutions of the Chartists. On June 14 Thomas Attwood introduced the Petition, and on July 12 there was a rather long discussion on the matter in the House of Commons. From an unprejudiced point of view, the National Petition was accorded a treatment incomparably more favourable than that shown to all the other petitions. The number of signatures, the comprehensive character of the Petition, and the violence of the agitation throughout the whole country enforced a respect for it which even the most conservative member could not refuse to give it. But all this did not alter the fate of the Petition in the very slightest degree.

On June 14, 1839, the petition was introduced. Several vans had brought it along. Attwood then unrolled a portion and laid it on the table. The Petition was read a first time and was printed as a parliamentary paper.

On July 12 Attwood proposed the second reading of the Petition and supported it in a long speech. He took the oligarchy severely to task, depicted the miseries of the working classes, and ascribed all their wretchedness to the gold currency and the resumption of specie payment (1819). The Birmingham men were well aware that a parliament elected by universal suffrage would commit excesses in reform, but as the present parliament was extremely Conservative, excesses in reform would redress the balance. The Petition was signed by the *élite* of the British working class and should therefore not be disregarded. A sympathetic treatment of the Petition would also have a soothing effect upon the minds of the working men, and would put an end to the policy of physical force, of which he had always disapproved.

John Fielden supported the motion in a short speech, in which he pleaded for the greatest possible restriction of indirect taxation and for the introduction of a property-tax. The House seemed always to favour the rich and to neglect the wishes of the poor. The adoption of the Petition was a necessary step ; it was equally necessary that the rich should take a larger part in bearing the burden of the State. Justice alone could avert the impending social catastrophe.

Lord John Russell replied on behalf of the government in a rather long speech. He congratulated Attwood on his refusal to identify himself with those who had recommended the use of arms and physical force, who under the pretence of promoting the " so-called " National Petition had used the most violent and revolutionary language—not exceeded in violence and atrocity in the worst times of the French Revolution—exhorting the people to subvert the laws by force of arms. The government were not opposed to the political views of the Petition and the Charter in favour of freedom, but to the menacing attitude of the Chartist leaders. The ministers could not conceive any form of political government or mode of legislation by which they could ensure to the whole community a perpetual state of prosperity, or by which, in a country, like Great Britain, depending very much upon commerce and manufactures, they could prevent that state of low wages and consequent distress which at all times affected those who were at the bottom of the scale, or prevent those alternate fluctuations from prosperity to distress which occur in every community of the kind. The United States of America already possessed all that the Petition demanded. Did that country never experience commercial crises, low wages, or want of employment ? The state of things in England, as depicted by the Petition, was grossly exaggerated. Look at the savings banks. Did they not furnish pretty good proof of the number of artificers in this country who were not only receiving adequate wages, but also looking forward to the future support of their families ? The member for Birmingham (Attwood) always held out only one cure for all our evils, viz., paper money. How did he know that a Parliament elected by Universal Suffrage would make use of this remedy ? The leaders of the General Convention, Mr. Feargus O'Connor, Mr. Lovett, Mr. Collins, Mr. Frost, and many others declared themselves against any such currency.

In conclusion, Lord Russell warned the Convention and the Chartists in general against the employment of ulterior measures, which could but lead to disturbance, confusion, and injury of the interests of the working men, whom he exhorted to turn their backs upon Chartism.

The Radical members and free trade leaders, Villiers, Hume, and Wakley, spoke in favour of sending the Bill to a committee, but the Conservatives, including Benjamin Disraeli, were opposed to it. Disraeli's speech was the only one which exhibited serious thinking and original views ; it bears evidence of a thorough knowledge of the first phases of Chartism. For the first time in its history parliament heard the voice of Conservative social reform and Tory democracy. He believed the rise of Chartism to have been due to the Reform Bill, which had transferred the political power from a small but efficient minority of socially-minded aristocrats to a commercial class, which was centralising the State and handing over the social duties to a soulless bureaucracy, while the new rulers were enjoying the rights and privileges which power conferred upon them. Corporate activity and help, protection of the poor, administration of justice, and organisation of defence—duties which the aristocratic minority had performed—were being neglected or restricted or put into the hands of paid officials and commissioners. The sympathetic connection between ruling class and people was severed. No wonder that that people had come to the conclusion that they themselves must look after their own interests Hence the Charter : " The Chartists are in hostility against the middle classes. They made no attack on the aristocracy nor on the Corn Laws ; they attacked the new class, but not the old. I am aware that this discussion is distasteful to both of the great parties of the House. I regret it and am not ashamed to say, however, that while I disapprove of the Charter, I sympathise with the Chartists. They form a great body of our working men ; nobody can deny that they labour under great grievances. Look at the House ; it has been sitting now for five months. What has it done for the people ? Nothing, the government sees everything in the brightest colours ; everything is the best in the best of worlds. The government is busy making peers, creating baronets, at the very moment when a social insurrection is at our threshold. Out of the destruction of our old Constitution trouble and dishonour will grow up to this realm."[1]

Attwood replied at the conclusion of the debate with a brief reference to Lord Russell's statements about the savings banks' deposits :—" In the English savings banks the deposits amount altogether to 22 million pounds, but of these only two millions

---

[1] *Cp.* Disraeli, *Sybil*, book 5, chapter 1.

consisted of deposits of sums under £20, and these alone can be ascribed to workmen and operatives."

The House then divided with the following result : Ayes 46, Noes 235. The Petition was therefore rejected.[1] All the Radicals and free traders voted with Attwood, whilst Disraeli voted with the majority.

This was Attwood's last service to Chartism. The riotous events in Birmingham, the opposition of the Chartists to his views on currency reform, and the predominance of the physical force party induced Attwood to resign his seat in parliament and to withdraw from the political arena. In a valedictory address, dated December 9, 1839, he surveyed his public life, his efforts and his want of success. "Exhausted, disappointed, and ailing," he resolved to leave it to other and more skilful hands to carry out his ideas on currency.

6.—THE CONVENTION AND THE GENERAL STRIKE

On July 10, 1839, the delegates returned to London, and on July 13 they resumed their deliberations. Usually only half out of the 53 delegates were present. Seven were in prison and about 20 were engaged in agitation or in a conspiracy and paid little attention to the affairs of the Convention. The Petition was rejected by such a decisive majority that all hope had to be abandoned of any parliamentary success. On the other hand, the delegates had witnessed the way in which the working men of Birmingham had displayed their power, and on the very day that the Convention reassembled in London the news arrived from Newcastle that 25,000 miners had gone on strike as a protest against the arrest of Taylor, Lovett, Collins, and Harney. The delegates were alive to the significance of these events : the power of Chartism lay not in parliament, but in the people. The Convention therefore set to work to mobilise the masses, and made the general strike, or the sacred month, the order of the day. The discussions on these matters lasted for several weeks. Pursuant to a resolution of the Convention, the secretary of the

[1] Hansard's *Parliamentary Debates*, Third Series, vol. 49, pp. 220–274.

Convention requested the delegates who were engaged in agitation to return to London immediately, so as to take part in the discussions and resolutions on the general strike, but for some time this request remained unheeded. It was only at the conclusion of the debate that some of them appeared in order to bring the matter to a conclusion. It was generally felt, but not openly expressed, that the rejection of the Petition had exhausted the functions of the Convention. Why did not the Convention dissolve? The answer seems to be as follows: Either the delegates lacked courage to admit their defeat or else they considered it advisable for the Convention to prolong its existence so as to become a Directory of the People in case of an insurrection. The latter consideration must have prevailed with the majority of the delegates.

On July 13 the Convention opened the discussion on the general strike. It did not, however, produce any thorough and comprehensive discussion. There was indeed no lack of time or of able thinkers and speakers, for the Convention continued to sit until the middle of September, and the two or three dozen delegates who regularly attended the meetings belonged to the *élite* of the movement. Most of the delegates, however, shared the conviction that the general strike was merely the prelude to a general insurrection of the people, and that it would not be the stoppage of work, but civil war itself, that would cut the Gordian knot. Most of the delegates were conversant with Benbow's pamphlet, which stated that a week's provisions would suffice to initiate the social revolution. The people would then be masters of the situation and would make use of all the accumulated wealth according to the decrees of the insurrectionary committees. The delegates who expected the matter to be solved by street warfare considered it unnecessary to discuss the possibility of the general strike or even the preparations for its accomplishment. For them the main point was to put before the movement the dilemma of ruin or street warfare. They believed in the justice of the people's cause and in the inevitable victory of justice. Victory implied warfare, and the only thing to be done was to organise the campaign. What was the use, therefore, of indulging in speculations on the general strike if this was merely to be the first move in the struggle? The delegates who held these opinions belonged to the most determined section of the Convention, and for a time carried the waverers along with them. O'Connor and his party belonged to the waverers. O'Brien was at first on the side of the advocates of a general strike and of street fighting, and subsequently opposed them. Lovett took no further part in this session of the Convention, for he was busy preparing for his trial, and was brought before the Assizes in August. Hetherington was ready for a general strike, but he was desirous of a clear and definite investigation of the situation. Most of the London men agreed with Hetherington as to the necessity for an exhaustive discussion of the nature and possibilities of the general strike, for they did not believe in street fighting.

About this time William Benbow suddenly appeared again on the scene. He was no longer in London, where his violent Radicalism found no response, but in Lancashire and Yorkshire, where he went about selling his pamphlet and holding meetings in the open air. We read that he spoke at Colne and Stockport, and exhorted the working men to lay out their money in procuring muskets and in preparing for the national holiday. On August 4, 1839, he was arrested, and on August 11 he was brought before the magistrates in Manchester. [1] It was only in April, 1840, that he appeared at the Assizes in Chester.

There can be no possible doubt that Benbow's pamphlet originated all the ideas of a general strike among the Chartists, and that the matter received no further thought. The following extracts from the *Charter* of July 21, 1839, give the gist of the debates and the final decision of the Convention on the subject.

On July 13, the day after the Petition had been rejected in parliament, the delegate Lowery moved the following resolution:

" The House of Commons, having refused to go into Committee on the prayer of the National Petition, it is vain to expect redress from the House; and it is therefore the opinion of the Convention that the people work no longer after the 12th of August next,

---

[1] *Charter*, August 18, 1839. Sir Charles J. Napier also mentions him in his diaries.

unless the power of voting for members of parliament, to enable them to protect their labour and their rights, is previously given or guaranteed to them."

After Lowery had moved his resolution, Moir (Scotland) declared that he would not vote upon the question, as he had received no instructions from his constituents, although he had requested them to inform him of their views; he must therefore consider that his work on the Convention had ceased. He added :—

" My personal opinion, however, is that the question before the Convention is one of the most important character. The sacred month is, in fact, nothing more nor less than the commencement of a revolution, the end of which no man can foresee. My opinion, therefore, is that before any such thing is recommended the organisation of the people should be carried out much more completely than it is now. It was not enough that some portion, some small portion, of the working classes should be willing to carry out the proposition for a national holiday; it must be adopted generally, if not universally, or evil and not good would be the result of it. I am of opinion that steps should be taken to get at least every large town to agree to act upon such a recommendation as that now asked for before such a recommendation can be given."

The delegates Neesom, Skevington, and Dr. Fletcher gave the assurance that Bury, Loughborough, Gloucester, Worcester, and Somerset were in favour of a general strike. The delegate of Rochdale opposed the resolution, saying :—

" The question we are discussing is most important. I must first ask, what is the meaning of the national holiday ? Are we to abstain from all manner of work ? If so, is the bread baked for a month ? Is the corn ground for a month ? I deny that is so. The people of Rochdale are of opinion that there is not food enough in South Lancashire to subsist the people for a fortnight. Failure in such a step would properly enough be looked upon as being a proof at once of folly and wickedness. It is of the utmost importance to consider not only the practicability, but also the consequences of such a measure as this. It had been called a bloodless effort. Those who said so knew better. They know that it must lead to both blood and plunder. I do not say I am against it, but I want to see beforehand what we are to gain by it, if even we are successful, and what we are to lose by it if unsuccessful. My mind is open to conviction, and although I am of opinion that a general strike is at once impracticable and foolish, the arguments to be brought forward may change my opinion."

Burns, who belonged to Taylor's conspiracy, declared :—

" It is no use now to cry ' Halt.' Whatever we may do now, we shall run great risks. The purpose of the national holiday is to show that if we ceased labour the government must cease to govern and the profitmongers to get their profit."

He was answered by William Carpenter as follows :—

" In proportion as I am impressed with a sense of the vast importance of this question is my embarrassment which I feel in addressing myself to it ; and I feel this the more, inasmuch as I know that every man who attempts to say or to do anything to repress the impetuosity of the more ardent spirits among us lays himself open to the imputation of timidity or cowardice, if not something much worse. A man's moral courage is much more seen in his daring to do right when he was liable to be vituperated and condemned, than blindly and heedlessly suffering himself to be carried along with the stream. We must discuss it then. But we have a right to expect that we should have a full convention, the day for the discussion having been fixed for some considerable time previously. We have about 30 members present out of 53. The absent delegates have been written to and urged, strongly urged, to be in their places. Where is O'Connor ? Where is O'Brien ? Craig, Dr. Taylor, and Frost ? . . . The fact is we have come to this subject without due preparation. All that has been said showed that we are alike ignorant of the probabilities of the order for the sacred month being obeyed and of the way in which the holiday should be turned to great account, even did the people obey and leave their work. Under these circumstances it would be a crime to do anything to bring about this crisis. It is true that the men

I F

of Newcastle and its neighbourhood are ready to obey the Convention, and if they were only a sample of the people generally I should not hesitate to vote for the holiday.   But this is not the case, and I would rather submit to misrepresentation than order a measure which would inevitably lead to the sacrifice of these brave fellows.   Friends, we are deceiving ourselves.   Glasgow is not ready, Ashton is not ready, Manchester has given no definite answer, nor has Sheffield.   Are we going to let loose hundreds of thousands of desperate and hungry men upon society without having any specific object in view or any plan of action laid down, but trusting to a chapter of accidents as to what the consequences should be ?   Is this a course worthy of a deliberate assembly ?   I have made up my mind.   I shall oppose fixing a day for the holiday until we have better evidence, first as to the practicability of the thing, or the probability of its being carried into effect ;   and next as to the way in which it is to be employed."[1]

In spite of the speeches against the general strike Lowery's resolution was carried on July 16.   The opposition to it, however, had not been in vain.   It brought Taylor, O'Connor, and O'Brien to London ;   a committee was formed of seven members with the object of discussing the most efficacious means by which a general strike could be carried into effect. The Convention at the same time held a secret consultation, which resolved to issue a manifesto on the general strike. M'Douall was desirous above all for the trade unions to be requested to co-operate with them in carrying out the ulterior measures.   The Convention was no longer so firmly convinced of the wisdom of the resolution of July 16, and sought for a means of escape from a difficult situation.

This was discovered by O'Brien.   On July 22, he made the following speech :—

" My absence from the Convention was excused by the circumstance that I was agitating in the North of England and Lancashire.   The people are well up to the mark, but I fear they are not ready yet for a general strike.   I strongly urge the Convention

[1] *Charter*, July 21, 1839.

not to precipitate matters. I should like to see great masses of the population keeping the holiday, but this could not be the case if it were fixed for August 12. At all events we ought to enquire into the facts and place them fearlessly before the people. I move the following resolution :—

" ' The Convention continues to be unanimously of opinion that nothing short of a general strike, or suspension of labour throughout the country, will ever suffice to establish the rights and liberties ; we nevertheless cannot take upon ourselves the responsibility of dictating the time or circumstances of such a strike, believing that we are incompetent to do so for the following reasons :—

" ' (1) Because our numbers have been greatly reduced by the desertion, absence, or arbitrary arrest of a large proportion of our number. (2) Because great diversity of opinion prevails amongst the remaining members as to the practicability of a general strike in the present state of trade in the manufacturing districts. (3) Because a similar diversity of opinion seems to prevail out of doors amongst our constituents and the working class generally. (4) Because under these circumstances it is more than doubtful whether an order from the Convention for a general holiday would be generally obeyed : in other words, whether a strike would not prove a failure. (5) Because, while we firmly believe a universal strike would prove the salvation of the country, we are at the same time equally convinced that a partial strike would only entail the bitterest privations and sufferings in all who took part in it, and in the present exasperated state of public feeling would not improbably lead to convulsion and anarchy. (6) Because, though it is the duty of the Convention to participate in all the people's dangers, it is no part of our duty to create dangers unnecessarily. (7) Because we believe that the working men themselves are the only fit judges of their right and readiness to strike work when they will, as also of their own resources and capabilities of meeting the exigencies which such an event would entail.

" ' Under these circumstances we decide that a committee of ten be appointed to reconsider the vote of the 16th inst. and to substitute an address, which shall leave to the people themselves to decide whether they will or will not commence the sacred month on the 12th of August next, at the same time explaining the reasons for adopting such a course and pledging the Convention to co-operate with the people in whatever measures they may then deem necessary to their safety and emancipation.' "

After a long discussion, O'Brien's resolution was adopted by a majority of six votes.[1]

The great majority of the delegates left London and returned to their constituencies. A central council of seven members was chosen to administer the affairs of the Convention. The ten members of the general strike committee also remained in London to receive the special reports from the provinces. The following declaration, based on these reports, was published by the committee on August 6 :—

" We are unanimously of opinion that the people are not prepared to carry out the sacred month on the 12th of August, 1839. The same evidence, however, convinces us that the great body of the working people, including those of most of the trades, may be induced to cease work on the 12th inst. for one, two or three days, in order to devote that time to meetings and processions, for deliberating on the present awful state of the country, and devising the best means of averting the hideous despotism with which the industrious orders are menaced by the murderous majority of the upper and middle classes, who prey on their labour. We, at the same time, beg to announce to the country that it is the deliberate opinion of this council that unless the trades of Great Britain shall co-operate as united bodies with their more distressed brethren in making a grand moral demonstration on the 12th inst., it will be impossible to save the country from a revolution of blood, which after enormous sacrifice of life and property will terminate in the utter subjection of the working people to the moneyed murderers of society. Under these circumstances we implore all our brother Chartists to abandon the project of a sacred month, as being for the present utterly impracticable, and to prepare themselves

[1] *Charter*, July 28, 1839.

forthwith to carry into effect the aforesaid constitutional objects on the 12th inst. We also implore the united trades, if they would save the country from convulsion and themselves from ruin, to render their distressed brethren all the aid in their power, on or before the 12th inst., towards realising the great and beneficent object of the holiday. Men of the trades! The salvation of the country is in your hands! " [1]

The manifesto reveals a feeling of despair. The discussions on the ulterior measures had alarmed the tradesmen, small shop-keepers, and manufacturers. The threats of the working men to make their purchases exclusively from Chartists and to undertake a general strike induced the shopkeepers and employers to apply to Lord John Russell for protection. On July 31, 1839, the latter issued directions to the magistrates to take energetic steps against any attempt to carry out the ulterior measures, to arrest all persons agitating for these measures, and to prosecute them, since the ulterior measures were " illegal and subversive of the peace." The arrests began in April and became more frequent : in August alone there were 130 Chartist leaders arrested.[2] Some of the delegates to the Convention were convicted, others were committed for trial and released on bail, viz., Vincent, Lovett, Collins, Brown, O'Connor, M'Douall, Taylor, Richardson, O'Brien, Carrier, Neesom, and Deegan.

It is also obvious from the manifesto that the trade unions were not inclined to enter blindly on a strike. Some members of the Convention had tried to induce them to form a secret organisation ; this can be inferred from a reference made by O'Brien in 1840 and 1842, without, however, giving any details.[3] The trade unions declined to entertain the suggestion.

For the time being the manifesto put an end to Benbow's plan, and the working men kept a holiday on August 12, and followed the advice of the Convention in holding large meetings and processions in almost all the manufacturing towns, causing

[1] *Charter*, August 11, 1839.
[2] *Accounts and Papers*, year 1840 (600), vol. 38, pp. 691 and *sqq*.
[3] *British Statesman*, November 5, 1842 ; *Southern Star*, January 26, 1840.

some disturbance of the peace in several localities. Delegates of the Convention visited most of the meetings and remained in the country until August 25. O'Connor went, at the instance of the Convention, to Glasgow, where a conference of 57 Scotch delegates was held. Their reports were opposed for the greater part to a general strike; the minority were in favour of arming, but the majority supported the policy of moral force.

On August 26 the Convention reassembled in London, but its functions were at an end. The Petition was dead, the general strike was abandoned, the lack of systematic organisation could no longer be denied, and there was no cessation of arrests and convictions. The failure of the Convention sowed dissension among the delegates, so that the public meetings of the Convention cast no credit upon anyone. On September 6 O'Brien moved in favour of dissolving the Convention. The motion was seconded by Taylor, and passed by 12 votes to 11. On September 14 the Convention finally dissolved. A few of the delegates, such as Carpenter and O'Brien, returned to journalism, O'Connor to agitation, Taylor, Frost, Burns, Cardo, and Bussey to conspiracy, and the tragic sequel of their activity will be dealt with in a later chapter.

One of the last acts of the Convention was the drafting of a " Declaration of the Constitutional Rights of Britons." In the course of the discussions on universal suffrage, annual parliaments, drilling and bearing of arms, meetings and assemblies, the Convention became aware of the fact that the constitutional rights of British citizens were undefined, and therefore liable to unfavourable legal interpretation. It resolved therefore to take the opinion of a constitutional lawyer. A German jurist, Schröder by name,[1] who had left his native country to find a new home in London, wrote his opinion in the form of a Declaration of Rights. He divided it into 39 articles —probably in imitation of the 39 Articles of Faith of the Church of England—set out the Chartist claims in paragraphs, and to each article he appended legal references, indicating a most exceptional degree of knowledge of English constitutional

[1] *Charter*, September 1, 1839.

literature. All the important statutes, charters, old codes and chronicles were utilised ; all precedents referring to these points, legal judgments and opinions of the great English lawyers and statesmen of the Middle Ages and recent times were pressed into the service of the Chartists.

The delegates were so delighted with the Declaration that they regarded it as the most important result of the Convention. They realised that their actions had not been founded on any solid basis, and that now they possessed a programme and a justification. The Declaration was closely studied by the leaders, agitators, and speakers of the Chartist movement. Ordinary workmen read the old statutes and the works of the great English lawyers, so far as they were available in English or in English translations. In the political trials of March and April, 1840, the accused quoted from these sources in order to demonstrate the legal and constitutional character of the Chartist agitation.[1]

[1] *Northern Star*, March and April, 1840.

V

CHARTIST REVOLT AND THE NATIONAL CONSCIENCE

I.—THE INSURRECTION IN SOUTH WALES

DURING the agitation of the Chartists and their volunteers in 1836, 1837, and 1838, the Whig government adopted a passive attitude. Neither the violent speeches delivered by Stephens, Taylor, Beaumont, and O'Connor nor the increasing number of Chartist advocates of physical force caused the government any anxiety. It was only the local authorities and the Conservative newspapers that were rather excited about it ; the former from the fear that the violent speeches might lead to breaches of the peace ; the latter from the motive of party policy, in order to discredit the Whigs throughout the country. Finally, in the autumn of 1838, the government was forced to take up a new attitude towards the agitation. On October 8, 1838, Lord John Russell, at a banquet given in his honour at Liverpool, delivered a speech on the general state of affairs and on the services rendered by the Reform Parliament, and he seized this opportunity to express his opinion on the Chartist agitation :—

" Public life pulsates strongly at present and is expressed by the numerous public meetings which are now in the course of being held in various parts of the country. There are some, perhaps, who would put down such opinions ; but such is not my opinion, nor that of the government with which I act. I think the people have a right to meet. If they had no grievances, common sense would speedily come to the rescue and put an end to those meetings. It is not from free discussion, it is not from the unchecked declaration of public opinion that governments have anything to fear. There was fear when men were driven by force to secret combinations. There was the fear, there was the danger, and not in free discussion."

This was the government's policy. Lord John Russell's attitude towards the Chartists was exceedingly humane; it was dictated by the sincere desire of avoiding bloodshed. Sir Charles Napier, who was in close communication with him, expressed the same opinion. But the increasing alarm of the local authorities, the growing violence of the Chartist leaders in the North of England, the bitter opposition of the Conservative press, which regarded the Reform Bill as the prelude of Chartism, as well as the fluctuating and diminishing majority of the Whigs in parliament, forced the government to adopt measures of suppression.[1]   On December 27, 1838, Stephens was arrested in Manchester and indicted for incitement to riot. He was indeed released on bail, but the excitement of the people in Lancashire, Yorkshire, and the whole of the North of England steadily increased.   What Stephens was to the North of England Vincent was to Wales and the West of England.   After some riotous scenes in Devizes and Llanidloes, Vincent was arrested on May 8, 1839.   In July, August, and September the arrests were so numerous that all the Chartist leaders of any importance were either in prison or awaiting trial.   But these prosecutions nowhere excited such bitterness of feeling as in Wales.

The simple, emotional, and enthusiastic nature of the Welsh working men was, and still is, averse from dilatory tactics and parliamentary methods ; it expects sensational deeds in any popular agitation.   Their temperament resembles that of the French proletariate, but it is nourished and stimulated by primitive Christian feelings rather than by logical inferences. The Welsh received the message of Chartism from the eloquent enthusiast, Henry Vincent, and regarded it as the embodiment of justice, liberty, and fraternity, for which their heart had been craving.   For their material condition was much better than that of most of the English workmen.   The industrial revolution was still scarcely known in Wales.   The actual proletariat consisted of coal miners and iron workers, who received relatively good wages.   Amicable, patriarchal relations regulated the

[1] A summary of the Conservative onslaughts on the government is given in the *Quarterly Review*, vol. 65, p. 290-314, 485.

questions of work and wages, whilst rich and poor met together
in the chapels, united by religious interests in common against
the Established Church. Chartism in Wales was a moral rather
than an economic movement. Its most important leader was
John Frost, a draper in Newport, who exerted an authoritative
influence on his comrades by reason of his position and personality. Since 1817 he devoted himself to the furtherance of
Radical doctrines, and in 1822 he brought upon himself a term
of imprisonment of six months. After the victory of the Reform
Bill and the introduction of new municipal government his
fellow-citizens elected him to the town council, and then he was
successively appointed, mayor, magistrate, and justice of the
peace. When Vincent brought Chartism to Newport in 1838,
Frost was justice of the peace. Nevertheless, he immediately
expressed his sympathy with the new movement, and allowed
himself to be elected a delegate to the Convention by the Chartists.
When the Convention assembled in London, Frost was denounced
by the Conservative press, and Lord John Russell in consequence
suggested to him the advisability of resigning the honourable
position of justice of the peace. Frost did so under protest, for
he regarded Lord John Russell's demand as a violation of
freedom of thought. The protest was published in the Chartist
press and made its author one of the most popular men of the
movement. Frost took no leading part in the public deliberations of the Convention, but he must have rendered great service
in committee meetings. Smarting under this treatment by the
government, and impelled by his own enthusiastic temperament,
he joined Taylor, and finally took part in his conspiracy for using
physical force.

Here we enter on a chapter of the history of Chartism which
is still to some extent wrapped in obscurity. All that is known
about it is derived from sources which are contaminated by
polemical passion.[1]

[1] *Northern Star*, May 3, 1845 ; Gammage, *History of Chartist
Movement*, p. 262 and *sqq.* ; William Lovett, *Life*, p. 238 and *sqq.* ;
Diplomatic Review, January 1872, p. 23 ; Thomas Frost, *Forty
Years' Recollections*, 1880, p. 109 & 297 (Thomas Frost was neither
related to nor acquainted with John Frost).

The following germ of truth may be extracted from all these accounts. When the Petition had been rejected and the peaceful policy of moral suasion had missed fire, the delegates, Taylor, Frost, Cardo, Bussey, Burns, and perhaps also Lowery, met in secret conclave and resolved to emancipate the working class by means of an insurrection. They considered Yorkshire, Lancashire, Birmingham, Sheffield, and Wales to be ripe or suitable for insurrection. The Pole, Major Beniowski, was sent down to Wales as military instructor, and old retired non-commissioned officers were appointed in some of the towns in the North of England and the Midlands for the purpose of drilling the workmen. It appears from Sir Charles Napier's diaries that most of these non-commissioned officers kept up relations with the military authorities and furnished them with information as to the preparations. The secret conspiracy was organised on the model of the United Irishmen, and the country covered by the Chartist agitation was divided into districts, in which the Chartists were classed in groups of 10, 100 and 1000 men with special leaders and captains. When Cardo was arrested in November, 1839, some of the plans of the organisation were discovered.[1]

In the meantime the Welsh became restive and urged that the time for action had arrived. The harsh sentences of imprisonment which had been passed upon the accused at Llanidloes, the prohibition of the right of assembly, and the confiscation of weapons, and finally Vincent's bad treatment at the hands of the prison authorities, roused Wales to a high pitch of bitter feeling. The working men and operatives were determined above all to set Vincent free by the use of force. Frost was no longer able to curb the people, and was obliged to put himself at their head. On the eve of the dissolution of the Convention he explained the situation in Wales to his more intimate friends, and declared that Chartism was compromised in that part of the country unless something was done without delay. But Wales could not take isolated action ; the North of England and the Midlands must also join in the insurrection at the same time.

[1] *Charter*, November 24, 1839.

Thereupon Bussey, the Bradford delegate, replied that he would stand by the Welsh and would rouse Yorkshire to insurrection. Frost returned home to set about the work, whilst Bussey did nothing and had no intention of doing anything. William Ashton, a local and influential labour leader in Yorkshire, who had been informed of the projected insurrection and who knew Bussey to be a braggart, foresaw the impending catastrophe and communicated with Hill, the editor of the *Northern Star*, to the effect that the Welsh were preparing an insurrection and were reckoning upon the assistance of Bussey, who would, however, leave them in the lurch. He requested Hill to acquaint O'Connor of the circumstance without delay, for O'Connor was the only man in a position to restrain the Welsh from their ill-fated intentions. Hill, as he asserted subsequently, carried out Ashton's request without delay and communicated the secret to O'Connor. O'Brien, too, learned of the course of events in Wales, and shared the same opinion that O'Connor would have to intervene immediately in order to avert misfortune from the Welsh. According to the account given by Hill and O'Brien in 1845, O'Connor took no steps towards rescuing the Welsh from their fate, and calmly went away to Ireland at the end of October ; nothing was heard of him until the Welsh insurrection had miscarried and its leaders were imprisoned. On the other hand, O'Connor asserted that neither Hill nor O'Brien had informed him of the secret conspiracy of the Welsh. It was in ignorance of the state of affairs that he left for Ireland, where he had business to attend to. O'Connor's account deserves more credence than that given by Hill and O'Brien. Whatever may be thought of O'Connor, he was certainly neither a coward nor a traitor.

This insurrection took the following course.

Towards the end of October, Frost, William Jones, a journeyman watchmaker, and Zephaniah Williams, an innkeeper, came to an agreement to march upon Newport with about a thousand men on the night of November 3, and to release Vincent from prison. The Chartists were mobilised and divided into three columns. A number of them were armed with old muskets, others with pikes and a number with clubs.   They marched and sang :

> " I have seen the poplars flourish fast,
>   While the humble briars bound them ;
> I have seen them torn up by the blast
>   Of elements around them.
>
> The lightning flashing through the sky,
>   The thunder loud roars after,
> O scorch, burn the oppressors !   Why ?
>   Because they withhold the Charter.
>
> Then rise, my boys, and fight the foe,
>   Your arms are truth and reason.
> We'll let the Whigs and Tories know
>   That union is not treason.
>
> Ye lords, oppose us if you can,
>   Your own doom you seek after ;
> With or without you we will stand
>   Until we gain the Charter."

On November 3 the columns converged upon Newport, but owing to the fact that the local circumstances were unfavourable, it was only early on November 4 that the insurgents entered the town.   The authorities had been well informed of this movement and kept in readiness a force of police, special constables, and 35 men of the 45th Infantry Regiment.   When the Chartists appeared in Newport, the policemen and special constables offered some resistance and then took to flight, running to Westgate Hotel, where the soldiers, under the command of a lieutenant, had taken up their positions at the windows and stood to arms.   To all appearance Frost and his colleagues had no knowledge of the presence of soldiers, and only knew that the magistrate was in the hotel.   The Chartist leaders marched up with their men to the hotel and demanded the liberation of the prisoners.   Suddenly there was a rattle of musketry, and in the space of twenty minutes ten Chartists lay dead and about fifty wounded in the square in front of the Westgate Hotel.   The rest took to flight.   The insurrection was at an end.   Among the dead Chartists there was a youth, only eighteen years old, George Shell by name, who had sent the following letter to his parents on the eve of the fight :

Pontypool, Sunday Night, Nov. 3, 1839.

Dear Parents,

I hope this will find you well, as I am myself at this present. I shall this night be engaged in a glorious struggle for freedom, and should it please God to spare my life I shall see you soon ; but if not, grieve not for me, I shall have fallen in a noble cause. Farewell !

Yours truly,

GEORGE SHELL.

Numerous arrests followed the suppression of the insurrection. Those arrested included Frost, Williams, Jones, and four other Chartists, who were indicted for high treason. The government sent a special commission of judges to Monmouth, where the trials began on December 31, 1839, and closed on January 13, 1840. Frost, Williams, and Jones were sentenced to death. The death sentence was also passed upon the other four Chartists, but with the intention of its being commuted to transportation for life. Owing to a technical error and still more probably owing to the great excitement of the people of Great Britain over the conviction of the three Welsh leaders, even the latter were reprieved and the sentences commuted to transportation for life. In 1856 they were granted a complete amnesty.

2.—WHOLESALE ARRESTS

From April, 1839, to June, 1840, 380 Chartist leaders in England and 62 in Wales were either arrested and acquitted or else condemned to terms of imprisonment, varying from three months to transportation for life; 425 out of the 442 arrested persons belonged to the working class : textile operatives, metal workers, and miners formed the main contingent; the remaining 17 belonged to the intellectual section and tradesmen.

On August 3, 1839, four of the men who had taken a leading part in the Birmingham riots of July 15 stood for trial at the

ssizes at Warwick.   Three of them were condemned to death,
ut their sentences were subsequently commuted to transporta-
on for life.   On August 6 and 7 Collins and Lovett stood before
ne same jury as accused persons.   Collins was defended by a
awyer, but Lovett conducted his own defence, which evoked
ne admiration of the public prosecutor and of the judge   The
nain points of the indictment included the authorship and
ublication of the resolutions of July 5, in which the London
olice and the local authorities at Birmingham had been censured
n the strongest possible terms.

Lovett did not withdraw a single word of these resolutions,
nd pointed out that the people had a right of assembly and free
iscussion.   The accused men were sentenced each to a year's
nprisonment, where they were treated as common criminals.
'n August 10 a number of Chartists and persons connected with
hartism stood their trial at the assizes at Chester.   J. R.
tephens and M'Douall were among the accused.   Stephens's
peech in his defence lasted for five hours, but there was nothing
hartist about it.   Stephens disavowed all connection with
hartism ; he denied that he had ever spoken in favour of
niversal suffrage, and he developed a conservative social pro-
ramme after the manner of Disraeli and Oastler, to which he
vas ready to devote his whole life.   His *volte face* was, however, of
ttle avail ; he was sentenced to 18 months' imprisonment,
ut he was well treated by the prison authorities, in striking
ontrast to Lovett and Collins.   Stephens's apostasy roused
esentment in Chartist circles.   He was accused of treachery,
ut O'Connor ascribed his change of opinion to the calumnies
which O'Brien had disseminated some months previously about
tephens, and in this way had made him an object of suspicion
o the people.

M'Douall was accused of incitement to procure arms and of
ncouraging fighting in the streets.   The speech he made in his
efence lasted also for five hours, and was practically an
xposition of the principles of Chartism.

Many of the great trials for high treason took place in March
nd April, 1840.   O'Connor was sentenced to 18 months' im-

prisonment for conspiring against the State ; Bronterre O'Brien received the same sentence [1] ; Benbow received 16 months ; his speech in his defence took over ten hours to deliver. He compared himself with Jesus, the Whigs with the Jews, and the judge with Pontius Pilate.[2]   Holberry, a spirit distiller, who was only 25 years old, had, in his romantic, revolutionary ardour, set himself the task of leading the Chartists against Napier and seizing Nottingham ; he received four years' imprisonment. Two years later he died in his cell, and was buried at Sheffield after an imposing funeral, in which 20,000 working men took part Harney delivered the funeral oration.

The speeches for the defence relied for the most part upon the law of nature, but in some cases speeches were made by ordinary workmen, which were devoid of all legal and pseudo-historical erudition, and gave most affecting descriptions of the distress among the working class. One of the accused, George Lloyd, a joiner, stood before the jury at Liverpool, and depicted such a harrowing scene of the sufferings and persecutions of the Chartist working men that the audience were moved to tears.

The wholesale arrests made great demands on the spirit of sacrifice of the Chartist and Labour movement. Money was collected for the families of the prisoners and a special maintenance fund was started. In spite of all this, the contributions were barely sufficient to alleviate the misery of the families involved. O'Connor devoted a part of the profits of the *Northern Star* to the support of the arrested men. The local organisations did much for their arrested leaders, and enabled them to obtain

---

[1] One of the witnesses against O'Brien was a shorthand writer who was employed as a reporter of the *Manchester Guardian* In his depositions he stated that O'Brien in his speech at Manchester on property divided land into three kinds of value : (1) original value ; (2) improved value (by cultivation) ; (3) improvable value by future improvements. This evidence of the stenographer is interesting. It is, word for word, the same division of values which is given by Ogilvie and which formed the central point of his land reform. *Cp. Northern Star*, April 11, 1840, p. 7, col. 1, and Ogilvie *Essay*, 1782, pp. 20-4.

[2] *Northern Star*, April 18 and 25, 1840.

better food in prison. The families of the more prominent leaders received a pound a week.[1]

Immediately after the tragic end of the insurrection in South Wales, Taylor withdrew from the agitation and died in a short space of time. Bussey was covered with ignominy and left home for America.

Further, the Chartist press suffered from the persecutions. In the year 1839-40 the following papers ceased publication : *True Scotsman, Operative, Charter, Champion, Southern Star, Western Vindicator*, and *Northern Liberator*. Their place was taken by the weeklies, *Scottish Chartist Circular* and *English Chartist Circular*. The latter appeared in London and existed until the end of 1843 ; it was well edited and contained a great store of materials for the history of the working classes and the revolutionary movements in Great Britain and Ireland ; it was also a supporter of the cause of temperance. In 1842 the weekly, the *British Statesman*, appeared in London, and was brilliantly edited by O'Brien in the latter half of the year.

The *Northern Liberator* (Newcastle), during the last months of its career, was, in addition, the organ of Lord Palmerston's opponents. The leaders of the anti-Palmerston agitation were David Urquhart and Charles Attwood (brother of Thomas Attwood).

3.—FIRST EFFECTS OF CHARTISM ON LITERATURE

" Delirious Chartism," wrote Thomas Carlyle at the end of 1839, " will not have raged to no purpose . . . if it have forced the thinking men of the community to think of this vital question."[2] The Charter, with its six points, the National Petition, with its five points, borne aloft on pikeheads and rendered glaringly visible to the people by the flaming torchlights of the nocturnal meetings, could not fail to force upon the national conscience the condition-of-England question The stirring events of 1837, 1838, and 1839 impressed, before all, the

[1] *Northern Star*, April 11, 1840.
[2] Thomas Carlyle, *Chartism*, 1839, chapter 1.

I G

imagination of writers and poets; they ushered in a literary
period distinguished by social reform novels, social economic
pamphlets, and revolutionary poetry. This literary movement
gained in strength and volume after the general strike in
the North of England in the autumn, 1842, but its origin
coincides with the upheaval of Labour in the years from 1833
to 1840.

The *Northern Star* gave, in 1837, long extracts from Dickens's
Oliver Twist. In 1839, Mrs. Trollope went to Manchester for
the purpose of investigating the real conditions of the factory
population. The result of her studies was the novel *Michael
Armstrong*. In 1841, Charlotte Elizabeth (Phelan) Tonna
published *Helen Fleetwood*, depicting " the vile, the cruel, the
body and soul murdering system of factory labour . . . the
prolific source of every ill that can unhumanise man." But,
while she also denounces Socialism as the " moral Gorgon " and
" the last effort of satanic venom," she pleads, with much force
and great sympathy, the cause of Labour, and exhorts the
Church to work for the welfare of the poor. However, the most
important writer of the period we are dealing with was Capel
Lofft, jun., who, in 1839, published a revolutionary epic, *Ernest,
or Political Regeneration*. It is the fanfare of Chartism.
It represents the growth, the heroic struggles, the triumph of the
Socialist and political Labour movement. Dean Milman, in a
long essay, regards it as the work of a dangerous genius, a poet
of extraordinary powers, whom he " entreats, exhorts, and
implores to consult his fame, his happiness, his life, his eternal
interests," and turn his gifts to more patriotic uses.[1] The book
had, however, by that time been withdrawn from circulation.
Ernest deals with the story of a peasants' revolt in Germany,
but the conditions and the atmosphere in the midst of which the
revolt is fought out are English. It is a struggle against
rapacious and oppressing landowners, for universal suffrage,
democracy, nationalisation of the land, and religious freedom
or primitive Christianity. The spiritual leader of the revolt is
a schoolmaster and Nonconformist preacher, who—

[1] *Quarterly Review*, vol. 65, p. 153 *sqq.*

> " . . . lit his torch from heaven, and with that torch
> Kindled all hearts—the poor look gladly on high ;
> Having scant comfort here. . . .
> . . . Faith, the gospel, and love
> These three he preached, leaving the mysteries
> Devised by man, for God's simplicity,
> And viewing the earth one commonwealth
> Level as is the ocean—so his word
> Waxed and took wings and flew forth wondrously."
>
> (*Ernest*, pp. 27–8.)

Then the young agitator gradually unfolds his system of regeneration :—

> " They who have toiled the ground, 'tis theirs of right
> To share it, and enjoy it, and thank God ;
> Sharing by rule of elders, duly ordained
> To make apportionment of labourers
> And judge all controversies of each farm.
> But for the landlord—'tis an impious name,
> By man usurped from God—so be it resolved,
> To make no further mention of his name,
> But let the State take their dominion,
> Paying them compensation lest they starve."
>
> (*Ibid.*, p. 146.)

Next in importance to land nationalisation is universal education, which should combine labour and art with letters, in order to enable the people to govern themselves and supply their needs by labouring and sharing in common.

Thomas Carlyle's *Chartism*, though it exhibits little knowledge of the essence of its subject, directed the attention of the nation to the discontent of the working classes. Its commonplace thoughts, clothed in super-Coleridgean phraseology, gave to it an air both of familiarity and profundity, and could, therefore, not fail to render it popular with educated newspaper readers.

Chartism had entered literature. It began to interest the thinking part of the population, yet very few intellectuals joined it. The gaps made in the ranks of the leaders by prosecution and imprisonment were not filled up. The Chartist movement subsequent to 1839 was poorer in capable thinkers than ever before. There was indeed no lack of young men who could deliver enthusiastic speeches on the rights of men, the corruption of government, and the merciless exploitation of labour, but no object would be gained by giving their names and biographies. Like bubbles they skimmed over the sea of Chartism, glittered for a time in its colours and burst unnoticed, to make place for others.   But Chartism suffered severely for want of independent and inquiring minds.   Yet the working men were eager to learn, attended mechanics' institutes, studied science, maintained halls for meetings, and spared no pains to educate themselves and to acquire knowledge.   In the industrial towns " you would see working men in groups discussing the great doctrine of political justice—that every grown-up, sane man ought to have a vote in the election of the men who were to make the laws by which he was to be governed ; or they were in earnest dispute respecting the teachings of Socialism." [1]

These words are more suitable of application to the years 1840 and 1842 than to any other period in the history of Chartism. At that time the expressions Chartist, Socialist, trade unionist, and working man were synonymous terms. In 1842 the standard of Chartism was actually the standard of the organised working men. Nevertheless, the movement comprised few intellectual adherents. The persecutions of 1839 and 1840 had driven many of the thinking workers away to North America, where they disseminated Ogilvie's and Spence's ideas of agrarian reform which they had acquired through Bronterre O'Brien. Many of them were repelled by O'Connor's methods of agitation and returned to local spheres of activity, others again joined the Anti-Corn Law League.

Among the Chartist leaders who joined the movement in the period from 1840 to 1842 only Thomas Cooper (1805-1892), the prototype of Kingsley's *Alton Locke,* deserves mention. Of all self-taught Chartists he was, next to Lovett, the most cultured and spiritual writer. By his indomitable will the young shoe-maker learned Latin, Greek, French, Italian, Hebrew, and wrote good English prose and poetry, though he never emancipated himself from the literary influences of Carlyle and Shelley. His

[1] Thomas Cooper, *Life,* ed. 1897, p. 393.

remarkable literary and oratorical gifts soon procured him the leadership for Leicester and the surrounding district. At first he sided with O'Connor, but from 1845 he became his opponent, in both cases with great vehemence, for Cooper had a contempt for half-measures. As an adherent of O'Connor, he brooked no opposition to him—as his enemy he had not got a single good word for him. He played a considerable part in the upheaval of 1842, and was sentenced to two years' imprisonment. His *Purgatory of Suicides*, which he dedicated to Thomas Carlyle, was written in prison. From 1845 onwards Cooper was for the absolute abandonment of physical force. He was mainly a literary man and a poet, and had only a slight knowledge of politics and political economy ; his socialism was hopelessly Utopian.

The following stanzas are taken from one of his best poems :—

> Truth is growing—hearts are glowing
>   With the flame of Liberty :
> Light is breaking—thrones are quaking,
>   Hark ! the trumpet of the Free !
>
> Long, in lowly whispers breathing,
>   Freedom wandered drearily—
> Still, in faith, her laurel wreathing
>   For the day when there should be
>   Freemen shouting—Victory !
>
> Now, she seeketh him that speaketh
>   Fearlessly of lawless might ;
> And she speedeth him that leadeth
>   Brethren on to win the Right.

VI

REORGANISATION AND ELECTORAL POLICY

I.—THE NATIONAL CHARTER ASSOCIATION (N.C.A.)

THE experience of the early years of Chartism impressed the leaders with the conviction that the loosely-knit local organisations were not favourable to unity of action. Organisation became a burning question and occupied the attention of all thoughtful Chartists. About the middle of the year 1840 the Chartist leaders entered into active correspondence on this subject—even the leaders who were in prison were able to correspond, or else found means to communicate their views to their comrades—and on July 20, 1840, 23 delegates from the Midlands and the North of England met in conference at Manchester, in order to devise a plan of organisation. The conference considered plans of organisation drawn up by Feargus O'Connor, O'Brien, Burns, M'Douall and Benbow. O'Connor was mainly in favour of strengthening the Chartist press by turning the *Northern Star* into a daily morning paper : " A Morning Star," he wrote, " will be specially devoted to producing a complete change in the circumstances of the working class by inducing it to return to agriculture." [1]

O'Brien's plan hinged upon the formation of electoral associations. M'Douall proposed to support Chartism by organising the different trades. Benbow's plan, comprising 28 closely written pages, was declared to be unsuitable and was not made public. As we shall see later on, Lovett and Collins drew up a plan of organisation, which was entirely based on educational associations.

[1] *Northern Star*, July 18, 1840.

The conference sat from July 20 to 24, 1840, and submitted the following proposal for organisation :—

The Chartists of Great Britain are incorporated in a National Charter Association. Its object is to obtain a Radical Reform of the House of Commons ; in other words a full and faithful representation of the entire people of the United Kingdom. The principles requisite to secure such a representation are : the right of voting for members of parliament by every male of 21 years of age and of sound mind ; no property qualification for members of parliament ; payment of members ; the ballot ; division of electoral districts, giving to each district a proportionate of representatives according to the number of electors ; annual elections. To accomplish the foregoing objects none but peaceable and constitutional means shall be employed, such as public meetings to discuss grievances arising from the existing system, and to show the utility of the proposed changes and to petition parliament to adopt the same. All persons will become members of this association on condition of signing a declaration, signifying their agreement with its objects, principles, and constitution, when they shall be presented with cards of membership, which shall be renewed quarterly and for which they shall each pay the sum of twopence. Wherever possible the members shall be formed into classes of ten persons, which classes shall meet weekly ; and one out of and by each class shall be nominated leader and appointed by the executive, who shall collect from each member one penny per week. Each town shall be divided into wards and divisions according to the plan of the Municipal Reform Act. Once a month a meeting of members of the said wards shall be held, when addresses shall be delivered and the society's business transacted. The leaders of the said classes shall attend the meeting and report about the state of the classes, in lawful and temperate language. At the first meeting of each ward or division a collector shall be nominated and appointed by the executive, to whom the class leaders shall pay the moneys collected from the class members. And the said collector shall hand over the money to the treasurer of the town at the weekly meeting of the council. Each principal town, with its suburban villages, shall have a council of nine persons including an assistant treasurer and secretary. The local council shall meet once weekly and shall have the power of appropriating half the moneys collected for local purposes. They shall also see that the recommendations of the executive be carried out. At the head of the N.C.A. there will be an executive of seven members, including the treasurer and secretary. The members of the executive shall be elected by the whole party and shall be paid for their work ; they shall be employed at the same time as missionaries. The general treasurer will publish a statement of accounts once a week in the Chartist newspapers.

This plan of organisation was adopted on July 24, 1840. It will be seen that the plan of organisation, as laid down by the conference, possessed a centralising character and was by no means legal, nevertheless it was adopted and carried out. The Chartist movement retained the name " National Charter Association " until the very end.

At the close of the conference the delegates issued an address to the Chartists, who were invited to join the organisation and to work for its objects within constitutional limits, above all to avoid forming secret societies, to further the cause of temperance and the diffusion of knowledge, and especially to support and to win subscribers for the Chartist press.

The plan of organisation was approved by their comrades in the country, but only about 20,000 joined the N.C.A.

The release of Lovett, Collins, M'Douall, and other Chartist leaders who had been sent to prison in 1839 contributed to revive the cause of Chartism in the summer of 1840, for they visited many towns in Great Britain, held meetings and took part in demonstrations. These meetings reunited the Chartists. The old hopes were aroused by the inspired words of the martyrs, who exhorted their followers to perseverance, to unity and to the unabated continuance of the struggle. The result of the manifesto must have been considerable, for even the Liberal press could no longer ignore it.[1]

[1] *Tait's Edinburgh Magazine*, 1840, p. 811.

2.—OTHER PLANS FOR ORGANISATION

During the last weeks of the London Convention of 1839 O'Brien came to the firm conclusion that the Chartist organisations could only escape the dangers of secret societies and conspiracies if they concentrated all their activity upon parliamentary elections and the diffusion of political knowledge. Therefore he proposed that the Chartists should bring forward their own nominated candidates at all parliamentary elections wherever possible, so as to give them the opportunity to expound the principles of the party. The Chartists should likewise attend election meetings of the other parties, take part in discussions and move amendments to the resolutions laid before these meetings. The aforesaid conference appended O'Brien's proposals to its plan of organisation and recommended the adoption.

M'Douall's plan of organisation was quite different in its character. He tried to group together working men who were already Chartists in Chartist associations on the basis of their trades, to permeate the trade unions with the Chartist spirit, so that they should eventually form the basis of the agitation. Organisation on these lines was carried out to a considerable extent both in London and Manchester. Combined Chartist and trade organisations existed in these districts down to the end of 1842. In the Chartist press of 1841 and 1842 we are continually finding mention of organisations called the Chartist association of shoemakers, of hatters, of joiners, of stockingers, etc.[1]

The scheme of organisation proposed by Lovett and Collins was based on educational associations, because they did not come within the limits of the Corresponding Act and therefore it would be possible to form a national organisation with branches. Whilst in prison at Warwick they wrote a pamphlet, entitled " Chartism," with this end in view. Both of them were convinced that above everything else the working classes were

[1] *Chartist and Republican Journal*, April 17, 1841 ; *British Statesman*, June 19, August 6 and 13, 1842 ; *Northern Star*, August 20, 1842.

lacking in education. It was only because they were uneducated
that they could fall into the hands of an O'Connor, an Attwood or
any other politician of the middle classes, who allied themselves
with the working men for their own ends and became their idol.
In a circular to the Chartists they declared :—

" You must become your own social and political regenerators
or you will never enjoy freedom. You must be intelligent and
moral, else no revolution will help you. Most of your grievances
are due to class legislation. Our agitation has been hitherto an
external one ; we appealed rather to the senses than to the
mind. Our public meetings have on many occasions been the
arenas of passionate invective, party spirit, and personal idolatry,
rather than public assemblies for deliberation and discussion,
dissemination of knowledge, and inculcation of principles. We
need political power to enable us to improve to any extent our
material condition, but we need also sobriety and moral culture.
Systematic education is necessary. . . . On the strength of
these convictions we have drawn up our plan, which is not
exclusive, but supplementary to the Chartist organisations
already in existence. Our plan is to form a National Association
for promoting the political and social improvement of the people.
Our plan is : (1) To establish in one general body persons of all
creeds, classes, and opinions who are desirous of promoting the
political and social improvement of the people. (2) To create and
extend an enlightened public opinion in favour of the People's
Charter and by every just and peaceful means to secure its
enactment, so that the industrious classes may be placed in
possession of the franchise—the most important step to all
political and social reformation. (3) To appoint as many missionaries as may be deemed necessary to visit the different districts
to enlighten and organise the people. (4) To establish circulating
libraries from 100 to 200 volumes each, containing the most
useful works on politics, morals, sciences, and history. (5) To
print tracts and pamphlets for circulation. (6) To erect public
halls or schools for the people throughout the kingdom. Such
halls to be used during the day as infant, preparatory, and high
schools. Such halls to have two playgrounds, rooms for cold

and hot baths, laboratory and workshops, where the teachers and the children may be taught science by experiments as well as the elements of trades. (7) Normal or teachers' schools, for the purpose of forming schoolmasters. (8) Agricultural and industrial schools, as may be required for the education and support of the orphan children of the association. If the members who signed the National Petition belonged to such an association, and paying about one penny per week, they would be able to effect the following important objects every year: (a) the erection of 80 district halls or normal or industrial schools at £3,000 each, or together £240,000; (b) 710 circulating libraries at £20 each, or together £14,200; (c) 4 missionaries at £200 a year, or together £800; (d) circulation of 20,000 pamphlets or flyleaves every week at 15 shillings per 1000, or together £780; (e) expenses for printing, postage, and salaries, £700. Sum total, £256,480. Since the income would amount to £257,180, there would be a small surplus of £700 for unforeseen expenses."[1]

Lovett's plan therefore was to found an organisation subordinate to the N.C.A., for the purpose of diffusing knowledge and of imparting education to the working classes.

At the same time that these plans were published the temperance or total abstinence movement made headway among the Chartists. Henry Vincent was its most zealous apostle. The *English Chartist Circular* bore the sub-title *Temperance Record*. Finally, Christian Chartists came forward in Scotland and Birmingham, carrying Chartism into the churches and instilling Chartist ideas into the Sunday sermons. O'Connor opposed these efforts and displayed great journalistic activity from his prison cell at York, writing an article on " Church Chartism, Teetotal Chartism, Knowledge Chartism," etc. He opposed the policy of permeating Chartism with religion, temperance[2] and knowledge. The greater part of his article was directed against Christian Chartism, whilst temperance and knowledge were

[1] Lovett and Collins, *Chartism*, 1841; *English Chartist Circular*, No. 16; Lovett, *Life*, 1876, p. 248.
[2] A year later O'Connor became a total abstainer, since most of the Chartists had declared in favour of temperance.

dismissed in a few sentences.[1] Soon, however, he took up the cudgels against Lovett, who was bold enough to write against hero-worship, that is to say, against the O'Connor cult and against exhibitions and rowdy meetings. O'Connor and his clique felt that the attack was directed against them, and regarded it as an attempt to stir up the people against them. They stigmatised Lovett, Hetherington, and James Watson as traitors and deserters, as tools of the Whigs and of O'Connell.[2] That was quite sufficient. Drilled by the *Northern Star* to regard O'Connor as infallible, the Chartists in many localities passed resolutions hostile to the London leader of the working men. Lovett made no rejoinder. Hetherington was the only one to take up the gauntlet, but it only resulted in unpleasant recriminations, rendering it quite impossible for the old rift between O'Connor and the London artisans ever to be healed. O'Connor again turned to " the fustian jackets, blistered hands, and unshorn chins," and instead of producing the proofs of treachery of Lovett and his friends which had been demanded, O'Connor merely heaped suspicion upon suspicion against his opponents.[3] It was the old contrast between the Irish agrarian revolutionary and the intelligent section of the working classes of the metropolis. O'Connor had learned nothing from the tragic events of the latter half of 1839. He was again full of boasting and threats of the invincible might and revolutionary power of the Chartists. A month after his crossing swords with Hetherington, O'Connor addressed the Irish landlords as follows :

" Well organised as we are, yet all hope failing of such immediate social change as we look for, we shall be left no alternative by your refusal but to experimentalise upon your properties. My Lords and Gentlemen ! We can rob you all in less than six weeks, though you had the Court, the Lords, and the Commons with you, and having done so, you would be thrown into revolution with the fundholder, the parson, and the usurer."

O'Connor tried to convince the Irish landlords in this manner

[1] *Northern Star*, April 3, 1841.　　[2] *Ibid.*, April 10 and 17.
[3] *Ibid.*, May and June, 1841.

that it would be more sensible and more advantageous for them
to nationalise their land or to lease it to small holders.[1]

Holding these opinions, he could only regard Lovett's plan
as an act of treachery and cowardice.[2]

3.—ELECTORAL POLICY

In 1841 the question of electoral policy became the order of
the day for the Chartists.   Among the middle classes there was
a distinct and growing tendency to make overtures to the
Chartists, and, on the other hand, among the Chartists there
was an undercurrent in favour of an alliance with the Radical
elements of the middle classes, in order to work together for the
cause of universal suffrage.   Among the Liberals the desire to
come into touch with the labour movement was fostered by the
courageous sacrifices of the Chartists, the speeches of the persecuted workers in their defence, the great extent of the agitation
in favour of the old ideals of Radicalism, no less than by the
forbidding attitude of the government to all further electoral
reform and its obstinate and decided opposition to the Anti-
Corn-Law League.   Since 1836 the people had shown that
they craved for political activity and were keenly interested in
parliamentary action, and they had created political organisations in order to obtain the Charter.   Why should the Liberals
keep aloof from a movement of this kind, which strove for civil
rights and constitutional liberties ?   The movement, to be sure,
still displayed considerable immaturity, but the Liberals ascribed
this to such adventurers as O'Connor, Taylor, etc.   A tendency
to meet this desire halfway was exhibited by some of the Chartist
leaders, such as Lovett, and somewhat later on by O'Brien.
The failure of the National Petition, the persecutions and excesses
of 1839 and 1840, induced the Chartists to proceed more warily
with the work, and to induce the intellectuals of the middle
classes to support the Charter.   This question had been mooted
even in the General Convention (1839), and an appeal was issued

---

[1] *Northern Star*, July 10, 1841.
[2] *Ibid.*, March 28, 1840 ; July 17, 1841 ; *cp.* also Thomas Frost,
Forty Years' Recollections, 1880, p. 173 and *sqq.*

to the intellectuals and the Radicals to declare in favour of the Charter.[1] In 1841 this idea came to life again, but there were few who had the courage to state the question openly and clearly for discussion. They were afraid of the people and they were afraid of O'Connor. For years the people had been warned against the middle classes. For years it had been drummed into their ears that the middle classes were their real enemies. How could anyone give the advice now to the people to enter into alliance with the middle classes? Would they not regard such counsels as treachery? The people hated the Whigs: " the vile, bloody Whigs," as the *Northern Star* called them. And were the Liberals any different from the Whigs? Better an open enemy than a false and treacherous friend! Better a Tory than a Whig! This was the view of the masses and this was O'Connor's mode of reasoning. But when it was a question of working in parliament for a Chartist petition, to whom did the Chartists address themselves? To the Liberals. And who voted for the petition? The Liberals. And who were subsequently opposed by O'Connor and the *Northern Star*? The Liberals.

It was only the leaders of the London working men who held a different opinion. " Unfortunately, the Chartists," said Hetherington in a public meeting, " have always most violently opposed those who approached nearest to them." [2]

In the midst of all these questions which cropped up the Liberals called a meeting at Leeds in order to arrive at an understanding with the Chartists. The following speakers were announced: Roebuck, Colonel Perronet Thompson, Sharman Crawford, Joseph Hume and Daniel O'Connell—all Radical members of Parliament who had co-operated in the production of the People's Charter. The meeting took place on January 21, 1841. Hume moved the following resolution :—

" That the great experiment made by means of the Reform Bill to improve the conditions of the country has failed to attain the end desired by the people, and a further reform having therefore become necessary, it is the opinion of this meeting that the united efforts of all reformers ought to be directed to obtain

[1] *Charter*, July 21, 1839.　　[2] *Northern Star*, January 28, 1843.

such a further enlargement of the franchise as should make the interests of the representatives identical with those of the whole country, and by this means secure a just government for all classes of the people."

The resolution was couched in general terms, for its object was to promote a coalition. The Radicals who had been announced to speak expressed themselves unreservedly in favour of Universal Suffrage. The Chartists who spoke comprised Moir from Glasgow, Collins and the Christian Chartist O'Neil from Birmingham, and Lowery from Newcastle. The resolution was carried unanimously and then found its way into the great wastepaper basket, where the majority of resolutions passed at meetings find their grave. Three months after this meeting a parliamentary by-election took place at Nottingham. Mr. Walter, the editor of the *Times*, was the Conservative candidate, a certain Larpent stood as the government candidate. The Chartists had a number of votes at their disposal in this constituency and threw themselves heart and soul into the election contest, working for Walter, who was returned by a majority of 278 votes on April 27. It was never known whether it was the Chartist votes that turned the scales, but it caused a great sensation : " The Chartists as allies of the Tories ! The Chartists a factor in elections ! "

This event gave the Chartists a real and living interest in discussions of electoral policy, which became all the keener since a dissolution of parliament could not be postponed longer. The Whigs had been at the helm since 1830, but from 1837 they had had no solid majority. The discontent in the country was frequently attributed to the Whigs. Fresh elections and a change of government were therefore imminent.

The Conservative leader, Sir Robert Peel, made use of this feeling, and on June 5, 1841, he moved a vote of censure on the government in order to force them to resign. His policy was successful, and the Whigs threw down the reins of government.

Before this resignation had taken effect a conference was held in London of twelve Chartist delegates to present a petition to parliament in favour of the liberation of the Chartist prisoners. M'Douall was the leading spirit of this conference, which sat from May 3 to 28, in order to canvass members of parliament in favour of the petition. The petition contained 1,348,848 signatures and was as comprehensive as its predecessor of July, 1839. According to all appearances, the conference also set itself the task of deliberating and deciding on electoral policy, for on May 15 it published an address to the Chartists, in which the delegates violently attacked the Whigs and recommended the following lines of action :—

" It is better at times to submit to a real despotism than to a government of perfidious, treacherous, and pretended friends. We are natural enemies to Whiggism and Toryism, but being unable to destroy both factions, we advise you to destroy the one faction by making a tool of the other. We advise you to upset the ministerial candidates on every occasion, to doubt their professions and disbelieve their hustings' promises. They even propose what they term a large extension of the suffrage. Be not deluded again—stand by your Charter, accept nothing less, and like the stern and independent Romans, rather bring your enemies under a despotism than be deluded with their treacherous professions . . . elect Chartists, or upset a ministerial hack."[1]

On May 27 the consideration of the Chartist petition was placed on the order of the day in the House of Commons. This extremely comprehensive document was carried into parliament by eighteen working men, and Thomas Slingby Duncombe, a Radical member, introduced it in a long speech and recommended it to the favourable consideration of the House. The attendance at the House was not nearly so great as on the occasion of the discussion of the National Petition in July, 1839. Nevertheless there was a debate, in which ministerialists spoke in favour of the petition. The vote was taken at the close of the debate : 58 ministerialists voted for the adoption of the petition, and 58 Conservatives voted against it, whereupon the Speaker gave his casting vote against its adoption. The petition was therefore rejected.[2]

[1] *Northern Star*, May 22, 1841.
[2] Hansard's *Parliamentary Debates*, third series, vol. 58, 1841, pp. 740–756.

This want of success was followed by the return of the delegates to their districts in order to take part in the election contests, which were fought in July and August, 1841.

The election policy of the Chartists lacked uniformity, in spite of the decision that had been laid down for their guidance at elections. The *Northern Star* and O'Connor were indeed in complete agreement with the resolution of the conference, but they lacked the courage to tell the Chartists in unequivocal terms that they were to work and vote for the Tories.

Under the heading " Dissolution of Parliament," the *Northern Star* of June 12, 1841, printed two leading articles. The first asked :—

" What's to be done ? The answer is clear. Let the great principle of universal suffrage be practically asserted. How ? In every city and borough let the people select their own men, qualified to sit, making the following the test of their principles : (1) The Charter ; (2) Immediate liberation of all Chartist prisoners and restoration of Chartist exiles to their homes ; (3) Repeal of the English Poor Law ; (4) Ten hours' work and a complete reform of the child-slaying factory system ; (5) Annihilation of rural police and the placing of town and borough police under the control of the inhabitants ; (6) Repeal of all laws fettering the press. Chartists ! The man who will vote for and do his utmost to accomplish the foregoing list of reforms—he is your man. Wherever by splitting with the Tories you can return your man, do so. Wherever by splitting with the Whigs you can return your man, do so. But where you cannot find a qualified man to start as your candidate, or where, owing to poverty, you dare not risk the expenses of a contest, then have your candidates, elect them by show of hands. This costs nothing. Select among you the honest and best talented. Let integrity be the first qualification, ability the second."

Then follows a second leader, which is a complete contradiction of the first. It is exclusively directed against the Whigs, whose defeat was regarded ás the supreme duty of the Chartists. The main object was no longer the Charter, nor the struggle for

Chartist principles; it was to fight against the ministerial candidates—against the Whigs and for the Tories:

"Wherever we cannot contest an election with our own resources, let us do our best to secure a defeat of the Whigs."

And since the Chartists were not strong enough in any single constituency to achieve success at the polls by their own efforts, O'Connor's advice practically amounted to the recommendation that the Chartists should give their votes and assistance to the Tories.

In addition to the foregoing electioneering advice, there were still other recommendations in the Chartist movement, viz., those of the London labour leaders and of O'Brien.

The views of the London labour-leaders on election policy were at the opposite pole to O'Connor's. They recommended the Chartists to support those Radicals and Liberals who pledged themselves to vote in parliament for the Charter and against all reactionary measures. In the opinion of the London men, the Chartists could not reckon upon running their own candidates. It would therefore be the best plan to work or to vote for those Radical and Liberal candidates who had supported the Chartist petitions and who had declared in favour of popular freedom on other occasions.

The third line of policy was advocated by O'Brien and his adherents. Their opinion was somewhat to the following effect :—

We have nothing to expect either from the Tories or the Whigs. The Tories are reactionary, out and out, and hate everything that is democratic. Their impending victory will chiefly be due to the circumstance that "public opinion" expects the Tories to persecute Chartism more ruthlessly and to stamp it out—that is to say, to accomplish what the Whigs were unable to accomplish. It is therefore impossible for Chartists to help the Tories to gain their victory. The recommendation by the conference and by O'Connor is therefore wrong. On the other hand, we cannot follow the policy of the London leaders, for Chartism has nothing to expect from the middle classes, since the interests of both are diametrically opposed. We must therefore make use of the elections mainly as a means for agitation. And the English methods of election lend themselves to this purpose in a high degree. We have nominations and polling. Every British inhabitant can take part in the nominations. The Chartists can therefore put up their own candidates, who will appear on the hustings with those of the other parties on the appointed days of nomination ; they will deliver their election addresses and will call upon the people to vote for them by a show of hands. There is no doubt that the people will vote on nomination days for Chartist candidates and will declare their intention of wishing to be represented in parliament exclusively by Chartists. When the voting by show of hands has come to an end and the Chartist candidate is elected, then the people must adopt a strongly worded resolution declaring that the candidates they have elected are the only representatives they will recognise, and when this is done they must instantly leave the hustings. The people do not, as a rule, participate in the polling, which takes place a few days later. But if the Chartists have a number of votes in many towns, which could turn the balance between Tory and Whig, then the Chartists may negotiate with either the Tories or the Whigs, for there is absolutely no difference between the two parties. If one of these parties declared itself prepared to support some of the Chartist candidates at the polls, and to ensure their return, then the Chartist voters may act in reciprocity by bestowing their votes upon them. The result of this policy will be twofold ; in the first place it will teach the working classes always and at all times to vote for their own candidates and to remain strictly in opposition to both Whig and Tory, for even when a Chartist votes for candidates prepared to compromise he is indirectly voting for his own representatives. In the second place the difference between the results of the nominations and of the polling will reveal the glaring wrong under which the British people is suffering ; they will show that the people are practically not represented.

O'Brien was also of opinion that the actual representatives of the people elected by nomination should form the National Council of the unrepresented people until the dissolution of parliament. O'Connor's election policy was pro-Tory ; that of the London leaders was pro-Liberal. O'Brien's was the policy of a relentless class war by a proletariate that was absolutely unable to convert its votes into political power.

These views on election policy brought O'Brien into collision with his leader, O'Connor. The opposition soon developed into enmity, for O'Brien did not mince matters, but plainly and openly declared that O'Connor must be either mad or dishonest.[1]

O'Connor's policy was, however, neither insane nor dishonest, but it was the logical consequence of a policy calculated on a quick, external success. O'Connor above all dealt only with parties engaged in parliamentary intrigues, and impelled by a craving for offices, honours, and highly paid posts. He neither knew nor appreciated the economic meaning of the social classes of which parties are the political expression. Thinking in this manner O'Connor believed that the position of the Chartists must remain a bad one so long as the Whigs were at the helm of the State—the fact of their being a governing party caused them to be averse from sweeping reforms. And since the Tories were in any case reactionary, it was obvious that the Chartists were opposed by a single reactionary and powerful body. But if the Whigs were beaten, they would then form the opposition and would adopt the language of liberty in order to return as soon as possible to the manger of government. The Whigs as the party of opposition would make advances to the Chartists and work in parliament in favour of their demands.

It was an easy task for O'Brien to dispose of these superficial views of parliamentary action ; in view of the fact that the Chartist agitation aimed at obtaining political power for the working classes as a means to a revolution of the rights of property in the interests of labour, it would be madness to allow Chartism to be deviated from its course by the game of intrigue between Tory and Whig and to wish to model the election policy of the productive classes upon it. O'Connor, in approving of a policy of this nature, was sacrificing principle to an illusory expediency.

[1] *Northern Star*, June 19, 1841.

O'Brien at the same time adversely criticised the policy of the London leaders, the "knowledge-mongers," who were included in the Radicals and Liberals.

All these controversies were written in the prisons where both leaders were immured.

In spite of O'Brien's mental superiority, the people adopted O'Connor's views. Their hatred for the Whigs was incomparably fiercer than for the Tories. The people had no longer any recollection of the acts of the Tories from 1812 to 1819, of the wholesale executions of January, 1813, the system of espionage and the manufactured insurrections of 1817, or of Peterloo and the Six Acts. They only knew that the Whigs had thrown the Chartist leaders into prison, had passed the new Poor Law and the treacherous Reform Bill. They did not take into account the events of the years 1838, 1839, and 1840, when half the working class had armed itself with muskets, pikes, and grenades, when the labour leaders incited the people to violent upheavals, and drew up plans and projects for insurrections, without the Whigs carrying out a single sentence of death. We may take it as a rule that social revolutionary movements hate the Liberals more fiercely than the Conservatives. An oppressed people demanding rights expects à priori more from Liberals than from Conservatives—Liberalism is so deeply permeated with abstract ideas of freedom that such expectations are naturally raised. But since the point of view of an oppressed class is social, and its aims are economic, while Liberalism deals, or dealt during the last century, mainly with constitutional changes and political freedom, it is inevitable that Liberals, when returned to power, should disappoint these expectations of the people. Fanned by the flames of disappointment, the opposition of the people to Liberalism in power is transformed into bitter hatred, which for a time darkens counsel and prevents clear thinking. The Liberals appear not only in the light of enemies, but also of traitors and cowards, who must be chastised and destroyed at all costs. Better an open enemy than a false friend! Better a Tory than a Liberal!

O'Connor was further influenced by an idea, which was not

in the minds of the people. O'Connor, who considered land to be the only true source of life, and in his revolutionary moments dreamed of the forcible expropriation of the landlords, merely regarded the Liberals as a buffer party standing between the people and the landowners, and therefore acting as a hindrance to a straight fight. His plan therefore was to destroy this buffer party so as to clear the battlefield between the two opposing armies of the robbers and the robbed. He considered the whole policy of the Whigs and Liberals to be to distract the Chartist army from marching straight to the field of battle.

During the election campaign of July and August, 1841, which returned the Tories to parliament with a considerable majority, the Chartists selected candidates at many places, but mostly for nomination purposes. In these cases the people voted everywhere by show of hands for the Chartist candidates, excepting at Leeds, the seat of the *Northern Star*, where both the Chartist candidates, Leach and Williams, were rejected by the people. There can be absolutely no doubt that if the people had possessed the franchise at that period they would have returned about a hundred Chartists to parliament as the representatives of the people. It was a matter of course for the operative of that time to regard the Chartist as his representative. It was quite different in the case of those elections at which the Chartist candidates went to the polls, that is to say, when they showed a real intention of becoming members of parliament. Such elections took place at Banbury, where Vincent stood as a candidate, at Nottingham, where M'Douall was a candidate in coalition with the Tories, at Marylebone and at Brighton. The number of votes cast for the four Chartist leaders at the polls was quite insignificant. The result of O'Connor's election policy was that the Chartists were accused of having allied themselves with the deadliest enemies of freedom. It was at this time, as already mentioned, that the breach occurred between O'Connor and O'Brien, which burst into open hostility in the early part of 1842, and exercised a baleful influence upon Chartism. It sowed mistrust and suspicion and discord, and it left the leadership of the Chartist masses exclusively in

O'Connor s hands. Lovett and O'Brien were cleared out of the way ; and they were the only men who could act as a counterpoise to O'Connor at conferences or could carry any weight with the people. Soon small cliques began to form among the Chartists, gathering round the wrangling leaders and poisoning party life by mischief-making, by the publication of private conversations and all manner of tittle-tattle.[1]

In August, O'Connor, O'Brien, and other prisoners were set at liberty, having served their sentences. The Chartists sent no less than 56 delegates to York to congratulate O'Connor on his release from prison. A triumphal car was specially built for this occasion, and O'Connor received—at his request—a suit of fustian, in order to symbolise his equality with the factory hands. The song, "The Lion of Freedom," resounded wherever the great leader showed his face. The meetings held by the liberated leaders throughout the country, as well as the defeat of the Whigs in the parliamentary elections, raised the enthusiasm of the people to its highest pitch in the later months of 1841 and the early months of 1842. The N.C.A. flourished as never before or since, yet the number of its enrolled members did not exceed 40,000, but Chartism possessed the unbounded trust of the labouring masses and of many trade unions.[2] There were hundreds of thousands of Chartists who refused to join the N.C.A., either because they regarded the organisation as illegal or because they felt no confidence in its leaders.

4.—CHARTISTS AND RADICALS

The questions of election policy to which the parliamentary elections of July and August, 1841, had given rise became even more acute in 1842. From the autumn of 1841 a serious industrial crisis prevailed in Great Britain, severely affecting a large part of the middle classes. The distress increased, and the fear became universal that the year 1842 might be marked by a social catastrophe. Nothing could be expected from parlia-

[1] *Northern Star*, May 14 (Report of the Convention of May 3), 1842.
[2] *Northern Star*, February 19, 1842.

ment. When even the Whigs had destroyed all hope of legislation for restoring trade and industry to a healthy condition, how
could any industrial remedy be expected from the Tories ? The
universal distress turned the thoughts of the educated middle
class in favour of reform. Counsels of despair were intermingled
with a friendly feeling towards reform. Surely nothing could be
worse than the present condition ; if universal suffrage were
granted, things might indeed be much better, for the Chartist
agitation, which had contributed so much to fostering enmity
between the working and the middle classes, would have attained
its object. Besides, whenever the economic catastrophe
arrived it would be met by a certain degree of understanding
between the working and the middle classes, which would
facilitate the inauguration of reforms with a view to the revival
of industry.

Joseph Sturge, of Birmingham, the universally respected friend
of humanity, stood at the head of this movement for parliamentary reform. He was also a member of the Anti-Corn Law
League, and at the same time worked for universal suffrage.
The project of effecting a reconciliation between the working
and the middle classes lay very near his heart. He attempted
to convince his friends that a class parliament is at the root
of most social ills and that there was no possibility of any
legislation in the direction of justice and happiness so long as
the working class was denied the franchise, and thereby the
capacity of transforming parliament into a truly national
parliament. Sturge and those of his friends who held the same
views founded for this purpose in the latter half of 1841
the weekly paper, *Nonconformist*, in which democratic principles
were advocated. This group of thinkers comprised, amongst
others, John Bright, who, in conjunction with Cobden, was about
to play such an important part in the agitation for free trade;
another leading member of it was the Rev. Thomas Spencer,
a progressive theologian and educationist, who regarded the
Christian Church as an organic growth, and therefore needing
reformation from time to time, an adaptation to external
environment. His nephew was Herbert Spencer, the philosopher

of evolution, who made his political *début* in a series of articles that appeared in the *Nonconformist* of August and September, 1841.

In the second week of February, 1842, Sturge convened a public meeting in London, in order to initiate a discussion on universal suffrage between the leading Chartists and Radicals. William Lovett accepted the invitation, and spoke in favour of the People's Charter and the abolition of the corn taxes. He explained to the Radicals how the suspicion had arisen among the Chartists that the Anti-Corn Law agitation was hostile to them, and expressed the opinion that the free traders could easily clear themselves from this suspicion by declaring unreservedly for the Charter.[1]

The discord in the Chartist ranks rendered Sturge's plan inestimable service. Many Chartists rallied round him so that a conference could be held in Birmingham from April 5 to 8, 1842, in which 103 delegates took part. Sturge, Bright, Spencer, Lovett, Collins, O'Brien, Vincent, J. R. Richardson and many other leaders appeared and discussed the question of founding an organisation to promote the six points of the People's Charter. All the delegates were united on the principles of the reform, and resolved to call another conference for the purpose of arriving at an understanding on the details of these principles. Among the Chartist delegates there were five from Bradford, who regarded the conference itself as an act of treachery directed against the working class, and as an attempt to weaken or obliterate the class war, and they sent secret reports to O'Connor against O'Brien. As soon as the conference decided to found an organisation, entitled the " National Complete Suffrage Union " (N.C.S.U.), the Bradford delegates were absolutely convinced of the correctness of their deductions and stigmatised O'Brien as a traitor. O'Connor and the *Northern Star* now possessed the material to hold up Lovett and O'Brien to the contempt of the people.[2] The N.C.S.U. appeared to them to be an organisation founded with the express intention of destroying the National Chartist Association, although Sturge had expressly stated that

[1] *Nonconformist*, February 16, 1842. [2] *Northern Star*, April 9, 1842.

the Chartists were not to give up their own organisations, since the N.C.S.U. had only been founded for those who could not join the Chartist organisations. O'Connor reprinted in the *Northern Star* an article from the *Poor Man's Guardian* directed against the middle classes, in order to demonstrate O'Brien's treachery in black and white.

The accused man was unable to reply to the attack before July, when he became editor of the *British Statesman* in London. His answer was as follows :—

" . . . Many of you looking back to our language in the *Poor Man's Guardian* and other publications of ours are apt to suspect that we have to some extent deserted your interests, because we do not come out in the *Statesman* with the same withering denunciations of the middle classes which formerly characterised our writing. Do not, good friends, judge us after this fashion. Judge us not by the epithets we use but by the principles we advocate, and by the tendency of our policy to promote your interests at a time of difficulties and dangers unexampled in our history.[1] The language which served you so effectually in 1834-1837 could not serve you now. . . . It was then necessary to rouse you, as with a rattling peal of thunder. The case is widely different now. You are wide awake ; you need no rousing now. The danger now is, not that you will not move, but that you will move too fast before your friends have been able to detach some of your enemy's forces from him and to make them either neutral or auxiliary to you in the coming conflict. In 1834 the middle classes treated us with scorn ; now vast numbers of them not only recognise us as an integral part of the body politic, but they have actually paid court to us. Never mind the motives of this. Never mind whether they act thus from policy or principle. Our business is to deal with them as we find them—to accept their advance and proffered aid in a frank and friendly spirit, to reciprocate such acts by every means at our disposal that involve no compromise of principle, and above all not to commit the suicidal folly of

[1] O'Brien seemed to have had a presentiment that an insurrection was being plotted in Lancashire, and it actually broke out in 1842.

confounding the honest portion of them, who would give us our rights, with the selfish knaves who would not—by involving the whole class in one indiscriminate cloud of abuse. Working men ! We appeal to your reason whether this be not an honest as well as a sound policy, and whether we are not justified in using a different language towards the middle classes now from what we used five, or even one year ago, when they were in open arms against us ? " [1]

We shall soon see what O'Brien meant by speaking of the coming crisis and of impending dangers. In the meantime we will continue the account of the activity of the N.C.S.U. This activity was so successful that even O'Connor adopted a friendly attitude towards it and supported Sturge. In August, 1842, a parliamentary by-election took place in Nottingham, where Sturge was the candidate of the Radicals and Walter (publisher of the *Times*) was the Conservative candidate. O'Connor and the best Chartist speakers now came to Nottingham to work for Sturge and against Walter. Only J. R. Stephens, whom O'Connor now dubbed " the renegade parson," spoke in favour of Walter. The latter was elected by a majority of 84 votes. He received 1,085 votes against 1,001 cast for Sturge.

At the same time the Chartists resolved to send delegates to the conference of the N.C.S.U. that was to be held in December. The conference sat from December 27 to 29, 1842. More than 300 delegates were present, and O'Connor was among their number. The chief debate turned on the following point : the committee of the N.C.S.U. had drafted a Bill containing the six points and moved for this draft to form the basis of discussion. The words Charter and Chartism were so repugnant to the middle classes that, although they were ready to declare for universal suffrage, they would have kept aloof from the agitation if they had been expected to declare for the Charter. The committee was of opinion that it would be all the same to the people whatever the name might be under which it accepted universal suffrage and the other demands ; the main point was that it accepted them.

[1] *British Statesman*, July 9, 1842.

Lovett, who belonged to the committee, had no idea, up to the moment of the meeting of the conference, that a Bill of this kind was going to be prepared; indeed, he was, on the contrary, under the impression that the People's Charter would form the basis of discussion. After the spokesman of the committee had made his proposal and moved the resolution, O'Connor and Lovett both rose and asked permission to speak. Although O'Connor had been the first to rise, he gave way to Lovett, who stated :

" I rise with considerable pain and anxiety to impress on the spokesman of the committee the necessity of withdrawing a few words of his resolution and substituting a few others. The words to be withdrawn are ' that the Bill to be presented by the N.C.S.U. to be the basis of the discussion,' and to substitute ' that the document entitled the People's Charter be taken as the basis of discussion.' " (Loud and prolonged cheering). " Impressed with the conviction that the present object of the N.C.S.U. was to effect, if possible, a cordial union between the middle and working classes, and not merely to conciliate one and neglect the other, I have joined the union. . . . The N.C.S.U. will never succeed in reconciling the working and middle classes if it is ashamed of the Charter. The people have made great sacrifices for the Charter ; in order to secure its enactment vast numbers of our countrymen have suffered imprisonment and transportation. I admit that the noisy agitation connected with the Charter has created a considerable degree of prejudice in the minds of the middle classes against the Charter. But after all, it is prejudice. If the middle classes are not strong enough to give up such prejudices, how can they be in the position of declaring in favour of universal suffrage ? Therefore I ask the committee to withdraw those words in the resolution. If this is not done, then I fear that the conference will lead to nothing."

The dispute between the Chartists and the leaders of the N.C.S.U. did not in any degree turn upon a question of words. Men of the standing of Lovett, Spencer, or Sturge do not quarrel about mere formalities. The real reason lay deeper still. The

People's Charter was not only the programme of the agitation for the five years since its publication, but it had become the symbol of social reform or revolution ; it was bound up with the hopes, the ideas, and the social, plans of the working class. To change it for another bit of paper would be to tear part of the soul out of the hearts of the people, or to change social democracy into mere political democracy.

O'Connor spoke after Lovett :—

" I do not regret my act of courtesy towards Mr. Lovett. I have never been more pleased in my life than to give way to Mr. Lovett, and never have I been better repaid than in listening to the admirable explanation he has given. It had been my intention to contrast the merits of the small Bill with the demerits of the large Bill. Those clauses which are valuable have been taken from the Charter, and those which are useless are at the same time injurious. I know that the so-called physical force stigma is attached to the Charter. But whose fault is it that the workmen use their rough and rude way in asking for their rights ? It is the fault of those who have kept the workmen in ignorance and who degraded them. . . . I don't lead; I am driven by the people. The people gave the lead to the agitation and we followed. It was a great consolation for me to find myself upon the platform of the Charter together with Mr. Lovett. I think the quarrels between us two have been due to the intermeddling of third parties, and I don't hesitate to express to Mr. Lovett my deep sorrow that I have ever mistaken his honesty and integrity. What was for me a task was for Mr. Lovett a duty, and I am glad that Mr. Lovett has availed himself of the opportunity of vindi-cating the principles and leaving me to follow him. For my part, I shall adhere to the course I have hitherto followed, and I would rather be a simple soldier in the battle for principle than a leader of an army in a battle for expediency."

Since neither the committee of the N.C.S.U. nor the Chartists could agree to a compromise, a vote was taken on the resolution and the amendment. Lovett's amendment obtained 193 votes, whilst the resolution of the committee obtained only 94 votes. This result implied a breach. The conference was practically at an end, and the N.C.S.U. had received a fatal blow. There was no reconciliation even between the Chartist leaders, for Lovett did not believe in O'Connor's sincerity.[1]

5.—THE SECOND NATIONAL PETITION

From April 12 to May 12, 1842, 23 Chartist delegates assembled in a convention at London, in order to arrange for and to supervise the introduction of the second national petition in favour of the Charter. It was signed by not less than 3,315,752 working men. London and suburbs contributed 200,000 signatures, Manchester 99,680, Newcastle 92,000, Bradford 45,100, Glasgow and Lanarkshire 78,062, Birmingham 43,000, Leeds 41,000, Norwich 21,560, Rochdale 19,600, Preston 24,000, Oldham 15,000, Bolton 18,500, Ashton 14,200, Leicester 18,000, Huddersfield 23,180, Sheffield 27,200, Liverpool, 23,000, Staleybridge 10,000, Stockport 14,000, Burnley 14,000, Brighton 12,700, Merthyr Tydvil 13,900. There was not a single industrial locality in all Great Britain in which a large number of the working men were not adherents of Chartism. And the second national petition was much more revolutionary and more sharply expressed than the first. It ran as follows :—

" To the Honourable the Commons of Great Britain and Ireland in Parliament assembled.

" Government originated from and was designed to protect the freedom and promote the happiness of, and ought to be responsible to the whole people. The only authority on which any body of men can make laws and govern society is delegation from the people. As government was designed for the benefit and protection of, and must be obeyed and supported by all, therefore all should be equally represented. Any form of government which fails to effect the purposes for which it was designed, and does not fully and completely represent the whole people, who are compelled to pay taxes for its support and obey the laws resolved upon by it is unconstitutional, tyrannical, and ought to be amended or resisted Your honourable House, as at present constituted, has not been elected by, and acts irresponsibly of the people ; and hitherto ha only represented parties, and benefited the few, regardless of miseries, grievances, and petitions of the many. Your honourable

[1] *Cp.* Thomas Cooper, *Life*, edition 1897, pp. 221–226.

House has enacted laws contrary to the expressed wishes of the people, and by unconstitutional means enforced obedience to them, thereby creating an unbearable despotism on the one hand and degrading slavery on the other. . . . In proof of their assertion your petitioners instance that your honourable House has not been elected by the people, that the population of Great Britain and Ireland is at present about 26 millions of persons, and yet out of this number little more than 900,000 have been permitted to vote in a recent election of representatives to make laws to govern the whole. The existing state of representation is not only extremely limited and unjust, but unequally divided and gives preponderating influence to the landed and moneyed interests to the utter ruin of the small trading and labouring classes. The borough of Guildford with a population of 3,920 returns to parliament as many members as the Tower Hamlets with a population of 300,000 ; Evesham with a population of 3,998 elects as many representatives as Manchester with a population of 200,000. . . . These being but a few instances of the enormous inequalities existing in what is called the representation of the people. Bribery, intimidation, corruption, perjury, and riot prevail at all parliamentary elections to an extent best understood by the members of your honourable House.

" Your petitioners complain that they are enormously taxed to pay the interest of what is termed the national debt, a debt amounting at present to 800 millions sterling, being only a portion of the enormous amount expended in cruel and expensive wars for the suppression of all liberty, by men not authorised by the people, and who consequently had no right to tax posterity for the outrages committed by them on mankind. And your petitioners loudly complain of the augmentation of that debt, after 26 years of almost uninterrupted peace and whilst poverty and discontent rage over the land. Taxation, both general and local, is at this time too enormous to be borne, and in the opinion of your petitioners is contrary to the Bill of Rights, where it is clearly expressed that no subject shall be compelled to contribute to any tax, tallage, or aid unless imposed by common consent in Parliament.

" In England, Ireland, Scotland, and Wales thousands of people are dying from actual want ; and your petitioners, whilst sensible that poverty is the great exciting cause of crime, view with mingled astonishment and alarm the ill provision made for the poor, the aged, and the infirm ; and likewise perceive with feelings of indignation, the determination of your honourable House to continue the Poor Law in operation, notwithstanding the many proofs which have been afforded by sad experience of the unconstitutional principle of the Bill, of its unchristian character and of the cruel and murderous effects produced upon the wages of working men and the lives of the subjects of this realm.

" Your petitioners would direct the attention of your honourable House to the great disparity existing between the wages of the producing millions and the salaries of those whose comparative usefulness ought to be questioned, where riches and luxury prevail amongst the rulers and poverty and starvation amongst the ruled. With all due respect and loyalty, your petitioners would compare the daily income of the Sovereign Majesty with that of thousands of working men of this nation ; and whilst your petitioners have learned that Her Majesty receives daily for private use the sum of £164 17s. 10d., they have also ascertained that many thousands of families of the labourers are only in receipt of 3¾d. per head per day. Your petitioners have also learned that His Royal Highness Prince Albert receives each day the sum of £164, while thousands have to exist on 3d. a day. Your petitioners have also learned with astonishment that the King of Hanover daily receives £57 10s. whilst thousands of the taxpayers of this country live upon 2¾d. per head per day. Your petitioners have with pain and regret also learned that the Archbishop of Canterbury is daily in receipt of £52 10s. per day, whilst thousands of the poor have to maintain their families upon an income not exceeding 2d. per day. . . .

" Your petitioners know that it is the undoubted constitutional right of the people to meet freely, when, how, and where they choose, in public places, peaceably, in the day, to discuss their grievances, and political and other subjects, or for the purpose of framing, discussing, or passing any vote, petition, or remonstrance upon any subject whatsoever. Your petitioners complain that the right has unconstitutionally been infringed, and 500 well-disposed persons have been arrested, excessive bail demanded, tried by packed juries, sentenced to imprisonment, and treated as felons of the worst description. An unconstitutional police is distributed all over the country, at enormous cost, to prevent the due exercise of the people's rights. And your petitioners are of opinion that the Poor Law bastilles and the police stations, being co-existent, have originated from the same cause, viz., the increased desire on the part of the irresponsible few to oppress and starve the many. A vast and unconstitutional army is upheld at the public expense for the purpose of repressing public opinion in the three kingdoms and likewise to intimidate the millions in the due exercise of those rights and privileges which ought to belong to them.

" Your petitioners complain that the hours of labour, particularly of the factory workers, are protracted beyond the limits of human endurance, and that the wages earned, after unnatural application

o toil in heated and unhealthy workshops, are inadequate to
sustain the bodily strength and to supply those comforts which are
so imperative after an excessive waste of physical energy. Your
petitioners also direct the attention of your honourable House to
the starvation wages of the agricultural labourer, and view with
horror and indignation the paltry income of those whose toil gives
being to the staple food of the people. Your petitioners deeply
deplore the existence of any kind of monopoly in this nation, and
whilst they unequivocally condemn the levying of any tax upon the
necessaries of life and upon those articles principally required by
the labouring classes, they are also sensible that the abolition of any
monopoly will never unshackle labour from its misery until the people
possess that power under which all monopoly and oppression must
cease ; and your petitioners respectfully mention the existing
monopolies of the suffrage, of paper money, of machinery, of land,
of the public press, of means of travelling and transit, of religious
worship, and of a host of other evils too numerous to mention, all
arising from class legislation, but which your honourable House has
always endeavoured to increase instead of to diminish.

" From the numerous petitions presented to your honourable
House we conclude that you are fully acquainted with the grievances
of the working men ; and your petitioners pray that the rights and
wrongs of labour may be considered with a view to the protection
of the one and the removal of the other ; because your petitioners
are of opinion that it is the worst species of legislation which leaves
the grievances of society to be removed only by violence or revolution, both of which may be apprehended if complaints are un-
attended to and petitions despised.

" Your petitioners complain that upwards of nine millions per
annum are unjustly abstracted from them to maintain a church
establishment . . . and entreat you to contrast the deeds of
the clergy with the conduct of the founder of the Christian religion,
who denounced worshippers of Mammon and taught charity, meek-
ness, and brotherly love.

" Your petitioners maintain that it is the inherent, indubitable
and constitutional right, founded upon the ancient practice of the
realm of England and supported by well-approved statutes, of every
male inhabitant of the United Kingdom, he being of age, of sound
mind and non-convict of crime, and not confined under any judicial
process, to exercise the election franchise in the choice of members
to serve in the Commons House of Parliament."

The petition then enunciates the remaining five points of
the Charter, and continues as follows :—

11

" Your petitioners complain of the many grievances borne by the people of Ireland, and contend that they are fully entitled to a repeal of the legislative union.[1]

" Your petitioners beg to assure your honourable House that they cannot within the limits of this petition set forth even a tithe of the many grievances of which they may justly complain ; but should your honourable House be pleased to grant your petitioners a hearing by representatives at the bar of your honourable House, your petitioners will be enabled to unfold a tale of wrong and suffering, of intolerable injustice, which will create utter astonishment in the minds of all benevolent and good men that the people of Great Britain and Ireland have so long quietly endured their wretched condition, brought upon them, as it has been, by unjust exclusion from political authority and by the manifold corruptions of class legislation.

" Exercising their constitutional right, your petitioners demand that your honourable House do remedy the many gross and manifest evils of which your petitioners complain, do immediately, without alteration, deduction or addition, pass into law the document entitled the People's Charter." [2]

On May 2, 1842, the petition was introduced by Thomas Duncombe, who spoke at length on the following day in its support. The speaker gave a fairly good survey, not however altogether devoid of inaccuracies, concerning the origin and the progress of the Radical movement in England from the seventh decade of the eighteenth century. He outlined the activity displayed by Cartwright, the Duke of Richmond, the London Corresponding Society, and the Radicals from 1817 to 1819, and then went on to speak about the violent agitation connected with the Reform Bill. The dissatisfaction of the people with the Reform Bill and the legislation of the Reformed Parliament had led up to the Charter, and now more than three million working men were petitioning for its introduction. Duncombe drew a vivid picture of the distress and desperate condition of the working class, and begged the House of Commons to allow the representatives of the petitioners to appear at the bar of the House and to present the case for the people by word of mouth.

[1] The Scotch and London delegates protested against the inclusion in the petition of the demand for the repeal of the union.

[2] Hansard's *Parliamentary Debates*, 1842, vol. 62, pp. 1376–1381.

Duncombe was of opinion that this request of the petitioners to be heard at the bar of the House was more practical and by far more important than their demand for the Charter to be discussed without delay and to be adopted without alteration.

Speeches on the same lines as that by Duncombe were then delivered by the Radicals and free traders, Dr. Bowring, Fielden, Roebuck, Wakley, and Joseph Hume. Both the Conservatives and the Whigs spoke in opposition to Duncombe. The discussion only produced two speeches worthy of notice ; both of these speeches proceeded from the Whigs : from Thomas B. Macaulay and Lord John Russell. The former attacked the communism of the petition, the latter opposed its dependence on natural law, which he traversed from the utilitarian standpoint taken by Bentham.

Macaulay stated :—

" I am opposed to universal suffrage. I believe universal suffrage would be fatal to all purposes for which government exists and for which aristocracies and all other things exist, and that it is utterly incompatible with the very existence of civilisation. I conceive that civilisation rests on the security of property. While property is insecure, it is not in the power of the finest soil, or of the moral and intellectual constitution of any country to prevent the country sinking into barbarism, while, on the other hand, so long as property is secure it is not possible to prevent a country advancing in prosperity. . . . Therefore, we can never, without absolute danger, entrust the supreme government of the country to any class, which would, to a moral certainty, be induced to commit great and systematic inroads against the security of property. The petition must be considered as a sort of declaration of the intentions of the body, who, if the Charter is to become law, will become the sovereign body of the State—as a declaration of the intentions of those who would in that event return the majority of the representatives of the people to this House. What is the petition directed against ? It is opposed to the national debt, monopoly in land, in machinery, and in the means of transit. · They find these to be the sources of the evils which must be stopped. What does

that mean ? It is an expression of opinion that a national
bankruptcy would be just and politic, that landed property,
machinery, means of transit, indeed the monopoly of property
in general should cease to exist. Can it be anything but a
sweeping confiscation of property which is contemplated ? . . .
The petitioners ask for supreme power ; in every constituent
body throughout the empire capital and accumulated property
is to be placed absolutely at the foot of labour. How is it
possible to doubt what the result will be ? Such a confiscation
of property and spoliation of the rich will produce misery, and
misery will intensify the desire for spoliation ; this will produce
desperate struggles which will bring some strong military despot
to the surface, who will give some security to the property that
will remain. . . ."

Macaulay's argument is transparently clear. Private property
was the basis of all civilisation and of all progress ; to be sure it
also included poverty, but this was a necessary evil, which was
fully counterbalanced by the blessings of civilisation. The abolition of private property would considerably increase the evil, and
destroy civilisation in the bargain ; communism was misery *plus*
barbarism, and that was the object of the petitioners who were
trying to attain it by means of universal suffrage. How could
any civilised and progressive politician be expected under these
circumstances to vote in favour of universal suffrage ?

Lord John Russell opposed the petition by making use of
another argument. He stated :—

" I am aware that it is a doctrine frequently urged, and I
perceive dwelt upon in the petition, that every male of a certain
age has a right, absolute and inalienable, to elect a representative
to take his place among the members in the Commons House of
Parliament. I never could understand that indefeasible and
inalienable right. It appears to me that that question, like every
other in the practical application of politics, is to be settled by
the institutions and the laws of the country of which the person
is a native. I see no more right that a person 21 years of age
has to elect a member of parliament than he has to be a jury-
man or to exercise judicial functions, as the people used in some

of the republics of antiquity. These things, as it appears to me, are not matters of right; but if it be for the good of the people at large, if it be conducive to the right government of the State, if it tend to the maintenance of the freedom and welfare of the people that a certain number, defined and limited by a reference to a fixed standard of property, should have the right of electing members of parliament, and if it be disadvantageous to the community at large that suffrage should be universal, then I say that on such a subject the consideration of public good should prevail and that no inalienable right can be quoted against that which the good of the whole demands. And as our society is very complicated and property very unequally divided, it might come that a parliament issued from Universal Suffrage might destroy or shake those institutions which are of the utmost value in holding society together. . . ."

Lord Russell's argument is utilitarian in theory. But whilst Jeremy Bentham used the same theory in support of Universal Suffrage and of democracy in general, Lord Russell, on the other hand, deduced from it the necessity for an oligarchy. The latter held the opinion that only the great patrician families possessed capacity for governing, and must therefore hold a dominant position in the State. For what was the use of equality if it was destructive of national power or the solidity of the State ?

Voting upon the petition then proceeded to take place, but it was not clear whether it dealt with Duncombe's proposal to hear the Chartist leaders at the bar of the House or with the adoption or rejection in principle of the People's Charter. To all appearance many members of parliament had the first of these requests in view, whilst others took the petition as a whole into consideration. The result was 287 Noes, 49 Ayes. The Radicals and free traders comprised the minority, and amongst them was Richard Cobden, who represented Stockport in parliament since the elections of 1841.[1]

Feargus O'Connor, however, positively revelled in the enormous numbers of the signatories to the petition, whom he regarded as adherents of Chartism ready for action :

[1] Hansard's *Parliamentary Debates*, 1842.

" We are 4,000,000, aye and more.   Never lose sight of the
fact that we are 4,000,000 and more.   How proud was I to call
you 2,000,000 just twelve months ago, when the prison walls
separated us, and how doubly proud must I now be to call you
4,800,000 ! " [1]

This was Catilinarian blustering in the worst sense, and it
boded ill for the future.   A leader of class warfare, who refuses
to weigh the value of the number of his own forces as well as
those that are opposing him, is but a leader of lost causes.

[1] *Northern Star*, May 21, 1842.

VII

THE CULMINATION OF CHARTISM

I.—ECONOMIC DISTRESS AND GENERAL STRIKE

THE month of August, 1842, will always be memorable in the annals of Chartism. It was the month in which the movement attained its zenith, it was the month of the general strike in the northern half of Great Britain and of the subordination of the trade unions to political Chartism. The nation was nearing a social cataclysm. The discontent and determination of the working class reached their highest point. Wages sank in spite of all trade unionist effort to keep them up to the level of 1839. The whole trade unionism appeared to the working class to be Sisyphean labour. Chartist speakers were able at that time to declare, without fear of contradiction or disapproval, in public meetings of trade unionists that economic action had proved utterly ineffective, and that the salvation of the people entirely depended on the passing of the Charter into law or on political power.[1] The crisis, so the workers believed, had reached a climax which must precipitate the catastrophe, bringing redemption in its train. Unfavourable reports from the markets caused rejoicings among the working men, whose cry was : " It is hastening the crisis ! " [2]

No one ventured to question the descriptions of the distress, and the staggering revelations of the labour of children and women in the mines, which led to Lord Ashley's Mines and Colliers Bill (1842), rendered any social palliation utterly impossible. In the mind of many a student of social problems the harrowing thought arose that industrialism itself might be a

---

[1] *Northern Star*, August 13, 1842 (leading article).

[2] Hansard's *Parliamentary Debates*, 1842, vol. lxiii., p. 23.

disease indicative of the decline and fall of the nation.[1]   Even in commercial circles the opinion began to prevail that " manufactures have failed to become a source of employment." [2]   The *Spectator* summed up the position in an article headed, " More factories—more pauperism."   An anonymous book, entitled *The Perils of the Nation* (1843), dealing with the industrial conditions, which were supposed to polarise society into a handful of magnates and masses of factory slaves, made a deep impression, particularly upon the leaders of the religious movements. And Gladstone, as vice-president of the Board of Trade, when speaking on the income-tax, frankly declared : " It is one of the most melancholy features in the social state of this country that we see beyond the possibility of denial that while there is at this moment a decrease in the consuming powers of the people, an increase of privation and distress of the labouring and operative classes, there is at the same time an enormous accumulation of wealth in the upper classes, a constant increase of capital." [3]   Finally, the Anti-Corn Law agitators redoubled their activities and roused the people to the miseries brought about by the taxes on bread.[4]   A gloomy social atmosphere was created, which lasted for several years and in which Thomas Hood wrote " The Song of the Shirt," Elizabeth Barrett Browning " The Cry of the Children," Carlyle *Past and Present*, Dickens the Christmas books, Disraeli *Sybil*.   There were many who believed England to be on the brink of a social revolution, whilst others hoped for a moral regeneration through Christianity.

In the midst of this general feeling of despair the hope of securing redemption by means of a general strike was once more revived.   Towards the end of July, 1842, the working men of Ashton, Stalybridge, and Hyde called meetings in order to deliberate on the state of affairs.   Most of the speakers recom-

[1] Charles Bray, Introduction to Mary Hennell's *Outline of Social Systems*, 1844.

[2] *Northern Star*, September 9, 1843.

[3] Hansard's *Parl. Debates*, third series, vol. lxvi., February 14, 1843, p. 480, and R. B. Seeley, *Perils of the Nation*, p. ix.

[4] W. G. Ward, *Ideal of a Christian Church*, 1844, pp. 27-30.   Kingsley, *Letters and Memories*, vol. i., p. 121.

mended a stoppage of work, first of all to prevent any further lowering of wages and then to raise wages again to the level of the year 1839.[1] On August 4 the operatives of Stalybridge joined the strike, and with cheers for the Charter, O'Connor, and the *Northern Star* they marched to Ashton and caused their comrades to join the strike. Marching from place to place they stopped the work of the factories everywhere; the number of the workers on the march grew to form a huge procession, which on August 9 converged upon Manchester. Outside the town they were met by the soldiers commanded by Colonel Wemyss, the successor and friend of Sir Charles Napier. The troops were also accompanied by a magistrate entrusted with the task of reading the Riot Act in case of need. The procession entered Manchester after conversations had been held between Colonel Wemyss and the leaders of the demonstration, who assumed all responsibility for the maintenance of public peace. Here it broke up into groups, proceeding from factory to factory, in order to induce the operatives to take part in the strike. In most cases the operatives willingly joined the strike. Force and intimidation were hardly necessary in Manchester. From Manchester as a centre the strike radiated outwards in all directions, embracing Lancashire, Yorkshire, Warwickshire, Staffordshire, the Potteries, and extended into Wales. At the

[1] Richard Pilling was the organiser of this strike movement. He was born in 1800, the son of a handloom-weaver, and followed his father's trade. He took part in the Peterloo demonstration and became a Radical from that time onward. The handloom was destroyed by the power loom. In 1833 Pilling entered the factory, which he hated from the bottom of his heart. He joined the ten-hour movement, read Cobbett, Sadler, and Oastler, became a trade union agitator and Chartist, and lost his berth in consequence in 1840. In 1841 he obtained work at Ashton, where a successive drop in wages reduced the weekly earnings of an operative to the sum of 7s. In 1842, when a further drop in wages was proposed, he organised strikes in Stalybridge and Ashton, which spread over the whole district and developed into a general strike. In May, 1848, he became a member of the Chartist National Assembly which met in London. On this occasion he related that in August, 1842, the strike funds amounted altogether to only 20s. (*Northern Star*, May 13, 1848).

same time the Scotch miners went on strike.   Even in London
nocturnal meetings were held by the Chartists in Lincoln's Inn
Fields to prepare for the fight.   In the second week of August
Benbow's dream seemed to be coming true.   The boilers grew
cold, furnaces were blown out, power looms ceased humming,
mines were deserted, factory bells were silent—every wheel stood
still.

It was not everywhere, however, that the working men's
holiday started so peacefully as at Manchester.   In many districts men willing to work were dragged by force away from the
workshops, the windows and doors of factories were smashed in,
the plugs of boilers were unscrewed, and manufacturers who
offered resistance were overcome by physical force.   On the
whole, violence was the exception.   Plundering, however, did
not take place anywhere and no property was wantonly
destroyed.   Starving operatives, in a state of civil war, poverty-
stricken insurgents of the working class remained for a whole
week in possession of the richest centre of the textile industry
without laying hands on the smallest article of value.   It was
with expressions of admiration that the leading newspapers
laid stress upon this circumstance.[1]

Conflicts between the strikers and the soldiers occurred at
Preston and Blackburn, where six workmen in all were killed
and several wounded.

A few days after the commencement of the strike the question
of wages passed into the background.   The idea was mooted
that the same exertion that was necessary for obtaining higher
wages would be sufficient to secure the Charter.   And when the
Charter was won, the scale of wages would not only improve, but
would be protected and secured, whilst a successful strike in the
best of cases could only be of a temporary nature.   The working
men argued on the following lines : " Even supposing that we
obtain an improvement in the scale of wages, what means are
then at our disposal for retaining this improvement and securing

---

[1] *Morning Chronicle*, September 27, 1842 ; *Examiner*, August 20,
1842, which quotes the *Times*, the *Manchester Times*, etc., with
reference to this point.

facilities for further action? Our trade unions have failed us. We have spent thousands of pounds for trade unionist purposes, and yet wages continue to fall. But if we obtain the Charter we shall be in possession of political power, with which we should be able to protect the fruits of our labour. Why then should the general strike be restricted to the question of wages?"

This was the opinion of the majority. To be sure, there were speakers at the meetings who opposed any mixing up of politics with the strike. The views of this minority were as follows: "So long as we restrict ourselves to the question of wages we shall possess the sympathy of many of the middle class and of all the friends of labour. We need this sympathy, for we shall not be in a position to protract the strike owing to our lack of funds. But if we make the Charter the main plank in our programme, we shall come into opposition with the Whigs and the Tories and all who are hostile to universal suffrage."

In the heat of the struggle the political and revolutionary idea gained the upper hand over the purely industrial view.

On August 11 and 12 the delegates of the trades of Manchester met in the Carpenters' Hall, and the following resolution was passed after a thorough review of the situation:—

"The trades pledge themselves not to sanction any illegal proceedings. They deprecate the late and present conduct of the employers who are reducing wages and by these means deprive the labourer of the means of subsistence and destroy the home trade; but at the same time we condemn all violence and destruction of property. We are also of opinion that until class legislation is entirely destroyed and the principle of united labour established, the labourer will not be in a position to enjoy the full fruit of his labours. It is the opinion of this meeting that the People's Charters contain the elements of justice and prosperity, and we pledge ourselves never to relinquish our demands until that demand becomes the law of the land."

This resolution of the leaders of the trades at Manchester

allows of no misunderstanding ; it demands democracy and socialism ; it declares for the People's Charter and for united or collective production.

On August 12 they issued the following appeal, which was printed in large red type and brought to the notice of the working men of Manchester by being placarded on the walls :—

" Justice, Peace, Law and Order !

" We, the delegates of all the various trades, having been duly and legally elected by our various trades, have again met in solemn conference, empowered by our constituents to watch over and to guard the interests of the people, do most earnestly implore you not to be led astray by the machinations of your enemies, but remain firm in your purpose to uphold your just rights, as set forth in the Carpenters' Hall on the 11th and 12th inst. We call upon you to be prompt in the election of your delegates to the great Delegate Conference which will be held on Monday, August 15.

" We most solemnly pledge ourselves to persevere in our exertions until we achieve the complete emancipation of our brethren of the working classes from the thraldom of monopoly and class legislation by the legal establishment of the People's Charter. The trades of Great Britain carried the Reform Bill. The trades of Great Britain shall carry the Charter."

On August 15 over 100 delegates from Lancashire and Yorkshire met at the large conference. Their mandates were examined with the utmost strictness, and only those were considered valid which were drawn up in the prescribed form by recognised trade organisations. Outside the hall of the conference thousands of workmen held meetings, but were dispersed by military patrols. The delegates sat until August 16, and were interrupted in their deliberations by the magistrates. The main subject of discussion was the question whether the general strike should retain its original character as a matter of wages or whether it should be transformed into a fight for the Charter. Most of the delegates held limited mandates ; only nineteen were instructed to vote with the majority in the question between wages and the Charter. The great majority of the speakers were in favour of the Charter, but there was very little deliberation devoted to the means for carrying out the general strike. The most ardent and eloquent of the speakers declared for the Charter ; a calm consideration of the general strike as a political weapon was rendered impossible not only by the excitement of the conflicts, but also by the pressure which the authorities exerted on the workers by the display of military force. The conference of the delegates was a replica of the general Convention of 1839. The belief in the power of universal enthusiasm proved stronger than any references to the necessity for long preparations. Two resolutions were proposed : one for keeping the wages question to the fore, the other for transforming the general strike into a fight for the Charter. Only seven delegates voted for maintaining the wages question of the general strike, whilst 58+19 voted for transforming the general strike into a national fight for the Charter. The 19 were the delegates already referred to, who had been instructed to vote with the majority.

Immediately after the adoption of the Chartist resolution the chairman of the conference issued the following appeal :—

" To the Trades of Manchester and surrounding districts.

" We hasten to lay before you the paramount importance of the day's proceedings. The delegates from the surrounding districts have been more numerous at this day's meeting than they were at yesterday's ; and the spirit of determination manifested for the people's rights has increased every hour. In consequence of the unjust and unconstitutional interference of the magistrates our proceedings were abruptly brought to a close by their dispersing the meeting, but not until in their very teeth we passed the following resolution :

" ' The delegates in public meeting assembled do recommend to the various constituencies which we represent to adopt all legal means to carry into effect the People's Charter. And further we recommend that delegates be sent to the whole of the country to endeavour to obtain the co-operation of the middle and working classes in carrying out the resolution of ceasing labour until the Charter be the law of the land.'

" Englishmen ! Legally determine to maintain the peace

and the well-being of the country, and show, by the strict adherence to our resolutions, that we are your representatives.

"ALEXANDER HUTCHINSON.
"CHARLES STUART.

"Manchester, *August* 16, 1842."

The general strike, the excitement it involved, and the disturbance of the public peace were not confined to Lancashire and Yorkshire. At the same time many miners in Scotland went on strike, and likewise in Staffordshire, where Thomas Cooper made a tour for the purpose of agitation. In the latter district serious disturbances broke out after one of Cooper's speeches, and were accompanied by the destruction of property and by incendiarism. His speeches he later summarised in the following stanzas :—

> " Slaves, toil no more !   Why delve, and moil, and pine,
>   To glut the tyrant-forgers of your chain ?
>   Slaves, toil no more !   Up from the midnight mine,
>   Summon your swarthy thousands to the plain ;
>   Beneath the bright sun marshalled, swell the strain
>   Of liberty ; and while the lordlings view
>   Your banded hosts, with stricken heart and brain,—
>   Shout as one man, ' Toil we no more renew,
> Until the Many cease their slavery to the Few !
>   We'll crouch, and toil, and weave, no more—to weep ! '
>   Exclaim your brothers from the weary loom :—
>   Yea, now they swear with one resolve dread, deep—
>   ' We'll toil no more—to win a pauper's doom ! '
>   And, while the millions swear, fell Famine's gloom
>   Spreads from their haggard faces, like a cloud,
>   Big with the fear and darkness of the tomb :—
>   How, 'neath its terrors, are the tyrants bowed !
> Slaves, toil no more—to starve !   Go forth and tame
>   the Proud ! "[1]

In the meantime a monument in commemoration of Henry Hunt was to be unveiled in Manchester on August 16, 1842, on the anniversary of Peterloo. For months preparations had

[1] Thomas Cooper, *Purgatory of Suicides*, 1845.

been made for this event. The Chartist organisations had elected delegates for this purpose, who intended to utilise this opportunity to deliberate on the state of the agitation, and especially on the dissensions which had arisen in the movement. The delegates were more than forty in number and met in Manchester on August 16. They were amazed at the appearance of the " town of the high chimneys." The stoppage of work was universal. " Not a single mill at work ! " exclaimed John Campbell, the secretary of the N.C.A. " Something must come out of this, and something serious too ! " [1]

On August 17 the Chartist delegates met secretly in a chapel. The original agenda of the conference, viz., the unveiling of the monument to Hunt and the dissensions in the movement, were dropped in order to discuss the new trade unionist struggle for the Charter. Most of the delegates were eager for an immediate mobilisation of the people. The declaration of the conference of the trades' delegates aroused indescribable enthusiasm among the Chartists.[2] They fully believed that " the time had come for trying, successfully, to paralyse the government." [3]

After the delegates had handed in their reports, M'Douall rose and proposed on behalf of the committee that the conference should identify itself with the resolutions of the trades, and that the general strike should be encouraged until the Charter had passed into law. Cooper seconded the motion, since the general strike could not fail to lead to a national struggle. A peaceful general strike was an impossibility, for the forces of the government would make an attempt to suppress and to persecute the strikers, and this could only be countered by the armed opposition of the people. The Chartists must now mobilise the masses of the people and render them irresistible. Several delegates spoke to the same effect as Cooper, thanking him for having expressed their secret thoughts. O'Connor opposed the motion . . . " We are not met here to talk about fighting. We are met to consider and approve the resolution of the trades."

[1] Thomas Cooper, *Life*, p. 206.
[2] Bronterre O'Brien in *British Statesman*, August 20, 1842.
[3] Thomas Cooper, *Life*, p. 208.

William Hill, the editor of the *Northern Star*, spoke against both Cooper and O'Connor :—

" I wonder that so a clear an intellect as Cooper's should dream of fighting. Fighting !—the people have nothing to fight with, and would be mown down by artillery if they attempted to fight. The strike has originated with the Anti-Corn Law League,[1] and we should simply be their tools if we helped to extend or prolong the strike. It could only spread disaster and suffering. I move an amendment that we entirely disapprove of it."

He was followed by Richard Otley, of Sheffield :—

" How could poor, starving weavers be expected to fight ? If we endeavoured to form battalions for fighting, the people would need food and clothing—they would need arms and powder and shot ; they would very likely have to bivouac in the fields— anyhow could poor weavers be expected to do that ? It would kill them in a few days."

Even Harney, our old friend of the *London Democrat*, the admirer of Marat, the friend of Major Beniowski, expressed himself against the policy of physical force.

When the vote was taken Hill's amendment received only six votes. The conference therefore resolved to range itself completely on the side of the trades, and passed the following resolution :—

" Whilst the Chartist body did not originate the present cessation from labour, the conference of delegates from various parts of England express their deep sympathy with their con- stituents, the working men now on strike, and that we strongly approve the extension and continuance of the present struggle till the People's Charter becomes a legislative enactment, and decide forthwith to issue an address to that effect, and pledge ourselves on our return to our respective localities to give a proper direction to the people's efforts."

[1] It was customary for Hill to ascribe everything to the free trade agitation ; he saw its influence everywhere, just as Cobden ascribed all his difficulties to the action of the Chartists and their alleged aristocratic supporters.

The conference issued not merely one address but two ; one was couched in fairly moderate language and signed by the executive ; the other was anonymous and was drawn up on the lines of the policy of physical force and insurrection.

The passing of the resolution and the issue of the addresses brought the action of the Chartist leaders to a close.

Was the position they adopted the right one ? Does it justify the conclusion that the Chartist leaders understood the significance of the situation ?

Let us examine the state of affairs. The industrial and commercial centres of the Midlands and the North of England were in a state of insurrection ; Scotland, Wales, and London could easily be mobilised, no longer for purely trade unionist purposes, but in support of the Chartist programme. The trade unions, the operatives, the working men of the whole country followed the standard of Chartism. What was, under these circumstances, O'Connor's duty and that of his lieutenants ? Their duty was to take over the supreme command. How often had not O'Connor said that he was ready to conquer or to die ? And could he hope for any more favourable opportunity of turning words into deeds ? The Midlands and North of England, Scotland, and Wales were waiting for their leader's word of command. But what did the leader do ? Absolutely nothing. He left all initiative to the people and returned to London. The throwing down of his weapons can only be interpreted as indicating that he foresaw the failure of the general strike. In this case it was clearly his duty to have supported Hill's resolution. There were only two alternatives : either Cooper was right or Hill. And since he did not share Cooper's views, it was his duty as leader to tell the people in explicit terms that they should adhere strictly to the question of wages, as they were not ready for an insurrection. And he should also have communed with himself and avowed that the whole policy of insurrection was a mistaken policy ; for, if it was impotent in the case of a national rising of the working men, it must inevitably be completely nugatory in the case of a partial rising.

I K

In the fourth week of August, 1842, the strike was obviously on the wane. Abandoned by their leaders, who dispersed; persecuted by the authorities, who made wholesale arrests; oppressed by misery, which was rendered more acute by the strike, the workmen gradually returned to the factories, but even at the end of September the strike still possessed a partial character. The whole moral advantage of the strike fell to the share of the Anti-Corn Law League, for many Whigs and Tories could no longer resist the conclusion that the people must be afforded cheaper means of subsistence in order to render it possible for them to make both ends meet with the low scale of wages.

The climax of Chartism was the commencement of the victorious career of free trade, but not of Chartism. Three and a half years later the Tory government introduced the Bill for the abolition of the Corn Laws, and on this occasion Sir James Graham, the Home Secretary, remarked :—

" We had the painful and lamentable experience of 1842—a year of the greatest distress, and now that it is passed, I may say, of the utmost danger. What were the circumstances of 1842 ? Allow me just to glance at them. We had in this metropolis, at midnight, Chartist meetings assembled in Lincoln's Inn Fields. Immense masses of people, greatly discontented and acting in a spirit dangerous to the public peace. . . . What was the condition of Lancashire ? . . . All the machinery was stopped. . . . It was my painful duty to consult with the Horse Guards almost daily as to the precautions that were necessary for the maintenance of the public peace. For some time troops were continually called on, in different parts of the manufacturing districts, to maintain public tranquillity. . . . For three months the anxiety which I and my colleagues experienced was greater than we ever felt before with reference to public affairs. . . ." [1]

The ministers who had been converted to free trade justified in this manner the change of their opinion.

[1] Hansard's *Parliamentary Debates*, February, 1846, vol. 83, p. 718 and *sqq.*

This was the state of affairs in August, September, and October, 1842, and O'Connor and his lieutenants left the working men in the lurch. O'Connor went to London to elaborate the plans for his so-called agrarian reform. M'Douall took to flight, and the remainder also did nothing, whilst O'Brien and Lovett were cut off from the working classes and were unable to express any effective criticism in opposition to O'Connor.

2.—TRIALS AND DISORGANISATION

Wholesale arrests on a larger scale than during the blackest period of the Whig government followed closely upon the retreat of the Chartist leaders and the failure of the strike. Arrest or arraignment was the lot of every leader or speaker among the Chartists or trade unionists, and of every working man suspected of complicity in the strike movement. An exact list of arrested men cannot be drawn up owing to the disorganisation of the Chartist press.

An estimate of 1,500 will not be far from the mark. About 800 were either released after a short space of time or sentenced in the police-courts, whilst 710 were tried at the assizes in York, Lancaster, Stafford, Chester, and Liverpool. The list of accused persons comprised working men differing most widely in age, from youths of 15 years up to an old man of 101 years! In October, 1842, about 651 prisoners appeared before the juries. Of this number only 125 were acquitted ; the remainder received sentences of imprisonment varying from a few months up to two years, whilst 79 were sentenced to transportation to the penal settlements in Australia. O'Connor and 58 of his comrades, comprising Hill, Harney, and Cooper, appeared only in March, 1843, before the assizes in Lancaster. By this time the dread of the general strike had been nearly forgotten, and both judges and juries gave milder sentences. Twenty-six of the accused were found not guilty, whilst the remainder received no more than the verdict of guilty; for the Court of Appeal, owing to a flaw in the indictment, quashed the trial, and no further proceedings were taken.[1] With the exception of M'Douall,

[1] Thomas Cooper was not so fortunate. After having been

who had taken to flight, O'Connor's fellow-prisoners comprised all those who had taken part in the Chartist conference of August 16, as well as the trade unionist leader, Richard Pilling who had started the strike in Stalybridge and Ashton. [1]

O'Connor conducted his defence with great skill, especially by his attack on the witnesses for the Crown, Griffin and Cartledge former Chartists who had entered the service of the prosecuting authorities.

Pilling's speech in defence was distinguished from all the rest by a particularly impressive description of the misery prevailing among the working men in 1841 and 1842.   He drew so harrowing a picture of the moral and domestic misery that followed in the train of the economic distress that he moved the jury and the court of justice to tears.   The public prosecutor left the court in order to conceal his emotion. [2]   After this speech neither judge nor jury could any longer shut their eyes to the fact that it was only the frightful misery that was responsible for the excesses during the strike, and that on the whole the workmen had displayed much patience and self-control.

Indications of the disorganisation of Chartism became apparent even in the autumn of 1842, that is to say immediately after the collapse of the general strike.   The prosecutions delayed the process of disorganisation to some extent, but after the assizes in March, 1843, the number of organised Chartists dropped to three or four thousand.

The circulation of the *Northern Star* steadily diminished, whilst misunderstandings increased daily among the leaders. The remnant of organised Chartism rallied round O'Connor, who embodied the movement.   In December, 1842, William Hill, the editor of the *Northern Star*, accused the whole executive of having been corrupted.   O'Connor took up the cudgels on behalf of the leaders, and appointed George Julian Harney to be assistant

acquitted, together with the 58 other defendants, he was sentenced to two years' imprisonment on account of his seditious speeches in Staffordshire.

[1] See *supra*, footnote, Part III., p. 141.

[2] *State Trials*, New Series, 1839 to 1843, vol. 4, p. 1097 and *sqq*.

editor. On July 8, 1843, Hill was dismissed and J. Hobson and Harney took over the editorial management.

There was now no end of tale-bearing. It was a crime to associate with a free trader; it was worse than a crime to express praise of Lovett and O'Brien. Treachery was suspected on all sides, and spies were continually on the look out for traitors.[1] The treasury of the National Charter Association was empty. O'Connor became the dispenser of funds, partly out of his own pocket, and partly from the considerable entrance fees and the collections which were made at his meetings. The most unmistakable sign of the apathy which had spread among the working class in the centres of industry was, however, the decision early in 1844 to remove the *Northern Star* to London. In subsequent years the trade unions still utilised the *Northern Star* for their appeals and communications, because it was considered to be the best source of information and the trade unions were still without a press of their own, but their minds were fast moving away from revolutionary experiments to the organisation of prosaic trade societies and co-operative stores.

In the meantime there was no lack of attempts at reorganisation. A conference of thirty delegates was held in Birmingham from September 5 to 8, 1843, in order to discuss a new plan of organisation, which proceeded from O'Connor, with the object of combining Chartism with agrarian reform. The two principal tasks which were now imposed upon the movement were to obtain the Charter and to found agricultural settlements. The delegate Marsden, one of the members of the General Convention of 1839. was present and protested against the attempt to buy land, since such a procedure would imply the recognition of the fact that the ground landlords had a right of possession, which had hitherto been regarded as a mere usurpation. The conference, however, decided in favour of the plan of organisation. A short discussion was also evoked by another point in the plan of organisation by which the lecturers should be appointed by the executive instead of leaving them in the hands of local committees. Marsden was of opinion it should never be forgotten

---

[1] *Northern Star*, April 27, 1844; December 28, 1844.

that there were two currents in the movement—the physical force and the moral force party. If the executive had to make the appointments of the lecturers, it would only appoint the lecturers who shared the same views as the executive. The conference, however, considered the former system to be prejudicial and voted for the new plan. This plan of organisation could not, however, be put into force, as the Chief Registrar declared it to be illegal.

At the conference held in the following year at Manchester, from April 22 to 26, 45 delegates were present for the purpose of deliberating upon a new plan of organisation. It was kept quite free from any agrarian reform, and its sole object was to consolidate the forces of Chartism. The *Northern Star* belauded this conference because the speeches were short, impartial and free from all irritating personalities. The new plan of organisation was adopted, but the mass of the Chartists kept aloof from the organisation, for their confidence in their leaders had been shattered.

In November, 1844, the editorial and publishing offices of the *Northern Star* were moved to London, where it came in touch with the international revolutionary movement through the political and communist refugees of the Continent. This does not indeed apply to O'Connor, who henceforth not only resisted new ideas, but gradually broke away from his traditions of agrarian revolution and became absorbed in experiments for turning the Chartists into small holders and peasants.

3.—O'CONNOR'S PLAN OF AGRARIAN REFORM

The years 1843 to 1845 signalised the decline of Chartism. Two events contributed especially to this result, viz., the collapse of the general strike of August, 1842, and the failure of the Owenite colony, Queenwood, in the summer of 1845. The first of these events broke the back of the movement in the North of England. Chartism as an ideal was indeed venerated by the people for a long time afterwards, but it remained, so to speak, in the air, because it had proved to be unserviceable as a policy in the field of operations. The second event deprived the Socialists of their last belief in the possibility of realising their ultimate aim. The most sanguine hopes of the Socialists of Great Britain had been bound up with the Queenwood colony. From 1842 they had watched its progress with eager anticipation. At first everything went swimmingly, so long as funds were in hand; and the *Northern Star* pointed with pride to the progress of Socialist production. When this last refuge of Owenite experiments had fallen to pieces, all belief in Socialism was abandoned.

O'Connor's falling away from agrarian Socialism is clearly revealed in the columns of the *Northern Star*. " In agitation," he explained, " there are three stages, viz. (1) the creation of public opinion; (2) the organisation of this opinion; (3) the direction of this opinion towards definite aims." For years he had worked for agrarian reform, now the time was ripe for organising adherents to agrarian reform. But what shape was this reform to take ? O'Connor replied :—

" Deposits to the amount of £207,270 lie in the savings banks of Leeds and its environs. We call upon the depositors to withdraw these deposits and to invest them in one of Owen's communistic colonies."[1]

Four years later he wrote in a similar strain.[2] And again in the early part of 1845 he exclaimed :—

" The land belongs to the people. It is the people's heritage. Kings, princes, lords, and citizens have stolen it from the people. The law of nature is on the side of the people. Usurpation is the work of the rich and powerful."

O'Connor now worked at the realisation of his agrarian plan. The agrarian plan received three titles in succession : (1) Chartist Co-operative Land Society ; (2) National Co-operative Land Company ; (3) National Land Company. This backsliding from Chartism and socialism to company promoting was completed between 1845 and 1846. In 1847 he already explicitly declared in so many words : " Peasant proprietorship is the best basis of

[1] *Northern Star*, June 16, 1838.
[2] *English Chartist Circular*, 1842, Nos. 68 and 69.

society." [1]   And he built upon this basis his Land Reform Joint Stock Company, which drew in and frittered away not less than £100,000 from Chartists, working men, and other reformers.

We can treat the history of these experiments in small holdings in a very brief manner, for it represented only an episode in the process of dissolution of the Chartist and Owenite period. A Chartist conference assembled in London in the fourth week of April, 1845. There were altogether only fifteen delegates present, including the members of the executive. The most important business of the conference was the founding of the Chartist Co-operative Land Society, with the following programme :—

Object : To purchase land on which to locate its members, in order to demonstrate to the working classes of the kingdom, firstly, the value of the land as a means of making them independent of the grinding capitalist ; and, secondly, to show them the necessity of securing the speedy enactment of the People's Charter, which would do for them nationally what the society proposes to do sectionally ; the accomplishment of the political and social emancipation of the enslaved and degraded working classes being the prominent object of the society.

Means : Good arable land may be rented in some of the most fertile parts of the country at the rate of 15s. per acre, and might be bought at 25 years' purchase, that is, £18 15s. per acre. And supposing £5,000 be raised, this sum would purchase 120 acres and locate 60 persons with two acres each, leaving a balance of £2,750 for building cottages, buying stock, etc. These allotments, with dwellings, might be leased for ever to the members of the society, at an annual rental of £5 each. The gross annual rental would thus be £300. The property, if sold at 20 years' purchase, would fetch £6,000, which sum, if expended in a similar manner to the first, would locate 72 persons ; these 72 allotments, sold at the rate of the first, would bring £7,200, and this sum, laid out in the purchase of other land, cottages, stock, etc., would locate 86 persons. This, sold again, would produce, at the original price, £8,600 ; with this capital the society could locate

---

[1] *The Labourer,* 1847, II., 149 ; *Reports on the National Land Company,* 1848, p. 172.

103 persons. These 103 persons would produce £10,317, and would locate 123 persons. Thus the original capital of £5,000 would more than double itself at the fourth sale ; and so in the same ratio, until the tenth sale would produce £37,324, which, if the project be taken up with spirit, might easily be effected in four years, and there would be 1,923 persons located with allotments of two acres. In the space of a few years a vast number of the " surplus labour population " could be placed in happiness and prosperity upon the soil of their native land.[1]

Shares were to be issued in order to raise the sum of £5,000 ; and a land bank was to be established for the purpose of enabling the members to purchase allotments, to deposit their savings and to obtain loans for trading purposes.

At first O'Connor attempted to register the Land Society as a friendly society, and he assured his readers that the Registrar of Friendly Societies could not refuse to register it ; if indeed he dared to refuse to do so he would be called to account. Nevertheless the registrar absolutely refused to register it on the grounds that the Land Society possessed the characteristics of a political society. O'Connor then attempted to bring his society within the range of the Joint Stock Company law, but the cost of registration was relatively high, for the fees for stamps and registering amounted to about £4 for every 100 shareholders, and the enrolment of members in O'Connor's colonising society was surprisingly rapid : from 1846 to the beginning of 1848 not less than 75,000 working men and Chartists joined the society. Every member had to take up on the average three shares of 26s. each and to pay for them by instalments. £96,000 pounds came in up to the early part of 1848 ! But owing to the fact that the society, which then already bore the name of National Land Company, was only provisionally registered, it possessed no legal status. The Chartists, however, did not trouble much about the illegality of their plan of emancipation and waited for O'Connor's Apocalypse. Violent attacks on the business management of the land reform venture were not lacking. Since there was no legal control and balance-sheets

[1] *Northern Star*, April 26 and May 3, 1845.

were published either in an incomplete form or at irregular intervals, there was ample material for hostile criticism on the part of O'Connor's opponents, among whom Thomas Cooper took a prominent position.[1] Yet the working men continued to stick to their old leader with his many plans, in spite of the fact that the results of his plan of reform were remarkably insignificant. During the two years when the fortunes of the land reform were in a flourishing condition only 230 persons out of the 75,000 shareholders were located on the land. An allotment comprised three acres on an average, and cost £300, including buildings, implements and stock. If it takes two years to locate 230 persons, how many years will be required to locate 75,000 persons ? Obviously 652 years. And if an allotment costs £300, how much will 75,000 allotments cost ? Obviously 22·5 million pounds sterling !

The Utopian character of O'Connor's plan could have been demonstrated by simple multiplication and division. Nevertheless the working men could not be induced to probe into O'Connor's plan. In June, 1848, parliament appointed a select committee to examine into the affairs of the National Land Company. O'Connor was elected a member of the committee. The investigation revealed a confused and extremely imperfect state of the account books, and two book-keepers and mathematicians appointed by the committee had to take a great amount of trouble and to make lengthy investigations before they could give a general outline of the state of the business. The committee adopted the following resolution as its final finding :—

" The books of proceeding of the National Land Company as well as the accounts of the company have been most imperfectly kept, and the original balance-sheets have been destroyed, and only three of them (from the end of September, 1847, to the end of March, 1848) have been produced ; but Mr. F. O'Connor having expressed an opinion that an impression had gone abroad that the moneys subscribed by the National Land Company had been applied to his own benefit, this committee are clearly of opinion that, although the accounts have not been kept with strict

[1] *Northern Star*, June 20, 1846.

egularity, yet the irregularity has been against Mr. O'Connor's interests, instead of in his favour, and that it appears there is due to Mr. O'Connor the sum of between £3,298 and £3,400. Considering that the company appears to have been carried on *bona fide*, it is the opinion of the committee that powers might be granted to the parties concerned to wind up the concern and to relieve them from the penalties to which they might have incautiously exposed themselves."[1]

The publication of these reports brought O'Connor's career to an end. The spell was broken, but a contributory cause to this result was the last London demonstration of April 10, 1848, to which we shall soon turn our attention, after making our acquaintance with some of the new men who entered the movement about this period.

4.—NEW LEADERS

During the last phase of Chartism several men came into notice who deserve a closer acquaintance. The most prominent among them was Ernest Charles Jones (1819-1869), born of British parentage in Berlin and educated in Lüneburg and London. After having been called to the Bar, he, in 1845, joined the Chartist movement. He was essentially a democratic poet and emotional social reformer. At first he came under the influence of O'Connor, was his co-editor of *The Labourer* and *Northern Star*. Since about 1850 to 1855 he learned a good deal from Karl Marx, unfortunately at a time when the latter, smarting under the defeat of the German and French revolutions of 1848, was too embittered to be able to think impartially. This influence is particularly noticeable in Jones's *Notes to the People* (1850-51) and in the first years of his *People's Paper*. And Jones himself, after his two years' prison (1848-50), to which he had been condemned in July, 1848, on account of his insurrectionary agitation, was in the same mood as his German friend. His political and social reform writings are of no importance. On the other hand, among his poems there are some of abiding value. The following is one of the best :—

[1] *Reports on the National Land Company, VI. Report,* 1848.

THE SONG OF THE LOWER CLASSES.

1.

" We plough and sow—we're so very, very low
That we delve in the dirty clay
Till we bless the plain—with the golden grain,
And the vale with fragrant hay.
Our place we know—we're so very low
'Tis down at the landlord's feet,
We're not too low—the bread to grow,
But too low the bread to eat.

2.

" Down, down we go—we're so very, very low,
To the hell of deep-sunk mines,
But we gather the proudest gems that glow
When the crown of the despot shines.
And whenever he lacks—upon our backs
Fresh loads he deigns to lay :
We're far too low to vote the tax,
But not too low to pay.

3.

" We're low, we're low—mere rabble, we know,
But at our plastic power,
The mould at the lordling's feet will grow
Into palace and church and tower—
Then prostrate fall—in the rich men's hall
And cringe at the rich man's door :
We're not too low to build the wall,
But too low to tread the floor.

4.

" We're low—we're low—we're very, very low,
Yet from our fingers glide
The silken flow—and the robes that glow
Round the limbs of the sons of pride.
And what we get—and what we give
We know, and we know our share :
We're not too low the cloth to weave,
But too low the cloth to wear."

A man of a different mentality was George Jacob Holyoake (1817—1906)—logical, rationalist, and essentially Liberal. He was rather an unattached Chartist, but he exercised some influence on the movement by his lectures and writings. He entered the Chartist ranks on the decline of Owenism and brought with him the idea of class solidarity and the conviction of the necessity for the working classes to co-operate with the Liberal party. He was one of the few working class leaders who saw that the ideas underlying Chartism were much too advanced for a nation which was just emerging from the domination of the landed interests. He felt that long years of triumphant Liberalism were required to prepare the minds of the people for democracy. Holyoake was acquainted with all the leading political refugees who found asylum in London, except with Marx and Engels.

The third man worth mentioning is Samuel Kydd (" Alfred "), who, in 1857, published a *History of the Factory Movement.* He was a Scotch shoemaker, who from 1846 onwards became prominent as a lecturer and writer. After the extinction of Chartism he studied law and was called to the Bar.

VIII

THE FINAL FLICKER AND EXTINCTION

I.—PARLIAMENTARY ELECTIONS OF 1847

FROM 1843 to 1847 Chartism only showed slight signs of life sometimes indeed barely perceptible. In 1844 O'Connor consoled his adherents and expressed the opinion that " Chartism is not dead, but sleeping."[1] And its sleep lasted until the middle of 1847, but it was the French February revolution that set it once again upon its legs.[2] Two events contributed to revive it in the year 1847, viz., in the first place, the parliamentary elections of the summer of 1847, which followed the victory of the free trade agitation, and, secondly, the agitation of the continental refugees in London.

In 1846 the Conservative leader, Sir Robert Peel, was converted to free trade, and obtained a majority in parliament for his new commercial policy. Strange to say, Peel's conversion was hailed as a wise, statesmanlike act by O'Connor and the *Northern Star*, which had always opposed the Anti-Corn Law League down to the end of 1845. O'Connor merely remarked that " free trade without free representation is sure to lead to revolution."[3] Peel's conversion demoralised the Conservative party, which had been in power since 1841; parliament was dissolved and new elections followed in July and August, 1847. The Chartists put forward several candidates, but they were only nominated, with the exception of O'Connor in Nottingham and Ernest Jones in Halifax. O'Connor formed an alliance with the

[1] *Northern Star*, July 27, 1844.
[2] *Ibid.*, April 1 and September 9, 1848.
[3] *Northern Star*, September 19, 1846. (This is an interesting number ; it contains a long account by O'Connor on the History of Chartism from 1836 to 1846.)

Conservatives in Nottingham and was elected, to the surprise of all.

The only other noteworthy candidate was George Julian Harney. Harney managed to be nominated at Tiverton in opposition to Lord Palmerston. From 1830 Palmerston had been regarded as the enemy of all freedom, more especially of oppressed nations, and as the servant of the Tsar. Harney now went down to his constituency and became a candidate in order to denounce Palmerston on the hustings, where all the candidates delivered their election addresses on the day of nomination. He spoke with much eloquence. Palmerston followed him in a speech of three hours' duration, taking Harney very seriously. When the vote was taken by show of hands, Harney obtained a majority, but he did not go to the polls, so that Palmerston was finally elected.

During these elections Robert Owen ran as a candidate for Marylebone with a programme of political reform. He was, however, only a nomination candidate, and received a considerable number of votes. One of Owen's political demands at this election was the substitution of a militia for the standing army. He was no anti-militarist, and in this he followed the earlier British Socialists and social reformers, like Sir Thomas More, Gerard Winstanley, and Thomas Spence. The only prominent anti-militarist was William Godwin ; but he was an anarchist, who believed that reason was the only legitimate and effective weapon ; and, therefore, condemned all force and struggle, either of individuals or classes and nations.

2.—CHARTISM AND THE INTERNATIONALS

In September, 1844, the idea arose among the German, Polish, and Italian refugees in London of founding a society to familiarise the English public with their aspirations. The society was started and was called the Society of Fraternal Democrats. Their place of meeting was at the German Communist Working Men's Club, which at that time held its meetings in Drury Lane. In 1845, at the request of Karl Schapper and the Pole, Louis Oborski, William Lovett drew up an appeal to the

Chartists to join the Fraternal Democrats. Harney, Jones, Cooper and others joined the society, and the *Northern Star* published at regular intervals accounts of its activity, giving full reports of the lectures that were delivered at its meetings. It used to celebrate the anniversaries of the French revolution and of the Polish insurrections, and discussions were held on European politics. The reports of these meetings introduced the Chartists into international politics, and they became a section of the revolutionary movement if Europe. Mazzini was active in a similar direction, but he never entered into any intimate relations with the Chartists who rallied round the *Northern Star*. Karl Schapper, a German revolutionary, was held in great esteem by the Chartists. Friedrich Engels stood in high favour with the intellectual section of the Chartists. From 1843 he was acquainted with the editors of the *Northern Star*. From 1845 he wrote for the paper at intervals about German affairs. In the summer of 1846 we read for the first time of the relations between Karl Marx and the Chartists. O'Connor had fought an unsuccessful by-election in Nottingham, whereupon the German Communists, living as refugees in Belgium, instructed Marx Engels, and Gigot to congratulate the Chartist leader on his fight. The writers praised the attitude of the *Northern Star* to British politics ; they told the British workmen that the real battle was between capital and labour, between the middle and the working classes, and that O'Connor and his organ fully appreciated these facts. The letter is dated Brussels, July 17, 1846 and published in the *Northern Star* of July 25. In November 1847, Marx and Engels came to London to attend the Congress of the Communists, and were commissioned to draw up the famous *Communist Manifesto*. At the same date a Chartist public meeting was held to commemorate the anniversary of the Polish insurrection of 1830. Among the speakers were Harney Jones, Marx, Engels, and Kydd. When the Polish business had been disposed of, the Fraternal Democrats directed their attention to working class politics. In a speech, delivered in German Marx declared :—

" I have been sent by the Brussels Democrats to speak with

the Democrats of London to call on them to cause to be holden *a Congress of Nations*—a Congress of working men, to establish liberty all over the world.   The middle classes, the free traders, held a congress in Brussels, but their fraternity was one-sided, and the moment they found that such congresses were likely to benefit the working men, that moment their fraternity would cease and dissolve.   The Democrats of Belgium and the Chartists of England were the real Democrats, and the moment they carried the six points of their Charter the road to liberty would be opened for the world.   Effect this grand object, you workmen of England, and you will be hailed as the saviours of the whole human race."[1]

By means of these inter-relations the readers of the Chartist newspapers were swept into the current of the European revolutionary tide and into the events of 1848.

At the same time the Chartists declared solidly in favour of the Irish revolutionists.   Chartist speakers were sent to Dublin, and in return Irishmen appeared at Chartist meetings and demonstrations.

A revolutionary International was in the course of formation. It was owing to this state of feeling that the *Northern Star* forgot all previous experience and wrote on January 1, 1848 :—" Moral force is moral humbug, unless there is physical force behind it." The Chartists understood the hint, and the old game of drilling and buying weapons began again in secret.   The enthusiasm of the Chartists, wrote the *Times* of March 28, grew to the same dimensions and heat as in the years 1839 and 1842.

Whilst these preparations were in progress news came of the outbreak of the French revolution in February, 1848.   A wave of feverish enthusiasm swept the ranks of the working men. Meetings and demonstrations were held all over the country. None of the halls in London were large enough to hold the masses who wished to attend the meetings.   Crowds assembled in the open air on Clerkenwell Green, Kennington Common, and in Trafalgar Square, etc., to hear the Chartist leaders and to adopt their proposals.   Serious breaches of the peace occurred

[1] *Northern Star* December 4, 1847.

in the provinces ; in Glasgow the unemployed marched through the streets shouting, " Bread or revolution ! " In Manchester crowds surrounded the workhouse and demanded the liberation of the inmates. In Bridgeton the soldiers fired on the working men and shot down several of them. Naturally, plenty of the usual Addresses to the French people were forthcoming. Harney and W. J. Linton [1] took Addresses over to Paris.

For the purpose of rallying the Chartists and estimating their strength, the committee of the National Charter Association resolved to present a petition to parliament for the introduction of the Charter and to get it widely signed. A National Convention had to be convoked, on the old lines, in order to superintend and to bring in the petition. But the government also adopted its former system of employing spies, concentrating soldiers, and swearing in special constables.

3.—THE PETITION AND APRIL 10, 1848

On April 1 O'Connor published the following appeal to the Chartists :—

" Onward, and we conquer,
Backward, and we fall !
The People's Charter and No Surrender !

" Old Guards ! As I believe in my soul that the time has now arrived when we are entitled to the fruits of our thirteen years' labour, I call upon you to perform that duty which your own order, ' the fustian jackets, the blistered hands and unshorn chins,' expect from your hands. It is impossible, as it would be immoral, that the labouring classes of England, the most oppressed of any country in the world, should allow the present manifestation of their order throughout the world to pass unnoticed or unimproved by them. . . . I would rather die than give up one particle of the Charter. Still, remember that our movement

[1] Linton was born in London in 1812. He was well known as a wood-engraver and a poet. His wife was Lynn Linton, the authoress of *Joshua Davidson*. He had taken part in the Chartist agitation since 1838. Walter Crane, the painter and socialist, was an apprentice in Linton's workshop.

is a labour movement, originated in the first instance by the fustian jackets, the blistered hands and the unshorn chins. Further, I would not give a fig for the Charter if we were not prepared with a solid, social system to take the place of the artificial one which we mean to destroy ; and it was good that we did not succeed earlier with the Charter, before we were ready with the new social system. Look at France ; the great trouble of the Provisional Government is the organisation of labour. And so will it be in Prussia, where the people are rejoicing over their victory over Frederick Wilhelm IV., while the latter is really laying the foundation for a stronger military power. But in addition to the Charter we have land reform, which will give bread to the working men when the Charter is carried. The Charter and the Land ! Those are our objects. Protect us in our work, People of England ! Sign the Petition ! "

At the same time O'Connor drew up a constitution of a peasant and democratic republic. He secretly hoped to become the first president of the republic. He told the Chartists that his uncle, Arthur O'Connor, who had been living in exile in Paris for fifty years, had an excellent prospect of being made president of the French republic, and that one of his brothers was prime minister of a South American republic.

There is hardly an article or a speech by O'Connor in the whole of the *Northern Star* that is so characteristic of his mode of thought or of his personal attributes as his manifesto of April 1, 1848, which has just been quoted. The date is, however, ominous.

On April 3, 42 Chartist delegates to the Convention assembled in an Owenite hall in John Street, Tottenham Court Road, for the purpose of considering the state of affairs and of taking charge of the petition which was to be taken and submitted to parliament by a vast procession on April 10. The petition was similar to the petition of 1842. It contained the following principles :

" Labour is the source of all wealth. The people are the source of all political power. The worker has the right to the produce of his labour. Taxation without parliamentary repre-sentation is tyranny. The resources and economic means of a country are best developed and administered most advantageously by means of laws which are made by the representatives of the working and the industrious classes. In recognition of these principles the Chartists demand that the People's Charter should become the law of the land."[1]

The members of the Convention, comprising Ernest Jones, George Julian Harney, and Bronterre O'Brien, reported on the situation and the state of feeling of the people. They were of opinion, with very few exceptions, that the people were ready to fight. The old watchword, " Peacefully if we may—forcibly if we must," resounded in nearly all the speeches. They were carried away again by violent talk ; all kinds of weapons were bought in secret, but not in accordance with any systematic plan ; and plots were hatched.

On April 7 the government published a proclamation, informing the public that the Convention was an illegally constituted body and issuing a warning against any participation in the procession of April 10. And the government did not let the matter drop. It turned London into an armed camp. The garrisons of the south of England were brought to London and the marines of the Home Fleet were kept in readiness. Extensive military preparations were made for the protection of the Tower and the Bank of England. Great numbers of special constables were in addition sworn in, among them being William E. Gladstone and Louis Napoleon. The published numbers of the strength of the troops, the police, and the special constables are extraordinarily high. In general, the figures of the military and police and of the Chartists and their friends on April 10, 1848, cannot be accepted with any confidence. Hope, fear, and a feverish imagination rendered it quite impossible for anyone to think soberly or to speak or write with any approach to exactitude.

The Convention sat daily, listened to speeches, and received the petition sheets with the signatures. No attempt, however, was made to examine and verify them or to count their number. Thus the fateful day, April 10, arrived. Many shops were shut.

[1] *Northern Star*, April 1, 1848 ; Hansard's *Parliamentary Debates,* third series, vol. 106, pp. 1268 and *sqq.*

Special constables stood at the doors of most of the houses. Bodies of police guarded the bridges over the Thames leading to the Houses of Parliament ; the soldiers stood under arms in the barracks or at the guns in the environs of the south of London. At nine o'clock in the morning the Convention in John Street opened its proceedings. Christopher Doyle, a member of the committee, read out a communication from the Chief Commissioner of the police, in which attention was drawn to the illegality of the intended procession to the Houses of Parliament. In the discussion that followed, O'Connor spoke, justifying the extensive military preparations of the government as being due to the violent speeches of the members of the Convention ; finally he stated he had heard from a trustworthy source that the police and the soldiers had received strict orders to fire on the Chartist leaders. At 10 o'clock the delegates left the council room and marched at the head of the procession. A richly-decorated wagon, drawn by four horses, was reserved for the petition. This was followed by a decorated carriage, drawn by six horses, in which the members of the committee of the National Charter Association sat. The procession passed through Tottenham Court road on their way to No. 144, Holborn, the office of the National Land Company, where the petition was kept. Thence the procession proceeded in a south-easterly direction to Black-friars Bridge, in order to reach the meeting on Kennington Common. On the way it was joined by groups of demonstrators from the north and east, in many cases with bands and banners. The road was lined by enormous crowds. Finally the procession reached the appointed place of meeting. The exact number of the demonstrators on Kennington Common cannot be determined ; the statements on this point vary enormously. Before the meeting could begin the Commissioner of Police, who was stationed in a public-house close by, sent for O'Connor and McGrath, a member of the committee, and told them the government had no objection to the meeting being held, but that under no circumstances would a procession be allowed to go to the Houses of Parliament. Even a semblance of intimidating parliament was a punishable offence ; and the government would hold O'Connor personally responsible. O'Connor and McGrath gave way and promised to break up the procession at the close of the meeting. In the meantime the rumour spread among the demonstrators that their leader had been arrested. Soon, however, he appeared in their midst and was greeted with continuous and stormy applause. But O'Connor was by no means at his ease. Ever since 1837 he had told the people he would knock at the gates of parliament with a petition in his hand, accompanied by a multitude of a hundred thousand determined fighters. Now his opportunity had arrived, and yet he found himself forced to send the people back to their homes. Now everything depended on his skill as an orator, and it did not fail him. He was followed by Ernest Jones, Harney, and other speakers. Then the petition was placed in three cabs and taken to the Houses of Parliament by the committee, whilst the people slowly and quietly dispersed.

O'Connor presented the petition, and stated that the number of signatures amounted to over 5·7 millions, whereupon it was handed over to a committee to be examined. The result showed that the number of signatures did not amount to over 5·7 millions, but only 1,975,469, furthermore that numbers of the names were in the same handwriting, finally, that many of the names were either imaginary or were not signed by their bearers.[1] This revelation turned the whole petition into a farce. And the imaginary names were so ridiculous that the reading of them produced an irresistibly comic effect. The tension which the fateful tenth of April had caused suddenly relaxed and shrieks of laughter followed as a natural reaction. After the terror came satire :—

THE CHARTISTS ARE COMING.

I.

" What a row and a rumpus there is I declare,
   Tens of thousands are flocking from everywhere,
   To petition the parliament onward they steer,
   The Chartists are coming, oh dear, oh dear,

---

[1] *Cf.* Charles Kingsley, *Alton Locke*, chapters 33–4, an exceedingly moving description of the death of Sandy Mackaye and his despair at the inefficiency of Chartist leadership on April 10, 1848.

To demand equal justice, their freedom and right,
Pump-handles and broom-sticks, lawk, how they can fight!
The nation, they say, is overwhelmed with grief,
A peck loaf for twopence and four pounds of beef!

Chorus.—Hurrah for old England and liberty sweet,
        The land that we live in and plenty to eat;
        We shall ever remember this wonderful day,
        See the Chartists are coming, get out of the way.

2.

" Such a number together was never yet seen,
Hurrah for the Charter and God save the Queen!
And when that Charter Old England has got,
We'll have stunning good beer at three-halfpence a pot;
A loaf for a penny, a pig for a crown,
And gunpowder tea at five farthings a pound,
Instead of red herrings we'll live on fat geese,
And lots of young women at twopence a piece.

3.

" The bakers and grocers, hark how they do laugh,
With dustmen and coal-heavers armed with a staff.
Five thousand old women, oh, how they do sing,
With frying-pans, fenders, and big rolling-pins.
There's Russell, and Bobby, old Nosey and Hume,
With pistol, bayonet, musket and broom,
Load away, fire away, chatter and jaw,
Shoot at a donkey and knock down a crow.

4.

" See the lads of Old Erin for liberty crow,
Repeal of the Union and Erin-go-bragh!
Peace and contentment, then none we can blame,
Plenty of labour, and paid for the same;
Some are rolling in riches and luxury too,
While millions are starving, with nothing to do,
Through the nation prosperity soon will be seen,
Hurrah for the Charter and God save the Queen!

5.

" Such constables there are in London, now mark,
Tailor and shoemaker, labourer and clerk,
Gaslightman, pickpocket, fireman too,
Greengrocer, hatter, pork-butcher and Jew;

Lollipop merchants and masons a lot,
And the covey that hollers ' Baked taters all hot.'
They are sworn to protect us and keep well the peace,
To frighten the Chartists and help the police."

The disgrace, however, clung to the petition, and the Chartists regarded O'Connor's behaviour on April 10 to have been the cause of its failure. The revolt against his leadership became general. His incapacity could no longer be denied. It was only after a lapse of fifteen months that the petition became the subject of debate in parliament. It was no longer treated seriously. On July 3, 1849, only 17 members voted in favour of the petition, whilst 222 voted against it. The year between the introduction and the rejection of the petition was a period of catastrophes for O'Connor. As already stated, his plans for the redemption of the land by small holdings collapsed in hopeless failure, and he was bound up in them with all his heart-strings. His heart broke and his mind began to give way.

4.—THE LAST STAGE OF CHARTISM

Chartism went steadily and visibly downhill after April 10, 1848. The Chartists felt that their movement had received a mortal blow, but few of them dared to admit it openly. The Convention, which had been convoked on April 4, continued its meetings and discussions until April 24, when it dissolved, only to be reconstituted on May 1 as a National Assembly, with the addition of new delegates. A plan of reorganisation was adopted, and some sensible speeches were delivered on the events of the last few years and on O'Connor's failure to play the part of the leader of the people. Militant tactics, however, still prevailed, furnishing the government with the excuse of giving Chartism its *coup de grace*. On May 13 the National Assembly was dissolved. The leaders, in disillusionment and desperation, left for the country, held mass meetings, delivered violent speeches, and threatened to organise a National Guard. In some places scenes of violence were enacted, in others spies and police agents manufactured secret conspiracies. These were followed by wholesale arrests. From May to October, 1848, a reign of terror swept over England. Altogether about ninety Chartist leaders were sentenced to varying terms of imprisonment, up to a maximum of two years, in London, Yorkshire, Lancashire, and Cheshire. Ernest Jones received the maximum term in July, and was treated at first like a common criminal in his prison, until O'Connor paid 5s. a week for him in order to secure better treatment and self-occupation.

The years 1849 and 1850 witnessed a remarkable intellectual revival of Chartism, probably in consequence of the influx of the foreign revolutionary leaders. A good press came into being, and was conducted almost exclusively by ordinary working men. It was, however, short lived. The *Spirit of Freedom* deserve special mention. It was edited by Gerald Massey, a poor, unschooled working man with a considerable and fertile talent for poetry. In the same year Harney left the *Northern Star* because O'Connor would not permit him to write in favour of a democratic and social republic. He successively founded the *Red Republican*, the *Friend of the People*, and the *Democratic Review*, and the three papers scarcely lasted two years. In the early part of 1852 he bought up the *Northern Star* for £100, changed its name to *Star of Freedom* in May, but the star went out in November, 1852. The great *Northern Star* ceased to exist after a stormy career of fifteen years. Its place was taken by Ernest Jones's *Notes to the People*, to which Karl Marx contributed several articles, and then by his *People's Paper*.

The fatal action of April 10, 1848, was meanwhile hastened by the collapse of O'Connor's plan of land reform and by the defeat of the European revolution. The British workmen never acquired a more international character than in 1848 to 1850. They knew the names of the revolutionary leaders in France, Prussia, Austria, and Hungary. They took the keenest interest in the victories of Paris and Berlin in February and March, 1848, and followed intently the course of the campaigns in Hungary. From all these movements they hoped for a beneficial reaction upon England. Then the bad news came and all the great hopes and expectations faded away. The quondam victorious leaders of the revolution fled from their country and sought asylum in England. Yet English Chartism was unable to offer them anything more than enthusiastic meetings and greetings.

A contributory factor in the increasing weakness of the movement was the continued splitting up into sects. Several organisations were formed in rivalry with the National Charter Association, *e.g.*, the National Reform League, by Bronterre O'Brien, the National Regeneration Union, the People's Charter Union, the Social Reform League, etc. They broke up the last remnants of Chartism until the leaders were left without an army.

In 1855 Feargus O'Connor died in London, after having spent two years in a lunatic asylum. About 50,000 working men took part in his funeral procession.

Three years later Robert Owen breathed his last in his native place, Newtown. To the very end he remained faithful to his convictions and adhered to his main principles. Shortly before his death the local clergyman came to his bedside to offer him religious consolation. Owen declined the offer in the most decided manner, and when the minister asked him whether he did not regret having wasted his life in fruitless efforts, he made the proud rejoinder : " My life was not useless ; I gave important truths to the world, and it was only for want of understanding that they were disregarded. I have been ahead of my time."

IX

MORAL INFLUENCE OF CHARTISM

I.—CONSERVATIVE SOCIAL REFORM MOVEMENTS

THE catastrophic break with the past, which marks the period from 1815 to 1848, staggered the conservative minds of the nation, and stirred them to action. With their eyes turned towards the past, round which Sir Walter Scott had woven a romantic veil of bewitching glamour, they believed the present to exhibit nothing but disintegration, social subversion, total eclipse of Church and State authority, with the giant of Labour mortally wounded and writhing at the bottom of chaos. Like Plato and Cicero in their times, the social students and patriots of Great Britain were pained to see the ruthless struggle of the classes, the division of the nation into hostile camps : " Two nations, between whom there is no intercourse and no sympathy, . . . as if they were dwellers in different zones, or inhabitants of different planets." [1] The cash nexus appeared not only unable to replace the old social bonds, but to aggravate the hostility which " the profit-and-loss philosophy " was engendering. " We call it a society and go about professing the totallest separation, isolation." [2] And Dickens puts into the mouth of Stephen Blackpool, the hero of *Hard Times*, the inarticulate wail, " It is all confusion." Although, as a rule, the moral philosophers and reformers knew little of the importance and meaning of Chartism, and probably very few of them saw the factory system at work, yet they could not help discovering that this movement " was the first open separation of interest, feeling, opinion, between the labouring portion of the commonwealth and all above them." [3] In the opinion of the conserva-

---

[1] Disraeli, *Sybil*, book ii., chap. 5.   [2] Carlyle, *Past and Present*.
[3] J. S. Mill, *Dissertations and Discussions*, Vol. II., p. 188–9.

tive thinkers it was capital that had brought the nation to that pass : " It is that the capitalist has found a slave that has supplanted the labour and ingenuity of man.   Once he was an artisan ; at the best, he now watches machines ; and even that occupation slips from his grasp to the woman and the child.   The capitalist flourishes, he amasses immense wealth ; we sink lower and lower. . . . And yet they tell us that the interests of Capital and Labour are identical." [1]   And in another passage he writes quite in the Coleridgean manner : " Since the passing of the Reform Act the altar of Mammon has blazed with triple worship.   To acquire, to accumulate, to plunder each other by virtue of philosophic phrases, to propose a Utopia to consist only of wealth and toil, this has been the breathless business of enfranchised England for the last twelve years, until we are startled from our voracious strife by the wail of intolerable serfage." [2]   Another conservative writer, whose book made a deep impression on the leaders of the Oxford Movement and on the future leaders of Christian Socialism, proclaimed to the country that encouragement for capital and prevention for the (labouring) population had been " the two leading ideas with statesmen and legislators for the last thirty years.   They have now succeeded in their object.   While the privations and distress of the labouring classes have increased, the wealth of the upper classes has been constantly accumulating, and the capital of those classes constantly augmenting." [3]

The dismay at the deplorable state of the nation was followed by ardent attempts at the reassertion of authority and restoration of social peace by means of legislative measures and private philanthropy.   " We owe to the poor of our land," said Lord Ashley in 1843, " a weighty debt.   We call them improvident and immoral ; and many of them are so ; but that improvidence and immorality are the results, in a great measure, of our neglect, and, in not a little, of our example." [4]   The Chartist struggles

[1] Disraeli, *Sybil*, book ii., chap. 13.   [2] *Id. op. cit.*, book i., chap. 5.
[3] Seeley, *Perils of the Nation*, 1843, p. xii.
[4] Hodder, *The Seventh Earl of Shaftesbury as Social Reformer*, p. 123.

and sufferings in the years between 1839 and 1842 were not fruit less. "The claims of labour," wrote Mill in 1845, "have become the question of the day, and even the Legislature is invited, in each Session and with increasing urgency, to provide that the labouring classes shall earn more, work less, or have their lot in some way alleviated. . . . The stream at present flows in a multitude of small channels; societies for the protection of needlewomen, of governesses,—associations to improve the buildings of the labouring classes, to provide them with baths, parks, and promenades, have started into existence. . . . But it is not in this spirit that the new schemes of benevolence are conceived. They are propounded as the beginning of a new moral order or an old order revived, in which the possessors of property are to resume their place as the paternal guardians of those less fortunate." [1] It was, however, by no means exclusively a time of social reform and philanthropy. Sadler, Lord Ashley, and their friends were not alone on the national scene. The attempts at restoration of authority in Church and State were even more strenuous, and they gave rise to fierce literary polemics, parliamentary duels, heated theological controversies, as well as to the repression of revolution by means of treason trials, imprisonment, and transportation. Looking behind all these various measures, one notices conservative thought brooding over the social chaos and searching for the kindly light to lead the country to permanent and stable order, based on the authority either of the laws of God, or of historic tradition, or of some heroic personality.

Pleiades upon pleiades of religious and moral philosophers, learned theologians, and stirring poets and novelists appeared on the horizon. Hurrell Froude, J. H. Newman and W. G. Ward, Carlyle, Lord John Manners and Benjamin Disraeli, Maurice, Kingsley, and Ludlow—all moving in the orbit of Conservatism, with Mill and Dickens as social Liberals and volunteers of the movement. All of them, without any exception, were either directly or indirectly under the influence of Coleridge. "Every Englishman of the present day," testified Mill, a close and

[1] J. S. Mill, *l. c.*

sympathetic observer of those critical years, " is by implication either a Benthamite or a Coleridgean ; holds views of human affairs which can only be proved true on the principles either of Bentham or of Coleridge." Bentham swayed Liberalism, Coleridge the thinking portion of Toryism. Mill forgot at that time the Chartists, who derived their principles neither from Bentham nor from Coleridge, but from Locke and Owen. A few years later, when writing and revising his *Principles of Political Economy*, he made ample amends for his oversight, as we shall see in a later chapter.

2.—THE OXFORD MOVEMENT AND YOUNG ENGLAND

The social elements of the Oxford Movement were subordinated to theology. Hurrell Froude, John Henry Newman, and W. G. Ward were mainly concerned with Church authority, and they believed to have found it in a return to Roman Catholicism. In retracing their steps to the origins of the Church, they rediscovered also the primitive Christian social and democratic spirit, the quasi-sacramental character of poverty, and the stigma of wealth. Their fierce opposition to Liberalism on account of its anti-dogmatic attitude, its corrosive and negative forces, and its respect for private and individual judgment soon led them to join issue with individualist political economy which was supposed to teach Capital to sacrifice everything to the production of wealth. " When the moral tone of the country is unchristianised," wrote Hurrell Froude, " it is all one whether the poor were serfs by law, or citizens by law. Their poverty in both cases is equally weak, contemptible, and ridiculous. It devolves on the Church, therefore, to assist in her own courts the rights of the poor. She must exhibit a picture of Christian equality, and put the poor and helpless in that honourable position, which shall render anything that injures or degrades them an obvious offence against the Church and shocking to the common feelings of Christians." [1] With characteristic boldness he expressed his sympathy with the French Christian Socialists " a High Church Party in France, who are Republicans, and wish

[1] Quoted in W. G. Ward, *Ideal of a Christian Church*, p. 31.

for universal suffrage, on the ground that in proportion as the franchise falls lower the influence of the Church makes itself felt ; at present the limits about coincide with those of the infidel faction." [1] The idea that an extension of the franchise would weaken the Liberal influence in Parliament was on the Continent quite common. The most outspoken opponent of Liberal political economy was Newman. When he learned that these doctrines were being spread in Oxford, he indignantly replied that they formed " a categorical contradiction of our Lord, S. Paul, S. Chrysostom, S. Leo, and all saints." The pursuit of wealth and gain, the endeavour to accumulate the means of future subsistence and enjoyment, were not, as the political economists were teaching, the great moral source of improvement, virtue, and happiness, but the root of all evil, " and the poor, on the contrary, are blessed, for theirs is the Kingdom of God." [2]

On parallel lines with the Tractarians moved Young England, whose ideal was a regenerated feudal order of society. They looked back wistfully to the time, when—

> " Each knew his place—king, peasant, peer, or priest,
> The greatest owned connection with the least ;
> From rank to rank the generous feeling ran,
> And linked society as man to man.

> " Gone are those days, and gone the ties that then
> Bound peers and gentry to their fellow men.
> Now, in their place, behold the modern slave,
> Doomed, from the very cradle to the grave,
> To tread his lonely path of care and toil ;
> Bound, in sad truth, and bowed down to the soil,
> He dies, and leaves his sons their heritage—
> Work for their prime, and workhouse for their age." [3]

The poet is yearning for Church and Noble rule, for seeing the Holy Church once more in unity, for there is more happiness under her wings, though clouds of incense load the air, than in

[1] Hurrell Froude, *Remains*, Vol. I., p. 312.
[2] John Henry Newman, *Idea of a University*, ed. 1873, pp. 91-3.
[3] Lord John Manners, *England's Trust*, p. 16.

some murky English street or alley, where science turns man's
energies to gain.   His indignation against capitalism, Liberal
legislation, and materialistic science reaches its most uncompro
mising expression in the famous lines—

> "Let wealth and commerce, laws and learning die,
> But leave us still our old Nobility."[1]

In practice, the men of Young England worked for social
reform legislation with Lord Ashley.   None of these movement
aimed at the subversion of private property, but were directed
against the excesses of unregulated wealth-production.

It was different with those ardent and tremendously seriou
Protestants, who created Christian Socialism. Maurice, Kingsley
Ludlow, Vansittart Neale, and their friends, really meant to
supplant the individualist and competitive system of property
by co-operative socialist production.

3.—CHRISTIAN SOCIALISM

The central figure of the remarkable group of men, who create
Christian Socialism in England, was Frederick Denison Maurice
" towering spiritually by head and shoulders over the rest."
In nobility and saintliness of character, in theological learning
and subtlety of intellect he may, perhaps, be compared with New
man.   But the spheres of their work were poles asunder.   Newman
was a great ecclesiastic, essentially mediaeval in temper an
intellect, while Maurice, by his religious and social philosoph
and intensely national feeling, represented one of the spiritual
forces of the nineteenth century.   As a Protestant and Englis
man, with a high political ideal, and more fully under the influence
of Coleridge than Newman was, he desired to see Christianit
not only a faith, but a deed.   The Kingdom of Christ was no
to come, but to be realised.   He believed that God had a
educational plan for the world, by which the perfection of th
individual and of the race was to be accomplished, that in th
development of that plan each age of human history had it

---

[1] *Ibid.*, p. 24.   [2] J. M. Ludlow, *Economic Review*, October, 1893.

own work to do, that there was a Christian ideal of society,—
nay, that the existing society, with its divinely created obligations, was the best, if man could only pay reverent homage to
those obligations.[1]   The Bible was not there only to be read and to
edify individually, but to form, as Coleridge taught, the manual
of the statesman.[2]   God's order was mutual love and fellowship,
while selfishness and competition were the direct results of man's
disorder : " God's order seems to me more than ever the anta-
gonist of man's systems : Christian socialism is in my mind the
assertion of God's order." [3]   This is a remarkable sentence ; it
translates a natural law doctrine into Christian terms.   " Human
society," he further proclaimed, " is a body consisting of many
members, not a collection of warring atoms ; true workmen must
be fellow-workmen, not rivals ; a principle of justice, not of
selfishness, must govern exchanges."   Such *dicta* might have been
enunciated by any of the leading Owenite writers.   But while
they would have based them on rationalist and secularist principles, Maurice found them to be rooted in the teachings of the
Gospel.   After a discussion in an Owenite and Chartist meeting,
in 1849, he wrote to Ludlow :—

" I never heard a stronger witness for the power of the will
to regulate and command circumstances than came from those
socialist worshippers of circumstances. I think they should be
made to feel that communism, in whatever sense it is a principle
of the New Moral World, is a most important principle of the
old world, and that every monastic institution—properly so-
called—was a communist institution for all intents and purposes.
The idea of Christian communism has been a most vigorous and
generative one in all ages, and must be destined to a full development in ours." [4]

Maurice's main idea was to socialise the Christian and to
Christianise the socialist. Socialism appeared to him to be

[1] Charles W. Stubbs, *Charles Kingsley*, 1899, Introduction.
[2] F. D. Maurice, *Kingdom of Christ*, ed. 1842 (Letter to D. Coleridge).
[3] F. Maurice, *Life of F. D. Maurice*, second ed. Vol. II., p. 44.
[4] *Ibid.*, p. 6–7.

I M

essentially the business of the Church and not of the State
" We want the Church fully to understand her own foundation
fully to work out the communism which is implied in her existence.
Church Reformation, therefore, in its highest sense, involves
theologically the reassertion of these truths in their fulness, apart
from their Calvinistical and Tractarian limitations and dilutions ,
socially the assertion on the ground of these truths of an actually
living community under Christ, in which no man has a right to
call anything that he has his own, but in which there is spiritual
fellowship and practical co-operation." [1]

It is impossible not to discern in these announcements distinct
traces of patristic and scholastic teachings.   Maurice's studies of
mediaeval philosophy evidently left deep impressions on his
mind, and predisposed him to look favourably on the effort of
the socialist propagandists of the Chartist period.   Indeed, as
far as the socialist form of economic life is concerned, there was
no difference between Maurice and the leading Owenites.   On
the other hand, he differed greatly from the political Chartists,
for he was no democrat and condemned the doctrine of the
sovereignty of the people as atheistic and subversive.   Maurice
was even prepared to serve, on the memorable April 10, 1848,
as a special constable.   He believed kingship to be of divine
origin.   We cannot help regarding Maurice as a spiritual descendant of John Wycliffe.

His friend and adherent, Charles Kingsley, stands far behind
his master in point of theological scholarship and socialist
thought.   He was essentially a poet, with the temperament of
an agitator,—fervid, vehement, inconsistent in his views, easily
moved by tales of misery and ready to attack any social evil
that met his eye.   But for his political principles, which somehow
were bound up with Conservatism, he might have been a revolutionary Chartist leader.   He publicly called himself a Chartist," [2]
although he was ready to eschew a thousand charters for the
French cry of " organisation of labour " into co-operative
workshops. Still, his revolutionary temper was unmistakable, and

---

[1] J. Maurice, *Life of F. D. Maurice*, p. 10.
[2] Mrs. Kingsley, *Letters and Memoirs*, Vol. I., p. 306.

he directed his mighty pen both against landed and capitalist
sweaters. His *Yeast* deals with the former :—

> " You have sold the labouring man, squire,
>   Body and soul to shame,
> To pay for your seat in the House, squire,
> And to pay for the feed of your game.
>
> *   *   *   *
>
> " When packed in one reeking chamber,
>   Man, maid, mother, and little ones lay ;
> While the rain pattered on the rotting bride-bed,
> And the walls let in the day.
>
> *   *   *   *
>
> " Our daughters with base-born babies
>   Have wandered away in their shame ;
> If your misses had slept, squire, where they did,
> Your misses might do the same." [1]

His *Alton Locke* is one great terrible indictment of the merciless
manufacturers. Kingsley, Maurice, and their friends, who
created Christian Socialism in England, were distinguished
from the men of the Oxford and Young England movement by
looking forward, and not backward. " My whole heart," wrote
Kingsley, " is set, not on retrogression, outward or inward,
but on progression. . . . The new element is democracy, in
Church and State. Waiving the question of its evil or its good,
we cannot stop it,—let us Christianise it instead." Yet, he
was no democrat in the usual meaning of the term. He thought
the real battle of the time was not Radical or Whig against
Peelite or Tory, but the Church, the gentleman, the workman
against the shopkeepers and the Manchester School.[2] His
devotion to the cause of Labour was boundless : " I would shed
the last drop of my life blood for the social and political emancipation of the people of England." [3] His knowledge of Chartism
was fairly wide. *Alton Locke* contains the history of this movement from 1844 to 1848, while Disraeli's *Sybil* is based on Chartism
of the years from 1838 to 1843.

[1] Charles Kingsley, *Yeast,* chap. 11.
[2] Mrs. Kingsley, *op. cit.*, p. 214–5.   [3] *Id.*, p. 184.

With Maurice and Kingsley worked J. M. Ludlow, who, having lived in Paris, possessed much knowledge of French socialism.   On March 2, 1848, he reported to Maurice that socialism was a real and very great power among the Parisian workmen, and that it must be Christianised or it would shake Christianity to its foundation, precisely because it appealed to the higher and not to the lower instincts of man.[1]

Among the other members of the Christian socialist movement may be mentioned E. Vansittart Neale, an ardent co-operator, who supplied the funds necessary for socialist co-operative experiments ;   Thomas Hughes, the author of *Tom Brown's Schooldays ;*   Charles Blackford Mansfield, a young scientist and mystic, who inspired Kingsley with the idea of sanitary reform ;   Charles Sully and Lloyd Jones, both socialist workmen, who organised co-operative shops and propagated the ideas of the movement among the working-men.[2]   .

They formed altogether a remarkable group of men—leaders and officers, but without any army behind them.

The first manifestations of the movement date from April 10, 1848.   On that memorable day Kingsley met Ludlow, who called upon Maurice to report to him the fate of the final struggle of Chartism.   Two days later Kingsley issued a manifesto to the London workmen, and on May 6, 1848, the first number of the weekly, *Politics for the People,* was issued.   Maurice wrote the prospectus, explaining their aim and end to consist in the establishment of a union between social life and Christianity. Under the pseudonym " Parson Lot," Kingsley contributed a letter to the Chartists : " My quarrel with the Charter is that it does not go far enough.   I want to see you free ; but I do not see how what you ask for will give you what you want.   You mistake *legislative* reform for *social* reform, or that men's hearts can be changed by Act of Parliament. . . . It disappointed me bitterly when I read it. . . . The French cry of Organisation of Labour is worth a thousand of it, and yet that does not go to

[1] F. Maurice, *Life of F. D. Maurice,* Vol. I., p. 458.

[2] Compare J. M. Ludlow, *Economic Review,* October, 1893, and January, 1894.

he bottom of the matter by many a mile." He complains that many of the Chartists were trying to do God's work with the levil's tools. Nevertheless, he believed that the time was near when those glorious old words were to be fulfilled: " Thou, Lord, hast heard the desire of the poor. Thou preparest their hearts, and Thine ear hearkeneth thereto, to help the fatherless and poor unto their right that the man of the world be no more exalted against Thee."

Although the paper was exceedingly well written, and had about 2,000 subscribers, its career was cut short after four months. The reason of its rapid extinction has never been explained. It must be assumed, however, that the vast majority of its subscribers were not workmen, for whom the paper was intended. The summer of 1848 was a time of severe persecutions of all revolutionary elements; the Chartist masses were not in a mood to take advice from clergymen and members of the upper classes. Among the contributors to *Politics for the People* were: Maurice, Kingsley (Parson Lot), J. M. Ludlow (John Townsend), Archbishop Whateley, Archbishop Trench, Bishop Thirlwall, Dean Stanley, Dr. Guy, Sir Edward Strachey. Most of them wrote anonymously or under a pseudonym. The editors consoled themselves—

> " There is no failure for the good and wise :
> What though thy seed should fall by the wayside
> And the birds snatch it ; yet the birds are fed ;
> Or they may bear it far across the tide,
> To give rich harvest after thou art dead."

In the year 1849 Maurice and Kingsley attended meetings of Chartists, and in 1850 they issued *Tracts on Christian Socialism*. The term " Christian Socialism " had not been used before that time. Maurice,[1] writing to Ludlow in January, 1850, declares : " We must not beat about the bush. What right have we to address the English people ? We must have something special to tell them, or we ought not to speak. *Tracts on Christian*

[1] F. Maurice, *Life of F. D. Maurice*, Vol. II., p. 35.

Socialism is, it seems to me, the only title which will define o
object, and will commit us at once to the conflict we must enga,
in sooner or later with the unsocial Christian and the unchristi
socialist."

The *Tracts* were no more successful than the *Politics*. (
November 2, 1850, the weekly, *Christian Socialist*, was starte
in which Ludlow developed the principles of the movemen
Socialism and Christianity were in their nature not hostile, b
akin to each other. Christianity, however feeble and torpid
might seem to many just now, was but as an eagle shedding i
worn-out plumage and putting on new (Socialism) to sprea
ere long its mighty wings for a broader and heavenlier fligh
" Socialism without Christianity, on the one hand, is as lifele
as the feathers without the bird, and therefore easily blown o
Christianity, on the other hand, when stripped of socialism,
chilly and helpless." The Christian gospel was wholly incom
patible with a political economy which proclaimed self-intere
to be the very pivot of social action. The principle of buyin
cheap and selling dear ; the system of trade, based on the ide
of taking more from our neighbour than we gave him, we
inimical to the teachings of Christianity. The aim of th
Christian socialist movement was to substitute fair prices an
living wages for false cheapness and starvation. Its watcl
words were, " Association and Exchange " instead of competitio
for profit.

The *Christian Socialist* expired at the end of 1851. In th
meantime a dozen small co-operative workshops were estal
lished, which could not withstand the impact of capitalis
competition. Besides, there is no worse human material t
experiment with than the remnants of a defeated revolutionar
movement. Embittered and demoralised, they are a thorn i
the side of their old friends as well as their new ones. The chie
speaker and missionary of the Christian socialists, Lloyd Jones
an old Owenite and tailor, was sent to Lancashire for the purpos
of winning adherents for the movement. In a protracted publi
discussion with Ernest Jones, the Chartist leader, he was utterl
defeated. The workmen flatly refused to pay any attentio

to the Christian socialist arguments.[1]   They were still clamouring for the Charter,—for political power in order to use it as an instrument for the socialisation of the means of production.

Their failure to gain adherents among the Chartists and the onslaughts levelled against them by Conservative writers[2] induced Maurice, Kingsley, and Hughes to change *The Christian Socialist* into *The Journal of Association* (1852) and to devote their energies to the dissemination of co-operative principles only. In 1854 the Christian socialist movement was at an end.   Their efforts were, however, not quite ineffectual.   They contributed to the legalisation of co-operative enterprise, to the promotion of sanitary reform, and to the furtherance of education among the London workmen by founding the Working Men's College, where some of the most famous men of art and science acted as teachers, among them being Ruskin, Tyndall, D. G. Rossetti, Madox Brown, and J. R. Seeley.

4.—J. S. MILL AND RICHARD JONES

The last years of Chartist class warfare and the ferment of 1848 have also left an indelible impress upon British economic literature.   An attempt was made to extend the bounds of political economy, so as to include sociological problems, or even to make economics the basis of sociology.   Two of its economic writers, John Stuart Mill and Rev. Richard Jones, were prompted to lend expression to sociological thoughts and speculations which were quite new in learned circles of acknowledged adherents of the existing order.

The disciple of Ricardo and Bentham was constrained to admit that all the mechanical inventions and general progress had hardly lightened the day's toil of the worker, and that they but enabled a greater number of people to live a life of drudgery and imprisonment, and an increased number of manufacturers and other middle class men to make fortunes (*Principles*, 1869, book iv.,

[1] An account of this debate is given in *Christian Socialist*, December 20 and 27, 1851.

[2] *Quarterly Review*, October, 1851, p. 523.

ch. vi., sec. 2 [1]).   Mill rightly discerned the effect of Chartism
when he declared that the working classes had now taken their
interests into their own hands, and were perpetually showing
that they thought the interests of the employers to be not
identical with their own, but opposite to them.   While reforms
and the organisation of the working classes might alter the
distribution of the produce to their advantage, the present class
relations could not permanently last.   " I cannot think," he
declares, " that the working classes will be permanently contented
with the condition of labouring for wages as their ultimate state
. . . In the present stage of human progress, when ideas of
equality are daily spreading more widely among the poorer
classes, and can no longer be checked by anything short of the
active suppression of printed discussion and even of freedom
of speech, it is not to be expected that the division of the human
race into two hereditary classes, employers and employed, can
be permanently maintained " (*Ibid.*, book iv. ch. 7).   These
relations were unsatisfactory both to the employers and employed.
An open or secret war raged between them, to the detriment of
the country.   On neither side was there any justice or fairness,
and it would sooner or later become insupportable to the employing classes to live in close and hourly contact with persons whose
interests and feelings are in hostility to them.   " Capitalists are
as much interested as labourers in placing the operations of
industry on such a footing that those who labour for them may
feel the same interest in the work which is felt by those who
labour on their own account " (*Ibid.*, book iv., ch. 7).

Mill was groping his way towards socialism.   He witnessed
the class war in Great Britain and France, and the rise of Labour
to importance, and arrived at the conviction that a tolerable
arrangement might be effected through some form of partnership of Labour as a means to the economic education of the
masses, as a stage in the process towards complete socialism.
" The form of association, however, which if mankind continue

[1] The *Principles* appeared in 1848.   The book was revised in
the successive editions, but not materially altered.   The changes
made in the second edition (1849) were all in favour of socialism.

to improve, must be expected in the end to predominate, is . . . the association of labourers themselves on terms of equality, collectively owning the capital with which they carry on their operations, and working under managers elected and removable by themselves," according to the theories found in the writings of Owen and Louis Blanc (*Ibid.*, book iv. ch. 7).

Even more interesting, from a theoretical point of view, are the observations of Rev. Richard Jones. He was the successor of Robert Malthus in the chair of political economy at the East India College at Haileybury, and may be regarded as the pioneer of the historical school of political economy in Great Britain. Unlike Mill, he wrote relatively little, but his literary remains bear the impress of an original mind. Probably owing to his position as professor and his relations with the Government of the period, he never allowed his thoughts and Celtic temperament full play. In his *Text-Book of Lectures*,[1] published in 1852, while dealing with capital and wages, he incidentally remarks : " The first capitalist employers—those who first advance the wages of labour from accumulated stock, and seek a revenue in the shape of profits from such advance—have been ordinarily a class distinct from the labourers themselves. A state of things may hereafter exist, and parts of the world may be approaching to it, under which the labourers and the owners of accumulated stock may be identical ; but in the progress of nations which we are now observing, we see . . . a body of employers who pay the labourers by advances of capital out of the returns to which the owners aim at realising a distinct revenue. This may not be as desirable a state of things as that in which labourers and capitalists are identified ; but we must still accept it as constituting a stage in the march of industry, which has hitherto marked the progress of advancing nations." [2]

Capitalism is thus but a stage in the economic development of mankind. Moreover, the great political, social, moral, and intellectual changes are inseparably connected with changes in

[1] Richard Jones, *Literary Remains*, edited by William Whewell, D.D. London, 1859, pp. 339–531.

[2] *Ibid.*, p. 445 (Lecture IV.).

the economic organisation of communities. Political economy is, therefore, not merely a science of capital, profits, rents, and wages, but the basis of social science. For, " economic changes necessarily exercise a commanding influence over the different political and social elements to be found in the populations where they take place ; that influence extends to the intellectual character, to the habits, manners, morals, and happiness of nations. . . . There is a close connection between the economic and social organisation of nations and their power of production." [1]

The whole Lecture IV. is very curious. It contains also the germs of that philosophy of social evolution which the Marxists call the Materialist Conception of history. It is a delicate balancing between capitalism and anti-capitalism. It is a strong reflex of the stirring events and thoughts of the Chartist period.

5.—CONCLUDING REMARKS

After a desperate contest of thirty years' duration, Chartism had come to an end. It had not been a struggle of a plebs for equal rights with the patriciate to spoliate and enslave other classes and nations, but a class war aiming at the overthrow of the capitalist society and putting production, distribution, and exchange on a co-operative basis. The working-class was apparently defeated.

Baffled and exhausted through erratic leadership, untold sacrifices, and want of proper mental munitions, they retired from the field of battle, bleeding and decimated, but little aware of the great results they had achieved. They only saw shattered ideals and broken hopes that lay strewn on the long path they had been marching and counter-marching from 1825 to 1855, not knowing that it was from the wreckage and *débris* of those shattered ideals that the material was gathered for building and paving the road of social progress.

The advance which Great Britain had made in those thirty years in social reform and democracy was enormous. The Chartist period witnessed the first real Factory Act (1833), the

Ibid., pp. 405–6.

first mining law for the protection of child and female labour (1842), the Ten Hours day (1847), the reduction of the newspaper stamp (1836), the abolition of the Corn Laws (1846), the repeal of the Corresponding Acts (1846). It bequeathed to the working classes the co-operative store and co-operative production, more successful trade unions, and international sentiments. It forced the thinking men of the nation to regard the labour problem as a serious subject for investigation and discussion. Finally, it imbued the thinking portion of the working class with the conviction that Liberalism must first do its work, before Labour could come into its own, both in the legislature and in the factory. In short, from the catastrophes of 1832, 1834, 1839, 1842, and 1848 the lesson emerged that the revolutionary policy of " all or nothing," of a sweeping triumph by one gigantic effort, of contempt for reform and of the supreme value of a total and radical subversion of the old order, were foredoomed to failure. The generation that succeeded Chartism went into Gladstone's camp and refused to leave it either for the social Toryism of Benjamin Disraeli or for the social revolution of Karl Marx.

PART IV

MODERN SOCIALISM
(1855-1939)

X

MAIN CURRENTS OF THE PERIOD

THE period with which we are now going to deal, while, on the whole, less stirring, is more complicated, and of much more vital importance than any of the foregoing periods. We are leaving, as it were, the antiquities of socialist speculation and the childhood of Labour, and are nearing the recent past and the immediate present. We have now to do with problems of modern society which are touching the very life of the nation. It might, therefore, be expedient, for a better comprehension of the totality of the period, to give, before entering into details, a broad outline of its tendencies and struggles.

From the angle of vision of the socialist historian the sixty-five years from 1855 to 1920 exhibit three distinct phases :

I.—ZENITH OF LIBERALISM

Unchallenged reign of liberal thought, and partly apathetic, partly active adherence of Labour to the existing order. The twenty years following upon the collapse of Chartism formed the golden age of middle class Liberalism. The glamour of its doctrines as set forth by Mill in his essay, *On Liberty*, the phenomenal growth of British trade and commerce, the unrivalled position of Great Britain as the workshop of the world, made British Liberalism the lodestar of all nations striving for freedom and wealth. Competition as the regulator of economic relations, free trade as the international bond of peace and goodwill, individual liberty as the sacred ideal of national politics, reigned supreme, and under their weight the entire formation of social revolutionary ideas of the past disappeared from view. The working classes formed a part of triumphant Liberalism.

Gladstone, surveying his hosts in 1866, appeared quite justi-fied in telling his Conservative opponents that there was no use fighting against the social forces, " which move onwards in their might and majesty and which . . . are marshalled on our side." [1] He might have addressed the same eloquent words to the leaders of the International Working Men's Association, who with Karl Marx at their head, were precisely at that time making a serious attempt to resuscitate Chartism and detach the masses from the Liberal Party. Socialism and independent labour politics came to be regarded as exotic plants which could never flourish on British soil.

The trade unions renounced all class warfare and merely tried to use their new citizenship (1867) and their growing economic organisation—the first trade union congress took place in 1869—with a view to influencing the distribution of the national wealth in their favour. Their aim and end was that of a class striving for equality with the possessing and ruling classes. It was, despite some struggle for the legalisation of trade unionism, a period of social peace, and it lasted till about 1880.

2.—LIBERAL LABOUR. BIRTH OF STATE SOCIALISM

The second phase is characterised by the rise of Labour to a junior partnership with the Liberal Party and the birth and growth of State and municipal socialism and new unionism. From 1875 the lustre of Liberalism began to grow dim, and in the years between 1880 and 1890 its inadequacy became apparent. The years 1873 and 1874 witnessed big strikes in mining, manufacturing, and agricultural districts ; they saw the entrance of working men into Parliament. On the heels of these ominous events came economic depression ; free trade had not secured prosperity. Competition had proved destructive not only of the unfit, but of the less favoured by fortune ; large capital crushed small capital, regardless of the qualities of their possessors. Foreign competition, mainly

[1] Quoted in John Morley's *Life of Gladstone*, ed. 1908, Vol. I. p. 627.

[2] *Cf.* John Morley, in *Fortnightly Review*, April, 1882, pp. 503-4 October, 1882, pp. 533-4.

American and German, fostered by protective tariffs, was making itself increasingly felt to British manufacturers and agricultural interests. Combination and mutual protection were gradually coming to be regarded as superior to the competitive systems. The propositions of orthodox political economy were seriously questioned. Land reform movements grew in strength. The term *Nationalisation* was created. Socialist organisations sprang up: the Social Democratic Federation, founded by H. M. Hyndman, propagating the Marxian doctrine of class war; the Fabian Society, with Sidney Webb as its foremost exponent, trying to apply socialism to practical politics; the Independent Labour Party, working with might and main, under the leadership of James Keir Hardie, to discredit the old Liberal-Labour leaders, to imbue the younger trade union officials with the spirit of socialism. They were years of a severe contest between liberalism and socialism for the soul of the working-class.

As long as Gladstone was active, the socialist efforts met with little success. Gladstone, on whose mind the social criticism of the early 'forties had left an indelible impression,[1] never lost sight of organised Labour, and whenever he saw it moving towards class warfare and socialism he spared no effort to lead it back to peaceful waters. He was the most potent personal force of Liberal Labourism. His influence among the trade unionists was amazing. And they received from him political recognition as soon as they became an indispensable part of Liberalism, that is, from 1886. It was Gladstone who raised working men to the rank of Ministers, thus inaugurating the era which has finally thrown open the gates of the Cabinet to Labour leaders and socialists. The growing strength of socialism and Labour politics since 1880 may be gauged by the treatment which prominent trade unionists and socialists received at various times at the hands of Liberal Governments. In 1834 William Godwin, the anarchist communist author of *Political Justice*, received an appointment as gentleman usher; in 1849 Samuel Bamford, the Radical weaver and one of the leaders of the

---

[1] See *supra*, Part III., p. 140.

I N

demonstration at Peterloo, was made doorkeeper at Somerset House.   Such was in those times the remuneration of socialists and labour leaders, whom the Governments delighted to honour. In 1886 Henry Broadhurst, the Labour lieutenant of Gladstone, was appointed Under-Secretary of State ; in 1892 Thomas Burt, Parliamentary Secretary ; in 1906 John Burns entered the Cabinet.   The difference between a doorkeeper of a Government building and a member of the Cabinet indicates the rise in the value of socialism and Labour politics from 1834 to 1906.

3.—INDEPENDENT LABOUR.   REVOLUTIONARY SOCIALISM

Liberal-labour was declining since 1900.   In that year the Labour Party was formed, and under the leadership of J. R. MacDonald, Hardie, and Pete Curran it rapidly developed.   In 1906 the Party entered Parliament as an independent political force.   Chartism revived, and the nation found itself soon in the grip of a widespread Labour unrest, which has been going on increasing in volume and revolutionary fervour, the motive power of which appears to be a more or less conscious striving for industrial democracy, for control of production,—an aim to be attained no more by State socialism or collectivism, but through direct action, through subordinating parliamentary methods to economic warfare.   The new phase has already produced a host of leaders and writers, the most prominent of whom is G. D. H. Cole.   The British Labour movement has never attracted so many intellectuals as at present.   Hands and brains are unitedly at work towards some shape of a socialist reconstruction of the economic foundation and governmental system of society.   They but form, under various names, a part of the general Labour unrest that is convulsing the civilised world.   The social crisis is practically universal.

The whole movement appears to be the inevitable outcome of the contrast between political and legal equality on the one hand and industrial dependence and insecurity of existence on the other.   Politically sovereign in the legislature, the workman is a mere hireling in the workshop ; he can make and unmake Governments, but has no say whatever in the arrangement of his

aily work. Political power without economic power is, there-
ore, in his eyes a mockery and dangerous delusion. He now
esires some part in the control of the production, just as he
esired, a half a century ago, a part in the making of the laws.
he mentality of the working classes is now passing from politics
) economics, and from economics to social ethics. They are
o longer willing to be treated as a commodity. The older
)cialists, as we know, used to argue against the wage system
n economic grounds ; they said that labour as a commodity
iffered from other commodities by not only affording value for
alue, but by producing surplus value. The present-day
)cialist or revolutionary trade unionists or guild socialists, while
greeing with their predecessors, are arguing that labour differs
om other commodities also by being inseparably bound up
ith a human soul. The working classes have grown in moral
nd intellectual stature, and are asking the nation to regard and
eat them as free personalities. It is an appeal on economic
s well as moral grounds.

Keeping this general outline in view, we shall now proceed to
eat the various phases in detail, describing the events and move-
ents as well as exhibiting the theories underlying them.

XI

INTERNATIONALISM AND LIBERAL LABOUR

I.—YEARS OF APATHY

THE ten years after the failure of Chartism were a period of calm. All efforts to revive the movement proved ineffectual. Moreover, the working classes seemed to have abandoned politics altogether, and turned their attention to trade unionism and co-operation. Radical politicians, like Cobden and Bright, deplored the political indifference of the working classes and confessed themselves powerless to stir them into activity. The ruling classes, mindful of the Chartist agitations, attempted to introduce moderate measures of franchise reforms, but they met with no response from the masses.[1] In 1861, Cobden complained that the working men were " so quiet under the taunts and insults offered them. Have they no Spartacus among them to head a revolt of the slave class against their political tormentors ? I suppose it is the reaction from the follies of Chartism which keeps the present generation so quiet." [2] Even in 1863 Cobden described the conditions of the workers as that of political inertia. Two years later, however, we find the working men in full activity for suffrage reform, and in 1867 in possession of the franchise !

This rapid transformation appears to have been the result of the stirring events in the sphere of international politics—the American Civil War and the Polish insurrection, and of the agitation of the International Working Men's Association. The thinking portion of the British working men retained as a legacy from the Chartist period strong sympathies for progressive movements abroad. During the American Civil War they

---

[1] John Morley, *Life of Gladstone*, popular ed., 1908, I., p. 623.
[2] John Morley, *Life of Cobden*, ed. 1903, p. 829.

demonstrated their sympathies for the Northern States ; in the time of the Polish insurrection of 1863 they were heart and soul with the Poles ; the Italians struggling to be free could always rely on the friendly feelings of British Labour, and when Garibaldi came to London they gave him a royal welcome. The working classes, once set in motion, were soon drawn into the agitation for suffrage reform. Under the auspices of the London Trades a Suffrage Association was formed in 1864, which was turned into the Reform League, the efficient instrument that caused the Government to introduce and carry the Second Reform Bill and change the United Kingdom into a Democracy. The close connection between internationalism and the reform agitation is most clearly exhibited by the fact that the same men who organised public meetings and demonstrations in favour of the anti-slavery Northern States, of the Poles and the Italians, were also the leaders of the Reform League—George Odger, W. Randall Cremer, and Robert Applegarth. They were likewise some of the most prominent members of the International Working Men's Association.

Internationalism was no less potent a factor in the economic sphere of the Labour movement. The sympathy of the advanced sections of the French working classes with Poland and Italy, coupled with the desire of their leaders to learn something of English trade unionism, caused them to utilise their visit to the International Exhibition in London in 1862 for entering into closer communication with the London Labour leaders. After an exchange of addresses in 1863, it was decided to convene a conference in London for the purpose of forming an International Association of Working Men. This conference took place in the fourth week of September, 1864, and settled the main question. In order to afford the London working men an opportunity of welcoming their foreign friends, and to seal the bond of friendship between the French and British working classes, it was resolved to hold a public meeting on September 28, and to invite the representatives of all working men's societies domiciled in London to attend either as guests or speakers. Among the representatives who accepted the invitation and

attended the meeting was Karl Marx, whose knowledge of worki
class economics and whose literary abilities predestined him f
the intellectual leadership of the new organisation.

2.—KARL MARX

Several circumstances have combined to render it necessa
to deal with Marx (1818–1883) as one of the decisive person
factors of modern socialism in Great Britain. First, the be
part of his life (1849–1883) was spent in London, where
gathered the elements of his economic system, partly from tl
writings of the Ricardian school and partly from the anti-capita
ist thinkers who in the first half of the last century directed the
critical shafts against the new social structure which arose out
the Industrial Revolution.[1] Marx gathered up their fragmentar
views, gave them logical coherence and sequence, and embodie
them into his system : he was the executor of the testament the
had left. Secondly, Chartism and British industrial life we
the inductive material from which he drew his sociologic
conclusions and upon which he based his hypotheses. Thirdl
the rise of modern socialism in Great Britain since 1882,
well as the whole Labour unrest since 1907, as far as their leade
have been attempting to give them a theoretical foundation, ar
inseparably linked to Marxism.

The teachings of Marx divide into three parts : (*a*) Sociologic
law of history, or the materialist conception of history ; (*b*) clas
warfare and its meaning ; (*c*) evolution of capitalism.

(a) *Materialist conception of history.*

Even a mere glance at human history shows that man, fro
period to period, has held different views of morality, religior
philosophy, law, government, trade, and commerce ; that he ha
had diverse and different social and governmental arrangements
that he has undergone a whole series of struggles, wars, an

---

[1] *Cf. supra*, Part II., pp. 245–70. In the last fifteen years of hi
life, Marx wrote a vigorous and brilliant English, even better tha
German. In his German writings of that period the English synta
predominates, which is sufficient proof that he no longer thought i
German, but in English.

igrations. What is the sufficient cause and reason of this baffling iversity and restlessness, of those various changes of human iought and action ? Marx raises that question not for the purpose f investigating the psychological origin of the ideas underlying iose arrangements and movements, but with a view to finding ie motive power that is causing the changes and revolutions f the essentials and forms of the mental and social phenomena. [e is much less interested in the origin and statics of things ian in their dynamics : he is searching for the dynamic law of istory.

Marx replies : The prime motive power causing the changes f human consciousness and, consequently, of the social arrange- ients, cannot be found in human reason nor in any transcendental lea or divine inspiration, but in the material conditions of life, that s, in the way in which man, as a social being, produces the means f life. Of all categories of the material conditions of existence he most important is production of the necessary means of life. This depends on the *forces of production*, which are partly in- .nimate (soil, water, climate, raw materials, tools, and machines) .nd partly personal (labourers, inventors, discoverers, engineers, .nd racial qualities). The foremost place among the productive orces belongs to the manual and mental labourers ; they are n the capitalist society the real creators of exchange-value. The next place of importance is taken by technology ; it is an :minently altering and revolutionising force in society. These orces are operating under *conditions of production*, that is, under .aws of property, political arrangements and class relations, iabits and manners, moral and intellectual conceptions, created by man in conformity with, and for the purpose of promoting the operation of the productive forces. Or in other words : In response to the stimuli of the productive forces man builds up the social order, government, religion, morality, art, philo- sophy, and science. The material production is the substructure or the groundwork, while the corresponding political, religious, moral, philosophical, and scientific systems are the superstructure, the upper stories of society. The substructure is material, the superstructure is the psychical reflex and effect.

It is well to keep in mind the two Marxist concepts : *productive forces* and *conditions of production*. The former are, in the main, gifts of nature, the latter are created by man, under the stimulus of the productive forces, according to his moral and intellectual qualities. Man, even the most heroic, is not the sovereign maker and lawgiver of social life, but its executive ; he can but comprehend the material forces operating in the groundwork of society and give their tendencies and requirements political, legal, institutional, intellectual, and emotional expression and effect.

When the productive forces expand and improve, in consequence either of the acquired greater skill and productive capacity of the workpeople through mechanical inventions and application of science to trade and industry, or of geographical discoveries and extension of the markets,—when, therefore, the productive forces are undergoing changes and the substructure of society is being altered, the old conditions of production (the laws, institutions, and systems of thought) gradually turn into impediments and cease altogether to satisfy the requirements of the productive forces and social life. For the old conditions of production were in harmony only with productive forces that are disappearing. With the unfolding of the new productive forces, the contrast, friction, and opposition between them and the old conditions of production grow keener. The superstructure ceases to respond to the new forces. Society is out of gear. A social crisis has arisen, since the institutions, class relations, and systems of thought are more conservative and cling to the old forms. Society enters on a revolutionary period, the symptoms and operating effects of which are the spread of dissatisfaction, unrest, class warfare, rise of new thinkers and prophets who in an apparently strange dialect and in accordance with their temperament, knowledge, and character attempt to interpret the crisis and to teach how to reorganise the conditions of production in the light of the new productive forces. The old social formation, however, does not go under unless and until the new productive forces have grown in volume and maturity, so as to form a solid groundwork for the new superstructure which is gradually being formed and erected in the storm and stress of class warfare, in the shock and clash of intellectual and moral controversies.[1]

The evolutionary view of society Marx acquired from Hegel, who regarded nature and history as being involved in a process of evolution inherently propelled by the Idea (a mystical God) to create and negate and recreate one stage after another, and each higher than the other, in eternal progression ; each stage creating its own antagonism which negates it, at the same time creating a new and higher stage. Hegel called this kind of evolution the *dialectical process*, and the three stages he named the *positive* (or *thesis*), the *negation* (or *antithesis*), and the *negation of negation* (or *synthesis*).

Marx adheres to this formula and regards the Hegelian dialectics as a true statement of the formal process of evolution, but in the place of the Idea he puts the economic forces as the predominant dynamic agency of human society and its history. He argues : " What else does the history of ideas prove, than that intellectual production changes its character in proportion as material production is changed ? The ruling ideas of each age have ever been the ideas of its ruling class. When people speak of ideas that revolutionise society they do but express the fact that within the old society the elements of a new one have been created, and that the dissolution of the old ideas keeps even pace with the dissolution of the conditions of existence. When the ancient world was in its last throes, the ancient religions were overcome by Christianity. When Christian ideas succumbed in the eighteenth century to rationalist ideas, feudal society fought its death-battle with the then revolutionary bourgeoisie. The ideas of religious liberty and freedom of conscience, merely gave expression to the sway of free competition

---

[1] Marx has nowhere given a systematic view of his sociology. The only attempt he ever made in this respect is to be found in the Preface to his *Critique of Political Economy*, 1859 (German). Aphoristic remarks on the subject are scattered in *Misère de la Philosophie*, 1847, *Communist Manifesto*, 1848, and in footnotes to the *Capital*, etc.

within the domain of knowledge." [1] Or again : " It is not the consciousness of man that determines his social existence, but quite the reverse ; it is his social existence that determines his consciousness." [2]

(b) *Class struggle and its meaning.*

Since the rise of private property, society has been divided into classes. Marx classifies the various elements of society according to their economic characteristics, since the economic factor is of commanding influence. A class is a group of persons who draw their means of livelihood from the same economic source. Modern society is, in the main, divided into two classes. The groups of persons whose source of living is labour-power constitute the working-class ; the groups of persons whose source of living is property (soil, houses, mines, factories, means of transport, commercial concerns) form the capitalist class. The fact that some members of the working-class draw dividends from their co-operative stores and copartnerships or interest from the savings bank, or that members of the capitalist class draw an income from payments and fees for superintendence, organising activity, or directorship, does not invalidate the classification, for, on the whole, the workman's main interest turns upon wages as the price of his labour power, while the main interest of the capitalist centres round his property and its profits. Of course, anyone is at liberty to classify society into other groups ; he may classify it into good and bad, philistine and artist, white and black, etc. ; but he must show that such classifications have a decisive effect on the development and dynamics of social life.

Society, then, consists, according to Marx, of two classes, one possessing labour-power only, the other the means of production. Between these two classes there is an irreconcilable opposition of interests. The opposition is, before all, of an economic nature. The wage-workers, as the possessors of labour power, desire to sell their only commodity for as high a price (wage) as possible,

[1] *Communist Manifesto*, English edition, 1888, pp. 20-21.
[2] *Kritik der Politischen Oekonomie*, 1859, preface.

while the possessors of capital endeavour to buy it for as low a price as possible. This opposition, being economic, is fundamental, but has, at first, no revolutionary influence on the mentality of the working classes. It is, apparently, an opposition like any other in civil life, between buyers and sellers of any commodity. At bottom, however, the difference is very great, for the possessor of the commodity labour-power is not in a position to bargain; if he does not sell his commodity he starves. The possessor of capital is thus able to starve the labourer into submission. The possession of capital reveals itself as a social power of the first magnitude.

This opposition and manifestation, which even Adam Smith clearly perceived, leads at first to the organisation of trade unions or to the incipient stage of class antagonism. There occur trade disputes and industrial conflicts, but these need not and will not assume the character of a class war, unless and until the working class recognise that their precarious condition is not incidental and transitory, but an inevitable effect of the capitalist system of society; that their economic inferiority cannot be mended as long as that system prevails; and, finally, that that system can be superseded by a different one, in which the means of production are in the control and possession of the whole society. In other words: only when the working-class learn to think socialistically do their sporadic and isolated disputes and trade union activities develop into a class war. The conviction is borne upon them that they cannot attain freedom and equality within the existing order of society, and that socialism only can emancipate them.

Even if that stage of mental development is reached, the working class will not pursue the struggle any further if they have not gained the consciousness that they are able or have got the power to achieve this emancipation themselves, and therefore look for some philanthropic saviour, for some heroic personality, to do for them what they think they cannot achieve by their own efforts. This was really the case at the beginning of the socialist movement, when the leaders of the working-classes saw quite clearly that the only way out of the social misery was the socialist mode of production, when the masses felt this is to be the road to their salvation, but were too weak to take their case into their own hands. That period was, according to Marx, the utopian stage of proletarian development. It was the time of Robert Owen in Great Britian, of Fourier in France, of the establishment of communist colonies in America, of many experiments with labour-exchanges and currency reforms. The Utopian stage was overcome through the economic development itself. With the growth and expansion of the capitalist system the working-class grew in numbers, strength, organising capacity, political importance, and self-consciousness. Particularly the concentration of industry gave them the power to paralyse through mass strikes, the whole fabric of civilised life, and to make the whole society realise that living labour-power was the soul of the whole social system. Moreover, the development of the capitalist system itself called the productive forces into being, and created forms of industrial organisation which rendered the transition to socialism easier than ever before. The Utopian stage was thus overcome, and a scientific view of social developments and socialist possbiilities was gained. To interpret this development and to bring it home to the working class was the mission of Marx. To that mission he devoted his life. It was his life-long endeavour to make the working-class conscious of their power, aims, and means. When they had grasped that, they impelled by their own interests and conditions of life, must take up the task of achieving socialism, their class war would lose all pettiness, all hesitation, all half-way measures, and would assume the character of a straight-aiming revolutionary struggle for their complete emancipation, for economic freedom, and equality of all.

The class war, far from being, as the Utopians thought, an impediment to socialism, was its most efficient locomotive. It was an integral part of the dialectical process of history. A glance at the evolution of European civilisation from the middle ages to the present day would confirm it. The feudal stage of society, impelled by its own economic necessities, promoted trade and commerce, and gave rise to a trading and commercial class, which gradually turned antagonistic to its parent, and out of the destruction of feudalism built up a capitalist society. The contests between manor and city, the conflicts between feudal usages and canon law on the one hand, and commercial law and trading interests on the other, not only were necessary, but contributed to the strengthening of the new rising class and to the awakening of their self-consciousness. The capitalist society, in its turn, was producing forces which were antagonistic, hostile, and subversive of its existence. It brought a propertyless working class into being, which, through the concentration of the means of production by Capital and the annihilation of the independent producers through the centralising factory system and the growth of the industrial concentration, was gaining in coherency, discipline, combination, and class consciousness. And this working class was necessarily antagonistic to the capitalist system, since the interests of Labour and Capital were absolutely opposed to and destructive of each other. Hence the class warfare, which was an inexorable historic necessity and an efficient instrument for the negation of capitalism and the furtherance of all new economic tendencies which were making for collective production and for social control of the means of production. Class warfare formed a revolutionary act of the utmost importance. The negating and recreating force of the last stages of capitalist society was the working class, whose vital interests were bound up with the abolition of capitalist control and with the transfer of the means of production to the whole society. Capitalism had destroyed production on a small scale by independent proprietors and rendered a return to the pre-capitalist form of production impossible. Now was the time to break the last chains of the institutions of private property and to expropriate the handful of the capitalist magnates in favour of the whole people. The working class was no more a motley of labouring poor, or a mob of helpless people, but a fighting class of producers—the master-builders of a new and higher stage of human society.

(c) *Evolution of Capitalism.*

From social philosophy Marx turned to economics, since our mental life was " nothing else than the material world reflected by the human mind, translated into forms of thought." [1] He then devoted some fifteen years of his life to the writing of the *Capital* (three volumes of about 700 printed pages each), the purpose of which was to analyse capitalist society, to show its genesis, its inner working, and its outcome, in the light he received from Hegel, Ricardo, and the British anti-capitalist school of 1820 to 1840. Marx had the ambition to continue and to accomplish the task left by those writers and by Chartism, or to discover the predominant dynamic laws governing modern society. His work deals with " the system of capitalist production which is based on the fact that the workman sells his labour-power as a commodity " (*Capital*, English edition, 1888, vol. i., p. 431). Following Ricardo he assumed that living labour only produced value, and that wages were the remuneration for the expenditure of labour power, and that wages and profit stood inversely to each other. Marx further assumed, with Ravenstone, Gray, Hodgskin, and Bray that capital was unproductive, and that profit, rent, and interest sprang from surplus-value or from that portion of the value produced by manual and mental labour which was not paid for and which was appropriated by the capitalist. This unpaid or embezzled or extorted labour was the main source of capital, hence the passion of the capitalist for surplus value.[2] This all-absorbing passion was the motive

[1] Marx, *Capital*, preface to the second German edition, 1883.

[2] The surplus-value extorted from the workmen does not flow directly to the employer, but is apportioned as profit, by means of competition, among the whole class of capitalists, according to their individual investments. Hence it follows that the surplus-value produced by the individual factory may considerably vary from the rate of profit which the individual employer as a member of the capitalist class receives under the operation of competition. However, the total amount of profit, interest, and rent, which accrues to the possessing classes, is equal to the aggregate amount of the surplus value extorted from Labour in the various workshops, factories, mines, and fields.

power of the capitalist class. In his striving for surplus-value, the capitalist imposed long hours upon the workpeople, and on their finally rebelling against health-destroying overwork, he searched for new methods of exploitation. In this search he introduced division of labour, closer co-operation of the hands in the workshops, better tools, more economic organisation of the process of production. On these methods proving inadequate to break the resistance of Labour, science was called in, machinery was invented which made the workers more amenable to work-shop discipline, and displaced many by woman and child labour. The impulse thus given to science and technology was enormous ; the workshop grew into a mechanical factory, the factory into a congeries of workshops. Work became automatic and intense ; this intensification more than compensated for the reduction of the working hours. The displaced workpeople formed a reserve-army to be called in in times of strike or in periods of prosperity, in order to enable capital to cope with the sudden extension of the markets. In this process the handicraftsmen and small masters were eliminated and thrown into the proletariate. Moreover, since it was manual and mental labour-power only that created value, and since machinery reduced the amount of living labour-power *per* commodity, the value of the commodity sank and with it the surplus-value or profit *per* commodity. Hence the tendency of the rate of profit to sink. With a view to compensate for the reduction of profit the employer extended production on an even larger scale, raised his capital, looked for more profitable markets, brought his machinery to the highest pitch of perfection in order to intensify and speed up labour, and to extort from it the last ounce of surplus value. Such a reconstruction and adaptation was only possible for big capital-ists, while the smaller ones were forced to give up the struggle and humbly leave the field to the giants of industry. Concentra-tion of capital grew apace, and in the same proportion its power. This expropriation is accomplished by the immanent laws of capitalist production itself, by the centralisation of capital. One capitalist always kills many. " Hand in hand with this expropriation of many capitalists by few develop, on an ever-

extending scale, the co-operative form of the labour-process
the conscious technical application of science, the methodic
cultivation of the soil, the transformation of the instruments
labour into instruments of labour only usable in common, th
economising of all means of production by their use as the mean
of production of combined, socialised labour, the entanglemer
of all nations into the net of the world-market, and with thi
the international character of the capitalist régime. Alon
with the constantly diminishing number of the magnates
capital, who usurp and monopolise all advantages of this proce
of transformation, grows the mass of misery, oppression, slavery
degradation, exploitation ; but with this, too, grows the revo
of the working-class, a class always increasing in numbers, an
disciplined, united, organised by the very mechanism of th
process of production itself. The monopoly of capital become
a fetter upon the mode of production which has sprung up
and flourished with and under it. Centralisation of the mean
of production and socialisation of labour at last reach a poi
when they become incompatible with their capitalist integumen
This integument is burst asunder. The knell of capitalist privat
property sounds. The expropriators are expropriated " (*Capita
vol. i., p. 788–789).

This is, of course, the social revolution. The victorious pr
letariate rises to political supremacy, and constitutes itself th
nation. Its main task is now to transform the institutions an
the laws in conformity with the social revolution. This ca
only be accomplished by the dictatorship of the proletariat
" The transition from capitalism to socialism will have as i
political organ the revolutionary dictatorship of the proletariate.
It will use its political supremacy, to wrest, by degrees, a
capital from the bourgeoisie, to centralise all instruments
production in the hands of the State, *i.e.* of the proletariat
organised as the ruling class, and to increase the total productiv
forces as rapidly as possible. " Of course, in the beginning, th
cannot be effected except by means of despotic inroads on th

[1] Marx, *Letter to the German Social Democratic Leaders*, in 187
Published in *Neue Zeit* (Stuttgart), 1891, No. 19 ; 1906–07, II, p. 16

rights of property and on the conditions of capitalist production, by means of measures, therefore, which appear economically insufficient and untenable, but which, in the course of the movement, outstrip themselves, necessitate further inroads upon the old social order, and are unavoidable as a means of entirely revolutionising the mode of production." [1]

Those are, in the shortest possible compass, the teachings of Marx.

It is impossible not to admire the enormous erudition and synthetic energy and intense labour embodied in his writings. He is, next to Plato and Thomas More, the greatest intellect in the annals of socialist thought. One feels mentally invigorated by a study of his works. They form an excellent intellectual discipline, particularly on their historical side. [2] His real achievement is not to be found in his economics, nor mainly in his sociology, but in his appreciation of the movement of the working class. He was the first socialist who grasped the importance and rôle of the proletariate. As to his errors, we may repeat here what we said concerning Adam Smith and David Ricardo, that the errors of great minds are but a degree less instructive than their truths. [3] There is much in Marx's works that is capable of stimulating thought and enlarging our outlook. There must be indeed something very vital in them, considering the fact that after so many refutations of their theories they are still the guiding star of the international revolutionary movement, which the world has now seriously to reckon with.

3.—ADDRESS AND RULES

The meeting of September 28, 1864, was held at St. Martin's Hall, Long Acre, London. It was convened by George Odger,

[1] Marx and Engels, *Communist Manifesto*, English edition, 1888, p. 21.

[2] As an introduction to the study of Marx may serve—*The Communist Manifesto*, 1848 ; the preface to *Critique of Political Economy*, 1859 ; *Capital*, Vol. I., chap. 32 ; *The Civil War in France*, 1871, chap. 3.

[3] *Cf. supra*, Part II., p. 199.

10

Randall Cremer, and other leaders of the London artisans Professor Edward Spencer Beesly was in the chair. The crowded meeting elected a provisional committee, consisting of London trade union leaders, old Chartists, Owenites, and others, to draw up a declaration of principles and rules. Drafts were subsequently prepared by a Mazzinian and an Owenite respectively, but failed to pass. Finally, Marx wrote the declaration of principles in the form of an *Address to the Working Classes*,[1] and also laid down the rules, which were carried unanimously. Both the Address and the Rules are written in the spirit of Chartism, in the traditions of which the founders of the International Working Men's Association (I.W.M.A.) had grown up. Marx's ideas of working class politics were largely in harmony with those of Chartism and his plan was to turn the I.W.M.A. into a nucleus organisation for the renewal of Chartism on a theoretical basis. Marx was a great admirer of the British working classes, of whom he thought that they but needed the capacity for generalisation in order to assume the leadership of the international Labour movement. He believed their greatest weakness to consist in their bent for empiricism, for fragmentary views and half-measures. He, therefore, threw himself heart and soul into the work of the I.W.M.A. in order to imbue it with a theoretical spirit.

In his Address, Marx reminded the working classes that notwithstanding the unprecedented growth of trade and commerce in the years from 1845 to 1864, the condition of Labour had not improved. In 1850, a moderate organ of the British middle classes, of more than average information, predicted that if the foreign trade of the United Kingdom were to rise 50 per cent. British pauperism would disappear. On April 7, 1864, the Chancellor of the Exchequer (Mr. William Gladstone) delighted his Parliamentary audience with the statement that the total foreign trade of the United Kingdom had grown in 1863 to nearly £444,000,000, which sum represented about three times the trade of 1843. With all that he was eloquent on poverty.

[1] This document is known as the *Inaugural Address*. A copy of it, probably the only one extant, is to be found in " George Howell's Collection " in the Bishopsgate Public Library, London, E.C.

n nine cases out of ten, human life was but a bare struggle for xistence. " The intoxicating augmentation of wealth and power is entirely confined to the propertied classes."

Marx then went on to amplify this striking sentence by adducing facts and figures, all extracted from official reports, and to paint a lurid background to Mr. Gladstone's financial statement, rom all of which he drew the inevitable conclusion that the rich were getting richer, and the poor poorer. Land and capital were undergoing a process of concentration ; the land question, in particular, was getting singularly simplified, as it had become in the Roman Empire, when Nero grinned at the discovery that half the province of Africa was owned by six gentlemen. Everywhere the great mass of the working classes were sinking to a lower depth of misery at the same rate at least that those above them were rising in the social scale. In all countries of Europe it had become a truth demonstrable to every unprejudiced mind that no improvement in machinery, no application of science to industry, no new contrivance of transport, no emigration, no opening of new markets, no free trade, nor all those factors put together, could do away with the misery of the productive classes, but that on the present false basis every fresh development of the productive powers of labour must needs tend to deepen the social contrasts and aggravate the social contradictions and conflicts. Death by starvation rose almost to the rank of a social institution, during that intoxicating epoch of industrial progress, in the metropolis of the British Empire. That epoch was marked in the annals of the world by the quickened recurrence, the widening compass, and the deadlier effects of that social pest called a commercial crisis.

Against that misery the generation o Chartism had been battling with most admirable perseverance for thirty years, and finally succeeded in getting the Ten Hours day, which led to an immense improvement, physical, moral, and intellectual, of British Labour. But there was something more in that triumph. The political economists had predicted that that measure would sound the death-knell of British industry. Capitalism, it appeared, could but live by sucking the blood of children, sacrificed to the blind rule of supply and demand. Instead o blind rule the Chartists had urged that production should b controlled by social foresight and humane consideration " The Ten Hours Bill was, therefore, not only a great practica measure ; it was a victory of a principle ; it was the first tim that in broad daylight the political economy of the middle classe succumbed to the political economy of the working class." A still greater victory was co-operative production undertaken b the despised " hands " ; they had shown, as Robert Owen ha taught them, that the capitalist was by no means an indispensabl factor of production. At the same time experience had prove that co-operative labour, if kept within the narrow circle of th casual efforts of private workmen, would never be able to arres the growth in geometrical progression of monopoly, nor eve perceptibly to lighten the burden of their miseries and wrong It had, therefore, become the great duty of the working classe to conquer political power and to make use of the machiner of the State to promote their interests. One element of succes they possessed—numbers ; but numbers weighed only in th national balance of power if united by combination and led b knowledge. This thought prompted the working men of differen countries who had assembled on September 28, 1864, in publi meeting at St. Martin's Hall, to found the I.W.M.A. Yet anothe consideration had swayed that meeting. If the emancipatio of the working classes required their international concurrence how were they to fulfil that great mission in the face of a foreig policy in pursuit of evil designs, playing upon nationalis and racial prejudices and squandering in piratical wars th people's blood and treasure ? " This has taught the workin classes the duty to master the mysteries of international politics to watch the diplomatic acts of their respective governments to counteract them, if necessary, by all means in their power and, when unable to prevent, to assemble in simultaneou demonstrations and to vindicate the simple laws of morality and justice, which ought to govern the relations of privat individuals as well as the intercourse of nations. To fight fo such a foreign policy forms a part of the general struggle fo the emancipation of the working classes. Workmen of all countries, unite ! "

The style and substance of the Address have a strong Chartist flavour, for Marx was indeed a Chartist, but equipped with a philosophical, economic, and political knowledge, to which no British Chartist could have laid claim.

The Rules he laid down were essentially as follows :

" The emancipation of the working classes must be achieved by the working classes themselves. The struggle for that emancipation means not a struggle for class privileges and monopolies, but for equal rights and duties, and the abolition of all class rule. The economic subjection of the man of labour to the monopoliser of the means of production or the sources of life is the foundation of servitude in all its forms, of all social misery, mental degradation, and political dependence. The economic emancipation of the working classes is, therefore, the great end to which every political movement ought to be subordinated as a means. The emancipation of labour is neither a local nor a national, but a social, problem, embracing all countries in which modern society exists, and depending for its solution on the concurrence, practical and theoretical, of the most advanced countries."

To arrange for such an international concert of Labour and to form a vitalising and guiding centre of working class activities was the task of the I.W.M.A. Marx advised the workmen to organise independent labour parties, to demand in Parliament social reform and factory legislation, to oppose all bellicose diplomacy, but to carry on a relentless class war, until they had conquered political power and nationalised the means of production.

4.—ACTIVITY AND FAILURE OF THE INTERNATIONAL

The I.W.M.A. held annual congresses in London, 1865, in Geneva in 1866, in Lausanne in 1867, in Brussels in 1868, in Berne, 1869, and in The Hague in 1872, when the organisation was practically dissolved. At first many British trade union leaders joined the I.W.M.A., among them being Henry Broadhurst, Robert Applegarth, George Odger,

Robert Hartwell, W. Randall Cremer, George Howell, but afte
the passing of the second Reform Bill the British unions graduall
withdrew their support, although the General Council of th
I.W.M. contained up to the end a majority of British member
The affiliation of many French, Swiss, German, Belgian, Italia
and Russian organisations turned the congresses into arenas
warring doctrines and sects, which, whilst in general agreemen
as to the socialist aim, were at loggerheads with regard to polic
and method, the main cleavage being the question of parlia
mentarism. Marx and his adherents advocated parliamentar
action, while many of the French, Italian, Spanish, and Russia
representatives were either for revolutionary economic action
or secret conspiracies for the purpose of insurrection. Marx
himself, in emphasising the superiority of economics to politics
and in attempting to permeate the working classes with the view
that the real source of all social evils was the monopoly of the
means of production, unwittingly contributed to the strengthen
ing of the anti-parliamentary tendencies that existed among
the Owenites, Proudhonites, and Anarchists. His economic
interpretation of history was, of course, the chief reason of his
strong leaning towards economic action, but the idea prevalent
at that time that the failure of Chartism was mainly due
to its one-sided political agitation must also have induced him
to redress the balance by giving increasing weight to the economic
and social side of the Labour movement. Marx was undoubtedly
an advocate of revolutionary trade unionism, as may be seen
from a resolution which he drafted for the congress of the
I.W.M.A., held at Geneva in 1866 :—

Trade Unions.—(1) Capital is concentrated social power,
whereas the workman possesses nothing but his individual labour
power. The contract between Labour and Capital can, therefore,
not be based on equitable conditions, even in the sense of
a society which ranges the possessors of all material conditions
on one side, and the living productive forces on the other.
The only social power on the side of the workmen is their number.
This power of numbers, however, is dispersed and weakened
through discord. The dispersion of the social power of Labour

is caused and maintained by the inevitable competition for a job. Trade unionism originated from the voluntary attempts of the workmen to resist the despotic behests of Capital and to prevent, or at least to keep in check, the mutual competition for an opportunity to labour, in order to obtain such conditions as would raise them above the level of simple slavery. The immediate aim of trade unionism is, for this reason, confined to the daily contests between Labour and Capital, or, in short, to wages and hours of labour. These activities of the trade unions are not only legitimate, but absolutely necessary; they cannot be dispensed with as long as the present system prevails. Moreover, they must be made general through an alliance of the workers of all countries. The trade unions have, however, unconsciously created centres of gravity for the whole working class, very much like the mediaeval guilds and corporations for the burgess class. If the trade unions, in their former capacity, are absolutely indispensable for the daily or guerilla warfare between Labour and Capital, they are, in their other capacities, all the more important as organised bodies for the abolition of wage-labour and of the capitalist domination.

(2) The trade unions have hitherto paid too much attention to the immediate disputes with Capital. They have not yet fully understood their mission against the existing system of production. They have kept aloof from the general social and political movement.

(3) Without flinching from their daily struggle against the encroachments of the capitalists, the trade unions must now learn consciously to act as the *foci* of the working classes, in the interest of their complete emancipation. They must support every social and political movement which has this aim in view; they should regard themselves as the champions and representatives of the whole class and carefully concern themselves with the interests of the unskilled or badly-paid workers, who on account of their miserable conditions are incapable of any organised resistance. Such actions will inevitably attract the great mass of unorganised workers and fill them with the conviction that the trade unions, far from being engaged in the pursuit of narrow,

selfish interests, are working for the emancipation of the down trodden millions."

The heroic and social revolutionary part which Marx assigned to the trade unions as the centres of economic action, and the subordination of parliamentary action as a means, were eagerly accepted by the anarchist and anti-parliamentary adherents of the I.W.M.A., who soon eliminated the subordinate means and laid stress on the main propositions. The result was an ever deepening and widening conflict between Marx and his friends on the one hand, and the Proudhonites, Owenites, and the Anarchists on the other. And when, in the course of the controversy, the theoretical considerations and differences were lost sight of, and suspicion, obloquy, and vituperation became the main weapons of the two opposing camps, the conflict broke out in all its fury and shattered the frail bark that had been launched in September, 1864. The various societies composing the I.W.M.A. separated and led for several years an obscure existence, until they completely disappeared.

The British Section issued, in March, 1872, a manifesto, which was quite in harmony with the Address which Marx had written in 1864, but with the following addition of principles: "The produce of labour ought to belong to the producer; the brotherhood of Labour should be the basis of society; the workers of all countries should unite for the emancipation of Labour and for the abolition of all class rule; Labour is of no country, for everywhere are they suffering from the same evils." The manifesto was signed by George Bennett, J. T. Blair, Alex. Clark, Thomas S. Sanders. In July, 1872, a national congress was held at Nottingham to consider the political situation and to adopt a definite programme for the federation. It was resolved to form a new political party, by means of which the workers could achieve their emancipation. A programme, drawn up by John Hales, Tyler, and G. B. Clark, contained the following demands: adult suffrage; proportional representation; free, compulsory, and secular education—primary, secondary, technical, and university; disestablishment and disendowment of all State Churches; abolition of hereditary titles and privileges and of unpaid justices of the peace; self-government for Ireland and a federal constitution for the British Empire; nationalisation of land, mines, and the means of production; establishment of a State Bank with a monopoly of note issue.[1]

The British Section of the I.W.M.A. lingered for some time and expired from exhaustion. The working classes had definitely abandoned all socialist agitation and class warfare, and not even the genius of Marx could bring them back to Chartism.

The improvement of the conditions of the skilled workmen in the years from 1846 onwards could not have failed to contribute to their appeasement. In the period from 1846 to 1866 money wages as well as real wages rose, as a result of the expansion of trade and the repeal of the corn-laws. According to Robert Dudley Baxter, whose social statistics are generally regarded as reliable, the population in 1867 amounted in round numbers to 30 millions, of whom 10 millions were men, women, and children depending on wages. The national income amounted to 814 million pounds sterling, out of which 325 million pounds fell to the share of the wage-workers, or in round numbers £30 per head of the working classes. These figures are averages. It may therefore be assumed that the organised workers in the staple industries obtained appreciably more than £30 a year. In comparison with the decades 1815 to 1845 such incomes meant a substantial amelioration.[2]

The reaction from the revolutionary idealism of the Chartist period was complete. The old Chartist, Thomas Cooper, who toured the North of England in 1869 and 1870 in the capacity of an evangelical preacher, found the working men there in a better material condition than in the years 1840–45, but he " noticed with pain that their moral and intellectual condition had deteriorated. . . . In our old Chartist time, it is true, Lancashire working men were in rags by thousands; and many of them lacked food. But their intelligence was demonstrated wherever you went. You would see them in groups discussing

[1] G. B. Clark, *Recollections of the International*, in *Socialist Review*, July-September, 1914, p. 253.

[2] Robert D. Baxter, *National Income*, 1868.

the great doctrine of political justice . . . or they were in earne
dispute respecting the teachings of socialism. *Now*, you w
see no such groups in Lancashire. But you will hear we
dressed working men talking of co-operative stores, and the
shares in them, or in building societies. And you will see other
like idiots, leading small greyhound dogs, covered with clot
in a string ! They are about to race, and they are betting mone
as they go ! . . . Working men had ceased to think, and wante
to hear no thoughtful talk ; at least, it was so with the great
number of them. To one who has striven, the greater part
his life, to instruct and elevate them, and who has suffered an
borne imprisonment for them, all this was more painful than
care to tell." [1]

After 1867 Marx expressed similar opinions of the British wor
ing classes, but he never accused the masses. His quarrel wa
with their leaders, whom he charged with being in the pay part
of Mr. Gladstone and partly of Mr. Disraeli. However, we sha
never understand the mental state of British Labour in th
period from 1850 onwards if we ignore the severe crises throug
which they passed in the years 1832, 1834–5, 1839–40, 184
and 1848.

5.—LIBERAL LABOUR ORGANISATIONS

Between the years 1866 and 1895 there existed thre
political organisations, whose object it was to obtain pa
liamentary representation of Labour ; the London Work
ing Men's Union (1866–8), the Labour Representatio
League (1869–80), and the Labour Electoral Associatio
(1886–95). They had nothing to do with independen
political action. Their dominant idea was rather as follows
Parliament, in its debates and legislation affecting labou
questions, required certain technical knowledge and experienc
which only Labour leaders could possess ; it was therefor
necessary to send some of these men to Parliament.

The Trades Union Congress which originated in 1868 and i
still in full vigour, belongs to the same category of organisations

[1] Thomas Cooper, *Life*, ed. 1897, p. 393–4.

its aim being to watch over the political interests of the organised working men. Its organ is the Parliamentary Committee, elected annually by the Congress for the purpose of carrying its political resolutions into effect, either by sending deputations to the Secretaries of State or by lobbying—by interviewing Members of Parliament who are in sympathy with Labour.

In February, 1866, the London Working Men's Union came into being. According to its programme the Union declared not merely in favour of universal suffrage, but for the direct parliamentary representation of working men for working men. Its secretary was Robert Hartwell, an old Chartist, who, as we may recall to mind, had presided over the great meeting of February 28, 1837, at which the movement for the People's Charter was set on foot. Hartwell made strenuous efforts to lead the new generation back to Chartist ideas. The Union, however, adopted his resolutions without carrying them into effect.

At the parliamentary elections of 1868 several Labour leaders came forward as candidates, among them being George Odger, president of the General Council of the I.W.M.A., Randall Cremer, formerly secretary of the same body, and Hartwell. Odger and Hartwell retired before the polling day, while Cremer obtained only 260 votes against 873 Liberal and 863 Conservative votes.[1]

The London Working Men's Union then disappeared from the scene and its place was taken by the Labour Representative League, which set itself the task of "avoiding Utopian theories and illusory phantoms and of bringing the interests of the working men into harmony with those of the whole of society." The league was evidently founded in opposition to the I.W.M.A. At the beginning of 1870 a parliamentary by-election had to take place at Southwark. The League's candidate was Odger, who was supported by J. S. Mill. He went to the poll and received 4,382 votes against 4,686 Conservative and 2,966 Liberal votes. This result, combined with the agitation of Labour for the legalisation of trade unionism, gave the League an impetus and made it for a time an influential political body.

[1] A. W. Humphrey, *History of Labour Representation*, 1912, p. 26.

It reached its highwater mark in 1874, when twelve Labour candidates were put forward, of whom, however, only the miners' leaders, Alexander Macdonald and Thomas Burt, were successful. The Liberals suffered defeat, and the Conservatives formed a Government under the leadership of Disraeli, who carried a trade union bill which satisfied the organised working classes. The League then declined, but the Trade Union Congress continued to pass resolutions for the increased parliamentary representation of Labour. These resolutions became hardy annuals which were moved and carried mechanically. At the general election of 1880 three Labour candidates were successful : Burt, Macdonald, and Broadhurst.

At the Trades Union Congress in 1885 the idea of forming a Labour Party was revived. During the years 1881 to 1885 the Social Democratic Federation, the Fabian Society and the Socialist League had come into existence and agitated in favour of socialism. The industrial depression also gave rise to much dissatisfaction in the ranks of Labour. These influences combined to create a desire for a more vigorous attitude of Labour in Parliament. In 1886, when as many as ten working men sat in Parliament, the Labour Electoral Association was formed. Its principles were formulated at the Trades Union Congress of 1886, by T. R. Threlfall in the following resolution :—

" This Congress views with satisfaction the growing intelligence of the masses to recognise in their emancipation the power they possess to demand the inalienable right of men in making laws to which they have to subscribe ; and in order to give practical effect to the various resolutions passed at previous Congresses on the question of Labour Representation it is essential to form an Electoral Labour Committee which shall act in conjunction with the Parliamentary Committee, the Labour Representatives in the House of Commons, and the friends of Labour Representation throughout the country."

In the same resolution Threlfall gave an outline of such an organisation, and the whole was carried by an overwhelming majority. The Labour Electoral Association worked from the outset in conjunction with the Liberal organisations, opposing socialist and independent Labour action. The weakness of Liberalism in those years and its defeat in 1895 proved fatal to the Labour Electoral Association. Before it expired the working men had already returned fifteen of their leaders to Parliament, including J. Keir Hardie and John Burns, who were elected in 1892, the former running as an independent Labour man, the latter as a social democrat. The terms " socialism " and " social reform " had lost well-nigh all terror in the eyes of Labour, and in the years from 1893 onwards it was an easy matter to carry at Trades Union Congresses social reform and even orthodox socialist resolutions. But the idea of Labour independence, directed alike against Liberals and Conservatives, was regarded by the bulk of trade unionists as the acme of revolutionary thought, as the most repellent expression of class warfare.

It would, however, be a mistake to conclude from the adoption of socialist resolutions by the Trades Union Congresses that British organised Labour had embraced socialism. There is no such thing to-day as a miraculous or wholesale conversion of masses by fiery speeches or decrees of assemblies. The favourable reception of those resolutions merely indicated that the working men were inclined to promote social reform through legislation. They knew that the socialist objective could never be embodied in a Bill to which the parties would have to adopt a definite attitude ; it was not practical politics and, therefore, not worth while opposing it and provoking long debates as to the feasibility of a sudden transformation of society. On the other hand, an independent labour party, in opposition both to Liberals and Conservatives, was an important living issue which could not be decided by a Congress resolution.

XII

REVIVAL OF SOCIALISM

I.—EXHAUSTION OF LIBERAL THOUGHT

IN the chapter dealing with the general characteristics of the last sixty years it has been pointed out that about the year 1880 Liberal thought found itself in the throes of a crisis. The conviction was beginning to gain in strength and volume that Liberalism was not in a position to perform what it had promised. The condition of the country was not satisfactory either in foreign or home affairs. The depression of trade grew worse and swelled the number of the unemployed. The political movement of the working classes, the appearance of trade union representatives in the House of Commons (1874), the organising efforts of the agricultural labourers, were regarded by the ruling classes as the beginnings of a new period of class warfare. Meredith's *Beauchamp's Career* (1875) mirrors the feelings and misgivings, as well as the hopes and longings of the incipient social rebellion : " The people are the Power to come. Oppressed, unprotected, abandoned ; left to the ebb and flow of the tides of the market, now taken on to work, now cast off to starve, committed to the shifting laws of demand and supply, slaves of Capital—the whited name for old accursed Mammon ; and of all the ranked and black-uniformed host no pastor to come out of the association of shepherds, and proclaim before heaven and man the primary claim of their cause ;—they are, I say, the power, worth the seduction of by another Power not mighty in England now : and likely in time to set up yet another Power not existing in England now." [1]

Another symptom of the decay of liberal thought was the assault on free trade. The movement in favour of fair trade came into being. Historians went to work to revise the liberal

[1] George Meredith, *Beauchamp's Career*, Vol. II., chap. 1.

views of empire and international relations. Professor Seeley's *Expansion of England* evoked an enthusiasm which would have been quite impossible a decade earlier. Ireland grew more determined to press her claim for Home Rule to a successful issue. Parnell on the political side, Michael Davitt on the social economic side, deployed their forces against the Union. The coercive measures employed by the Liberal Government against the Irish roused much dissatisfaction in the Radical ranks. The war against Egypt, the South African tangle, and the situation in India and Afghanistan, deepened the discontent of all the Radical elements in Great Britain. The failure of Liberal governance, the exhaustion and impotence of Liberal thought could no longer be concealed.

It was, therefore, quite natural that the orthodox political economy, the ideology of Liberalism, should be assailed. And the converging assault came from the Marxists, the land reformers, and the new school of social science. J. S. Mill, Alfred Russel Wallace, David Syme, Cliffe Leslie, J. K. Ingram, H. M. Hyndman, Sidney Webb, Belfort Bax, who, while belonging to various schools of social economics, were endeavouring each in his own way to create new currents of thought calculated to favour either social reform or the social revolution.

2.—MARX AND HYNDMAN

Turning our mental gaze retrospectively on those years we see H. M. Hyndman, Belfort Bax, Sidney Webb, William Morris, George B. Shaw, busily engaged in their investigations and re-examinations. Visits were paid to Karl Marx ; Mill's writings received new attention ; Henry George was acclaimed ; the old Chartist pamphlets and periodicals were diligently studied, and the activities of the German social democracy closely examined. These were stirring years of disquisition and discussion, the charm of which can only be imagined by those who, after having wrestled with doubt and uncertainty, finally arrive at a working hypothesis.

Marx's doctrines were only accessible to those Englishmen who read either German or French. In 1880 two articles on

Marx appeared in English monthly magazines, one in favour of the other in opposition to, his doctrines. The former was written by E. Belfort Bax, who, from his intercourse with the refugees of the Paris Commune and from a study of the *Capital*, had embraced socialism. At the same time Henry M. Hyndman began the study of the French edition of *Capital*, which had been recommended to him by Butler-Johnstone, the Turcophile and Conservative member of Parliament. He lost no time in making the personal acquaintance of its author and often paid him visits in order to obtain further instruction from him by word of mouth.[1]

The impression which Marx's vigorous intellect made on Hyndman was enormous and has proved indelible ; on the other hand, the impression which Hyndman left on Marx was anything but favourable. And this was due to the following circumstances. Marx, in his way, was a proud mental aristocrat, having been descended, both on his paternal and maternal sides, from a long line of Rabbis and Talmudic scholars of great repute, and he was related, by marriage, to the high Prussian bureaucracy, his wife being a Baroness Von Westphalen, a sister of the Prussian Home Secretary of the same name, and related to the Argyles. Likewise, his revolutionary past and severe persecutions at the hands of the Prussian, French, and Belgian Governments, were not calculated to assuage his temper. Finally, his enormous erudition and socialist pioneering work gave him a strong feeling of personal superiority. The late Professor Edward S. Beesly, who had known him since 1867, told me, in a conversation I had with him in the winter of 1902, at St. Leonard's, that " Marx was a walking encyclopaedia, in knowledge of history, economics, and philosophy, having had hardly any equal." And Beesly said that, after Marx had the temerity to tell him that Comte, as a thinker, was very inferior to Hegel. To that proud, self-conscious intellect, Hyndman came, as a young Roman patrician, aspiring to the tribunate, might have come to a poor expatriated Greek scholar, say a Polybios, to learn something from him about Hellenic communist movements, and to use this knowledge for

[1] H. M. Hyndman, *Record of an Adventurous Life*, Vol. I., p. 268 *et sqq.* Cf. Sorge's *Briefwechrel*, Stuttgart 1896, p. 180–81.

the purpose of keeping the proletariate within the folds of Roman politics, and to teach his countrymen how to avoid the revolutionary pitfalls which had proved so destructive to Hellas. Of course, Polybios, utterly tamed by Roman power, would not have objected to such a procedure. But it was quite different with Marx. Neither the Prussian State Prosecutors, nor the French Governments before and after 1848, nor English hospitality and " killing with kindness " could tame him. In the autumn, 1880, Hyndman called several times upon Marx, who gave him information about the prospects of the revolutionary movement on the Continent. Hyndman then sat down and wrote a paper under the heading, " The Dawn of a Revolutionary Epoch," which was published in the *Nineteenth Century* (January, 1881), and in which Marx's information was made use of in an anti-revolutionary sense. From that time onwards Marx looked with suspicion upon Hyndman, and regarded him as a news-hunting busybody. Then occurred another incident, which rendered a final breach between the two men inevitable. In June, 1881, Hyndman thought to have progressed far enough to interpret Marxism to his countrymen. He published his *England for All*, in which he embodied the essential doctrines of his master on Capital and Labour, and in the preface he stated that " for the ideas and much of the matter contained in chapter 2 and 3, I am indebted to the work of a great thinker and original writer," whose works he hoped would soon become accessible to the majority of Englishmen. Hyndman, knowing the prejudices of Englishmen against foreigners and, at that time, particularly against Marx, avoided mentioning his name and the *Capital*. But he was quite unaware of the inordinate desire of Marx for public recognition of his work. This great revolutionist had spent years of labour on the writing of *Capital ;* no amount of privation, distress, and suffering would deter him from elaborating its main ideas or from searching for some recondite quotation which might support them. His whole being came finally to be bound up with the fate of his book; any one who disregarded it was sure to be looked upon by its author as a know-nothing or a weakling.

P

After the publication of his *England for All*, Hyndman had no chance with Marx, Engels, and their friends. He was not long in perceiving his mistake or in attempting to remove it. In 1883 he wrote his best book, *The Historical Basis of Socialism*, a comprehensive study on the origin of capitalism, the Labour movement and socialism from the fifteenth century down to the nineteenth. He quoted Marx, Engels, Rodbertus and the whole German school of socialism, but the breach between him and the German Marxists has never been completely repaired. A certain soreness has remained on both sides, which has sometimes been aggravated by the general lack of mental sympathy betwen Englishmen and Germans. Still, it is due to Hyndman that Marxism has found some footing on British soil. For, although Webb, Shaw, and Morris have also been more or less influenced or rather stimulated, by the writings of Marx, it was Hyndman who became his English disciple and spread his views in season and out of season,[1] and even created an organisation which is based on the doctrines of Marx.

For this work Hyndman was severely taken to task by the *Quarterly Review* in a paper of remarkable ability, the writer of which treated Hyndman as an incendiary.[2] But a Catiline he never was. For all his Marxism and internationalism, he has remained what he was in the 'seventies—a patrician, aspiring to the tribunate, a sort of an English Tiberius Gracchus, exhibiting the same characteristics as his Roman predecessor, who, according to the description of Appian, was a patriot, burning with zeal to see all his countrymen, the scions of a great race, well-fed, well-housed, and warlike, having a stake in their world-wide Empire, the boundaries of which they should be prepared to defend and to extend.[3]

---

[1] Hyndman, *op. cit.*, p. 251 *sqq.*; Archibald Henderson, *Life of G. B. Shaw*, 1911, pp. 98, 160, *sqq.*; J. W. Mackail, *Life of William Morris*, ed. 1911, Vol. II., p. 97; *Fabian Tracts*, No. 41, p. 16.

[2] *Quarterly Review*, October–December, 1883, p. 352, *sqq.*

[3] Appian, *Civil Wars*, book i., ch. 11.

3.—THE ASSAULT ON ORTHODOX POLITICAL ECONOMY

The theories propagated in Great Britain by Adam Smith, David Ricardo, and their interpreters and commentators, were essentially the ideology of the business interests of the British manufacturing and commercial classes, or what the socialists call the modern *bourgeoisie*. The cardinal error of those theorists was that they regarded man as a constant factor, that they identified him with the business man, and believed political economy to furnish an eternal model to civilised society. Man and, therefore, society were thought to have always been actuated by the desire of gain, by the wish to improve their material condition, and if left unhampered by State intervention and mediaeval traditions, they would surely attain to that happiness which everybody was striving after. The individual, sovereign and freely competing in a free market, was the centre of the universe.

The commercial crises, the distress and misery, Chartism and the general dissatisfaction gradually undermined those theories, and we saw J. S. Mill straining at the leash put upon him by his father, the orthodox interpreter of Ricardo. In the 'seventies the authority of the Ricardians was gone. A new school was arising, a school which made a great effort to make political economy one of the departments of social science or sociology, to have it looked upon only as a phase in the evolution of human society, and to subordinate the whole to ethics. This new British school of social science, whose pioneers were Ruskin, Cliffe Leslie, David Syme, J. K. Ingram, Toynbee, and Cunningham, owed its theoretic origin partly to the influence of the Christian Socialists of the earlier decades ; partly to Comte and the English Positivists ; and partly to the German historical school of Knies, Roscher, Kautz, and Schmoller. It was assisted by the spread of biological knowledge, which suggested many, though superficial, analogies between a biological organism and social life. Herbert Spencer was the pioneer of this kind of speculation in Great Britain.

John Stuart Mill formed the connecting link between the

old and the new school, for he was, as he relates in his *Auto-biography*, " a mind always pressing forward, equally ready to learn either from his own thoughts or from those of others," and he learned a good deal from French socialism. His mental crisis was caused by reading its works as well as those of Comte. And Comte himself was under very great obligation to the socialists,[1] he having been the collaborator of St. Simon.   John Ruskin's *Unto this Last* and *Munera Pulveris* were undoubtedly the effect of having for a time been associated with Maurice, Kingsley, and Ludlow in the 'fifties ; his social economic sermons led in the same direction, though to a more definite goal than Mill's,—namely, to the subordination of the individual to society, the substitution of social service and co-operation in the place of individual gain and competition.   Cliffe Leslie, who learned from the German historical school, was befriended by Mill, David Syme by Leslie, while Ingram, a Comtist himself, tried to view the history of political economy from the standpoint of his master.   Many of these impulses and currents operated on Arnold Toynbee, Cunningham, Ashley, Foxwell, Hewins, and Alfred Marshall, who attempted to create a British school of economic history,directed against the orthodox political economy. The latter point is the common measure of all those factors mentioned above.   The rise of this movement in all its ramifications, which took place in the United Kingdom (Leslie and Ingram were Irishmen) between 1860 and 1890, would well deserve of special treatment,[2] but we cannot do here more than indicating those features which are relevant to our subject.

Comte was introduced to the British public by the indefatigable Miss Harriet Martineau and G. H. Lewes.   But it was J. S. Mill who brought Comte's influence to bear upon political economy.

---

[1] Cf. Alfred Marshall, *Principles of Economics,* third edition, p. 64.
[2] Professor W. J. Ashley, in his *Address to the British Association* at Leicester, August 1, 1907, made such an attempt, but it is very meagre and misses the historical significance of the movement.   I am told that Professor Foxwell also published a paper on the subject in the *Quarterly Journal of Economics,* Boston, 1887, but I could not get it.

While studying the *Cours de Philosophie Positive* he could not but be struck by the sneers of its author at the futile and scholastic squabbles of the political economists, on the one hand, and by his treatment of economics as a department of social science, on the other. Mill found there certain ideas which reminded him of the Germano-Coleridgian school,[1] as well as of Richard Jones. Comte showed him human society in a process of evolution, in which the various groups of phenomena were connected with one another, so that changes in one group led to modification in other groups. He further taught him that the path of social reform lay in the subordination of life to ethics, in the training of the sympathetic impulses, which, by the way, also, Adam Smith was quite aware of, when dealing not with material wealth, but with moral sentiments. The English Positivists, a very conservative body, were spreading the same views.

The German historical school, partly from their organic view of social development, partly from an antipathy against modern industrialism and unrestricted competition,—an antipathy which originated in their veneration of the State as the supreme moral authority in social life, was averse from the classical English political economy and turned to the analysis of the diverse forces which operated in the various periods of the civilised nations, and which gave rise to social problems, legislative acts, and political arrangements. Social relations, according to that school, are not a natural phenomenon, but the creation of human volition and controlled by the ethical concepts and views of man under various historical conditions. This school, for the purpose of strengthening the weak and keeping society together, favoured social reform legislation, corporate or State organisation with a view to prevent society being atomised or broken up by conflicts.

The three currents of thought—Christian socialist teachings, (as spread by Ruskin), Comtism, and German ethical and historical economics, converged in the 'seventies of the last century and affected British economics in two ways.

The one effect was the revival and prosecution of historical

[1] Cf. *supra*, Part II., p. 272–73.

and social studies, to which, in the United Kingdom itself, Jones, Maine, and Stubbs had imparted a strong impulse. The beginning of the 'eighties witnessed the publication of Cunningham's *Growth of English Industry and Commerce*, Seebohm's *Village Community*, Hyndman's *Historical Basis of Socialism*, Toynbee's *Industrial Revolution*, Belfort Bax's and William Morris's *Socialism : Its Growth and Outcome*, Booth's *London Life*, leading up to the Webbs' *History of British Trade Unionism, Industrial Democracy*, and other historical and social studies, connected either with the Fabian Society and the London School of Economics or with the socialist movement in general.

The other effect was a new tendency in British economic theory, which endeavoured to dethrone the orthodox political economy. The foremost representative of the new tendency was Cliffe Leslie, whose acute intellect and great learning predestined him to do for the new school what Adam Smith had done for the old one. He was, however, prevented by bad health from achieving his purpose. He only left a collection of essays and some papers in the *Fortnightly Review*, all of them exceedingly suggestive and stimulating. His leading idea was : " The whole economy of every nation . . . is the result of a long evolution in which there has been both continuity and change, and of which the economic side is only a particular aspect or phase. And the laws, of which it is the result, must be sought in history." [1] He saw the time coming when democratic legislation would intervene in directions not in accordance with the doctrines to which the interests of the great capitalists and landowners were attached. Ideas of social obligation would play a much greater part in the economic sphere than they have ever done since Adam Smith based a complete economic code on the desire of every man to better his own condition. [2]

A more systematic attempt to formulate the views of the new tendency was made by David Syme, a friend of Cliffe Leslie. His leading idea is : " The (old) economists insist that the

[1] Cliffe Leslie, *Essays in Pol. and Moral Philosophy*, Dublin and London, 1879, p. 227.
[2] *Id.*, *Fortnightly Review*, November, 1881, pp. 658–9.

individual is the best judge of his own interests. The doctrine is one that I am not disposed to dispute. All that I insist upon is that the principle should have a more general application and that society should in regard to ability of judging as to its own interests, be put upon the same footing as the individual." [1] The tone and mode of expression are quite Fabianesque. The right of society to protect its own interests would of course mean the subordination of the interests of the individual to those of the community at large. It would mean co-operation in the place of competition. Indeed, the best criticism of competition came from Syme. He anticipated the movement towards syndicates, pools, and trusts, as a result of competition. He argued : The object of the producer in engaging in any branch of industry being profit, he would naturally take all the means at his command to increase that profit to the utmost. And this was only possible if he had the whole market to himself and were not compelled to share it with others, for as a rule, the greater the amount of competition in a given market, the smaller the profit to be divided among the competitors. It would thus become the object of every competitor to reduce the number of his rivals. In other words, in order to render competition successful, a monopoly must be established, either by causing the economic death of a great number of competitors or by command of a large capital, that is by the amalgamation of the strongest competitors who refused to get killed. In that process those competitors would succeed who were not troubled with any moral principles. " Competition leads to the destruction of all morality, and nobody appears to be ashamed of it." [2] The whole economic system of to-day was such that the less consideration a man needed the more he got, and the more he needed the less was shown to him. " In the economic world honesty counts as nothing, and help comes in the inverse order of a man's needs." [3] Syme condemned the British commercial policy in India, and showed that the British commercial supremacy in the 'fifties and 'sixties was often due to dumping. Altogether, Syme's final

[1] David Syme, *Outlines of an Industrial Science*, London, 1876, p. 168.   [2] *Ibid.*, p. 83.   [3] *Ibid.*, p. 53.

view was that ethics was the real foundation of social science, one department of which was economics.[1]

What Syme was teaching by means of cold, clear reasoning, Ruskin was preaching with supreme moral fervour and found a large audience among the young men and women who became dissatisfied with conditions which, as Matthew Arnold then declared, had created a materialised upper class, a vulgarised middle class, and a brutalised lower class.[2] Ruskin won able followers in Patrick Geddes and John A. Hobson. Likewise on its biological and philosophical side, the new school of social science has produced some good work—Karl Pearson's *Socialism in Theory and Practice* (1884), Ritchie's *Darwinism and Politics* (1889), Bonar's *Philosophy and Political Economy* (1893). H. G. Wells, an amazingly prolific literary craftsman, who gave to the socialist movement *New Worlds for Old* (1908), started as a biologist, and J. Ramsay MacDonald, one of the leaders of the Labour Party, had a biological training.

Far less satisfactory, from the socialist point of view, has been the work of the University professors. Some of them have used the historical method to defend Protection, the tariff movement, and Imperialism; their assault on orthodox political economy has meant an assault on free trade, international peace, and socialism. Only the greatest among them, Professor Alfred Marshall, has remained true to the new school, but owing to his constitutional dread of generalisation and decisive action, his *Principles of Economics*, which ought to have been the *Novum Organum* of the British historical school, is, for all its learning, breadth of views, and mastery of method, a disappointing performance. All that has been left of the storm and stress of the 'seventies and 'eighties is a polite bow to " the ethical forces, of which the economist has to take account," [3] a generous compliment to the German Jews for the

[1] *Ibid.*, p. 175.

[2] Matthew Arnold, *The Future of Liberalism*, in *Nineteenth Century*, July, 1880, p. 17.

[3] Alfred Marshall, *Principles of Economics*, third edition (Preface to the first edition).

many daring speculations as to the conflict of interests in society,[1] and an acknowledgment to the socialists, " among whose wild rhapsodies there were shrewd observations and pregnant suggestions from which philosophers and economists had much to learn."[2]

Still, from the new school of British economics have come many men and women to the socialist movement, particularly to the Fabian Society.

4.—THE INFLUENCE OF MILL AND THE LAND REFORMERS

Besides the work of the International Working Men's Association and the new economics, social criticism was kept alive in the 'sixties and 'seventies by the land reformers, and they based their theories not only on the law of nature but increasingly on economic grounds.

David Ricardo's theory of value forms the starting-point of Marxist economics, and Ricardo's theory of rent forms the foundation of the modern theories of land and taxation reform. According to Ricardo rent was the result of the general progress of civilisation, or, as Ricardo thought, of the activity of Capital, yet it only served to enrich the landlords who did nothing for the progress of mankind. Ricardo considered that the remedy lay in free trade ; as a staunch adherent of the existing state of society and of *laissez-faire*, he had no inclination whatever to tilt against the institution of private property, but rather to remove the impediments or neutralise the cross-currents which he believed were vitiating the beneficent workings of private enterprise and the operations of the inherent laws of social life. But he was succeeded by reformers who combined his theory of rent with the doctrines of laws of nature and of the rights of man, as expounded by Locke, Spence, Ogilvie, and Paine. They demanded heavy taxation of ground rent or its complete extinction by the agency of taxation or by land nationalisation.

Many social reformers went still further and formulated the demand that all incomes which bore the character of rent should

[1] *Ibid.*, p. 51 ; Marshall means evidently Marx and Lassalle.
[2] *Ibid.*, p. 64.

be turned into the main source of taxation.   This is the doctrine of " unearned increment," which J. S. Mill, following a suggestion of his father, worked out.   For the period from 1848 to 1880 Mill was, in theory, as authoritative as Smith, Bentham, and Ricardo had been from about 1780 to 1848.   He was the philosopher and political economist of the transition from *laissez-faire* to social reform.   His inconsistencies and oscillations were admirably adapted to a period which was to all intents and purposes liberal, but contained elements working for a new conception of social organisation.   Everybody could find in Mill's writings what he was looking for.

Mill's concept of landed property is akin to that of socialism. Such a right of property, he thought, was an expediency ; it was not as " sacred " as property in movables, for " no man made the land ; it is the original inheritance of the whole species." [1]   Rent he considered to be the effect of a natural monopoly and a fit subject of special taxation.   " Suppose," he says, " there is a kind of income which constantly tends to increase, without any exertion or sacrifice on the part of the owners ; those owners constituting a class in the community, whom the natural course of things progressively enriches, consistently with complete passiveness on their own part.   In such a case it would be no violation of the principles on which private property is grounded, if the State should appropriate this increase of wealth, or part of it, as it arises.   This would not properly be taking anything from anybody ; it would merely be applying an accession of wealth, created by circumstances, to the benefit of society, instead of allowing it to become an unearned appendage to the riches of a particular class.   This is actually the case with rent.   The ordinary progress of a society which increases in wealth, is at all times tending to augment the incomes of landlords. . . . They grow richer, as it were, in their sleep, without working, risking, or economising.   What claim have they, on the general principle of social justice, to the accession of riches ?   In what would they have been wronged

[1] J. S. Mill, *Principles of Pol. Economy*, sixth ed., book II, chap. 2, § 6.

if society had, from the beginning, reserved the right of taxing the spontaneous increase of rent, to the highest amount required by financial exigencies?" The arguments advanced by Mill have been adopted by all land reformers. The remedy he proposes is taxation of land values. "The first step," he proceeds to declare, "should be a valuation of all land in the country. The present value of land should be exempt from the tax; but after an interval had elapsed, during which society had increased in population and capital, a rough estimate might be made of the spontaneous increase which had accrued to rent since the valuation was made."[1]

We shall see later on how the principle of rent and the inferences drawn from it have been applied to unearned increments of industrial and financial wealth, thus forming the basis of British social reform[2]. For the present we shall confine ourselves to the subject of ground-rent and to the reform schemes connected therewith.

Two years after the publication of Mill's *Principles* a Scottish reformer, Patrick E. Dove, developed a theory of land reform which culminated in the Single Tax scheme. He argued that the land was the heritage of mankind, and that it ought not to be turned into private property nor divided into separate holdings. Common ownership was a right principle. On the other hand, the events of 1848 had demonstrated that communism was unattainable. If, then, division and private ownership were wrong and men were not yet fit for communism, how could the use of the earth be made accessible to all? Dove replied that by means of the nationalisation of rent the income derived from this source would be sufficient to defray the expenditure of government and enable the nation to abolish all other taxes. There were but two sources of taxation, land and industry. The taxes on industry or labour, the true source of property, was robbery pure and simple; the industrious were

[1] *Ibid.*, book v., chap. 2, § 5.

[2] An indication of this line of reasoning is given *supra*, Vol. I., p. 151; compare Mill, *Principles of Pol. Economy*, book iii., chap. 5, § 4.

deprived of a portion of their property and freedom and weakened
in their initiative. On the other hand, the earth was not made
by man, but given to mankind for the benefit of all, and was
therefore the proper source of taxation. Trade and industry
liberated from the incubus of taxation, would then be able freely
to develop to the advantage of the whole nation.[1]

Dove's theory implies unrestricted competition in manufacture
and commerce; freedom from taxation for the middle and
working classes; and inviolability of private property as the
product of personal efforts. It resembles in its results the
doctrine of Thomas Spence, and it entirely anticipates Henry
George's schemes.

In the post-Chartist period land reform was increasingly
popular with Liberals. Even Herbert Spencer, the most anti-
socialist of all political and evolutionary philosophers of the
second half of the nineteenth century, could not shake himself
free from these ideas.[2] In *Reynolds's Newspaper*, Bronterre
O'Brien published from time to time, until his death (1864),
articles on land reform, which were collected by his disciples
and published in 1885 under the title *Rise and Progress of
Human Slavery*. And to the present day the doctrines concerning taxation of land values, nationalisation of rent,
and even of the land have found zealous advocates among politicians and reformers who decline to have anything to do with
socialism. In the Land Tenure Reform Association, founded by
Mill in 1870, many of the most prominent Liberal theorists and
politicians worked together with social reformers and members
of the International Working Men's Association, as may be seen
from the following names: Professor Thorold Rogers, John
Morley, Sir Henry Fawcett, Peter A. Taylor, M.P. Professor
Cairnes, Professor Cliffe Leslie, Sir Charles W. Dilke, Alfred Russel
Wallace, Cowell Stepney (Treasurer of the I.W.M.A.), W. Randall
Cremer (first secretary of the I.W.M.A.), George Odger, Benjamin
Lucraft, T. Mothershead, John Weston. Also the last mentioned
four Labour leaders were members of the I.W.M.A., and repre-

[1] Patrick E. Dove, *Science of Politics*, 1850, Vol. I., p. 387.
[2] Herbert Spencer, *Social Statics*, 1851, chap. 9.

sented a large section of the working people of the metropolis. "An active and influential portion of the working classes," Mill remarks, " have adopted the opinion that private property in land is a mistake, and that the land ought to be resumed and managed on account of the State, compensation being made to the proprietors." [1]

The Land Tenure Reform Association was by no means a milk-and-water organisation. It claimed the " unearned increase of the land and the produce thereof for those who were its real authors," that is, society as a whole. It urged upon the nation to take control of the land, for " the State has exactly the same right to control it that it has to control, for instance, the railways."[2]

Similar remarks apply to the Land Law Reform Association, the Land Nationalisation Society, the English and Scottish Leagues for the Taxation of Land Values, and many other organisations which have been connected with land reform, since Mill set the movement on foot, and Henry George's lecturing tours in Great Britain and Ireland in the years 1882 and 1884 inspired it with new life. They have all been more or less Liberal but opposed to complete socialism.

How is this apparent contradiction to be explained ?

Liberal political economy is based on competition, on the unrestricted efforts of the individual to promote his welfare. It presupposes equality of opportunity, equality of external advantages. All restraints of trade, all monopolies of economic goods are repugnant to it. Such restraints and monopolies ought to be mended or ended, if man is to attain to happiness and to a full development of his capacities. Land, however, is *per se* a monopoly,[3] since it cannot be multiplied and it is absolutely indispensable to human existence. If, in addition to its monopolistic nature, it is handed over, by legal monopoly, into the power of the few, a state of things is created which constitutes

---

[1] J. S. Mill, *Programme of the Land Tenure Reform Association*, London, 1871, pp. 6–7.

[2] *Id., Dissertations and Discussions*, Vol. IV., pp. 280–3, 239–88.

[3] *Id., Principles of Pol. Econ.*, book ii., chap. 15, § 1.

the gravest danger to society. Land, therefore, is an economic
good to which the rule of competition or liberal doctrine cannot
apply. It is an exception, and must be dealt with as such.
Individualism must stop short of the land ; it ought to be
controlled by the nation as a whole, and not by any individual
or group of individuals. Land is a proper and legitimate subject
of State interference. The laws and regulations proposed for
this purpose have nothing to do with the system of socialism.

To these arguments the socialist may fairly reply: If the
absence of competition or the existence of monopoly justified
national control of the land, why should not the same arguments
hold good with regard to industrial and commercial monopolies
which resulted from competition ? The course of modern economic
life had amply demonstrated that the result of competition was
not the diffusion of wealth and independence among the greatest
number, but on the contrary the monopolising of the sources of
life by the few,—by syndicates and trusts of multi-millionaires,
and dependence and wage labour of the many. Capital was now
assuming the character of a monopoly, and there would soon be
no difference in this respect between capital and land.

This line of reasoning, based on Marx's theory of the concentration of capital as a result of unrestricted competition,[1] may
serve as an indication of the process of transition from land reform
to socialism, which actually took place in the years between
1880 and 1890, when young intellectuals and intelligent working
men passed from the meetings addressed by the American land
reformer, Henry George, to those addressed by H. M. Hyndman
and Sidney Webb.

In 1879 Henry George published his book *Progress and Poverty*,
which had a large and immediate sale. He at once gained
great popularity as a reformer, as if American and British public
opinion had been waiting for his coming. His fame spread to
the United Kingdom, where Mill's land agitation and the Irish
Land League had prepared the way for the leader of the single-
tax movement. In 1882, when his book had attained a circula-

[1] This argument was brought forward independently by David
Syme, as shown *supra*, p. 235.

tion of about 100,000 copies in the United Kingdom, he came to London and went on a lecturing tour to Ireland. He was accompanied by J. L. Joynes, an Eton master and journalist, who later joined the Social Democratic Federation, popularised Karl Marx, and wrote revolutionary poetry. The Government, scared by the Irish unrest and the Land League agitation, had them both arrested. They were soon set at liberty, and George returned to London, where he delivered lectures on the single tax, which enjoyed much popularity.

George's book contains nothing new to English readers. Its leading ideas are natural rights, Ricardo's and Mill's theory of rent, and the schemes of Spence and Dove. But it is written in a popular and eloquent style, and therefore could not fail to attract the attention of all those who at that time were searching for theories and schemes of social reform. George argued that nowhere in the civilised world did labour receive its just wage. Everywhere was Labour haunted by unemployment. Many people ascribed these phenomena to over-production, others merely designated them as economic crises, others again thought them to be due to over-population. These explanations were wide of the mark. Over-production could not possibly exist as long as there were men suffering from hunger, wearing bad clothes, and living in ramshackle houses. There was no lack of opportunity for work, so long as so many human needs cried for satisfaction, and there were so many hands ready to create the necessary goods. The fundamental cause of the whole evil was to be sought in the fact that the people were shut off from the land, which, combined with human labour, formed the source of all wealth. The most important condition for their existence was monopolised by the few. All men came into the world with equal rights, and all had an equal right to the most indispensable source of life. Men laboured at enriching this source, and yet they were debarred from the free use of it ; the more diligently they toiled in increasing the value of this source, the more it flowed into the pockets of the land monopolists who contributed nothing to the increase. The question, therefore, arose, How could man recover his natural rights ?

George supplied two answers to this question, one for new countries, the other for the Old World. In a newly-opened country it was best to regard the land as belonging to all, and to permit everyone to take possession of and cultivate as much as he required. If parts of the land thus taken possession of had special advantages, then their possessors should pay a rent to society. Similarly, if several people were to apply for the possession of such favoured plots of land, the bidder of the highest rent should get them. In old countries, however, the taxation of rent was the best remedy. All taxes on labour industry, and trade were a burden and an impediment to their free development and should be abolished. Taxation of rent would thus form the single tax.

George further maintained that socialism was incompatible with personal freedom, the greatest good of man. In order to allow everyone to enjoy it to the fullest degree without prejudicing the freedom of his fellow-man it was but necessary to abolish the land monopoly ; such a measure would gradually eradicate the social evils from which Labour was suffering.

Simultaneously with Henry George's agitation, Alfred Russel Wallace published his *Land Nationalisation* (1882), which went through two editions. It is an appeal to the working classes of Great Britain to make a serious effort for the nationalisation of the land, " the birthright of the British people," as the best means towards an amelioration of their miserable condition. Wallace directs his keen criticism at " the fundamental error shown to exist in our social system," to be found in " the leading idea which has governed all social and industrial legislation for the last fifty years . . . that whatever favours and assists the production of *wealth* and the accumulation of *capital* by individuals, necessarily advances the well-being of the whole community. That idea pervaded the whole legislation." But none of these legislative acts have resulted in a diffusion and equalisation of wealth, or in a diminution of the large class ever hovering on the verge of pauperism. . . . The increase of the number of very wealthy people or of any great capitalists (which is what legislation favours), so far from being beneficial, is, in every respect, antagonistic to the well-being of the community at large." [1]

Wallace proposes, in the main, that the State shall assume the ownership of the land and that the holders shall be the cultivators. " Every one," he declares, " must hold land from the State, subject to whatever general laws and regulations are made for all land so held. The State must in no way deal with the individual land-holders, except through the medium of special courts, which will have to apply the laws in individual cases. Thus no State *management* will be required." [2]

However, it was not Wallace's appeal that attracted the attention of the incipient socialists, but Henry George's books and lectures. They stimulated many of the younger generation of intellectuals and working men, and caused them to turn their attention to economics. Four-fifths of the socialist leaders of Great Britain in the 'eighties had passed through the school of Henry George. [3]

In 1884 Henry George came once more to London. A public discussion of single-tax and socialism between him and H. M. Hyndman was held at St. James's Hall. By that time socialism had already two organisations in London, whose members and friends attended that meeting and evinced marked sympathy with the views so ably and eloquently advocated by the socialist opponent of Henry George.

[1] A. R. Wallace, *Land Nationalisation*, second edition, 1882, pp. 11–13.
[2] *Ibid.*, p. 193.
[3] Archibald Henderson, *Life of G. B. Shaw*, p. 115; compare Sidney Webb, *Socialism in England*, p. 19 *sqq.*

I Q

XIII

SOCIALIST ORGANISATIONS

I.—THE DEMOCRATIC FEDERATION

In the history of the socialist revival since 1880 we have assigned one of the foremost places to Henry M. Hyndman. He has been the first to unfurl the banner that had fallen from the hands of the Chartists and the leaders of the International Working Men's Association. His leading ideas are the result of the teachings of Karl Marx, Bronterre O'Brien, and Benjamin Disraeli, all anti-liberal and anti-capitalist, and these ideas have been operating on an intensely English mind in revolt against commercialism. His organising activity began in 1881, when he had many meetings and conferences with various well-known men and women whom he thought to be in sympathy with his own aspirations, or in revolt against official Liberalism. He met Professor Edward Spencer Beesly, Helen Taylor (the stepdaughter of J. S. Mill), Joseph Cowen, Herbert Burrows, and several old Chartists and members of the I.W.M.A. Some of them entered into relations with the Radical working men's clubs and Irish associations in London, and finally decided to form a new Party. It was with this objective in view that Hyndman wrote his *England for All*—a manifesto embodying the principles of English democracy. It was first published in June, 1881, and republished three months later in a cheap popular edition. It distinctly points towards social democracy. It is written with great ability and verve, and it reveals the author as a serious politician actively engaged in forming his own opinion on all the leading political questions of the country. The author was conscious that the task he undertook was difficult and that it demanded many sacrifices; but he thought that the circumstances were favour

ble, for the whole economic life was moving in the same
direction.

On June 8, 1881, a conference of the founders of the new Party
took place, on which the Democratic Federation was formed.
Only a few of its members were clear in their minds as to their
aims. Hyndman was aiming at the creation of a proletarian
movement with the view of continuing the " great work of Spence
and Owen, Stephens and Oastler, O'Connor and O'Brien, Ernest
Jones and George J. Harney." [1] He had discussed with Marx
the Chartist movement and inquired of him whether it would be
advisable to revive it. Marx was in sympathy with the idea,
but doubted its practicability.[2] Hyndman, however, dauntless
and pertinacious as he is, went ahead and worked with might
and main for the new organisation which he had called into being.
He formulated the following programme : (1) Universal suffrage ;
(2) Triennial Parliaments ; (3) Equal electoral divisions ; (4)
Payment of members ; (5) Corruption and bribery of the electors
to be punishable as criminal offences ; (6) Abolition of the House
of Lords as a legislative body ; (7) Home Rule for Ireland ; (8)
Self-government for the Colonies and Dependencies ; (9) Nationalisation of the land.

The latter demand was the only one of a socialist nature,
and was at that time better known and more popular than any
other. The membership of the Democratic Federation increased
but slowly, and was never large. On the other hand, the most
prominent socialists of the country gradually joined its ranks,
among them being Ernest Belfort Bax, a philosophical writer
of much originality; J. L. Joynes; William Morris, a poet and
artist of great renown ; Eleanor Marx, the daughter of Karl Marx ;
among its working men members were John E. Williams, James
Macdonald, and Harry Quelch (1856–1913), editor of *Justice*
from 1892 to his death. In 1883 they published a small pamphlet,
Socialism made plain, which had a circulation of about 100,000

[1] *Justice*, April 19, 1884; March 21, July 25, September 27,
November 21, 1885; Hyndman, *Record of an Adventurous Life*.
Vol. I., p. 294.

[2] *Ibid.*, p. 273.

copies. Its arguments may be thus summarised : social an
political power was monopolised by those who lived on the labo
of their fellow-men ; up to 1832 the landlords had the upp
hand ; from 1832 to 1846 landlords and capitalists jointly rule
and governed, but differed on the subject of free-trade ; ev
since 1846 all difference between them had disappeared and the
took it in turns to govern the country. What was the result
this dominion ? Poverty for the working classes, luxury for tl
few, misgovernment in Ireland, ruin in India. The value of tl
annual production of the United Kingdom amounted to 1,30
millions sterling ; of this sum the few received 1000 millio
in rent, profit, and interest ; the workers obtained 300 millio
only. And yet all wealth was due to labour and ought to l
the reward of labour. This just demand would never be realise
so long as the means of production were monopolised, or so lon
as the system of wage-labour continued to exist. They demande
therefore, the socialisation of the sources of life. The productio
of wealth had already a social character ; it was the produc
of collective work ; all they were asking now was that exchang
and distribution should also be put on a collective basis. Th
Democratic Federation was founded for the purpose of spreadin
these views among the working classes. It had been charge
with attacking private property. No ! It only attacked th
private property of the few who were robbing the many of thei
well-earned property.

The masses were then urged to work for the following measures
(1) Erection of healthy dwellings by the central or local authori
ties and letting them at low rents to working men ; (2) Fre
and universal education and at least one free meal for schoc
children ; (3) An Eight-Hours Day ; (4) Progressive taxatio
on incomes of over £300 ; (5) Establishment of national bank
and gradual abolition of private banking ; (6) Nationalisatio
of railways and land ; (7) Organisation of the unemployed unde
State control on co-operative principles ; (8) Rapid redemptio
of the National Debt.

At the end of 1883 the members of the Federation resolve
to publish a weekly paper. Edward Carpenter placed th

ecessary funds at their disposal, and on January, 1884, the first
umber of *Justice* appeared, with the sub-title, *Organ of Social
Democracy*. Since that date the paper has been issued with
he utmost regularity, but it has never paid its way. The self-
acrifice of a few socialist writers has kept it going. The services
t has rendered to the propaganda of Marxist views in Great
Britain have been considerable.

From the outset the chief agitator has been Hyndman, who
s also a remarkable speaker and writer of a vigorous and trenchant English. It is owing mainly to his tireless energy and un-
flinching courage that the Federation continued to exist, under
various names, up to the Great War. But he also imparted
o it a dogmatic, fierce, and anti-liberal spirit. His most
famous co-worker in the first years was William Morris,
who had been introduced into the Federation by Ernest Belfort
Bax. His devotion to the movement knew no bounds. He
defrayed the first year's deficit of the *Justice*; he delivered
lectures on socialism at street-corners, in the parks and at
working men's clubs, and he played the part of a newspaper-boy
and pushed the sale of the organ of the Federation. He called
upon the masses to join the new movement :—

> " Come, shoulder to shoulder, ere the earth grows older !
>   The Cause spreads over land and sea ;
> Now the world shaketh and fear awaketh,
>   And joy at last for thee and me."

The path, along which William Morris entered the sphere of
revolutionary socialism, took its point of departure in a vague
sentiment of repulsion to the triumphs of commercial civilisation,—a sentiment, born of his study of human history, of his
deep love of life, of his passion for the practice of art. Looking
backwards at the efforts, struggles, and achievements of mankind,
and comparing them with the dull squalor of the mechanical
civilisation around him, he asked himself, " Was it all to end in
a counting-house on the top of a cinder heap, with Podsnap's
drawing-room in the office, and a Whig committee dealing out
champagne to the rich and margarine to the poor ? " Had the
Promethean struggles of mankind produced nothing but this

sordid, aimless, and ugly confusion ?   In this mood, Rusk
was his master towards a new social ideal, while the reading
Carlyle's *Past and Present* merely intensified his disconte
with the present conditions.   Mill's posthumous papers o
socialism, although containing anti-socialist arguments,[1] co
vinced him that socialism was necessary and that it was possib
to bring it about in our own days.   He became a socialist, joine
the Federation, and tried to learn something of the econom
side of the movement.   He tackled Marx's *Capital*, the historic
part of which he thoroughly enjoyed, but suffered agonies o
confusion of brain over reading its pure economics.   Pric
to his conversion to socialism he was for a short space of tim
a Radical.   His views on the failure of Radicalism are embodie
in two letters which he addressed, in 1883, to a Radical frien
and which afford an insight into the mental development o
Morris during that crisis.   Morris wrote :—

   " For my part I used to think that one might further rea
socialistic progress by doing what one could on the lines o
ordinary middle-class Radicalism :   I have been driven of lat
to the conclusion that I was mistaken ;   that Radicalism is o
the wrong line, so to say, and will never develop into anythin
more than Radicalism ;   in fact that it is made for and by th
middle classes and will always be under the control of rich capi
talists ;   they will have no objection to its political development
if they think they can stop it there ;   but as to real social changes
they will not allow them if they can help it ;   you may see almos
any day such phrases as ' this is the proper way to stop the sprea
of socialism ' in the Liberal papers, the writer of the phras
never taking the trouble to find out what socialism meant. . .
Meantime I can see no use in people having political freedom unles
they use it as an instrument for leading reasonable and manlik
lives. . . . .   I cannot help thinking that the workmen will b
soon finding out that for themselves ;   it is certain that Henry
George's book has been received in this country and in America
as a new Gospel.   I believe that Socialism is advancing, and wil
advance more and more as education spreads, and, so believing

   [1] Published by Helen Taylor in the *Fortnightly Review*, 1879.

find my duty clear to do my best to further its advance. . . .
he contrasts of rich and poor are unendurable and ought not
) be endured by either rich or poor. Now it seems to me that,
eling this, I am bound to act for the destruction of the system
hich seems to me mere oppression and obstruction; such a
ystem can only be destroyed, it seems to me, by the united
iscontent of numbers; isolated acts of a few persons of the
iiddle and upper classes seem to me quite powerless against it;
i other words the antagonism of classes, which the system has
red, is the natural and necessary instrument of its destruction.
he system of chattel slavery had to give place to the feudal
ystem of seigneur and serf; and this has been swept away
i favour of our present contract system between rich and poor,
nd this in turn will give place to socialism." [1]

Morris was extremely serious in his socialist views and prepared,
: necessary, to offer his life to the cause he embraced :—

Hear a word, a word in season, for the day is drawing nigh
When the Cause shall call upon us, some to live and some to die !
He that dies shall not die lonely ; many a one hath gone before ;
He that lives shall bear no burden heavier than the life they bore.
Nothing ancient is their story, e'en but yesterday they bled,
Youngest they of earth's beloved, last of all the valiant
    fled. . . . "[2]

In those days British socialists still believed that socialism
vould have to be won by means of physical force. Morris
vas ready to undergo even this ordeal. The speeches of some
if the leaders of the Federation bore a violent character. They
vere reminiscent of Chartist times, and boldly proclaimed the
ild Chartist battle-cry, Peacefully if we may—forcefully if we
nust. At that time the following historical parallel was popular
vith some members of the socialist movement: " Gunpowder
ielped to sweep away feudalism when new forms arose from the
lecay of the old ; now far stronger explosives are arrayed against

[1] J. W. Mackail, *Life of William Morris*, ed. 1912, Vol. II., p.
(09 *sqq.*

[2] This moving poem was written on the occasion of a public
lebate between Hyndman and Bradlaugh on April 17, 1884. It is
published in *Justice*, April 19, 1884.

capitalism, whilst the ideas of the time are rife with revolution as they were when feudalism fell.   To obviate anarchy we must organise and educate the masses."[1]

The concluding sentence lends to this striking parallel a peaceful and statesmanlike aspect, but the catchword of gunpowder against feudalism and dynamite against capitalism was used by unscrupulous adversaries of socialism.

From the commencement of 1884 Eleanor Marx, Dr. Edward Aveling, Henry H. Champion, Walter Crane, and Hunter Watts took an active part in the movement in addition to Hyndman, Bax, Morris, Andreas Scheu, Burrows, and Joynes.   George B. Shaw was very near joining the Federation, but he finally decided in favour of the Fabian Society.

On August 4, 1884, the Federation held its fourth annual conference, at which, on the motion of Burrows and Williams, it adopted the name Social Democratic Federation (S.D.F.), and it retained this name down to 1907.

Until the end of March, 1884, the members of the Federation worked together in harmony and comradeship. Gradually discord and dissension began to make themselves painfully noticeable. As usual the discord was ascribed to personal factors, particularly to the domineering temper of Hyndman. In reality the cause was not so simple.   Unity prevailed during the initial stages of the Federation, owing first to the hope of a speedy success among the working men, secondly to the general want of clearness as to the nature of the means by which socialism could be achieved.   Enthusiasm, hope, and indefiniteness formed a mist which concealed the sharp and jagged outlines of the field of operations.   In the spring of 1884 the failure of the agitation was apparent : the Radical working men's clubs refused to join the Federation ; at the same time the members had to some extent attained to clearer views as to matters of policy.   Schism and discord were the inevitable result.   It was evident that the Federation consisted of heterogeneous elements —parliamentary social reformers, revolutionary social democrats, anti-parliamentary socialists, and pronounced anarchists.

[1] *Justice*, April 19, 1884.

The result was a foregone conclusion. By the end of December, 1884, the disruption was complete. Morris, Crane, Bax, Eleanor Marx, Scheu, and others left the Federation and formed the Socialist League, while Hyndman, Champion, Joynes, John Burns, Hunter Watts, H. W. Lee, Quelch, Williams, Burrows, and others remained in the Federation.

2.—THE SOCIALIST LEAGUE

Before continuing the history of the Social Democratic Federation it is advisable to give an account of the Socialist League, for it was but an episode in the revival of socialism during the last quarter of the nineteenth century. The Federation emerged from the split as a reduced body, crippled both in financial and intellectual resources, but it had gained homogeneity. Its leaders were Hyndman and Champion, who stood head and shoulders above all other members in authority, knowledge, and ability. It was easy for them to impress their views upon the whole organisation. The Socialist League found itself in a quite different position. It lacked unity of views and aspirations ; some of its members had turned their backs upon the Federation, because they mistrusted Hyndman ; others were convinced that it was premature for a socialist organisation to perform the duties of a political party, and that the most urgent task consisted in the dissemination of socialist ideas with the object of gradually educating the working men to independent political action ; others again had a low opinion of parliamentary action or were avowed anarchists.

At that time William Morris belonged to the anti-parliamentarians. His arguments were somewhat as follows : the socialists hoped to see society transformed into something quite different from what it was. They were looking for a revolution, for a radical change of the social institutions. On the other hand, the object of parliamentary institutions was the preservation of society in its present form, and to mend the defects of the political machinery in order to keep it going. Liberal legislation—and there was no other, for the Tories also were forced to legislate in a Liberal sense—meant yielding what was absolutely necessary to popular demands in the assured hope of whittling them down to their lowest minimum, so that the fleecing of the people might never come to an end.[1]

Strictly considered, this argument is directed not only against parliamentary action, but against every kind of reform short of revolution. It may be applied to factory legislation, to social insurance, to trade unionism, and generally to all measures that are aiming at amelioration. The error into which Morris fell lay in regarding society as a mechanical contrivance and reform as a sort of patching up of some defective parts of the machine. This mode of viewing society allows of no other remedy than the complete removal of the old machine and its replacement by another of a quite different pattern. In reality society is not a mechanical contrivance, but a living organism in constant change and development, an organisation capable of being developed into a higher form by legislative and other measures granted to a new class rising in importance and power in society. At first the influence of such reforms on the social structure may be imperceptible, but with the increase of the quantity of reforms the alteration in the quality of society grows apace, until it amounts to a revolutionary change visible to all. Great social upheavals which are designated revolutions are the effect of the inrush of economic and ethical transformations into the region of politics, or of the peremptory demand of a large portion of the nation to give legal effect to them and re-distribute political power accordingly. The real revolution had been going more or less silently for a long time anterior to the upheaval, but, as it had been split up in particular changes and reforms effected during long intervals, there was no considerable resistance to its growth. The revolution, in its dramatic or sensational form, is but an attempt to add up the particular changes and reforms and bring out the sum total. The revolutionary character of a reform does not depend on its volume and sweep, but on its direction and nature. In our time, for instance, any reform is revolutionary which tends to strengthen the

---

[1] *Commonweal*, 1885, p. 61.

working class and to give them control of the means of pro
duction, distribution, and exchange.

Socialists and anarchists who have not yet overcome the
mechanical conception of society would no doubt reject that
definition of revolutionary reform and would maintain that
everything which tended to intensify the dissatisfaction of the
working classes and influence them against the existing order
was revolutionary, while social reform but tended to render
them less dissatisfied and less rebellious and was therefore
anti-revolutionary in its effect. According to this view the
condition of the working classes must grow worse before it
would grow better, while according to the biological view the
condition of the working classes must gradually improve in order
to fit them for the higher duties of social citizenship.

However, Morris hardly speculated upon these questions. He
was undoubtedly of a heroic mould of character, and, like Sir
Thomas More, would cheerfully have mounted the scaffold and
laid down his head on the block. But, unlike Sir Thomas More,
he was infinitely more of an artist and humanitarian than of a
sociologist and statesman. After he had left the Federation
he fell into the hands of anarchists.

It would be hard to find a socialist organisation which exhibited
so much talent and self-sacrifice and at the same time so little
organising and executive capacity, as the Socialist League.
Morris gave it his best, poems of great excellence, newspaper
articles, utopian romances of imperishable beauty of language and
imagination, like the *Dream of John Ball* (1888) and *News from
Nowhere* (1890), and large money contributions. Belfort Bax
was the theorist of the League. With them worked Eleanor
Marx-Aveling, who in energy and devotion equalled her father ;
Dr. Edward Aveling, who translated a part of *Capital*
into English ; Andreas Scheu, an Austrian socialist, of whom
Morris had a high opinion, was one of the agitators ; Frederick
Engels was the adviser of the parliamentary socialists of the
League. In February, 1885, they founded the *Commonweal*,
which was first published monthly, and then weekly. The ablest
members of the League wrote for it. Morris was the editor, and

no paper has ever been directed by a man of greater genius. From 1886 to 1888 Belfort Bax and Morris wrote for it a series of essays under the heading *Socialism : its growth and outcome,* which appeared later in book form ; they are a paraphrase of the *Communist Manifesto,* but based on English economic and political history. From a financial point the paper was never a success ; it suffered from a chronic deficit. The League itself made no progress. Its largest membership only amounted to a few hundred, and even this number was mainly the result of the unemployed agitation and other political demonstrations which were arranged in 1886 and 1887 by the Social Democratic Federation and by the London Radical clubs in favour of the Irish or of free speech, leading to disturbances of the public peace, which will be treated in a later chapter. About the middle of 1887 the anarchists began to gain the upper hand in the League and rendered it impossible for Morris to work with any chance of success for a reunion with the Social Democratic Federation. From that time the League commenced to show signs of disintegration. The parliamentary socialists withdrew in 1888 and either returned to the Federation, or took up the work of organising the unskilled working men and of promoting " New Unionism." In 1889 the victory of the anarchists in the League was complete. They deprived Morris of the editorship of the *Commonweal* and handed it over to Frank Kitz, an anarchist workman, while Morris was patiently defraying the deficits of the paper, which amounted to £4 weekly. In the meantime he had learned much wisdom. He confessed that anarchism was an impossibility and that the anarchists, against their will, taught him that lesson, just as John Stuart Mill, also against his will, had taught him that socialism was necessary.[1] In the autumn of 1890 Morris decided to withdraw from the League, and in November he sent a valedictory letter to the *Commonweal,* in which he summed up his socialist views and his attitude towards the anarchists. He drew attention to the fact that notwithstanding the short space of time of seven years,

[1] J. W. Mackail, *op. cit.*, p. 232 ; compare *How I became a Socialist,* p. 17 *sqq.*, published by *Justice.*

the small number of socialist agitators and their slight mental equipment, the progress of socialist ideas was considerable. He had hoped the working men themselves would produce leaders from their midst. This hope had not been realised. And in the League itself much time and energy had been wasted by petty squabbles, lack of deliberation and of unselfishness, though there had been evidence of courage and readiness for making sacrifices. In spite of all this, socialism had increased in influence, simply because the apparently impregnable edifice of modern society was now on the verge of its downfall. Owing to the knowledge that the victory of socialism was inevitable, there was at present a good deal of discussion as to the proper policy to be adopted. The policy of physical force was senseless and only recoiled on the heads of its advocates. The policy of social reform would lead to State socialism and was equally undesirable. But there could be no gainsaying the fact that the spirit of the time was favourable to the policy of reform. At a period when reforms were being demanded on all sides it was the duty of all true socialists to confine themselves to preaching socialism. Only when a greater number of people professed socialism would it be time to discuss policies and lines of action.[1]

In the last years of his life Morris took no active part either in the S.D.F. or in the anarchist movement. A small group of men and women formed at Kelmscott House the Hammersmith Socialist Society, where Morris used to lecture or to attend the lectures of his friends. The Society published a few pamphlets and signed also the *Joint Socialist Manifesto*, drafted by the representatives of the S.D.F. and the Fabian Society on May 1, 1893.

A deep insight into the character of Morris is given by G. D. H. Cole : " Morris passed from art to socialism, because he saw that under capitalism there could be no art and no happiness

---

[1] In the summer of 1895 Morris invited me to Kelmscott House. In a conversation on Socialism I defended parliamentary action, while Morris thought such action to be of little use in Great Britain. Grant Allen, then famous for his book *The Woman Who Did*, was present and appeared to support the views of Morris.

for the great majority. . . . He saw clearly that, so long as men are in thrall to the industrial system, there could be no good art and no good life for the mass of the people. Perhaps he did not see so clearly the way out—that was less his business. What he did was to put clearly before the world the baseness and iniquity of industrialism, and its polluting effect on civilisation despite the increase of material wealth. . . . He wanted passionately that the things men had to make should be worth making— a joy to the maker and to the user." Those who desire to understand Morris should start with reading his *Hopes and Fears for Art*, " in which he set out clearly his conception of the relation of art to the social system." Then let them read the *Dream of John Ball*, a message of a free England, in which men count as comrades and not as "hands" in a profit-making system. Morris, more than any other prophet of revolution, " is of the same blood as national guildsmen, freedom for self-expression, freedom at work as well as at leisure, freedom to serve as well as to enjoy —that is the guiding principle of his life. Or as Morris sang :

> Ours is the host that bears the word
> *No master high or low—*
> A lightning flame, a shearing sword,
> A storm to overthrow.[1] "

Morris's influence, as we see, is still active ; it is being felt among the Guild Socialists, the Church Socialist League, and literary men who are inclined towards socialism, like Clutton Brock and John Drinkwater.

3.—THE SOCIAL DEMOCRATIC FEDERATION

The S.D.F. began its career in 1885 as a small group, impaired by the defection of the men and women of the Socialist League, and immediately threw itself into the fray of parliamentary action in spite of its numerical and financial weakness. The political situation of the country appeared most favourable to this attitude ; the dissolution of parliament and a general

[1] G. D. H. Cole, *Self-Government in Industry*, third edition, pp. 120–21, 302 (Bell & Sons, London, 1917).

election were imminent. In the previous year the agricultural labourers had obtained the franchise ; the Gladstone Cabinet which had directed the affairs of the country since 1880 had lost much of its prestige on account of the Irish unrest and the Egyptian war ; the Radical wing of the Liberal party was in open rebellion. The end of the old Liberal period, which had become apparent since 1880, was now an established fact. Neither the Conservatives nor the Liberals, for the most part, had any clear idea as to their future policy. Disraeli was dead, and his place as leader of the Conservative party was taken by Lord Salisbury, who was essentially a Whig. The Liberalism of old had been so completely victorious that there was nothing more left for it to do, and it had therefore to disappear from the political arena. What, however, was the Liberal party to do ? The only politician who had an answer ready was Joseph Chamberlain, the member for Birmingham and the idol of his fellow-citizens, just as Thomas Attwood was in his time. In August, 1885, Parliament was dissolved. Chamberlain started his agitation and delivered aggressive speeches on social reform. Liberalism had to be set on its legs again by means of a popular programme. Inequality in the distribution of national wealth was the chief evil that had to be remedied. Free and universal education ; a graduated income-tax ; land reform ; the transformation of the agricultural labourers into owners of small holdings ; an extension of municipal self-government in order to facilitate the enactment of these reforms by the municipalities ; Ireland also would have to obtain a scheme of local autonomy. Lord Salisbury expressed alarm at this programme and dubbed its author " Jack Cade." Indeed, Chamberlain's memorable " Ransom " speeches were reminiscent of natural law doctrine. The whole country was in a state of excitement.

To high-spirited politicians like Hyndman and Champion, the state of affairs seemed to be particularly propitious for the S.D.F. to come forward as a political factor. Both of them attempted, first of all, to negotiate with Mr. Chamberlain, but he bluntly refused to consider their suggestions. Thereupon Champion applied to his friend, Mr. Hudson, the soap manu-

facturer, who provided him with the funds for the candidatur
of John Burns. The Conservative Party, apprehensive of th
victory of the Jack Cades, attempted to split the Liberal vot
and supplied the funds for two other social democratic candidate
The S.D.F. was now able to enter upon its electoral campaig
John Burns contested Nottingham, John E. Williams Ham
stead, and John Fielding Kennington. The elections took plac
in November, 1885. Burns obtained 598 votes, Williams 2
votes, Fielding 32 votes. Socialism was evidently still too wea
for the *rôle* of a political party. The result of the electior
proved for the S.D.F. all but fatal. It lost many of its members
the subscriptions decreased to an alarming extent; the pres
began to ignore its very existence. But this eclipse of the S.D.I
was soon overcome. In 1886 the demonstrations of the unen
ployed and the Radical agitation in favour of the Irish gave th
leaders of the S.D.F. an opportunity for attracting notice an
regaining prestige, and they were not long in seizing it.

The economic depression which began in 1875 reached it
lowest depths in 1886. The number of the unemployed ha
greatly increased; discontent spread in an ever-widening circle
the dissatisfaction with free-trade found expression in th
movement for fair-trade. In addition, the disruption of th
Liberal Party, consequent upon Mr. Gladstone's Home Rul
Bill, deepened the general unrest which had been gathering sinc
1880. The materials for agitation were all ready to hand, and i
was therefore an easy matter to arrange huge demonstratior
in London. In the provinces also, in Manchester, Birminghan
Leicester and elsewhere, unemployed processions were organised
The years 1886 and 1887 were in general characterised by inter
national unrest. Disturbances, strikes, and street fighting too
place in Holland and Belgium; the violent agitations in som
parts of the United States, led by anarchist communists, reache
their climax in the tragic dynamite outrage in Chicago. Alto
gether, it was a most favourable time for the deployment c
popular forces and for arraying them against the existing orde

The leaders of the S.D.F. marshalled the London unemploye
in processions, arranged deputations to various poor law gua

dians, and held open air meetings. In one of these meetings Champion declared that he wished the capitalist class had only one neck, so that the misery of the people could be ended by a single stroke. Hyndman was of opinion that the prayers of the unemployed would only gain the ear of the public if a rich man were to be sacrificed on the grave of every poor man. The S.D.F., however, had not the field to itself. It found a competitor in the movement for fair trade or protective tariffs, into which also some labour leaders had drifted, and which decided to arrange counter-demonstrations with the view of attracting the masses and teaching them that the real cause of their misery was free trade and not capitalism, and that the true remedy was protection and not socialism. Towards the end of January, 1886, the leading men of the S.D.F. learned that the protectionists were thinking of holding a demonstration in Trafalgar Square. The S.D.F. at once decided to arrange a counter-demonstration on the same day and at the same place. On February 8, both the protectionists and the social democrats converged on Trafalgar Square. Under these circumstances a disturbance of the peace could hardly be avoided. The police, therefore, requested the leaders of the S.D.F., in the interest of public order, to transfer their demonstration to Hyde Park. John Burns then seized the red flag, and, with his stentorian voice, called upon the crowd to follow him. Hyndman, Champion, and Williams marched at the head and the crowd followed them. When the demonstration reached the streets in the neighbourhood of Pall Mall, some of the rich young men of the fashionable clubs appeared at the windows and doors, and provoked the crowd by derisive gestures and taunts. A shower of stones against the windows was the prompt reply of the demonstrators. The excitement rapidly increased in intensity, and soon the unemployed attacked the large shops and looted them until the police rushed up and scattered the mob. Hyndman, Burns, Champion, and Williams were arrested and soon released on bail. This, however, was not the only result of the demonstration : in the course of a few days the Lord Mayor of the City of London raised about £75,000 for the unemployed. The newspapers,

I R

which depend for their existence on creating sensations and scares, did their very best to magnify the powers of the S.D.F a thousandfold and to exaggerate its harmfulness to an absurd degree. On April 5, 1886, the four accused socialist leaders were brought before a jury. Burns delivered a great revolutionary speech, while Hyndman was the real counsel for the defence. On April 10 all the defendants were acquitted. In the latter half of 1887 trade improved, and the opportunity for work was more plentiful, so that the unemployed agitation lost its hold upon the masses. The police began to look upon such demonstrations as a nuisance to be checked and took stringent measures against them. On October 18, 1887, the police broke up one of these meetings in Trafalgar Square, and arrested twenty persons. A similar occurrence took place in Hyde Park. The change of Government must also have contributed to the change in the police attitude towards the unemployed demonstrations. The Liberals had been defeated and the Conservatives came in, whose Home Secretary prohibited all meetings in Trafalgar Square. This measure, which was regarded as an attack on free speech, aroused great dissatisfaction among the Radicals in London, who were willing to make common cause with the Socialists in defence of liberty. In addition, the Liberals were dissatisfied with the treatment which Mr. William O'Brien, the Irish member of Parliament, who was then undergoing a term of imprisonment, received at the hands of the prison authorities. The Radicals of London therefore decided to demonstrate in favour of O'Brien on Sunday, November 13, 1887, in Trafalgar Square. At first they tried to induce the Home Secretary to give them the use of the Square. With this object in view they sent to him a deputation headed by Cunninghame Graham, the socialist and Scottish member of Parliament. The Home Secretary received the deputation, but refused their request, whereupon the Radicals and socialists resolved to defy the Government. Sir Charles Warren, at that time Commissioner of the Metropolitan Police, closed the square both with police and military troops. All the bridges leading from the south of London to the Square were guarded by soldiers, and the police formed an iron ring

ound the Square. Contingents of demonstrators from the
outh of London attempted to rush the sentries at Westminster
Bridge, but were repulsed; several of them were wounded,
nd had to be transported to Charing Cross Hospital. The
contingent from the North of London approached under the
leadership of Cunninghame Graham and John Burns. Both of
hem made a determined attempt to force a way through the police
cordon for their men, but were badly handled by the police,
especially Graham, who bled profusely. Both Burns and Graham
were then taken into custody. These events were subsequently
known as "Bloody Sunday." On February 28, 1888, another
demonstration took place, at which a workman, Sinnell by name,
was mortally wounded by the police. The socialists of London
arranged an imposing funeral at which William Morris and Harry
Quelch were the chief speakers. This event coincided with the
conclusion of the period of unemployed demonstrations. Graham
and Burns were arraigned before a jury and sentenced each to
six weeks' imprisonment. Their counsel for the defence was Mr.
H. H. Asquith, at that time a barrister, but at the present
day (1914) Prime Minister, with John Burns as his colleague
in the Cabinet (till August, 1914) !

In casting our glance back upon this period, apparently a time
of great ferment and excitement, we must refer to the
apocalyptic hopes to which it gave rise. Although it was the
product of unorganised and practically aimless movements and
agitations, it was regarded by some of the socialist leaders as the
eve of the social revolution. Morris and Champion indeed uttered
warnings against rash measures, but they were both of opinion
that these events had a revolutionary significance. Morris
drew from them the lesson that the task of the socialists consisted in the " education of the people for the revolution," whilst
Champion called attention to the inefficiency of the traditional
fighting by means of barricades. Champion was a soldier and
knew a good deal of military service, which affords an excellent
training for thinking in revolutionary realities. He wrote :

" The recent labour troubles in the United States, Belgium, and
Holland, show the bitterness of the spirit of revolt now aflame

in the hearts of the working classes and the readiness with whic
their enemies call in the assistance of brute force. The firs
object of a general is to get the initiative, to keep in hi
own hands the choice of place and time of fighting. We hav
seen that rioters and even revolutionists have nearly alway
neglected this elementary precaution. Invariably the Goverr
ment selects the occasion and the position. There is no excus
for such fatal blunderings. It seems to arise in this way. I
peaceful times the Socialists of all shades are usually hard a
work denouncing social injustice. Some incidents occur tha
arouse popular indignation, and the revolutionists are suddenl
called upon to make good their words. Too often they hav
not the courage to say : ' This is not the time nor are you pre
pared. Go home and organise victory.' Usually they have beer
goaded by taunts into premature action, with the result ; ruthles
white terror, imprisonment, disorganisation. Nor do some o
our comrades seem to have realised the full meaning of moderr
improvements in weapons of war. In previous times barricade
may have been successful. In the face of our modern arms o
precision and quick-firing guns, barricades are of no use. To b
successful in street-fighting we must have either better weapon
or the positive assurance that the soldiers will refuse to obey
their officers. If we should do it we are just like savages, who
with their arrows and bows, array themselves against Gatling
and Nordenfeldt guns. The *rôle* of street-fighting is over." [1]

It must not be supposed, however, that Champion, in giving
utterance to these wise reflections, renounced the policy of
physical force. On the contrary, he was careful to point out
at the same time that street-fighting would have to give place
to dynamite—dynamite in the hands of small groups of determined men, acting in secret. Nevertheless, Champion must
not be counted among the decided adherents of physical force.
He did not believe in violence as a principle. He was merely
sick and tired of futile demonstrations and doctrinaire discussions.
Successful parliamentary action would have completely satisfied
him. In 1887 he left the S.D.F., and joined the staff of the

[1] *Justice*, August 14, 1886.

Nineteenth Century, working at the same time for the creation of an independent Labour party. The rise of the New Unionism, which may be regarded as one of the results of the ferment of 1886 and 1887, favoured such an idea. In 1889 Champion placed at the disposal of the dockers' strike his military knowledge of deploying and exercising large bodies of men and posting of sentries. He edited the *Labour Elector*, to which he gave a social conservative tendency. In this he was influenced by Maltman Barry, a Conservative disciple of Karl Marx and a writer of ability and great *savoir faire*, who was never appreciated at his true value by his party friends.[1] Champion left England definitely in 1894 and settled in Australia, where he has been active in the interest of social democracy.

Still, the year 1887 was remarkable enough. Its stormy events suggested to the *Westminster Review* the following thoughts : " The community should address itself to the great social questions which every day are knocking more loudly at our doors. The ' convincing statistics ' of official optimists like Mr. Giffen betray a significant miscalculation of the factors and forces in modern society. It may be true, as he is always telling us, that there is not more poverty or misery in England than there used to be. But he omits to state that there is infinitely less disposition on the part of the poor to put up with their poverty. . . . This movement is common to the whole world, and in this country has been largely forwarded by the agitation of the S.D.F., which the general public has alternately ignored and gone into panics over. The effects of the agitation, however, are too patent by this time for it to be sneered at or suppressed." The paper relates further how Champion was invited by the Church Congress to lecture before them on social-

[1] In 1902, on the occasion of the London Trade Union Congress, Mr. (later Sir) Randall Cremer and M. Jean Longuet introduced me to Maltman Barry. On my question as to his opinion about Marx, he gave me the following reply : " As a Conservative, I dislike naturally three things : Atheism, the Jewry, and Germany. Marx united in himself all the three. Yet, when I stood before him, listening to his words, I forgot my idiosyncrasies and I had but one feeling—veneration."

ism, how the Northumberland miners, on the instigation of th
socialists, refused the Parliamentary salaries to their leader
Messrs. Burt and Fenwick, and carried a resolution in favou
of an eight hours' day. " This is the first victory of th
new socialist section, but will not be the last." [1] The auth
of that paper proved a true prophet. The year 1887 saw als
in the northern parts of Great Britain the rise of independer
Labour politics, but there it was Keir Hardie and not Hyndma
who was throwing the ferment into the trade union movemen

Towards the end of 1887 the S.D.F. possessed thirty branche
mainly in London and Lancashire. *Justice* was increased i
size. The S.D.F. began to gain in strength owing to the rise o
New Unionism in 1888, and the successful dockers' strike in 188
The chief leaders in that memorable movement, viz., Ben Tillet
Tom Mann, John Burns, William Thorne, Herbert Burrow
Annie Besant, and Eleanor Marx, either were members of th
S.D.F. or had close relations with it. Ever since that ever
the general interest in socialism has been keener. The establish
ment of the London County Council, the rise of municipa
socialism, the revival of the International Working Men
Association in 1889 at the congresses in Paris and Brussels, th
celebration of May Day, and the general election of 1902, hav
all greatly contributed to the dissemination of socialist idea
The S.D.F., however, had only a membership of about 5,000 i
1894 and about 9,000 in 1900, rising in the first decade of th
present century to about 12,000. Its influence has always bee
an indirect one. It has stimulated action both by its criticis
and by its positive proposals. In parliamentary elections i
has always been unsuccessful. In 1892 it put forward two candi
dates, in Salford and in Bethnal Green, and they received onl
659 votes in all. In 1895 its four candidates polled a total o
3,730 votes. In the general election of January, 1906, it ha
eight candidates, but not a single one was successful. Thei
total number of votes amounted to 22,000, including 4,932 cas
for Hyndman in Burnley, but this number fell to 3,810 in th
December elections of 1910.

[1] *Westminster Review*, December 1887, pp. 1063-64.

4.—PROGRAMME AND ELECTORAL POLICY OF THE S.D.F.

The federation has had two programmes since its foundation. The first, which was adopted in October, 1884, ran as follows :—

Labour is the source of all wealth, therefore all wealth belongs to labour. The object of the S.D.F. is the establishment of a free society, based on the principles of political equality, with equal social rights for all and complete emancipation of Labour. Our demands are : all officers or administrators to be elected by universal suffrage ; legislation by the people ; abolition of the standing army ; establishment of a militia ; the people to decide upon peace and war ; free, secular, and compulsory education ; free justice ; Home Rule for Ireland and the Colonies ; the production of wealth to be regulated by society in the common interest of all ; the means of production, distribution, and exchange to be declared as collective property.

This is followed by the programme adopted by the Democratic Federation.

The programme has been extensively amended since 1893 and took shape as follows :—

OBJECT.—Collective ownership of the means of production, distribution and exchange managed by a democratic State in the interest of the whole commonwealth ; complete emancipation of labour from the domination of capital and landlords ; establishment of social and economic equality between the sexes.

This is followed by the demands which are identical with those of the former programme. Finally the following measures are demanded as palliatives or temporary reforms "in order to alleviate the evils of existing society" ; public authorities and corporations to build healthy houses for the people, the rents solely to cover the cost of building and maintenance ; free, secular, and technical education, to be compulsory for all classes ; likewise free feeding and clothing of children in all national schools. Child-labour is forbidden until the age of sixteen years ; employers are to be severely punished for any violation of these measures. The normal working-day consists of eight hours or less, but not more than forty-eight hours in the week ; any breach of this law is to be punished. Cumulative taxation all incomes over £300 a year. Nationalisation of railways; municipalisation of gas, electricity, and water ; organisation of road-traffic in towns and of similar public monopolies in the interest of the whole commonwealth. Extension of the Post Office Savings Banks, so as to absorb all private institutions drawing profits from banking transactions. Repudiation of the national debt, collective ownership of land, organisation of agriculture in the interest of working men by the State and the municipality on the basis of co-operative principles. Disestab- lishment of the Church. Pensions for aged and invalid workers. Every person of the age of fifty to be released from the obligation to work, and granted the right to be supported by the State Erection of municipal hospitals. Municipal control of the supply of coal and foodstuffs. Abolition of the present system of the maintenance of the poor, and the unemployed to be provided with useful work. State control of the lifeboat service. Pay- ment of members of Parliament and municipal officials ; election expenses to be defrayed by the State. Universal suffrage, annual parliaments, proportional representation, abolition of plural voting, abolition of monarchy and the House of Lords, self- government for all parts of the Empire.

It is manifest that the programme grew up by successive ad- dition of all kinds of reform measures, as opportunity demanded The members of the S.D.F. have, as a rule, attached little importance to the palliative measures. They regarded them as being only capable of alleviating the social evils, but not of radically curing them. At the best they could but serve as a stimulant to the ailing, and give them a chance of pulling through the crisis. There was, however, a section of the S.D.F. who regarded palliatives as positively injurious, since they were calculated to render the existing order more bearable, to lull the people and keep them quiet. The argument used by this section was that the task of the socialist was to allow the existing state of things to grow as bad as possible in order to aggravate class warfare, and cause it to rise to the intensity and volume of a social revolution. But even those members of the S.D.F.

who expressed approval of palliative measures failed to see that they were well worth fighting for, that the struggle waged on their account must lead to two results—first to a moral and intellectual improvement of those who are engaged in the battle for reform, secondly to a change in the social structure.

The attitude of the S.D.F. towards social reform was not much in advance of that of Chartism. It drew up an extensive programme of reforms in order to depreciate it. Its annual conferences recommended palliative measures and they were haunted by the fear that they might postpone the revolution. This ambiguity led to misunderstandings and contradictions, which in 1903 and 1905 caused members in Scotland and London to secede from the S.D.F. and call rival organisations into being. They faced the consequences and condemned all propaganda for reform, devoting their energies to the spread of uncompromising, revolutionary socialism. The Scottish secessionists organised themselves into the Socialist Labour Party (1903) after the model of the American Socialist Labour Party, led by Daniel De Leon (d. 1914), a professor of international law at the Columbia University, New York, and an extreme Marxist, who in the last years of his life embraced syndicalist views, without however rejecting Parliamentary action. The London secessionists formed the Socialist Party of Great Britain (1905), and with much perseverance and self-sacrifice have been disseminating Marx's views on economics and political class warfare.

The lack of clearness concerning the relation between reform and revolution, the faith in the efficacy of carrying theoretic resolutions and programmes, and the misinterpretation of Labour politics, have prevented the S.D.F. from developing into a great Socialist Labour party, or bridging the gulf between pure sublimated theory and the complexities and crudities of social life.

The S.D.F., for the same reason, was never able to reach a complete unanimity with regard to electoral policy. Its principles, which were the outcome of the theory of class-war, consisted in adopting the same attitude to the Liberal as to the Conservative party, with a spirit of enmity to both of them. No alliance, no compromise with outside bodies. Independent action as social democrats in opposition to all non-socialist candidates, whether the latter belonged to the capitalist class or to the working class. It was not merely the capitalist, it was the non-socialist who had to be opposed. In practice, however, it was not possible to give effect to these principles. At elections the members of the S.D.F. displayed the tendency to vote for the Radicals in constituencies where no social democrat candidates had been put forward. The violation of this principle caused much discontent. This was increased by the old Chartist tradition that the Whigs (the Liberals) were the real enemies who had to be swept out of the way. These fluctuations in opinion were expressed in the eighteenth and nineteenth annual conferences (1898 and 1899). At the former conference the following resolution was proposed by the committee :—

" This Conference is of opinion that the votes of members should be consistently used for opposing Liberal candidates. Wherever no social democrat candidates are standing, our members should at all times vote for the Tories, excepting in the case of candidates who belong to the extreme Radical section of the Liberal party, and are ready to work for the realisation of our immediate demands."

After Hyndman and other delegates had spoken in favour of the resolution, Dan Irving, the delegate from Burnley, moved the following amendment :—

" In view of the fact that capitalists and landlords show the tendency at elections to combine in injuring the interests of the people, the Conference urges upon the Executive Committee to induce the members to cast their votes against both Liberals and Conservatives and to keep solely in view the interests of socialism, except in cases where the candidates are extreme Radicals."

The difference between the two resolutions is sufficiently clear. The former resolution was particularly directed against Liberal-ism, whose destruction is considered as the most important task of the socialists as voters. This policy of the S.D.F. is an exact, though unconscious, repetition of Feargus O'Connor's attitude in 1840–41. The other resolution is strictly social revolutionary and coincides with Bronterre O'Brien's views at that period.

The Executive withdrew its resolution in favour of Irving's, which was passed unanimously. Nevertheless, a year later the Executive reaffirmed its belief in the resolution it had withdrawn and placed it before the annual conference. It provoked a keen discussion. Irving and Burrows spoke against it. The latter declared that the Federation had neither the power to injure the Liberals nor the mandate to force social democrats to vote for Tories. Finally, the resolution was adopted by 51 votes to 31, but it possessed merely an academic value.

5.—THE RELATION BETWEEN THE S.D.F. AND TRADE UNIONISM

In September, 1884, the S.D.F. defined its attitude towards British trade unionism. John Burns was the chief agitator against the trade unionist leaders who had relapsed into Liberalism. He accused them of venality and lack of principle, and called upon working men to rouse themselves from the slumber in which they had been sunk since 1848.[1] Two months later the Executive Committee of the Federation published a manifesto to the Trade Unions, reproaching them with having forgotten how to fight and with having made peace, or even concluded an alliance, with capitalism. They made no reference to the class struggle that really existed and must go on between Labour and Capital. They proclaimed by silence a truce where there was no truce. The trade unions represented only the merest fraction of the workers. Yet they pretended to speak for Labour. The trade unions unhappily only thought of improving the social position of the more favoured few affiliated to their body, and they were blind to the misery of the masses. They failed to see that it was not improvement but revolution that was wanted. The raising of wages, the shortening of hours, were the loftiest things for which they strove. The trade unions must understand that it was the wage-system that must be fought. Private property in the means of production must cease, and associated

[1] *Justice*, July 19, 1884.

labour with equitable distribution of its produce must take its place.[1]

This manifesto inaugurated the era of hostility between the Trade unions and social democracy, which lasted for more than a decade, and gave rise to polemical excesses on both sides. The social democrats condemned trade unionism root and branch, while the old trade unionist leaders proclaimed themselves the bulwark against revolution. Gradually, however, these excesses and enmities ceased. With the rise of the New Unionism and the formation of the Independent Labour Party, both camps, socialism and Labour, arrived at a better and truer appreciation of their respective spheres of action. A current of ideas more friendly to trade unionism set in among the S.D.F. societies in the North of England, whose members began to urge a revision of the S.D.F. views concerning trade unionism. At the seventeenth annual conference (1897) of the S.D.F. the Executive recommended all members of the Federation to join trade unions and co-operative societies, because these were organisations tending to the improvement of the conditions of the working classes. At the same time the members were called upon to do their best for the education of the trade unionists in socialism, and to extend their political support to trade unionists and co-operators as a means to the promotion of the socialist aim and end. The mover of this resolution, Dr. Edward Aveling, speaking in support of it, declared that it was high time to make an authoritative declaration on the relation between the S.D.F. and trade unionism, Everyone was aware that the opinions of the Federation on this matter were divided. It was the duty of socialists to permeate the trade unions and co-operative societies with collectivist views, since the ideas of the organised working men were moving in a socialist direction. The resolution was seconded by Dan Irving, who stated that the opinions of some social democrats were repellent to trade unionists. After a rather lengthy discussion, in which all views found expression, the resolution was carried by 46 votes to two.[2]

[1] *Justice*, September 6, 1884.
[2] Report of XVII. Annual Conference of the S.D.F., 1897, p. 20.

At the twenty-second annual conference (1902) the question of the relation of the S.D.F. to trade unionism received further elucidation. Harry Quelch, editor of the *Justice*, moved the following resolution on behalf of the Executive :—

" In view of the increasing tendency of the Trade Unions to enter into politics[1] . . . the Conference recommends all members of the S.D.F. to become active members of their trade unions so far as possible, and to bestir themselves to lead their political activities into socialist channels. Whilst expressly laying stress on the view that the collective ownership of the means of production, distribution, and exchange must be the objective of every actual movement of the working class, and that this object can only be attained by an energetic class-war until the working class has achieved its emancipation from class-rule—the Conference again confirms the friendly attitude of the S.D.F. to trade unionism and similar organisations and recognises them as corporate bodies of working men, who have combined in order to fight the capitalists. Whilst we decline to form an alliance with the trade unions which might bind us to support men and measures with which the S.D.F. cannot agree, we recommend the affiliated societies to cultivate friendly relations with the trade unions, and we assure the trade unions that we sympathise with them in their fight for better conditions and are ready to work hand in hand with them as soon as they are willing to adopt socialist measures." [2]

The theoretical phases, through which the S.D.F. passed in the years between 1894 and 1902, already indicate that in the meantime considerable political changes must have occurred in Great Britain, and particularly in the ranks of Labour. It is indeed not possible to continue the history of the S.D.F. from 1901 onwards without continually referring to the other socialist organisations, social reform societies and Labour politics, with the history of which we have still to deal.

[1] The Labour Party was formed in the year 1900.
[2] Report of the XXII. Annual Conference, 1902, p. 19–20.

XIV

THE FABIAN SOCIETY

I.—ORIGIN AND NAME

AMONG the many societies for social reform, which came into existence in the years from 1870 to 1890, none has exercised so marked and beneficial an influence on educated public opinion and on legislation as the Fabian Society. In 1882 several persons met in London for the purpose of the study of ethics. The leading spirit was Professor Thomas Davidson, who was born in Scotland, worked as an educationist in the United States of America, and from time to time visited Great Britain. He was essentially an ethical anarchist communist, basing all improvement on self-reform. He gained a small group of adherents in London, to whom he submitted the plan of forming a Fellowship of the New Life with the view of reconstructing human life on the principle of highest morality. After a few months the majority, altogether a dozen men, came to the conclusion that social reform through legislation was at least as important as self-reform through ethical contemplation. They left the Fellowship and settled down to a study of social questions. The outcome of their studies was the formation of the Fabian Society (F.S.) in January, 1884. The Society adopted the name Fabian after Fabius Cunctator, the Roman general, whose tactics, which they undertook to imitate, they defined as follows : " For the right moment you must wait, as Fabius did most patiently when warring against Hannibal, though many censured his delays ; but when the time comes you must strike hard, as Fabius did, or your waiting will be in vain, and fruitless." The author of this motto was Frank Podmore. The F.S. has been from the outset socialist, although its socialism was indefinite, or at least of no special mark. Its members had been stimulated by the agitations of Henry George and H. M. Hyndman as well as by the writings of John Stuart Mill and the whole current of the new school of social science. None of the original members were distinguished by particular talents which could have raised them above the leaders of the Democratic Federation or of any of the social reform societies which then existed. A few months after its formation the F.S. began to attract the attention of two young intellectuals who were in search of light rather than heat, and who were destined to impart to the new organisation a special character. These men were George Bernard Shaw and Sidney Webb. Shaw was at that time an obscure journalist and budding novelist, Webb held a clerkship in the Colonial Office. To these two members the F.S. owes its importance in the history of British socialist thought. They were ably supported by Sidney Olivier, Graham Wallas, Mrs. Annie Besant, Hubert Bland, and William Clarke. All of them brought fresh, open, and critical minds to bear upon economic and social questions, and all of them were conscious that they had still a good deal to learn, before they could teach and act. They read Marx, Lassalle, Proudhon, Owen, as well as the English economists, Smith, Ricardo, Mill, Cliffe Leslie, and Cairnes, and gradually shook themselves free from the old socialist traditions. This period of study and preparation lasted from 1884 to 1887. It began with a rather mild disapproval of the " statements and phrases " of the Democratic Federation,[1] and it ended with a complete separation from the doctrinal bases and propagandist methods of all socialist organisations. These were years in which the leading Fabians took the offensive against the main doctrines of Marx, Owen, and Chartism. The leader of this campaign was Sidney Webb, an essentially constructive mind, and therefore more fitted for the council chamber and lecture room than for agitation and public demonstration. He found a most responsive and efficient spokesman in George Bernard Shaw, a born fighter and formidable controversialist. Were his ardent temperament and dour determination not counterbalanced by an analytical

[1] *Fabian Tracts*, No. 41, p. 21.

intellect averse from all romanticism, Shaw would have been a revolutionary leader.

Under the guidance of these men the Fabians have endeavoured to do as much for British socialism as was done for British liberalism, in the first decades of the nineteenth century, by the philosophical radicals with Jeremy Bentham and James Mill at their head.[1] The philosophical radicals were not a political party, and yet they succeeded in exercising a permanent influence on the reform movements and on the legislation of that period. Why should not the Fabians, then, be able to perform a similar function in their time ? Theoretically, Bentham's efforts were directed against the system of law of nature, whose most famous exponents at that time were the followers of Rousseau. In a like manner Webb and Shaw brought their critical powers to bear upon the socialist deductions from Ricardian economics, as expounded by Marx and his disciples. In all the writings of the Fabian leaders up to the end of the nineteenth century, even in those that have no direct connection with socialism, the echoes of those battles are still audible. Further, Bentham's practical activities were directed against the landed oligarchy and in favour of democracy. Similarly, Webb and Shaw have always been opposed to the capitalist-liberal oligarchy. Bentham's formula was, " The greatest happiness of the greatest number." The Fabian formula is, " The greatest efficiency of the greatest number." The analogy is still closer. The philosophical radicals, for all their opposition to Rousseauism, arrived at the same conclusions as Rousseau. For all practical purposes it makes no difference whether democracy is deduced from the social contract or from utility. Similarly, it makes no difference whether socialism is to be established by reasoning from the labour value theory and class struggle or from the theory of rent and collective effort.

The analogy between philosophical radicalism and the Fabian Society renders it easier to define the character of the latter. The Fabian Society is neither a socialist party nor pre-eminently a school of socialist doctrines, but a group of men and women who

[1] *Fabian Tracts*, No. 51, p. 6.

are endeavouring to spread practical views on the immediate
and pressing social problems, and to indicate the way for their
embodiment in legislative or administrative measures. According
to these views socialism is not a revolutionary movement of the
working classes for the purpose of establishing some new form of
society, nor is it an anti-parliamentary and an extra-national
system of co-operation. It is the result of a long series of
national problems, which have arisen out of the manifold
economic, social, and spiritual changes that were taking place in
the last century, and which must be dealt with by the nation
if it desires to raise its efficiency and to continue its upward
progress.

2.—FROM OWEN AND MARX TO WEBB

It has just been stated that Sidney Webb must be regarded
as the real pioneer of Fabianism. He has been greatly assisted
by the analytical powers and dialectical skill of G. B. Shaw,
and to a higher degree by the social knowledge, ethical fervour,
and great literary gifts of Mrs. Sidney Webb. His achievements
are thus the result of the co-operative efforts of several minds.
But so are the achievements of any inventor, discoverer, or philosopher and scientist. No man creates *ex nihilo*, but out of the
materials supplied to him by his predecessors, his contemporaries,
and his own experience. Yet, people are wont to trace back
particular thoughts and actions to a particular man or woman
who expressed or performed them in the most acceptable or
satisfactory manner or at the proper time. In this sense do we
speak here of the pioneering work of Sidney Webb with regard
to Fabianism, though the assistance and contributions of G. B.
Shaw and Mrs. Sidney Webb must by no means be ignored.

We shall be able the better to appreciate the work of Webb,
if we compare it with that of his illustrious predecessors, Owen
and Marx.

At the time when Owen entered on his socialist propaganda
the working classes were not organised and not conscious of the
strength which unity could give them, and they were on the whole
uneducated and helpless. The State was entirely oligarchic and

an instrument of oppression and repression,—a machinery for war, police, and taxation. Anything in the nature of welfare, improvement, and social justice, was not regarded as the business of the State. Under these circumstances Owen could not help coming to the conclusion that the salvation of the people must come from some self-sacrificing redeemer, some heroic educator and organiser, who would use the new resources, which were unlocked by science, for the benefit of the working classes. Parliamentary action was futile, since the State had nothing to do with the welfare of the masses. Trade union action was of no avail, since the possessing and ruling classes were united against the people ; capital, machinery, and soldiery, would defeat any effort the working classes might make towards improving their condition. Besides, the rich as well as the poor were basing their ideas, feelings, laws, and aspirations on an error,—on the cardinal error that man made his own character, whereas in reality the character of man was made for him by circumstances. These circumstances were created by private property and competition, and therefore resulted in social evil. A change of circumstances was necessary—a change from private property and competition to communism and co-operation ; and this change could only be achieved by a hero of rationalism, who has won the respect and the hearts of the people.

When Marx, armed with the evolutionary philosophy and positive science of his age, appeared on the scene, the working classes formed already an army, valiantly fighting against heavy odds for political and economic emancipation. The landed oligarchy, too, was engaged in a losing fight against the rising tide of middle-class liberalism. The State was gradually assuming the character of a protector of child and female labour, while the adult working population was being left to the tender mercies of competition, of supply and demand and the struggle for life, without any direct power to influence legislation or the conditions of labour, and this in an era of enormous accumulations of wealth and the accession to political power of the middle classes. Marx's theories are the adequate expression of this period ; they epitomize the conditions created by a fiercely

competitive economic life, non-democratic constitution, and a
society split up in antagonistic warring classes.

Between the years 1865 and 1885 Great Britain entered on a
period of change. Thought was moving away from its old
moorings. The rise of the working classes could no longer be
denied ; their influence on legislation and the wage-contract
was visibly on the increase. They had obtained the franchise
and the legalisation of trade unionism. The British Constitution
was turned into a democracy. Old liberalism, with its doctrine
of individual interest as the best guide to happiness, was giving
way to the collectivist theory of State and municipal action for
social reform.

It must, however, not be supposed that these changes were
clearly defined and manifest to all. They were tendencies rather
than accomplished facts,—tendencies often neutralised by old
modes of thought and action. But Webb saw them clearly
enough. Experience is, after all, not a passive mental reflection
of the external world, but the product of external phenomena
and of the operations of mind according to its capacity and equipment. At any rate, it appeared to Webb that it was no longer
admissible to allow a socialist theory which was grounded on
past conditions to continue unchallenged and unrevised. A
democratic State which was prepared to take upon itself social
reform duties, a working class with economic influence and power,
a nation with a growing social conscience, could not be treated
from the standpoint of revolution and class struggle. The
fundamental socialist concepts needed a new basis and new
methods more in harmony with new conditions. Socialism had
to be adapted to democracy. This adaptation has been performed by Sidney Webb. It represents the transition from
Marxism to Fabianism, or from social revolutionary doctrine to
social practice.

Rightly understood, the pre-democratic socialists of the
Chartist or Marxist type could not but think of a revolution,
since they had first to sweep away the old State in order to create
a political mechanism for a collectivist re-organisation of society.
In a democratic society, and in a State which acknowledges the

duty of carrying social legislation, there was no need for a revolu
tion in order to create a new political mechanism, for it was in
existence and needed but to be used. The real question, there
fore, was, How was this State to be used in order to get systematic
social reform ?

The Owenites went outside the State for the purpose of building
up a co-operative commonwealth, and they elaborated its general
outlines, and even its details, by pen and pencil. The Marxists
scorned all sketches and all questionings for the details of the
future State, but urged upon the working classes to fight against
the existing order, to obtain political power, to seize the State for
the purpose of the abolition of the capitalist system which
obstructed the birth of the new society, or rather the collectivist
forces which the present society created ; this constituted the
real mission of the socialists. Webb investigates the particular
evils of society, points out the remedy for each of them in accordance with the general principles of socialism, and endeavours to
persuade the nation that those remedies are practicable and
suitable for legislation. The mission of the socialists was therefore to acquire knowledge by means of specialised research into
the various manifestations of economic and social life, to acquaint
themselves with the machinery of legislation and administration.
and to put their knowledge and experience at the disposal of
all political agencies. There was no reason for socialists to wait
for the social revolution. The realisation of socialism had
begun from the moment when the State became accessible to
social reform ideas, and the employers of labour admitted collective bargaining and submitted to State and trade unionist
intervention.

The Owenites advised the working men to abandon political
and trade unionist action, and to devote their energies and
funds to collective production. The Marxists advised the working
men to conquer political power and to use their trade unions for
social revolutionary purposes. Webb asks the working men to
vote straight and send social reformers to Parliament in sufficient
numbers to form a majority and to assume the reins of government. He further advises them to work for the extension of

the principles of democracy to factory, workshop, mine and field.

Owenite socialism was idyllic ; Marxist socialism was revolutionary and theoretical ; Fabian socialism is everyday politics for social regeneration.

The key of Owenism is the doctrine of circumstances in relation to the formation of human character. The philosophy which served Marx in his analysis of capitalist society and in the mobilisation of the working class for socialism, consists of the labour-value theory with class warfare as the dynamic force. The socialism of Webb is based on the extension of the theory of rent and on the growth of the social conscience of the nation.

Webb stands on the shoulders of J. S. Mill. He is the direct mental descendant of the last great Utilitarian. He has taken up the work of socialism where Mill left it—namely, half-way between individualism and social reform, and has carried it a good distance further. We have seen how Mill was groping for a theory of social reform by means of the law of rent, but did not go beyond land reform. Webb, on the other hand, went on and crossed the sphere of movable capital. Looking back over the record of human progress there appeared to him one main economic characteristic underlying every form of society. As soon as production was sufficiently advanced to furnish more than maintenance, there arose a struggle for the surplus product. The individuals or classes who possessed social power had at all times, consciously or unconsciously, made use of that power for the purpose of appropriating the surplus product and leaving to the great majority of their fellows practically nothing beyond the means of subsistence according to the current local standard. This surplus product possessed the character of rent. In relation to agriculture it was fertility, mineral contents, position, or even the mere presence of human beings, that combined to make the net advantages of one piece of land very different from that of another. This differential advantageousness, rising in scale from the very margin of cultivation to the most superior sites, accounted for the phenomenon of economic rent. It was this law of rent that formed the economic ferment of our generation.

Under unrestricted private ownership and free competition, with the motive of pecuniary self-interest in full play, the man in possession of any position economically superior to the very margin of cultivation or to the very limit of advantageousness was finding himself able to retain for himself the whole differential advantage of that position over and above the yield of the worst in use. This law of rent held good not of land only. All productive labour was but man's method of earning a living; and in economics, "as Whately long ago observed, rent is a genus, of which land rent is but one species." Alike in all capitalist enterprise—in manufacture, in transport, in distribution, as well as in agriculture—the factors of production were different one from another in net advantageousness no less than the land itself. The world of business was as diverse in its productivity as the various classes of soil of a farm. In one industry every operative would be using, on an average, a thousand pounds worth of plant and machinery. In another, carried on in the very same street, the operatives work with a total plant worth perhaps a few pounds. A census of production would show striking differences in the output per head of the working people in the same branches of industry. The differences between the qualities of land would find their analogy in the difference between the sites of the factories and commercial offices, use of inventions and discoveries, raw materials and tools, forms of organisation and management. And as the wages and prices were determined by marginal labour the differential advantages of the more favoured establishments consisted of enormous industrial rents, the greatest portion of which was unearned increment, since the special advantages which resulted in the differential rents were not the effects of the mental and bodily efforts of the capitalists, and their rewards bore no relation whatever to their social services.

The advantages which capitalists enjoyed were the effects of social effort. All who were rendering services to society contributed to the growth of civilised life, to the achievements of science, to the increase of wealth, and more efficient forms of organisation. This did not, however, imply that the distribution of the produce should be effected on the principle of equality. But every worker should be guaranteed a minimum of civilised existence, and the more able should receive a higher remuneration as rent of ability. As long as the social conscience of the nation was not yet developed enough to cause men to perform their duty to society without regard to the degree of remuneration, equality of distribution was impossible. Meanwhile it was but bare justice to afford every willing worker a minimum of bodily and mental existence, corresponding to the existing level of civilisation, in order to keep him in efficiency and to render him capable of rising in the scale of social life and earning a rent of ability.

From these considerations follows a social policy which is different from that of both Owen and Marx. (1) The struggle is not to be fought out between rationalist and theological views, nor between the capitalist class and the working class, but between the overwhelming majority of the nation and the appropriators of differential rent—between those who make inventions and discoveries, or who are busy with scientific and social research, who organise industries, design machinery, perform bodily labour, and those who grow rich on these social services merely because they invest capital ; (2) Since differential rent or unearned increment is the result of social labour and general development it ought to be utilised for the good of the whole society ; (3) A government which is seriously bent on social reform must therefore turn its attention to the industrial and agricultural rent and use it in the interests of the whole community, partly by means of taxation, partly by municipalisation and nationalisation.[1]

Webb, being always in contact with social realities, has never ceased to study socialism. He professes no dogmas or final truths ; he has no theory from which he would separate with regret. He brings an open mind to every new development of socialist and economic theory. He has been, for instance, one of the very small number of State socialists whom syndicalism has

[1] *Fabian Tracts*, Nos. 7, 15, 41, 51, 70, 108, 159 ; *Fabian Essays*, 1889 ; *New Statesman*, April–July, 1914. (Compare H. G. Wells, *New Worlds for Old*, 1908, Chapter xii., §1.)

not frightened into an *a priori* condemnation of its tenets and tendencies, but who have made an impartial study of it.

Only in one respect Webb appears to have committed an error. He has not appreciated to the full the historic mission of the working class in bringing about socialism. His mental descent from Mill and the new school of political economy on the one hand, and his implicit belief in British democratic institutions on the other, have not allowed him to see the kernel of truth which the Marxist theory of class warfare contains. Marx has not idolised nor idealised the proletariat ; he took the working class for what they really are—an oppressed class, to whom the avenues of art and science and all mental culture are closed ; but he saw quite clearly that the material interests, needs, and efforts of a social class, when in conformity with the general development of society, are a powerful lever of progress. It is only from this consideration that Marx has appealed to the proletariat and endeavoured to make them conscious of their conditions and efforts. From this, and from no other, point of view can independent Labour politics and a socialist Labour programme be justified.

3.—AIM AND POLICY OF FABIANISM

The clearest insight into the aims and policy of the Fabians is afforded by their official report to the International Socialist and Trade Union Congress in London (1896). The object of the Fabian Society was to persuade the nation to make their political constitution thoroughly democratic, and so to socialise their industries as to make the livelihood of the people entirely independent of capitalism. The Fabian Society, far from holding aloof from other bodies, was urging its members to join them and was permeating them with Fabian ideas. Almost all organisations and movements contained elements making for socialism. The Fabian Society was constitutional in its attitude, and its methods, which were those usual in political life in England. It stood for democracy, which meant simply the control of the administration by freely elected representatives of the people. It repudiated, however, all conceptions of democracy as a system by which all the technical work of national administration and the appointment of public officials should be carried on by means of the referendum or by any other form of direct popular election. Socialism, as understood by the Fabians, meant the organisation and conduct of the necessary industries of the country, and the appropriation of all forms of economic rent of land and capital by the nation as a whole, through the most suitable public authorities, parochial, municipal, provincial, or central. The United Kingdom now possessed an elaborate democratic State machinery, graduated from the parish council up to the central government, which could be used for the purpose of carrying socialist measures. The difficulty was not to secure more political power for the people, but to persuade them to make proper use of the power they already possessed. The Fabian Society did not direct its appeals to any particular class, but to men and women of all classes who saw the evils of society and desired to remedy them. It was, therefore, endeavouring to rouse social compunction by making the public conscious of the evil condition of society under the present system. This it was doing by collecting and publishing authentic and impartial statistical tracts, compiled from official sources. Socialism needed light rather than heat. The Fabians discarded such phrases as " the abolition of the wage system." Socialism by no means involved the abolition of wages, but was aiming at the establishment of standard allowances for the maintenance of all workers of the community in its own service, as an alternative to wages fixed by the competition of destitute men and women working for private employment, as well as for commercial profits, commissions, and all other speculative and competitive forms of remuneration. The Fabian Society opposed all pretensions to hamper the socialisation of industry with equal wages, equal hours of labour, equal official status, or equal authority for everyone. Such conditions were not only impracticable, but incompatible with equality of subordination to the common interests. The Fabians steadfastly discountenanced all schemes for securing to any person or any group of persons " the whole product of their labour." Moreover they recognised that wealth was social in its origin and must be social in its distribution, since the evolution of industry had made it impossible to distinguish the particular contribution that each person made to the common product, or to ascertain its value.

These declarations make it easier to understand the programme and methods of the Fabians.

4.—PROGRAMME AND METHODS

The declaration of principles on the " basis " of the Fabian Society is as follows :—

" THE FABIAN SOCIETY consists of socialists.

" It therefore aims at the re-organisation of Society by the emancipation of land and industrial capital from individual and class ownership, and the vesting of them in the community for the general benefit. In this way only can the natural and acquired advantages of the country be equitably shared by the whole people.

" The Society accordingly works for the extinction of private property in land and of the consequent individual appropriation, in the form of rent, of the price paid for permission to use the earth, as well as for the advantages of superior soils and sites.

" The Society, further, works for the transfer to the community of the administration of such industrial capital as can conveniently be managed socially. For, owing to the monopoly of the means of production in the past, industrial inventions and the transformation of surplus income into capital have mainly enriched the proprietary class, the worker being now dependent on that class for leave to earn a living.

" If these measures be carried out, without compensation (though not without such relief to expropriated individuals as may seem fit to the community), rent and interest will be added to the reward of labour, the idle class now living on the labour of others will necessarily disappear, and practical equality of opportunity will be maintained by the spontaneous action of economic forces with much less interference with personal liberty than the present system entails.

" For the attainment of these ends the Fabian Society looks

to the spread of socialist opinions, and the social and political changes consequent thereon, including the establishment of equal citizenship for men and women. It seeks to achieve these ends by the general dissemination of knowledge as to the relation between the individual and Society in its economic, ethical, and political aspects."

The leaders of the Fabian Society, believing that it was possible to turn the whole power of British political action in the direction of distinctly socialist reforms, are urging upon the members to exercise continuously their full influence in local political affairs. The work of the Board of Guardians, the County, Town, District or Parish Council, the local political associations or clubs, would offer to Fabians many opportunities not only for valuable socialist propaganda, but also for important work in carrying socialist principles into practice. The Fabians should therefore join some local political association, and endeavour to become a member of its executive council and one of its representatives to the central political bodies for London and the United Kingdom respectively. In short, active political work and full exercise of citizenship in the interest of social reform is the duty of the Fabians. It is therefore particularly important that they should make themselves acquainted with the actual machinery of public administration in the districts in which they reside, and with the parliamentary constituency in which they are electors. Finally, the Fabians should cultivate friendly relations with, and afford all possible assistance to, the other socialist organisations in their districts.

The Fabian Society appears to form an institute for social engineering. It always combines an ounce of theory with a ton of practice. Having learned from experience that socialists cannot have their own way in everything any more than any other people, the Fabian Society recognises that in a democratic community compromise is a necessary condition of social progress.

These methods differentiate the Fabian Society from any other socialist organisation in the United Kingdom. For the first time in the history of socialism we see socialists who do not desire to separate themselves from the nation by forming communistic or ethical colonies or by organising the working classes into a State within the State, but who are endeavouring to leaven the national life with their ideas and strengthen the State with their practical measures. Their work is social citizenship pure and simple. The nation having arrived at a new phase of its development, in which it needs new ideas and measures for its existence, the Fabian Society has voluntarily trained itself for this national mission.

The Fabian Society was instrumental in forming the Labour Party and has been represented on its executive by one delegate. Although the Fabians, as has been shown, are averse from forming a political party of their own and, least of all, a class party, they promoted the idea of an independent Labour party by their two Tracts, entitled *A Fabian Election Manifesto* (1892) and *A Plan of Campaign for Labour* (1894). Several of the leading men of the Fabian Society have of late largely identified themselves with the Labour Party and the socialist Labour movement.

There is, of course, no complete unity of thought and aims in the Fabian Society. Since 1906, when H. G. Wells, the foremost sociological novelist of Great Britain, who was then a member of the Fabian Society, raised the banner of revolt, a certain amount of opposition to the old policy has been growing. Some of its members have been advocating its transformation into a socialist party. Others have been asking for a closer identification with the Labour Party. In the last few years some of the younger members, mostly University men and publicists who are in touch with syndicalism and industrial Unionism, have been working for guild socialism, with the importance of which we shall deal in a later chapter.

5.—LITERARY AND SCIENTIFIC WORK

The first fruits of the economic and historical studies and researches of the leading minds of the Society were the *Fabian Essays in Socialism*, published in 1889, republished since several times, reaching a total number of 40,000 copies. Three of the essays, which Sidney Webb and Bernard Shaw contributed, stand forth as masterpieces of socialist thought and economic reasoning.   Webb excels in economic history, Shaw in elucidation of some economic categories and in summarising British socialist history.   The *Essays* form the groundwork of Fabianism. While the latter are calculated to influence the educated, the *Fabian Tracts* are meant to instruct all intelligent men and women who desire either a good summary of some socialist question or guidance in carrying out social reform measures. They are published in the form of pamphlets of about twenty-four pages at the price of one penny.   There are now about 190 Tracts published, the total circulation of which must have reached by now far over one million copies.   Most of them were written by experts.   The following deserve special mention : *Socialism, true and false*, by Sidney Webb, explanatory of the meaning of modern socialism ; *Facts for Socialists*, a statistical survey of the distribution of the national income amongst the classes, and of the resulting conditions of the people ; *Socialism and Superior Brains*, by Bernard Shaw, arguing both against the crude notion of equality of income and against the appropriation of surplus social labour by the owners of capital ; *Rent and Value*, by Bernard Shaw ; *The necessary Basis of Society*, by Sidney Webb ; *Public Service versus Private Expenditure*, by Sir Oliver Lodge ; *The Moral Aspects of Socialism*, by Sidney Ball ; *Capital and Land*, pleading for socialism against single-tax ; *Twentieth Century Politics*, by S. Webb ; *The Fabian Society, its early history*, by Bernard Shaw ; *The Case for a legal Minimum Wage*, by Mrs. Sidney Webb ; *State Control of Trusts*, by H. W. Macrosty ; showing the tendency towards concentration of capital ; *State Purchase of Railways*, by Emil Davies ; *The War and the Worker*, by Sidney Webb, dealing with some immediate measures to prevent unemployment and relieve distress.

But the *magnum opus* of Fabian reform is the *Minority Report*, written by Mrs. and Mr. Sidney Webb, as the *Report of the Minority of the Royal Commission on the Poor Laws*, 1909.   It constitutes a code of social measures for the abolition of the immediate causes of poverty and the assistance of the destitute in order to enable them to become more efficient and useful members of society. It is a code of practical social reform, which in peaceful, slowly moving times, might have been read and used all over the civilised world, with a view to drafting reform measures, even as Jeremy Bentham's penal codes and constitutional outlines were consulted in the first quarter of the nineteenth century. Time is, however, out of joint. After the overthrow of such eminently retarding and conservative factors as the Russian and German Empires, social evolution is moving and will move at an accelerating rate, despite some occasional stoppages and breaks. It is, on the whole, no more a question of palliating poverty, but the reformation of the whole system of social life.

6.—FABIAN (LABOUR) RESEARCH DEPARTMENT

Modern socialism, the starting point of which is social experience, naturally implies investigation into the economic structure of society. Still, so long as socialism bears a doctrinal character and is aiming at a catastrophic subversion of the capitalist system, its investigation and research work is extensive rather than intensive ; its scientific object being the attainment of broad generalisation. As soon, however, as socialism has overcome the doctrinal stage, or as soon as modern socialists in a democratic State find an opportunity for starting practical work, their investigations and researches become specialised or confined to particular phenomena. Socialism turns into a series of social reforms, each of which must be thoroughly examined. The socialist agitator gives place to the social investigator. The Fabians have long felt the need for a special research department, but only in the last years has a start been made to meet it. In 1912 the Fabian Research Department was established which began an exhaustive examination of all the existing forms of control of industry, apart from mere capitalism ; of trade unionism in all its developments ; of the co-operative movement ; of the organisation of industry by public authorities ; and of land and rural problems.

In 1916 the Research Department opened its membership to all socialists and trade unionists. At the same time it invited affiliation from Labour bodies. Its connection with the Fabian Society thus became nominal or personal only. In 1918 its constitution was altered ; it placed half control over the work into the hands of Labour bodies, and its name was changed to Labour Research Department. It is now (1919) the main armoury of the advanced trade unions, and the sociological department of the British Labour movement. Young Fabianism has thus removed the reproach from the Fabian Society of superciliously deprecating the Marxist theory of class warfare.

Since its rise in 1912, the Research Department, with the assistance of the Webbs and the older school of Fabianism, as well as under the stimulus of the younger socialist and Labour Fabians, like G. D. H. Cole, W. Mellor, and R. Page Arnot, has accomplished an enormous work.

The main problems of the Research Department divide under two heads,—first, to examine into all experiments in collectivist production, distribution, and exchange which have in the last years been made not on a pre-arranged socialist plan or with the idea of carrying socialism into practice, but rather in consequence of the growing need of society to escape from the baleful effects of individualism, such experiments bearing testimony to the gradual and unconscious evolution of society toward collectivist economies ; secondly, to examine into the activities of the various societies of the working class which are either fighting for the control of the means of production and distribution, or are engaged in peacefully reorganising production and distribution on co-operative lines.

On all these subjects a very extensive collection of material has been made and is being prepared for publication. There are now four sub-committees at work. Sub-committee I. has undertaken a careful inquiry into the feelings and desires, objects and methods, of all the English Syndicalists to whom access could be obtained. A detailed study has been made (chiefly from documents and books) of French syndicalism ; and a less elaborate one of the United States varieties of syndicalism and " Industrial Unionism." A report has been drawn up by G. D. H. Cole on " What Validity does our Enquiry show Syndicalism to Possess," and another by H. J. Gillespie and W. Mellor on the nature and extent of syndicalism in the United Kingdom.

With regard to trade unionism, a complete survey has been made of trade union organisation in the United Kingdom in relation to the question of amalgamation or federation of unnecessary separate unions. A personal inquiry has been made into the organisation of trade unionism in Germany, with special reference to the relation of local branch to head office and of sectional craft to the industry as a whole. An elaborate memorandum on this has been prepared by W. Stephen Sanders. Personal enquiries into the organisation of trade unionism in Belgium and France have been made, and memoranda prepared, by C. M. Lloyd. Schemes for the improvement of trade union organisation in Great Britain have been prepared, and are being considered and revised by detailed enquiries.

The well-known attempts (1913-4) of the miners, railway men, and transport workers of the United Kingdom to form an alliance for purposes of common defence may show the importance of such investigations. The triple alliance of the miners, railwaymen, and transport workers could, in the event of a well-prepared but suddenly declared general strike, paralyse the economic life of the country.

Sub-committee II. is studying the real constitutions and position of all the associations of producers (self-governing workshops) existing in the United Kingdom. A list has been made, and particulars obtained, of all those that have failed within the last twenty-five years. Studies have been made (from books) of similar associations in France, Belgium, and Italy. An elaborate memorandum of provisional conclusions as to these associations in England has been prepared by Mrs. Bernard Drake. Profit-sharing and Industrial Co-partnership schemes have been re-examined and submitted to the detailed criticism of trade unionists and other workmen, economists, and employers.

Sub-committee III. has for its task the study of the actual workings and results of the co-operative societies. A report on the features thus revealed has been prepared by Mrs. W. P. Reeves.

Municipal trading forms the subject of sub-committee IV. The relation of trading municipalities to their employees has been investigated in detail. The actual organisation and working of the manufacturing operations of a large Government Department have been personally studied. The statistics of the trading operations of all the municipalities in the United Kingdom have been analysed for further investigation. A detailed monograph on the comparative results of municipal and joint stock enterprise with regard to electricity has been prepared by C. Ashmore Baker.

The land and rural problem, which may be regarded as one of the most important for Great Britain, has been investigated by a special committee and a report prepared by H. D. Harben. Likewise, the subject of workmen's insurance, either by State or private agencies, is being carefully enquired into by the Research Department.

For the Committee of Enquiry into the Control of Industry, the Webbs drafted Reports on *Co-operative Production and Profit Sharing* (1914), *State and Municipal Enterprise* (1914), *Professional Associations*, four parts (1917), which were published as supplements to the *New Statesman*, a weekly journal, founded in 1913 by some leading Fabians. The financial problems resulting from the War were dealt with in a volume *How to Pay for the War*, which was edited by Sidney Webb.

The researches into the latest developments of trade unionism have been under the guidance of G. D. H. Cole, whose *Introduction to Trade Unionism* (1918), *Payment of Wages* (1918), and *Self-Government of Industry* (fourth edition, 1919) have brought the economic movement of the British working-class into connection with the most recent tendencies of socialist thought. Under his stimulus the theory of trade unionism has extended its boundaries far beyond the region which the Webbs had marked out for it. Cole has found able collaborators in Page Arnot and Margaret I. Postgate.

The Research Department is also publishing *Monthly Circulars*, dealing with all matters of interest to Labour and socialism from a national as well as international point of view, and *Labour Year*

I T

Books (1916, 1918), giving reviews of the whole Labour and socialist movement at home and abroad.

7.—EDUCATIONAL WORK AND WOMEN'S MOVEMENT

Increased attention has been given to the organisation of educational work among the socialists themselves. In 1906 a Fabian Summer School was established. Three or four times a year for periods varying from one week to three months, the School is filled with members and their friends, who are using their holidays for the purpose of attending lectures on economic, social, and political subjects, and for arranging conferences to discuss special problems connected with the Research Department. Another educational development has been the organisation of classes in economics, industrial history, and local government for the members of the socialist societies.

This growth of educational work has given to the various University Fabian societies their real mission. They are no more satisfied with debating sociological questions, but are endeavouring to bring the Fabian Society into closer touch with the newer currents of the Labour movement and to destroy the prejudices of some of the older Fabians against the so-called proletarisation of socialism. More and more they are coming to regard socialism, trade unionism, and Labour politics as the streams of one great movement towards the reorganisation of society on a collectivist and democratic basis. The University Fabian Societies of Oxford, Cambridge, London, Edinburgh, Glasgow, Manchester, Birmingham, Aberystwith, Liverpool, and Sheffield organised themselves into a Federation, governed by an executive consisting of one representative from each society together with two national representatives. The University Socialist Federation (U.S.F.) forms the backbone of the Fabian Research Department.

Finally, the female members of the Fabian Society, believing that the emancipation of women constituted an integral part of socialism, formed in 1908 a Fabian Women's Group. Its promoters were of opinion that there was a close analogy between the advance of women and the growth of socialism, and that this connection needed to be made clear. They held that the complete political and economic emancipation of women was essential to any real socialisation of our national life. They looked forward to a time when each individual should be economically independent, with ever-widening personal freedom. Its main object is to study and to strengthen the economic position of women and to bring them into line with men in the advance towards paid work for all, for the equal advantage of all. It asks for equality of opportunity for women as for men : it asserts that if half the community is to remain in a weak economic position, progress for the other half must, in the nature of things, be retarded. By " equality of opportunity " Fabian women do not necessarily mean " similarity of opportunity," either as between the sexes or as between individuals. It seeks to clear up the present popular confusion of judgment, which at one moment exaggerates the nature of the essential disabilities of the woman-worker, and the next ignores those disabilities altogether when determining the social burden to be imposed upon her. Its object has been, and is, to discover how far difference of sex-function must necessarily cause a difference of mental outlook and a differentiation of work. Lack of knowledge of existing conditions, their causes and history, insufficient data upon which to base theories or demands—these were the first wants it was necessary to supply. It was felt that, if women are to be freed from political and economic subjection, they must examine their position for themselves and express their needs from their own standpoint.

The subject first investigated was that of women's natural disabilities as workers. An endeavour was made to discover the differences in ability for productive work involved in difference of sex-function, first in women not actively engaged in child-bearing, and secondly in mothers with their special disabilities. The next step was to investigate the position of women as workers and as consumers in this country in former ages. The Group has begun its study of women as producers and consumers in this country at the present time. Eighteen lectures of this series have been given, and it was decided to produce a series of books of which the papers and discussions of the Group meeting should form the nucleus. The first volume, *Women Workers i Seven Professions*, is the first of this series.

Several Women's Group pamphlets, dealing with socia questions from the woman's standpoint, has been published b the Fabian Society :

(1) *The Working Life of Women*, by Miss B. L. Hutchins. / collection of statistics, showing the relative age and numbers o women workers. (2) *Family Life on £1 a week*, by Mrs. Pembe Reeves. The now well-known collection of family budgets which has since formed the nucleus of *Round About a Pound Week*, a book recently published. (3) *Women and Prisons*, b Mrs. Charlotte Wilson and Miss Helen Blagg. This pamphle utilises the information obtained by a sub-committee of th Group from suffragist prisoners. It deals with the English pena system for women and makes suggestions for its reform. (4) *Th Economic Foundation of the Woman Movement*, by Miss Mabe Atkinson ; and (5) *Women in Agriculture* : *their Work an Payment*, a historical survey by Mrs. Charlotte Wilson.

Besides the above, the Group published two summaries of th lectures upon the Disabilities of Women as Workers, and upon th Disabilities of Mothers as Workers.

Thus in various ways the members of the Fabian Women' Group are working strenuously for the economic independenc which they believe to be the sole remedy for various social ills they are endeavouring to establish, as the result of economic investigation, that this solution must ultimately be accepted b all those who believe in equality of opportunity for all citizens irrespective of sex.

All this work has been accomplished, or is being accomplished by a numerically small society. In 1914 the number of members was less than 3,000 ; its income, apart from that of the Research Department, was about £4,000. During the war (1914–1918 the lecture propaganda of the Fabian Society practically ceased and the income suffered considerable diminution, but some compensation for this was a large increase in the sale and distri- bution of its pamphlets and books.

Earlier or later a social historian may arise who will do with regard to the Fabian Society what Leslie Stephen has so admirably accomplished for the English Utilitarians. Meanwhile, these lines will perhaps show that the subject is worthy of the attention of all who take an interest in social reform. The future historian will find some guidance for his work in the *History of the Fabian Society* (1915), published by E. R. Pease, who, since the inception of the Society till 1912, was its secretary.

XV

INDEPENDENT LABOUR POLITICS

I.—ONSLAUGHTS ON LIBERAL LABOUR

It became increasingly clear ever since the last of the great unemployed demonstrations in 1887 that neither the Social Democratic Federation (S.D.F.) nor the Socialist League (S.L.) had made any impression on the organised working class of Great Britain. Out of the turmoil and travails of those years no socialist Labour party arose ; only the economic action of the unskilled London workmen received a temporary access of strength. Independent socialists and Labour leaders gradually took stock of the situation and arrived at the conclusion that it was much less important to emphasise the aim and end of socialism than to organise the working men for independent Labour politics. The S.D.F., it appeared, had put the cart before the horse. The German socialist, Frederick Engels, who had spent the better part of his life in England, wrote in May, 1887, that the immediate question of British socialism was the formation of a Labour party with an independent class programme, which, if successful, would thrust the S.D.F. and the S.L. into the background.[1] The Fabian, E. R. Pease, wrote at that time of his society : " The chief aim of our plan is the formation of a distinct Labour party in Parliament."[2] Similar ideas were growing in Scotland and the North of England. James Keir Hardie, speaking as delegate of the Ayrshire Miners at the Trade Union Congress in 1887, strongly protested against Labour representatives identifying themselves with the Liberals, who " are in direct antagonism to the working classes."[3] Since

[1] *Sorge's Briefwechsel*, p. 263 (H. W. Dietz Verlag, Stuttgart).
[2] *To-Day*, 1887, p. 171.
[3] Frank Rose, *The Coming Force*, p. 47.

1887 sporadic attempts at organising local labour associations in opposition to Liberal Labour were made in Yorkshire. It was in Scotland and in the North of England that the idea of independent Labour politics took practical shape. Since 1832 it has been increasingly manifest that London may be able to produce socialist and Labour ideas, but is incapable of carrying them into effect, while the North of England and Scotland possessed both originating and executive capacity. In 1888 a parliamentary by-election took place in Mid-Lanark, where Hardie, ably supported by H. H. Champion, Robert Smillie, Dr. G. B. Clark, and other socialists, came forward as an independent Labour candidate in opposition both to the Liberals and Conservatives, and polled 712 votes. Arising out of this contest, the Scottish socialists, led by Cuninghame Graham, Dr. Stirling Robertson, George Gerrie, and Keir Hardie, met a few months later at Glasgow and formed the Scottish Labour Party, which adopted the following programme :—

" Adult suffrage with abolition of plural voting. Triennial Parliaments ; elections to be all held on one day. Simplification of registration laws, so as to prevent removal from one constituency to another disfranchising an elector. Payment of members by the State, and of official election expenses from the rates ; second ballots. Home Rule for each separate nationality or country in the British Empire, with an Imperial Parliament for Imperial affairs. Abolition of the House of Lords and all hereditary offices. Nationalisation of land and minerals. Labour Legislation : an Eight Hours Bill ; abolition of the present Poor Law system and substitution of State insurance to provide for sickness, accident, death, or old age ; arbitration courts, with power to settle disputes and fix a minimum wage ; weekly payment of wages ; homestead law to protect furniture and tools to the value of £20 from seizure for debt ; application of the Factories and Workshops Acts to all premises, whether public or private, in which work is performed. Prohibition of the liquor traffic. No war to be entered upon without the consent of the House of Commons. Free education ; Boards to have power to provide food for children. Disestablishment. Reform in the system of civil government, and abolition of sinecure offices and pensions. Simplification and codification of civil and criminal law. State acquisition of railways, waterways, and tramways. National banking system, and the issue of State money only. Cumulative income tax, beginning at £300 per annum."

Thanks to the work of socialist and Labour organisations most of the foregoing demands may appear to-day to bear a commonplace character, while some of them have actually found their embodiment in legislation, having been imposed by the independent socialist and Labour movement on the Liberal Government. But a quarter of a century ago no Liberal would have given countenance to them ; indeed, they were opposed by Liberal speakers and the Liberal press, and ridiculed either as leading to State slavery or to Utopia.

A manifesto was issued to the workers of Scotland explaining the objects of the new party, and the following extracts may give an idea of the lines upon which it was intended to proceed :—

" Hitherto the workers of Scotland have been kept divided in the political field, fighting against each other under the banners of Whig or Tory for party objects which, with the exception of such Acts as those already mentioned, have been of no real value to Labour. If any workman doubts this let him figure out how much his actual condition would be improved if the whole programme of the Liberals or of the Conservatives, or both together, were made law to-morrow. Some may argue that by and by the so-called " party of progress " will adopt Labour reforms as part of its policy, as it has adopted Home Rule for Ireland. Our reply is that when men die of hunger, as they are doing to-day, no delay can be permitted, and that if the workers of Scotland want Labour legislation they must, as the Irish have done, form themselves into a concrete political party, and give the other political parties no rest and peace until their demands are conceded.

" The first step to this end is the formation of a distinct, separate, and *Independent Labour Party*, which will rally at the polls the forces of the workers and of those who sympathise with our efforts. . . .

" It has been by acting in this way that the Irish people have secured the almost undivided attention of Parliament, and have obtained relief from some of their greatest grievances. It is by acting in this way that we in Great Britain shall make Parliament alter the present condition of affairs, in which every twentieth inhabitant is a pauper, a million of men are out of work, one-fifth of the community is insufficiently clad, what are known as starvation diseases are rife amongst large classes, and in which one-third to one-half of the families of the country are huddled together six in a room. In the name of those who suffer from these evils we call on you to enrol yourselves in the Scottish Parliamentary Labour Party, and to assist it in carrying its programme at the next election in your division." [1]

The first independent Labour organisation of any size in England was The Labour Union in Bradford, which came into being as the result of an extensive local strike in the winter of 1890. The propaganda was carried on by Ben Tillett, Robert Blatchford, and Joseph Burgess, who as writers or speakers exercised considerable influence in the North of England. Even London began to feel the effect of their work. At the general election of 1892 Keir Hardie was successful in South-West Ham, John Burns in Battersea, J. H. Wilson in Middlesbrough, all of whom had stood either as independent Labour or as socialist candidates, while Ben Tillett, the parliamentary candidate in Bradford, polled 2,749 votes against 3,306 obtained by the Liberal. The Fabian Society had published an *Election Manifesto*, in which the workmen were urged to quicken the pace of reform by the straightforward action of a genuine Working Class Party. [2]

The electoral campaign of 1892 made a deep impression on thoughtful politicians of the two great parties. Lord Randolph Churchill, writing to a friend, declared that the contests which Labour was now carrying on were significant and instructive. It had treed itself to a great extent from the mere mechanism of party politics. Its struggle was no longer for wages, but for

[1] *Socialist Review*, April, 1914. [2] *Fabian Tract*, No. 40.

political power. Labour was now seeking to do for itself what the landed interests and the manufacturing capitalist interests did for themselves, when each in turn commanded the disposition of State policy. The land laws were framed by the landed interests, for their own advantage. Political power passed very considerably from the landed to manufacturing capitalist interests, and the fiscal system was shaped by this latter power to its own advantage, foreign politics also being made to coincide. The nation was coming fast to a time when Labour laws would be made by the Labour interests for the advantage of Labour, but it had to face strong and numerous forces—social, professional, and journalistic—and the many prejudices and resources which those forces could array against it.[1]

In the autumn of 1892 measures were taken to unite the various independent labour organisations into one party. On January 13 and 14, 1893, a conference was held in Bradford, which resulted in the formation of the Independent Labour Party (I.L.P.).

2.—FORMATION OF THE I.L.P.

About 120 delegates, under the chairmanship of Keir Hardie, assembled at Bradford. They included five from the Social Democratic Federation (S.D.F.) and twelve from the Fabian Society (F.S.), among them being G. B. Shaw, who, on their behalf, declared at the commencement of the proceedings that they regarded themselves but as guests, since their organisations were not inclined to join the new party. The deliberations of the conference with regard to the object of the formation of the party apparently showed a certain want of clearness. The great majority of the delegates, if not all of them, were convinced socialists, and yet they were engaged in forming a rival organisation to the S.D.F. Moreover, they were socialists and nevertheless declined to give their new organisation a socialist name. They felt, however, how the land lay.

The problem before the delegates was, in short, as follows.

[1] Joseph Burgess, *John Burns*.

In Great Britain there existed a social democratic organisation and a Liberal Labour organisation. The former had not succeeded in winning over the working class ; the latter had failed to pursue a Labour policy. What was the reason of these failures ? In the case of the S.D.F. the want of success was caused by the separation of the socialist aim from the Labour movement ; it spurned all compromise between theory and the actual mental condition of the working class ; it endeavoured to impose the truth instead of allowing the working classes to educate themselves through error to truth ; it failed to see that in order to convert the heathen and the sinners we must act like St. Paul and not like St. Peter ; the fiery apostle from Tarsus abandoned the laws of Moses and worshipped the spirit of Christ. The S.D.F., for all the emphasis it laid on the importance of class warfare, was not organised on class lines, but on the basis of theory—of socialist theory, on the acceptance of which depended the admission to its membership. The organised workman, who by means of his trade union was fighting against Capital, or the co-operative workman, who was assisting in organising distribution on collectivist lines, were not regarded as comrades by the members of the S.D.F., simply because those workmen lacked the capacity of thinking out where their activities led them to. In the case of the Labour Electoral Association the cause of failure was both intellectual and moral ; the Association sacrificed the political independence of Labour ; it simply failed to be Labour and formed but a branch of the Liberal Party. Therefore it was essential to found a party which should avoid both the over-righteousness of the one and the laxity of the other. Its main task appeared to consist in detaching the working classes from Liberalism and showing them that political Labour could not constitute a branch of Liberalism any more than trade unions could join the employers' associations. In fact, an independent Labour party was nothing else but the political counterpart to trade unionism.

It cannot be said that the delegates who had assembled at Bradford were fully conscious of the task they were undertaking. But there is no doubt that most of them were actuated by

sentiments of this nature, for after the discussions of the proposals concerning the name of the new party they rejected the
name Socialist Labour Party, which was favoured by some, and
adopted the name Independent Labour Party, because they felt
that if they succeeded in detaching the trade unions from
Liberalism the reform activities of Labour must inevitably
move in the direction of socialism.

The conference then adopted a socialist programme. Its objects
were the collective ownership and control of the means of production to be achieved through parliamentary action, social reform,
protection of Labour and democracy in central and local government.

No difference could be detected between the programmes of
the I.L.P. and the S.D.F., but marked divergencies existed
between them in their attitude towards the trade unions and in
the tone of their propaganda. From the very beginning the
I.L.P. adopted a sympathetic attitude towards the trade unions
and never swerved from it. At the second annual conference
(1894) it was laid down as the duty of every member of the
party to join a trade union, and, when Trade Union Congresses
were sitting, to hold in the evenings socialist demonstrations
and to bring the delegates along with them. The main argument
of the I.L.P. consisted in showing the necessity for the trade
unions to transfer their independent economic action to the
political field, for it would be illogical to strike against Liberal
employers and to vote for them at parliamentary elections, thus
making them legislators and masters of the laws that govern
strikes. The speakers of the I.L.P., in their educational work
among the trade unionists, hardly ever referred to revolution
and class-warfare, but started from the ethical, Nonconformist,
and democratic sentiments which appeal most to British workmen. Nevertheless the old trade union leaders adopted a hostile
attitude to the new party. They knew Keir Hardie and his friends,
who had waged war against the Liberal Labour men at the Trade
Union Congresses since 1887. Also the S.D.F. was for a long
time against the I.L.P., and regarded it as an organised attempt
at splitting and dispersing the socialist forces of Great Britain.

In 1894 the I.L.P. took part in three parliamentary by-elections and polled a total vote of 9,209. As a beginning the results were most promising. This relative success induced the I.L.P., only two years old, to make a large electoral experiment in 1895.

3.—PARLIAMENTARY AND MUNICIPAL ELECTIONS

The Liberal Government of Gladstone and Rosebery, which had come into " power " as the result of the general election of 1892, was exploded by the cordite vote in June, 1895. In the few years of its precarious existence it democratised parish administration, established the death duties, and brought in a Home Rule Bill. Weakened by dissensions consequent upon the retirement of Gladstone, and attacked by friend and foe, it rapidly grew weary of the burden of office and seized the opportunity of the vote of censure against the Secretary for War, Sir Henry Campbell-Bannerman, and retired. Parliament was dissolved on July 8, 1895, and the election campaign commenced. The I.L.P., led by Hardie and Tom Mann, put up twenty-eight candidates—decidedly too many for a young and numerically small party. The campaign required a minimum expenditure of £9,000. At that time the membership of the I.L.P. stood at a little over 6,000. The financial burden was great, but it was shouldered. Much more difficult was it for the party to get sufficient speakers, organisers, agents, canvassers, and all those various helpers who are indispensable for success at British elections, the mechanism of which has been designed by the rich and for the rich. Every one of the twenty-eight I.L.P. candidates was unsuccessful ; the total vote they polled amounted to 44,320 ; even Hardie lost his seat in South-West Ham. The elections turned out badly for all the elements of progress ; the Liberals as well the Liberal Labour candidates suffered defeat after defeat. The Conservatives obtained a majority of 152 votes and took office. The work of the I.L.P. candidates was, however, not quite fruitless : it prepared the ground for the successes of 1906.

The members of the I.L.P., on finding that they were debarred from parliamentary honours, devoted their energies to municipal government and trade union propaganda. Here they were able to achieve signal successes. In a short space of time about 800 members of the party were elected to the various local bodies ; in the municipal elections of November, 1897, 38 per cent. of the total votes cast were for the I.L.P. candidates in the districts where they were standing. The more active trade unionists came more and more into touch with the I.L.P., applying to its leaders for advice and information on political matters or electing them as secretaries of the unions. Harmonious relations were being gradually established between the economic and political wings of the Labour movement, although the old trade union leaders grew all the more determined in their hostility to the new party. The following instance may serve to show to what lengths this hostility could proceed: In 1897 a parliamentary vacancy occurred at Barnsley, a mining district in Yorkshire. Pete Curran, one of the organisers of the Gas Workers' and General Labourers' Union and one of the ablest leaders of the party, ran as the I.L.P. candidate. He was opposed by a Liberal employer and a Conservative captain. Ben Pickard, the general secretary and chief leader of the miners, worked day and night for the Liberal ; the whole press was on the side of the latter, whilst Curran was stoned by the miners and mobbed by their women and children, whistling and yelling and shouting him down. Nevertheless he polled 1,091 votes. Ten years' later, Curran was elected member of Parliament for Jarrow ; and in 1908 the Miners' Federation joined the Labour Party, and has since been growing more and more independent. A similar by-election was fought out in March, 1897, at Halifax, with Tom Mann, the secretary of the I.L.P., as the Labour candidate in opposition to both Liberals and Conservatives. Although the old trade union leaders, Broadhurst and Fenwick, spoke on behalf of the Liberals, Tom Mann obtained 2,000 votes. Events of this nature must be kept in view in order to arrive at a clear understanding of the history of the political Labour movement and of the enormous progress in the union and consolidation of the working class from the time of the formation of the Labour Party in 1900, with which we are now going to deal. As far as personal forces shape history, the new developments must be ascribed mainly to the leading men of the I.L.P., though the work of the S.D.F. and the Fabians was, of course, of much assistance to them, as also was that of the writers of the *Clarion*, who at that time had not yet felt the mission of teaching the nation the principles of strategy, tactics, and Imperialist politics.

4.—THE "CLARION" AUXILIARIES OF THE I.L.P.

The editor of the *Clarion*, Robert Blatchford, had been instrumental in forming the nucleus of the I.L.P. at Bradford. Born and brought up in a working class family, he learnt the meaning of poverty and the indignities of wage-labour in the hard school of experience. He was, at first, a brushmaker, then a soldier, and finally turned to journalism, advocating democracy and land reform, but adversely criticising socialism. In 1890 he was converted to the new collectivist theories after having read a pamphlet written jointly by Hyndman and Morris. Blatchford, who in his self-taught way had been groping for a scheme of social reform, saw directly that the collectivist idea was the very thing he had been looking for, that it was at once juster, simpler, and more perfect than his own plan, and that it was very different from what he had thought socialism to be. He left the *Sunday Chronicle*, became an avowed socialist, and, with his friend, A. M. Thompson, founded the *Clarion* (1891), a weekly newspaper, in which socialism and independent Labour politics have found clear expression, easily grasped by intelligent working men who have no time or training to read the works of socialists and political economists. The *Clarion* writers are not strict party men ; they are volunteers rather than members of the I.L.P., with the policy of which they are not necessarily in agreement, though they accept its main principles.

The numerous socialist pamphlets and books, published by Blatchford and his co-workers, have enjoyed a large circulation. The best representation of socialism, as taught by the *Clarion*, is *Britain for the British*, written by Blatchford in the years 1900-02, at the crucial time of the entrance of the trade unions into independent Labour politics. The author declares that at present Britain did not belong to the British, but to a few of the British, who employed the bulk of the population as servants or as workers. It was because Britain did not belong to the British that a few were rich and the many were poor ; that the owning class lived in a state of useless luxury and pernicious idleness, and the working classes in a state of drudging toil, of wearing poverty and anxious care. This state of affairs was contrary to justice, reason, and Christianity. It was bad alike for the rich and for the poor ; it was against the best interests of the British nation and the human race. The only remedy for this evil was socialism, which simply meant Britain for all the British. After an exposition of the evils of the present social system, of the sources of the social evils or the causes from which they arose, of the true meaning of socialism, of the answers to the principal objections commonly raised against socialism, the author deals with the need for a Labour party. The chapter devoted to this subject forms the culminating point of the book. " My chief object in writing this book," Blatchford tells the British workman, " has been to persuade you that you need a Labour party." He argues from the point of view of the anti-socialist, who was constantly declaring that not altruism, but self-interest, was the strongest motive of mankind. For the sake of argument Blatchford agrees and goes on to say : " If self-interest be the leading motive of human nature, does it not follow that when a man wants a thing done for his advantage he will be wise to do it himself ? " Indeed, it had been so in political life. The upper classes used political power for their own interests ; the middle classes had done the same. If, therefore, the working class desired their interests to be attended to, they must take to heart the lesson contained in those examples and form a working class party. Neither the Tories nor the Liberals could do as much for Labour as Labour could do for itself. " Is not self-interest the ruling passion in the human heart ? Then how should any party be so true to Labour and so diligent in Labour's service as a Labour party would be ? " He then takes up the analogy between trade union and Labour party and says : " What is a trade union ? It is a combination of workers

o defend their own interests from the encroachments of the
employers. Well, a Labour party is a combination of workers
o defend their own interests from the encroachments of the
employers or their representatives in Parliament and on municipal bodies. Do you elect your employers as officials of your
trade unions? Do you send employers as delegates to your
Trades Union Congress? You would laugh at the suggestion.
You know that the employer could not attend to your interests
in the trade union, which is formed as a defence against him. Do
you think the employer is likely to be more useful or more
disinterested in Parliament or the County Council than in the
trade union? Whether he be in Parliament or in his own
office, he is an employer, and he puts his own interest first and
the interest of Labour behind. Yet these men, whom as trade
unionists you mistrust, you actually send as politicians to make
laws for you. A Labour party is a kind of political trade union,
and to defend trade unionism is to defend Labour representation."

Blatchford, without ever having read a single line of Marx or
studied the theory of class warfare, proceeds with his argument,
which is a perfect application of those doctrines: " If an employer's interests are opposed to your interests in business, what
reason have you for supposing that his interests and yours are not
opposed in politics? If you oppose a man as an employer, why
do you vote for him as a member of Parliament? His calling
himself a Liberal or Tory does not alter the fact that he is an
employer. To be a trade unionist and fight for your class
during a strike, and to be a Tory or Liberal and fight against
your class at an election, is folly. During a strike there are no
Tories or Liberals amongst the strikers; they are all workers.
At election times there are no workers, only Liberals and Tories.
. . . We want Britain for the British. We want the fruits of
labour for those who produce them. We want a human life for
all. The issue is not between Liberals and Tories; it is an
issue between the privileged classes and the workers." Socialism, rightly understood, was the logical conclusion of trade
unionism. The latter was helping the workman to resist the

I U

capitalist, the former desired to get rid of him altogether. Efficient defence implied attack, and for this purpose the work-men needed a strong and united Labour party that would fight for Labour in and out of Parliament, and would stand for Labour apart from the Liberals and the Tories. [1]

5.——KEIR HARDIE AND HIS COADJUTORS

The propaganda carried on by the I.L.P. was pervaded by the spirit of James Keir Hardie, who represented all that is best in the British working class. Socialism and Labour politics were not subjects for him to be reasoned and dogmatised upon. He had little tuition, but a great deal of intuition. A deeply religious, even mystical nature, although born of freethinking, rationalist parents, he had something in him of the primitive Christian, and he rebelled against the injustice flowing from the division of society into rich and poor, and the disintegration of mankind into hostile nations and warring States. Socialism and the brotherhood of man—these were his religious tenets, and to these he attached himself with all the spirituality that his rich Celtic nature was capable of. As a self-taught and self-centred man, he had his peculiarities and *bizarreries*, which earned for him the nickname " Queer Hardie " (a nickname given to him by Daniel De Leon), but they never interfered with the life work he had mapped out for himself. Undisturbed by success or failure, by taunts or eulogies, he was serenely wending his way, destroying Liberal-Labourism and giving the British working class an independent political existence.

Hardie was born on August 15, 1856, in Lanarkshire. His father was a shipwright. His mother taught him reading, and that was his whole tuition. At the age of nine years he had to earn wages as a mining boy and worked underground for some sixteen years, spending his leisure hours in reading and studying. Gradually he ascended the scale of offices which his trade union, the Ayrshire Miners' Association, offered him. Eased from hard bodily work, he could devote more time to study, and he read Carlyle, Ruskin, and Mill, became for a time a member of the

[1] Robert Blatchford, *Britain for the British*, chap. 17.

Evangelical Union, and was then caught by the land reform agitation of Henry George (1882–1884), as so many brave spirits were, who at that time attempted to revive socialism in Great Britain. But, while Hyndman and Webb and Morris were engaged in socialist propaganda, Hardie intuitively felt that the beginning must be made with throwing the Liberal rider off the trade union horse. His first national appearance in this *rôle* was at the Swansea Trade Union Congress (1887), when he assailed Henry Broadhurst, the secretary of the Parliamentary Committee and Labour lieutenant of Gladstone, for supporting capitalist candidates at elections. From that time onwards we see Hardie moving along his chosen path, swerving neither to the right nor to the left. We see him as an independent Labour candidate in Lanarkshire, then as independent Labour M.P. for South-West Ham, as founder of the I.L.P., and we shall see him in the following pages as the co-founder and first Parliamentary leader of the national Labour Party. The official organ of the I.L.P., the *Labour Leader*, is also his creation. Its parent was the *Miner*, a small monthly journal founded by him in 1887; its title was afterwards changed into the present one, and since 1893 it has been published as a weekly. Hardie owned and edited it himself till 1904, when it was transferred to the Party. It has been successively edited by J. Ramsay MacDonald, J. Bruce Glasier, J. T. Mills, Mrs. Bruce Glasier, and A. Fenner Brockway. So he worked on, for socialism and the brotherhood of nations, by pen and speech, guided by his inner light, until overwork and the war took him away from us on September 26, 1915.[1]

Among Hardie's friends, who were intimately connected with the rise of the I.L.P. and its ideas, Bruce Glasier deserves the first place. He was the best successor to Hardie as editor of the *Labour Leader*. He enjoyed a much better school training than his political leader, and he came to socialism not as a working man, but as an ethical and intellectual student; both of them belong, however, to the same spiritual cast, which is

[1] *Cf.* J. Bruce Glasier, *James Keir Hardie, A Memorial.* National Labour Press. Manchester and London, 1916.

religious and mystical. For, also, Glasier's socialism is no materialistic or political; it has for him the meaning of an ethical religion, a practical love and service of humanity, rather than any capture of political power and change of State administration. In his latest book, which is the final outcome of his life and experience as a socialist writer and speaker, he sums up his faith: " Historically, socialism is more closely related to religious than political propagandism. It is from the prophets, apostles, and saints, the religious mystics and heretics, rather than from statesmen, economists, and political reformers, that the socialist movement derives its example and ideals. . . . Socialism means not only the socialisation of wealth, not only the socialisation of the means of production and distribution, but of our lives, our hearts—ourselves. . . . Socialism, when finally resolved, consists not in getting at all, but in giving; not in being served, but in serving. . . . Its ultimate moral, as its original biological justification, lies in the principle, human and divine, that ' as we give, so we live,' and only in so far as we are willing to lose life do we gain life." [1]

Next to Glasier stands James Ramsay MacDonald, who from a Scottish pupil-teacher and London journalist has risen to the front rank of writers and leaders of the socialist movement. His favourite studies were biological. Spencer's works and Ritchie's *Darwinism and Politics* appear to have influenced him most; his experience was mainly political; his writings bear indelible traces of both. Although now well over fifty years of age his mind is still very active and open to new currents of thought. He joined the I.L.P. in 1895, where he received his Labour education, which enabled him to take over the duties of the secretaryship of the Labour Representation Committee (or Labour Party) at its foundation in 1900 and to carry them out with conspicuous ability. He contributed greatly to the growth of the Labour Party, and in giving his best to the movement he has been adding much to his own intellectual stature. He is a prolific writer. Among his many books and pamphlets his

[1] J. Bruce Glasier, *The Meaning of Socialism*, concluding chapter. National Labour Press. Manchester and London. 1919.

Socialism and Society (1905) and *Socialism and Government* (1911)
contain his views on the practical problems of the socialist
Labour movement.   In regarding society as an organism analogous to the animal organism, he rejects class warfare and revolutionary action.   " The watchword of socialism is not class
consciousness, but community consciousness " (*Socialism and
Society,* p. 144).   The proper organ for accomplishing socialism
was the democratic State, which meant the organised political
personality of a sovereign people.   The State was not the organ
of a class, but of the whole society.   Indeed, " socialism could
not be defined better than as that stage of social organisation
when the State organises for society an adequate nutritive
system ; and democratic government is the signal that the
change is taking place" (*Socialism and Government,* i. 33).
Socialism would come through Parliament or it would not come
at all (*Syndicalism,* p. 8).   Under socialism the State would
reach a degree of organisation and importance in the community far greater than it could possibly attain under a *régime*
of competition.   The land and all the means of production
would belong to the State.   Still, there must be no confusion
between the State and society.   " The State is but one of the
organs of the community, all of which together form the organism
society " (*Socialism and Government,* i. 37).   Of the other
organs he only mentions the Church.   Had he proceeded further
and shown that also other organisations, for instance, trade
unions, employers' federations, teachers' associations, and other
bodies, were as much organs of society as the State was, he
would have arrived at guild socialism.   At any rate, it is quite
evident that MacDonald is a social reformer, averse from all
struggles, believing society to be moving by its inner development, as expressed and assisted by the human mind, from
lower to higher stages of organisation, more and more in accordance with the interests of the whole community.   He, therefore,
is of opinion that no well-defined socialist party, no dogmatic
programme, is needed and that it is quite sufficient to have a
broad socialistic movement which would consider all public
questions from the point of view of socialism as that stage to

which we are approaching (*Socialism and Government*, ii., 12–13). With these views as his guide, MacDonald was the best possible secretary of the Labour Party in the first years of its existence. The trade unions, which had to be gradually weaned from Liberalism, were essentially of the same opinion, though they could not have expressed it in biological terms. All they wanted was social reform and democracy. They could not have stood yet a clear-cut socialist programme, based on the theory of class warfare or on any other doctrinal substructure.

Hardie was also very proud of his comradeship with Philip Snowden, who has proved the best socialist Budget speaker and financial writer. Robert Smillie, now President of the Miners' Federation of Great Britain, was a life-long friend and co-worker of Hardie. The same may be said of Frank Smith.

Among the earliest members of the I.L.P. and friends of Hardie were Fred Jowett (who had risen from a simple factory hand to one of the best Labour journalists), J. R. Clynes, George N. Barnes, and G. H. Roberts. Indeed, several of the labour leaders who in the last years of the war occupied Ministerial positions had served their political apprenticeship in the I.L.P.

XVI

FORMATION OF THE LABOUR PARTY

I.—ABORTIVE STRIKES AND THE SUBVERSION OF TRADE UNION LAW

IT is a matter of doubt whether the founders of the I.L.P. were satisfied with the results of the first years of their work. After all, the new party proved to be merely an improved edition of the S.D.F. The main object, namely, to enlist the masses of the organised workers to the cause of independent politics, was not attained. The progress made by the I.L.P. in the ranks of the more alert trade unionists was, indeed, encouraging, but the masses failed to respond to the new propaganda. This was clearly demonstrated during the parliamentary elections and by-elections in the years from 1895 to 1898. The polling results were but moral victories and as such could make no impression on the masses. The leaders of the I.L.P. had therefore to search for other methods, or to watch for opportunities which would assist them in their efforts. And they had not long to search and wait for them. Events were shaping themselves in the trade union world which could not fail to promote the objects of the I.L.P. In 1897 and 1898 the engineers and the Welsh miners came out on strike for better conditions of labour, and after a stubborn fight lasting for many months were discomfited. In 1898 Gladstone died, and with him one of the main pillars of Liberal Labourism disappeared from British politics. Simultaneously the Trade Union Acts, 1871, 1875, 1876, which were regarded by Labour as its charter of liberty, were being shattered. By decisions of the law courts the right of picketing was gradually curtailed and the freedom from collective responsibility nullified. The process of shattering trade union law began in 1896, but failed to attract much attention at the time owing to the insignificant nature of the actions. The Taff Vale decision (1900–1) was but the sensational revelation of an accomplished fact. At the beginning of the twentieth century the organised working men, the pick of British Labour, became conscious of the fact that the strike was a blunt and clumsy weapon and that even this weapon was no longer available. At the same time the controversies on the South African War threatened the existence of the Liberal party, which the bulk of the trade unionists regarded as their political representative. The accepted methods of economic and political action, by which the trade unions had set so much store, proved a bundle of dry and broken faggots fit only for the fire. The Liberal Labour period was manifestly nearing its end.

This was the state of affairs at the ringing out of the old and the ringing in of the new century.

2.—THE TRADE UNION CONGRESS OF 1899

In the summer of 1899 the trade unions made preparations for their annual congress, which was to be held at Plymouth during the first week in September. The leaders of the I.L.P., unless they were wage-workers or paid trade union officials, were not allowed to be elected as delegates to the Congress, since a resolution to this effect had, at the instance of John Burns, been adopted by the Trades Union Congress of 1895, in order to free the delegates from the influence of " socialist adventurers." The leaders of the I.L.P. had therefore to look for indirect methods to make their voices heard in the Labour parliaments. In the office of the *Labour Leader*, the organ of the I.L.P., a resolution was drafted for the purpose of promoting Labour representation and handed over, through the executive of the Amalgamated Society of Railway Servants, to James Holmes, the organiser of the Taff Vale strike and one of the delegates to the Trade Union Congress. The resolution ran as follows :—

" This Congress having regard to the decisions of former years, and with a view to securing a better representation of the interests of Labour in the House of Commons, hereby instructs the Parliamentary Committee of the Trade Union Congress to invite the co-operation of all the Co-operative, Socialist, Trade Union, and other working class organisations jointly to co-operate on lines mutually agreed upon in convening a special congress of representatives from such of the above-mentioned organisations as may be willing to take part to devise ways and means for the securing of an increased number of Labour members to the next Parliament."

Holmes moved the resolution, and he was followed by James Sexton, a clever and eloquent Irishman, the delegate of the Liverpool dockers, who seconded it. The old trade union leaders opposed the resolution. Their spokesman, Thomas Ashton, the secretary of the spinners in Oldham, was of opinion that it was sheer waste of time to have long debates on this resolution; not one trade unionist in 10,000 would give it a moment's attention; trade unionism would altogether come to grief if it were to be turned into a political party. Nevertheless the resolution was discussed and passed by 546,000 votes to 434,000. It laid the foundation-stone of the Labour Party.

The mere adoption of the resolution by the Congress at Plymouth naturally did not accomplish much. It would have led to just as little result as earlier resolutions, or as the Labour Representation League and the Labour Electoral Association. It was therefore necessary above everything to withdraw the practical application of the resolution from the Trade Union Congress and its traditionally Liberal organ, the Parliamentary Committee, and to place it in the hands of the I.L.P. This was a relatively easy matter, for the Parliamentary Committee had no belief in the success of the resolution. A committee was appointed for this purpose, consisting of four members of the Parliamentary Committee: Sam Woods (Liberal), W. C. Steadman (Radical and Fabian), William Thorne (Social Democrat) and R. Bell (at that time with socialist learnings), further, of two members each from the I.L.P., S.D.F., and the Fabian Society—Keir Hardie, J. Ramsay MacDonald, Harry Quelch, H. R. Taylor, G. B. Shaw and E. R. Pease (secretary of the Fabians). The socialists were in the majority on the committee and they were far superior to the trade unionist members in intelligence, energy, and knowledge of their aims. The committee held several meetings and decided to convene a general conference. As a basis for the deliberations of the conference they drew up the following eight resolutions and rulings :—

1. *Object of Conference :* A resolution in favour of working class opinion being represented in the House of Commons by men sympathetic with the aims and demands of the Labour movement.

2. *Labour Members in the House of Commons :* A resolution in favour of establishing a distinct Labour group in Parliament, who should have their own Whips and agree upon their policy, which must embrace a readiness to co-operate with any party which, for the time being, may be engaged in promoting legislation in the direct interest of labour, and be equally ready to associate themselves with any party in opposing measures having an opposite tendency.

3. *Constitution of Committee :* The committee shall consist of twelve representatives from trade unions, ten from the co-operative societies, provided they are represented as a body at the conference, two from the Fabian Society, two from the I.L.P., and two from the S.D.F.

4. *Duty of Committee :* This committee should keep in touch with trade unions and other organisations which are running Labour candidates.

5. *Financial responsibility :* The committee shall adminster the funds which may be received on behalf of the organisation, and each body shall be required to pay 10s. per annum for every 1000 members or fraction thereof, also that it shall be responsible for the expenses of its own candidates.

6. *Reporting to Congress :* It should also report annually to the Trades Union Congress and the annual meetings of the national societies represented on the committee, and take any steps deemed advisable to elicit opinion from the members of the organisations to which the committee is ultimately responsible.

7. *Basis of Representation :* Societies, by whatever name they may be known, shall be entitled to one delegate for every 2,000 members or fraction thereof, and they must pay 10s. for each delegate attending the conference, and forward their names and

addresses seven days prior to the date fixed for the meeting. No credential card shall be issued to any society not having complied with the foregoing conditions.

8. *Voting :* The method of voting shall be by card, to be issued to the delegates of trade societies according to their membership, and paid for on the principle of one card for every 1000 members or fractional part thereof represented.

All the organisations in question were invited by the committee to send delegates to the general conference. With the exception of the co-operative societies many organisations accepted the invitation, and the committee made the necessary preparations for the conference.

3.—THE LABOUR REPRESENTATION COMMITTEE

On February 27 and 28, 1900, exactly sixty-three years after the meeting of the London Working Men's Union at which the People's Charter was formulated, 120 delegates met in London, representing more than half a million working men belonging to trade unionist and socialist organisations, for the purpose of inaugurating a new Chartist movement. The chair was taken on this occasion also by a London working man—W. C. Steadman, who had already represented a London constituency in the House of Commons. John Burns, member of Parliament for Battersea, was likewise present, but not much attention was paid to him.

Steadman opened the conference and stated :—

" I am one of those trade unionists who believed, until the last ten years, that the workers of this country could attain their object in securing better conditions by voluntary efforts through their trade organisations. But the dispute which occurred in my own trade ten years ago for a reduction of the hours of labour had convinced me that the leaders of the advanced movement who believed in political action were right and I was wrong. I give way to no man in my desire to see Labour better represented in the House of Commons than it was to-day."

The conference then proceeded to deliberate upon the resolutions drawn up by the committee. The debate that ensued disclosed three main lines of thought. The first desired to include among the working class candidatures all those " who are sympathetic with the aims and demands of the Labour movement " ; the second that the labour candidates should be restricted to those belonging to the organisations represented on the committee ; the third that they should be restricted to social democrats who advocated class warfare and the collective ownership of the means of production. The first aimed at a rapprochement between the committee and the Radicals ; the second desired a strict Labour policy ; the third was in favour of the identification of the committee with the Social Democratic Federation. John Burns supported the first view and expressed the opinion :—

" I am getting tired of working class boots, working class trains, working class houses, and working class margarine. I believe the time has arrived in the history of the Labour and social movement when we should not be prisoners to class prejudice but should consider parties and policies apart from all class organisations."

The advocates of the second trend of thought were George Barnes, Pete Curran, James Sexton, and Keir Hardie, who for the most part aimed at an independent Labour party and a harmonious co-operation between trade unionists and socialists. Harry Quelch and James Macdonald supported the third line of policy.

The views of the second current of opinion corresponded on the whole to the feelings and wishes of the conference, and they were adopted by large majorities. The conference elected a Labour Representation Committee (L.R.C.), consisting of seven trade unionists, two members of the I.L.P., two members of the S.D.F., and one of the Fabian Society. James Ramsay MacDonald, a member of the I.L.P., was elected secretary, and immediately set to work to enlist the sympathies of the trade unions for the L.R.C. Yet in 1900 only 375,931 trade unionists and socialists affiliated, among them being 13,000 members of the I.L.P., 9,000 of the S.D.F., and 861 of the Fabian Society.

The admission to the membership of the L.R.C.[1] was, at that time, not open to individuals, but to Labour and socialist organisations ; the unit of membership was not the individual, but the trade union or socialist society. As a rule it was effected in the following manner :—Some of the members of a union or a trades council or a socialist group proposed that the organisation should join the Labour Party. A general vote was taken and the decision lay with the majority. The case, therefore, easily arose that powerful minorities of trade unionists who were either Liberals or Conservatives and therefore not in agreement with the essentials of the Labour Party were nevertheless reckoned as its members. The method, which is in use for purely trade unionist purposes, was made applicable to politics. In exclusively trade unionist questions, for instance, in strikes, a decision is rarely unanimous, and yet the decision to quit work has to be obeyed by all ; the minority has to subordinate its wishes to those of the majority. In the same manner, a decision to vote Labour against Liberals and Conservatives was to be binding on all. The difficulty, however, was that, whilst a strike forms an integral part of trade unionist action, the political vote was for a long time a matter of party. The conversion of trade unions to a national Labour Party in opposition to all other parties was bound to give rise to difficulties. In the course of our narrative we shall see what were the problems and conflicts which resulted from the new phase of the British Labour movement. But in the first few years they were scarcely noticeable, and the L.R.C. was able to obtain a surprising measure of success without being involved in internecine struggles.

4.—GROWTH OF THE L.R.C.

In September, 1900, Parliament was dissolved and in October the general election took place. The L.R.C., though young and hardly prepared for an election campaign, sent fifteen candidates into the field, of whom two only were successful—Richard Bell

[1] From 1906 onwards the L.R.C. assumed the name of Labour Party, but the latter term was also used, though not officially, from the time it was formed.

in Derby and Keir Hardie in Merthyr Tydvil. In the fifteen constituencies 177,000 votes were cast for all parties, 62,700 of which were given to Labour candidates. In 1901 the number of trade unions affiliated to the L.R.C. amounted to sixty-five, while that of the socialist organisations fell to two, the S.D.F. having withdrawn in the summer of the same year from the L.R.C. The total membership stood at that time at 455,450. In 1902 the membership was doubled—it rose to 861,200. The meaning of the Taff Vale decision was beginning to be thoroughly understood by the organised masses ; political action became the leading question, for the trade unionists saw that new legislation was necessary in order to remove the paralysis which had overtaken their organisations in consequence of the Taff Vale decision. In June, 1902, a parliamentary vacancy occurred at Clitheroe. The I.L.P. was prepared to put up Philip Snowden as the socialist candidate, but gave way to David J. Shackleton, the secretary of the textile workers, who came forward as an independent Labour candidate and was returned unopposed. In 1903 the Labour group in Parliament was increased by two more members—William Crooks and Arthur Henderson. Crooks was elected in Woolwich, having polled 8,687 votes against 5,458 cast for the Conservative, while Henderson carried Barnard Castle against both Liberals and Conservatives. In 1904 the Labour group in Parliament was joined by Thomas Richards, member for West Monmouthshire, who defeated his tariff reform opponent. Meanwhile, the Taff Vale decision imposed heavy burdens on some of the trade unions. In 1903 the Railway Servants paid to the Taff Vale Company damages and costs to the amount of £23,000, and judgment was delivered against the South Wales miners, who were mulcted in £50,000. It may incidentally be remarked that only in Wales did the employers have recourse to the Taff Vale decision, while English and Scottish employers suffered the grave inconveniences which industrial conflicts imply rather than aggravate the tension between Capital and Labour by onslaughts on the trade union funds. This may, to some degree, explain the syndicalist and revolutionary tendencies among the Labour organisations in South

Wales. To the end of 1905 the Labour group in Parliament consisted of four members, Richard Bell having returned to the Liberal camp. Indeed, Bell had never felt quite at home as secretary of his union, or as member of the I.L.P. and the L.R.C. When paying the above-mentioned damages and costs to the Taff Vale directors at a special dinner which he arranged for them, he ate humble pie by delivering a very contrite speech and winding it up by expressing his best wishes for them. In the same year (1903) a bye-election took place at Norwich, with George H. Roberts as I.L.P. candidate. Roberts was then a fiery socialist and internationalist. Many of the Labour leaders, notably David J. Shackleton and Arthur Henderson, fresh from the field of glory, supported him, while Richard Bell sent his best wishes to the Liberal candidate and urged the electors to vote " yellow." The disloyal action of Bell created a ferment in the movement and led finally to the great discussion on the question of independence, which, as we shall see in one of the next chapters, was subsequently settled at the Newcastle L.R.C. conference in the same year.

During all those years the Conservative Government made no serious attempt to amend trade union law or to arrive at any compromise with the working men. Their whole attention was concentrated on the tariff reform movement, which Joseph Chamberlain, the Colonial Secretary, set on foot in May, 1903, and which resulted in a crisis in the Conservative Party. The L.R.C. received scant notice from the press and the public, though the election of William Crooks caused the *Daily Telegraph* to remark that a new Chartist movement was in the course of formation. This shrewd remark was not followed up. Tariff reform and the growing tension of Anglo-German relations soon diverted the thoughts of politicians and publicists from Labour problems. No wonder, then, that the results of the elections in January, 1906, struck them as a bolt from the blue.

In December, 1905, the Conservative Government resigned and Sir Henry Campbell-Bannerman, who had led his party from defeat to victory, formed a Liberal Cabinet, in which John Burns was appointed President of the Local Government Board.

The general election took place in January, 1906. The L.R.C., scarcely six years old, had a membership of 900,000, and sent fifty candidates into the electoral campaign, twenty-nine of whom were successful. The total vote cast for all the parties in the fifty constituencies amounted to 860,000, of which 323,200 were given to Labour. The Miners' Federation, represented in Parliament by fourteen members of their own, was the only one of the larger trade unions which remained outside the L.R.C. At that time the representatives of the miners belonged to the Liberal Party.

The Labour successes formed the sensation of the year. Newspapers and clubs, drawing-rooms and country houses, forgetting for a time the crushing defeat of Toryism and tariff reform, discussed hardly anything else but the political uprise of the working classes. The spirit of the nation was stirred to its depths, and the remarkable thing was that the speakers and writers occupied themselves less with Labour than with socialism, although the L.R.C. was not socialist. A whole literature dealing with the history and essence of socialism came into existence with lightning rapidity ; the socialist weeklies, *Justice*, *Labour Leader*, *Clarion*, *Forward*, etc., gained a large circulation ; everybody seemed to be anxious to get some knowledge of the new power which had so unexpectedly made its appearance. The nation grasped somehow the truth that an independent Labour Party meant a reorganisation of society on socialist lines.

The L.R.C., henceforth officially known as the Labour Party (L.P.), held its sixth annual conference in the middle of February, 1906, in London. Its deliberations were exceedingly cordial. Socialists, like Keir Hardie and Pete Curran, trade union leaders, like Shackleton and Henderson, regarded each other as comrades in a spirit of candour and cheerfulness. The conference celebrated the reconciliation of Labour and Socialism. The scenes of enthusiasm occurring during the conference and the declarations of solidarity of all the Labour forces vividly recalled the best moments of Chartism. The mass demonstration which was held at the Queen's Hall on the evening of February 16,

1906, in honour of the conference delegates, left an indelible impression on all who took part in it. At last the effects of the past defeats of Labour seemed to have vanished for ever !

The first-fruits of the victory of the Labour Party was the reversal of the Taff Vale decision. The Party imposed upon the Campbell-Bannerman Cabinet a Trade Disputes Bill, which secured to the organised workers the right of picketing and freedom from collective responsibility. In the House of Lords a current of opinion was manifested in opposition to the Bill, the great majority of the peers sharing the opinion of many lawyers and judges that this measure raised the trade unions to a privileged position before the law of the land. But Lord Lansdowne, appreciating the revolutionary effect of the Taff Vale decision on the working classes, considered that the Trade Disputes Bill was not a favourable battleground for the Conservatives, and therefore advised them to execute a strategic retreat. The Bill was passed.

The signal victory of the small Labour group over the strongest Liberal Government and the House of Lords, as well as over capitalists and lawyers, raised the hopes of the working classes and the socialists to a higher degree than ever before. Altogether the year 1906 was one of the most remarkable in the annals of British democracy and Labour. There was nothing like it since 1831-2 ; moreover, as far as Labour was concerned, the counter-currents and disappointments were somewhat longer in coming than in 1832. In July, 1907, two sensational by-elections took place. At Jarrow, Pete Curran, the socialist and Labour candidate, carried the constituency in a four-cornered or "square" fight ; in the Colne Valley, Victor Grayson, a young, inexperienced socialist, curiously recalling the type of the young Chartist agitators of 1840, was successful on a purely socialist programme. On the other hand, the parliamentary session of 1907 proved barren of social legislation, and gave rise to much dissatisfaction among the working classes. Disillusionment was gradually setting in, and it was intensified by the defeat of the Society of Railway Servants. After long and laborious preparations the railwaymen were determined to give

I W

battle for better condition of labour, and particularly for the recognition of their union by the Railway Companies. In the autumn of 1907 the prospect of a disastrous struggle thoroughly alarmed the public, and the Government was urged to interfere. Lloyd George, then President of the Board of Trade, appeared on the scene, and finally succeeded in forcing upon the men's leaders a scheme of conciliation and arbitration boards. On November 6 the conflict was declared to have come to an end. In reality, it was merely postponed, for the railwaymen regarded the result as a defeat, and many of them even thought it to have been the result of a betrayal of the men by their leaders. The railway men were " welshed," as the editor of the *Justice* remarked.[1]

The reaction from parliamentarism and conciliatory industrial methods gradually manifested itself in rebellions of the trade unionists against their leaders, and, finally, in revolutionary trade unionism or anti-parliamentary syndicalism, which will be dealt with in a later chapter. Meanwhile we must turn our attention to the problems of independent politics and organisation which troubled the Labour Party.

[1] Compare G. D. H. Cole and R. Page Arnot, *Trade Unionism on the Railways*, 1917. pp. 21, 110-113.

XVII

PROBLEMS OF THE LABOUR PARTY

I.—LABOUR POLITICS AND SOCIALISM

IN the latter half of the nineteenth century the organised workers were overwhelmingly Liberal, though as trade unionists they were nominally neutral. They supported, from their funds, parliamentary representatives, as a rule Liberal Labour members ; and they defrayed the expenses of the Trade Union Congress, which has always had a good deal to do with politics. In fact, the political neutrality of the trade unions was the result of the absence of any strong and definite opposition to Liberalism, the Conservative minorities of the trade unions forming a negligible quantity. With the exception of one or two Conservative trade union leaders, the officials of the Labour organisations belonged to the Liberal Party.

With the affiliation of an increasing number of trade unions to the L.R.C. or Labour Party, an examination into the principles on which political parties are based became inevitable. For, if the L.R.C. was Liberal, there was no need for it. Seeing, however, that it existed and flourished, it must needs have adopted principles different from those of Liberalism. What were they ? These examinations, questions and discussions were taken in hand as soon as the L.R.C. came into being. They were carried on mainly by the members of the I.L.P. and the S.D.F.

The members of the S.D.F. advocated the prompt and immediate transformation of the L.R.C. into a social democratic party, and attempted to force upon it the recognition of the ultimate aim of socialism, with its method of class warfare. Even if this resulted in a split, nothing would be lost. What could a Labour Party accomplish without an ultimate aim ?

Nothing. On the other hand, much could be accomplished by a small social democratic party possessing a definite programme. At the conference, at which the L.R.C. was formed (1900), James Macdonald, the delegate of the S.D.F., moved :—

" That the representatives of the working class movement in the House of Commons shall form there a distinct party . . . based upon a recognition of the class war, and having for its ultimate object the socialisation of the means of production, distribution, and exchange. The party shall formulate its own policy for promoting practical legislative measures in the interests of labour, and shall be prepared to co-operate with any party that will support such measures, or will assist in opposing measures of an opposite character."

A similar resolution was submitted a year later (1901) by Harry Quelch, editor of *Justice*. All the delegates of the trade unions and the I.L.P. spoke against binding the L.R.C. candidates to socialism. On the other hand, the conference adopted the resolution moved by Keir Hardie :—

" That this conference is in favour of establishing a distinct Labour Group in Parliament, who shall have their own Whips, and agree upon their policy, which must embrace a readiness to co-operate with any party which for the time being may be engaged in promoting legislation in the direct interest of labour, and be equally ready to associate themselves with any party in opposing measures having an opposite tendency."

This resolution outlined the policy of the party in Parliament. It aimed at the formation in the House of Commons of a Labour Party having its own policy, its own Whips, and acting in all that concerned the welfare of the workers in a manner free and unhampered by entanglements with other parties. Each of the affiliated organisations would be left free to select its own candidates without let or hindrance, the one condition being that, when returned to Parliament, the candidate should agree to form one of the Labour Group there, and act in harmony with its decisions. In this way they would avoid the scandal, which in the past had pained earnest men on both sides, of seeing trade unionists opposing socialists, and *vice versa*.

As to the economic principles of the new party, the conference adopted the resolution which James Sexton, the delegate of the Liverpool dock labourers, moved on behalf of his union :—

" That this conference declares that in view of the combinations of capital and the federations of employers it is necessary for the trade unions of the country to use their political power to defend their existence and secure their demands, and while it deprecates the introduction of mere party politics into the trade union movement, it urges upon trade unionists the necessity of combining on an independent platform for the following purposes : (1) The defence of the legal rights of combination. (2) The passing of such laws as will put an end to a system under which the producer of wealth has to bear an enormous burden in the shape of rents and profits which go to maintain large classes of non-producers."

The resolutions of Keir Hardie and James Sexton respectively contain essentially the same demands and principles as the resolutions of James Macdonald and Harry Quelch, but the former are free from dogmatic formulæ and were therefore more acceptable to the trade union delegates. Nevertheless, the S.D.F., at its annual conference in 1901, decided to withdraw from the L.R.C. A resolution to that effect was adopted by fifty-four to fourteen votes. The withdrawal of the S.D.F. delegation from the L.R.C. had two unfavourable effects. In the first place it gave rise to hostile recriminations between the organs of the S.D.F. and the I.L.P., and widened the gulf between the two socialist bodies whose co-operation was necessary for the success of socialism in Great Britian. Secondly, the two vacant places on the L.R.C. were filled by Liberal Labour trade unionists. The socialist influence was weakened and frittered away at a moment when the affiliation of trade unions to the L.R.C. was proceeding at a great rate—in 1902–3 the membership rose from 455,450 to 847,315. The new movement was filled with masses of recruits who needed training in independent Labour politics and social reform, while the S.D.F. members who could have undertaken that training made strenuous efforts not to let their doctrines pass into the hands of the heathen. The relatively small number of socialists on the L.R.C. were faced with the task of protecting the new organisation from being swamped with Liberal Labourism. We shall see presently how they attempted to solve the problem. In the meantime we may observe that, although the S.D.F. as a body was no longer in a position to send delegates to the conferences in an official capacity, several of its members attended them annually as delegate of trade unions affiliated to the L.R.C. Their exertions, however, suffered from the suspicion that they were attempting to smuggle in the ideas of an organisation which was not in sympathy with the L.R.C. They moved social democratic resolutions at the annual conferences of the L.R.C., which, when taken *seriatim*, were rejected, as the annual conferences were not inclined to pledge their parliamentary representatives to socialism. On the other hand, the social democratic resolutions were adopted, when they were meant merely as an invitation to socialists to act in concert with the British Labour movement. Both cases occurred at the eighth annual conference (1908), held at Hull. On the discussion of the amendments to the constitution of the Labour Party, William Atkinson, the delegate of the paper stainers and a member of the S.D.F., moved that it was the aim of the Labour Party—

" To organise and maintain a Parliamentary Party, with its own Whips, whose ultimate object shall be the obtaining for the workers the full results of their labour by the overthrow of the present competitive system of capitalism and the institution of a system of public ownership and control of all the means of life."

In support of this amendment he declared that no Labour Party worth the name ought to be satisfied with a mere wage system. It was no use to hide the fact that most of them were already persuaded that the socialist position was the right position.

He thought that if the Labour Party desired to maintain an onward march, and make that march quickly, it was more likely to accomplish it by declaring to landlords and capitalists that it was not afraid of its convictions and that it intended to realise them at an early date.

Atkinson was supported by R. Davis, delegate of the society of ironfounders, then by V. Grayson, at that time member of Parliament, finally by Harry Quelch, the social democratic leader, who attended the conference as a delegate of the London Trades Council, and by J. Gribble (Boot and Shoe Operatives' Union). The amendment was opposed by J. Bruce Glasier, delegate of the I.L.P., who wished to draw the attention of the conference to the important fact that the resolution did not simply consist in a declaration in favour of socialism, but it actually meant that if it was passed every trade unionist would be excluded from the party if he was not prepared to declare in favour of socialism. On behalf of the I.L.P. he declared that it had no wish to impose socialism on those who were not prepared to accept it ; he and his fellow delegates from the I.L.P. wished to say that they rejoiced to work with the trade unionists, as owing to that alliance the Labour Party had been so successful in Parliament. Glasier was followed by J. R. Clynes, M.P. (Oldham Trades Council), one of the most persuasive speakers of Labour, who declared that he believed in the public ownership and control of all the material things needed for the maintenance of life. But so far as they took part in politics they ought to be careful not to sharpen the weapons of the enemy. He believed that if they forced this declaration of objects upon the organised million represented in the party the effect would be harmful. The party subsisted at present on an alliance. The conditions of the alliance ought to be respected. The success of the alliance ought not to be ignored. He was more in favour of preaching to make converts to socialism in the country than of seeking in the conference to fasten the socialist label upon the large mass of organised workers who were not socialists at all. They were not out, as a matter of fact, for ultimate objects ; they were out for Old Age pensions ; they were out for immediate industrial legislation ; they were out for some kind of effective and helpful legislation on the subject of unemployment ; and at the same time they were out in the country preaching ideals to the people.

A. H. Gill, M.P., said that as one of the old type of trade unionists he wished to oppose the amendment. It was because he was anxious to maintain the alliance as it at present existed that he opposed the amendment. They wanted to get something done at the present time and they could not afford to wait to realise the whole of the programme that the extreme men or advanced men were going in for.   Trade unionists were not all socialists yet, and until they became all socialists they would not be prepared to pay their levies for the purpose of supporting a socialist party. There was no difficulty at the present time in the House of Commons in the two wings of the party working together. He thought for the next twenty years those two sections could work hand in hand and they could have useful work done. If it had not been for the alliance between the trade unionists and the Socialists in the House of Commons they would not have had a Trades Disputes Act passed ; they would not have had the Compensation Act passed in the way it was.   Instead of trying to find points of difference the policy should be to find points of agreement, and there were many points about which they were all agreed, although some were not prepared to go the whole hog. He ventured to say that if the amendment were carried the trade unions would be forced out of the party and thus wreck it.

Pete Curran, M.P. (gasworkers), said that nine years ago the socialist trade unionist and what might be called the old-timer trade unionist joined hands in an open and honourable alliance, in accordance with the resolution passed at the Plymouth Trade Union Congress. They joined hands for political purposes on strictly independent lines, and at that time the S.D.F. came in. But then the younger and more turbulent spirits, the men who did all the shouting and little work, forced the Federation out of the alliance, and now members of the Federation attended the Labour Party conferences representing other organisations. It was grieving to those who left the party to find that it was successful even in their absence. In the House of Commons Mr. Gill and the other men who represented the more moderate side of the trade union movement on all questions since he had been there had been as loyal and as independent as any socialist could be. The carrying of the amendment would do more to help the London *Daily Express* and *Daily Mail* in disrupting the movement than anything else that could be done. They had the trade unionists to-day working under conditions that they refused to work under twelve, thirteen, and fourteen years ago. They were willing to admit that at that time they did not see the wisdom of independent political action, and what had brought them to see it was the force of circumstances, legal tyranny, and the educational propaganda of the socialists in the trade union movement. They wanted to work with them openly and honourably, and he believed that with the process of evolution they would come right along as far as desired, but they should not be driven nor forced.

The amendment was then put up and the vote was as follows :— for the amendment 91,000, against 951,000.

The same conference, however, carried, two days later, a socialist resolution, because it was understood that it was proposed for the purpose of eliciting an expression of opinion. J. J. Stephenson (Engineers) moved :—

" That in the opinion of this Conference the time has arrived when the Labour Party should have as a definite object the socialisation of the means of production, distribution, and exchange, to be controlled by a democratic State in the interest of the entire community ; and the complete emancipation of Labour from the domination of capitalism and landlordism, with the establishment of social and economic equality between the sexes."

He said he was going to attempt to speak to this resolution from the experience of a trade unionist. The organisation responsible for the motion came into existence fifty-six years ago to protect the interests of those under its jurisdiction. But had their aspirations been realised ? We had unemployed to-day in the engineering community and we had a standard of living far short of that which our forefathers desired. He wanted to say that it was not the purpose of the Engineers' Society to drive away any members in the coalition which formed the party. When they had carried our remedial legislation as far as it was possible they would still be confronted by inequalities that could only be removed by the commonwealth having charge of all the forces of the commonwealth and owning them. Consider the scenes that were presented in the large cities : Piccadilly in London at midnight, the East End at midday, the unemployed at Tower Hill and on the Embankment ; in Hull, Carr Lane from six in the evening, and the dock gates from six in the morning. To what were these spectacles due but to the private ownership of the means of life ? Take another illustration with which they are familiar. The latest triumphs of shipbuilding and engineering were the " Lusitania " and the " Mauretania." Go down for an hour into the stokeholds and see how men earned their bread. Here was the distribution of wealth exemplified. For every penny the coal-trimmers get as wages for their hard work, the landlord receives 35s. royalty rent on the coal. Landlords and employers when they had control of the Legislature passed the laws in their own behalf. The founders of his organisation fifty-six years ago put the memorable words in the preface of the Rule Book that they hoped the interests of the workers would be promoted by their trade unions until some more general principle of co-operation should be acknowledged in society, guaranteeing to every man the full enjoyment of his labour. He was one of those who believed that they must have an ideal in their politics ; that ideal being in this case the absolute removal from their midst of all that makes crime and vice rampant.

Only two delegates took part in the discussion, one speaking for, the other against the resolution, which was then put and carried by 514,000 votes to 469,000.

The results of the discussions of socialist resolutions at the Hull conference were unmistakable. The Labour Party stood for social reform—for a socialistic reorganisation of society by gradual steps, but it was not social revolutionary ; it had no final goal, but immediate aims ; it did not occupy itself with theories, but with practical measures.

2.—LABOUR'S DECLARATION OF INDEPENDENCE

The growth of the L.R.C. in 1902-3, the swamping of the organisation with Liberal Labour men, and the attempt on the part of some Labour leaders, like Richard Bell, John Ward, and he old trade union officials to beat a hasty retreat to the Liberal camp, induced the I.L.P. members of the L.R.C. to define, in unambiguous terms, the conception of Labour independence, and to cause the L.R.C. to embody it in an authoritative declaration. At the third annual conference (Newcastle, 1903) Pete Curran, in accordance with the recommendation of the Standing Orders Committee, moved the following resolution :—

" In view of the fact that the L.R.C. is recruiting adherents from all outside political forces, and also, taking into consideration the basis upon which the committee was inaugurated, this conference regards it as being absolutely necessary that the members of the Executive Committee and officials of affiliated organisations should strictly abstain from identifying themselves with, or promoting the interests of, any section of the Liberal or Conservative parties, inasmuch as if we are to secure the social and economic requirements of the industrial classes Labour representatives in and out of Parliament will have to shape their own policy and act upon it regardless of other sections in the political world ; and that the Executive Committee report to the affiliated association or bodies any such official acting contrary to the spirit of the constitution as hereby amended."

Curran declared that the delegates would remember the resolution brought forward at the Trade Union Congress at Plymouth (1899) by the Society of Railway Servants declaring that the time was ripe for a parliamentary Labour group to act independently. That resolution was passed by the Congress, and the following January a special conference met in London to form this representation committee. The constitution, as then drafted, was admittedly weak because of the infancy of the movement that they were then inaugurating. To-day the movement had grown even beyond the anticipations of the most sanguine. They were to-day in Newcastle, historical so far as programmes were concerned, representing nearly a million organised workers throughout the length and breadth of this country. The newspapers every morning were telling them to be good boys, informing them that they should go on the path of political virtue and righteousness ; in fact, the papers were condescending to tell them that the possibility was that they (the press) might see their way to help. He made bold to say that the time had arrived when the working class movement could stand politically upon its own legs ; that there were enough people represented at this conference to form a movement—not necessarily antagonistic to other parties, but outside and independent—to formulate their own policy and carry it into the House of Commons, and try to obtain there for it due support. He said that if this line were not adopted the movement had no mission. Why did they call it into existence if they could find redemption through either party ? But most men at this conference were convinced in their heart of hearts that no political party in the State to-day outside their movement would grapple with those deep-rooted evils which we desired to see eradicated. It was because they were convinced of this that they were there to strengthen and solidify their movement. Calling upon the responsible officials of affiliated organisations to abstain from identifying themselves with other parties was only the necessary and logical sequence of the meeting there that afternoon, if they were going to have a movement, solid, acting together in and out of the House of Commons. They were only weakening themselves if they strengthened other parties. He wanted to say that they had lessons in history why they should act on the lines suggested. Over half a century ago the old Chartist movement originated among the hills of Durham. Yet the Chartist movement became weak enough to be absorbed in one of the political parties and so became useless. The Labour Electoral Association existed in this country, and had within its ranks some of the best trade unionists that could be found, and many of them were present. It attached itself to the tail end of one of the parties, and was to-day extinct. Let them take a lesson, and let them strengthen their constitution in a way that would not tie down the trade unionist to socialism, nor the socialist to trade unionism, but both to Labour. By so doing they would keep the best men in the ranks, and be able to accomplish those valuable reforms that they aspired to accomplish at the earliest possible moment.

John Hodge, M.P. (Steel Smelters), seconded the resolution.

After an exhaustive discussion, in which Bell, Ward, and other opponents of independence had spoken and endeavoured to show that independence was tantamount to isolation and destruction of the movement, Keir Hardie rose to argue that the opponents of independence really meant to bring Labour back to a policy of weak and unprincipled opportunism. In reality there was but one weapon which would stand the test of time and prove effective : adhesion to an honest principle. Any departure from that would ruin their Labour movement. They all, Liberal, Tory, and socialist alike, rejoiced at the magnificent conference got together in that hall. What was the principle that enabled them all to come together and discuss this matter ? Independence. If they, the socialists, had insisted that all should be socialists, there would be no such gathering. Had the Liberals insisted that all should be Liberals, they would have had the like result. They had fixed upon a common denominator that, when acting in the House of Commons, they should be neither socialists, Liberals, nor Tories, but a Labour party. They were seeking by the resolution to prevent individuals from disrupting the movement. What the resolution said was that the officials of this conference should not, on their own initiative, and because of certain political predilections of their own, give this movement a bias which would affect it to its foundations. The Parnell movement was organised on an independent basis. Every Irish branch was a strictly non-political organisation, holding its force in reserve to use in any way the council told it. They desired their forces to be used in the same way. If some stood as Liberals, and others as Tories, and others as socialists, the divisions that now rent Labour would be continued. When a man who represented a trade union, who was being paid by a trade union, passed over the Trades Council and the organised trade unions of a constituency, in order to have himself selected by a Liberal or Tory organisation, he was not playing the game straight. Let them beware lest they surrender themselves to Liberalism, which would shackle them, gag them, and leave them a helpless, discredited, and impotent mass. Let them have done with Liberalism and Toryism and every other " ism " that was not

Labourism, and let them give the rank and file a straight and honest lead, and if that were done the rank and file would support them.

Hardie's speech, in which the term " Labourism " was coined, was followed by speeches from Ben Tillett and Curran, who clinched the argument for independence. The resolution was then put and carried by a card vote of 659,000 to 154,000. It was embodied in the constitution of the L.R.C. and formed the so-called " pledge " of the Labour Members of Parliament to abide by the decisions of the Party. The revised constitution, or the " Newcastle Programme " of the Labour Party, ran as follows :—

I.

The Labour Representation Committee is a federation of trade unions, trades councils, the Independent Labour Party, and the Fabian Society. Co-operative societies are also eligible for membership.

II.—OBJECT

To secure, by united action, the election to Parliament of candidates promoted, in the first instance, by an affiliated society or societies in the constituency, who undertake to form or join a distinct group in Parliament, with its own Whips and its own policy on Labour questions, to abstain strictly from identifying themselves with or promoting the interests of any section of the Liberal or Conservative parties, and not to oppose any other candidate recognised by this Committee. All such candidates shall pledge themselves to accept this constitution, to abide by the decisions of the group in carrying out the aims of this constitution or resign, and to appear before their constituencies under the title of Labour candidates only.

III.—THE EXECUTIVE

The Executive shall consist of thirteen members, nine representing the trade unions, one the trades councils, one the Fabian Society, and two the Independent Labour Party. The members shall be elected by their respective organisations at the Annual Conference.

IV.—DUTIES OF THE EXECUTIVE

The Executive Committee shall appoint a chairman, vice-chairman, and treasurer ; shall transact the affairs of the Committee, and make proper arrangements for the payment of permanent officers when necessary.

It shall keep in touch with trade unions and other organisations, local and national, which are running Labour candidates, and on the approach of a general election it shall prepare a list of candidates run in accordance with the constitution, shall publish this list, and shall recommend these candidates for the support of the working class electors. The members shall strictly abstain from identifying themselves with or promoting the interests of any section of the Liberal or Conservative parties.

It shall report to affiliated organisations if the chief officials of any affiliated body publicly oppose the approved candidates of the Committee, or if any member of this Executive, Member of Parliament or candidate, who has been endorsed by the Committee, act contrary to the spirit of this constitution.

The revised constitution worked fairly well up to the end of 1908. The pledge was not too strictly applied, the Labour members having been left free to vote, in matters of conscience, as they thought right, but on the whole the party showed a united and unbroken front. From 1909 onwards the constitution has been weakened from the following causes : In the first place, the miners' federation, the largest British alliance of unions, numbering over a half a million, joined the Labour Party and brought with them a strong minority of Liberal Labour men and fourteen Liberal Labour members of Parliament. The infusion of so many Liberal elements into the party acted necessarily as a solvent on the mental cohesion and discipline of the new movement. Secondly, the growing national crisis caused by the Liberal Finance Bills and the conflict between the Commons and the Lords could not fail to induce the Labour Party to support the Liberals and to restrain its criticism of the Government. It was simply impossible for the Labour members to maintain their independence and to attack a Government which was engaged in a battle for democratic and social reform progress

Finally, in addition to those disturbing factors, the action of W. V. Osborne *v.* the Amalgamated Society of Railway Servants threatened the financial resources of the party and for a time all but paralysed its activities.

3.—THE OSBORNE DECISION

The penal laws, actions, and law court decisions against organised working men up to 1906 had for their aim either the destruction of the trade unions or the restraining of their activities and methods. It was the economic combination and procedure of the wage earners which were regarded as illegal. The Trade Disputes Act, 1906, closed the period of trade union disabilities and rendered the collective economic action of the working classes perfectly legal. At the very moment of their decisive victory the trade unions were confronted with a new legal problem. The rise of the Labour Party meant the conversion of the economic organisations of Labour into a vast political confederation. The economic class had grown into a political class—economics as its basis, politics as its superstructure. The Trade Union Acts, 1871, 1875, 1876, and 1906, had undoubtedly economic objects in view, and only these were legalised. The entrance of the unions as such into politics produced a series of new facts, for which no legal regulations existed. The British Labour Party was not at that time an organised collection of individuals having similar political views, but a confederation of trade societies which by virtue of a majority vote were supposed to act politically in concert. The party, according to its constitution, pursued an independent Labour policy with the view of acquiring political power or obtaining a majority in Parliament over the Liberals and Conservatives. The manner in which affiliation took place necessarily left a number of Liberal and Conservative minorities which were, none the less, pledged to make financial contributions towards the upkeep of a party which is opposed both to the Liberals and Conservatives. Hence the opposition of Liberal working men to the compulsory levies and to the use of trade union funds for political purposes. They argued somewhat in the following manner:

It was indeed true that in purely trade union questions they submitted to the decisions of the majority, but they could not be expected to do violence to their conscience and pay contributions for socialist objects or for a policy directed against the Liberals. To these objections the party replied : The object of trade unionism was to promote the interests of the workers ; for nearly half a century the trade unions had been acting on the generally accepted view that these interests were to be promoted not only by economic methods, but also by parliamentary action ; until 1900 they believed that the furtherance of the interests of Labour could, politically, be best attained by acting as auxiliaries of the Liberal Party. Gradually, however, the conviction had been borne in upon them that a separate Labour Party was necessary for this purpose ; the levies which they were now demanding were therefore destined for trade union objects. Were they to permit minorities to take up an independent position directly opposed to that of the party as a whole, then no organisation whatever would be possible and each member of the working class would suffer in consequence. It had been happening often enough that trade unionist minorities went into a strike, though they could not, conscientiously, approve of it. Human arrangements were never perfect ; and so long as anarchism was an impossibility, the least defective mode of organisation was democracy or the submission of the minority to the majority.

The first conflict of this kind arose in 1905, when the plumbers' union in Canning Town asked for the return of their contributions paid for political purposes. The disagreement was settled amicably. Still, the leaders of the Labour Party, foreseeing future difficulties that might arise from the opposition of militant minorities, took the opinion of the two eminent lawyers, Sir Robert Reid (now Lord Loreburn) and Sir Edward Clarke. Both of them gave it as their opinion that the Trade Union Acts were no obstacle to political action. The leaders of the Labour Party then approached the Chief Registrar of Friendly Societies, who gave a decision on this point in favour of the trade union majorities, but urged that appropriate alterations should be made in their rules in order that the trade unionists should be made acquainted with the political purposes of their organisations. The matter was then thought to have been finally settled.

In 1908 the whole question was brought up again by a Liberal railway servant, W. V. Osborne (Walthamstow), and taken to the law courts. In his plea he stated that compulsory levies by trade unions for political purposes were *ultra vires*. In the first instance, Justice Neville dismissed the application. The case was carried to the higher courts, and the Master of the Rolls and finally the Law Lords delivered judgment to the effect that a trade union, as defined by the Trade Union Acts, acted *ultra vires* in raising compulsory levies for political purposes. One of the judges also pointed out that the " pledge " was unconstitutional.

At one stroke the financial resources of the Labour Party, or of the political action of the trade unions, appeared to have been cut off. It was even doubtful whether it was legal for trade unions to finance municipal elections, or to defray the expenses of the Trade Union Congress or of their deputations to the various Secretaries of State. The Liberal and Conservative minorities were not slow in taking advantage of the new legal situation. They applied to the law courts for injunctions against the levying of political contributions, and, as a rule, obtained them. The party suffered financially in 1909 and 1910 —at a time of great national excitement which was caused by the Lloyd George Budget and the constitutional crisis, when two general elections took place within twelve months. It must, however, be remarked that the Osborne judgment raised comparatively little indignation in the ranks of Labour. It came at a moment of political disillusionment among the most active elements of the organised workers, who were fast turning to economic action and even to a modified syndicalism, while the revolutionary socialists thought the Osborne judgment to be favourable to their cause, since it might induce the party to shed Labourism and make the adherence to socialist principles the test of membership. Still, there remained a good many trade unionists and socialists, among them being the Parliamentary Labour Party, who sincerely desired a reversal of the Osborne judgment and the legalisation of the political activities of the trade unions. They brought as much pressure to bear upon the Liberal Government as they could, and they succeeded in exacting from it, first, payment of members of Parliament by the State; secondly, the Trade Union Act, 1913, which represents a fair compromise between the contending parties. A trade union may henceforth use its funds for political objects, provided a majority of members voting on the question so decide. It does not matter how small the number may be who vote; the majority of even a minority of members is sufficient. The Act further safeguards the liberties of the dissenting minorities by giving them the right of exemption from political contributions if they give notice that they object to contribute; they may ask, and the trade union is under the obligation to return to them, *pro rata*, the monies spent for political objects. Above all, the Act practically obviates all possibilities of law court actions in this matter by setting up the Chief Registrar as umpire between the contending majority and minority. The Act was the work of Sir Rufus Isaacs (now Lord Reading), who was at that time Attorney-General.

On the other hand, the party, at the end of September, 1910, decided to abandon the " pledge " in order to remove the objections which had been raised against it on constitutional grounds. A resolution to that effect was carried by the Labour Party conference in 1911.

In pursuance of this Act the trade unions had to take ballots on the question of using trade union funds for political action. Up to the end of May, 1914, sixty-three unions took a ballot of their members as to political objects. In the aggregate they showed 678,063 votes in favour of such objects and 407,356 against. Only three small unions had each a majority of votes against. Many other unions were carrying out the procedure under this Act, but the results were not made public, since the War diverted the attention of Labour from party affairs.

	Votes in favour.	Votes against.
Miners' Federation of Great Britain ..	261,643	194,800
National Union of Railwaymen	102,270	34,953
Amalgamated Society of Locomotive Enginemen and Firemen	7,839	3,841
Railway Clerks' Association	15,496	1,340
Amalgamated Society of Engineers ..	20,586	12,740
Amalgamated Weavers' Association ..	98,158	75,893
National Union of Gasworkers	27,802	4,339
National Union of Dock and Riverside Workers	4,078	501
National Union of Boot Operatives ..	6,085	1,935
Union of Co-operative Employees ..	11,130	11,967
National Union of Clerks	1,844	540
Prudential Assurance Agents	1,304	313

Owing to the outbreak of the War, the matter was not further pursued. Armageddon pushed all such questions into the background, and changed, in its course, also the complexion and constitution of the Party. These changes will be dealt with in the concluding chapters.

XVIII

THE SOCIAL REVOLUTIONARY FERMENT

I.—ECONOMIC AND POLITICAL INFLUENCES

THE future historian, poring on his records and materials and calling upon his constructive imagination to draw a true picture of Great Britain in the period from 1908 to 1920, will gradually behold the unrolling of a series of social revolutionary developments, with the Great War but an episode and the various reform measures as so many concessions wrested by the working class and democracy. For the arrangements of society, constitutional and institutional, appeared to have lost well-nigh all stability. Ferment and unrest spread throughout all ranks. The accepted views on commercial policy and public finance, on the relation between the Commons and the Lords, on the position of woman in political life, on trade unionism and socialism were fiercely assailed and more or less shaken. Even conservative minds, usually averse from popular agitation, were thinking and speaking of revolutionary methods and rebellious acts. Educated and refined women had recourse to terroristic and conspiratory deeds. And masses of workmen, organised and unorganised, used the weapon of the strike on an unprecedented scale. Capital and Labour moved in phalanxes against one another. The whole nation was in movement, as if driven by elemental forces. Taking drama as a mirror of the time it may be said that the nation moved within the short space of ten years (1898–1908) from Pinero's *Gay Lord Quex* to Shaw's *Major Barbara* and Galsworthy's *Strife*. The most salient feature of this amazing chapter of contemporary history was the appeal to economic facts and needs and to new social ethics. Economics, social statistics, prices and cost of living, trade and commercial re-organisation, taxation, and social reform legislation filled the minds of the nation.   Behind all constitutional, legislative, and popular questions stood everywhere the economic factor and the ethical problem.

British industrial life has since 1880 been undergoing profound changes.   Under the pressure of the German and American advance the leaders of British industry, trade, shipping, and commerce have gradually adopted new methods of organisation, which are aiming at the regulation of competition by mutual agreements and combines for the purpose of securing economies in production, distribution, and exchange, as well as of gaining greater control of labour.[1]   Administrative centralisation, scientific management, constant improvement of machinery have cheapened production and gradually enabled British industry to face foreign competition.   The new methods of production and distribution could not fail, however, to press upon the working and lower middle classes.   Since the beginning of the new century British Labour has been raising its voice against the "speeding-up" methods, and the lower middle classes have been living in dread of losing their independence.   Indeed, since 1880 and in a more pronounced degree since 1900 a new factory system has arisen which bears the same relation to the factory system of the beginning of the nineteenth century as intensive cultivation to extensive agriculture, or, better still, as the modern armies to the old ones.   The constantly growing mechanisation of the processes of production and locomotion, as well as the enormous development of land and sea traffic, brought a host of unskilled workmen, unused to the discipline of old trade unionism, into close proximity to skilled labour or gave them an equal status with it.   The traditional gulf between the two categories of labour was gradually bridged.   The skilled workers felt their privileged and protected position seriously threatened, and many of them began to learn the lesson of the solidarity of Labour—namely, that the interests of the wage earners, as a whole, no matter what their special crafts or trades or professions might be, were

[1] *U.S. Industrial Commission Report*, Vol. XVIII., p. 15 *sqq.*, quoted in Carter, *Tendency toward Industrial Combination*, pp. 3–4.

inseparably interwoven with one another.   Sectionalism is dis-appearing, Labour alliances are being formed, hand and brain workers are coalescing.

In commerce and finance a similar process has come into operation.   The wholesale traders are reducing the retail traders to the rôle of distributive agents working on commission.   And the great manufacturers are gaining control both over the wholesale and retail trade.   The great departmental store, the large importers, and the co-operative societies have been dis-placing great numbers of small shopkeepers.   The tendency of modern times appears to be the displacement of the independent lower middle class by a salaried class of clerks, salesmen, officials, and civil servants.   This process of concentration in commerce and finance could not escape the observation of a sociological writer like H. G. Wells.   " Shopkeeping, like manufactures," he declares, " began to concentrate in large establishments, and by wholesale distribution to replace individual buying and selling . . . The once flourishing shopkeeper lives to-day on the mere remnants of the trade that great distributing stores or the branches of great companies have left him.   Tea companies, provision-dealing companies, tobacconist companies, make the position of the old-established private shop unstable and the chances of the new beginner hopeless.   Railway and tramway take the custom more and more effectually past the door of the small draper and outfitter to the well-stocked establishments at the centre of things ; telephone and telegraph assist that shopping at the centre more and more. . . . And this is equally true of the securities of that other section of the middle class, the section which lives upon invested money.   There, too, the big eats the little.   Through the seas and shallows of investment flow great tides and depressions, on which the big fortunes ride to harbour while the little accumulations, capsized and swamped, quiver down to the bottom." [1]

Finally, the two most popular political leaders of the first decade of the new century, Mr. Joseph Chamberlain and Mr. Lloyd George, taught the masses to think in economics.   The

[1] H. G. Wells, *New Worlds for Old*, 1908, ch. viii. § 1.

tariff reform movement, initiated by the former in May, 1903, not only stimulated economic thought but brought the condition of England question before the nation. In working class meetings the tariff reform leaders spoke of the problem of unemployment, of loss of wages, and of the relatively bad condition of Labour. The most fundamental aspects of manufacture and agriculture were discussed and investigated. Indeed, not since the Anti-Corn Law agitation in the 'forties of the last century did the working classes receive so thorough an economic education as during the tariff reform controversy. The reply to the tariff reform movement was a Liberal campaign against landlordism, mining royalties, and the House of Lords. After the general election of 1906, Liberal speakers continued to press social economic questions to the front. Dismayed by the rapid growth of the Labour Party and still believing in the peril of tariff reform, Lloyd George came forward as the chief defender of Liberalism against both the tariff reformers and the socialists. Speaking on October 11, 1906, at Cardiff, he declared :—

" You must remember that up to the present there has been no real effort to counteract the socialist mission amongst the workmen. When that effort is made you may depend it will find it adherents even amongst working men. Common sense bids Liberals and Labour to get along together as far as w can to-day, and not to block the road of progress by standing on it in groups to quarrel about the stage we hope to reach the day after to-morrow. We want the assistance of Labour to give direction to the policy of Liberalism and to give nerve and boldness to its attack. If the able men who now think that they are best serving the cause of progress by trying to shatter Liberalism were to devote their energies and their talents to guide and to strengthen and to embolden Liberalism, they would render higher and more enduring service to progress. But I have one word for Liberals. I can tell them what will make this independent Labour Party movement a great and sweeping force in this country. If at the end of an average term of office it were found that a Liberal Parliament had done nothing to cope seriously with the social condition of the people, to remove the national degradation of slums and widespread poverty and destitution in a land glittering with wealth, that they had shrunk to attack boldly the main causes of this wretchedness, notably the drink and this vicious land system, that they had not arrested the waste of our national resources in armaments, nor provided an honourable sustenance for deserving old age, that they had tamely allowed the House of Lords to extract all the virtue out of their Bills, then would a real cry arise in this land for a new party, and many of us here in this room would join in that cry.   But if a Liberal Government tackle the landlords, and the brewers, and the peers, as they have faced the parsons, and try to deliver the nation from the pernicious control of this confederacy of monopolists, then the independent Labour Party will call in vain upon the working men of Britain to desert Liberalism that is gallantly fighting to rid the land of the wrongs that have oppressed those who labour in it."

The leading ideas of this speech form the keynote of the subsequent work of Lloyd George as Chancellor of the Exchequer. The rise of the Labour Party meant the end of the Liberal Party, and it was the duty of the Liberal leaders to enlarge and strengthen their creed by adopting those socialist reform measures which they thought to be practicable.   The region of Liberalism having become arid was to be made fertile by irrigation from the rivers of socialist thought.   The Finance Bills of the years 1908 to 1914 were the result of these efforts.   The distinction made between earned and unearned incomes ; the transformation of the Budget into an instrument of social reform ; the heated discussions to which the new financial measures gave rise ;   the impassioned and inflaming oratory of Mr. Lloyd George at Limehouse (London, E.) and other working class centres ;   the land reform agitation, with its inevitable references to the fundamental tenets of socialism ;   finally, the constitutional struggle between the Commons and the Lords, which necessarily carried the mind of the nation back to the great conflicts and crises of English history, added a force to the social agitation and unrest.

Another aggravating factor was the continual rise of prices, which began in 1896 and was growing increasingly pronounced since 1907 and which resulted in a considerable reduction of the real wages.   As far back as 1909, the Labour Party Executive, in their Report to the Ninth Annual Conference at Portsmouth drew the attention of the delegates to those facts : three years later, the *Fifteenth Abstract of Labour Statistics of the U.K.* (London, 1912, Cd. 6228) showed that in the years 1900–1911 in the five principal trades (building, mining, engineering, textiles, agriculture) the increase of wages amounted to 0.31 per cent., the wholesale prices of foodstuffs rose by 11.6 per cent., and London retail prices by 9.3 per cent. ; and in 1913 the *Board of Trade Report on Wages* confirmed the painful discrepancy between wages and prices, and thus supplied official material for the revolutionary agitation.[1]   The electoral victories and the usual trade union methods, it appeared, resulted in an economic defeat.   Revolutionary writers and speakers did not fail to point the moral and draw the lesson against parliamentary action and old trade union leadership.   The light of State socialism began to pale before the rise of syndicalism, guild socialism, and direct action.

The Great War accelerated or matured all those tendencies and movements.   The dilution of labour, the employment of masses of unskilled and woman workers in skilled trades, the rapid increase of automatic machinery, and the latitude accorded to the manufacturer to draw tighter the net of scientific management, formed a demonstration *ad hominem* that the privileged position of the upper strata of Labour has vanished.   Women's work penetrated, with surprising success, even into the closely guarded domain of the engineering industry.   " In particular the Bristol exhibition was remarkable for the many hundreds of specimens of work wholly or mainly done by women.   Apart from the still larger range covered by the photographs, fourteen separate groups of samples were shown, dealing respectively with aircraft engines, motor-car engines, magnetos and other accessories of internal combustion engines, locomotives and stationary engines, guns and gun components, small arms, gauges,

[1] *Cf.* S. G. Hobson, *Guild Principles in War and Peace,* London (Bell & Sons), 198, pp. 17–18.

cutters and allied work, drawing dies and punches, welded and other aircraft fittings, aircraft framing and structural parts, projectiles, miscellaneous engineering, and optical and glass work. The list is long, but its very length summarises no more than fairly the variety of applications that are being made of women's services in one work or another. A similar variety was seen in the composition of most of the individual groups." [1]   War finance and commerce favoured the process of economic amalgamation and concentration. Joint stock banks, shipping companies, chemical works, coal, iron, and steel concerns formed alliances or were linked up with one another. The rich grew richer and the position of the middle classes grew more precarious.[2] Liberalism, which Mr. Lloyd George had expected to rid the land of socialism and independent Labour politics, was finally shattered by the war. A part, however, of his Cardiff prophecy came true. He had warned his audience that " if at the end of an average term of office it were found that a Liberal Parliament had done nothing to cope seriously with the social condition of the people, to remove the national degradation of slums . . . to arrest the waste of our national resources in armaments . . . then would a real cry arise for a new party, and many of us would join in that cry." Many Radicals not only joined in that cry, but joined the Independent Labour Party and other socialist organisations ; the idealists among the intellectuals have even taken the lead in the social revolutionary movements. The influence of the War on the rise of prices is too obvious to need any further remark. And the accumulated effect of all those developments has been the accentuation of the economic factor and the cleavage between the classes on the one hand, and the weakening of Parliamentary action and purely political democracy, on the other. Here we touch Bolshevik ground.

[1] *Times Engineering Supplement*, June 29, 1917.
[2] " For every 20s. which the Government spent during the war they borrowed 16s. This system of financing Government expeditions tends to accumulate more and more wealth in the hands of the well-to-do." (Sidney Webb, in *Labour Year Book*, 1919, p. 68.)

2.—EDUCATIONAL INFLUENCES

Meanwhile, the education of the upper strata of the working classes grew apace. Elementary education, continuation schools, debating societies, cheap reprints of some of the best books, socialist propaganda, the classes conducted by the Workers' Educational Association, which was founded in 1903, and to which 1,071 trade unions, trade union branches, and trades councils, and 384 co-operative societies and committees are now affiliated, and Ruskin College at Oxford have produced a young generation of working men responsive to the mental currents of the time. Great Britain possesses now what it never possessed—Labour intellectuals with a healthy desire for the study of economics, social history, and science. In the 230 University Tutorial Classes, organised by the Workers' Educational Association, there are now some 4,000 students engaged in courses of study lasting for not less than three years, and in the shorter classes which it has established, several thousand more. Ruskin College, founded by two Americans in 1899, has been preparing annually from thirty to forty of the ablest engineers, miners, railwaymen, and textile workers for further studies and self-education by imparting to them the elements of political economy, evolution, logic, industrial history, and sociology. Students of Ruskin College were among the first Labour intellectuals who responded to the syndicalist teachings which originated in America (Industrial Workers of the World or I.W.W.) and in France (*Confédération Générale du Travail* or C.G.T.). As far back as May, 1905, when I called at the College to prepare a report on this institution for the Berlin *Vorwärts*, I noticed a certain dissatisfaction among some students with the economic teaching of the College professors. The students desired to be taught economics from Marx's *Capital*, particularly the labour theory of value, instead of the Jevonian theory of marginal utility. After the election of 1906, with the sudden surging up of social economic problems, the dissatisfaction ripened into a conflict. The dissatisfied students formed a separate organisation called the Plebs League and finally seceded in 1909. They established an institution of their own, the Central Labour College (now the Labour College), at first at Oxford, then in London. The spirit and aim of this institution may be gathered from the following guiding principles : " (1) The College to be based upon the recognition of the antagonism of interests between Capital and Labour. (2) The aim to be the imparting of education of a definitely utilitarian character, viz. the training necessary to equip workers to propagate and defend the interests of their class against the dominant ruling class ideas and theories prevalent in capitalist society. (3) The college to be owned and controlled by the representatives of organised Labour, viz. the trade unions, socialist and co-operative societies." The main props of the Labour College are the South Wales Miners' Federation and the National Union of Railwaymen, while the Plebs League, consisting of students, ex-students, and sympathisers, are controlling the curriculum and the spirit of the teaching, so as " to further the interest of independent working class education as a partizan effort to improve the position of Labour at present and ultimately to assist in the abolition of wage slavery." [1]

Revolutionary working class schools were established in Scotland, South Wales, and the Midlands, where the works of Marx, Engels, Dietzgen, Kautsky, Lenin, and Trotsky were studied and discussed. The materialist conception of history and the labour value theory were favourite subjects. The Scottish Labour College had, in 1919, an income of over £1,000. A small section of the British working class were being imbued with a spirit of generalisation. John Maclean, W. Paul, W. W. Craik, Noah Ablett, Walton Newbold acted as their teachers and writers in various parts of the country.[2]

Of the many books published on the eve of the Labour unrest none had so notable an effect as Sir Leo Money's *Riches and*

[1] *Oxford Chronicle*, October 20, 1911 ; Ruskin College, *Manifesto to the Students*, July, 1909 ; Plebs League, *The Democratic Control of Ruskin College*, Leicester, 1909 ; *The Plebs Magazine*, Sheffield (monthly), *Labour Year Book*, 1919, p. 294-5.

[2] *The Call* (London), December 11, 1919.

Poverty. The statistics showing the growth of the national income and its very unequal distribution could not fail to intensify the dissatisfaction which sprang from the general tendencies of the economic and political developments mentioned above. The statistical tables had come very opportunely to throw the dry light of facts and figures on a situation full of ferment and excitement. They were used by socialists and Labour speakers all over the country in a similar manner as Colquhoun's statistical table was used in the time of the incubation and rise of Chartism. [1]

3.—REVOLUTIONARY TRADE UNIONISM : DIRECT ACTION

The syndicalist movement or revolutionary trade unionism is differentiated from State socialism or collectivism by the emphasis it places (a) on the economic factor as the primary formative agent of social arrangements and social ethics, (b) on the economic antagonism between Capital and Labour, (c) on the direct action and struggle of the working class for its emancipation from the wage basis of livelihood and for the control of the means of production by Labour itself, (d) on the trade union and not on the electoral district as the focus of Labour power. Syndicalism, therefore, is averse from conciliation boards and industrial agreements between employers and employees ; it recognises no social peace or even truce as long as the wage basis prevails ; it is opposed to Parliamentary politics being made an integral and important part of the Labour movement ; it scorns social reform by Liberal or Conservative or Labour legislation ; it refuses to believe in the efficacy of a Labour policy acting through Parliamentary representatives and Labour officials. The syndicalist movement is pre-eminently revolutionary ; the socialist movement is largely reformist. The former puts itself deliberately outside the present system of society in order the better to get hold of it and to shake it to its

[1] *Cf. The Highway* (monthly), W.E.A. Year Book; A. Mansbridge, *University Pictorial Classes ; Oxford and Working Class Education,* 1908. R. H. Tawney, " An Experiment in Democratic Education," in the *Political Quarterly,* May, 1914. (Compare *Times,* January 14, 1914, note on the meeting of the Historical Association.)

very foundations ; the latter is working within the present order of society with the view of gradually changing it. The syndicalist knows therefore of no compromise ; class warfare, relentless and continual, is his supreme means. Starting from the premise (a) that economics rules social relations and shapes social ethics, (b) that the economic antagonism between Labour and Capital is irreconcilable, the syndicalist cannot arrive at any other conclusion.

These principles and inferences may be termed the syndicalist form of Marxism.

It must not be supposed, however, that the syndicalists are materialists on principle. There are among them profoundly spiritual thinkers ; but they believe that capitalist society is materialist and that no spiritual uplifting of the people, no social justice and individual salvation are possible unless capitalism, with money and financial success as the measure of all things, has been laid by the heels.

The first body to spread syndicalist views in Great Britain was the Socialist Labour Party in Scotland, whose members originally belonged to the Social Democratic Federation, but gradually came under the influence of the Socialist Labour Party in the United States of America and finally seceded from the S.D.F. in 1903. The leader of the American Socialist Labour Party was Daniel De Leon, a University lecturer and a strict adherent of Marxism, who for a long time worked on the application of Marxist theories to the American Labour movement. Disgusted with the corrupting influences of American politics, which, as he believed, rendered all Parliamentary action of socialist and Labour parties nugatory and corrupted the trade union leaders, he turned to the economic action of trade unionism organised for relentless class warfare and for the socialist objective.[1] Similar

---

[1] In November, 1899, when I went to New York on a lengthy visit to my parents, I was at once introduced to Daniel De Leon, with whom I remained on friendly terms till September, 1900. He was one of the straightest Marxists I had ever come across. Two years later, when I met Ulianov (Lenin) in London and enjoyed his friendship for over a year, I could not help being struck by the great similarity of character and views of both revolutionary leaders. De Leon believed literally in every word Marx had written.

views were, since 1903, springing up amongst socialist trade union leaders of the Marxist type and led in 1905 to the formation of the Industrial Workers of the World (I.W.W.), which declared itself to be guided by the following principles :

" (1) There can be no peace so long as hunger and want are found among millions of working people, and the few who make up the employing class have all the good things of life ; (2) the working class and the employing class have nothing in common ; (3) between these two classes a struggle must go on until all the toilers come together on the political as well as on the industrial field and take and hold that which they produce by their labour through an economic organisation of the working class without affiliation with any political party."

Parliamentary politics were not altogether eliminated, but were made strictly subservient to the economic action of Labour. Later on party politics were dropped and the I.W.W. turned anti-parliamentarian, since parliamentary action involved Labour in compromise with the political parties of the employing class. The leaders of the I.W.W. further argued that the economic organisation of Labour into multitudinous trade unions was obsolete, for the trade union originated in the relatively simple and individualist conditions of manufacture, whereas at the present day manufacture was developing on a vast scale and was based on national and international combines. The modern form of manufacture required not trade unions but industrial unions—Labour organisations as vast and combined as capitalist industry itself. The miners and all the workpeople employed about the mines, be they engineers, firemen, or general labourers, should form one comprehensive mining union ; the transport workers one single transportation union, instead of being split up and scattered in hundreds of local, district and trade societies, with their multifarious offices, officials, and consequent waste of energy and money, leading to inefficiency and failure. Concentra-

He held the materialist conception of history, the class war, and even the iron law of wages to need as little defence as the multiplication table. His capacity for work and his devotion to the cause won him the admiration even of those who were opposed to him on the score of his flint-like orthodoxy and his fanatical intolerance.

tion of the organised forces of Labour had become an urgent necessity, should the working class be able to face the combined forces of Capital.   The extension of the local and district strikes to the general strike is but a corollary of the proposed new form of industrial organisation, or Industrial Unionism.

These views, propagated by the Socialist Labour Party in Scotland, gradually penetrated to the more intelligent or more alert members of the British trade unions and added to the fermentation which was dealt with in the foregoing section.   The first symptoms of the operation of the new spirit manifested themselves in the rebellion of many trade unionists against their officials ; from 1908 onwards it became a difficult matter for the officials of many trade unions to obtain from their members the ratification of agreements and settlements entered into by them with the employers.   The British workman, generally loyal, began to refuse to follow his leader.   It was partly under these influences that the formation of the Plebs League at Ruskin College took place.   The League formed a section of the Industrial Workers of the World.[1]

The ideas of Industrial Unionism streaming from America through Scotland into England were supplemented and strengthened by the current of syndicalism coming from France. After the excitement of the Dreyfus affair and the disappointment with the socialist Minister Millerand, some of the Marxists and anarchists coalesced and turned the French *syndicats* or trade unions into the revolutionary *Confédération Générale du Travail*.[2] French syndicalism has been more theoretical and philosophical than American Industrial Unionism, but in essence both of them represent the same revolt against socialist and Labour parliamentarism and official-ridden and petty trade unionism.

[1] *The Preamble of the I.W.W.*, published by the Socialist Labour Party, Edinburgh ; *Industrial Unionism*, by G. Harvey, Edinburgh ; David Evans, *Labour Strife in the South Wales Coalfields*, Cardiff, 1911; *English Review*, March, 1912 (R. Kenney, " The Brains behind the Labour Revolt ").

[2] An account of the rise of French Syndicalism is given by G. D. H. Cole in his *Self-Government in Industry*, 3rd edition, pp. 303–321, London, 1917.

The French influence was brought to bear on the British Labour movement by Tom Mann, a staunch trade unionist and socialist, with a golden heart and mercurial brain. He is one of the best known figures and most effective speakers in the International Labour movement. In the oratorical tournament which took place at the International Socialist Congress in London, 1896, and in which Jaurès, Millerand, Bebel, and Hyndman participated, Tom Mann's intervention on behalf of the admission of the anarchist delegates made a deep impression. Like most of the British socialist leaders, Mann was stimulated by Henry George's propaganda tour in the United Kingdom in 1882 and 1884, and soon became one of the main forces of British trade unionism, and together with John Burns organised the London strikes in 1887–1889. He joined the S.D.F., afterwards the I.L.P., whose general secretary he was from 1895 to 1898. Disheartened by the slow progress of the social revolution in Great Britain, he left for Australia, where he was active in the Labour movement until 1910, when he returned to his native country, and in order to study the French syndicalist application of Marxist theories to trade union strife, he, in June, 1910, went to Paris. He " was much impressed with the attitude of the revolutionary comrades in France, who had been able to accomplish a magnificent work by permeating the unions and forming the C.G.T." [1] The journey to Paris was, however, by no means the *hegira* of Mann. Unknown to himself, he had imbibed in Australia the spirit of the American I.W.W. His studies among the French workmen were but the finishing touches to his conversion. After his return from Paris he at once set to work to permeate the British trade unions, which, as Mann admits, for some five or six years previously had carried on " an agitation for the closer combination of the unions and for the adoption of different tactics." With the assistance of Guy Bowman, a socialist journalist who knows the French language, he edited, from July, 1910, to June, 1911, a monthly series of syndicalist booklets, entitled the *Industrial Syndicalist*, in which the need and means for better organisation

[1] Tom Mann, *From Single Tax to Syndicalism*, 1913, p. 64.

were outlined.   Some of them are ably and effectively written, and all of them had a good circulation.   On November 26, 1910, a conference of syndicalists took place in Manchester, which was attended by some two hundred delegates representing sixty thousand workers.   As a result of this conference the Industrial Syndicalist Educational League was formed, under whose auspices the monthly paper *Syndicalist* was edited from the beginning of 1912 to the middle of 1914.   Apart from these monthly booklets, the best of which was the *Miners' Next Step*, there appeared from time to time special periodicals like *The Syndicalist Railwayman*, *The Transport Worker*, and fly-sheets to the miners.   The main idea of all those publications and activities was the class struggle as expressed through direct action and the general strike.   Parliamentarism should not be altogether abandoned, but made subservient to economic action, or the " best English Club " should be transformed into the best platform for revolutionary agitation.   Behind the Labour politician should always stand the revolutionary trade unionist and dictate his attitude in the House of Commons, since the politician was apt to forget the class character of the State and to talk of the General Will, where in reality there was but the special interest of the capitalist class.   The utmost such a politician or old trade union leader could look for, was State socialism, which really signified State capitalism, while the revolutionary trade unionist was always conscious of the fact that Government was but the executive of the possessing classes, and that the emancipation of Labour could only be effected by the working class themselves, by their own ceaseless fighting on the economic battlefield. Nationalisation and municipalisation could not release the proletariate from the grip of the capitalists and their Government tools.   Hence, instead of State socialism, the proletariate must work for the control and administration of the means of production by and for Labour.

Meanwhile, other and far abler champions of revolutionary socialism entered the political arena.   The *New Age*, a weekly review, founded in 1907 by members of the Fabian Society, and edited with great literary ability and intellectual freedom by A. R. Orage, was transformed into a centre of educated revolutionary criticism ; its weekly notes on current political and Labour affairs, though often one-sided because written in the midst of battle and with the view of provoking thought and controversy, formed a running commentary on contemporary British history. But a still more ambitious journalistic venture was undertaken by the publication of the *Daily Herald* (April, 1912, suspended on account of the war in September, 1914), which from the beginning of its career formed a platform for all heterodox opinions and rebellious minds. It was a thorn in the side of the Labour Party and a fearless critic of Liberalism. It often mistook the mob for the people and vulgarity for vigour ; but it atoned for these errors of judgment by a profoundly spiritual attitude towards the Labour and socialist problems. The *Daily Herald* contained some of the basest epithets in the English language, but also some of the noblest aspirations of the human mind. During the war *The Herald* appeared as a weekly and was one of the best trade union papers ; its writers on this subject were G. D. H. Cole and W. Mellor. At the beginning of 1919 *The Herald* reappeared in its old form as a daily, under the editorship of George Lansbury.

These movements against the existing social order and against Parliamentarism and political democracy were indirectly strengthened by Hilaire Belloc and Cecil Chesterton, whose literary activities bore the same relation to the British ferment as those of Brunetière, Faguet, Maurras, and Chéradame to the French syndicalist philosophy of Sorel and Lagardelle. The years from 1909 to 1913 witnessed in France a veritable torrent of invective against democracy. Nationalists, chauvinists, and revolutionary syndicalists vied with each other to represent democracy as a sink of corruption and imbecility, as a confederation of freemasons, Jews, Protestants, and aliens, whose main purpose was to ruin France or to sell her to Germany. French democracy was on its trial for life.[1] Hilaire Belloc, with his French literary

[1] Those who desire to learn something of the French anti-democratic literature prior to the war will obtain much information from Georges Guy-Grand, *Le Procès de la Démocratie*, Paris, 1911 (Colin).

training, transferred those Parisian creations to London and found a fervent coadjutor in Cecil Chesterton, who, after having been successively an admirer of Sidney Webb and H. M. Hyndman, embraced Roman Catholicism and joined Belloc in his crusade against British democracy. Their pamphlets, *The Party System* and *The Servile State*, as well as their journalism in *The New Witness*, strengthened the hands of the British syndicalists in their assault on political democracy and added much turbid matter to the social ferment of the years 1911–1913.

4.—THE MASS STRIKE MOVEMENTS

The most striking effect of all those various factors was the Labour unrest, which found expression in the rapid growth of trade unionism and the national strikes. The aggregate membership of the British trade unions, which in 1899 was 1,861,000, and 2,369,000 in 1909, amounted in 1920 to over six millions ! The trade union statistics of the last twenty years may be summed up by saying that the years 1899–1905, when the Taff Vale decision was paralysing trade union activities, were a period of stagnation or decline ; the years 1906–1910, when parliamentary action culminated, formed a period of slight revival ; and the years since 1910, with their increasingly syndicalist character, have been marked by a growth which is, in a comparative sense, extraordinary. Moreover, the tendency has manifestly been towards larger and fewer societies, or towards the combination of smaller societies into larger and better managed trade organisations. Labour has been marshalling its forces and imbuing them with a spirit of solidarity and battle :—

TRADE DISPUTES

Year.	No of workpeople directly involved.	Aggregate duration in working days.
1907	100,728	1,878,679
1908	223,969	10,632,638
1909	170,258	2,560,425
1910	385,085	9,545,531
1911	831,104	7,620,367
1912	1,233,016	38,142,101

In the first three years of the war (1914–1916) the strike movement abated, but in 1917 it revived, the number of workpeople involved amounted to 821,000, and the aggregate number of strike days amounted to 5,514,000. Some of these strikes bore a social revolutionary character, to which we shall refer in a later chapter.

The years 1911–1913 will ever be memorable in the annals of British Labour. The United Kingdom witnessed for the first time a class war in which all its component parts were involved. English, Welsh, and Scottish miners, English railwaymen and Irish transport workers were joining hands across the borders and seas. Robert Smillie, Tom Mann, James Larkin, and James Connolly, all born fighters, marshalled and led the new forces in battle array. Nothing like it had ever happened before : neither in comprehensiveness nor in numbers had that Labour upheaval any parallel in British social history. A comparison of this strike movement with that of the years 1839–42 exhibits in an unmistakable manner the enormous advance British Labour has made in organising and executive capacity.

The upheaval of 1911–1913, though apparently defeated, profoundly affected British social and political history. The Irish transport strike disclosed the misery of the Dublin proletariate, but also their dour determination and revolutionary fervour. The manifestoes of Larkin and Connolly were distinguished by a high spirit of Labour solidarity and socialist self-sacrifice. They laid the foundation of that remarkable coalition between revolutionary Labour and nationalist Sinn-Fein, as well as of the " Citizen Army," both of whom played their part in the Irish Easter tragedy of 1916. Connolly, the author of *Labour in Irish History*, fell in the insurrection.[1]

Another effect, likewise pregnant with social revolutionary portents, was the formation, in April, 1914, of the Triple Industrial Alliance of miners, railwaymen, and transport workers, with an aggregate membership of 1,500,000. Moreover, Robert Smillie, President of the Miners' Federation of Great Britain and the brain of the Alliance, expressed the opinion that, while the scheme at the moment was not intended to include more than the

[1] Concerning Connolly's views on Socialism and Labour, compare S. and B. Webb, *History of Trade Unionism*, 1920, pp. 655-657.

three trades referred to, " it may well be found advisable later on to extend the scope of the Alliance in the general interests of Labour as a whole." [1]   The miners, forming the main strength of the industrial alliance, have been agitating for the nationalisation of the mining industry, and have tried to educate public opinion to the necessity of such a measure.   One of the most striking means used for that purpose was the Coal Commission which, under the menace of a general strike, was held in London in the spring, 1919, under the chairmanship of Justice Sankey. The representation of Labour on this Commission was remarkable, having embodied the coalition of hand and brain workers, viz. Robert Smillie, Herbert Smith, and Frank Hodges (miners), Sir Leo Money, R. H. Tawney, and Sidney Webb.   The evidence and the discussion ranged from wages, profits, and hours of work to the origin of property, land nationalisation, and Marxism.   It was a landmark in social development.   The Sankey Report was a victory for Labour.   The first Report, signed by Mr. Justice Sankey and three business men, declared that " even upon the evidence already given, the present system of ownership and working in the coal industry stands condemned, and some other system must be substituted for it, either nationalisation or a method of unification by national purchase and (or) by joint control." [2]

Nationalisation has become a burning question.   We shall see in one of the next chapters the meaning of it.

5.—RISE OF GUILD SOCIALISM

Notable attempts at interpreting and guiding the Labour ferment were made in the pages of the *New Age* (1907–1914) by Arthur J. Penty, S. G. Hobson, and G. D. H. Cole, resulting in the creation of a socialist Guild movement.   Penty, a thoughtful mediævalist and Christian social writer of outstanding ability, must be regarded as the pioneer of the modern Guild idea, but it was Hobson and Cole [3] who adapted it to current socialist philosophy.   Cole sees in the new Labour movement the inchoate

[1] Robert Smillie, *Labour Year Book*, 1916, p. 103–04.
[2] R. Page Arnot, *Facts from the Coal Commission*, 1919.

expression of the desire of the more intelligent and alert workmen for the control of production. He argues that socialist
and Labour parties and collectivist schools had been regarding
the social problem first and foremost as a problem of distribution of the division of the national income. A more equitable distribution in the interest of Labour being impossible
under the capitalist system of economics, the socialists and
advanced Labour leaders proposed the transfer of the means of
production from the private capitalist to the State. Nationalisation of the monopolies was their policy. They looked forward
to an impartial State, controlling and organising industry,
securing for the worker an adequate share in the wealth he
produces, laying charges on industry for the benefit of the weak
and incapable, and in other respects carrying on production
much as it is carried on now, with a State Department in place of
a limited company or combine and a bureaucrat in place of a
managing director. On the other hand, syndicalism claimed
for the worker not merely higher wages, but also something which
it termed "control of industry." It demanded that men be
regarded not as citizens and consumers only, but primarily as
producers, that their work be recognised as the central fact of
their lives. This tendency manifested itself even in the older
trade unions, for whilst wages were still the dominant question
of disputes with employers, another set of disputes was coming
to the front which concerned conditions of labour, limitation of
hours, employment of non-unionists—questions, in short, which
touch the process of production or what had long been regarded
as the exclusive sphere of the master class. This tendency
towards transforming the trade union from a wage-bargaining
into an organic unit of production should be developed and
brought to maturity. From this point of view the trade unions
represented the germs of the future organisation of industry. The
trade union should do for modern industry what the guild did
for the mediæval arts and crafts. Collectivism would form an
industrial bureaucracy; syndicalism—an industrial democracy.
Pending the consummation of this supreme end and aim, the
workers, if they desired an improvement of their condition,

should co-ordinate their forces, organise on the basis of industrial unionism, and use the weapon of the strike, since political action could achieve little, if anything at all. The Liberal reforms in the years from 1906 onwards, for all the praise bestowed on them by politicians, had done practically nothing to raise the condition of Labour. The strike period from 1911 to 1913 had raised wages, improved the conditions of labour, and increased the respect for the organised working class far beyond any so-called social reform legislation could have done. Where the strike failed it was due to the obsolete form of trade union organisation. The day of the small union had passed. Large industry must be confronted with greater unionism. The small trade union was wasteful. Labour parliamentarism, as at present consti- tuted, was a costly delusion.

While Cole devotes much space to a review of Labour in France, America, and Germany with a view to tracing the new tendencies, the author of *National Guilds* deals exclusively with Labour and economic conditions in Great Britain. Its author and editor have drunk deep from the source of Marxism and have acquired method and system, which give to their work a logical sequence and unity not often to be found in English writings. The book must be regarded as one of the most important docu- ments of the Labour unrest which dominated British home affairs in the years 1908 to 1913 Its critical apparatus is grounded on the syndicalist form of Marxism, and it is followed up with that relentless logical force which characterises the writings of Karl Marx. Its positive contribution contains several British elements—it envisages the nation rather than a class and it presents an outline of the practical applica- tion of syndicalist ideas to British economic life. Its main ideas, negative and positive, contained in *National Guilds* and in the *New Age*, 1912-3, may be summarised as follows :—

For three generations British Labour had been engaged in a struggle for emancipation, but it had never grasped the full meaning of its object. It had not realised that emancipation meant the rescue from oppressed or evil living and the inauguration of a healthy way of life.   The foundation of social life was labour.   Hence it followed that if the conditions that governed labour were evil the whole way of life must needs be evil, and that the real emancipation consisted in replacing those conditions by a new scheme of labour.   The conditions that had been governing labour formed the wage system or wagery, which was one of the species of the genus slavery.   A struggle for emancipation must therefore aim at the abolition of the wage system.   Instead of which the working men frittered away their energies on a struggle for higher wages and for the improvement of the wage system of labour.   Even the socialists, whether as members of the Social Democratic Federation or of the Fabian Society or of Independent Labour Party, had never fought consistently against the wage system.   Some of them even went so far as to deprecate the economic action of Labour and to seek salvation in Parliament— political power should lead to economic power—utterly oblivious of the most salient lesson of history that economics precede politics.   The grand experiment in Parliamentary Labourism had been made in the last ten years.   In the first flush of satis- faction that followed the general election of 1906, and in conse- quence of the marked respect paid to the Labour Party at that time, a great number of workmen seriously believed that emanci- pation was nigh.   In the first two sessions of Parliament the Labour representatives were treated with exceptional deference ; in the third session a change manifested itself—the sentiments of the House were distinctly hardening against the Labour Party, and since 1910 they had been practically ignored.   The Labour movement outside Parliament had become a much more serious factor than inside.   What was the meaning of this transforma- tion ?

In the years from 1900 to 1910, or during the first decade of the history of the Labour Party, in spite of all so-called social reforms and Labour victories on the parliamentary field, profit, interest, rent, cost of living were rising and real wages were falling, and even the rate of the increase of nominal wages fell far short of that of profits.   According to the report of the Board of Trade, 1913, giving particulars of rents, retail prices, and wages in 1905 and

1912, prices advanced 13.7 per cent., wages between 2 and 5.5 per cent., while the capitalists increased their income by 22.5 per cent. per annum. This was a period of Labour triumphs in Parliament, a period of Liberal social reform which was claimed by its authors to be unprecedented in the annals of legislation.

The contrast between political triumphs and real failure, with its immediate consequence in the total eclipse of the Labour Party in Parliament, had not taken the syndicalist or guild socialist unawares, for he knew beforehand that Parliament always responded to economic power and ignored economic weakness. If the working class desired political power it must first acquire economic strength in factory, mine, and field. Those who owned and controlled the sources of wealth commanded also the labour which produced the wealth, and in commanding labour they controlled the foundation of society and its political superstructure. Labour could never acquire any power if it left the wage system untouched. This system of remunerating labour was the most potent factor in the upholding of capitalist domination. Wages were not the equivalent of the produce of labour ; they were not paid to workmen as human beings who contributed their quota to the welfare of society, but for the purpose of being able to subsist while the employer exploited their inherent force of labour, just as he exploited a mine, a field, or a river, regardless of the fact that labour possessed the particular quality of vitalising the materials offered by nature to man, rendering them capable of being assimilated by the social body and thus enhancing their value and multiplying wealth. Labour was being bought for a subsistence wage, while all the wealth produced by it went to the employer, so that one-half of the national income was swallowed up by one-fifth of the population. And it was in wealth, in property, that economic power, and with it all political and social power, resided. How, then, could a Parliamentary Labour Party, which failed to assail the wage system, acquire power ? Manifestedly, it could not.

There was only one way to destroy the wage system, and that was the determination of the workman never to sell their labour for wages. Let the workmen stop spending money on political action and on strikes that aimed merely at mitigating the evils of capitalism; they should spend it on a great effort to organise themselves as completely as possible and to acquire a monopoly of labour. Trade unionism and manual and mental labour should be co-extensive. There would then be on one side the army of workers in complete possession of living, value-creating labour; on the other, the capitalist class possessing the dead machinery of production. Such a situation would lead to a deadlock and to a long and arduous struggle, in which the majority, well organised, skilfully led, and completely united, would finally be victorious. The owners of the dead means of production would yield them up to the State for a compensation consisting of a reasonable annuity for two generations. The State, as trustee for the whole community, would then lease the means of production to appropriate guilds, about fifteen in number, covering the vast majority of manual and brain workers. They would produce, administer, and exchange their products, referring all difficulties and questions to a general committee of the federated guilds, elected by the annual congress of the guilds. The nuclei of such guilds already existed—the trade unions. They needed but to concentrate their energies on (a) the organisation of all who work in industrial unions, as a means and as nuclei of guild socialism; (b) the abolition of the wage system and the vesting of all industrial assets in the State, as the end and aim of unionism.

Before proceeding further with the elaboration of the theories of Guild Socialism, it may be useful to define the nature of a National Guild. This is " a combination of all the labour of every kind, administrative, executive, and productive, in any particular industry. It includes those who work with their brains and those who contribute labour power. Administrators, chemists, skilled and unskilled labour—everybody who can work —all are entitled to membership. Numerically considered, the trade unions must form the bases of these National Guilds; but they, in their turn, must merge into the greater body." [1]

[1] S. G. Hobson, *Guild Principles in War and Peace*, 1908, p. 26-7.

The theory of guild socialism gained much strength from Cole's new book, *Self-Government in Industry* (1917), which presents an advance on his first book, but also savours of Utopia, as may be gathered from its millennial outlook referred to at the end of this chapter. His *World of Labour* appears to have been a sort of reconnaissance anterior to a general assault on State socialism. His *Self-Government in Industry*, in the chapters dealing with the nature of the State, contains quite original, though fragmentary, views, a full development of which may, at the first blush, make the State of the Social Democrat or Fabian appear quite an obsolete affair.

Differing from the Marxists who hold that the State is but the Executive of the ruling class and that with the overthrow of capitalism the State will disappear, and unlike the Anarchists who, in consonance with the philosophy of the law of nature, think the State as such to be the root of evil, Cole defines the State as the political and governmental institution of the citizens as consumers. The community, whose governmental organisation is the State, consists of a certain number of individuals, inhabiting a certain geographical area ; they are, territorially, neighbours to one another, who desire to use and to enjoy all those things that affect them in an equal way as consumers ; the State has to see to it that they should be able to satisfy that desire. In municipal life the view of the citizen as a consumer and the rôle of the local government unit as the communal representative of the inhabitants as consumers, are quite evident. The case, argues Cole, is the same with the national State. Parliament, in so far as it is democratic, represents men as users or enjoyers in common, this time on a national instead of a local basis (pp. 71-8). If, then, the State is a sort of an association of the citizens as consumers only, the proper function of which is to safeguard their interests, it can have neither the qualification nor the powers for dealing with the interests of the citizens as producers or as believers. " The State," declares Cole, " is not equally qualified in those matters which affect men differently according as they are miners or railwaymen, Catholics or Protestants." (p. 79). The question naturally arises : Why should the State be qualified to deal with consumers and not with producers ? The answer to this pertinent question, if I understand the author aright, is, that the citizens as consumers have identical interests ; they all desire to pursue, without disturbance, their business, to use the means of locomotion, to exchange their services and products, to enjoy the opportunities for worship or entertainments, to satisfy their bodily and mental needs ; on the other hand, the citizens as producers or adherents of religious beliefs have by no means identical interests, therefore they cannot have the same organisation or the same machinery for regulating their affairs ; as a matter of fact, the citizens as producers are divided into various and diverse groups and have or may have each their own associations, specially qualified to deal with their respective interests. The State thus appears to be really one of the many organisations of the community ; it may be the most extensive, but on no account the supreme one. And since economic power controls politics,and the State is a political association, it follows that the State may even be regarded as subordinate to the associations of production. At any rate, the State is not the supreme institution of society. If it is not supreme, " the theory of State sovereignty falls to the ground." The nation, as we see, resolves itself into a certain number of autonomous associations, with their own rights and powers, owing allegiance to nobody but their own members. " In all this diversity of human association, the State can claim an important place, but not a solitary grandeur " (pp. 80–3).

Cole's reasonings on the subject are challenging and suggestive. His point of departure is evidently the Liberal and Nonconformist view of the State as the big policeman, as Lassalle might have said. Its main duty is a negative one—to prevent disturbances and disorders. But, while Liberalism, as the philosophy of the capitalist middle classes, acknowledges State sovereignty in order to have a powerful stick to keep the exploited classes down, Cole, as the advocate of Labour, attempts to divest the State of its sovereignty, thus reopening the old and ever new controversy between State and Church, State and manor, State and individual, but no more for the purpose of adjudging supremacy to the one or the other. He is rather striving to put all national associations on a footing of equality or to obtain for the National Guild the same rights and powers of which the State has been deemed the only repository. It is a revolutionary theory, and it is catching, too.

Let us now try to apply this theory to the practical problems with which Great Britain has to deal. Stripped of the phraseology of the various Socialist schools, the problem is: How is the economic life of the nation to be arranged, so as to produce an abundance of wealth, social peace, and freedom for all?

With the social reformer the Guild Socialists will have no parley, since all his measures are rendered nugatory by the economic power of the capitalist class. To the Collectivist or State Socialist, the Guildsman will point out that the function of the State is not production, but consumption. And the Syndicalist, who works for the supremacy of the trade union in all matters, is dismissed by them with the remark that the purely industrial sovereign is no advance on a purely political sovereign. What, then, is the solution?

The nation, which, for the purpose of the revolutionary struggle, has been divided into opposing camps of Capital and Labour, will now, with a view to reconstruction, divide into producers and consumers, having each their proper national association. The State should own the means of production; the Guild should control the work of production. The former is to regulate the prices of commodities and, generally, take charge of the interests of the consumers so as to prevent the producers from exploiting the community or dictate to it what it shall consume. State and Guild will form a partnership of equals, " not the revocable concession of a benignant and superior State, and, to make it real, the Guilds must be in a position to bargain on equal terms with the State. The conditions upon which the producers consent to serve and the community to accept their service, must be determined by negotiation between the Guild and the State. The Guild must preserve the right and the economic resource to withdraw its labour ; the State must rely, to check unjust demands, on its equal voice in the decision of points of difference, and on the organised opinion of the community as a whole " (pp. 109–110, 86–7). In case of conflict between the two associations, "we must look for our ultimate sanction to some body on which all the citizens in their various activities are represented " (p. 87). This division and co-operation of powers implies the establishment of two legislatures— the Guild Congress and Parliament, the former for all matters concerning production, including science and technical education, the latter for all other matters ; there will thus be Guild laws and State laws (pp. 97–8).

The process of production, based on complete self-government of the Guild and thus freed from private and State oppression, will henceforth go on without friction and will yield abundant wealth. Social peace will reign, for, the capitalist class and State bureaucracy being abolished, there can be no antagonism of classes or accumulation of dissatisfaction. And these two facts combined will give the producers freedom at work and at leisure, freedom for self-expression in their handiwork, and instead of the deadening machine drudgery of the wage-slave for the capitalist, there will be the joyful creation of beautiful things by free men for the use of the whole community.[1]

6.—NATIONALISATION AND CONTROL OF INDUSTRY

The first outcome of the social revolutionary ferment has been the demand of organised Labour for the control of industry combined with nationalisation. This demand represents a compromise between social democracy and syndicalism. It is a British product. It began to make itself noticeable during the last war and has been growing in volume and importance. What

---

[1] *Cf.* A. R. Orage, *An Alphabet of Economics* (T. F. Unwin, London); Cole and Mellor, *The Meaning of National Guilds*, Allen & Unwin, London ; A. J. Penty, *Old Worlds for New ; Id. Guilds and the Social Crisis.* National Guilds League Leaflets, *A Catechism of National Guilds ; Id. A Short Statement of the Principles of the N.G.L. ;* Reckitt and Bechhofer, *The Meaning of National Guilds.*

this demand signifies and how far it has modified the older socialist thought, we shall see presently.

Since the revival of socialism in 1880 till about 1909, the main object and the final goal of all socialist propaganda was nationalisation of the land and the other means of production. This demand was put forward in general terms, few socialists having taken the trouble to define the term nationalisation and its practice. While there was, as a matter of course, a general consensus of opinion that the means of production should be owned by the State as the representative of the nation, socialists, with few exceptions, were not clear or differed on the question as to who should organise and conduct the process of production.

The first trace of this demand, not in the form of a Utopia, but as a practical proposition, is to be found in the revolutionary ferment of 1649, when Peter Chamberlen called for the nationalisation of certain landed properties and mines. The meaning of nationalisation was at that time quite clear; it was in conformity with the principle of the Elizabethan poor law. The Commonwealth was asked to manage, through its officials, the nationalised properties and unearned increments in the interest of the labouring poor, and should assume the duties which employers performed.[1] The authority of the State was still unshaken. It was the Leviathan. The next advocate of nationalisation was Charles Hall, who demanded that the State should be the only legitimate owner of the land and should divide it in equal shares among the farming population or the overwhelming majority of the nation. Hall, however, does not appear to have favoured State management; he but desired that the rents should be paid to the State.[2] The same remarks apply to Bronterre O'Brien's nationalisation programme, which was based on the plan of buying out the landlords and settling the land with farmers who would pay their rents to the State, which, resting on manhood suffrage, would form a Democracy.[3]

From 1882 onwards, the term Nationalisation came into

[1] See *supra*, Part I., p. 72–73.   [2] See *supra*, Part II., p. 130.
[3] See *supra*, Part III., p. 20; *cf.* Bronterre O'Brien, *Rise of Human Slavery*, 1885, pp. 118, 128.

I Z

popular use.   In that year, Alfred Russel Wallace published his treatise *Nationalisation of the Land*, and H. M. Hyndman republished Spence's Newcastle lecture and gave it the title *Nationalisation of the Land*, although Spence would have demurred to it, since he desired to see the communes the owners of the land, and not the State.   Wallace distinctly declared that he only desired to see the State as landlord, but not as manager of agriculture.[1]   Hyndman and his organisations, the Democratic Federation and the Social Democratic Federation, were evidently not clear as to the meaning and scope of nationalisation.   In their various programmes, published between 1881 and 1885, nationalisation was used both in the meaning of State ownership and management as well as ownership only.   The S.D.F. programme used also the term " Socialisation," meaning, however, " control by a Democratic State."   Indeed, the Social Democratic knew no difference between nationalisation and socialisation.[2]   The clearest definition of nationalisation was given by the Fabian Society, who declared that " socialism means the organisation and conduct of the necessary industries of the country . . . by the nation as a whole, through the most suitable public authorities, parochial, municipal, provincial, or central." [3] The Independent Labour Party and the Labour Party, in matters of theory, were dependent either on the Fabian Society or the writings of J. Ramsay MacDonald, who, as we have seen, were State socialists.   Control of industry by Labour was not thought of.   The control of the Democratic State and municipality by the voters was believed to constitute an adequate safeguard against oppressive measures on the part of the managing authorities.

The agitation of revolutionary trade unionists and adherents of direct action, as well as the propaganda of the guild socialists and the activities of the Webbs since about 1910, have changed the concept of nationalisation and the tenets of State socialism The demand for the control of industry by the workers them-

---

[1] See *supra*, p. 268.   [2] See *supra*, p. 285.
[3] Fabian Society, *Report to the International Socialist Congress*, London, 1896.

selves, through shop committees and industrial councils, has been rapidly popularised. Nationalisation and State socialism have come to be regarded as another, and by no means better form of capitalism, unless combined with joint control of industry by organised Labour, " both in relation to workshop management and the question of discipline." [1] The last war, which strengthened the revolutionary movements all over the world, contributed a great deal to the rapid popularisation of the demand for the control of industry. The shop steward movement is partly the expression of this demand. The Clyde strike in February, 1915, was the first manifestation of the new spirit. The strike committee turned into a workers' committee, and this model was imitated in other industrial towns ; workers' committees and shop steward committees took the place of the old trade union executives and formed the centres of the extensive strike movements in 1917. The Clyde strikers, the pioneers of the new economic organisation of the proletariate, were largely under the influence of the leaders of the Socialist Labour Party, who, as it has been shown on the preceding pages, are adherents of revolutionary trade unionism or of the primacy of economic action.[2]

The importance of the new demand is shown by the partial and reluctant recognition it found in the Whitley Report upon Works Committees (Cd. 9001) and the Garton Foundation *Memorandum on the Industrial Situation after the War*.[3] The Whitley Report recommended the co-operation of employers and employed in certain workshop matters, and the Garton Memorandum proposed the establishment of joint boards composed of representatives of the employers' associations and the trade

[1] G. D. H. Cole, *Introduction to Trade Unionism*, p. 99.

[2] *Cf.* J. T. Murphy, *A Workers' Committee*, Sheffield, 1918 ; William Paul, *The State*, 1919 ; both authors are prominent writers of the S.L.P.

[3] For a socialist criticism of the Whitley Report see J. T. Murphy, *Compromise or Independence ?* Sheffield, 1918 ; *Labour Year Book*, London, 1919, pp. 253–256. On the Garton *Memorandum* see S. G. Hobson, *Guild Principles in War and Peace*, 1918, pp. 76–126 (Bell & Sons).

unions. But, while the authors of those reports, having had mainly in view the reconstruction of the economic life after the war, may have regarded their proposals as an industrial expediency rather than a new social principle, the Trades' Union Congresses since 1915 onwards have taken up the question of control in the sense of a forward move of Labour towards a higher conception of social justice. At the Bristol T.U. Congress (1915), on the motion of the Post Office Associations, the following resolution was carried unanimously :—" This Congress expresses the opinion that nationalisation of public services is not necessarily advantageous to the employed and the working classes unless accompanied by steadily increasing democratic control, both by the employed and the Parliamentary representatives of Labour." At the Birmingham T.U. Congress (1916), the chairman, Harry Gosling, in his opening speech, inveighed against industrial autocracy and, in demanding for Labour a share in the management of the workshop, declared that industrial democracy was the only means to social peace. The same Congress called upon the Government to nationalise the railways and to grant to the trade unions concerned " such a share in the management of the railway system as will enable the railway workers to have a real voice in the control of the conditions of their life and work." The National Union of Railwaymen demanded, in 1917, that the nationalised railways shall be jointly controlled and managed by the State and the railwaymen's representatives. A similar demand was put forward by the Annual Conference of the Miners Federation in 1918, when the following resolution was carried :— " The time has arrived in the history of the coal mining industry when it is clearly in the national interests to transfer the entire industry from private ownership and control to State ownership, with joint control and administration by the workmen and the State." The Nationalisation of Mines and Minerals Bill, 1919, drafted by the Miners' Federation, was based on the same principle : the State and Labour as joint managers of the mining industry. Thus, the demand for nationalisation and control of industry has been the positive outcome of the turmoil of the last ten years.

XIX

LABOUR IN POLITICS

I.—ACHIEVEMENTS OF PARLIAMENTARY ACTION

THE economic action of Labour is the soil of revolutionary ideas ; it touches the elemental divergences of the classes in modern society ; it is apt to pit power against power ; it vibrates with the very life and its struggles for advance and renovation, and runs full tilt against traditional forms of thought and speech. In leaving its heated atmosphere for Parliamentary action, we soon find ourselves again connected with the chain of continuity and in the midst of peaceable discussions, in familiar terms, concerning improvement of conditions, removal of grievances, and introduction of reform measures. The contrast is striking. And we shall realise it presently.

The reform measures of the Liberals (1906–1913), as expressed in the Trade Disputes Act, 1906, Workmen's Compensation Act, 1907, Old-Age Pension Act, 1908, Miners' Eight Hours Act, 1908, Trade Boards Act, 1909, National Insurance Act, 1911, Coal Mines Act, 1912, Parliament Act, 1912, and Trade Union Act, 1913, naturally weakened the independence of the Parliamentary Labour Party and exposed it to the criticism of the syndicalists and revolutionary socialists. The Party, composed of Labour-Liberals, social reformers, democrats, and socialists, could not help abandoning its opposition to a Liberal Government which year after year put some reform measure on the Statute Book. Although the various Acts mentioned above were sharply assailed by the revolutionary elements of the socialist Labour movement, many trade union leaders regarded them as beneficial to the working class and would have disapproved of any serious opposition on the part of the Labour representatives in

Parliament. And it can hardly be doubted that the reforms enacted in the years from 1907 to 1913 resulted in an improvement of the condition of Labour. There are some statistical data on this point which may be quoted. Sir Hugh Bell, in a speech addressed to the shareholders of Bell Brothers (Limited), on April 9, 1914, gave the following illustrations :—

" Going back twenty years to 1893, the Cleveland miners earned 25s. 3d. per week and lost 10½ per cent. of their time. Ten years later the figures stood, earnings 30s. 1d., time lost 13½ per cent. In 1913, earnings 34s. 9d., time lost 16¼ per cent.

" With regard to the tons per man, the question is complicated by various circumstances. In the first place, the stone being more distant from the face and poorer in quality, and consequently requiring cleaning, involves the employment of a larger number of off-hand men in proportion to the actual number of miners. On the other hand, very considerable improvements in mining implements have taken place within the twenty years. Bearing these facts in mind the following table is very significant and worthy of consideration :—

		Tons worked per actual miners employed.	A fall of Per cent.	Tons worked per man of total number employed.	A fall of Per cent.
1893	..	1,848	—	912	—
1903	..	1,740	5·84	793	13·04
1913	..	1,516	17·96	671	26·42

" You will note that wages have gone up from 25s. 3d. in 1893 to 34s. 9d. in 1913, or say upwards of 35 per cent., while the time lost has increased more than 50 per cent.—viz., from 10½ per cent. to 16¼ per cent. . . . In 1899 we were at the beginning of that process of social reform (as it is called) which has made such remarkable progress in the fifteen years which have elapsed. From that year legislation for the advantage, not of the community generally, but of individuals in your employment, began to take great proportions. As instances of what I mean I may mention the Workmen's Compensation Act and the Insurance Act. In 1899 we paid £1,229 in compensation, and there were no other items to compare with the other five items I am going to mention. In 1913 we paid for workmen's compensation £7,566, and the figure still grows. In respect of workmen's insurance, comparatively a recent piece of legislation, the full extent of which we are only beginning to feel, we paid £3,836.' In the way of mining Acts, the Eight Hours Act was passed in 1908, very much against the better judgment of the miners and mine-owners in the counties of Northumberland and Durham, and in spite of their strong representations to the contrary. It cost us last year £7,949. The Rescue and Aid Act cost us £319. The Coal Mines Act of 1911 cost us £7,583, the Minimum Wage Act £3,130. These figures total £30,383. Add to this £30,383 the increase in local rates amounting to £10,680 and you get upwards of £41,000 added to the cost of production. The figures are even more striking if I reduce them to the ton of pig iron. In 1899 the total of these amounts represented 6d. per ton on our make of pig iron and in 1913 2s. 5d. per ton, a most serious change in the position of matters." [1]

These and similar improvements which have resulted from the long series of Labour and Factory legislation enabled the working classes to build up formidable organisations, to form industrial alliances, and to conceive far-reaching plans for the future. Their whole standard of life, material, moral, and intellectual, has risen. Index numbers of the rise of the cost of living do but touch one side of human life, and not even the most important one, since they are not directly concerned with the movement of moral values.

The charge levelled, in 1908–1913, against the Labour Party of having had a political *entente* with the Liberals was not baseless. Of the thirty-nine members then composing the Parliamentary Labour, the majority had been elected with the assistance of Liberal votes. The weaning of Labour from Liberalism was a long and painful process.

The weakest point of Labour is their journalism. From October, 1912, the Labour Party had an organ of its own, the *Daily Citizen*, published in Manchester and London, and edited by Frank Dilnot. It was mainly a trade union political paper

[1] *Times*, June 23, 1914.

skilfully defending the interests of the workpeople in their disputes with the employers. In politics it stood for democracy, in industrial matters for social reform, but it was not well supported by the labouring masses. It finally stopped publication at the beginning of June, 1915. It left no gap, for it had no distinctive feature of its own.

During the last war, Parliamentary Labour assisted in putting on the Statute Book some of those hardy annuals or long-standing resolutions of the Trade Union Congresses and Labour Party Conferences, notably concerning the creation of a Ministry of Labour, agricultural minimum wages, and democratisation of the suffrage. The Ministry of Labour (December, 1916) is destined to form, earlier or later, the statistical and research centre for all questions touching socialisation ; the importance of this office depends on the capacity and views of its holder. The agricultural minimum wages (July, 1917) have already raised the standard of life of a class of workers who, left to themselves, could do very little to improve their condition and status. The Representation of the People Act (February, 1918) has all but completed the democratic revolution, initiated in 1688, demonstrated for at Peterloo, 1819, and fervently striven for by the Chartists. The century between Peterloo and the last suffrage Act tells an impressive tale of the rise of Labour. The same remark applies to the attitude of the ruling classes towards Labour during the Napoleonic Wars and the last war. A century ago the working classes, treated as helots, were forbidden to volunteer ; in the years 1915–1918 the representatives of Labour were Cabinet Ministers, members of Government, official envoys, and controllers of the nation's food. At the formation of the Coalition Government (May, 1915), Arthur Henderson, the leader of the Labour Party in the House of Commons, was appointed President of the Board of Education, William Brace (miners) Under-Secretary at the Home Office, and G. H. Roberts (compositors) Junior Lord of the Treasury. In December, 1916, at the reorganisation of the Government, with Lloyd George as Prime Minister, Arthur Henderson entered the War Cabinet, John Hodge (steel smelters) became the first

Minister of Labour.   In the summer, 1917, Henderson was sent
to Russia as special envoy, carrying with him the contingent
appointment as British ambassador, but having found in Petro-
grad his Damascus, resigned office, which was then taken by
George N. Barnes (engineers).   Finally, in July, 1918, J. R.
Clynes (gas workers) was appointed Food Controller.   This
triumphant political march of Labour has been mainly the effect
of the industrial development of the nineteenth century.   How
prophetic were the words of that Conservative writer who, in
1826, declared : " The age which now discloses itself to the view
promises to be the age of industry . . . and the age of the
people." [1]   It rendered all those democratic achievements
possible, aye, necessary.

2.—ATTITUDE TOWARDS FOREIGN AFFAIRS AND THE WAR

In all questions of foreign relations and war and peace, the
organised working class has followed the tradition of Mid-
Victorian Radicalism, striving for peace, international good-will,
disarmament and arbitration, denouncing armaments and war-
diplomacy, and demonstrating in favour of oppressed nationalities.   Jean Jaurès used to speak with pride of the action of
British working class leaders in fraternising, during the Fashoda
crisis (1898), with the French trade unionists. [2]   In 1903 the
Labour Party joined the International Socialist Bureau.   A few
years later, when the relations between the German and British
Governments entered a critical stage, British working class
delegations visited Germany and German delegations attended
British Trades Union and Labour Party Congresses.   The Parliamentary Labour Party watched with growing apprehension the
fatal development of the tension between the two nations.   On
the XII. Annual Conference of the Labour Party, held in the
last week of January, 1912, at Birmingham, the subjoined
resolution was carried.

[1] Cf. supra, Part II., p. 283.
[2] For similar remarks compare Renaudel's speech in London,
June, 1918, reproduced in Report of the 18th Annual Conference of
the Labour Party, London, 1918, p. 55.

" That this Conference, believing the anti-German policy pursued in the name of the British Government by Sir Edward Grey to be a cause of increasing armaments, international ill-will, and the betrayal of oppressed nationalities, protests in the strongest terms against it. The Conference is of opinion that this diplomacy has led the present Government to risk a war with Germany in the interest of French financiers over Morocco, to condone the Italian outrage in Tripoli, the Russian theft in Mongolia, and in joining hands with Russia in making an assault on the independence of Persia." [1]

These were the views which animated the Party up to the first week of August, 1914. Ramsay MacDonald, the chairman of the Parliamentary Party, replying to Sir Edward Grey's memorable statements of August 3, 1914, on the general European situation, strongly urged that everything should be done to preserve British neutrality. On August 7 the Executive Committee of the Labour Party issued the following letter to its constituent bodies :—

" We beg to inform you that a special meeting of the National Executive of the Labour Party was held on August 5 and 6, to consider the European crisis, when it was decided to forward to each of the affiliated organisations the following resolutions :—

" That the conflict between the nations of Europe in which this country is involved is owing to Foreign Ministers pursuing diplomatic policies for the purpose of maintaining a balance of power ; that our national policy of understanding with France and Russia only was bound to increase the power of Russia, both in Europe and Asia, and to endanger good relations with Germany. Further, that Sir Edward Grey, as proved by the facts which he gave to the House of Commons, committed, without the knowledge of our people, the honour of the country to support France in the event of any war in which she was seriously involved, and gave definite assurances of support, before the House of Commons had any chance of considering the matter.

" That the Labour movement reiterates the fact that it has

[1] *Report of the XIIth Annual Conference of the Labour Party*, London, 1912, p. 98.

opposed the policy which has produced the war, and that its duty is now to secure peace at the earliest possible moment on such conditions as will provide the best opportunities for the re-establishment of amicable feelings between the workers of Europe.

" That without in any way receding from the position that the Labour movement has taken in opposition to our engaging in a European war, the Executive of the Party advises that . . . . all Labour and socialist organisations should concentrate their energies meantime upon the task of carrying the resolutions . . . detailing measures to be taken to mitigate the destitution which will inevitably overtake our working people while the state of war lasts."

On August 7 the Party decided to make no pronouncement on the vote of credit, whereupon Ramsay MacDonald resigned the chairmanship, and Arthur Henderson took his place. It may be said that from that day onwards the Party rallied to the support of the cause of the Allies with practical unanimity, the few dissentients making hardly any impression on the political life of Labour. On August 24, 1914, an industrial truce was de-clared by a resolution passed in a meeting of representatives of the trades unions and the Labour Party, which recommended " that an immediate effort be made to terminate all existing trade disputes, and whenever new points of difficulty arise during the war period a serious attempt should be made by all con-cerned to reach an amicable settlement before resorting to a strike or lock-out." The truce was fairly kept till 1917, when both an extensive strike and peace movement made themselves noticeable in the ranks of Labour owing largely to the news of the Russian Revolution. That, none the less, the ranks were not broken was mostly due to the social reform activities of the War Emergency National Workers Committee appointed by a Special Conference of the various Labour organisations which took place, on the invitation of the Labour Party Secretary, on August 5th, 1914. The Committee pursued both critical and constructive aims. It formulated and pressed upon Government and municipal authorities carefully worked out measures for the protection of the labouring population against food speculators, rent-racking, evictions, unemployment, underfeeding of school children, in short, against the vicissitudes and hardships which the war might bring in its train and unduly aggravate the conditions of the have-nots. The Committee met, at first, several times weekly, then weekly and fortnightly, and dealt, besides, with military allowances and pensions, import of wheat, distribution of shipping, war finance, and labour problems after the war. The Committee included all sections of the movement, moderate reformers and left wingers, adherents of war policy as well as pacifists. Discussions on military policy and purely trade union questions were, however, ruled out of consideration. Arthur Henderson was its first chairman, and after his joining the Coalition Government he was succeeded by Robert Smillie. J. S. Middleton, Assistant Secretary of the Labour Party, acted throughout as secretary. But the constructive brain of the Committee was Sidney Webb, who for the first time came into actual contact with the inner workings of the Labour movement ; owing to his proposals the Committee was constantly ahead of Government policy on all social measures affecting the daily life of the civilian population. Throughout the period of the war the Committee served as a direct channel of communication with the various local bodies of the country, and, therefore, as the centripetal force which kept the working class from splitting up into opposing sections, despite the growing differences of opinion as to war policy, Munition Acts, Peace, etc. The consequence was that by 1918 the Labour Party, unlike most socialist and working class Parties in Europe and America, remained united and was in the right frame of mind to respond to the necessity of its being reorganised into a Socialist Labour Party, setting up of individual members' section, developing the women's side of the Party. and taking the lead in the Socialist and Labour International

XX

REORGANISATIONS OF THE SOCIALIST PARTIES

I.—THE BRITISH SOCIALIST PARTY

THE unrest which overtook Labour since 1908, caught also the various socialist bodies. The Social Democratic Federation (S.D.F.) was seething with discontent some years before. In 1903 several Scottish branches seceded, in 1905 some London branches followed suit and formed separate organisations. The leaders of the S.D.F., trying to exorcise the spirit of unrest, changed in 1908 the name of their organisation to Social Democratic Party (S.D.P.). Even in the ranks of the I.L.P. much dissatisfaction was manifested with the alleged complicity of the I.L.P. leaders with the spiritless attitude of the Parliamentary Labour Party towards the Government. Several branches of the I.L.P. seceded and entered into communication with the S.D.P. and other dissatisfied socialists, notably of the *Clarion* group, and in their confabulations conceived the idea of forming a new socialist party. In 1909 a committee for socialist representation was formed in Manchester, who gradually succeeded in convening a large conference with a view to forming a united socialist party. This conference took place on September 30 and October 1, 1911, in Manchester, and the British Socialist Party (B.S.P.) was called into being. In the last week of May, 1912, the B.S.P. held its first annual conference in Manchester and adopted a programme which was partly social democratic and partly revolutionary trade unionist. The old traditions and the old leaders proved too strong for the new spirit to assert itself. The B.S.P. was substantially the old S.D.F., or the old S.D.P.

When the war came, the B.S.P., like most socialist parties of the belligerent countries, hauled down the red flag. Its policy consisted, at first, of vague affirmations of internationalism, rather more definite denunciations of Prussian militarism, and a quite decided insistence on an immediate policy to ensure the proper supply of food and the alleviation of distress caused by the war. Gradually, however, opinions in the Party consolidated into two main groups. One, led by H. M. Hyndman, Dan Irving, H. W. Lee, and the older members, took up a definitely patriotic attitude, affirmed the necessity for national defence and the "will to victory," while still maintaining a critical attitude towards the Government in all its dealings. The other section, whose opinions were voiced by E. C. Fairchild, John Maclean, A. A. Watts, and the Secretary, Albert Inkpen, declared for an international agreement between the workers of all lands to end the war at the earliest possible moment. It declared its belief that the war was the inevitable outcome of modern capitalist development in the mad race for markets, and that all the Powers were equally responsible for its outbreak. In the early part of 1915 a number of divisional conferences were held at which each of the two sections struggled to obtain mastery, but without definite result. But at a National Party Congress, held at Salford at Easter, 1916 (the first since the war), the crisis came to a head. The feeling among the delegates was so obviously and overwhelmingly against the "will to victory" section that, on a minor matter of procedure, about 20 delegates representing that section, including H. M. Hyndman, withdrew from the Conference, and eventually from the Party. It should be said that the Executive of the Party had been acutely divided on main principles right away through 1915, the internationalists being in a majority of one. It had been decided, for instance, much against the wishes of the Hyndman section, to send a delegate to the first Zimmerwald Conference.[1] The proposal fell

[1] The first International Conference of Revolutionary Socialists during the war took place in the first week of September, 1915, at Zimmerwald (Switzerland). Delegates were present from Germany, France, Italy, Russia, Poland, Rumania, Bulgaria, Sweden, Norway, Holland, and Switzerland. The most prominent among them were

through, however, owing to the refusal of passports by the Government, but a referendum of the branches subsequently endorsed a resolution expressing the adherence of the B.S.P. to the Zimmerwald platform.

From the Salford Conference onwards, the B.S.P. was definitely ranged with the left wing of what remained of the Socialist International. The secession of Hyndman, Thorne, Bax, and others did not materially affect its strength. They were the better known names, it is true, but not the really virile elements of the Party. Lesser known men stepped into their places. Tom Quelch (son of Harry Quelch) wielded a trenchant pen in the columns of *The Call*, which had been started as the official organ of the Party, after the defection of the privately-owned *Justice* to the ranks of the secessionists.

On the outbreak of the second Russian revolution (November, 1917), which brought Lenin and Trotsky into power, the B.S.P. definitely ranged itself on the side of the revolutionary working class and peasantry in Russia, organised under the banner of the Bolsheviks. From that attitude it never swerved. At its Easter Conference in 1918 a message of appreciation was read from M. Litvinoff, at that time acting as Bolshevik plenipotentiary in Britain, and the whole Conference was solidly behind the new régime. Later in the year, John Maclean, an Executive member, who had already served a sentence of eighteen months' imprisonment for anti-war propaganda, was sentenced to three years' penal servitude, largely because of his enthusiastic advocacy of the Bolshevik cause. The 1919 conference at Sheffield still further emphasised the pro-Bolshevik attitude of the B.S.P. It declared that " the world war is bound to give birth to a world revolution, in which the hitherto exploited and oppressed classes in all countries would seize the reins of power, overthrow the rule of the capitalist and landlord classes, establish the direct

Lenin, Ledebour, Bourderon, Merrheim, Modigliani, Lazzari Racovski, and Höglund. They declared themselves for an immediate peace without annexations and indemnities, for the self-determination of the nationalities, against the industrial truce, and for the revolutionary class war.

rule of the workers and peasants by means of Soviets, and wind up the capitalist order of society." A referendum of the Party was taken on the question of adhesion to the Third (Communist) International, established at Moscow. By an overwhelming majority (only four branches dissenting) it was decided to secede from the Second and join up with the Third International. The B.S.P. is definitely in favour of Sovietism as a form of government to supersede capitalist parliamentary democracy. But it adheres to the parliamentary weapon in its prosecution of the class struggle. It is prepared, indeed, to use any weapon available as occasion demands or exigencies determine. It does not expect the social revolution through Parliament, but regards it as a point of vantage from which to attack the capitalist system.

Just before the outbreak of the war, the B.S.P., which for over twelve years, under various names, had remained outside the Labour Party, decided to reaffiliate to that body. This affiliation took actual effect at the Annual Conference of the Labour Party in Manchester in 1917, and since that time the B.S.P., with the assistance of many local trades councils and labour parties, has constituted the revolutionary left wing of the Labour Party. At the General Election of November, 1918, the B.S.P. had some twenty-five parliamentary candidates running under Labour Party auspices. None were successful, but all polled as well as, and some of them considerably better than, the average Labour Party candidate.

It is, however, doubtful whether the B.S.P. has definitely shed those fissiparous tendencies which marked the career of its predecessors, the S.D.F. and the S.D.P., for it can hardly be assumed that the whole Party is in favour of the Soviet system.

2.—THE NATIONAL SOCIALIST PARTY

Upon the secession from the B.S.P., Hyndman, William Thorne, Dan Irving, Hunter Watts, H. W. Lee, J. Jones, John Stokes, and Joseph Burgess (formerly I.L.P.), formed the National Socialist Party. Their organ is the old weekly *Justice*. Hyndman, who, as Parliamentary candidate, had for so many

years nursed Burnley, had the satisfaction to see his friend and
disciple, Dan Irving, elected as member for that constituency
at the general election in December, 1918. Also " Colonel "
William Thorne and J. Jones were successful, so that the young
and small Party was represented in the House of Commons by
three members. The Party is affiliated to the Labour Party.

3.—THE INDEPENDENT LABOUR PARTY

In the years of unrest, the I.L.P. went through a severe crisis.
In 1913 the Party appeared to have weathered the storm. Its
" Coming of Age " conference at Bradford, April, 1914, was
attended by fraternal delegates from abroad as well as by delegates of the Labour Party, the Parliamentary Committee of the
Trade Union Congress, the Co-operative Societies, the Fabian
Society, and the British Socialist Party, as a recognition of the
work of the I.L.P. At that time, seven of its nominees, J. R.
Clynes, Keir Hardie, F. W. Jowett, Ramsay MacDonald, James
Parker, Tom Richardson, and Philip Snowden sat in Parliament
as part of the thirty-nine members constituting the Parliamentary Labour Party. It was a well-merited tribute to the
achievements and inspiration of the I.L.P.

During the first years of the last war, the Party, owing to its
pacifist attitude, suffered an eclipse, the effects of which manifested themselves in the general election in December, 1918,
when even its most prominent members, Philip Snowden, J.
Ramsay MacDonald, and F. W. Jowett, lost their seats. As a
compensation for the losses, the Party gained four new Parliamentary representatives, Ben G. Spoor (Bishop Auckland), Neil
Maclean (Govan), W. Graham (Edinburgh), and Tom Myers
(Spen Valley). Since 1918 the membership increased to a very
considerable extent, the Party having become the refuge of all
those men and women of influence, reputation, and learning,
who had lost faith in the Liberal Party and who would like
to see humanity and righteousness the foundation stones of
government.

In 1910, under the auspices of the Party, a printing and
publishing agency, the National Labour Press, Ltd., was estab-

2 A

lished in Manchester, which has proved a growing and profitable concern. The Labour Press publishes the *Labour Leader*, the official weekly organ of the party. It is also responsible for the publication of the *Socialist Review* (quarterly), edited by J. R. MacDonald. In 1905 the party inaugurated the publication of a socialist library, which includes the following volumes : Ferri, *Socialism and Positive Science* ; MacDonald, *Socialism and Society* ; Jaures, *Studies in Socialism* ; Oliver, *White Capital and Coloured Labour* ; Bernstein, *Evolutionary Socialism* ; MacMillan, *The Child and the State* ; K. Kautsky, *Dictatorship of the Proletariat* ; Bruce Glasier, *Meaning of Socialism*. Various party writers, notably Sir Leo Money and E. D. Morel, have been publishing, from time to time, instructive pamphlets on the questions of the day.

The questions of the dictatorship of the proletariat and the Soviet form of government, which have been agitating some portions of British Labour and socialism, occupied the attention of the I.L.P. at the end of 1919, and it dealt with them in a *Memorandum*, explaining its attitude towards them. The party had to record a decline of the authority of Parliament in Great Britain, owing—

" (a) To the fact that the Conservative reactionaries supported the threatened rebellion in Ulster against Parliament in 1913–14 ;

" (b) To the deterioration of politics in Great Britain under the influence of Mr. Lloyd George, as was seen at the election in December, 1918 ;

" (c) To the predominance of the Executive, especially since the war, and the corresponding refusal of the House of Commons to discuss important questions concerning the welfare of the country ;

" (d) From the point of view of democracy, the most serious result is that the House of Commons is now felt to respond too slowly to the real needs and wishes of the nation, and some of the more hasty spirits amongst the working class, which in its workshops and at its firesides continues to experience its economic and other grievances, are disposed to turn to " direct action and other forms of extra-Parliamentary pressure for protection."

The real cause of the decline of Parliamentary government or democracy was to be looked for not in any inherent weakness of Parliamentarism, but in the insufficient education of the people and the imperfect state of socialist propaganda. The efforts of the socialist must therefore be directed towards removing that cause. Given persistent and systematic education and propaganda, democracy would work well, even in the transition time from capitalism to socialism. A revolutionary dictatorship of the proletariat, therefore, need not be necessary, " but whether it has to be resorted to or not depends solely upon the policy of the capitalists themselves and not upon the political necessities of Socialism. Socialists ought not to allow capitalist interests and designs to divert Socialist propaganda and methods. That in most politically democratic countries will only strengthen the hands of the reaction, and in countries well equipped with modern military weapons will only lead to massacre not to revolution."

The party rejected, likewise, the Soviet system, for the conditions under which it had been established in Russia were abnormal and the system itself had not reached yet any finality. Therefore, the party saw no reason for departing from its old position that until socialist propaganda influenced public opinion and until socialists were chosen as representatives on public bodies, no secure foundation for the socialist State could be laid.

As to " direct action," the party was of opinion that neither economic action nor parliamentary action alone could do the work which socialism demanded ; both were necessary, and each must be given its proper place in a full attack all along the line by democracy upon capitalism. The party was of opinion " that direct action for political purposes is essentially different in its nature from direct action for industrial purposes, and that the risks of failure of the former are so great that its political practicability is slight. The threats and fears of direct action, taken along with a general state of working class unsettlement such as exists to-day, do, however, contribute materially to the influences which curb the policy of reactionary governments. The party, therefore, rejects direct action as a substitute for Parlia-

mentary action, but considers it as one of the several weapons
which the reaction may compel the working classes to use. Thus
used it may be regarded as a means of restoring representative
government and not of destroying it."

4.—THE SOCIALIST LABOUR PARTY

The Scottish members of the S.D.F., who seceded in 1903,
formed, after the model of the American Socialist Party, an
organisation of their own which was practically but a branch of
the American Party. For the first eight years its activities were
mainly propagandist and limited to spreading the class war
doctrines of Marx, according to the interpretation of Daniel De
Leon. They denounced, in the style of their master, all other
working class organisations, both socialist and trade union, as
" non-militant " and " non-class-conscious," and their leaders as
" fakirs " ; they refused to be mixed up with those bulwarks of
capitalism ; they indicted industrialism from the point of view
of the Labour theory of value. It was an abstract agitation
which had little relation to the actual conditions in Great Britain.
After 1911 its members, caught by the general unrest and
militant tactics of Labour, began to be active in strikes and thus
to grapple with realities ; they mixed with the trade unions and
deviated from the rigidity of their earlier views. During the
first year of the war, several of their members, knowing the
theory of direct action, became shop stewards in the engineering
industry, and to them must largely be credited the Clyde strike
in February, 1915, the strike in March, 1916, when several shop
stewards were deported from the Clyde, finally, the great engineering turn-out in May, 1917.

The S.L.P., well versed in Marx's materialist conception of
history, had no difficulty in recognising the economic motives
of the last war and regarding it as the extreme expression of the
industrial and maritime competition between Great Britain and
Germany. Their members were all anti-war. At the general
election in December, 1918, three candidates were put forward—
Arthur MacManus, J. T. Murphy, and William Paul—and each
polled several thousand votes.

The S.L.P. theories came nearest to those of Lenin and Trotsky. The triumphs of the Bolshevik revolution gave, naturally, much encouragement to the S.L.P. Its organ is the *Socialist*, and its views dominate more or less such papers as the *Worker, Solidarity,* and the East London *Workers' Dreadnought,* while the Central Labour College shows much affinity with the S.L.P., and there is hardly any difference between the latter and the B.S.P.

5.—VARIOUS ORGANISATIONS

The London secessionists from the S.D.F. in 1905, with Fitzgerald at the head, formed the Socialist Party of Great Britain. It was very active in spreading Marxist theories and it opposed all other political parties, no matter whether they were calling themselves socialist or Labour. It emphasised the importance of proletarian political action on strictly social revolutionary lines. Its organ is the *Socialist Standard*.

The Socialist Sunday School movement, for which A. P. Hazell, one of the oldest members of the S.D.F. and one of the best students of Marxist economics in England, had done much, contributed a good deal towards the propaganda of socialism. The *Young Socialist*, founded by Archibald Russell at Glasgow, was the special organ of the Socialist Sunday schools.

The youngest socialist organisation is the National Guilds League. It was founded in 1915, with William Mellor as secretary. It is mainly a propagandist body and looks less for numbers than for effective writers and speakers in sympathy with guild socialism. Among its several members may be mentioned Bertrand Russell, R. H. Tawney, Clifford Allen, George Lansbury, W. N. Ewer, Mrs. Townshend, H. J. Gillespie. The League has published a number of ably written pamphlets on the guild idea, based on Marxist economics, the best among them being *A Catechism of National Guilds*.

On the whole, the educational activities of the socialist, industrial unionists, and guildsmen immediately before the war and in 1918 and 1919, were on an unprecedented scale. Moreover, they were able to reach the organised working classes. The formation of the Labour Party in 1900 by trade unionists and socialists rendered it possible for intellectuals to come in touch with the mass of trade unionists. Something like an alliance between Labour and social knowledge was established. These activities and developments, combined with the effects of the war, the Russian revolution, and the Representation of the People Act, led to a recasting of the Labour Party constitution and to a revision of its aims and objects.

XXI

REORGANISATION OF THE LABOUR PARTY

I.—CAUSES OF THE REORGANISATION

THE Labour Party consisted, up to the beginning of 1918, of bodies of the best organised wage-workers, with a slight admixture of middle class socialists. At party gatherings and conferences, the socialists as such played no part whatever ; in the deliberations and councils of Labour their voices were scarcely heard. Indeed, the Labour Party conferences were little else than second and by no means improved editions of the trades union congresses. Cotton and coal controlled both. The constitution of the party was limited to the formation of a separate Parliamentary representation, .with no other programme than the hardy annuals transmitted from one annual conference to the other. The Labour Party was an extended Parliamentary Committee of the Trades Union Congress.

The social revolutionary ferment, with its symptomatic unrest and strike fever, and the fiery cataclysm which shook Europe for the last years and laid bare the foundations of modern civilisation, rendered a reconstruction of society necessary and prompted the leading minds of the working classes to make the Labour Party the political instrument of that reconstruction. For, as Marx taught, the time must needs arrive when the class struggle turns into a political struggle—political, not only in the narrow meaning of Parliamentarism, but in its true, Greek meaning of social—of all matters concerning the constitution of society. That this work of reconstruction could only proceed on socialist lines, few contested, since the whole evolution of economic life tended in that direction. Individualism was dead, and its organ, the Liberal Party, was decaying, while the other parties

395

had no other remedies but digging up the skeletons of past policies and clinging to shattered idols. Moreover, the last war turned the State into the largest producing and distributive agency of the nation ; the Government controlled, directly or indirectly, production and distribution. It revealed, further, the enormous wealth of modern society and showed that poverty was altogether an unnecessary and preventible evil. " The real cause of the manifest unrest among the workers in connection with social matters," declared a moderate Labour leader in 1918, " was the recognition by the working classes of the causes of their misery and degradation. While they used to be content when told that any reform costing a few millions a year would mean bankruptcy to the State, the most ignorant people now understood that if the State could spend eight millions a day on the destruction of humanity, they could at least find some millions for the reconstruction of humanity." [1]

For the reconstruction on socialist lines, the Labour Party stood in need of social economic knowledge. And there were men and women with that knowledge, middle class intellectuals, who had cut themselves adrift from their class and sought admission to the Labour Party, but whose strait gate did not allow them to enter freely, since the old constitution of the Labour Party has been made mainly for manual workers. Things shaped themselves as Marx foresaw when he declared that " in times when the class struggle is nearing the decisive hour . . . a portion of the middle class ideologists, those who have raised themselves to the level of comprehending theoretically the historical movement as a whole, joins the revolutionary class, the class that holds the future in its hands." [2] To allow them to join the Labour Party and supply the necessary knowledge to the proper instrument of reconstruction, a reorganisation or a new constitution of the Labour Party was necessary. The need was all the more imperative as the democratisation of the

[1] Labour Party, *Report of the 18th Annual Conference*, London, June, 1918, p. 43 (speech by J. H. Thomas, M.P.).
[2] Marx and Engels, *Communist Manifesto*, English edition, 1888, p. 14.

suffrage extended the basis of party life to the limits of the nation. The whole British nation became sovereign. The political programme of Chartism was now the law of the land, and it was henceforth the mission of the grandsons of the Chartists to take in hand the " ulterior motives " [1] of their grandfathers.

2.—THE ESSENTIALS OF THE NEW CONSTITUTION

In August of the memorable year 1917, the Labour Party appointed a sub-committee to prepare a scheme of reorganisation. The work was soon taken in hand, the constitution drafted and submitted to the Labour Party Special Conference on February 26, 1918, which adopted it. The gates of the party were thrown open to the intellectual proletariat, and the British working classes given a socialist programme. Sidney Webb, in his commentary on the aims and objects of the reorganised Party, heads the last chapter with the apophthegm " More light—but also more warmth ! " [2] While, in 1896, he told the London International Socialist and Labour Congress that " socialism needed light rather than heat," [3] he now declared that it needed warmth as much as light.

The most important changes of the constitution concerned the ultimate aim of the party and the enrolment of members, as may be seen from the following :—

" 3. (d) To secure for the producers by hand or by brain the full fruits of their industry, and the most equitable distribution thereof that may be possible, upon the basis of common ownership of the means of production and the best obtainable system of popular administration and control of each industry or service.

" (e) Generally to promote the political, social, and economic emancipation of the people, and more particularly of those who depend directly upon their own exertions by hand or by brain for the means of life."

The other important change concerned membership. While

[1] *Cf. supra*, Part III., p. 45.
[2] Labour Party (Sidney Webb), *Labour and the New Social Order*, London, 1918, p. 23.
[3] *Cf. supra*, Part IV., p. 285.

up to the beginning of 1918 the Labour Party was a confederation of trade unions and socialist bodies, which were affiliated
each by a majority vote of its members, the new constitution
provided also for the enrolment of individual members, and it
afforded special facilities to women electors to join the party.
The party has thus been organised on the double basis of national
Labour or socialist bodies and constituency organisations, the
latter enrolling individually men and women who subscribe to
the party constitution and programme.

The Party, by embodying into its constitution the declaration
of common ownership of the means of production, has become a
socialist Labour party.

3.—THE CONSTRUCTIVE PROGRAMME

The constructive work was outlined, on behalf of the Party,
by Sidney Webb in his *Labour and the New Social Order*. He
looked upon the last war as the final collapse of an industrial
civilisation, which the workers would not seek to resuscitate.
The war had destroyed the very basis of the individualist system
of capitalist production. It proved economically far from
efficient and morally indefensible. The new social edifice would
be erected on four pillars : (*a*) the universal enforcement of the
national minimum ; (*b*) the democratic control of industry ;
(*c*) the revolution of national finance ; and (*d*) the surplus wealth
for the common good. The first principle of the Labour Party
was the securing to every member of the community, in good
times and bad alike, of all the requisites of healthy life and
worthy citizenship. It would do this by enforcing the universal
application of the policy of a prescribed minimum of health,
leisure, education, and subsistence by the extension of such
legislation as the Factory Acts, Public Health Acts, Housing
Acts, Education Acts, Trade Boards Act, and by various measures
against unemployment.

The principle of control of industry demanded the progressive
elimination of the private capitalist from the control of industry
and the scientific reorganisation of the nation's work on the basis
of common ownership of the means of production and equitable

distribution of the produce. The railways, mines, and electrical power should be immediately nationalised. In order to remove the evils of centralisation and the drawbacks of bureaucracy, the party would work for the fullest possible extension of the scope of democratically elected local governing bodies. Special care should be devoted to the democratisation of education and to the development of agriculture.

With regard to national finance, the party would raise the greater part of the revenue by direct taxation of the incomes above the necessary cost of family maintenance ; a very substantial part of the National Debt should be paid off by a special levy on capital.

The absorption of the wealth of the community by individual proprietors must be stopped ; the arising surplus wealth should be secured on the one hand by nationalisation and municipalisation and on the other hand by the steeply graduated taxation of private incomes and riches. The surplus wealth should be used for the perpetual improvement of the means of production and transport, for scientific research, and for the maintenance of the aged, sick, and infirm.

The party, in its Imperial policy, would repudiate all forcible domination of other races and countries ; it would develop a system of Home Rule and democratic self-government within the Empire. Its foreign policy would rest on a universal league of nations, with suitable machinery for judicial arbitration and conciliation.

With these social reforms and political aspirations, the labouring population is being imbued and organised into a vast national party, which within the next ten years might be called upon to form a Government. Still, socialism will have no easy triumph. It will meet with dexterous manœuvring and stubborn resistance on the part of the possessing classes and their adherents. For, capitalism, as a purely economic force, has not collapsed ; the leaders of industry, commerce, and finance do not at all feel like a bankrupt or effete class. Modern society has accomplished industrial wonders ; it has called into being productive forces and possibilities of wealth-creation beyond the dreams of all scientific Utopias. And this is its justification and its title to existence. It will, therefore, not readily abdicate. And yet, it is being seriously challenged for it has utterly failed in the domain of social ethics. Its very success, its most marvellous achievements have been bound up with the destruction of human solidarity and social service. In its pride of wealth and science it has looked upon the *civitas terrena* as the real order of the universe. It has turned religion and ethics into handmaids to minister to its bodily comforts. The contrast between material efflorescence and moral stagnation is the root cause of the disharmony of modern humanity. From this hellish chasm springs the world tempest.

Socialism is called upon to redress the balance of material and moral power, to help mankind to attain to an equilibrium of the main forces of life. Its instruments are the poor and the lowly, as in the days of old. But they must take up their mission with clean hands and pure hearts, and not to try to do God's work with the devil's tools. Worldly power, the formation of Labour and socialist governments, must be strictly subordinated not only to the socialisation of the means of production, but to the socialisation of man, to the restoration of the moral order of the world.

XXII

GREAT BRITAIN IN TRANSFORMATION, 1917-28

I.—FROM INDIVIDUALIST TO CORPORATE ENTERPRISE

THE twelve years from 1917 to 1928 witnessed even more profound changes in the social structure of Britain than the twelve years from 1903 to 1914. The new industrial revolution, of which the nation became conscious only in the years 1927 and 1928, began in the first decade of the new century. Until then the workshops and factories, the mercantile and financial houses of the country, were largely controlled by individual firms or families, and in the great majority of cases were carried on on a comparatively modest scale. Big industry was in the minority ; trustification was just starting on its career ; individual management formed still a potent factor in industrial life.[1] The second decade, with the pressure of German and American competition on British manufactures, with its four years of war and post-armistice prosperity, considerably accelerated the process of amalgamation of smaller and middle-sized undertakings into large-scale works and business concerns. The third decade, with its revolutionary changes in applied science, manufacturing processes, and means of transport—further, with its flaming conflicts between Capital and Labour in transport, engineering, and mining, which expanded to national dimensions—imparted the final stimulus to the amalgamating tendencies so characteristic of the industrial life of modern civilisation. On top of these unprecedented alterations in the economic structure and methods of production, transport, and exchange came the crisis in the basic industries which used to supply the bulk of British exports.

[1] *Cf.* Hewins, *Trade in the Balance* (London, 1924), pp. 16, 66–67.

Owing partly to a redistribution of the industrial activities of the nations, and partly to a shrinkage of the demand of certain countries—effects which were practically all due to the Great War (1914–18)—British coal, cotton, iron, and steel met everywhere, at home and abroad, with severe competition. The percentage of unemployment rose since 1921 to critical heights, with the consequent pressing down of the standard of living of large sections of the working population. The annual average percentages unemployed among members of trade unions making returns were—1911 : 3.0 ; 1912 : 3.2 ; 1913 : 2.1 ; 1919 : 2.4 ; 1920 : 2.4 ; 1921 : 14.8 ; 1922 : 15.8 ; 1923 : 11.3 ; 1924 : 8.1[1] ; 1925 : 10.5 ; 1926 : 12.2. And this state of things in the staple industries appears to assume a chronic character. Such a series of rapid changes and violent dislocations in the material conditions of a highly complicated and delicately poised national system were bound to generate widespread unrest, to release dissolving elements, and to quicken the desire either for the restoration of tranquillity and " normalcy "—that is, the *status quo ante*, with corresponding reforms, with the view of stabilising the essentials of the old society—or for a more or less bold advance towards a new form of social production and distribution, for a different social order, more in accord with the new industrial forces which were distinctly tending to collective ownership and responsibility. The idea " that the existing industrial system is only a stage in our economic evolution " began to penetrate into the circle of the great captains of industry.[2] Furthermore, with the younger generation of British historical and social students, the recognition of the economic and collectivist factor is visibly displacing the political and parliamentary, personal, and

[1] The improvement was due to the French occupation of the German Ruhr valley, which paralysed German coal and metal industries, and thus benefited the corresponding British industries.

[2] The quotation is taken from the speech of Sir David Milne-Watson, at the Mond-Turner Conference, held on January 12, 1928. (*Report to the 60th Annual Congress of the British Trades Unions*, London, 1928, p. 137.)

heroic interpretation of national developments. One may venture now to predict that the coming historians of Britain will be much more occupied with researches into industrial changes, and their attendant social collisions, than with conflicts between kings and barons, between personal monarchy and parliament, or between theology and enlightenment, religion and science.

No social class and no political party escaped the effects of the changes and vicissitudes to which Britain was exposed in the last decade. What those effects were may be easily surmised from the foregoing reflections. The people of substance, with a stake in the country, and those who were dependent on them, or those who from temperament and conviction saw the salvation of the country in the adherence to traditional ways of life, turned to the Conservative Party. Men and women, born after 1871, caught sight of the ghost of revolution for the first time in their lives in the years 1917, 1918, and 1919, and could not forget it. They eschewed all Radical phraseology and took refuge under the wing of the traditional party of law and order.

The working people, with nothing but their labour capacity, and organised in trade unions, as well as men and women not belonging to the wage-earning class, but who from temperament and conviction, from intellectual and moral considerations, saw the solution of the crisis in the enactment of social reform measures became socialists and joined the Labour Party. The conversion of organised Labour to socialism was one of the phenomena of the years 1917–28. Henceforth trade union history forms a part of socialist history.[1]

---

[1] There were, of course, socialists among the trade unionists as far back as the 'nineties of the last century ; and Trades Union Congresses carried sometimes socialist resolutions ; but these were sporadic and informal affairs, not binding on anybody. It was only in 1918 and 1924 respectively that political and industrial Labour adopted socialist programmes, with the full knowledge of their significance.

Both parties grew at the expense of the Liberals, whose voting strength dwindled in the same measure as economic individualism was losing ground in the centres of industry and commerce. The parliamentary and municipal elections of the decade 1918–28 bore witness to the political regroupment of the nation on the new economic lines. The eclipse of the Liberal Party must, however, not be taken to signify the extinction of liberalism. Indeed, the Liberal Party might ultimately be crushed between the upper millstone of Conservatism and the nether millstone of social reform Labour, and yet liberalism as an attitude of mind would remain one of the controlling factors in British politics and a considerable obstacle against any advance of either fascism or bolshevism. The individualist and competitive phase of capitalist enterprise generated out of its material conditions and interests the ideas of toleration, freedom of thought, respect of the individual conscience and judgment, and bequeathed it as a spiritual legacy to posterity. More or less of its substance was gradually woven into the mental texture of various strata of the nation, and liberalised them. The great majority of the British people may truly say, " We are all liberals now, but each of us with some adjective which marks us off from the Liberal Party." And nowhere has liberalism been more completely assimilated than by the Labour Party.[1] It is the method of Labour democracy. This is the watershed between the social democratic Labour movement and the communist Labour movement.

[1] " We Young Liberals," writes one of them in the *Manchester Guardian*, November 13, 1924, "find our ideals in the Labour Party." And E. B. Schofield writes (*ibid.*, November 5, 1924), " We young people are joining the Labour Party in large numbers, but we remain essentially liberal at heart." The Hon. R. D. Denman and E. G. Armstrong are pleading for merging the Liberal Party in the Labour Party, since everything essentially liberal is to be found in the Labour Party (*ibid.*, November 12, 1924, and November 7, 1924). The correspondence columns of the *Manchester Guardian*, in October–November, 1924, and again in September–October, 1928, on labour and liberalism are of great sociological value.

2.—GENERAL VIEW OF ORGANISED LABOUR, 1917–28

The first quarter of the century (1903–26) was characterised by an increase of disputes unprecedented in the number of workers involved and the aggregate duration in working days. In the six years 1903–08 the total number of workpeople involved in disputes amounted to 952,000 ; the aggregate duration in working days 22,100,000. In the six years 1909–14 the respective figures were 4,136,000 and 83,290,000, though in the last five months of the year 1914, owing to the war, all disputes ceased. In the years 1915 and 1916 the industrial truce was fairly observed. In the six years 1917–22 the respective figures were 8,868,000 and 174,781,000. In the four years 1923–26 the respective numbers were 4,193,000 and 189,281,000. The rise of the social temperature in 1917–26 was alarming, and symptomatic of the revolutionary changes which were going on in industrial and political life. Still, not all the disputes were of the same nature. From the point of view of the economic action of organised Labour, the years 1917–26 divide into two periods —*viz.*, 1917–21 and 1921–26. The years from 1927 onwards fall into a different social category, and will be dealt with later on.

In the four or five years from 1917 till the " Black Friday " (April 15, 1921) the trade unions were animated by a fighting spirit, and took the offensive, not merely for strictly industrial aims connected with wages and hours of work, but for larger social objectives, as control of industry, nationalisation. The disputes assumed national dimensions, the unions not directly involved were ready to take sympathetic action and to solidarise themselves with the strikers. While not succeeding in their larger objectives, the disputes brought many advantages to Labour. Wages rose, the weekly working hours decreased, the care for the unemployed and the necessitous came to be regarded as a national duty, expenditure on social reform measures and benefits increased considerably. Nineteen-twenty marked the peak year in the advance of the working class ; its share in the national income of 1919–20 was probably larger than ever before or after.[1] Those achievements cannot, however, be ascribed exclusively to trade union activities and policy. They appear to have been partly due to the fear of revolution—a sort of insurance premium against social conflagrations and breakages, paid by the propertied classes—and partly the effect of the post-bellum prosperity, which allowed more liberal remuneration all round. The prestige of trade unionism was likewise greatest in 1920, when its membership amounted to 6.5 millions, or about 50 per cent. of the number of industrial and mercantile workers, a figure never reached before nor after. It was, too, in 1920 that industrial and political Labour formed a Council of Action to bring pressure to bear upon the Government to desist from attacking Russia. British Labour was then full of optimism and ready to pass any revolutionary motion. In one of the greatest speeches ever delivered by J. H. Thomas, we find the following memorable words :

" During the past few weeks (August, 1920) we have gone through what is, perhaps, the most momentous period of the Trade Union and Labour Movement in our long history : a period which found, for the first time, a united and determined working-class effort to challenge the existing order of Parliamentary Government. . . . That our course was bold none can deny ; that it definitely challenged the Constitution there can be no doubt . . . but it was justified by the result. . . . Our only object was to prevent another war against Russia. So far we have succeeded, but the danger is not yet over, and cannot be over until a complete peace and understanding is arrived at with the Russian Government. Our action does not carry with it an acclamation of the Soviet method of Government. We can, by unity and by the exercise of our political powers, determine our own form of Government, and if the Russian people prefer the Soviet system it is their business." (*Report of T.U. Congress*, 1920, pp. 62–63).

This utterance of J. H. Thomas adequately characterised the sentiments of Labour in 1920.

---

[1] " Wages reached their highest level in December 1920." (*Times*, October 19, 1928, *sub* " Rises in rates of wages.") The high rate of wages and the very low percentage of unemployment, amounting to 2·4 only, may be taken as the justification of the above assumption.

The second period embraced the years from the spring of 1921 to the end of 1926. In this period, trade unionism was driven into a defensive position. All it could do was to strive for maintaining and safeguarding the achievements of the immediate past. All the great contests which organised Labour fought in those memorable years on the industrial and political field, while unparalleled in magnitude and far-reaching in their bearing on the course of British history, were but actions of defence and resistance. The struggles which occurred in the years between the " Black Friday " and the National Stoppage in May, 1926, lacked the aggressive character. The same remark applies to the electoral efforts of Labour in the years 1923 and 1924, as well as to the measures of the first Labour Government in 1924. Organised Labour fought with determination, with exasperation, and some groups with revolutionary fervour, not for the overthrow or transformation of the existing order, but against being deprived of the advantages gained in the years 1917–20. A. J. Cook's cry during the miners' struggle in 1926, " Not a penny off the pay and not a second on the day," epitomised the feelings and views of the overwhelming majority of the trade unions in the period 1921–26. Yet many of the achievements were lost ; the hopes for control of industry vanished ; all guild experiments, undertaken in 1920–22, failed through shortage of capital. The situation appeared desperate, and it favoured the spread of social revolutionary ideas. The Communist Party, established in 1920–21, began only in 1923 to gain adherents in working-class circles ; in 1924 the Anglo-Russian Advisory Council was formed, and Bolshevik delegations from Moscow were heartily welcomed on the Trades Union Congresses in Hull (1924) and Scarborough (1925)—indeed, the whole atmosphere of the Scarborough Congress was charged with revolutionary aspirations. There was a great contrast between the daily struggles for immediate interests and the revolutionary sentiments and theories that swayed the Congresses and meetings.

The two periods of aggression and defence, or the ascending and descending curve of the aspirations of Labour, found their counterpart in the rise and decline of the trade union membership. The number of members represented on the Trades Union Congress, 1905, amounted to barely a million; in 1910 to 1,647,715; in 1917 to 3,082,352; in 1918 to 4,532,086; in 1919 to 5,283,676; in 1920 to 6,505,482; in 1921 to 6,417,910; in 1922 to 5,128,648; in 1923 to 4,369,268; in 1924 to 4,328,235; in 1925 to 4,350,982; in 1926 to 4,365,691; in 1927 to 4,163,994; in 1928 to 3,900,000.

The year 1927 inaugurated a new period which promised to be marked by an armistice, and even friendly co-operation, between Capital and Labour, with a view to reconstructing the industrial organisation.

3.—THE MINING INDUSTRY AS STORM-CENTRE

In the years 1917–26 there occurred several large or national disputes, such as in the railway service in 1919, which involved 517,000 persons and caused a loss of 4,200,000 working days; in engineering, etc., in 1922, which involved 369,000 persons, causing a loss of 17,484,000 working days; in the building trade in 1924, which involved 115,000 persons, causing a loss of 3,145,000 working days. None, however, could compare in the remotest degree in point of importance and consequences with the chain of conflicts in the coal industry. There were several causes which accounted for the unsettlement of the conditions in the coalfields. First, the predominantly obsolescent, small scale, and wasteful way of coal getting. Secondly, the unwillingness of the Government to recognise the principle of nationalisation, and to accept in letter and spirit the Sankey Report. Thirdly, the transition from war to peace : during the war years the British coal industry was under State control and enjoyed on the markets of the European Allies a quasi-monopoly, earning and accumulating large profits, from which also the miners benefited ; on the signing of the Versailles Peace the monopolist advantages gradually disappeared. Coal exports declined and prices fell. French and Belgian mines revived ; German industry was getting on its legs again, and, being under the necessity of providing not only sustenance for its own population, but heavy reparation payments for the Allies, it strained all its energies to raise production and push the export trade to its utmost limit ; moreover, the Spa Agreement (July, 1920) imposed upon Germany the obligation of delivering two million tons of coal monthly to France, which, in its turn, disposed of it in other markets. The autumn of 1920 was actually the beginning of the crisis in the British coal industry. The same date may be fixed for the abrupt termination of the post-armistice industrial prosperity in Britain and the setting in of the trade depression, with its consequent rapid, even catastrophic, rise of unemployment. The causal connection between the two series of phenomena—the revival of German industry, spurred on by the bayonet-point of the Versailles Treaty and Spa Agreement on the one hand, and the sudden collapse of the British " boom " on the other—is shown in the following table :

Percentage unemployed among members of British and German trade unions, 1920–22

	GREAT BRITAIN [1]			GERMANY [2]		
MONTH	1920	1921	1922	1920	1921	1922
June	1.2	20.6	15.6	4.0	3.0	0.6
Dec.	6.0	16.2	13.8	4.2	1.6	2.8

In the same measure as the unemployment figures rose in Great Britain, they fell in Germany. The growing depression of British industry reacted unfavourably on the home demand for coal. In the course of the latter half of 1920 the British miners felt all security slipping from under their feet. Their long-standing demand for nationalisation[3] had to give way to

[1] *Nineteenth Abstract of Labour Statistics of the United Kingdom*, 1928, p. 79.

[2] *Statistisches Jahrbuch f. d. Deutsche Reich*, 1926, p. 304.

[3] Robert Smillie, in moving a resolution on the T.U. Congress, 1919, in favour of nationalisation, remarked, " I find that since the year 1882 this Congress has actually passed no less than forty-two resolutions in favour of the general principle of nationalisation. . . . It is over twenty years since the Congress first passed a resolution affirming the principle that the mineral wealth of the country ought to be the wealth of the State, and not of individuals." (*Report of the T.U. Congress*, 1919. pp. 259–60.)

less radical proposals, and, finally, nothing was left to them but to carry on a prolonged, costly, and, withal, hopeless battle for a living wage. In their despair, the miners downed tools on October 18, 1920, whereupon the Government moved for an Emergency Powers Act, and carried it on October 28. The Act has become one of the most powerful weapons in the hands of Government authority, equal to the old-time Suspension of the Habeas Corpus Act, which served Pitt and Lord Sidmouth against the English Jacobins and working-class Radicals in the last years of the eighteenth and the first quarter of the nineteenth centuries. On November 3 the stoppage was settled by compromise, which merely postponed the *dénouement* of the crisis. It was but the end of the first act of the tragedy which was to occupy the public stage up to the end of 1926. It called forth the whole heroism which British workmen are capable of and entailed immense suffering on millions of men, women, and children. The tragedy rolled on. On February 15, 1921, the Government announced decontrol of coal, which took effect on March 31, 1921. The owners got back the full control of the mines, and at once proposed drastic wage reductions and settlement by districts. The miners rejected the proposals and were locked out. The sympathy of the whole working class went out to the miners ; the Triple Alliance was stirred to action. A stoppage of the whole traffic by land and water was fixed for Friday, April 15, 1921. The Government mobilised all available armed forces, and declared a State of Emergency ; there was tension in London, and an intervention of the Government in favour of the miners seemed likely. In the last moment, however, at midnight April 15, Frank Hodges, the miners' secretary, threw a plank over the yawning gulf and *pourparlers* with both parties were opened, which enabled the leaders of the railwaymen and the transport workers to recede from the participation in the stoppage. There was no doubt that the masses were ready to respond to the call for a general strike, but the spell was broken. There were charges against the leaders of having betrayed the militant working class, and the Friday, April 15, 1921, was black marked in the calendar of advanced Labour, and became known as "Black Friday." The miners, however, with their indomitable perserverance, fought on till June, when starvation forced them into submission. Henceforth, with the exception of one day ("Red Friday," July 31, 1925), the initiative was with the owners. In the second half of 1923, owing to the French occupation of the Ruhr Valley (the main German coalfields) and the consequent paralysis of the German metal industry, the depression in the British coal and metal industries somewhat lifted, and in 1924 the miners succeeded in getting their minimum wage raised. With the re-opening of the Ruhr coalfields the British coal crisis reasserted itself. The owners knew no other remedy but wage reductions and the increase of the weekly working hours, and gave notice to terminate the agreement of 1924 on July 31, 1925. The miners, led by A. J. Cook, the successor of Frank Hodges, argued—and in this they used the arguments of the whole Labour movement—that worsening of the labour conditions would not mend matters, and that the remedy was to be found in a reorganisation of the industry on rational lines which would increase its productive efficiency and competitive power, and, pending the results of re-construction, the State should grant a subsidy to the in-dustry. The owners and the Government spurned the miners views. The Prime Minister (Mr. Baldwin) set his face against the subsidy, but recommended the setting up of a Royal Com-mission to inquire into the coal industry. The miners, remem-bering the fate of the Sankey Commission, fought shy of further inquiries. Both parties then prepared for the worst. Interviews and negotiations having proved abortive, the General Council stepped in, and on July 30, 1925, the leaders of the railway and transport workers issued notices to refuse to handle coal after midnight of Friday, July 31. The publication of the notices had an electric effect on the Prime Minister : the general strike was, after all, going to materialise. After an interview with the miners on Friday, July 31, he granted the subsidy and requested the owners to suspend the notices ; on the other hand, the miners withdrew their opposition to the Royal Commission.

The victory of the miners and the solidarity of the trade union world manifested on Friday, July 31, or " Red Friday," was regarded in some quarters as a humiliating defeat of all Government authority, and it was felt desirable to render any similar attempt on the part of Labour impossible. The nine months of the subsidies (August 1, 1925, to April 30, 1926) allowed time enough for preparations. In September, 1925, the Organisation for the Maintenance of Supplies (a purely voluntary organisation) was instituted. In October most of the Communist leaders were imprisoned for six and twelve months respectively. In November, 1925, local authorities were circularised and their duties in the event of a strike explained. Stocks of coal were laid in, adequate for a five months' stoppage; and large additions were made to the police.[1] The Communists urged the formation of proletarian Defence Corps, propaganda in the Army and Navy, agreement with the co-operative societies for supplying the miners with food—finally, assumption by the Trades Union Congress of Government functions : that is, the organisation of a Soviet Government. The General Council, however, was from the outset determined not to give cause for prosecutions or persecutions, hoping that organised Labour would succeed in getting the Prime Minister to continue the subsidy. Meanwhile the Government had set up a Royal Commission, under the chairmanship of Sir Herbert Samuel, which issued on March 6, 1926, an exhaustive and instructive Report, recommending thorough reconstruction of production and marketing of coal, discontinuance of the subsidy, retention of the seven hours' day, and a wage reduction. Neither the owners nor the miners accepted the Report. The general strike again loomed on the horizon, but this time the Government and the propertied classes were fully prepared for any emergency. Indeed, for an economically dependent class, a chance victory over a powerful ruling class, is more dangerous than a defeat : the Roman slave rebellion under Spartacus, and the English peasant war under Wat Tyler are the classic examples of that

[1] *The British Public and the General Strike*, by Kingsley Martin, London, 1926, pp. 55–56.

lesson. The Government and the influential men and women of the ruling class conceived the general strike as an attack on constitutional government, on law and order, and as leading to ruin and anarchy. (Mr. Baldwin, in the *British Gazette*, May 6, 1926.) On the other side, the leaders of Labour thought of nothing else than a few days manifestation of working-class solidarity with the miners' cause, as the noblest expression of loyalty to their long-suffering brethren in the coalfields, in order to impress upon the Government the urgent necessity of continuing the subsidy until reorganisation of the mines was well under way. From the middle of April, 1926, innumerable meetings, interviews, and conferences were held between the miners and the General Council, between the latter and the Government ; a Special Conference of the Executives of all important unions sat since April 29, 1926, in London ; but no peaceful solution of the crisis was in sight. The owners insisted on an extension of the working day and a wage reduction ; the Government refused to continue the subsidy ; the miners defended the *status quo*. The battle was joined. It needed but a slight incident to cause the guns to go off. On April 30 the King signed a Proclamation declaring a State of Emergency ; the Government departments were busy with mobilising the armed and civil forces ; on May 1 the lock-out of over a million miners took effect ; on the same day the special Conference of the Union Executives approved by 3,653,529 votes to 49,911 the proposal for a general stoppage to begin at midnight of May 4. The negotiations with the Government were still going on the whole of May 3, when, late in the night, the fatal incident happened. The machine workers of the *Daily Mail* refused to print an article which, in their opinion, was a gross libel on the trade unions, calculated to inflame public opinion and set class against class. Mr. Baldwin, informed by telephone of that incident, declared this to have been " the first move in the general strike " and broke off all negotiations.

On May 4, 1926, the general or national strike began. The response of the workers surpassed all expectations. The best paid categories of employees obeyed the call of the General Council.

The industries that were to be included in the strike were transport, railway service, printing and newspaper business, metals, building (except sanitary, health, and food services). But only transport, railways, Press, metal workers, and gas and electrical workers concerned with the supply of power for industry or a total of 1,580,000 persons, besides the miners, were called up as the first line of defence. They were eventually to be joined by the electricians, gas-workers, etc., as second line, who would have done their duty by the miners. The General Council decided, however, not to go to the length of stopping light, food distribution, etc. From the number of persons involved in the stoppage it could not reasonably be called a general strike, but the absence of traffic and daily papers created the impression that the whole national life was brought to a standstill. Most of the daily papers did not appear at all, and some only in a considerably reduced size. The Government established the *British Gazette* as its organ ; the General Council the *British Worker*; the Communists issued typewritten bulletins. In these papers the Government and Labour gave their views and news concerning the stoppage. The *British Gazette* informed the public that the strike meant civil war ; the *British Worker* assured that it was nothing of the kind, but an industrial dispute which from particular circumstances assumed larger dimensions than former strikes. Towards the end of the first week, when, owing to a shortage of raw materials or fuel, other workshops and factories began to shut down and the stoppage threatened to become really general, Sir Herbert Samuel hurried back from Italy to London, and, after having an interview with the Minister for Mines, approached the General Council and submitted to them a memorandum embodying the conditions which were believed to be susceptible of forming a basis for a resumption of negotiations. The General Council, after discussing and altering the memorandum, agreed with Sir Herbert that a basis for negotiations was formed and decided to terminate the stoppage. Two members of the General Council called at noon, May 12, 1926, on Mr. Baldwin, who, accompanied by half a dozen State Secretaries and Ministers, received the *surrender*—so the *British*

Gazette expressed it—of the Labour leaders.   The General Council issued an order to strikers to return to work.   The railwaymen, transport workers, compositors and printers gradually obeyed the order, but the miners rejected the memorandum ; the lockout continued during the long summer and autumn, for over six weary and terrible months, until it accomplished the work of attrition.   Poor relief, borrowings from co-operative societies, contributions from trade unions, British and foreign—the Russians sent over £1,100,000—fell far short of satisfying the most elementary needs of the locked-out families. At the beginning of November, 1926, their endurance was at an end. Starved and broken, the miners surrendered at discretion, leaving some hundred thousands of them to penury and acute distress.

Apart from the misery in the mining districts, the national strike and the mining dispute left their mark on the Statute Book of the Realm.   In 1927 the Government carried the Trade Disputes and Trade Unions Act, which brands as illegal general and sympathetic strikes, restricts picketing, makes the law courts the final arbiters of the legality or illegality of strike activities, and tends to upset the financial basis of the Labour Party by the contracting-in clause :   only those trade unionists may contribute to the political fund (that is to the fund of the Labour Party) who declare in writing on a special form that they are willing to be levied for that purpose.   The income of the Labour Party for the year 1927–28 was thereby seriously reduced.

4.—REFLECTIONS ON THE GENERAL STRIKE AND LABOUR

The attitude and utterances of some of the propertied classes and their newspapers during the general strike afforded sufficient evidence of the existence of large and influential circles in Great Britain who still look on the working population as lower orders and on their independent actions as rebellious.   This bodes ill for the future of a country which is involved in a new industrial revolution, with all its consequent dislocations, disturbances, and necessarily painful readjustments.

The nine days national stoppage disclosed the strength and

determination of the masses to go ahead with the fight. There is much potential revolutionary feeling among the British working class ; they will one day, as the new industrial revolution unfolds itself, rise up again and change their leaders and organisations, unless there is a change of attitude of the upper classes and higher officialdom, and rationalisation proves capable of satisfying the needs of the working population. A study of the last British general strike, such as attempted by Kingsley Martin in his *British Public and the General Strike*, or as rhapsodically given by H. G. Wells in his *Meanwhile*, is well worth undertaking and pondering over.

On the other hand, there is no reason to concur in the charges of treason and cowardice levelled at the men of the " Black Friday " and May 12, 1926. As a matter of fact, the trade union leader can do nothing with the idea of a revolutionary general strike ; this is, in his eyes, if at all practicable, an eminently political affair, involving ultimately the taking over of Government by the Labour Party. He thinks in industrial terms, he deals with labour conditions and not with social problems. His proper function, he has come to learn, is negotiating with employers, and not overthrowing Capital. His ambition is to be a successful negotiator, to pit his intellect against that of the big industrial employer, and outwit a board of directors. In this state of mind, leaders are not likely to respond with alacrity when called upon to marshal the men into battle array and fight to a finish. The more the antagonistic nature of the dispute asserts itself, the more is their mind inclined to turn towards some solution which affords negotiating and mediating free scope. This happened towards the end of the first week of the general strike, when Sir Herbert Samuel appeared on the scene with his memorandum. There is no betrayal in such a turn of the dispute ; it proceeds logically from the inclination and conviction of those leaders; far from thinking that they are betraying the cause of Labour, they themselves feel betrayed by those who manœuvre them into a general strike. This was the feeling of the General Council (except A. J. Cook) all along during the nine days from May 4 to 12, 1926. And the same feeling swayed the leaders of the Labour Party. They all went into the fight actuated by a sense of loyalty, and not by reasoned conviction. The leading men of the Trades Union Congress and the Labour Party are moving now on parallel lines, because their respective spheres are being clearly defined. Harmony reigns between the political and industrial wing of the organised working class. Both wings have been co-ordinating their measures against the Left opposition, the Minority movement and the Communists. It has taken three years (1925–28) of patient effort to make the trade unions conform to the anti-Communist resolutions of the Labour Party.

5.—RISE OF THE COMMUNIST PARTY

One of the symptoms of the struggles in the years 1917–21 was the rise of a Communist Party which instituted itself as the British Section of the Third (Moscow) International. Its direct influence has not been commensurate with its efforts ; even in the years 1925–26, which were quite favourable to the growth of a revolutionary working-class party, the ultimate increase of its membership was disappointing. The number of its members was in 1928 about 3,000 to 4,000 in all. But its indirect influence on all those trade union elements who have been dissatisfied with an industrial leadership which shuns fighting has been considerable, though here, again, many of those elements have kept aloof from the Communist Party, and have formed organisations or movements of their own. The opposition to the Labour Party policy or trade union leadership—such as the Left Wing, the Minority Movement, the Cook-Maxton conferences—while in contact with, or promoted by, the Communists, consists in the main of non-Communists. But, small in number as they are, the Communists have everywhere been in the thick of the battle. The Labour Party Executive, in rejecting the application of the Communist Party for affiliation, stated that the " energy and enthusiasm of the Communists is undoubted." (*Report of the Annual Conference of the Labour Party*, 1924, pp. 38–39.) And in

H. G. Wells's *Meanwhile* it is said of the Communists, in connection with the general strike of May 16, 1926, " The only people in all the tangle of affairs who seem to have any life in them and any real go are—don't be startled—the Communist Party. They can take risks and sacrifice themselves—quite horrible risks they will face." Yet they are far from growing into a mass movement, and could not do their work without the financial backing from the Communist International. Maybe that their day will arrive when a Labour Government, backed by a majority of its own, disappoints the hopes of the working class. This will be the crucial time of the British Labour movement.

The Communist Party was established in 1920–21. On July 31 and August 1, 1920, a conference of the British Socialist Party, the Scottish Socialist Labour Party, and similar groups took place in London, with the view of forming a Communist Party. The main discussion turned on two questions : adhesion to the Third International ; affiliation to the Labour Party. The first question was soon settled : a resolution in favour of adhesion to the Third International was carried by acclamation. The second question gave rise to a serious difference of opinion ; a strong minority argued against affiliation. It was only at the end of January, 1921, that the representatives of the above-mentioned organisations, assembled in conference at Leeds, arrived at a decision in favour of affiliation and formed the Communist Party of Great Britain (C.P.G.B.). The Party Executive applied for affiliation to the Labour Party. The matter came up for final decision at the Labour Party Annual Conference, 1924. After an exhaustive debate, a card vote was taken on the following three resolutions: " 1. That the application of the Communist Party for affiliation be refused." Carried by 3,185,000 votes to 193,000. " 2. That no member of the Communist Party be eligible for endorsement as a Labour candidate for Parliament or any local authority." Carried by 2,456,000 to 654,000. " 3. That no member of the Communist Party be eligible for membership of the Labour Party." Carried by 1,804,000 to 1,540,000. A year later the Annual Conference of the Labour Party passed a resolution by 2,870,000 votes to 321,000 asking the trade unions to refrain from sending members of the Communist Party as delegates to Labour Party conferences or meetings. Slowly but surely the trade union executives conformed to the request of the Labour Party. They could not proceed against the Communists on the same grounds as the Labour Party, since eligibility for union membership does not depend on political or any other views, but on the industrial status. The trade unions can only proceed against members who are endangering the interests of the organisation. In 1927 and 1928 the Communists were, so to speak, reduced in rank, because, in the opinion of the executives, their speeches and actions had the tendency or the effect of splitting the unions or reducing their membership. The Communists and their adherents and sympathisers in the Minority Movement or Left Wing were in many cases disqualified from being elected as delegates or holding any office or any position of authority in the trade unions. The ban on the Communists is all but complete.

Up to 1928 the Communist electoral policy was friendly to official Labour candidates. As a rule, they supported them at elections and refrained from running candidates against them. Only in constituencies where there was no Labour candidates did the Communists put up their own. At the general election of October, 1924, they contested eight seats, with the following results : Saklatvala (Battersea), 15,096 votes—increase against 1923, 2,755 votes; Stewart (Dundee), 8,340 votes—decrease 2,000 ; Wall (Streatham), 3,204 votes ; Vaughan (Bethnal Green), 6,024 votes—increase 773 ; Tom Mann, 2,605 votes ; William Paul (Rusholme), 5,328 votes—increase 38 ; Geddes (Greenock), 7,590 votes—decrease 3,000 ; Dunstan (Birmingham), 7,158 votes. The eight candidates polled a total of 55,345 votes.

The year 1928 marked a turning-point in the Communist electoral policy. The Communist International decided that the Communists should everywhere put up candidates against Social Democracy or Labour Parties. This decision was put to the test for the first time at a by-election in North Aberdeen (August, 1928), with the following result : Wedgwood Benn (Labour), 10,640 votes ; Sandeman (Con.), 4,696 ; Ferguson (Communist), 2,618 ;

Rutherford (Lib.), 2,337 votes. At the next general election (1929) 15 to 20 Communist candidates will run against some of the most prominent Labour leaders. Ramsay MacDonald, the Parliamentary and spiritual leader of the Labour Party and parliamentary candidate for Seaham Harbour, will be opposed by the Communist, Harry Pollitt (boilermaker), the most persuasive and respected speaker of the Communists.

The main Communist organ is the *Labour Monthly*, always notable for Palme Dutt's comments on the current events in the Labour Movement.

6.—LABOUR PARTY, ITS GROWTH AND POLICY, 1918–28

The growth of the voting strength of the Labour Party has been proceeding without interruption and without reverse, as may be seen from the following table :

General Election.	Seats Contested.	Members returned.	Labour Vote.
1918	316	57	2,244,945
1922	414	142	4,236,733
1923	427	191	4,348,379
1924	514	151	5,487,620

The number of members oscillates round three millions, but this is not so reliable a gauge as the voting strength. The party draws its votes mainly from the trade union world ; probably 90 per cent. of the party voters have been working men and women, and only 10 per cent. professional men and women. The electoral progress of the party has been most marked in the industrial and commercial centres, while in the counties there are large stretches of land not touched yet by political Labour.

There is no doubt that the party will in the future turn its attention more and more to the agricultural districts, where, however, it will meet with the rivalry of the Liberals and the entrenched positions of the Conservatives.

The organisation of the working women is being carefully attended to by the chief woman officer, Dr. Marion Phillips. At the annual conference of the labour women held at Portsmouth in May, 1928, there were 663 delegates, representing 476 women's sections, 71 divisional and local Labour Parties, and 116 trade unions, co-operative and socialist societies. The organ of the movement is the monthly *Labour Woman.*

The most important event in the political history of the last decade was the assumption of Government office by the Labour Party at the end of January, 1924. Although it lasted only to the end of October—about nine months in all—and although it had no majority of its own, it has left an indelible impression on social thought. The grandchildren of the " labouring poor," as the working class was called at the end of the eighteenth century, and the children of the " lower orders," as the working class was known in the middle of the nineteenth century, controlled—as far as any Government can control—the destinies of Great Britain and, to a large extent, the British Empire. The mere thought of it would have staggered or convulsed with laughter the statesmen of a century ago. The deeds and measures of the Labour Government are of much less importance than the fact of its existence. The year 1924 is an epoch-making one in British history. Our grandchildren, from their more favourable angle of vision, will get a truer perspective of the magnitude of the event.

Linked with this event are—Ramsay MacDonald as Prime Minister and Foreign Secretary, Philip Snowden as Chancellor of the Exchequer, John Wheatley as Minister of Health, and Sidney Webb as President of the Board of Trade.

The stabilisation of international peace was partly attempted, partly promoted, by the MacDonald Government through the recognition of the Russian Soviet Government, the Dawes Plan, the Geneva Protocol, and the draft agreement of commerce and

2 C

amity with the Soviet Government. The Imperial interests were safeguarded through a policy of continuity in relation to Egypt, the Mossul dispute, India, etc., whereby strategical and commercial considerations were its motives. The leader of the Labour Party and British Prime Minister disillusioned the leaders of the revolutionary nationalist elements in Egypt, Turkey, and India. And Mr. Snowden's Budget was in the best Radical "breakfast table" tradition. In home affairs, Wheatley's Housing Act, the improvement in Unemployment Insurance, the preliminary work for widows' and orphans' pensions, and for the extension of the suffrage to young women, were greatly to the credit of the Labour Government. The year 1924 was, besides, the only one in the series from 1921 to 1928 in which the total increase of wages overbalanced the total decrease. Most beneficial of all was the influence of the Labour Government on the progressive movements in Europe.

In the first week of October, 1924, through a combined Conservative-Liberal action, the position of the Labour Government became critical. The refusal of the Government to assent to the appointment of a Committee to inquire into the quashing of the prosecution of J. R. Campbell, the editor of the Communist weekly paper, resulted in its defeat. On October 9, MacDonald dissolved Parliament. After twenty days of a most passionately fought electoral campaign—in which the so-called Zinovieff Letter, and in reality the fight against the British-Russian draft agreement, played a sinister part—the election took place on October 29, 1924, and resulted in an overwhelming victory of the Conservative Party.

The nine-months Labour Government strengthened, on the one hand, the reformist tendencies of the leaders of the Labour movement as against the revolutionists, while, on the other hand, they produced much dissatisfaction in advanced Labour and socialist circles, who had expected the Government to stand in trade disputes by the trade unions, instead of which they were amazed to hear that a Labour Government must be, and was indeed, prepared to have recourse to the Emergency Powers Act against the workers. The trade union weeklies and monthlies—

particularly the railwaymen's, engineers', woodworkers', and foundry workers'—were filled with closely reasoned discussions of socialist policy, class struggle, Marxism, communism, which exhibited a very high level of social and economic thinking. The national organisations of both the Minority Movement in the trade unions and the Left Wing in the Labour Party were formed in that memorable year 1924.

7.—THE ESSENCE OF LABOUR PARTY AND TRADE UNIONIST POLICY

The great majority of trade unionists and Labour members, however, accept in the main the policy of their leaders, which may be thus formulated :

There is no collapse of the capitalist system, but it cannot be denied that it is dangerously out of gear, that there is a serious disproportion between the various industries and between production and consumption, between supply and effective demand, resulting in chaotic conditions which make themselves painfully felt in the life of the workers in the shape of unemployment and decreasing wages. A reconstruction of the system of production and distribution is necessary. This is recognised on all hands ; enlightened and progressive employers are ready to undertake it. But there is another important factor to be considered : the working classes have grown into a great political power : they can make and unmake governments ; they can promote or prevent reconstruction. To this the workers may retort : " It is not at all our business to help reconstruct a system that exploits and degrades us ; let it perish, and we shall rebuild an industrial system on socialist lines for ourselves." The leaders' reply is as follows : " Socialist society cannot be erected on the ruined capitalist system, but on its fullest development ; the reconstruction which is wanted means rationalisation and amalgamation ; the small scale, wasteful undertakings are eliminated ; the productive forces raised ; the sources of wealth are made to flow abundantly. At the same time the number of independent employers decreases, while the number of workers increases, and not only in number, but in organisation, knowledge, and executive ability. The whole process amounts, indeed, to a gradual, orderly progress towards socialism. Continuity and gradualness, and not, as Marx thought, revolution and catastrophes, will lead us to emancipation. We ask you, therefore, to co-operate with the captains of industry in the great task of reconstruction ; but you must have a voice in the management ; you must influence the course of reconstruction in your own interests, material as well as moral. This will be a step forward in the democratisation of industry, and will constitute one of those reforms which are in their very nature socialistic—that is, in full conformity with our aim. Furthermore, if you give us a majority in Parliament we shall legislate for all those reforms which are calculated to protect you from excessive exploitation, and which are promoting socialisation, such as nationalisation of the mines, railways, etc. Your work in the factory and in the council chamber with the capitalists, and our work in Parliament—industrial and political action—will be complementary to one another. In short, our aim and end is socialism through democratic reforms and constitutional methods. The nature of the British Constitution operates in our favour. It knows no finality. It is flexible. Any part of it may be changed by Act of Parliament. Born in the struggle for freedom, it is broadening down, as Dicey demonstrated, from political to social precedent."[1]

This is the essence of the Labour Party policy, expressed in the various resolutions and in the new programme *Labour and the Nation*, and approved by the Annual Conference of the Labour Party in Birmingham, October, 1928. And this is the meaning of the new trade unionist policy as expressed in the Mond-Turner conferences.

The years 1927–28 marked the beginning of a new period of trade union policy. If the years 1917–21 formed a period of trade union offensive and the years 1921–26 of trade union defensive, the years 1927–28 initiated a period of industrial armistice and even co-operation, with strong concentration of the Labour forces on electoral and parliamentary activity. The

[1] *Cf.* Dicey, *Law and Opinion in England*, ed. 1924, pp. 211–302, and John Morley, *Life of Cobden*, I., pp. 302–03.

Anglo-Russian Advisory Council was discontinued and the relations with the Russian trade unions were broken off. The new policy took its start from a suggestion of George Hicks, who, as president of the General Council in 1926–27, opened the Fifty-Ninth Trades Union Congress in Edinburgh (September, 1927) with an address in which the following passage occurred. " Our trade unions have not yet reached the limit of their development. Rather I would say that we are just at the beginning of their constructive period. . . . Practically nothing has yet been done to establish effective machinery of joint conference between the representative organisations entitled to speak for industry as a whole . . . and who have responsibility for the conduct of industry and know its problems at first hand. . . . Discussion on these lines would bring both sides face to face with the hard realities of the present economic situation, and might yield useful results in showing how far and on what terms co-operation is possible in a common endeavour to improve the efficiency of industry and to raise the workers' standard of life." While the whole Press welcomed the suggestion of Hicks, the employers' organisations remained indifferent, until Sir Alfred Mond (now Lord Melchett) took the initiative and, in a letter of November 23, 1927, invited the General Council to a conference with the view of discussing questions concerning the entire field of industrial organisation and industrial relations. The General Council accepted the invitation, and on January 12, 1928, the first full joint conference of twenty-seven of the most prominent British employers and the General Council took place. The leader of the employers' group was Sir Alfred Mond, the leader of the General Council was its president for 1927—Ben Turner. There were in the months January—July, 1928, a dozen conferences, presided over alternately by Sir Alfred Mond and Ben Turner. The discussions dealt with the finance and management of industry, new developments in technology and organisation, methods of rationalisation, means for assuring the security of the workers and for setting up a National Industrial Council and conciliation machinery for settling disputes. The employers declared that reconstruction had become a vital necessity, which, however, needed the co-operation of the workers; changes in the industrial system were inevitable, and in order that they should be brought about in a constitutional, peaceful manner, national arrangements for a constant and friendly exchange of views between Capital and Labour were to be instituted. The trade unions were thus not only recognised as a bargaining factor in collective agreements regarding wages and hours of work, but as national organs in the reconstruction and management of industry. Next to Lord Melchett, Lord Weir, Sir David Milne-Watson, and George Hicks, though the latter does not like all the implications of the new policy, the initial success of the Mond-Turner conferences is due to Walter Citrine, the general secretary of the General Council, and to J. H. Thomas.

Some leaders of Labour regard the new development as an important step in the direction of industrial democracy, of raising the industrial status of Labour to the political level. The Mond-Turner Conferences were approved by the Sixtieth Trades Union Congress in Swansea (September, 1928) by an overwhelming majority. Both the Labour Party and the Trade Union Congress look upon the present as a transition period from capitalism to socialism. The co-operation in industry is the counterpart to the political coalition of the social democratic Labour Parties with the progressive parties in Parliament and Government. Here is one of the most salient differences between them and the Communists. The former regard industrial co-operation with enlightened Capital, and political coalition with progressive parties, as the appropriate and most beneficial policy of Labour in the transition period from capitalism to socialism; while the Communists regard the dictatorship of the proletariat as the proper government during the transition period, in which capitalist society will be transformed into a socialist society. The Communists argue that there can be no co-operation between Capital and Labour for the benefit of the latter; no equality of status of the proprietors and the proletariat is possible, since those who possess the means of life are the masters of those whom they can starve; no matter how strong democratically minded Labour is, it will always get the worst, unless it adopts revolutionary

methods. The Communists, the Left Wing, the Minority movement, the Cook-Maxton opposition,[1] are, however, numerically
too weak to deflect labour frnm its strictly evolutionary course
mapped out for it by Sidney Webb in his writings since 1884,
and by Ramsay MacDonald in his *Socialism and Society* (1905).

[1] Cook and Maxton, *Our Case*, London, 1928 ; *Socialist Review*,
monthly organ of the I.L.P., edited by J. Strachey, who keeps the
reader well informed on these questions.

XXIII

THE YEARS 1929–39

I.—THE DIFFICULTIES OF LABOUR GOVERNMENTS

THE British Labour organisations, both in the form of trade unions and of electoral bodies, exhibit a certain rhythm in their movement for the amelioration of the social conditions of the wage-earners. Whenever their weight as trade unions proves insufficient to achieve their purpose, they concentrate, in constituency and municipality, on their political power as democratic citizens, and *vice versa*. This rhythm has increasingly manifested itself since the second Reform Bill (1867) and the Local Government Act (1888).

The years 1926–28, following the defeat of the national stoppage and the prolonged contest of the miners, formed a period of trade union decline and deterioration of the labour conditions. It was therefore not difficult to foresee that the main efforts of the Labour organisations would soon be directed towards political action, in order to bring their voting power to bear upon Parliament, with a view to abrogation of the Trade Disputes Act (1927) and to obtaining social reform laws, particularly in favour of the miners and the unemployed.

The political propaganda against the Baldwin Government proved very popular in Labour circles and resulted in surprisingly large successes at the General Election of 1929. The votes polled by the Labour candidates rose from 5,487,820 in 1924 to 8,362,594 in 1929, and the number of members of the Parliamentary Labour Party increased from 151 to 289, against 269 Conservatives and 59 Liberals. The Labour Party thus emerged from the election as the strongest single Party, but could only form a Government with the co-operation of the Liberals. Mr. Ramsay MacDonald, the leader of the Labour Party, took over the Premiership.

The real difficulties of Labour and Socialist Governments, as the post-war events amply demonstrated, always and everywhere begin after the victory, no matter whether the victory is the result of a revolution or of constitutional methods. The difficulties arise from two sources: (i) the exaggerated hopes and the urgency of the demands of the working classes for immediate improvements; (ii) the opposition of the propertied classes to any policy of far-reaching economic reform advocated by Socialists. With these difficulties a Labour Government has seriously to reckon and to provide for even in case of having an absolute majority; and the difficulties grow quite formidable if it has to depend for a majority on another Parliamentary party. The MacDonald Government was in the latter position in 1929–31, as it had been in 1924.

The experience of the difficulties in 1924 might have hardened and strengthened the determination of Labour Leaders of the type of Keir Hardie and John Wheatley to move boldly forward and not to be daunted in their effort to implement the electoral programme as far as the immediate needs of Labour are concerned. Those men loved the common people; and their love was the unerring and driving motive of their Socialist activities. The effect of the experience of 1924 on Ramsay MacDonald and Philip Snowden was the opposite: it weakened their faith in social reform as demanded by the labouring masses, and it strengthened their respect for the wide economic knowledge and financial dexterity of the captains of commerce and industry.

The nine months of office of MacDonald and Snowden in 1924, disclosed to them a world, not at all corresponding with that which they, as old propagandists of Socialism, had been wont to theorise upon and to subject to severe criticism. On the assumption of their high offices in 1929—one as Prime Minister, and the other as Chancellor of the Exchequer—they were chastened and timid men, and their dependence on Liberal co-operation was surely not calculated to fill them with courage.

The Labour Government could thus neither carry the repeal of the Trade Disputes Act nor improve the condition of the miners or effectively amend the Unemployment Insurance Act, for which the trade unions were clamouring. After the first twelve months of the Labour Government, disappointment was growing among the labouring masses, for the percentage of unemployed was rising. In 1929 it amounted to 10·4 of the insured workers; in 1930 it rose to 16·0. At the Nottingham Trades Union Congress (1930) the work of the Labour Government found many severe critics among the delegates, to whom Mr. (later Sir) Ben Turner replied:

" In recent days there have been a number of our own people both in the Trade Union and the political world who have been decrying the present Labour Government for their alleged inefficiency and ineffectiveness, and who have been prophesying that in the next election we are going to be down and out. I want to repudiate all such notions " (*Trades Union Congress Report*, 1930, p. 289).

The events of 1931 proved that the prophets had not prophesied in vain, but none of them could have foreseen the calamitous nature of the fulfilment of the prophecy, for none could then have foreseen the reactions of the American industrial crisis and the financial catastrophe in Austria and Germany on British politics.

2.—THE ECONOMIC CRISIS

The post-war years were in the U.S.A., and partly also in Central and Western Europe, a period of vast economic activities, industrial reconstruction and technical re-equipment, generally known as rationalisation. In the years 1924 to 1929 all those countries enjoyed great prosperity. The effective demand was everywhere large, particularly in the U.S.A., and came not only from exporters but from the home market. Agriculture and manufacture grew prodigiously and, outstripping even the constantly increasing consumption, finally resulted in the U.S.A. in overproduction of commodities and in over-speculation in industrial and financial securities. In the autumn of 1929 came the collapse of prices and profits, with its inevitable restriction of production, rapid increase of unemployment, runs on the deposit banks, and suspension of payments. The collapse of the American economic structure, which had been deemed to be impregnable, shook the whole complicated, yet finely balanced, fabric of international credit.

The distrust communicated itself to the financial centres of Europe, and soon made itself most painfully felt in Central Europe—in Austria and Germany—for, in addition to their financial weakness, the rapid rise of the Nazi Party was paralysing trade and commerce. The Nazis made no secret of their determination to repudiate all War Reparation payments, to destroy the Versailles Treaty, and to outlaw the Jews. Their programme meant war against the beneficiaries of the Versailles Treaty, and revolutionary changes at home. In September 1930, at the General Election in Germany, the Parliamentary representation of the Nazi Party rose from fourteen to over a hundred members, and disorder became the order of the day. German public life appeared to lose all stability.

The effect of the Nazi successes at the September election (1930) proved disastrous. Foreign creditors, mainly American, French and Dutch, who had advanced short-term loans to Germany, urgently called for speedy settlement; home depositors of local banks withdrew as much as they could obtain, so that even the largest banking establishments were being gradually depleted of their liquid resources. In July, 1931, one of the leading Berlin banks—the Darmstädter Bank—closed its doors, after having been compelled to repay to foreign creditors some 500 million marks within four or five months.

At this point we must return to British affairs, for in no other financial centre was the reaction of the German calamity so severely felt as in London, and this from two reasons. First, a large part of London's sterling resources was immobilised in long-term loans in Germany. Second, the general loss of confidence, caused by the American crisis, the German disintegration, and the fear that London was to a large extent involved in the German financial calamities, induced foreign creditors, who had considerable gold balances in London banks, to call them in. The Bank of England honoured its obligations and was losing much of its gold, until in the summer of 1931 the drain became unbearable, so that the Governors had to appeal to New York and Paris for gold advances. This signal of distress added to the general nervousness and filled some people with fear for the stability of the pound sterling and with forebodings of British insolvency.

3.—THE LABOUR GOVERNMENT IN CRISIS

The effects of the American industrial crisis, the Austrian and German financial calamities and political unrest, and the rationalisation of British industry in post-war years, combined to make unemployment, for the time being, the most crucial of all problems for the British working classes. Towards the end of 1930 the number of unemployed increased to over 2,300,000, and in 1931 unemployment of the insured workpeople amounted to 21 per cent, and in some important industries to 25 per cent. The expenditure on unemployment insurance benefit rose proportionately and gave the opponents of Labour the opportunity for discrediting the Labour Government.

In December 1930 the Government appointed a Royal Commission on Unemployment, before whom a Treasury officer, Sir Richard Hopkins, declared that unemployment benefit was being paid with borrowed money. This and similar evidence, as well as the gold outflow and the fear for the stability of the pound sterling, led to launching an economy movement with a view to calling a halt to public expenditure and to saving the country from bankruptcy. The financial difficulties, though caused mainly by the external causes mentioned above, were laid at the door of the Labour Government.

The economy movement seems to have greatly impressed the Prime Minister and the Chancellor of the Exchequer, for on

February 11, 1931, the latter told the House of Commons that, without drastic and disagreeable sacrifices from all, it would be impossible to balance the Budget. An Economy Committee on National Expenditure was set up under the chairmanship of Sir George May, whose Report—the so-called May Report—was issued at the end of July, 1931, and gave its opinion that the Budget for 1932 would show a deficit of £120 millions, which would have to be met by economies (about £90 millions) and fresh taxation (about £30 millions).

"The wide publicity given to this Report greatly intensified the fears existing on the Continent and elsewhere. The British Press took up the cry and alleged that the economic position was alarming. . . . The result was to increase still further the withdrawal of gold from London" (*Trades Union Congress Report*, 1931, p. 512–513).

The fears were, in fact, greatly exaggerated. The alleged deficit included the provision of £50 millions for the Sinking Fund, and a loan of £40 millions for the Unemployed Insurance Fund. Now, the Sinking Fund could have been suspended, and the loan for the Insurance Fund would be repaid as soon as employment improved, so that there remained only a deficit of £30 millions—a sum which Britain had been spending in four or five days during the Great War (1914–1918).

Nevertheless the impression made on MacDonald and Snowden was decisive, and they spoke of the "dread realities" which Labour refused to face. They demanded sacrifices, to which neither the Party nor the trades unions could agree. The latter made counter-proposals—suspension of the Sinking Fund and increased taxation—which the majority of the Cabinet rejected. So the things stood on August 21, 1931, and no other consultation took place and no further communication passed between the Cabinet and the Executives of the Party and the Trade Unions. "We heard nothing more," relates Mr. (Now Sir) Walter Citrine, "until, on Monday, August 24th, we heard that a National Government was being formed" (*Trades Union Congress Report*, 1931, p. 83).

MacDonald, Snowden, and Thomas deserted their Party,

joined the leaders of the Conservatives and some Liberals, and
formed on that day the "National" Government with a view
to restoring the national credit by carrying into effect the economies recommended in the May Report, namely, cuts in salaries,
wages, and unemployment benefit.

4.—DEFECTION AND DEFEAT

The Party and the trade unionists bore with quiet dignity the
insult offered to them by their most prominent political leaders.
The defection of trusted officers caused some painful disappointment, but no disarray among the rank and file.

Ramsay MacDonald, who had grown in political stature with
the growth of the Labour Party, forfeited the love which many
good men and women had cherished for him, and he failed to
win the respect of the Conservatives.   He was allowed to continue
in office as Prime Minister for a few years, but he evidently felt
a beaten man; there was neither zest nor happiness in his heart
any more.

Philip Snowden, who was rewarded with a Viscountcy, enjoyed
much popularity in the North of England, but neither he nor the
Party was any the worse for his defection.   It was, somehow,
hard to think of him as a comrade with whom one could talk
intimately on Socialist and trade union matters, and still less on
international Labour politics, and on all those questions which
formed controversial topics on Socialist Congresses or Conferences.
He was essentially a free-trade English Radical, with friendly
feelings towards the labouring people as long as they agreed
with him.

Among the more prominent leaders who remained true to the
Party and to his Trade Union comrades was Arthur Henderson,
Foreign Secretary in 1929–1931, and formerly Party Secretary.
He was henceforth sure to be received with hearty and demon-
strative cheering whenever he put in an appearance on Labour
Conferences.   He was one of the finest products of British trade
unionism and Gladstonian tradition; genial and loyal as a co-
worker, a model chairman, tactful, sympathetic, and never at

a loss for a shrewd reply to an opponent; a man of peace and reform, and disposed to settle differences by friendly discussion. One could not have wished for a better man at the head of a Labour Government.

The National Government, in the two months from the end of August to the end of October 1931, initiated its policy of economies, which caused much unrest amongst the wage- and salary-earning classes. At the same time the Government took the pound sterling off gold and reduced its nominal value by about 33 per cent. The pound sterling sank to the nominal value of a medieval English silver mark. The " dreadful prospect " of the fall of the pound to the level of the German inflation mark in 1923, with which MacDonald and Snowden had tried to frighten the trade unions into accepting the cuts of wages and salaries, failed to materialise. The National Government was particularly lucky. The exceptionally low level of American commodity prices in 1931, which was partly the effect of the general economic crisis and partly the cause of its long duration, prevented the British prices rising in proportion to the devaluation of the pound sterling, and thus warded off the lowering of the standard of life of the fully-employed working-people, which would have inevitably followed the cuts of wages. The real trouble was that the number of unemployed, those, that is, who depended on unemployment benefit, was so abnormally large and that the policy of economies hit the poorest so hard.

In the midst of the complications of everyday life and the perplexities of the currency problem it was by no means so easy to grasp the causative sequence of events as we do it now *post factum* on paper. The policy of economies as regards wages, salaries, and unemployed benefit, and particularly the fall of the pound, the abandonment of gold, and the borrowing of gold in Paris and New York, caused much perturbation and gave rise to deep misgivings about the position of the country. Some even feared or expected that the final collapse of the capitalist system was rapidly approaching. A good many people ascribed all their private worries and troubles to the Labour Government, to the alleged unfitness of Labour to govern. Into this unrest and disquiet came the dissolution of Parliament, and the General Election took place at the end of October 1931.

The electoral method of Britain takes on, in times of public excitement and tension, the irrationality of a lottery. The Labour Party which in 1929 polled 8,360,000 votes and elected 287 members, obtained now in round figures 6,500,000 votes but got only 52 members elected. The loss of votes had nothing of a sensational character, but the loss of 235 members was a staggering blow and looked like an overwhelming and irreparable defeat, like a knock-out. The triumph of the National Government was indeed complete. No effective opposition seemed possible. Britain turned into a quasi-totalitarian state.

5.—REVIVAL AND STATEMENT OF POLICY

The first reactions to the severe lessons of 1931 were unfavourable to a continuation of the policy of " gradualism." The advocates of a more decisively Socialist attitude had for a time the upper hand. At the Party Conference at Leicester, in October 1932, a resolution, moved by Sir Charles Trevelyan, was carried, which instructed the Parliamentary Labour Party and the next Labour Government to promulgate definite Socialist legislation, and to stand or fall on the principles in which they had faith. Of equal determination was the Socialist spirit which animated the proceedings of the Trades Union Congress at Newcastle, in September, 1932. The opening address of the chairman, John Bromley, was a rousing plea for the inauguration of a Socialist policy as the only remedy against the evils of an economic system that proved unable to adjust consumption to overflowing production, or which allowed poverty and under-nourishment to exist in the midst of plenty.

The revolutionary wave, however, was of comparatively short duration. The organised working classes—with the exception of the small minorities which formed the Independent Labour Party (I.L.P.), the Communist Party, the Socialist League, etc. —returned to their faith in gradual reform, and steadfastly refused to allow any scope to the Communist Party or any Left

Movement to influence their policy. Of the smaller bodies which advocated a more determined Socialist policy, the Communists were undoubtedly the more important, and yet, for all their ability, zeal, and self-sacrifice, they failed to make any impression on Labour.   The critical years 1930–1932 were, indeed, putting the Communists to the crucial test, and they were found wanting. At the General Election in 1931, their twenty-six candidates polled the grand total of 74,824 votes, an average of less than 3,000 votes for each candidate.   From these facts we draw the lesson: If a Communist Party, after ten years of ardent propaganda, is unable to make headway at a time when " gradualism " is visibly falling into discredit, when the feeling is widespread among organised Labour that capitalism is on the decline, and when unemployment is putting 20 to 25 per cent of the insured workpeople on the " dole," then the conclusion is inescapable and the argument irrefutable that there is no hope for a Communist Party in Britain.

A similar consideration applies to the I.L.P. which in the autumn of 1932 severed its connection with the Labour Party. Socialists, who for one reason or another separate themselves, or are kept separated, from the organised Labour Movement, are doomed to become sectarians, that is, self-constituted guardians of the purity of doctrine, without influence on the main currents of social life.   This was for many years a weakness also of the Social Democratic Federation, which, as I learn while writing these lines, closed its existence at the end of October 1939, after two generations of Socialist propaganda.   Founded in the years 1881–1883 by H. M. Hyndman and his friends, it lived to see the rise of the Fabian Society, the New Unionism, the I.L.P., the Labour Party, and the adoption of Socialist principles by organised British Labour. ·

Ever since the end of 1932 a gradual revival of the Labour forces has manifested itself.   Their participation in Municipal elections and Parliamentary by-elections brought them considerable successes, and boded well for the General Election of 1935. The hopes of Labour were not deceived.   It regained its voting strength of 1929 in polling 8,330,000 votes, though

2 D

not its Parliamentary strength, the number of elected members amounting to only 154 *plus* 4 I.L.P. members.

From 1935 onwards the same tendency has been operating in Municipal Elections and Parliamentary By-elections. In the London County Council the Socialists came to power in 1934, and, led by Herbert Morrison, have earned the confidence and respect of all classes of the metropolis.

The policy of the Labour Party or Socialist Party—the latter appellation is coming more and more into use—can now be clearly stated. From the experience of the first and second Labour Governments the Party drew the following lessons: (i) Not to ally itself to any other organisation, no matter whether it calls itself " United Front," " Popular Front," " Left Unity Campaign "; (ii) To refuse any invitation to join or to form a Coalition Government, but to remain strictly a Labour Party, based on a Socialist programme of a gradual reconstruction of society through democratic methods; (iii) To concentrate all its efforts on gaining a solid majority at the next General Election.

As to its policy during the war, which began in September 1939, the Parliamentary Labour Party is to act as a responsible and constructively-minded Opposition, criticising or supporting the Government measures on their merits, while preserving complete independence and preparing for the day when it will itself be called upon to form a Government.

INDEX

(PARTS III. AND IV.)